Handbook of
Evidence Based Management
Practices in Business

Handbook of
Evidence Based Management
Practices in Business

Edited by

Satyendra Kumar Sharma

Associate Professor, Department of Management,
Birla Institute of Technology & Science (BITS), Pilani

Praveen Goyal

Associate Professor, Department of Management,
Birla Institute of Technology & Science (BITS), Pilani

Udayan Chanda

Associate Professor, Department of Management,
Birla Institute of Technology & Science (BITS), Pilani

Routledge
Taylor & Francis Group

New York London

First published 2023
by Routledge
4 Park Square, Milton Park, Abingdon, Oxon OX14 4RN

and by Routledge
605 Third Avenue, New York, NY 10158

Routledge is an imprint of the Taylor & Francis Group, an informa business

British Library Cataloguing-in-Publication Data
A catalogue record for this book is available from the British Library

ISBN: 978-1-032-54216-4 (pbk)
ISBN: 978-1-003-41572-5 (ebk)

DOI: 10.4324/9781003415725

Typeset in Times LT Std
by Aditiinfosystems

Contents

PART II   Evidence Based Human Resource Management

Handbook of Evidence Based Management Practices in Business – Satyendra Kumar Sharma et al. (eds)
© 2023 Taylor & Francis Group, London, ISBN 978-1-032-54216-4

List of Figures

List of Tables

Preface

Part-I Evidence Based Management in Finance

In the paper titled "Insurance Buying Motives for Sustainable Financial Goals" Dhannur and Kusane studied the influence of emotional buying motives of life insurance policies using Factor analysis and SEM modeling. They found that consumers act irrational and buy polices due to emotional motives resembling commitments, trust, friendships and other factors.

In the paper titled "Fintech payments as a facilitator of value co-creation - a theoretical framework" Singh and Dutta developed a framework for value cocreation for fintech payment services by utilizing service-dominant logic. This study's main aim includes applying for fintech payment as an example and developing a framework to explain how this technology may be combined with operant and operand resources to create value that benefits both users and service providers.

In the paper titled "Lack of Evidence Based Management (EBM) of Non-Performing Assets (NPAs) in Regional Rural Banks (RRBs)" Chauhan conducted an Empirical study on the current status of NPA management in rural banking and how EBM can evolve a more effective tool to strategize efficient NPA management.

In the paper titled "Empirical Investigation of Heckscher Ohlin Theory on India's Foreign Trade" Prakash and Dhir found whether the exports and imports of the Indian economy conform to the Heckscher-Ohlin (H-O) theorem of international trade. Their work exclusively focuses on the growth and trade of the Indian economy from 2000 to 2021.

In the paper titled "Indicators of Risk Management in Banking Sector" Kaur studied the significant risks faced by banks by comparing the ratios of two Indian public sector banks, namely Dena Bank and the State Bank of India, for five years, from 2013-14 to 2017-18.

In the paper titled "Implied volatility, risk premium and option mispricing: An examination of information efficiency of options market" Sharma and Bhatia examined the information contents and forecasting accuracy of implied volatility in determining future realised volatility. Their study is conducted on world's largest option index i.e., CNX Nifty Index option to test the information efficiency of Nifty Index options in Indian capital market. Ordinary least square regression and ARCH-LM model has been used to analyse the call and put implied volatility data.

In the paper titled "Determinants of working capital efficiency of Indian MSME's: An Empirical evidence." Tripathi and Chadha gathered insight into working capital management (WCM) practises and the factors that influence of its efficiency. Their paper used panel regression methodologies on 578 micro small and medium enterprises (MSME's).

In the paper titled "Financial Inclusion and Pradhan Mantri Jan Dhan Yojana : Evidence From Durg District." Tripathi et al. evaluated one of the financial inclusion policies "Pradhan Mantri Jan Dhan Yojana" announced by the Indian government. . The condition of infrastructure (such as the quantity of roadways) was shown to be the most influential factor. Other influences were employment, poverty, and geographical disparities.

In the paper titled "Comparative Analysis of the Financial Structures of Germany and Japan" Gupta made a comparative analysis of the similarities and differences in the financial structures of Germany and Japan and concluded there is a need for regulatory authorities to ensure not only effective implementation of macro-prudential regulations, but also to take active steps in response to financial innovations such as securitization and cryptocurrency so that regulatory power may not implicitly get diluted.

In the paper titled "Effects of Digitisation on Banknote Durability" Asthana et al. investigated the durability of banknotes during pre and post demonetisation period in relation to their withdrawal for circulation in order to satisfy fundamental requirements. In the paper titled "Assessing Investment Attractiveness- Developing Economies Perspective" Kaushal attempts to rank the major emerging Asian economies as potential destinations for the "plus one" country. According to their findings of the aggregate ranking methodology, India is the most appealing destination for outgoing MNCs. In the paper titled "Sustainable FDI Inflows in Emerging Economies-Indian Perspective" Kaushal aims to investigate sustainable FDI inflows in India, employing an augmented gravity framework in the panel data set. Their findings suggest that GDP, economic and social stability, EPU, good governance, and sustainable energy consumption significantly and positively attract FDI in India from the top 15 FDI origins.

In the paper titled "A Descriptive study of the role of microfinance in sustainable development and its challenges" Kalpana found that there is a positive as well as a negative role of microfinance in sustainable development and found some major challenges. The research states performance of microfinance in sustainable development brings out stability in the social, economic and environmental and challenges faced by them. In the paper titled "The impact of cryptocurrency on the growth prospect of indian economy" Rithul and Srivastava research looked at cryptocurrency platforms and discovered a slew of difficulties and roadblocks that put the financial system at risk. Their study finds that the lack of legislations has exposed the cryptocurrency market to a great deal of risk which discourages the investors. In the paper titled "Economic burden of non-communicable diseases and challenges of health insurance coverage: Insights from primary survey" Shukla and Arora examined the association between health insurance on healthcare utilization and the burden of OOPE among people with reported NCDs. The findings of the study are based on the primary data analysis collected through a web-based survey. Through descriptive and regression analyses, the study presents evidence on awareness, and decision-making process in the insurance uptake, therefore, providing a behavioral approach for policy design to expand insurance coverage.

In the paper titled "Interconnectedness between foreign portfolio investors and market returns: Evidence from asymmetric Exponential GARCH model" Usmani and Shaikh recommended that nations adopt policies that would promote long-term flows. India needs to be well-equipped to compete with the global economic powerhouses and position itself as an open, globally competitive economy as it has been asserted that foreign portfolio investments, particularly short-term flows, raise volatility.

In the paper titled "Impact of Bitcoin Price on the Energy Consumption and Further Estimating its Carbon Footprint" Sapra and Shaikh in their study found an increase in the price of bitcoin leads to an increase in the amount of energy that is consumed when mining bitcoin, which further increases the amount of carbon emissions. Their study helps to illustrate how an increase in the market-driven price of bitcoin as a crypto asset may result in a larger carbon footprint from bitcoin mining by collecting data from the Bloomberg database.

In the paper titled "Causality between defence expenditure and Economic growth in India" Vadikar and Shaikh analysed the causality between defense spending and Economic growth in India, from 1981 to 2018. The author does not find a significant long-run relationship between defense spending and economic growth, but in the short run, there is a uni-direction relationship between defense spending and economic growth.

In the paper titled "A Study on Financial Literacy amongst the Rural and Urban Area of Surat District" Gondaliya and Shah focussed on the level of financial literacy amongst people of Rural and Urban areas of Surat District using 426 samples. The result revealed that there is fair financial literacy among the household of the rural and urban areas of Surat district.

In the paper titled "Portfolio management using OPM% based dynamic allocation strategy" Sharma looked at two equity investment schemes for creating an investment portfolio. The author also examined an investment strategy based on an equal-weighted portfolio performs better than dynamic allocation based on OPM%-weighted portfolios. The result reveal that dynamic allocation strategy based upon OPM-dependent weightage to selected companies generates better returns than the equal-weighted investment strategy.

In this paper "A Brief Appraisal on Tourism Finance Corporation of India "by Kurma Sankara Rao outlines the overview, vision and mission of TFCI and provides capital for new projects through term loans, structured finance, investment banking and MSME finance

In this paper "Bibliometric Analysis of Behavioral Finance with Vos viewer: Last Twenty-Five Year" by Dinesh garg and Seema Takhurused Bibliometric analysis to compile a summary of the scientific research that has been done on behavioral finance. In this literature review, the Scopus database was utilized. Using the clusters as a starting point, we analyzed 1052 papers using the Vos viewer software to identify the research gaps and suggest new study ideas

Part-II   Evidence Based Management in Human Resources

Evidence-based human resources (HR) decision-making is the practice of making decisions supported by evidence, scientific findings, and reliable data to drive people management decisions to achieve organizational goals effectively. In the following section of this book, we present some contemporary studies on Human Resources.

The chapter "Changing Paradigms in Training Methods: A Bibliometric Review" by A. Naga Ramani and Jayashree Mahesh, used the bibliometric analysis method to understand the most relevant training techniques in this volatile, uncertain, complex, and ambiguous (VUCA) work environment. The research identifies the most effective training methods to utilize in various sectors in India.

The next chapter, "How Emotions Experienced at Home Impact Employee's Stress at Work: A study on Indian Working Professionals Working in India" by Shridhar Gokhale and Raina Chhajer, discusses the reverse spill-over effect for Indian working professionals working in India. The study restated the existence of the reverse spill-over effect, which people generally try to suppress. The authors argued that this study could help HR professionals to design positive psychological interventions to reduce perceived stress in the workplace and induce positivity.

The chapter "Unwrap the Roles of Green Human Resource Management Practices with the Mediating Role of Green Innovation" by Jyoti Kamboj and Eronimus A, attempted to establish whether green human resource management practices can foster green innovation among employees. The authors also identify the factors that mediate the relationship between green innovation and green HRM. Authors argued that green innovation and environmental strategy could improve environmental performance by adopting appropriate policies and procedures and employees' willingness to participate in sustainable activities.

In the following chapter "An integrative framework of employees' flourishing-at-work" by Meera Peethambaran, Mohammad Faraz Naim and Saurabh Sugha, presented a conceptual framework to understand the association among empowering leadership, employee work passion, and flourishing-at-work. Authors suggested that empowering leaders can encourage employee work passion, contributing to employees' well-being.

The chapter "Does Learning Enhance the Psychological Well-Being of Employees at Work? A Pilot Exploration" by Anurag Chadha and Raina Chhajer, explored the association between learning and psychological well-being. The authors inferred that learning and psychological well-being have a positive correlation. The authors argued that this study has direct implications for employees, leaders, and organizations to improve employee performance.

In the next chapter, "Effect of Human Resource Practices on Employees' Behavioral Outcome In Neyveli Lignite Corporation (NLC) India Ltd, Neyveli" by R.Ramachandran discusses the existing practices of human resource management at NLC, Neyveli, affecting employees' behavioral outcomes. The accomplishment of Neyveli Lignite Corporation (NLC) India Ltd in recent years can be attributed to the employees' work commitment.

The chapter "Dark Tetrad and Work-Life Balance: A Case Study on Married Doctoral Students" by Akash Dubey, Rajneesh Choubisa and Jerin V Philipose, validates the measurement tools of personality and work-life balance of of doctoral students in India and investigates the relationship between these two variables. The authors identified a significant influence of dark personality on the work-life balance of doctoral students.

The chapter "Academic Adjustment and Gratitude in College Students: A First-Hand Evidence from a Psychological Perspective" by Jerin V Philipose, Rajneesh Choubisa and Akash Dubey, discussed the mechanism that explains whether academic adjustment leads to the development of gratitude or vice-versa or whether there is a third explanation behind this thesis. The authors suggested that this research can help to implement meaningful interventions that can enhance academic achievement, gratitude, or both.

The next chapter, "Work Environment: A Review of Established Scales from 50 Years of Literature" by Shipra Pandey and Jayashree Mahesh, review the scales related to the work environment domain and identifies their significance in the literature. The authors suggested that the similarities and differences in scales depend on the context, industry, and research domain.

The chapter "Role Stressors and Burnout: Examining the mediating role of Rumination" by Nidhi S. Bisht and Arun Kumar Tripathy, examines whether role stressors - role ambiguity and role conflict are related to burnout for researchers and practitioners in Indian higher education institutions. The authors recognize that both job stressors were positively associated with burnout, and the faculty's tendency to ruminate mediated the relationship between job stressors and burnout.

Part-III   Evidence Based Management in Marketing

Marketing Practitioners require the support of evidence in order to make effective decision making. This evidence will help them establish the relationship between the variables. The evidence may come from the consumer survey, observation, experience of practitioners, theoretical support, review of existing literature, or from financial data. This section of this book presents various studies focusing on supporting evidence-based decision-making in marketing.

The chapter "Performance Prediction of Amazon Ad Campaigns through past Performance Data using Machine Learning" by Pratyut Sharma focuses on identifying and explaining the changes of the user-controlled variable for a given advertising campaign on its output evaluative parameters. The model proposed by the author gives a holistic approach to break down KPIs for each level of the funnel and uses Amazon Ads' calculation methods, thus calculating the expected profitability accordingly.

In the chapter "Social Media Influencer as a Winning Strategy for Influencing Purchasing Decision of Teenage Segment" by Nidhi, Preeti Thakur, and Rakesh Kumar Gupta, the authors focuses on how can companies use Social Media Influencer as a Winning Strategy for Influencing Purchasing Decision of the Teenage segment? This study provides various instances of different brands using various social media influencers on the buying decision of the teenage segment.

The chapter "Interaction Behavior of Customers in Viral Marketing: An Analysis of its Impact on Customer Opinions" by Amrit Kaur, Dr. Harmeen Soch, and Dr. Sunpreet Kaur aims at understanding the interaction behavior of customers concerning viral content and its impact on customers opinions towards content. The study's findings support that content characteristics and source credibility are the significant factors driving content virality.

The chapter "Talking the Walk: Conceptualizing Antecedents and Consequences of Greenhushing" by Dr. Anand Thakur, Kavita Singla, and Kamini Singla focuses on critically examining the role of green perceived risk (functional risk, financial risk, hedonic risk, and self-image risk), perceived consumer skepticism, fear of greenwashing, pure altruism, and environmental certification in the green hushing practice.

The chapter "A Bibliometric review of Greenwashing research by using Co-occurrence Analysis and Bibliographic Coupling" by Sakshi Goyal, Harshika Sondhi, and Praveen Goyal provides a review of the literature on Greenwashing. The study's authors used Bibliometric Analysis techniques to explore the growth of the literature in this field of study. The outcome of this study provided evidence of significant growth in studies across the globe to understand greenwashing.

The next chapter, "Marketing metrics and advertisement campaign budget: A VECM approach" by Venkat Narasimhan R, Udayan Chanda, and Yashvardhan Sharma, used multivariate time series model to investigate the effect of impulse shocks on a specific keyword and its performance. According to the model, authors observe the impact of these sudden, impulsive shocks on impressions, clicks, and conversions that define the efficiency of an advertising campaign, a short-run equilibrium among these metrics, and the evolving nature of the keyword in paid search advertisements, and forecast the metrics using the vector error correction estimates.

Next chapter, "An Analytical Study on Green Skin Care Products: Impact on Consumer Purchase Intention" by Anu Grover and Hareesh Kumar T. The study aims to assess the influence of various antecedents like health consciousness, price sensitivity, and promotional efforts on consumers' purchase intention towards green skin care cosmetics products. The result indicates a positive influence of health consciousness and price sensitivity on consumers' purchase intention towards green skin care products.

The chapter "An Analytical study on the Usage of Debit card and Credit card in Indian Economy" by Dr.Ruchi Gupta, Muskan Diwan, and Dr.W Ramana Rao is an Analytical study on the Usage of Debit cards and Credit card in the Indian Economy. In this study, authors used secondary data to find the correlation between debit cards and credit cards using mean, min, max, standard deviation, correlation, and regression. The result shows that there is a negative correlation between the usage of debit cards and credit cards.

In the chapter "Experiential Perspective and Technology Adoption of Digital Educational Ecology amid Pandemic Context" by Virendra Singh Nirban, Tanu Shukla, and Mounika Prashanthi Vavilala, the authors focused on measuring the Technology Adoption behavior of students from higher education institutions broadly divided into either rural or urban geography. he results also indicate that there are significant differences among moderating categories with respect to Accessibility, Affordability, and Tech-Entanglement of Digital Educational Ecology.

The chapter "Impact of seed type and fertilizer on pearl millet yield: A descriptive study in selected districts of Rajasthan" by Nikita Dhankar, Srikanta Routroy, and Satyendra Kr. Sharma focuses on various input factors for cultivation practices adopted in the upstream supply chain. Seed quality, fertilizer use, rainfall, temperature and farmer awareness play an important role in maximizing the pearl millet yield. The findings of the current research will be useful in developing different policies related to pearl millet and Stover yield and will be a valuable addition to the upstream pearl millet supply chain in specific.

The chapter "Adoption and Usage of the Electronic National Agriculture Market: A Literature Review" by Nirankush Dutta, Udayan Chanda, and S.R. Singh, focuses on reviews of existing literature on the adoption of the e-NAM platform across different Indian states to highlight the status of adoption and acceptance by its various stakeholders.

The next chapter, "Agro-tourism: A Literature Review", by Praveen Goyal, Saurabh Chadha, and S.R. Singh, presents a review of the literature in the field of agro-tourism. The literature for the study was collected from the Scopus database using specific keywords. Research studies published in the last 20 years were collected for the review. The study results show a significant growth in the literature in the field of agro-tourism across the globe.

The next chapter, "Performance of Farmer Producer Organisations in Rajasthan: An Empirical Assessment" by Krishna Muniyoor, Sabhya Yadav, Rajan Pandey, Satyendra Kumar Sharma, and Srikanta Routroy focuses on evaluating the financial performance of FPOs registered in Rajasthan. The analysis of this study is mainly based on the primary data collected from the registered Farmer Producer Organisations in the state of Rajasthan.

The chapter, "Greenwash Perception and Sustainable Consumer Purchase Behavior", by Bharti Ramtiyal, Paras Garg, and Gunjan Soni, examines how corporate greenwashing and stakeholders' environmental concerns affect sustainable consumer behavior. Further, this study also focuses on This study also examines Green Word of Mouth and Green Brand Loyalty as mediators of Greenwash perception and Sustainable Purchase Behavior.

Part-IV Evidence Based Management in Operations

The use of Evidence-based decision-making in the field of operations management and Information Technology can increase the effectiveness of the managerial decision-making process. Evidence-based decision-making uses unbiased information, scientific findings, and reliable evidence to make decisions in the organization's best interest while meeting customer needs. In the following section of this book, we present some of the contemporary studies made in Operations Management and Information Technology.

In the chapter "Retailer's Ordering Policy under the influence of Inflation and Dynamic Potential Market Size in a Supply Chain System" by Alok Kumar and Udayan Chanda, the authors argued that the optimal ordering policy of technology products in inventory research is significantly influenced by those parameters which are relevant and essential for a business. The authors introduced the dynamic potential market size and inflation in the light of innovation diffusion theory to develop the retailer's optimal ordering policy.

The chapter "Designing a robust Supply Chain Model for the distribution of – COVAXIN" by Ankur Roy, Imlak Sheikh, and Satyendra K Sharma discusses a robust and agile supply chain model for the distribution of COVAXIN vaccine across India and abroad. The proposed model is designed to achieve a seamless and robust supply chain model for the distribution of Covid vaccine in India in a very cost-effective way.

In the chapter "Identification and Extraction of Retailer's Expectations in the Last-Mile Delivery" by Krishna Veer Tiwari, Leela Rani and Satyendra Kumar Sharma, presented an extensive review of the literature to identify the evolution of retailer's expectations, including the role of sustainability aspect to meet the Sustainable Development Goals (SDGs) in future delivery models. The authors used keyword cluster analysis to study the main enablers of evolving trends in Last-Mile Delivery (LMD) from the standpoint of different stakeholders, such as retailers, and their respective expectations. Based on the literature review, the authors concluded that future studies on LMD should focus on a specific location-based optimization technique.

The chapter "Supply Risk Indicators to Assess Location and Environmental Risk" by Ankur Roy, Imlak Shaikh and Satyendra K Sharma, analyzed the supply risk associated with the location using a risk assessment model. Authors used Analytical Hierarchy Process based on subjective assessment, intuition, and expert statements. Based on the study, the authors observed that if there is Disease Outbreak, a supply chain will have low total risk with maximum weightage for risk due to operational contingencies and lowest weightage.

The next chapter, "An Indian approach to AI policy : A comparative study between three sectors" by Anand R Navaratnaa and Deepak Saxena, discusses India's policy approach towards Artificial Intelligence (AI) by considering three emerging sectors: Information Technology and Information Technology Enabled Services (IT&ITES), Telecommunications and Biotechnology through an evidence-based approach. Authors suggested that the 'time frame for setting up a central agency to empower an emerging domain', 'the need for a central department/ ministry or nodal agency to enable focused growth of emerging sector', and 'regulatory authority' are the three common factors that work as a catalyst for the expansion of Artificial Intelligence (AI) in the above three sectors.

The chapter "CTR Prediction: A Bibliometric Review of Scientific Literature" by Arti Jha, Yashvardhan Sharma and Udayan Chanda, reviewed scholarly literature on CTR prediction using bibliometric analysis of 1051 publications from journals indexed by Scopus. The outcome of this literature evaluation will aid future researchers in gaining a deeper comprehension of the scientific studies around CTR prediction.

The chapter "An Investigation Into Understanding Consumer Opinion About Adoption of Electric Vehicles Using Machine Learning" by Pooja, Abhishek Tripathi and Yatish Joshi, tried to comprehend consumer opinion and emotions about the adoption of electric vehicles in India. Using consumer sentiment analysis from Twitter data, the authors recognize the positive views of the customers about electric cars.

The chapter "Click-Through Rate: An Overview of Scientific Research in Management" by Venkat Narasimhan R, Udayan Chanda and Yashvardhan Sharma, examined click-through rate evolution from an empirical standpoint using the bibliometric methods, reviewing 596 articles from the Scopus index. The click-through rate is the ratio of the number of impressions to the number of clicks of an advertisement. Through this scientific review, authors identified the most influential articles, authors, and journals, serving as a baseline for future research, and mapping the topic's evolution over the last decade.

The next chapter, "Consumer's Safety Concerns on fire hazards and readiness of Electric Vehicle Batteries (EV) in India" by Vikash Joshi and Payal Phulwani, highlights the current safety concerns and describes the way forward for a much safer Electric Vehicle battery ecosystem within the country. The authors tried to identify the consumers' concerns regarding the capacity and safety of electric vehicle batteries. Authors suggested that the major causes of fire in EV batteries in India are Internal & External short circuits, overcharging, exposure to high temperature & mechanical deformation & impact.

The chapter "Policy uncertainty and Purchasing managers' index" by Imlak Shaikh, attempted to predict the Purchasing Manager's Index (PMI) of the USA, China, and Japan with the help of a neural network and regression technique. The PMI helps forecast several vital economic variables and is used widely to indicate various economic trends. The author found that the regression technique gave better results than the neural network technique due to the availability of fewer data points.

The chapter "Food Waste Management in BITS Pilani" by Ujjwal Aggarwal and Arkya Aditya, investigates the food waste management system and its implementation at Birla Institute of Science and Technology (BITS) in Pilani, Rajasthan, a renowned engineering college in India. The authors analyzed the problem from the viewpoints of managers, staff, and workers in messes and eateries on the issue of food waste management. They provided insight into the institute's current food waste management practices.

The chapter "Assessment of EVs adoption in India using AHP-BWM approach" by Sudhanshu Ranjan Singh, Abhijeet K. Digalwar, and Srikanta Routroy , explored the catalyze of electric vehicles (EVs) adoption in India. The authors investigated the crucial factors of EV adoption. They validated them using hybrid multi-criteria decision-making methods, including the best-worst method (BWM) and the analytic hierarchy process (AHP).

The next chapter, "Identification and Analysis of Health Parameters for the Development of a Mobile app and Sensor Based Wearable Health Band" by Mayuri Digalwar, Abhijeet Digalwar, Dinesh Tundalwar, and Rashmi Pandhare, discusses the design and development of an integrated mobile app and sensor-based wearable device that can identify and analyze the health parameters in a community during and post Covid scenario. The study's findings show an immense need for designing and developing an interactive mobile app and sensor-based wearable device to help people overcome their health-related problems.

The next chapter, "Risk Propagation Modelling for Agri-Food Supply Chain: An Indian perspective" by Khalid Hussain Ansari, Shailender Singh, Srikanta Routroy, and Krishna Muniyoor, identified the to create a tool for assessing and determining the risk exposure to AFSC in India risk factors. The risk network proposed in this chapter demonstrates the basic framework of associated risk factors in AFSC in India.

The following chapter, "Impact of External Risk Factors on Indian Road Construction Supply Chain Performance" by Anubhav Tiwari, Shailender Singh, Srikanta Routroy and Prasanta K. Sahu, examined the impact of external risk on the performance of construction supply chain management for Indian road projects. Based on this study, the authors concluded that project management risk significantly impacts the Indian road construction project.

The chapter "Analysis of impetus for formal E-waste management system in India" by Varun Kumar, Om Ji Shukla and Saurabh Tripathi, attempts to identify the causes and the contributing factors for the formal E-waste management system in developing countries. The authors argued that this study's outcome can help e-waste collection policymakers and efficient e-waste management systems in a developing nation.

The chapter "Long term Business Planning to mitigate ill-effects of Natural Calamities" by Rajkumar Sharma and Satyendra Kumar Sharma, examined the impact of natural calamities on small-scale businesses in big cities. The authors suggested that the frameworks discussed in this chapter can help eliminate risk from natural calamities to MSMEs.

The next chapter "Analyzing the Impact of Agri Supply Chain Management Strategies on Farmers' Incomes" by C V Sunil Kumar and M L N Rao , analyzes how the agricultural supply chains (ASCs) processes can boost the farmers' income to reduce this gap and better meet the needs of the end customers. According to the authors, farmers' incomes can rise in tandem with their efforts to meet the demands of consumers by providing high-quality produce.

Part-V   Evidence Based Management in Strategy and Entrepreneurship

The chapter "Winner-Take-All Strategy in Digital Platform Market: A Theoretical Exposition" focuses on the findings from literature and real-life cases that show a shift in the platform market dynamics such that winner-take-all is no longer the standard in digital platform markets. To achieve the objective of this paper existing research papers on digital platforms from the field of strategic management and case studies from Harvard Business Review, Fortune, and Business Week were referred. The present study will help managers to employ significantly different strategies than those that were successful in the past.

The chapter "Business Networks and Strategic Orientation help firms navigate the Dynamic nature of business, leading to Product Innovation" examines the effect of business networks and strategic orientation on a firm's ability to handle the highly vulnerable and changing environment by developing dynamic capabilities like upcoming technologies, flexible strategies, and strategic partnerships, which leads to Product Innovation. The hypotheses are tested using Covariance-based structural equation modeling. The study surveyed 270 respondents working in the manufacturing and service sectors.

The chapter "Sustainability Practices: A case study of State Bank of India" presents the case of the State Bank of India (SBI) to identify and differentiate various sustainability practices of SBI for the year 2020-21on the basis of Global Reporting Initiatives (GRI) and Business Responsibility Reporting (BRR). It aims to fill the gap in the literature by comparing GRI standards with BRR principles. The data has been collected from the sustainability report and annual report with the help of content analysis. To quantify the results of content analysis, four points scale has been framed ranging from "No Evidence" to "Full Compliance of Standard".

The chapter "Value Appropriation in Inter-firm Coopetitive Alliances: Case of the Indian Pharmaceutical Industry" is a qualitative study, intending to inform research about configurations of value appropriation by identifying the determinants of value appropriation in interfirm coopetitive alliances. The study proposes a framework based on determinants influencing value appropriation in coopetitive interfirm alliances in the IPI. Overall, the results provide unique insights into how pharmaceutical firms in a coopetitive dyadic alliance perceive value appropriation, and how different factors influence value appropriation and guide managers on what factors or mechanisms can help in appropriating value in a coopetitive alliance.

The chapter "DIVA'S of Enterprise: A study of Constraining Factors Affecting Women Entrepreneurs in India" aims is to study the challenges and barriers faced by women entrepreneurs in India while setting up their businesses. For this study, an exploratory research methodology has been adopted wherein a literature review of 125 research articles was done and ten themes (challenges and barriers) faced by women entrepreneurs were found. This paper will help women entrepreneurs to know the issues they can face and accordingly prepare themselves to solve those problems.

The chapter "Bibliographic Analysis and Strategic Management Research in India" examines the existing literature regarding strategic management research in India based on the bibliometric approach used as a means of supplementing the subjective evaluation of bibliographic literature reviews. A total of 245 research publications were extracted from the Scopus database and bibliometric techniques using the Vows viewer, which includes sources, authors, organizations, keywords, and citation analysis.

The chapter "Enabling sustainable entrepreneurial intentions through the fintech ecosystem and entrepreneurship education ecosystem: Does sustainable orientation matter?" addresses and attempts to bridge the gap in the literature by providing a roadmap to a sustainable entrepreneurial career. This paper adopts the lens of knowledge spillover theory and empirically investigates how ecosystem actors of the fintech industry (blockchain, venture funding, crowdfunding) impact the entrepreneurship education ecosystem (EEEs) determinants (institutional settings, curriculum structure, incubators) to influence youth's sustainable intention to pursue an entrepreneurial career path.

The chapter "Opinion of Students Pursuing Higher Education on Online Learning During COVID-19 Pandemic: Review of Literature and a Sample Survey" tried to know the students' perceptions of online learning by reviewing the literature of research done by different researchers. The chosen research papers for review examined the pros, cons, and overall effectiveness of online education in various institutions.

The chapter "Exploring a mediating role of Entrepreneurial Passion between Individual Entrepreneurial Orientation and Social Entrepreneurship linkage: A Conceptual Framework" analyses the connections between Individual Entrepreneurial Orientation (IEO) and Social Entrepreneurial Intention (SEI) and presents a theoretical framework to fill this gap by utilizing the conceptual viewpoints of Indian university students.

The chapter "Evidential insights: factors affecting higher education readiness" introduces a framework of Higher Education Readiness with the conceptualization of skills that can foster STEM learning in the transitioning young population of India. It aims to investigate the differences in the readiness ability along the demographic lines of gender and spatial reference by using the Higher Education Readiness test. Data from the district with a high literacy rate was collected to address the objectives of the study. The findings of the study would help in the transformation of educational management towards vocationalisation and increasing productivity levels in the learning individual.

The chapter "Choice of Expansion modes: A Capabilities Perspective" focuses on the choice of expansion modes of a firm. This paper argues that the choice of expansion mode of firms is based on the firm's present level of capabilities and the level of capabilities required to address its future market opportunities. The paper also presents a framework is that links a firm's expansion mode to its capability creation process.

The chapter "ESG Disclosures and Firm Performances – Evidence from India Inc." examines whether the Environmental, Social and Governance (ESG) performance (proxied by ESG and governance score), a supposed contributor to shareholder wealth creation, is leading to the better financial performance of the firms in an emerging market like India. With help of the Governance and ESG Scores of the BSE 500 constituent companies in India and employing a panel regression model, the study attempts to test its two research hypotheses.

Handbook of Evidence Based Management Practices in Business – Satyendra Kumar Sharma et al. (eds)
© 2023 Taylor & Francis Group, London, ISBN 978-1-032-54216-4

Foreword

The Birla Institute of Technology & Science, BITS Pilani, is an all-India Institute for higher education. The primary motive of BITS is to "train young men and women able and eager to create and put into action such ideas, methods, techniques, and information." The institute is a dream come true of its founder late Mr. G.D. Birla - an eminent industrialist, a participant in the Indian freedom struggle, and a close associate of the Father of the Indian Nation, late Mr. Mohandas Karamchand Gandhi (Mahatma Gandhi). What started in the early 1900s as a small school blossomed into a set of colleges for higher education, ranging from the Humanities to Engineering, until 1964, when all these colleges amalgamated to culminate into a unique Indian University of International standing. This university was christened as the Birla Institute of Technology and Science, Pilani, known to many as BITS, Pilani.

Over the years, BITS has provided the highest quality technical education to students from all over India admitted based on merit. Its graduates may be found worldwide in all areas of engineering, science, and commerce. BITS symbolizes the maturing of Indian technical ability and "can-do" entrepreneurial spirit, especially as derived from the private sector. BITS has five campuses located at Pilani, Dubai, Goa, Hyderabad and Mumbai.

BITS mission is to advance knowledge and educate students in science, technology, and other areas of scholarship that will best serve the nation and the world in the 21st century. The institute is committed to generating, disseminating, and preserving knowledge and working with others to bring this knowledge to bear on the world's great challenges. BITS is dedicated to providing its students with an education that combines rigorous academic study and the excitement of discovery with the support and intellectual stimulation of a diverse campus community. We seek to develop in each member of the BITS community the ability and passion to work wisely, creatively, and effectively for the betterment of humankind.

The Management group at BITS, Pilani, was established in 1971. It initially offered the two-year Master of Business Administration (MBA) programme but later in 1973, when the institute created an integrated educational structure, MBA evolved into the integrated first-degree programme MMS- Master of Management Studies, which is a blend of engineering and management. This programme was successfully offered for a time period of three decades. Based on the industrial demands, the course was restructured as MBA in the year 2006. The Management programme in BITS was ranked by Asia week as one of the Top 30 Best Full-Time MBAs. The programme has also been profiled by Business Week Online (the Best B Schools). The latest survey done by Outlook India for 2018 ranks the Department of Management, BITS Pilani, in the top 10 Private B-Schools of India.

Catering to contemporary industry demands, BITS Pilani, introduced an MBA in Business Analytics in 2021-22. Over the years, BITS Pilani has stressed the importance of experience as a part of the education process by ensuring that its programs interface strongly with industry and provide opportunities for students to engage in independent experiential learning. The MBA in Business Analytics curriculum is an optimum combination of core, electives, and industrial components/research in the form of Practice School/dissertation. The pedagogy ensures that at least 50% of the sessions are devoted to cases/projects /simulations/laboratories / other experiential components.

BITS Pilani is consistently ranked within the top 30 over-all among educational institutes in India as per NIRF. Management education in BITS Pilani is ranked within the top 500 globally by QS (2021)

The book is a collection of selected high-quality research papers presented at the 4th International Conference on Evidence-Based Management (ICEBM) 2023, held at Birla Institute of Technology & Science, Pilani, Rajasthan, India, during February 24–25, 2023. It has 76 chapters written by various scholars focusing on evidence-based management practices in different functional areas of management with the application of theory and empirical techniques. I am sure that the outcomes of the studies presented in this book will be helpful to practitioners, academicians, scholars, and policymakers.

Thanks to all researchers for their excellent research contributions, and congratulations to the conference organizing team for their efforts in bringing out this edited book in time. Thanks to CRC press for publishing this edited book and being part of the successful organization of the conference.

February 2023

Pilani

Sudhirkumar Barai, PhD

Director, BITS Pilani, Pilani Campus

About the Editors

Satyendra Kumar Sharma

Dr. Satyendra Kumar Sharma is BE, MBA from MNIT Jaipur and PhD from BITS Pilani. Dr. Sharma carried out his Phd research on Supply chain risk management. He has more than 2 years of experience in industry and 14 years in academics. Currently he is working as a Associate Professor in Department of Management. He has served as Nucleus member of planning cell in Practice school division, BITS Pilani. Currently he is also heading Center for Innovation, Incubation and Entrepreneurship (CIIE). His research interest areas are Supply Chain Risk Management, Project Risk Management and Multicriteria Modelling. He has successfully completed two sponsored R & D Projects. He has published more than 50 papers in international journals of repute, and more than 22 papers in international conferences and four Case studies. He has guest edited tow special issues of Emerald Publishing. He has conducted several MDP's. He is a member of professional bodies like Society of operations and production management and AIMS international.

Praveen Goyal

Dr Praveen Goyal is an Associate Professor at the Department of Management, Birla Institute of Technology & Science (BITS), Pilani. He holds a PhD from the Department of Management Studies, Indian Institute of Technology (IIT), Roorkee. He has published various papers in the area of CSR, Corporate Sustainability and Consumer Behavior in the journals of international repute most of which are ranked and indexed by Australian Business Deans Council (ABDC), Scopus and Social Science Citation Index (Clarivate Analytics) like Management Decision; Journal of Non-profit and Public Sector Marketing; Benchmarking: An International Journal; Journal of Business & Industrial Marketing; Sustainable Production and Consumption, etc

Udayan Chanda

Udayan Chanda is currently working as an Associate Professor in the Department of Management, Birla Institute of Technology & Science, Pilani. Earlier, he was associated with the Industrial Statistics Lab., Department of Information & Industrial Engineering, Yonsei University, as a Post Doctoral Fellow and Department of Operational Research, University of Delhi, as an Assistant Professor. He received his Ph.D. in Marketing Models and Optimization from the University of Delhi. He has published numerous research articles on Marketing Models, Optimization, Software Reliability, and Inventory Management in international journals of repute.

PART I

EVIDENCE BASED FINANCIAL MANAGEMENT

Handbook of Evidence Based Management Practices in Business – Satyendra Kumar Sharma et al. (eds)
© 2023 Taylor & Francis Group, London, ISBN 978-1-032-54216-4

Chapter

Insurance Buying Motives for Sustainable Financial Goals

Vijaykumar Dhannur[1]
Assistant Professor, Dept. of Management Studies,
Visvesvaraya Technological University, Belgaum, Karnataka

Shubham Mohan Kusane*
Full Time Research Scholar, Dept. of Management Studies,
Visvesvaraya Technological University, Belgaum, Karnataka

ABSTRACT: Although Covid-19 pandemic has been an awakening force towards eminence of life insurance policies and with insurance penetration in India has witnessed momentum increase. This leads to us to a critical question, that is are we all rational while buying life insurance policy? The current prevailing literature insists irrationality among policy buyers. This study aims to understand the influence of emotional buying motives of life insurance policies. For this study primary data is collected using a structured questionnaire with Cronbach's alpha of 0.803. Factor Analysis and Structural Equation Modeling have been utilized to study the relationship among the variables. This study also illustrates the significance of buying insurance at early age for higher life cover at lower premium. The results suggests that consumers act irrational and buy polices due to emotional motives resembling commitments, trust, friendships and other factors. In rational motives tax savings play a significant role. Individual tend to prefer LIC's policy over other competitor.

KEYWORDS: Buying motives, Emotional buying, Life insurance policy and decision making

1. Introduction

Over the last 40 years, life insurance has grown in importance as a component of the financial industry, offering a variety of financial services to clients and becoming a significant source

---

*Corresponding Author: kusaneshubham1@gmail.com
[1]vijaykumar.d@vtu.ac.in

DOI: 10.4324/9781003415725-1

of capital market investment (Thorsten Beck, 2003).Having acknowledged the facts life insurances primarily can help foresee the adverse risk arising due premature death of bread earner and disrupts the family's financial planning. Insurance companies often use emotional appeal in advertisements to tap in people to buy policy's (WARC, 2018). Years ago our policy agents would list down our identical career milestones such as retirement planning, children's education and marriage expenses, live cover and the added tax benefits under section 80C. Despite the fact that insurance brands must address product features and relevance, producing optimistic emotion is what will make the most difference, especially in a highly illogical market. However, as they get older, their acquired fortune may be enough to cover their basic requirements, and they are less likely to have dependents to cater for (Gianni Brighetti C. L., 2014). Even though life insurance policy provides enormous opportunities and benefits to the policy holder, according to the recent statistics of 2021 only three percent of the Indian population have life cover (Statista.com, 2022).With the prospective of making risky or probabilistic decisions making similar to buying a life insurance policy it is often seen than people deviate from rationality and act to be irrational. Covid-19 Pandemic might have been an eye opener for the people as the deadly virus claimed around 5.28L lives and in several cases those were single bread winners for their families. The fear of the deadly virus and the uncertainty will surely be a crucial factor in growth of term life insurance in years to come. Covid-19 has managed to a miracle which advertisements of life insurers have failed in previous decades by bringing the life insurance penetration rate equally to the global standards of 3.2% in the year 2020 from prevailing 2.82% in 2019 (Kumar, 2022). According to a recent consumer survey from TATA AIA Life insurance which claims that consumers have started to appreciate insurance as a financial security (Dhanorkar, 2021).

1.1 Life Insurance as Investment?

As we discuss about investment, the commonly preferred investment avenues are FDs, Gold, Real Estate, SIP and Equity. For generations insurance has been viewed as an instrument that could save our loved once in case of any unfortunate event that might occur to the insured or person. However, life insurance are not limited to only this core effort. Different policies like Endowment, ULIPs, and Money back policy's offer a wide range of benefits with promising returns with endowment(ICICI, 2020).(Parrish, 2019) In an interview with Forbes tells how insurance is an investment and how he has been reaping benefits of insurance at later phase of life. Life insurance can act as a great investment and can help one in estate planning, retirement planning and tax planning. Proper insurance mapping can lead to a smart investment by providing crucial benefits like peace of mind, habit of disciplined investment, tax benefits, a supplement to retirement benefits, dealing financial liabilities and achieve long term financial goal. Thus while planning for personal finance insurance can play a critical and major role. It can also play a bigger role than just a risk protection plan(Groww, 2022). The question remains if insurance has so much to offer what stops Indians from buying one?

The metamorphosis between the awareness and ownership is a marginally high, for instance 59% of the respondents had awareness about the term life insurance however only 28% of the respondents poses the ownership of term life insurance. This disparity in the figures shows exactly how underrated life insurance policy is among the consumers in India. Few of the reasons why Indians avoid buying insurance policies are, lack of foreseeing and understanding the risk, lack of proper knowledge towards the policies, procrastination and company cover (HDFClife, 2021). Problems involving the purchase of insurance coverage appear to be an intriguing and possibly lucrative subject for the application and testing of risk bearing theories (Mossin, 1968). Growing studies in behavioralfinance depicts how biases effecting the decision making similar study by (Anek Belbase, 2015) reveal majority of purchases of life insurances happen because of life events like having a child or getting married. Also, determining the right cover remains a tricky part so they end up buying based on the fair premium prices. In a study to understand(Gianni Brighetti C. L., 2014)the psychological variables on the demand for the life insurance policies show positive traits of emotions on the possible insurance demand. In some cases, the entire set of behavioral variables greatly increases socioeconomic information; in others (health and indemnity insurance), it does not significantly increase the predictive potential of models. (Palmer, 1984) Foreseen the significance of driving factors behind households buying the insurance policies. Lack of brand loyalty among the insurance players creates a growth opportunities and healthy competition among the players. Product Quality and Brand Image has been a crucial factors to determine purchase decision (Singh, 2012). The Future of Insurance is based on our understanding of consumer and corporate behavior to provide solutions to both narrow and large problems. What information could be offered to assist consumers in deciding what forms of coverage to consider purchasing? What methods may insurance companies take to continue offering coverage at reasonable premiums even after huge losses? How should capital markets be designed so that insurance companies can provide coverage for the largest possible range of events while charging premiums that both investors and consumers find appealing?(Howard C. Kunreuther, 2013). According to a report by (Deloitte, 2015) ownership of policies are hugely and positively linked with the life events, in a survey it was concluded that married, retired and parents show positive signals compared to unmarried individuals. However (Chugh, 2019) decodes the modern day generation and enlists various reasons so as to why the younger generations are different than the previous as they look at insurance as an instrument to fulfill their career and financial goals and not simply for protection.

Demand for life insurance are also driven by demographics variables, significant level of savings and financial literacy among the people was considered to be irrelevant in defining the demand for the insurance (Victorian, 2013). Financial literacy also plays a pivotal role in financial planning and wealth accumulation. There lays a direct and substantial relationship between literacy and retirement planning through sound financial decision (ANNAMARIA LUSARDI, 2010).Multiple factors impact sound decision making among households buying life insurances, the refraining factors include lack of awareness, savings, risk perceptions and procrastination (Muhammad Mehedi Masud, 2020). To choose or not to choose an insurance policy was examined in terms of financial resources over time. (Gabriela-Mihaela MUREŞAN, 2016). Several arithmeticmodelling in particular justify that to maximize profits from the life insurance business, insurance companies should gradually increase the loading factor from single to double (Ye, 2007). (Schlesinger, 2014) Illustrates the importance of developing a behavioral grasp of the underlying decision processes before developing policy recommendations based on genetic information. Households with higher loss aversion, many children, substantially higher income but smaller loadings demand more life insurance. Also the relationship between age, mortality and wealth is unjustified (Wang, 2019). Households with children and commitment level are more likely to be found with the ownership of life insurance policies, thus showing rational motives overridden by emotional motives (Sauter, 2014). One should have the awareness of a sustainable insurance coverage one should have derived based on the annual income, claim settlement ratio, premium term and other important factors (Menon, 2017).

Table 1.1 Impact of age factor on insurance premium

Policy	Life Cover	Premium when Age is below 25	Premium when is between 25 to 30	Premium when age is Above 30
Exide Life	1 Cr	12,542	13,199	15,754
Kotak Life	1Cr	10,620	11,210	13,216
HDFC Life	Basic: 30 Lac With additional benefits: 1Cr	11,336	11,766	13,410

Source: Data derived from Policybazar.com

From the above Table 1.1 shows how the policy premium increases in the three time segment i.e, below twenty five, twenty five to thirty and thirty & above. A twenty five percent rise in the cost of premium does justify why insurance is the first ever investment one should make. However, awareness and literacy about insurance and its benefits at early stages of career has to be inculcated among the younger generations.

2. Research Methodology

2.1 Literature Gap

The current literature persists with regards to the perception and awareness towards the life insurance and health insurance policies. This paper attempts to determine the study the influence of emotional and rational motives while considering and buying polices. Factor Analysis and structural model has been utilized to construct relationship among latent and observed variables to derive out conclusion

Objectives:

1. To study the impact of emotions on insurance buying motives.
2. To determine factors influencing life insurance buying decisions.
3. To observe irrationality in decision making.

Sources: The study relies on primary source of data collected using questionnaire.

Cronbach's alpha: is measured at 0.803.

Sampling Design: convenience sampling

Statistical Tools: SPSS, SPSS Amos and Excel.

Sample Size: 168 respondents

3. Empirical Results

Head starting with some descriptive statistics from the survey, 68% respondents were male and 32% were female, only 43.1% of the population have life insurance ownership, out of those who enjoys ownership only 26% of the respondents follow the thumb rule of life cover (i.e., the total life cover is over 10-15% of their annual salary). Roughly 29% of the respondent aged 18-30 have ownership of life insurance policy.

Table 1.2 Factor analysis demonstrating reasons for buying policy

Sl. No	Factors	Rotation I	Rotation II
1	To save for future needs like children's education & retirement.	.292	.866
2	To save some amount regularly so that I don't spent it all	.131	.795
3	It helps to secure the future of my family in case of death.	.686	.206
4	To save income tax	.582	.302
5	Life insurance purchase was needed in order to get some loans/ services from the bank.	.768	.214
6	Knowing the life insurance agent socially, I felt a social obligation to invest in an insurance policy.	.805	

Source: Author's compilation

From the Table 1.2 the major factor that influences buying decision is because of social obligation as for decades the policies are offered by friends and families. The second factors that adds up to is that respondents consider buying life insurances to secure the future needs like retirement and children's education. The influence of agents pushing to buy policy has also seen to be a crucial factor. Over many years this has been sole reasons why people actually buy insurance because they perceive knowing the agents personally puts then in a moral obligation to purchase from them. To reassure the above results structural equation model is created to analyze the factors determining rational and emotional buying motives. The above aspects of the questionnaire were designed based on the research of (Giri, 2018) and data was collected and analyzed thereafter.

The constructs from the model (Fig. 1.1) show positive constructs among latent and observed variables. Knowing insurance agents adds to the social and emotional variables as the estimates are dominant, pandemic fear also remains among the most contributing factors while buying and creating demand for policies. Another crucial factor are commitments like marriage, children etc. Among the rational appeal tax savings, children's education and securing futures for the family adds up to the buying motives (refer Table 1.3). All the factors considered for the study have shown positive influence on insurance buying motives. Thus it is fair to conclude that the buyers act irrationally while buying insurance policies.

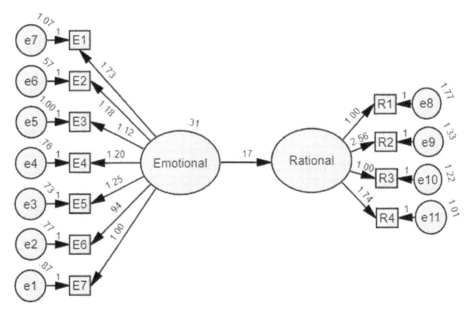

Fig. 1.1   Structural model depicting emotional and rational motive

Source: Author's compilation

Table 1.3   Regression weights: (group number 1 - default model)

			Estimate	S.E.	C.R.	P Label
Rational	<---	Emotional	.174	.206	.841	.400
Commitments	<---	Emotional	1.000			
Emotional buying	<---	Emotional	.943	.195	4.837	***
Death	<---	Emotional	1.251	.229	5.467	***
Pandemic Fear	<---	Emotional	1.199	.224	5.347	***
Emotional Ads	<---	Emotional	1.123	.228	4.930	***
Trust	<---	Emotional	1.178	.211	5.568	***
Friends and Relatives	<---	Emotional	1.731	.305	5.673	***
Children's Education & Retirement	<---	Rational	1.000			
Tax Saving	<---	Rational	2.556	3.183	.803	.422
Savings	<---	Rational	.995	1.529	.651	.515
Secure future in case of Death	<---	Rational	1.738	2.235	.778	.437

Source: Author's compilation

3. Conclusions

This study investigates the emphasis of buying motives with reference to life insurance products, the results of the study thus show traces of deviation from rationality and act irrational especially when insurance buying is prospected. These are the following derived conclusion from the study firstly lack of awareness among the younger generations towards buying insurances at early stages of life and career is prominent, and provides a scope for improvement and further research. Secondly consumer believe personally having a relationship with the policy agent puts them in a social obligation to consider buying a life insurance, and they are more likely to buy policies if being offered by their friends or family members. Even though the insurance penetration is matching up to the global mark due to the fear stigma of covid-19 pandemic, the role of Life Corporation of India (LIC) and Insurance Regulatory and Development Authority (IRDA) would remain crucial in decades to come as respondents happen to trust LIC over other insurance providers. Insurance companies have to move from emotional appeal of advertisements to rational appeal and create awareness towards how to actually compare and select best coverage for their loved ones without overburdening the consumer's pocket with hefty premium amounts. It can easily be claimed that life insurance market in India is decently dependent on emotional beliefs, commitments like marriages, birth of children and less towards achieving a sustainable retirement and financial goals arising out of duly sketched out financial plans. Off course Life Insurance and General Insurance would thus remain hot research areas for decades to come, limitation of this particular study is that it prevails largely towards life insurance and avoids other forms of insurance which gives further scope for researchers to explore up on.

REFERENCES

1. Anek Belbase, N. B. (2015). Overcoming Barriers to Life Insurance Coverage: A Behavioral Approach. *Center for Retirement Research at Boston College*.
2. Annamaria Lusardi, O. S. (2010). Financial Literacy among the Young. *The Journal of Consumer Affairs*.
3. Chugh, T. (2019, December 30). *Brands*. Retrieved from Business Insider: https://www.businessinsider.in/advertising/brands/article/how-consumer-behavior-has-evolved-in-the-life-insurance-sector/articleshow/73031056.cms
4. Deloitte. (2015). *Life insurance consumer purchase behavior.* UK: Deloitte Touche Tohmatsu Limited.
5. Dhanorkar, S. (2021, April 06). *Life Insurance*. Retrieved from Economic Times: https://economictimes.indiatimes.com/wealth/insure/life-insurance/10-common-mistakes-people-commit-when-buying-life-insurance-and-how-to-avoid-them/articleshow/81883327.cms
6. Gabriela-Mihaela MUREŞAN, G. A. (2016). Trust – The Intangible Asset of Policyholder Behavior on Insurance Market. *Scientific Annals of Economics and Business*, 125–136.
7. Gianni Brighetti, C. L. (2014). Do emotions affect insurance demand? *Review of Behavioral Finance*, 136–154.
8. Gianni Brighetti, C. L. (2014). Do emotions affect insurance demand? *Review of Behavioral Finance*, 136–154.

9. Giri, M. (2018). *A Behavioral Study of Life Insurance Purchase.* Indian Institute of Technology Kanpur.

10. Groww. (2022, March 17). *Personal Finance* . Retrieved from Groww.in: https://groww.in/blog/how-smart-an-investment-is-life-insurance

11. HDFClife. (2021, August 04). *Insurance Basics.* Retrieved from HDFClife.com: https://www.hdfclife.com/insurance-knowledge-centre/about-life-insurance/reasons-why-people-dont-buy-life-insurance-in-india

12. Howard C. Kunreuther, M. V. (2013). Insurance and Behavioral Economics: Improving Decisions in the Most Misunderstood Industry. *Cambridge University Press.*

13. ICICI. (2020, Dec). *Life Insurance.* Retrieved from ICICIprulife: https://www.iciciprulife.com/life-insurance/life-insurance-investment.html

14. Kumar, N. (2022, January 31). *Personal Finance* . Retrieved from Economic Times: https://economictimes.indiatimes.com/wealth/personal-finance-news/covid-brings-life-insurance-penetration-in-india-to-global-levels/articleshow/89243583.cms

15. Menon, P. (2017, December 29). Retrieved from News18.com: https://www.news18.com/news/india/5-things-to-consider-when-buying-an-insurance-policy-1617765.html

16. Mossin, J. (1968). Aspects of Rational Insurance Purchasing. *Journal of Political Economy*, 553–568.

17. Muhammad Mehedi Masud, N. A. (2020). A conceptual framework for purchase intention of sustainable life insurance: a comprehensive review. *Int. J. Innovation and Sustainable Development.*

18. Palmer, J. J. (1984). Examining Life Insurance Ownership through Demographic and Psychographic Characteristics. *The Journal of Risk and Insurance*, 453–467.

19. Parrish, S. (2019, Jul 9). *Retirement.* Retrieved from Forbes: https://www.forbes.com/sites/steveparrish/2019/07/09/is-life-insurance-an-investment/?sh=3dafd8f432b4

20. Sauter, N. (2014). Bequest Motives and the Demand for Life Insurance in East Germany. *German Economic Review*, 272–286.

21. Schlesinger, A. R. (2014). Behavioral insurance: Theory and experiments. *Journal of Risk and Uncertaint*, 85–96.

22. Singh, D. D. (2012). Demographic Analysis of Factors Influencing Purchase of Life Insurance Products in India. *European Journal of Business and Management.*

23. Statista.com. (2022, July 21). *Insurance.* Retrieved from Statista.com: https://www.statista.com/statistics/655395/life-and-non-life-insurance-penetration-india/#:~:text=In%20financial%20year%202021%2C%20India's,over%20four%20percent%20in%202021.

24. Thorsten Beck, I. W. (2003). Economic, Demographic, and Institutional Determinants of Life Insurance Consumption across Countries. *the world bank economic review*, 51–88.

25. Victorian, N. S. (2013). The Determinants of Life Insurance Demand: A Focus on Saving Motives and Financial Literacy. *Asian Social Science*, 274.

26. Wang, N. (2019). The demand for life insurance in a heterogeneous-agent life cycle economy with joint decisions. *The Geneva Risk and Insurance Review*, 176–206.

27. WARC. (2018, December 19). *MetLife taps power of emotional ads.* Retrieved from WARC.com: https://www.warc.com/newsandopinion/news/metlife-taps-power-of-emotional-ads/41479

28. Ye, S. R. (2007). Optimal life insurance purchase and consumption/investment under uncertain lifetime. *Journal of Banking & Finance*, 1307–1319.

Handbook of Evidence Based Management Practices in Business – Satyendra Kumar Sharma et al. (eds)
© 2023 Taylor & Francis Group, London, ISBN 978-1-032-54216-4

Chapter

Fintech Payments as a Facilitator of Value Co-Creation—A Theoretical Framework

Saumya Singh[1]
Professor, Department of Management Studies,
IIT ISM Dhanbad, Dhanbad, India

Antora Dutta[2]
Department of Management Studies,
IIT ISM Dhanbad, Dhanbad, India

ABSTRACT: Fintech payments as a facilitator of value co-creation- a theoretical framework. The purpose of the study is to explore how the service-dominant logic (S-D logic) (Karpen, Bove and Lukas, 2012) can be extended to fintech payment services to assist create value for both users and organizations. This study takes the perspective of S-D logic by perceiving fintech payment modes as a technological application by which both users and organizations incorporate their operant and operand revenues to accomplish payment activities and thereby generate enticing value. The study develops a theoretical framework to describe this value co-creation process (Lacoste, 2016) by integrating task-technology fit as a mediator between the vendor's resources and the value established, and expectancy-value theory as a mediator between the user's resources and value established. A co-creation of value between users and vendors may be feasible with the help of this approach. S-D logic and the existing theories have been paired in very few studies to analyse the fintech payment usage behaviour. Therefore the foremost finding of this study is the conceptual framework that is developed. By adopting such a model, the fintech payment value chain can thrive as a type of ecosystem with shared institutional mechanisms and collaborative value generation via customer service experience. This will help to broaden the value chain's scope in future research by fully integrating it into the value chain.

KEYWORDS: S-D logic, Fintech payments, Value co-creation, Customer service, Cashless payment

[1]saumya@iitism.ac.in, [2]antora.20dp0172@ms.iitism.ac.in

DOI: 10.4324/9781003415725-2

1. Introduction

(FSB 2017) defined Fintech as "digitally enabled financial innovation that may result in new business models, applications, processes or products with a tremendous influence on financial markets and systems along with the provision of the financial sector." According to the principle of S-D logic, fintech technology can function as both operand and operant resources, yielding benefits for users and service providers. Value is primarily recognized by merchants as profits from transactions and the expected business value rests on the users' preferred mode of fintech payment (Lim et al., 2019). For consumers, value is something that users experience rather than something inherent in the products/services they use (Gil, Berenguer, and Cervera 2008).

The primary users of fintech technology who define the benefits of stakeholders for co-creation in the value chain are users and merchants. According to S-D logic, all actors interact with each other by participating in mutual service-for-service interactions with additional and complementary resources (Akaka, Vargo, and Lusch 2013). However, there is little evidence from prior studies to investigate how fintech payments encourage users and service providers to co-create value.

Therefore the purpose of this study is to address this gap by exploring how fintech payments may contribute to mutually creating value for users and service providers. This study adopts S-D logic by interpreting fintech payments as a potential application by which users and service providers merge their operand and operant resources to accomplish the transactions and thereby co-create value.

2. Service-Dominant Logic (S-D Logic) and Value Co-Creation

S-D logic posits interaction and cohesiveness between the service provider and user wherein they collaborate to manage resources for the creation of mutual value and is based on an actor-to-actor orientation (Laud et al. 2015). According to S-D logic, value can be speculated during the usage process and is based on the functional perspective of the product rather than its production phase (Woodruff and Flint 2014). It is revealed that the value co-creative concept with the customers' point of view is validated by S-D logic (Goi, Kalidas, and Yunus 2022). Consumers and vendors can function together to co-create value by using their professional knowledge and expertise to contribute significantly to the conception, manufacturing and delivery of tailor-made solutions as well as through knowledge transfer and integrated production (Torfing, Sørensen, and Røiseland 2019). It endorses a customer-oriented approach as opposed to a production approach which indicates that users are co-creators of value and utilise operand and operant resources to provide 'service'(Merz, He, and Vargo 2009). Technology can be described as an operant resource in S-D logic that enables sharing of information both within and between the service infrastructure (Lai, Jackson, and Jiang 2017). Businesses and service providers can integrate knowledge assets in conjunction with app services to co-create value. Technology serves two roles: one as an operand resource that requires some action to be done to be valuable and the other as an operant resource that may be utilised to act on other resources (Weiß et al. 2018).

3. Fintech Payment Value Chain

Fintech is a digital financial innovation that provides innovative products, processes and business strategies that may have an impact on how financial services are provided, how the financial sector develops, and how market competition and service reputation are fostered (Zhao, Tsai, and Wang 2019; Chandler and Krajcsák 2021). The recent boom in the fintech sector has made it possible to high quality, user-friendly and secure online banking services (Bhat, AlQahtani, and Nekovee 2022). In recent decades, payments have undergone significant digitization and decentralization which has raised their informational authenticity and accessibility (Kurpjuweit et al. 2021; Makhdoom et al. 2019). Even if businesses don't process payments themselves, using Fintech payments generates verifiable information about potential users outside of financing relationships that can be easily accessible and exploited by tech-savvy institutions (Zalan and Toufaily 2017). The established synergy in utilising and forming external data sources implies a joint growth of Fintech lending and cashless payments and promotes the creation of an alternative banking model devoid of relationships in the conventional sense. Figure 2.1 illustrates all the different entities participating in the fintech payment value chain through which they work together to co-create value.

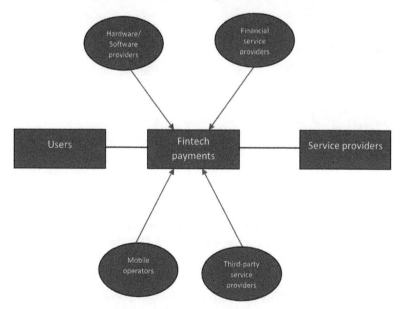

Fig. 2.1   Fintech payment value chain

Source: Author's compilation

Collaboration between several service providers and financial institutions is necessary to bring fintech payments to the public. Service providers must supply secure connections. A lot of financial institutions have either formed strategic alliances with fintech start-ups or have acquired them, even though they are gaining market share in certain business lines (Panetta 2018). To boost their digital strategies, financial institutions are doing this by integrating fintech services into their value chains. The development of fintech payment solutions has also demonstrated that the emphasis has shifted away from intra-organizational solutions and toward customer-oriented business-to-business, customer-to-customer and business-to-business inter-organizational methods (Ofori et al. 2020).

4. Conceptual Framework of Value Co-Creation by Fintech Payment Services

Every day, individuals engage in a wide range of activities, each of which composes several tasks to satisfy their diverse demands. The completion of each task will undoubtedly produce value for users, whereas service providers will benefit from users doing their tasks (Humphreys and Grayson 2008). The S-D logic promotes value co-creation in this manner as shown in part B of Fig. 2.2. Profits can be achieved by businesses as an outcome of the benefits. For the users, value is referred to as customer-perceived value (Marciuska, Gencel, and Abrahamsson 2013). Generally, this value is thought of as the trade-off between rewards and costs involved.

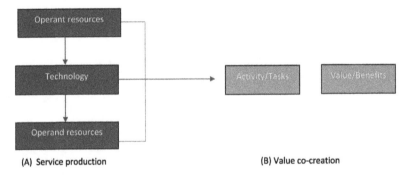

Fig. 2.2 Service production for value co-creation

Source: Author's compilation

Customers' perceptions of value are typically complex, reliant on several contexts and dependent on the methods used to process, advertise and supply products or services to the user (Lapierre 2000). The value-in-context concept in S-D logic is consistent with a value that is context-dependent in this way. Fintech payment can be used as a tool for immersing users in co-creation activities regardless of time and location (Fernandes 2020).

Users need the assistance of service, which is composed of operant resources, technology and operand resources from the service providers to accomplish each task of a given activity (Hsiao 2019). For example, digital banking users should have mobile, required apps and knowledge of how to use the digital payment apps (operant resources). The actors then collaborate to develop a service that supports task completion by integrating all of the operant and operand resources with technology (Adams et al. 2014), demonstrated in part A in Fig. 2.2

Technology in S-D logic can act as both an operant resource (link U1) which acts as an initiator to generate new operand resources (Hollebeek, Srivastava, and Chen 2019) and also as operand resources (link U2) which enables users to complete their activities. On one hand, technology makes it possible to share and integrate resources and expertise to encourage service innovation and on the other, it plays a vital role in the innovation itself (Barrett et al. 2015).

This study establishes a theoretical framework shown in Fig. 2.3 outlining the numerous ways that users and service providers might use fintech payment services to complete the payment task and accomplish the desired value which signifies that is intended for a specific purpose. For users part (A), these resources assist them in determining the technology to be used and owned (link U1) . Examples of these resources include knowledge and experience acquired by using fintech payment services. Then both decide which operand resources they will utilize (link U2); which precisely implements the core concept from portion A in Fig. 2.2.

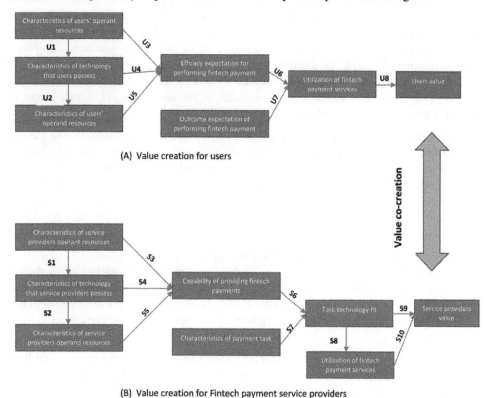

(A) Value creation for users

(B) Value creation for Fintech payment service providers

Fig. 2.3 Theoretical framework for value co-creation by fintech payment services
Source: Author's compilation

Users would be able to use fintech payment options if they had access to all of these resources, including operant resources, operand resources and technology. Such a skill can be viewed as a form of efficacy expectation or the belief that users can successfully carry out the actions required to create the outcomes (Bandura 1977). To put it another way, effectiveness expectation is the person's confidence in his or her ability to complete a task i.e., making a fintech-based payment as opposed to outcome expectancy, which is the confidence that a certain action will result in a specific result (Bandura 1977). It can be anticipated that users' efficacy expectations, but not outcome expectations, for using fintech payment services, would be controlled by operant and operand resources, and technology (link U3,U4,U5).

According to the expectancy-value model (Wigfield and Eccles 2000) of achievement motivation, efficacy expectation and result expectancy are the primary factors that encourage users to use fintech payment services (link U6, U7). Utilizing fintech payments results in customers receiving value (link U8). Such a value can be the customer perceived value in the context of consumer decision-making, the outcome of the user's subjective evaluation of the cost and advantage associated with the exchanges (Wu et al. 2014).

For service providers and businesses, their operant resources govern the technology that will be used by them (link S1), which in turn determines the operand resources(link S2). This is illustrated in part A of Fig. 2.2. The Resource-based theory claims that firm resources are the primary factor in determining a firm's performance and a significant source of competitive advantage resource (Kozlenkova, Samaha, and Palmatier 2014). (Wirtz and Ehret 2009) relied on this theory and made the assumption-similar to S-D logic- that enterprises' information system capabilities depend on their resources such as human capital, IT infrastructure and information system flexibility link (S3, S4, S5).

Fintech payments are an application of technology that facilitates the completion of payment tasks. The Task-technology fit model (Goodhue and Thompson 1995) states that to be included and have a positive impact (link S8) on user performance(link S9, S10), information technology should be a good match with the tasks it supports (link S6, S7). This model analyses usage effects, evaluates task and technology features and determines how information technology influences performance. This performance is the accomplishment of a person's portfolio of tasks (Cane and McCarthy 2009).

As an early attempt to incorporate the central principle of S-D logic into the existing models discussed, Fig. 2.3 needs to be further validated. It is difficult in particular to measure technology's characteristics in line with the S-D logic and operand resources' features. Therefore, the traits of users' operant resources may be those that mirror their personal traits such as age, gender, and income which are indices of their knowledge and experience (Nguyen Hau and Thuy 2016).

The individual qualities of employees that reflect their knowledge and expertise, might be the features of merchants' operant resources. These qualities of the technology merchants can be used as a gauge of an organization's information technology capabilities when it comes to the efficiency of the business with which operations can be improved. While considering socioeconomic environmental factors, the features of merchants' operand resources can serve as an indicator of an organization's financial capacity to make and implement financial management decisions. Therefore, the users and the service providers of fintech payment can acquire their resources and work towards co-creating their values.

5. Conclusion

This study includes the application of fintech payment as an example and developed framework to explain how this technology may be combined with operant and operand resources to create value that benefits both users and service providers. The task fit technology model and S-D logic have been combined to analyse fintech payment usage behaviour. Therefore the foundational framework this study establishes becomes its main contribution. However Fig. 2.1 demonstrates that more entities than just users and merchants are participating in the fintech payment services value chain. As a result, a value chain's value co-creation process may be far more complex than what is depicted in Fig. 2.3. A service ecosystem defined as a largely self-adjusting network of resource-integrating players has been described in the literature to reflect the complexity and dynamics of what happens among intermediaries exchanging services (Lusch, Vargo, and Gustafsson 2016). By adopting such concept, the value chain for fintech payment may also be viewed as a type of ecosystem which is connected by shared institutional arrangements and the development of mutual value through service trade (Gozman, Liebenau, and Mangan 2018).

REFERENCES

1. Adams, Frank G., Robert Glenn Richey, Chad W. Autry, Tyler R. Morgan, and Colin B. Gabler. 2014. "Supply Chain Collaboration, Integration, and Relational Technology: How Complex Operant Resources Increase Performance Outcomes." *Journal of Business Logistics* 35 (4): 299–317. https://doi.org/10.1111/jbl.12074.
2. Akaka, Melissa Archpru, Stephen L. Vargo, and Robert F. Lusch. 2013. "The Complexity of Context: A Service Ecosystems Approach for International Marketing." *Journal of International Marketing* 21 (4): 1–20. https://doi.org/10.1509/jim.13.0032.
3. Bandura, Albert. 1977. "Self-Efficacy: Toward a Unifying Theory of Behavioral Change." *Psychological Review* 84 (2): 191–215. https://doi.org/10.1037/0033-295X.84.2.191.
4. Barrett, Michael, Elizabeth Davidson, Jaideep Prabhu, and Stephen L. Vargo. 2015. "Service Innovation in the Digital Age: Key Contributions and Future Directions." *MIS Quarterly: Management Information Systems* 39 (1): 135–54. https://doi.org/10.25300/MISQ/2015/39:1.03.
5. Bhat, Jagadeesha R., Salman A. AlQahtani, and Maziar Nekovee. 2022. "FinTech Enablers, Use Cases, and Role of Future Internet of Things." *Journal of King Saud University - Computer and Information Sciences*, September. https://doi.org/10.1016/j.jksuci.2022.08.033.
6. Cane, Sheila, and Richard McCarthy. 2009. "Analyzing the Factors That Affect Information Systems Use: A Task-Technology Fit Meta-Analysis." *Journal of Computer Information Systems* 50 (1): 108–23. https://doi.org/10.1080/08874417.2009.11645368.
7. Chandler, Nick, and Zoltán Krajcsák. 2021. "Intrapreneurial Fit and Misfit: Enterprising Behavior, Preferred Organizational and Open Innovation Culture." *Journal of Open Innovation: Technology, Market, and Complexity* 7 (1): 1–16. https://doi.org/10.3390/joitmc7010061.
8. Fernandes, L. 2020. *The Perspectives of Product Managers on Co-Creation Through Customer Involvement in the Product Development Process Within the Information Technology ....* Proquest. https://www.proquest.com/openview/3b10f8d912528a6f8fe3fb4085b7dff9/1?pq-origsite=gschola r&cbl=51922&diss=y.
9. FSB. 2017. "FinTech - Financial Stability Board." Financial Stability Board. 2017. https://www.fsb.org/work-of-the-fsb/financial-innovation-and-structural-change/fintech/.
10. Gil, Irene, Gloria Berenguer, and Amparo Cervera. 2008. "The Roles of Service Encounters, Service Value, and Job Satisfaction in Achieving Customer Satisfaction in Business Relationships." *Industrial Marketing Management* 37 (8): 921–39. https://doi.org/10.1016/j.indmarman.2007.06.008.

11. Goi, Mei Teh, Vigneswari Kalidas, and Norzita Yunus. 2022. "Developing and Testing a Customer Value Co-Creation Model of Higher Education Institutions." *Journal of Marketing for Higher Education*. https://doi.org/10.1080/08841241.2022.2076275.

12. Goodhue, Dale L., and Ronald L. Thompson. 1995. "Task-Technology Fit and Individual Performance." *MIS Quarterly: Management Information Systems* 19 (2): 213–33. https://doi.org/10.2307/249689.

13. Gozman, Daniel, Jonathan Liebenau, and Jonathan Mangan. 2018. "The Innovation Mechanisms of Fintech Start-Ups: Insights from SWIFT's Innotribe Competition." *Journal of Management Information Systems* 35 (1): 145–79. https://doi.org/10.1080/07421222.2018.1440768.

14. Hollebeek, Linda D., Rajendra K. Srivastava, and Tom Chen. 2019. "S-D Logic–Informed Customer Engagement: Integrative Framework, Revised Fundamental Propositions, and Application to CRM." *Journal of the Academy of Marketing Science* 47 (1): 161–85. https://doi.org/10.1007/s11747-016-0494-5.

15. Hsiao, Ming Hsiung. 2019. "Mobile Payment Services as a Facilitator of Value Co-Creation: A Conceptual Framework." *Journal of High Technology Management Research* 30 (2): 100353. https://doi.org/10.1016/j.hitech.2019.100353.

16. Humphreys, Ashlee, and Kent Grayson. 2008. "The Intersecting Roles of Consumer and Producer: A Critical Perspective on Co-Production, Co-Creation and Prosumption." *Sociology Compass* 2 (3): 963–80. https://doi.org/10.1111/j.1751-9020.2008.00112.x.

17. Kozlenkova, Irina V., Stephen A. Samaha, and Robert W. Palmatier. 2014. "Resource-Based Theory in Marketing." *Journal of the Academy of Marketing Science*. Springer Science and Business Media, LLC. https://doi.org/10.1007/s11747-013-0336-7.

18. Kurpjuweit, Stefan, Christoph G. Schmidt, Maximilian Klöckner, and Stephan M. Wagner. 2021. "Blockchain in Additive Manufacturing and Its Impact on Supply Chains." In *Journal of Business Logistics*, 42:46–70. John Wiley & Sons, Ltd. https://doi.org/10.1111/jbl.12231.

19. Lai, Chia Tai (Angus), Paul R. Jackson, and Wei Jiang. 2017. "Shifting Paradigm to Service-Dominant Logic via Internet-of-Things with Applications in the Elevators Industry." *Journal of Management Analytics* 4 (1): 35–54. https://doi.org/10.1080/23270012.2016.1259967.

20. Lapierre, Jozée. 2000. "Customer-Perceived Value in Industrial Contexts." *Journal of Business & Industrial Marketing* 15 (2/3): 122–45. https://doi.org/10.1108/08858620010316831.

21. Laud, Gaurangi, Ingo O. Karpen, Rajendra Mulye, and Kaleel Rahman. 2015. "The Role of Embeddedness for Resource Integration: Complementing S-D Logic Research through a Social Capital Perspective." *Marketing Theory* 15 (4): 509–43. https://doi.org/10.1177/1470593115572671.

22. Lim, Se Hun, Dan J. Kim, Yeon Hur, and Kunsu Park. 2019. "An Empirical Study of the Impacts of Perceived Security and Knowledge on Continuous Intention to Use Mobile Fintech Payment Services." *International Journal of Human-Computer Interaction* 35 (10): 886–98. https://doi.org/10.1080/10447318.2018.1507132.

23. Lusch, Robert F., Stephen L. Vargo, and Anders Gustafsson. 2016. "Fostering a Trans-Disciplinary Perspectives of Service Ecosystems." *Journal of Business Research* 69 (8): 2957–63. https://doi.org/10.1016/j.jbusres.2016.02.028.

24. Makhdoom, Imran, Mehran Abolhasan, Haider Abbas, and Wei Ni. 2019. "Blockchain's Adoption in IoT: The Challenges, and a Way Forward." *Journal of Network and Computer Applications*. Academic Press. https://doi.org/10.1016/j.jnca.2018.10.019.

25. Marciuska, Sarunas, Cigdem Gencel, and Pekka Abrahamsson. 2013. "Exploring How Feature Usage Relates to Customer Perceived Value: A Case Study in a Startup Company." In *Lecture Notes in Business Information Processing*, 150 LNBIP:166–77. https://doi.org/10.1007/978-3-642-39336-5_16.

26. Merz, Michael A., Yi He, and Stephen L. Vargo. 2009. "The Evolving Brand Logic: A Service-Dominant Logic Perspective." *Journal of the Academy of Marketing Science* 37 (3): 328–44. https://doi.org/10.1007/s11747-009-0143-3.

27. Nguyen Hau, Le, and Pham Ngoc Thuy. 2016. "Customer Participation to Co-Create Value in Human Transformative Services: A Study of Higher Education and Health Care Services." *Service Business* 10 (3): 603–28. https://doi.org/10.1007/s11628-015-0285-y.

28. Ofori, D. A., P. Anjarwalla, L. Mwaura, R. Jamnadass, P. C. Stevenson, P. Smith, Wojciech Koch, et al. 2020. "FINTECH VS TECHFIN: A NEW FORM OF COOPETITION, DETAILED COMPARISON BETWEEN FINANCIAL TECHNOLOGY FIRMS." *PEARSON JOURNAL OF SOCIAL SCIENCES & HUMANITIES* 2 (1): 1–12. http://clik.dva.gov.au/rehabilitation-library/1-introduction-rehabilitation%0Ahttp://www.scirp.org/journal/doi.aspx?DOI=10.4236/as.2017.81005%0Ahttp://www.scirp.org/journal/PaperDownload.aspx?DOI=10.4236/as.2012.34066%0Ahttp://dx.doi.org/10.1016/j.pbi.201.

29. Panetta, Fabio. 2018. "Fintech and Banking: Today and Tomorrow. Speech by the Deputy Governor of the Bank of Italy." https://www.bancaditalia.it/pubblicazioni/interventi-direttorio/int-dir-2018/panetta-120518.pdf.

30. Torfing, Jacob, Eva Sørensen, and Asbjørn Røiseland. 2019. "Transforming the Public Sector Into an Arena for Co-Creation: Barriers, Drivers, Benefits, and Ways Forward." *Administration and Society* 51 (5): 795–825. https://doi.org/10.1177/0095399716680057.

31. Weiß, Peter, Andreas Zolnowski, Markus Warg, and Thomas Schuster. 2018. "Service Dominant Architecture: Conceptualizing the Foundation for Execution of Digital Strategies Based on S-D Logic." In *Proceedings of the Annual Hawaii International Conference on System Sciences*, 2018-Janua:1630–39. https://doi.org/10.24251/hicss.2018.204.

32. Wigfield, Allan, and Jacquelynne S Eccles. 2000. "Expectancy-Value Theory of Achievement Motivation." *Contemporary Educational Psychology* 25: 68–81. https://doi.org/10.1006/ceps.1999.1015.

33. Wirtz, Jochen, and Michael Ehret. 2009. "Creative Restruction - How Business Services Drive Economic Evolution." *European Business Review* 21 (4): 380–94. https://doi.org/10.1108/09555340910970463.

34. Woodruff, Robert B., and Daniel J. Flint. 2014. "Marketing's Service-Dominant Logic and Customer Value." In *The Service-Dominant Logic of Marketing: Dialog, Debate, and Directions*, 183–95. Routledge. https://doi.org/10.4324/9781315699035-25/MARKETING-SERVICE-DOMINANT-LOGIC-CUSTOMER-VALUE-ROBERT-WOODRUFF-DANIEL-FLINT.

35. Wu, Lei Yu, Kuan Yang Chen, Po Yuan Chen, and Shu Ling Cheng. 2014. "Perceived Value, Transaction Cost, and Repurchase-Intention in Online Shopping: A Relational Exchange Perspective." *Journal of Business Research* 67 (1): 2768–76. https://doi.org/10.1016/j.jbusres.2012.09.007.

36. Zalan, Tatiana, and Elissar Toufaily. 2017. "The Promise of Fintech in Emerging Markets: Not as Disruptive." *Contemporary Economics* 11 (4): 415–30. https://doi.org/10.5709/ce.1897-9254.253.

37. Zhao, Qun, Pei Hsuan Tsai, and Jin Long Wang. 2019. "Improving Financial Service Innovation Strategies for Enhancing China's Banking Industry Competitive Advantage during the Fintech Revolution: A Hybrid MCDM Model." *Sustainability 2019, Vol. 11, Page 1419* 11 (5): 1419. https://doi.org/10.3390/SU11051419.

Chapter

Lack of Evidence Based Management (EBM) of Non-Performing Assets (NPAs) in Regional Rural Banks (RRBs)*

D. S. Chauhan**

HR-Organisational Behaviour,
Lal Bahadur Shastri Institute of Management, New Delhi, India

ABSTRACT: Prologue: The banking industry, dominated by government owned Public Sector Banks (PSBs) in India, is historically beset with the ever spiraling and compounding problem of managing 'bad loans'. Thus an efficient management of NPAs is high on their priority. The low levels of recovery of loans and advances and the bad health of the assets has severely affected the profitability of these financial institutions. The advent of Basel III and IV norms have further put pressure to curtail NPAs and keep them to the desirable level of 3% or below of the total loans and advances. The importance of availability of capital towards socio-economic development of the country led to creation of RRBs to cater the financial requirements of rural India. The micro-credit segment of these banks which generally cater to priority sector lending (PSL), which in turn is a 'directed lending' is also adversely affected by NPAs.

The effective NPA management starts right from the starting point of the process of initiating the loan product. The customer profiling, loan application appraisal, pre and post disbursement monitoring and corrective mid-term measures are required to stop the loan from turning 'bad'. The absence of data base, especially at the branch levels, in spite of information technology advances hinders these banks from evolving an effective and efficient NPA management.

Scope of Paper: An Empirical study on the current status of NPA management in rural banking and how EBM can evolve a more effective tool to strategize efficient NPA management.

Methodology: Collection, collation and analysis of primary and secondary data to be collected through branch level survey formats and questioners and available literature and documents respectively. Experiential inputs from real life situations will be an added research tool.

*The views expressed are solely of the author and do not reflect the views, policy or the interpretations of the RRB concerned or author's Ex-employer, NABARD.

**dush_chn@yahoo.com

Universe of the Study: Forty-four (44) branches of a Regional Rural Bank (RRB) operating in district Mainpuri of Uttar-Pradesh, India.

Sample Size and Sample Profile: 5 branches (10% of the universe), 5 branch managers, 5 other branch officials, 5 supervisors and 250 account holders (customers).

Sample Selection: Based on the analysis of secondary data available so as to have a fair representation of the universe.

Conclusion: The availability of a model based on big data analytics to the lending points (branches) of the RRBs will greatly help the branch managers and recovery officials in evolving a topical and effective strategy in asset management, especially the NPAs.

KEYWORDS: Agricultural credit, Asset liability management (ALM), Capital, Credit appetite, Credit appraisal, Credit due diligence, Customer appraisal, Customer profile, Doubtful assets, Erosion, Evidence based management (EBM), Kisan credit card (KCC), Know your customer (KYC), Loss assets, Net profit, Non-performing assets, Post disbursal monitoring, Pre-sanction appraisal, Provisioning, Recovery management, Regional rural banks (RRBs), Scheduled banks, Standard assets, Sub-standard assets, Systematic study, Working capital

1. Introduction

The ever growing Non-Performing Assets (NPAs) in scheduled banks operating in India has been adversely impacting their profitability and financial stability. A loan, is an asset for a bank, as it earns the interest charged thereon and is therefore a source of income and resultant profitability for the bank. However, if the borrower fails to repay the loan along with the interest charged thereon, in full or part thereof then it is termed as Non-Performing Asset (NPA). The Reserve Bank of India (RBI) has defined the NPAs as those assets for which principal or interest payment remains overdue for a period of ninety days from the due date of recovery. The RBI has classified three types of assets within the category of NPAs— Substandard assets, Doubtful assets, and Loss assets[1]. A NPA account reduces the Return on Assest (RoA)[2,3,4] which leads to loss of income which adversely impacts the profitability of the bank[5,6]. Further to it, the loss of asset i.e. failed recovery of the principal amounts leads to erosion of the bank's capital base and has serious consequences of termination of the banking license by Reserve Bank of India (RBI) as the bank may fail in its obligation to safeguard the interest of its depositors and maintain its prescribed paid-up capital.

The Regional Rural banks (RRBs) were opened in 1975 onwards and were created to specifically cater to the needs of rural India. RRBs, along with Rural Cooperative Banks (RCBs), were mandated to meet the credit demands of the rural populace and act as formal credit channelizing agencies so as to achieve 'development through credit' by promoting farm and off the farm livelihood activities. As on 31/12/2022, there are 43 RRBs operating in the country through their 23,507 banking outlets[7].

One of these 43 RRBs, is operating in Uttar Pradesh through its 22 regional offices overseeing the functioning of its 1362 branches. As on 31/03/2022, the total deposits of the RRB stood at Rs. 311162.10 Million and its total loans & advances outstanding were recorded at Rs. 225336.53 Million. The bank posted a net profit of Rs. 626.67 Million in the financial Year (FY) 2021-22 and created a provision of Rs. 7199.69 million to cover its NPAs worth at Rs. 202135.25 million. Thus the profit lines of the bank were adversely impacted by Rs. 7199.69 million on account of provisions created[8].

2. Evidence Based Management (EBM)

The actions of human beings are related to their behaviour and the science of management indicates that behaviour is not random and it is defined by a set of conditions the ecosystem provides to a person[9]. Thus, in order to predict the behaviour with accuracy the concept of systematic study has been underlined in managerial sciences. The systematic study is defined as 'looking at relationships, attempting to attribute causes and effects, and drawing conclusions based on scientific evidence[10]. EBM complements systematic study by basing managerial decisions on the best available scientific evidence.

3. The Study

This study is an attempt to have a systematic study on the causes and effect of occurrence of NPAs and draw conclusions based on the scientifically collected and collated evidences.

3.1 Methodology

Collection, collation and analysis of primary and secondary data collected through branch level survey formats and questioners and available literature and documents respectively. Experiential inputs from real life situations will be an added research tool.

3.2 Universe of the Study

Forty-four (44) branches of a Regional Rural Bank (RRB) operating in district Mainpuri of Uttar Pradesh, India. GBA, as on 31/03/2022, has 44 branches in the Mainpuri region with total deposit of Rs. 7860 million, loans outstanding at Rs. 6232 million and total NPAs at Rs.783 million respectively. The region has posted a profit of Rs. 359 million during the FY 2021–22[6]. Almost 85% of the loan accounts were under Crop loan (agri sector), where loans were disbursed through Kisan credit Cards (KCCs) for the working capital requirements of the farmers to undertake crop husbandry and for activities allied to the farm i.e. animal husbandry, minor irrigation etc. The remaining loans were for undertaking retail trade activities, consumption and housing purposes. The majority of the customers fall under Small (SF) and Marginal farmer (MF) category. A small farmer is one who owes 1 to 2 hectares of farm land while the marginal farmer is one who owes upto 1 hectare of farm land respectively.

3.3 Sample Size

5 branches (10% of the universe), 5 branch managers, 5 other branch officials, 5 supervisors and 250 account holders (customers) who have availed loans from these 5 branches. Out of

the 250 customers selected for the purpose of the study, 125 customers were having non NPA accounts while the remaining 125 customers' loan accounts have turned as NPAs.

3.4 Sample Profile and Selection

In order to have a fair representation of the sample, the secondary data collected for all the 44 branches in respect to deposits, loans outstanding, profitability and amount of NPAs was analysed and the 5 branches viz. Aong, Baranhal, Kurra, Ouncha and Shajhanpur were selected for the study having highest incidence of NPAs as on 31/03/2022.

Table 3.1 Sample profile

(Rs. In Million)

Branch name	Deposits	Loans O/S	NPAs	% NPAs to loans	Profit
Agra road	327	131	19	15	10
Aliganj	187	98	6	6	11
Alipur Khera	159	89	12	13	7
Aong	**69**	**77**	**19**	**25**	**1**
Ashokpur	64	92	10	11	3
Ashrohi	91	155	23	15	7
Baranhal	**112**	**95**	**27**	**28**	**7**
Beelon	113	71	4	6	3
Bewar	463	230	11	5	19
Bhanwat	120	135	3	2	6
Bhogaon	541	172	20	12	21
Bichwan	265	310	10	3	15
Chacha	225	78	4	5	9
Chityan	93	224	24	11	8
Dihuli	131	172	12	7	9
Ghiror	127	180	16	9	6
Jagatpur	122	65	13	20	5
Jasmai	140	109	7	6	6
kalhore	92	174	13	7	7
karhal	301	210	10	5	16
Karhal road	425	158	37	23	15
Kisni	267	281	52	19	15
kuraoli	308	189	26	14	16
Kurra	**69**	**206**	**61**	**30**	**3**

Branch name	Deposits	Loans O/S	NPAs	% NPAs to loans	Profit
Kushmara	102	106	13	12	5
Lekhrajpur	96	156	11	7	7
Madhan	117	173	16	9	10
Mainpuri	526	171	18	11	21
Nanamau	122	78	7	9	5
Nawaterha	141	151	16	11	8
Ouncha	**202**	**181**	**52**	**29**	**8**
Paronkha	122	156	19	12	8
Ramnagar	155	190	46	24	9
Ratanpurbara	73	58	2	3	2
Ratibhanpur	129	199	18	9	9
Rausinora	124	43	3	7	3
Sahara	181	117	12	10	7
Shahjahanpur	**72**	**257**	**71**	**28**	**6**
Station Road	545	199	25	13	15
Vyotikhurd	95	47	10	21	2
Kosma muslemeen	30	69	3	4	1
Nabeeganj	125	94	1	1	6
Partapur	63	54	1	2	2
Saung	29	32	0	0	0.02
	7860	6232	783	13	359.02

Source : Gramin Bank of Aryavat (GBA), Annual Audited Balance Sheet & Report, FY 2021-22

4. Data Collection and Collation

Empirical evidences in form of data were collected through structured and pre-tested questioners, analysis of secondary data and formatted interviews. The data so collected has been analysed with help of bivariate tables and is summarised below.

4.1 Responses from the Borrowers

- **Customer Appraisal**: Customer appraisal is one of the most important aspect in credit appraisal and due diligence. Studies have shown that a thorough customer appraisal leads to a better credit approval decision and which in turn helps the banks in mitigating the credit risk[11] .Question posed to the control group as also experimental group was if the bank officials have visited their habitat, neighbourhood or the place of activity to find about their credentials before loan approval was granted. The response is tabulated below:

Table 3.2 Response on customer appraisal

Control Group (Non NPA)			Experimental Group (NPA)		
Yes	No	Total	Yes	No	Total
74 (59%)	51(41%)	125 (100%)	27 (22%)	98 (78%)	125 (100%)

Source: Author's compilation

- **Activity Appraisal**: Appraising the activity for which loan application has been submitted so as to assess the viability of the project and to ensure adequacy of credit is one of the important step which assists in taking a correct decision[12]. Question posed to the control group as also experimental group was if the bank officials have discussed, analysed the nuances of the activity for which loan has been applied for, with specific reference to its technical and financial viability. The response is tabulated below:

Table 3.3 Response on activity appraisal

Control Group (Non NPA)			Experimental Group (NPA)		
Yes	No	Total	Yes	No	Total
52 (42%)	73(58%)	125 (100%)	18 (14%)	107 (86%)	125 (100%)

Source: Author's compilation

- **Credit Adequacy:** Availability of required credit is another important aspect which determines the project implementation. Inadequate financing may lead to infructuous activity, while the over financing adds to the interest burden and resultant distortion in cash inflow and outflow in the project, leading to its non viability. Thus, both under and over financing may result in bad recovery of dues and the resultant NPA[13]. The question posed to both the groups was if they have been provided adequate credit support from the bank. The response is tabulated below:

Table 3.4 Response on adequacy of credit provided

Control Group (Non NPA)			Experimental Group (NPA)		
Yes	No	Total	Yes	No	Total
81 (65%)	44 (35%)	125 (100%)	47 (38%)	78 (62%)	00%)

Source: Author's compilation

- **Borrowings from informal sources such as moneylenders, chit funds and friends:** It has been pointed out that the credit appetite of a borrower should have a link with her repaying capacity. The higher is the household debt, the more is the credit risk for the banks[14.] The question posed to the respondents was if they have an unpaid liability towards money lenders, chit funds or friends. The response is tabulated below:

Table 3.5 Response on borrowing from Informal sources

Control Group (Non NPA)			Experimental Group (NPA)		
Yes	No	Total	Yes	No	Total
32 (26%)	93 (74%)	125 (100%)	89(71%)	36 (29%)	125 (100%)

Source: Author's compilation

- **Timely disposal of loan applications**: A hassle free and timely disposal of loan applications by the banks create a healthy relationship between the bank and the customer, which promotes reduction of NPAs[15.] The question posed to the respondents was if their loan application was disposed within a reasonable time period and ease of financial transaction was experienced by them. The response is tabulated below:

Table 3.6 Response on timely disposal of loan application

Control Group (Non NPA)			Experimental Group (NPA)		
Yes	No	Total	Yes	No	Total
73 (58%)	52 (42%)	125 (100%)	41 (33%)	36 (67%)	125 (100%)

Source: Author's compilation

- **Intensity and quality of Monitoring (post disbursal visits, MIS etc):** Post disbursal monitoring in order to ensure proper end-use of credit, timely project completion & implementation, verification of asset/s created out of the loan availed and provide hand holding support, if required, is pivotal towards recovery management and reduced NPAs[16]. The question posed to the respondents was if the bank officials continue to monitor and follow-up and provide hand holding support, if required. The response is tabulated below:

Table 3.7 Response on quality of monitoring

Control Group (Non NPA)			Experimental Group (NPA)		
Yes	No	Total	Yes	No	Total
94 (75%)	31 (25%)	125 (100%)	43 (34%)	82 (66%)	125 (100%)

Source: Author's compilation

- **Effect of loan waivers and freebies:** various studies of pointed out that although the agri-credit sector, due to its inherent risk profile and generally unfavourable terms of trade being faced by small and marginal farmers, requires financial support, in the form of loan waivers etc. but announcements and implementation of such freebies vitiates the repayment ethics of the farmers and it leads to wilful defaults in repayment of loans and it results in increased NPAs[17]. The question posed to the respondents was if they expect and wait for loan waiver schemes before making repayments to the banks. The response is tabulated below:

Table 3.8 Response on effect of loan waivers and freebies

Control Group (Non NPA)			Experimental Group (NPA)		
Yes	No	Total	Yes	No	Total
60 (48%)	65 (52%)	125 (100%)	89 (71%)	36 (29%)	125 (100%)

Source: Author's compilation

4.2 Response from the Bankers

15 bank officials who manned the 5 sample branches were interviewed to elicit their response on the reasons which they foresee for increased NPA levels. The %age distribution in terms of the priority assigned towards the reason on a scale indicating most responsible, is tabulated below.

Table 3.9 Response from bank officials on various parameters

Reason	Weightage (%) assigned in terms of intensity
Weak Customer Appraisal	06
Lack of data bank on the customers	02
Weak Activity appraisal	04
Weak Monitoring	16
External Pressure to lend	10
Cumbersome mechanism for recovery of bad debts	12
Loan waivers etc.	50

Source: Author's compilation

5. Conclusion

Based on the data analysis the following evidences emerge.

- Weak customer and activity appraisal can be co-related to higher incidence of NPAs.
- Lax monitoring and weak MIS may also contribute towards higher NPAs
- Banks endeavour towards timely disposal of loan applications and providing customer friendly ease of business platform can be leveraged to reduce the credit risk and resultant NPAs.
- Households having disproportionate debt, specially from informal sources are more likely to default in their dues to the bank.
- Government sponsored schemes leading to loan waivers etc have a potential to vitiate the recovery ecosystem of the banks.
- IT enabled monitoring systems and maintenance of relevant historical data on potential and existing customers can help the branch officials in better decision making.
- Strong, vibrant and simplified versions of recovery tools such as Debt Recovery tribunals and methodologies to initiate punitive actions on wilful defaulters will act as deterrent towards creation of NPAs.

REFERENCES

1. RBI: Master Circular - Prudential Norms on Income Recognition, Asset Classification and Provisioning pertaining to Advances, http://www.rbi.org.in>Scripts>NotificationUsers
2. Islam Md and S, Nishiyama S (2016), The determinants of bank profitability: Dynamic panel evidence from South Asian countries. Journal of Appl Finance Bank 6(3):77–97
3. Kannan R, Narain A, Ghosh S (2001) Determinants of net interest margin under regulatory requirements: an econometric study. Econ Polit Wkly 36(4):337–344
4. Kohlscheen E, Murcia A, Contreras J (2018) Determinants of Bank Profitability in Emerging Markets. BIS Working Paper, No.686
5. Berger AN, DeYoung R (1997) Problem Loans and Cost Efficiency in Commercial Banks. J Bank Finance 21(6):849–870
6. Ozurumba BA (2016) Impact of Non-Performing Loans on the Performance of Selected Commercial Banks in Nigeria. Res J Finance Account 7(16): 95–109
7. Key statistics & Financial Statements of RRBs as on 31/03/2022, NABARD, Mumbai, July, 2022
8. Gramin Bank Of Aryavat (GBA), Annual Audited Balance Sheet & Report, FY 2021–22
9. Pareekh U., Understanding Organisational Behaviour, 2021, 3rd Edition, Oxford University Press, New Delhi
10. Stephin P. Robbins, Timothy A. Judge & Neeharika Vohra Organisational Behaviour, 2022, 18th Edition Pearson India education ltd., Chennai,
11. Bhaatacharaya H. Banking Strategy ,Credit Appraisal and Lending decisions, 2011, 2nd edition, Oxford India
12. Agarwal R., Mehra Y. S., Project Appraisal & Management, 2021, Taxman, India
13. Ibid
14. Vivek kaul, Bad Money, 2020, 1st edition, Harper Business, USA
15. Kumar A., Sharma A.K., komma G., Banking Industry and Non Performing Assets, 2018 Ingram, USA,
16. Mukherjee D. D., Credit Monitoring, Legal Aspects & Recovery of Loans,2018, Snow White, India
17. Gine X., Kanz M (2017), The Economic Effects of a Borrower Bailout: Evidence from an Emerging Market, The review of Financial Studies

Chapter

4

Empirical Investigation of Heckscher Ohlin Theory on India's Foreign Trade

Shri Prakash[1]

Professor of Eminence (retd.),
BIMTECH, Greater Noida, India

Sonia Anand Dhir[2]

Associate Professor,
JIMS, Rohini, New Delhi, India

ABSTRACT: The focus of this study is to check whether the exports and imports of the Indian economy conform to the Heckscher-Ohlin (H-O) theorem of international trade. H-O theorem states that the trade of a nation is governed by its factor endowments. This theorem assumes a static economic framework. Hence, it is assumed that neither factor endowment nor economic and trade structures change through time. This assumption violates the changes brought about in economies in a dynamic state of flux due to the continuous process of growth. The production structure, factor endowment and trade of an economy change due to the economic growth process. The export and import basket of a nation are consistent with the factor endowment of the nation in the initial phases of economic growth. But both trade and factor endowment start to diverge from each other due to the process of growth. The initial factor endowment of developing economies determines their trade in a manner such that capital-intensive goods are imported and labour-intensive goods are exported. Such exportable goods are generally produced by primary and simple manufacturing activities like textiles. But the accumulation of capital due to a rise in savings and investments and expansion of education in developing economies tend to change both factor endowment and economic structure due to the priority given to manufacturing for growth. The paper empirically tests the hypothesis relating to changing economic structure, trade and factor endowment due to the process of growth. But the paper exclusively focuses on the growth and trade of the Indian economy from 2000 to 2021.

KEYWORDS: Heckscher-Ohlin theory, Factor endowment, India exports and imports

[1]shri1j@gmail.com, [2]soniadhir01@gmail.com

DOI: 10.4324/9781003415725-4

1. Introduction

According to the Heckscher-Ohlin (H-O) theorem, factor endowments of a nation determine the trade of its commodities with other nations. The export basket of a labour-abundant economy would comprise labour-intensive goods while that of a capital-abundant economy would comprise capital-intensive goods. This further governs the exporting nation's production structure as it tends to specialise in the production of goods which are determined by its factor endowment (Ohlin, B.,1967). According to the theorem, a labour-abundant nation like India would import capital-intensive goods as the production structure of such goods does not conform to the nation's factor endowments, India being a labour-abundant economy. Import of heavy and basic industrial goods has had the largest share in India's imports since independence as against primary goods which are largely labour-intensive have had a significant share in Indian exports (Economic Survey). In line with the classical theories of trade, the theorem is based on a static analytical framework and does not take dynamic economic changes into consideration. One of the important assumptions of the theorem is the constant factor endowment of the trading nations. This implies that the since there is no change in the factor endowment of the nation, therefore, there is no change in its pattern and composition of trade (Prakash S, Sharma A, 2011; Prakash S, Dhir S.A., 2014). According to Leamer (1995), traded goods comprise factors of production bundled together leading to an indirect arbitrage of these factors through an inter-country exchange of the tradable commodities. This also causes a transfer of services of immobile factors from abundant areas of their prevalence to scarce areas (Leamer, 1995). The theorem also assumes that though goods are mobile between nations, the factors of production are immobile between the nations, but mobile within the nations. This implies that there is a fixed supply of factors like labour and capital which cannot be changed for a nation inspite of its trade with other nations. It further means that the factor endowment of a nation remains constant and is not altered by the economic growth of a nation (Prakash S, Sharma A, 2011; Prakash S, Dhir S.A., 2014). No economy, however, tends to remain fixed in the dynamic economic environment. Its factor endowment as well as the production structure tend to transform due to the dynamic growth process and this in turn leads to changes both in the magnitude and direction of trade in an economy (Helpman,1984; Prakash S, Dhir S.A., 2014; Mallick, J., 2017). Such change may lead to change in the structure of trade itself over a period of time. A nation's export and import basket which, according to H-O theorem, is in accordance with its factor endowment may diverge away from it over a period of time due to the growth process. (Prakash S, Dhir S.A., 2014, Che X. N., 2012). Moreover, factor endowments of industrialising developing economies tend to change with time(Tandon, A., 2020).

2. Economic Growth, Factor Endowment and Trade

The total consumption and savings of a nation tend to grow during the growth process of the nation. The production structure of an economy itself may change due to the strategy adopted by the policymakers to influence the growth of a nation and to fill up the observed gaps (Prakash S, Sharma A, 2011; Prakash S, Dhir S.A., 2014). Developing nations like India exhibit such a model of the growth process. India adopted an import substitution strategy in order to replace foreign with domestic production and gave centre stage to industrialisation keeping heavy and basic goods industries in focus as a part of the development process (worldbank.org, 2018). This impacted the trade structure of the nation as both the export and the import basket of the nation changed over a period of time, more so after the adoption of the policy of globalisation, liberalisation and privatisation during the 1990s. All such macroeconomic changes led to the replacement of certain imports by domestically produced goods and the addition of new manufactured goods to the export basket of the country. Trade structure, therefore, changes as a result of the growth process (Krueger A, 1985; Prakash S, Dhir SA,2014). This is additionally supported by the fact that in order to boost exports and achieve its trade policy targets, the Indian government under the Atmanirbhar Bharat scheme, has announced Production Linked Incentive Scheme, Make In India, Digital Bharat, Gati Shakti Yojna etc. Such plans announced by the government will lead to specialisation in the production of both traditional and new goods which enter the export basket. The quantum of exports will rise and result in the transformation of the production structure in favour of sectors contributing to exports.

There is thus, mutual inter-relation and positive linkage between the trade and production structure. Due to the rapid growth of the Indian economy, a transformation of the production and trade structure has taken place (Fairweather, Z., and Sutton M., 2020). Both keep impacting each other in the dynamic economic environment during the process of growth. These actions and reactions between the two further lead to a change in the demand and supply of both physical, financial and human capital of the nation (Prakash S, Sharma A, 2011; Prakash S, Dhir S.A., 2014). Leontief Paradox (1953) led researchers to examine the validity of the H-O theorem with respect to the Indian economy and other economies around the world. Since none of the studies has found evidence to refute the H-O theorem for the Indian economy, it thus forms the theoretical backdrop of this study.

3. Objectives of the Study

The study seeks to find whether the change in factor endowment of the country has brought about a change in its economic structure and trade over the period of the last two decades, also ascertaining the magnitude of change in trade due to the change in the economic structure of the country and to find out the magnitude of change in the factor endowment and the trade basket of the country over the time period of the study, if any. The sector-wise data relating to gross value added, employment, capital stock, exports and imports are taken from Economic Survey, Ministry of Finance, Govt. of India, CSO, Ministry of Labour, Govt. of India. The sectors have been broadly classified into the following categories: primary, mining and quarrying, manufacturing and services. The period of study is from the year 2000 to 2020.

4. Models and Methods

The paper has employed econometric models for analysis. Growth curves and multiple regression models are estimated by Ordinary Least Squares. Dickey-Fuller Test is used to evaluate the stationarity of the time series. Factor endowment relates to capital employed per unit of labour in secondary and tertiary sectors of the economy. While value added by manufacturing plus services per unit of total value added in the economy and proportion of exports/ imports of manufactured and services in total exports/imports are taken as the economic and trade structure indicators. Besides, the absolute values of sector-specific exports and imports are also considered separately.

5. Analysis of Empirical Results

The empirical results are discussed in this section whereby first and foremost the results of the test of stationarity of the time series used in the study are discussed. Thereafter, the results of the inter-relation between exports of secondary and tertiary sector goods and primary goods, current factor endowment and current economic structure of the country are discussed and lastly, the results of the inter-relation between imports of secondary and tertiary sector goods and primary goods, current factor endowment and current economic structure of the country are discussed. The OLS estimates of the Dickey-Fuller test applied to test the stationarity of the time series are discussed below.

Table 4.1   Results of Dickey-Fuller unit root test

Endogenous variable	ρ	R^2
$\Delta \ln ES_t$	-0.079 (2.153)	0.196
$\Delta \ln FE_t$	-0.146 (1.542)	0.111
$\Delta \ln EXP_t$	-0.073 (0.792)	0.032
$\Delta \ln IMP_t$	-0.517 (2.715)	0.279

Source: Author's own calculations

The OLS estimates of the Dickey Fuller Unit Root test (refer Table 4.1) applied to the time series of the endogenous variables used in the study suggest that the time series of factor endowment and total exports are non-stationary as the value of the coefficient attached to their lagged value is not significant. However, the time series of economic structure and imports are found to be stationary on grounds of the Dickey-Fuller test since the value attached to the lagged variable is both negative and significant and thus is away from the unit root circle. Non-stationarity of the time series necessitates validation of the functions using such series for the test of cointegration. Hence, the Engel Granger test for cointegration has been applied to the functions wherever necessary.

The OLS estimates of the inter-relation between economic structure and factor endowment and change in factor endowment over the time period of study are given below:

Table 4.2   Inter-relation between economic structure and factor endowment

		a_0	$\ln FE_t$	T	R^2	F	F sig	d
1	$\ln ES_t$	-0.319 (5.77)	0.040 (2.95)	0.003 (7.30)	0.954	197.104	0.000	0.974
2	$\ln FE_t$	4.078 (97.59)		0.025 (7.71)	0.748	59.443	0.000	

Source: Author's own calculation

Where, $\ln ES_t$ is the log value of the current economic structure indicated by the ratio of the value added of secondary and tertiary sectors and total value added; $\ln FE_t$ is the log value of the current factor endowment indicated by the ratio of capital per unit labour employed in manufacturing and tertiary sectors of the Indian economy. T represents the time period.

Table 4.2a   Engel Granger test result: function 1

ΔU_t	U_{t-1}	R^2
Function 1	-0.434	0.174
	-2.055	

Source: Author's own calculation

The OLS estimates of functions in Table 4.2 show that both coefficients are statistically significant in function 1. The value of the coefficient of determination indicates that the data fit well to the function. The total amount of change explained in the dependent variable i.e. economic structure is 95% by both the explanatory variables, factor endowment and time. Corresponding to a one per cent increase in factor endowment, economic structure changes by 4%. Even if factor endowment remains constant, economic structure changes by 0.3%. The results imply that the strategy of growth brings about a change in the economic structure. The growth strategy brings about an annual compound rate of change of 0.3% in the economic structure. The significance of the negative intercept implies that some excluded variables exercise a negative influence on economic structure. All coefficients being significant including intercept imply no multicollinearity in the function. The function is acceptable on grounds of Durbin Watson d statistic calculated to rule out autocorrelation. Also, all variables are found to be well-cointegrated. The same is verified through the Engel Granger test for cointegration (results displayed in Table 4.2a).

Function 2 in Table 4.2 fits the data reasonably well as the total variation explained by the explanatory variable in the dependent variable is 75%. There is a significant change in factor endowment over a period of time. Corresponding to 1% change in time, factor endowment changes by 2.5%. This indicates that the total value added per person employed in the manufacturing and service sector is increasing in the positive direction.

Table 4.3   Inter-relation between exports, economic structure and factor endowment

Function No.	Endogenous variable	a_0	$\ln ES_t$	$\ln FE_t$	R^2	F	Fsig.	d
3	$\ln EXP(SM)_t$	7.533 (11.38)	13.759 (14.66)	0.038 (0.3)	0.985	606.72	0.000	1.44
4	$\ln EXP(SM)_t$	7.721 (177.2)	13.946 (36.89)		0.986	1361.23	0.000	1.57
5	$\ln EXP(SM)_t$	-1.5 (1.86)		1.755 (9.5)	0.819	90.24	0.000	1.04
6	$\ln EXP(A)_t$	6.667 (2.64)	16.35 (4.57)	0.151 (0.3)	0.877	63.88	0.000	1.232

Function No.	Endogenous variable	a_0	$\ln ES_t$	$\ln FE_t$	R^2	F	Fsig.	d
7	$\ln EXP(A)_t$	7.435 (42.65)	17.337 (11.58)		0.876	134.08	0.000	1.28
8	$\ln EXP(A)_t$	-4.072 (3.08)		2.192 (7.23)	0.733	52.26	0.000	0.82

Source: Author's own calculations

Where, $\ln EXP(SM)_t$ is the log value of total exports of manufactured and tertiary goods; $\ln EXP(A)_t$ is the log value of total exports of primary goods.

Table 4.3a   Engel Granger Test results: functions 3-8

ΔU_t	U_{t-1}	R^2
Function 3	-1.286 5.66	0.628
Function 4	-1.214 5.48	0.601
Function 5	-0.527 2.71	0.27
Function 6	-0.549 2.195	0.202
Function 7	-0.57 2.26	0.212
Function 8	-0.357 1.75	0.138

Source: Author's own calculations

Where, ΔU_t is the first difference value of the errors of the function and U_{t-1} is the lagged value of the error of the function.

Table 4.3b   Growth Curves of Sector-Wise Exports

		a_0	T	R^2	F	F sig
9	$\ln EXP(SM)_t$	5.521 (130.86)	0.056 (16.63)	0.936	276.513	0.000
10	$\ln EXP(A)_t$	4.686 (59.17)	0.071 (11.20)	0.868	125.431	0.000
11	$\ln PS(A_{EXP/TEXP})_t$	-0.890 (15.95)	0.012 (2.61)	0.264	6.814	0.017
12	$\ln PS(SM_{EXP/TEXP})_t$	-0.055 (3.09)	-0.003 (2.25)	0.211	5.073	0.036

Source: Author's own calculations

Where, $lnEXP(SM)_t$ is the total exports of manufactured and tertiary sector goods; $lnEXP(A)_t$ is the total exports of primary goods; $lnPS(A_{EXP/TEXP})_t$ is the proportionate shares of primary goods exports in total exports and $lnPS(SM_{EXP/TEXP})_t$ is the proportionate shares of manufactured and tertiary goods taken together in total exports.

The OLS estimates in Table 4.3 show that the total variation explained in the exports of secondary and tertiary goods by economic structure and factor endowment taken together as explanatory variables in function three is more than 98%. The coefficient attached to economic structure is found to be significant, though the one attached to factor endowment is not found to be significant. Such a result may be attributed to multicollinearity in the function and necessitates step-wise regression to rule out multicollinearity. The results of step-wise regression performed show that the value of the coefficient of determination improved slightly in function four indicating a significant impact of economic structure on exports of secondary and tertiary goods. However, the total variation in the dependent variable was found to be much lower (81%) in function five where only factor endowment was included in the function as the explanatory variable. It is inferred from the above results that the structure of the economy has influenced the exports of the secondary and tertiary sectors more than factor endowment. Function six in Table 4.3 is found to fit the data well as the total variation explained in the total exports of primary goods by both economic structure and factor endowment is almost 88%. The coefficient attached to economic structure is found to be significant, however, the coefficient attached to factor endowment is not significant. In order to rule out multicollinearity stepwise regression was done. The OLS estimates thus obtained show that there is no improvement in the value of the coefficient of determination when economic structure alone is used as the explanatory variable in the function (function seven) and it's value further deteriorates when factor endowment is the only explanatory variable in the function (function eight).

Such results indicate that primary sector exports depend exclusively on economic structure and change in factor endowment has not affected the dominance of primary exports in the total exports of the country. Change in factor endowment has not affected the structure of exports. The export basket of India was dominated by primary commodities and still continues to do so. The exportable surplus of the secondary and tertiary sectors though has increased but not to an extent greater than that of primary goods exports. Despite a significant change in factor endowment, Indian exports continue to be dominated by primary goods. This also indicates that the secondary and tertiary sectors have still not reached the maturity stage. Consequently, these results are also supported by the OLS estimates obtained from functions eleven and twelve shown in table 3b which indicate that the proportionate share of primary goods exports in total exports is rising at the compounded annual rate of one point two per cent, however, the compounded annual rate of growth of proportionate shares of exports of secondary and tertiary goods in total exports is found to be decreasing at the rate of point three per cent. Notwithstanding the fact that the total exports (absolute value) of both secondary and tertiary goods are significantly increasing at compounded annual rates of five point six per cent. This indicates that though the exports of secondary and tertiary sectors are increasing, these sectors have not been able to generate exportable surpluses large enough to surpass primary sector exports.

Table 4.4 Inter-relation between imports, economic structure and factor endowment

		a_0	$\ln ES_t$	$\ln FE_t$	R^2	F	Fsig	d
13	$\ln IMP(SM)_t$	7.65 (6.63)	15.333 (9.37)	0.009 (0.04)	0.963	240.896	0.000 0.000	1.766
14	$\ln IMP(SM)_t$	7.697 (96.84)	15.394 (22.55)		0.964	508.509	0.000 0.000	1.764
15	$\ln IMP(SM)_t$	-2.421 (2.43)		1.923 (8.41)	0.788	70.732	0.000	1.06
16	$\ln IMP(A)_t$	7.519 94.58)	14.695 (6.31)	0.019 0.06	0.925	110.251	0.000	1.248
17	$\ln IMP(A)_t$	7.614 (67.33)	14.817 (15.25)		0.925	232.705	0.000	1.25
18	$\ln IMP(A)_t$	-2.132 (2.04)		1.853 (7.7)	0.757	59.333	0.000	0.9

Source: Author's own calculations

Where, $\ln IMP(SM)_t$ is the total imports of manufactured and tertiary sector goods; $\ln IMP(A)_t$ is the total imports of primary goods; $\ln PS(A_{IMP/TIMP})_t$ is the proportionate shares of primary goods imports in total imports and $\ln PS(SM_{IMP/TIMP})_t$ is the proportionate shares of manufactured and tertiary goods taken together in total imports.

Table 4.4a Engel Granger test results: functions 13-18

ΔU_t	U_{t-1}	R^2
Function 13	-0.832 2.68	0.275
Function 14	-0.831 2.68	0.274
Function15	-0.528 2.61	0.264
Function 16	-0.583 2.498	0.247
Function 17	-0.585 2.503	0.247
Function 18	-0.416 2.068	0.183

Source: Author's own calculations

Where, ΔU_t is the first difference value of the errors of the function and U_{t-1} is the lagged value of the error of the function.

Table 4.4b   Growth curves of sector wise imports

		a_0	T	R^2	F	F sig
19	lnIMP(SM)$_t$	5.288	0.060	0.870	127.021	0.000
		79.31	11.27			
20	lnIMP(A)$_t$	5.268	0.060	0.908	186.996	0.000
		95.49	13.67			

Source: Author's own calculations

The OLS estimates of functions in Table 4.4 indicate that the total variation explained in the imports of secondary and tertiary goods by both economic structure and factor endowment taken together as explanatory variables in function thirteen is more than 96%. The coefficient attached to economic structure is found to be positive and significant, and the coefficient attached to factor endowment is not found to be significant. The reason for the non-significance of factor endowment could be due to multicollinearity in the function. The results of step-wise regression thus performed show that the value of the coefficient of determination improved slightly in function fourteen though its value decreased in function fifteen. This makes factor endowment a redundant variable in determining a change in imports of secondary and tertiary goods in the country. Imports of secondary and tertiary goods are found to be significantly influenced exclusively by economic structure. Corresponding to a one per cent change in the economic structure, the imports of secondary and tertiary goods increased many times more than a hundred per cent.

The total variation explained by the independent variables in the dependent variable was found to be almost 93% in function sixteen. Whereas the economic structure was found to be positively and significantly impacting the imports of primary goods, the coefficient attached to factor endowment was not found to be significant. Again to rule out multicollinearity, step-wise regression was performed. The OLS estimates of functions seventeen and eighteen indicate that the coefficient of determination does not improve when economic structure alone is considered as the explanatory variable and the value of the coefficient further decreases to 76% when factor endowment alone is taken as the dependent variable. This makes factor endowment a redundant variable in determining the change in imports of primary goods. The economic structure is exclusively determining the imports of primary goods in the economy. Though the output of primary, secondary and tertiary goods in the economy has been increasing it has been unable to replace imports of primary, secondary and tertiary goods to fulfil the domestic demand yet. This is supported by the fact that import demand for primary goods and secondary and tertiary goods rising at an annual compounded rate of growth of six per cent as shown in Table 4.4b. All functions were found to be valid on grounds of Durbin Watson test for autocorrelation and Engel Granger Test for cointegration (results displayed in Table 4.4a)

6. Conclusion

- There is a significant change in factor endowment of Indian economy over a period of time. This indicates that the total value added per person employed in the manufacturing and service sector is increasing in the positive direction.
- The structure of the economy has influenced the exports of the primary, secondary and tertiary sectors more than factor endowment.

- Despite a significant change in factor endowment, Indian exports continue to be dominated by primary goods. Change in factor endowment has not affected the structure of exports. The export basket of India was dominated by primary commodities and still continues to do so.
- The exportable surplus of the secondary and tertiary sectors though has increased but not to an extent greater than that of primary goods exports. This also indicates that the secondary and tertiary sectors have still not reached the maturity stage. This indicates that though the exports of secondary and tertiary sectors are increasing, these sectors have not been able to generate exportable surpluses large enough to surpass primary sector exports.
- Imports of primary, secondary and tertiary goods are found to be significantly influenced exclusively by economic structure alone. Though the output of primary, secondary and tertiary goods in the economy has been increasing it has been unable to replace imports of primary, secondary and tertiary goods to fulfil the domestic demand yet.

REFERENCES

1. Krueger, Anne O. 1985. Import substitution versus export promotion. Finance & Development, p. 56, Volume 22: Issue 002, International Monetary Fund, DOI: https://doi.org/10.5089/9781616353612.022
2. Bharadwaj, R. 1962. Factor Proportion and Structure of Indo U S Trade, Indian Economic Journal, vol 10
3. Fairweather, Z., and Sutton M. 2020. Economic Developments in India, Bulletin – December 2020, Global Economy, Reserve Bank of Australia, www.rba.gov.au/publications/bulletin/2020/dec/economic-developments-in-india.html
4. Helpman, E. 1984. The Factor Content of Trade. The Economic Journal. Vol. 94, no. 373, pp. 84-94
5. India's Growth Story Since the 1990s Remarkably Stable and Resilient. press release. March 14, 2018, worldbank.org
6. Key Indicators for Asia and the Pacific. 2022. Asian Development Bank. kidb.adb.org
7. Leamer, Eric. 1995. The Heckscher-Ohlin Model in Theory and Practice. Princeton Studies in International Finance. No. 77, February 1995
8. Mallick J. 2017. Structural Change and Productivity Growth in India and The people's republic of China. ADBI Working Paper Series. No. 656, February 2017. www.adb.org/sites/default/files/publication/226566/adbi-wp656.pdf
9. Natasha Xingyuan Che.2012. Factor Endowment, Structural Coherence, and Economic Growth. IMF Working paper. https://www.imf.org/external/pubs/ft/wp/2012/wp12165.pdf
10. Ohlin, Bertil.1967. Interregional and International Trade. Harvard Economic Studies. Vol. 39. Cambridge, MA: Harvard University Press.
11. Prakash Shri, Sharma Amit. 2011. Balancing factor Endowments and Structure of Exports, Paper presented in The 19th International Input-Output Conference, Alexandria, USA, 13-17 June 2011
12. Prakash S., Anand S. 2014.Impact of Growth on Factor Endowment and Structure of India's Trade. IOSR Journal of Economics and Finance. Volume 5, Issue 5. (Sep.-Oct. 2014), PP 53-66
13. Tandon, A. 2020. Revisiting Factor Proportions in the Indian Economy A Study of Tradable Sectors. Economic and Political Weekly, volume 55, issue no 3
14. Wassily, Leontief. 1953. Domestic Production and Foreign Trade; The American Capital Position Re-Examined. Proceedings of the American Philosophical Society. 97 (4): 332–349. JSTOR 3149288

Handbook of Evidence Based Management Practices in Business – Satyendra Kumar Sharma et al. (eds)
© 2023 Taylor & Francis Group, London, ISBN 978-1-032-54216-4

Chapter

Indicators of Risk Management in Banking Sector

Gaganpreet Kaur*

Research Scholar, Guru Nanak Dev University

ABSTRACT: The most crucial component of a firm, whether it is financial or not, is risk management. An institution can sustain over long run with adequate risk management capabilities. To control a company's risk, management must establish an appropriate risk regulatory framework. Banks are more accountable for risk management since they deal with public funds. The objective of the study is to pinpoint significant risks faced by banks by comparing the ratios of two Indian public sector banks, namely Dena Bank (merged with Bank of Baroda in 2019) and the State Bank of India, for five years, from 2013-14 to 2017-18. Using 24 accounting ratios, this study examines various risk categories. Further, using the Mann Whitney U test, it was discovered that only 10 out of 24 ratios were capable of recognizing the differences in the banks' risk management. Comparing Dena Bank with State Bank of India, whose risk assessment is effectively handled, allows us to see the primary risks that contribute to the efficient management of the bank in India because Dena Bank was unable to sustain its risk and was eventually merged.

KEYWORDS: Basel, Commercial banks, Financial risk, Liquidity risk, Market risk, Operational risk, Risk management

1. Introduction

Since banks handle the public's money and are responsible for managing risk, better transparency and risk management have become even more crucial after the 2008 financial crisis (Subbarao, 2009).

*gaganpreet27@gmail.com

DOI: 10.4324/9781003415725-5

For the banking industry to operate effectively, risk management is essential. All Indian banks, public and private, must manage their risk by Basel 3 norms which RBI introduced in 2013 (Datey and Tiwari, 2014). Along with other risks like credit, operational, and market risks, Basel 3 strongly emphasizes liquidity risk. Additionally, bank reports should have more risk disclosure (Kaur and Kapoor, 2015). By imposing a Prompt corrective action (PCA) mandate and limiting their varied activities, the RBI takes strict action against banks that do not manage their risk appropriately (Narasimhan, 2021; Bhusan et al., 2022). Therefore, liquidity, credit, market risk, and operational risk are currently the main risks that banks need to maintain (Kaur and Kapoor, 2015). This paper aims to find the major factors that impact the risk management capabilities of public sector banks. For this reason, the paper is divided into various sections, including an introduction to the subject of the study, a review of relevant literature, a discussion of the goal and methodology of the study, an analysis of the results, and a conclusion.

2. Review of Literature

The preliminary studies on risk management are of Al-Tamimi (2002) and Hassan (2009), which studies risk management of banking sector. Throughout the course of their study, it was discovered that banks' risk management procedures had improved. The risks posed by banks can be calculated using various ways, including content analysis, primary research utilising questionnaires, and accounting ratios. The estimate of risk in the banking industry was done using accounting ratios by Sensarma & Jayadev (2009), Zhang et al. (2013), and Sarkar et al. (2018). Further, some studies studied the effect of individual risks. In their study, Sharifi et al. (2018) looked at credit risk and how it affects the banking sector's operations and found that non-performing assets are the root cause of credit risk in banks. The effectiveness and capability for accepting risks of the banking sector are significantly impacted by risk management (Abid et al., 2021). In their study, Das and Ghosh (2004) discovered that smaller banks had more capital for the risk they faced than larger banks. Additionally, Sharifi et al. (2016) focused on operational risk and its impact on banks in their research and found similar outcomes. Therefore, the study uses a variety of accounting ratios to evaluate the banks' ability to manage risk.

3. Objective

The objective of the study is to identify significant risks faced by banks by comparing the ratios of two Indian public sector banks, namely Dena Bank (merged with Bank of Baroda in 2019) and the State Bank of India.

4. Methodology

The study is conducted over a five-year period, from 2013–14 to 2017–18. The information used was secondary information obtained from the bank's annual reports. Further, the Mann-Whitney U test is used to analyse the data in SPSS software.

5. Data Analysis and Interpretation

5.1 Credit Risk

As shown in Table 5.1, the Mann-Whitney U-test indicated that the following ratios with p-values less than 0.05 affected the banks' credit risk.

Table 5.1   Credit risk test statistics

	Capital adequacy ratio (CAR)	Gross Non-performing assets (NPA) to Gross Advances (%)	Net Non-performing assets (NPA) to Net Advances (%)	Allowance For Loan Loss to Gross Loans	Loan Loss Reserve to Total Assets	Debt-Equity Ratio	ROA Based Z Score
Mann-Whitney U	.000	9.000	5.000	9.000	9.000	.000	.000
Wilcoxon W	15.000	24.000	20.000	24.000	24.000	15.000	15.000
Z	-2.611	-.731	-1.567	-.731	-.731	-2.611	-2.611
Asymp. Sig. (2-tailed)	.009	.465	.117	.465	.465	.009	.009
a. Grouping Variable: bank name							

Source: Author's compilation

5.2 Market Risk

As shown in Table 5.2, the Mann-Whitney U-test indicated that the following ratios with p-values less than 0.05 affected the banks' market risk.

Table 5.2   Market risk test statistics

	BV Of Equity to Total Assets	Total Derivatives to Total Assets	Interbank Borrowings to Total Borrowings	Market Return	Beta
Mann-Whitney U	.000	5.000	.000	4.000	8.000
Wilcoxon W	15.000	20.000	15.000	19.000	23.000
Z	-2.611	-1.567	-2.611	-1.776	-.940
Asymp. Sig. (2-tailed)	.009	.117	.009	.076	.347
a. Grouping Variable: Bank Name					

Source: Author's compilation

5.3 Liquidity Risk

As shown in Table 5.3, the Mann-Whitney U-test indicated that the following ratio with p-value less than 0.05 affected the banks' liquidity risk.

Table 5.3 Liquidity risk test statistics

	Gross Loan to Total Assets	Liquid Assets to Deposits	Liquid Assets to Total Assets	Equity to Loan	Current Assets to Total Assets
Mann-Whitney U	7.000	.000	8.000	8.000	8.000
Wilcoxon W	22.000	15.000	23.000	23.000	23.000
Z	-1.149	-2.611	-.940	-.940	-.940
Asymp. Sig. (2-tailed)	.251	.009	.347	.347	.347
a. Grouping Variable: Bank Name					

Source: Author's compilation

5.4 Operational Risk

As shown in Table 5.4, the Mann-Whitney U-test indicated that the following ratios with p-values less than 0.05 affected the banks' operational risk.

Table 5.4 Operational risk test statistics

	Risk Weighted Assets (RWA) for Operational Risk to Total Assets	Operating Expense to Net Operating Income	Risk Weighted Assets (RWA) for Operational Risk to Operating Expense	Risk Weighted Assets (RWA) for Operational Risk to Net Operating Income	Equity to Total Assets	Operating Profit to Total Assets	Operating Expenses to Total Assets
Mann-Whitney U	.000	9.000	.000	.000	5.000	.000	11.000
Wilcoxon W	15.000	24.000	15.000	15.000	20.000	15.000	26.000
Z	-2.611	-.731	-2.611	-2.611	-1.567	-2.611	-.313
Asymp. Sig. (2-tailed)	.009	.465	.009	.009	.117	.009	.754
a. Grouping Variable: Bank Name							

Source: Author's compilation

It is evident from analysing the mean values of the relevant ratios in Table 5.5 that the bank's main risk was an operational risk. The bank's declining profitability and increased operational costs ultimately resulted in its merger. In addition, Dena Bank was more risk-averse than the State Bank of India.

6. Conclusion

It was found that all types of risks included in the study impact banks to some extent. The main source of concern, however, was the operational risk. Credit risk was not the primary concern

Table 5.5 Mean values of significant ratios

Serial No.	Ratio	Mean values	
		Dena Bank	State Bank of India
1	CAR	11.11	12.65
2	Debt-Equity Ratio	4.59	5.80
3	ROA Based Z Score	12.75	36.59
4	Liquid Assets to Deposits	0.76	0.91
5	BV Of Equity to Total Assets	0.06	0.003
6	Interbank Borrowings to Total Borrowings	0.18	1.99
7	RWA for Operational Risk to Total Assets	0.003	0.005
8	RWA for Operational Risk to Operating Expense	0.23	0.36
9	RWA for Operational Risk to Net Operating Income	0.04	0.07
10	Operating Profit to Total Assets	0.010	0.018

Source: Author's compilation

for Dena Bank, but rising operating costs and declining profitability had a substantial impact on its performance, eventually leading to its merger. Bankers must control their operating costs and improve profitability in order to stay in business and avoid financial and reputational losses.

REFERENCES

1. Abid, Ammar, Ammar Ali Gull, Nazim Hussain, and Duc Khuong Nguyen. (2021). Risk governance and bank risk-taking behavior: Evidence from Asian banks. Journal of International Financial Markets, Institutions and Money 75: 101466.
2. Al-Tamimi, Hussain A. Hassan. (2002). Risk management practices: an empirical analysis of the UAE commercial banks. Finance India 16(3): 1045.
3. Bhusan, Soumik, Angshuman Hazarika, and Naresh Gopal. (2022). Time to Simplify Banking Supervision—An Evidence-Based Study on PCA Framework in India. Journal of Risk and Financial Management 15(6): 271.
4. Das, Abhiman, and Saibal Ghosh. (2004). The relationship between risk and capital: Evidence from Indian public sector banks. RBI Occasional Papers Summer 22: 1–21.
5. Datey, Rachanaa, and Kavita Tiwari. (2014). Basel III norms and Indian banks–A new definition of risk management. International Journal of Advanced Research 2(7): 894–905.
6. Hassan, Abul. (2009). Risk management practices of Islamic banks of Brunei Darussalam. The Journal of Risk Finance 10(1): 23–37.
7. Kaur, Mandeep, and Samriti Kapoor. (2015). Adoption of Basel norms: a review of empirical evidences. Journal of Financial Regulation and Compliance 23(3): 271–284.
8. Narasimhan, A. L. (2021). Prompt Corrective Action (PCA). Reserve Bank of India. (March). https://www.rbi.org.in/scripts/NotificationUser.aspx?Id=1099.

9. Sarkar, Sanjukta, Rudra Sensarma, and Dipasha Sharma. (2018). The relationship between risk, capital and efficiency in Indian banking: does ownership matter?. Journal of Financial Economic Policy. 11(2): 218–231.

10. Sensarma, Rudra, and M. Jayadev. (2009). Are bank stocks sensitive to risk management?. The journal of risk finance. 10(1): 7–22.

11. Sharifi, Sirus, Arunima Haldar, and SVD Nageswara Rao. (2016). Relationship between operational risk management, size, and ownership of Indian banks. Managerial Finance. 42(10): 930–942.

12. Sharifi, Sirus, Arunima Haldar, and SVD Nageswara Rao. (2019). The relationship between credit risk management and non-performing assets of commercial banks in India. Managerial Finance. 45(3): 399–412.

13. Subbarao, Duvvuri . (2009). Ethics and the World of Finance. Conference at Sri Sathya Sai University, Prasanthi Nilayam, Andhra Pradesh, August 28.

14. Zhang, Jianhua, Chunxia Jiang, Baozhi Qu, and Peng Wang. (2013). Market concentration, risk-taking, and bank performance: Evidence from emerging economies. International Review of Financial Analysis. 30: 149–157.

Chapter

Implied Volatility, Risk Premium and Option Mispricing: An Examination of Information Efficiency of Options Market

Vijay Kumar Sharma*

FICWA(ICAI), Pursuing PhD (IIFT, New Delhi);
Ph.D. Research Scholar (Finance) Indian Institute of Foreign Trade,
New Delhi, India

Satinder Bhatia[1]

Professor (Finance) & Dean,
Indian Institute of Foreign Trade,
New Delhi, India

ABSTRACT: The primary role of equity derivatives is price discovery of underlying. For this price discovery in derivative market, implied volatility must have capacity to predict future realised volatility. Implied volatility is the major component for the asset pricing models such as Black-Scholes model. This study examines the information contents and forecasting accuracy of implied volatility in determining future realised volatility. This study is conducted on world largest option index i.e., CNX Nifty Index option for the period 2012 to 2021 to test the information efficiency of Nifty Index options in Indian capital market. To test the information efficiency of implied volatility ordinary least square regression and ARCH-LM model has been used to analyse the call and put implied volatility data. The outcome of this study indicates implied call and put volatility subsumed information to predict the future realised volatility and the implied volatility contains information about futures realized volatility.

KEYWORD: Information efficiency, Implied volatility, Future realised volatility, Black-scholes, Equity options

---

*Corresponding Author: cma.vijay2011@gmail.com, Vijay_phdmp19@iift.edu;
[1]satinderbhatia@iift.edu

DOI: 10.4324/9781003415725-6

1. Introduction

Price discovery is a major function of derivative market. Option prices reflects market expectation on the distribution of the future value of underlying assets. The derivatives market uses all the information available to it to form its expectations about future volatility. Therefore, the option price displays the market's volatility estimate. Implied volatility of options considered as the option market's forecast of the volatility of future returns volatility over the remaining life of the option. It is assumed that in an efficient market implied volatility is the best possible forecast, which subsumed all necessary information generated by other explanatory variables to explain future realized volatility. However, the existing literatures has produced a mixed result on this. At one end it documents stocks with higher implied volatilities also have higher ex-post realized volatility. In contrast, Gwilym and Buckle (1999), who studied S&P 100 index options for the period 1985-1989 conclude that implied volatility is biased and inefficient predictor about future volatility. Today researchers are more focused on examining the information contents of implied volatility in a dynamic environment i.e., whether the implied volatility of an option predicts the ex-post realized volatility over the remaining life of the option.

Indian equity derivatives market has many unique features that provide a good setting to investigate the pricing efficiency of the options at all levels. Apart from the large size and liquidity, the unfragmented market structure is expected to result in more efficient pricing of derivatives. This may channel leverage-hungry informed speculators into its highly liquid option market, unlike most developed markets like Unites States of America. In this context, the objective of this study is to investigate the pricing efficiency of the equity options market of India (NSE) and examining the relationship between the estimated smile-adjusted implied volatility (IV) and the realized volatility (RV) across underlying strikes. Most of the existing literatures from across the world indicates that IV exceeds RV for all options. This difference has been attributed to mispricing and risk premium dynamics. The study examined the extent of mispricing of options in NSE by identifying the absolute difference between calculated price using implied volatility curve and actual market price in the market. On the other side, realised volatility has been computed and compared with the implied volatility to test the efficiency of option market to predict risk premium and option price.

The rest of the structure of this study is as follows: section 2 discussing the existing relevant literatures and research gaps, section 3 research methodology and data analysis process, section 4 results of the analysis and section 5, conclusions of the study.

2. Review of Literatures

In existing literatures, mixed evidence is observed on implied, and futures realised volatility. Since implied volatility is the expectation of future in market, any differences between implied and realised volatility indicates the market inefficiency. Cao, and Semin (2020) find that the S&P 500 (USA) implied volatility is 3.3% higher than realised volatility from 2011 to 2015. They argued that market volatility increased sharply when market is in stress and at the time of negative market returns. This increases the option premium and buyers are willing to pay higher premium. This indicates a higher implied volatility and options mispricing. Similar evidence is also observed by and Deb, (2020). Pathak, and Deb, (2020) show evidence of mispricing in equity derivatives market in several stock exchanges across the world. Bekiros, *et.* al (2017) use twenty single stock option closing prices from 2012 to 2013 from Australian equity derivatives market to examine the overpricing and expiry day effects on option premium. Luo, and Qin (2017) investigates the relationship between realised and implied volatility in Chinese stock market to check the effect of price shocks and market efficiency of implied volatility. His results indicates that the implied volatility index have negative and significant effects on the Chinese stock market while the effect of realised volatility shocks is negligible. Park *et.* al (2017) examined the micro-efficiency of realised and implied volatility in Korean stock market (KOSPI 200) and it is observed that dynamic conditional correlation exists between the volatility at moderate level, especially during the financial crisis period. In another study, a positive relationship between implied and historical has been observed and positive predictive power of implied volatility (Dai *et.* al, 2020). Liang *et.* al (2016) examined the predictability of implied volatility in five developed economies (UK, Japan, USA, France and Germany) for the period 2012 to 2017. The sample results indicates that stock market implied volatility is efficient in predicting the futures realised volatility in short run. In another study by (Park *et.* al ,2017) it is found that implied volatility outperforms historical as well as realised volatility of futures and subsumed the information content of past volatility is short period.

One justification focuses on how index option markets process volatility information inefficiently. Given the liquidity, depth, and trading activity in the options market, this explanation is, nevertheless, doubtful. A second possibility is that the Black and Scholes (1973) option pricing model, which is used to compute implied volatility, cannot be used to price index options because of prohibitive transaction costs associated with hedging of options in the cash index market (Vagnani, 2019). This justification is also incomplete, though. The Black *and* Scholes model does not necessarily require continuous trading in cash markets. In a study it is reported that implied volatility is an efficient though biased, predictor of future return volatility (Narain, *et.* al, 2016). Implied volatility was more biased before the crash than after, at least partially due to a poor signal-to-noise ratio prevalent prior to the crash, and perhaps also due to learning by market participants in the wake of the crash. It is found that historical volatility has much less explanatory power than implied volatility (Kumar Singh, 2020).

Research gap: The implied volatility of options is an important component in option pricing and its valuation. Traders, hedgers, and investors are highly concerns on implied volatility of options before and after taking any position in stock market. Option premium, risk and movements in derivatives market is highly influenced from implied volatility. However, the information efficiency of options is less explored in Indian derivatives market. Thus, scope is available to study the efficiency of implied volatility to predict the futures realised volatility and changes in option premium and risk patterns with volatility dynamics.

3. Research Methodology

The present study has been conducted on Nifty 50 Index options, which represents 65% of the total float-adjusted market capitalization at National Stock Exchange (NSE) and the most highly liquid index option market in the world. The study period covers ten years from January 2012 to December 2021. Secondary data has been collected from the NSE website such as Nifty Index options daily and monthly settlement price (spot), call and put option strike price and premium etc.; 91 days T-bills rate used for the risk-free rates etc. To reduce bias due to a synchronicity and stale prices between the option prices and the underlying Index option, all options contracts whose market prices lies outside the Black model's arbitrage bounds have also been removed. Our sample of minute-matched futures and options potentially reduces the number of options violating the arbitrage bounds due to pure a synchronicity.

 Implied volatility (IV), which is the major component of asset pricing Black-Scholes (BS) Model, computed from BS formulae for the Nifty 50 Index options. The realised volatility (RV) of options computed by standard deviation of daily return of remaining life of options. If the daily closing price on the day of remaining life left for expiry is "P_i" and "i" each trading day, then continuously compounded daily return (R) will be.

$$R = \ln\left(\frac{pi}{pi-1}\right)$$

The annualised realised volatility of option can be.

$$RV = \sqrt{\frac{252}{n-1}\sum_{i=1}^{n}(Ri,t - Rt)^2}$$, Where Rt denotes mean value of R.

Historical volatility (HV) of options is computed as annualized standard deviation of daily continuously compounded return of the period going back t days (i.e.,30 calendar days)

$$HV\ t - i = \sqrt{\frac{252}{t-1}\sum_{i=1}^{n}(Ri,t-1 - Rt-1)^2},$$ where R_{t-1} denotes the mean of daily continuously compounded return during the period t-1.

Augmented Dickey Fuller (ADF) test has been applied to test the stationery of data from implied volatility (IV), realized volatility (RV) and historical volatility (HV). After that Ordinary Least Squared (OLS) method, and ARCH LM (autoregressive conditional heteroskedasticity - Lagrange multiplier) test has been used to examine the relationship between IV, RV and HV.

To examine the efficiency of implied volatility and information contents over realised volatility, the following two equations has been used.

$$RV = \alpha + \beta_c.IV_{c,t} + \varepsilon_{c,t} \tag{1}$$
$$RV = \alpha + \beta_p.IV_{p,t} + \varepsilon_{p,t} \tag{2}$$

4. Results

Descriptive statistics of the implied volatility (IV) indicates mean value of put implied volatility is higher than call implied volatility. Skewness of the call and put implied volatility indicates positively skewed from the right tail and kurtosis is leptokurtic shape (grater than 3). Jarque-Bera statistics indicates implied volatility of put and call implied volatility are not normally distributed as it is far from zero. In case of historical (HV) and realised volatility, their standard deviation is very close to each other. Skewness and kurtosis are representing normality of the series. Jarque-Bera statistics are showing it RV and HV both are not normally distributed.

Table 6.1 Descriptive analysis

Particulars	Implied Volatility		Realised Volatility	Historical Volatility
	Call	Put		
Mean	0.2628	0.2742	0.2376	0.2348
Maximum	0.7580	0.7916	0.6693	0.6623
Minimum	0.1327	0.1307	0.1019	0.0988
Standard Deviation	0.1042	0.1107	0.1159	0.1132
Skewness	1.7841	1.6505	1.3961	1.3911
Kurtosis	7.8296	7.1939	5.1556	5.1986
Jarque-Bera	147.98[a]	116.96[a]	51.05[a]	51.60[a]

Source: Compiled by the author from result on e-views 12

Augmented Dickey-Fuller (ADF) test (Table 6.2) was applied to check the time series data are stationery or not at 5% level of significance where,

H_0 (Null hypothesis): time series data is non-stationary

H_A (Alternative hypothesis): time series data is stationary

The null hypothesis was rejected and the result shows that all three volatilities are stationary.

Table 6.2 Augmented Dickey-Fuller (ADF) test

ADF Test	Call implied Volatility	Put implied Volatility	Historical Volatility	Realized Future Volatility
CNX Nifty Index Options	-3.2966[b]	-3.5097[b]	-4.3591[a]	-4.3895[a]

Source: Author's compilation

Realised volatility was regressed on implied volatility using OLS method Eq. (1) for booth call and put options. The slope of the co-efficient (β_{call} or β_{put}) of IV call options is significant at 5% level of significance. Now, if the implied call or put implied volatility contains information on future's realized volatility, then co-efficient ($\beta_{c/p}$) should be significant or non-zero figure. In Table 6.3, coefficient of implied call and put volatility are significant and contains information about realized volatility of future. F statistics are used to test the significance of regression (OLS) which is significant at 5% level of significant.

Table 6.3 Regression analysis

Particular	α_0	$\beta_{c/p}$	Adj R^2	F-statistics
RV on IV call	0.0188	0.8256[a]	0.57	118.27[a]
RV on IV put	0.0264	0.7710[a]	0.56	123.66[a]
RV on HV	0.0782[a]	0.6675[a]	0.46	82.34[a]

Source: Compiled by the author from result on e-views12

In the second step, realized volatility was regressed on historical volatility and the slope of the coefficient was found to be significant at 5% level of significance. F-statistics also significant at 5 level of significance. The overall result from Table 6.3 indicates implied volatility contains information about futures realized volatility.

Table 6.4 ARCH-LM test result

Panel A: ARCH LM test on residual from the regression		
Particular	F-statistic	p-value
Nifty index call options	1.1056	0.2964
Nifty index put options	1.3583	0.2503

Source: Author's compilation

Here ARCH-LM test is conducted to test the implied volatility of call and put are informational efficient predictor of future realised volatility or not. The F-statistics results for call and put are 1.1056 and 1.3583 respectively and are insignificant. Thus, null hypothesis is accepted, and it can be concluded that implied call and put volatility are efficient predictor of future realised volatility

5. Conclusions

This study was conducted to study the movements and relationship between implied volatility and futures realised volatility of Nifty 50 Index options and to examine the information contents of implied volatility which indicates its efficiency to predict the future volatility in India derivative market. The study was conducted during the period January 2012 to December 2021. This study is based on monthly options data and descriptive statistics indicates that mean of put volatility is higher than call options. This may be due to buying pressure on put options for hedging purpose. Implied volatility of put options is higher than call options which indicates put options are more volatile. It is also observed that historical volatility is slightly higher than the future's realised volatility. The mean of implied volatility (call & put) is higher than historical and realised volatility. This may be due to Black-Schole option price is overpriced for call and put options. According to the result of regression analysis, implied call and put volatility subsumed information to predict the future realised volatility. The implied volatility contains information about futures realized volatility.

REFERENCES

1. Gruber, P. H., Tebaldi, C., & Trojani, F. (2021). The price of the smile and variance risk premia. *Management Science.* https://doi.org/10.1287/mnsc.2020.3689
2. Simlai, P. (2010). What drives the implied volatility of index options. *Journal of Derivatives and Hedge Funds, 16*(2), 85–99. https://doi.org/10.1057/jdhf.2009.20
3. Pe~ Na, I., Rubio, G., & Serna, G. (1999). Why do we smile? On the determinants of the implied volatility function. In *Journal of Banking & Finance* (Vol. 23). www.elsevier.com/locate/econbase
4. Narain, Nigam, N. K., & Pandey, P. (2016). Behaviour and determinants of implied volatility in Indian market. *Journal of Advances in Management Research, 13*(3), 271–291. https://doi.org/10.1108/JAMR-09-2015-0062

5. Han, Q., Liang, J., & Wu, B. (2016). Cross Economic Determinants of Implied Volatility Smile Dynamics: Three Major European Currency Options. *European Financial Management*, 22(5), 817–852. https://doi.org/10.1111/eufm.12072

6. Kumar Singh, A. (2020). *Determinants of Option Moneyness 163 ã Indian Institute of Finance FINANCE INDIA ã Indian Institute of Finance* (Issue 1, 2020).

7. Vagnani, G. (2009). *The Black-Scholes model as a determinant of the implied volatility smile: A simulation study.* 72(1), 103. https://doi.org/10.1016/j.jebo.2009.05.025ï

8. Latané, H. A., & Rendleman, R. J. (n.d.). American Finance Association Standard Deviations of Stock Price Ratios Implied in Option Prices. In *Source: The Journal of Finance* (Vol. 31, Issue 2).

9. Park, S. Y., Ryu, D., & Song, J. (2017). The dynamic conditional relationship between stock market returns and implied volatility. *Physica A: Statistical Mechanics and Its Applications*, 482, 638–648. https://doi.org/10.1016/j.physa.2017.04.023

10. Dai, Z., Zhou, H., Wen, F., & He, S. (2020). Efficient predictability of stock return volatility: The role of stock market implied volatility. *North American Journal of Economics and Finance*, 52. https://doi.org/10.1016/j.najef.2020.101174

11. Bekiros, S., Jlassi, M., Naoui, K., & Uddin, G. S. (2017). The asymmetric relationship between returns and implied volatility: Evidence from global stock markets. *Journal of Financial Stability*, 30, 156–174. https://doi.org/10.1016/j.jfs.2017.05.006

12. Cao, C., & Simin, T., (2020). Predicting the equity premium with the implied volatility spread. *Journal of Financial Markets*, 51. https://doi.org/10.1016/j.finmar.2019.100531

13. Christensen, B. J., & Prabhala, N. R. (1998). The relation between implied and realized volatility. In *Journal of Financial Economics* (Vol. 50).

14. Day, T. E., & Lewis, C. M. (1992). Stock market volatility and the information content of stock index options. In *Journal of Econometrics* (Vol. 52).

15. Dixit, A., & Jain, S. S. P. K. (2010). Informational efficiency of implied volatilities of S&P CNX Nifty index options: A study in Indian securities market. *Journal of Advances in Management Research*, 7(1), 32–57. https://doi.org/10.1108/09727981011042847.

16. Gemmill, G. (1986). The forecasting performance of stock options on the London Stock Exchange. In *Journal ownings Finance @Accounting* (Vol. 13, Issue 4).

17. Gwilym, O. A., & Buckle, M. (1999). Volatility forecasting in the framework of the option expiry cycle. *International Journal of Phytoremediation*, 21(1), 73–94. https://doi.org/10.1080/135184799337190

18. Luo, X., & Qin, S. (2017). Oil price uncertainty and Chinese stock returns: new evidence from the oil volatility index. *Finance Research Letters*, 20, 29–34. https://doi.org/10.1016/j.frl.2016.08.005

19. Christensen, B. J., & Hansen, C. S. (2002). New evidence on the implied-realized volatility relation. *European Journal of Finance*, 8(2), 187–205. https://doi.org/10.1080/13518470110071209

20. Pathak, J., & Deb, S. G. (2020). Stylized patterns in implied volatility indices and stock market returns: A cross country analysis across developed and emerging markets. *Cogent Economics and Finance*, 8(1). https://doi.org/10.1080/23322039.2020.1723185

21. Hansen, C. S. (n.d.). *The relation between implied and realised volatility in the Danish option and equity markets.*

22. Bali, T., Hu, J., & Scott, M. (n.d.). *Option Implied Volatility, Skewness, and Kurtosis and the Cross-Option Implied Volatility, Skewness, and Kurtosis and the Cross-Section of Expected Stock Returns Section of Expected Stock Returns.* https://ink.library.smu.edu.sg/lkcsb_research

23. Claessen, H., & Mittnik, S. (n.d.). *Forecasting Stock Market Volatility and the Informational Efficiency of the DAX-index Options Market Forecasting Stock Market Volatility and the Informational Efficiency of the DAX-index Options Market *. http://www.ifk-cfs.de

Chapter

Determinants of Working Capital Efficiency of Indian MSME's: An Empirical Evidence

Deepak Kumar Tripathi*, Saurabh Chadha[1]

Department of Management, Birla Institute of Technology and Science,
Pilani, Pilani Campus, India

ABSTRACT: This research aims to gather insight into working capital management (WCM) practises and the factors that influence of its efficiency inside the Indian micro small medium enterprises (MSME's) manufacturing sector using organisation variables by examining two efficiency models, namely cash conversion cycle (CCC).

For the research, the paper used panel regression methodologies on 578 micro small and medium enterprises (MSME's) of the most important production and manufacturing industries from 2012 to 2021. Several firm-specific variables, including leverage (lever), tangibility (Tangib), firm size (Fsiz), profitability(Prof) , Human capital (HCap), Asset Turnover ratio (ATR), Firm Growth (FG) have significant effect on Working capital management efficiency (WCE), whereas Age of the firm(AGE) and salary expenses (sal) were having insignificant effect on working capital management efficiency. This study explores WCM efficiency comprehensively by including organisation factors in Indian manufacturing MSME's utilising efficiency metrics, i.e. cash conversion cycle (CCC), the findings of which revealed as the solution to an appropriate Working capital management (WCM).

KEYWORD: Working capital efficiency, MSME's, India, Cash conversion efficiency, Cash conversion cycle, Manufacturing.

1. Introduction

In today's dynamic corporate landscape, corporate survivability drives an enterprise to outperform its competitors. Sustainability in the current era will be attainable if a company has

---
*Corresponding Author: p20210036@ pilani.bits-pilani.ac.in
[1]saurabh.chadha@pilani.bits-pilani.ac.in

DOI: 10.4324/9781003415725-7

adequate financial resources to confront its future and existing commitments. Management of working capital is a crucial aspect of financial management. The success of a business in a given period is contingent on its working capital management efficiency. Consequently, working capital management has assumed the center stage in contemporary business growth. Today's businesses concentrate on the two fundamental linkages of operation and investment (Liu et al., 2021). Working capital efficiency (WCE) is a metric that quantifies how well a company manages the funds trapped in trade receivables with its payables on the acquisition of inventories. Specifically, this metric compares enterprises of a similar kind (e.g., size, industry, etc.) depending on the proportion of capital deployed to fulfill their regular operating requirements.(Aktas et al., 2015). In addition, the WCE of a company indicates its credibility and influences an investor's perception of the company's financial health. High working capital efficiency reduces short-term borrowing and enables the business to prepare for long-term borrowing when growing or investing in new projects. Sustaining desirable aspects of working capital efficiency compels firm managers to make quick judgments regarding investments in current assets and short-term Finance. Such choices are crucial components of working capital management (WCM) (Prasad et al., 2019). WCM has been a quasi-concern in businesses, with many financial planners finding it challenging to identify the critical variables of working capital and determine the ideal liquidity position. Most research on the working capital practices of enterprises from industrialized countries, whereas only a handful of studies represents the same for firms from growing economies, for example, India.

Finance management has long been the lifeblood of businesses. Consequently, financial decisions have always been considered by the body's head. Capital Structure (Financing) Decisions, Investment/Capital Budgeting Decisions, and Working Capital fall under the Long-term category of corporate financial decisions (Kasozi, 2017). Working Capital represents the difference between an organization's current assets and current liabilities. It has been recognized for some time that, considering the significance of Finance, less theoretical progress has been made on the subject of Working Capital. (Arunkumar & Sonwaney, 2019) states that the omission of working capital has been the cause of numerous corporate failures to date. Thus, paying close attention to this area can aid in maintaining liquidity and paying off existing bills, thereby ensuring timely payments. The available literature on Working Capital Management has been conducted with larger corporations in mind, with data accessibility being the most critical and apparent reason (Abbadi & Abbadi, 2012; Mutua Mathuva, 2014; Yousaf et al., 2021)

Despite the presence of work in the field of working capital on larger corporate houses, it would not aid in overcoming the issues encountered by SMEs, as the smaller enterprises have fewer ways to receive funds, necessitating the efficient and effective use of their limited funds (Padachi et al., 2012).

The Make in India project - "Atmanirbhar Bharat Abhiyan" - has considerably boosted smaller businesses, increasing India's domestic manufacturing industry. Under this effort, Micro, Small, and Medium-Sized Businesses (MSME) are the backbone of the Indian economy. Analyses on the importance of working capital for Micro, Small, and Medium-sized businesses (MSME) are lacking in the extant literature on Working Capital Management of SMEs. According to numerous studies, the performance of larger companies differs from that of SMEs. Likewise, the versions of Micro, Small, and Medium-sized businesses differ.

Our current study evaluates the effect of determinants of working capital management components such as cash conversion efficiency, cash conversion cycle, and inventory holding period for micro small and medium-sized businesses. Firm characteristics include Firms age, tangibility of assets, financial leverage, asset turnover ratio, salary, Human capital, and firms size. Over time, a sample of MSMEs has been examined.

The MSMED Act of 2020 defines "micro, small, and medium enterprises as follows: an enterprise whose investment in plant and machinery or equipment does not exceed Rs. 1 crore and whose turnover does not exceed Rs. 5 crores is classified as a micro-enterprise; an enterprise whose investment in plant and machinery or equipment does not exceed Rs. 10 crores and whose turnover does not exceed Rs. 50 crores are classified as a small-enterprise whereas an enterprise whose turnover does not exceed more than 250 crores and investment in plant and machinery is less than 50 crores is termed as medium enterprise."

Government, financial institutions, banks, and other interested organizations will be aided in formulating policies/schemes by the size disparity and working capital management practices of these firms.

2. Literature Review

2.1 Determinants of Working Capital Efficiency

Size: Numerous studies support that size of the firm affects the working capital efficiency. Larger firms have more efficient working capital than smaller firms(Dalci et al., 2019). In order to increase sales, larger businesses either invest more in working capital or use their size to strengthen their relationships with suppliers, which results in lower working capital investments(Kieschnick et al., 2006). In addition, the most significant advances and digitalization in supply chain management systems make it easier for corporations to engage in such processes, communicate with all stakeholders, and efficiently administer each system, including WCE (Seth et al., 2020). Small organizations may find it challenging to apply such practices due to a lack of resources, funding, and knowledge.

Subsequently, smaller businesses are more likely to fail than bigger ones since the latter are much more diverse (Baños-Caballero et al., 2016). Because large companies are subject to increased analyst scrutiny and have less information asymmetry than smaller businesses, this impacts the trade credit (Hill et al., 2010). Similarly, (Niskanen & Niskanen, 2006) claims that companies will grant better credit facilities if they have greater funding opportunities and can manage their cash flow. They discovered that the firm's size impacted the amount of trade credit issued.

(Elbadry, 2018) highlighted large enterprises can accept flexible inventory and receivables policies due to low financial limitations, reduced information asymmetry, and significant borrowing capacity. Smaller enterprises face higher funding costs when investing in current assets, which hurts their working capital efficiency. Due to more substantial financial constraints or fewer funding sources, small businesses also use trade credit through their vendors as a source of funding, which benefits the CCC.

As a result, it is anticipated that size and WCM efficiency are negatively correlated. The study employs SIZE as a proxy for firm size.

Firm Age: A company's age reveals how well it can compete with and outperform its competitors. Investor confidence and a company's age are positively correlated. This is so because more seasoned employees and business partners tend to work for older companies, which increases their efficiency. Customers also like the more established businesses. This has an impact on the company's credibility with its stakeholders as well. Comparatively speaking, older businesses have better access to working capital than newer ones, reducing the cost of acquiring working capital, thereby enhancing efficiency (Niskanen & Niskanen, 2006). Similarly (Seth, Sharma & Chadha, 2020) discovered age's favorable and significant effect on the firm's working capital efficiency.

Firm age has a positive effect on working capital.

Growth opportunity: Growth opportunities can be expressed in terms of growth in sales of the firm compared with last year's sales (Nyeadi et al., 2019). Sales growth can be achieved by extending credit on their products, increasing the investment in receivables, and, consequently, their working capital.(Singh & Kumar, 2017) proposed a positive relationship between sales growth and working capital. The pecking order theory suggests that organizations anticipating greater demand need more significant investment and, thus, greater internal Finance (Seth, Sharma, & Chadha, 2020). This expectation would lead businesses to increase their cash and short-term investments. In addition, companies may amass massive inventories in anticipation of expansion possibilities, which would offset the effects of trade credit. However, the association between overall sales and working capital may be subject to endogeneity issues, as sales volumes stimulate working capital and affect sales growth (Hill et al., 2010). Similarly, (Kieschnick et al., 2006) demonstrated that potential sales growth has a favorable impact on a corporation's CCC and thus suggested that firms may increase their inventory levels in expectation of future overall sales. Consequently, it is anticipated that a positive association will exist among Growth Opportunities represented by sales and working capital efficiency

Asset tangibility: Prior studies show that investment in fixed assets negatively affects the efficiency of working capital(Baños-Caballero et al., 2010; Kieschnick et al., 2006; Singh & Kumar, 2017). They reasoned that, in the case of financial restrictions, increased expenditure on tangible fixed assets reduces the available funds for working capital. Consequently, SMEs must implement an active policy toward working capital. This result is consistent with (Jaworski & Czerwonka, 2022; Yousaf et al., 2021), finding an inverse relationship between tangibility and CCC.

Accordingly, we can say that tangibility is inversely related to working capital efficiency.

Leverage: The ratio of total debt to capital is the financial leverage (Kieschnick et al., 2006). Due to the cost of debt element, leverage has a detrimental effect on a company's profitability(Mutua Mathuva, 2014). Moreover,(Baños-Caballero et al., 2013) highlighted that firms with increased costs from external funding tend to have a short CCC, as they will suffer greater interest expenses due to their borrowing. Consequently, the cost of investment in working capital would also increase. Small and medium-sized enterprises are frequently harmed by asymmetric information, which reduces the opportunities for acquiring debts. Since small and medium-sized enterprises (SMEs) have a more challenging time obtaining long-term loans than multinational corporations, they are compelled to maintain their expenditure on current assets as low as feasible; reported that SMEs tend to support a low CCC to minimize outflows of cash in the form of interest costs to reduce the cost of external borrowing. Thus, with the increased bulk of research levels, an effective WCM will assist these businesses in avoiding increased capital needs that trigger external funding (Moussa, 2019). The overwhelming research has discovered an inverse relationship between Debt Level and Working Capital efficiency (Abbadi & Abbadi, 2012; Akinlo, 2012; ur Rehman et al., 2017). Therefore, we anticipate a negative relationship between leverage and CCC. Firms with a high level of external financing have trouble obtaining the funds necessary for day-to-day operations, leaving borrowings as their only option for meeting their requirements.

CCC: Several researchers have investigated CCC as a metric for quantifying working capital efficiency (Abbadi & Abbadi, 2012; Baños-Caballero et al., 2013; Chauhan & Banerjee, 2018; Moussa, 2019). CCC gauges the period between cash inflow from finished goods sales and cash outflow for inventory purchases. A longer cash conversion cycle (CCC) improves the enterprise's earnings since it gives customers more time to pay off their debts, providing them with the asset of time and increasing sales. In addition, assisting businesses in gaining customers over their competitors(Nunn, 1981), developing a further beneficial relationship between a firm's profitability and CCC (Sharma et al., 2020). However, depending on the situation, a negative association can also be observed between firm performance and CCC (Hill et al., 2010; Mutua Mathuva, 2014; Singh & Kumar, 2017). If CCC is reduced, there will be less demand for cash, which will lessen the need for external borrowing. This reduces the cost of financing(Baños-Caballero et al., 2010). In contrast, (Aktas et al., 2015), the potential of both a negative and positive association demonstrates the presence of set-off or trade-off, indicating a nonlinear relationship between CCC and the profitability of SMEs.

We infer from that there is bi-directional association among the CCC and exogenous variables.

Human Capital: Human capital is important dimension for measurement of any firm performance. Two firms having same economic resources may differs in terms of social resources. Firm which invest more on their human resources get sustainable benefits over a future period of the time. Very few studies(Seth, Sharma, Ruparel, et al., 2020) have explored the effect of Human capital as the determinant of working capital, still it has been proved from the literature as one of the most important dimension for differentiation among competing firms.

We in this studies have taken training and development expenses as the proxy of firm performance assume that Human capital significantly affect the efficiency of working capital.

There is need for measuring Human capital and firm efficiency especially in MSME's in India given limited physical and economic resources.

We assume that there is bi directional association among the HCap and WCME denoted by CCC

3. Data and Methodology

The sample consists of 578 micro, small and medium manufacturing enterprises of India, of which are 59 micro-enterprises and 296 and 223 are small and medium enterprises, respectively. The sample comprises industries: industrial, chemical, energy , consumables, real estate, discretionary, etc. The data were collected from Prowess IQ, a data fetching tool from CMIE prowess data base. Initially, we fetched results for 1064 companies in India. Still, due to the non-availability of data in some variables, we excluded 486 companies from our data set. Finally, we derive a sample of 578 enterprises with 5780 observations for ten year's time period.

4. Variables Interpretations

CCC and CCE are the significant model terms used to measure the Working capital efficiency of India MSME's manufacturing enterprises. CCC is computed by Summing up closing inventory and accounts receivables(AR) and deducting accounts payables (AP) with the sum (Moussa, 2019). This study examines the connection amongst working capital management (WCM) efficiency and the firm's external factors. Age of the firm denoted as firms life compared to current year, tangibility, borrowing level denoted by leverage, firm size denoted by Total assets of the firm, profitability, firms' growth by denoted by difference between current and past year sales, salary expenses calculated as total expenses in salary of employees, and asset turnover ratio is the ratio of total income to asset comprise the collection of predictor factors.

Table 7.1 shows the variables used in this study. All explanatory variables in this study's equation are subjected to the redundancy test to determine their reliability. The redundancy test findings demonstrated that all explanatory factors are statistically meaningful and therefore must be incorporated into the formula. Table 7.1 also shows the outcomes of tests for multicollinearity

Table 7.1   Variables and corresponding variance inflation factor

Variables	Source	VIF
sal	Kieschnick et. al. (2006)	1.165
FSiz	Naseer et. al. (2012)	1.914
Hcap	Sapra and jain (2019)	1.33
Prof	Habib and Haung (2018)	1.213
Lever	Amr Ahmed Moussa (2019)	1.055
Tang	Panda (2012)	1.048
AGE	Salehi (2012)	1.04
ATR	Vaidya (2011)	1.026
FG	Naseer et. al. (2012)	1.01
CCC	Ahmed et. al (2017)	—

Source: Author compilation

of causal variables. Variance Inflation Factor (VIF) is used to assess multicollinearity (Habib & Kayani, 2022) The fact that the VIF test results are less than 2 suggests that there is no significant correlation between the independent variables (Habib & Mourad, 2022) and that multicollinearity does not exist.

Additionally the results of test for heteroskedasticity in both the model shows that the data is Homoskedasticity as the *p* value is more than 0.05.

White's test for Ho: homoskedasticity

against Ha: unrestricted heteroskedasticity

$$chi2(65) = 79.75$$

$$Prob > chi2 = 0.1030$$

Cameron & Trivedi's decomposition of IM-test

Table 7.2 Heteroskedasticity test

Source	chi2	df	p
Heteroskedasticity	79.750	65	0.103
Skewness	6.460	10	0.775
Kurtosis	-1.20e+08	1	1.000
Total	-1.20e+08	76	1.000

Source: Author compilation

5. Results and Discussion

The descriptive statistical analysis of all the predictor factors analysed in this study utilising data from all companies are provided in Table 7.3. The findings of descriptive and inferential statistics reveal high variation in the data, that requires further analysis.

Table 7.3 Pairwise correlation

Variables	(1)	(2)	(3)	(4)	(5)	(6)	(7)	(8)	(9)	(10)
(1) CCC	1.000									
(2) Lever	-0.346	1.000								
(3) Tang	0.433	0.144	1.000							
(4) Fsiz	-0.242	-0.143	0.117	1.000						
(5) Prof	-0.287	-0.317	-0.363	-0.010	1.000					
(6) Hcap	-0.266	-0.522	0.528	0.366	0.428	1.000				
(7) sal	-0.143	-0.464	0.335	0.670	0.250	0.493	1.000			
(8) AGE	-0.239	0.348	-0.451	-0.257	0.143	0.217	0.583	1.000		
(9) ATR	0.431	0.226	-0.123	-0.374	0.349	-0.259	-0.346	0.458	1.000	
(10) FG	0.461	0.476	0.118	-0.129	0.231	-0.312	-0.149	0.239	-0.235	1.000

Source: Author compilation

The pairwise correlation is shown in Table 7.4. The correlational analysis illustrates the association between all the variables employed in this study. It is potent instrument for summarizing a data and discovering correlation coefficients for predictor factors in the model.

Table 7.4 Descriptive statistics of independent variables

Variable	Obs	Mean	Std. Dev.	Min	Max
Leverage	5780	.303	.407	1.64	3.5
Tangi	5780	.311	.208	.232	.972
Fsize	5780	6.01	1.582	.095	9.737
Prof	5780	-1.315	59.918	-28	386
Hcap	5780	-.043	1.717	-4.711	5.455
sal	5780	2.829	1.747	-2.303	6.765
ATR	5780	2.006	4.861	-.006	103.167
AGE	5780	3.111	.524	.693	4.344
FG	5780	19.562	41.606	-2.039	132

Source: Author compilation

Table 7.5 shows the results of Hausman test where we found that the *p* value is less than 0.05 rejecting the null hypothesis and using fixed effect model for estimation.

Table 7.5 Hausman (1978) specification test

	Coef.
Chi-square test value	53.323
P-value	0

Source: Author compilation

Table 7.6 illustrates the corrected R-squared values for MSME's sector as a whole, as determined using linear regression with pooled data fixed effect analysis for CCC. Observing Table 7.6 , it can be noticed that the r-square for the MSME's sectoral data are substantial, indicating that the prediction models adopted in this research have significant explanatory power. Additionally we found most of the variables including leverage, firm size, firm growth, tangibility, Human capital to be significant at five percent level of significance whereas profitability and asset turnover ratio is significant at 1 percent and 10 percent level with model 1 represented in Table 7.6 which implies that tangibility, leverage, firm size, profitability, expenses in Human capital, ATR, and firm growth affect the cash conversion cycle in both positive and negative ways. Salary and age of the firm were not significant from the result shown in table.

Leverage and CCC are having negative association, so we can infer from this that increase in debt level in firm will reduce the efficiency of the working capital. This finding is supported by previous research (Seth, Sharma & Chadha, 2020). This can be supported from the fact debt level enhances the burden by reducing the firm liquidity as businesses have to make the timely payment of interest which reduces the cash and bank reserves from the business.

Table 7.6 Regression results from CCC

CCC	Coef.	St.Err.	t-value	p-value	[95% Conf	Interval]	Sig
Lever	-1460.519	634.994	-2.30	.022	-2706.117	-214.92	**
Tangib	1421.125	637.989	2.23	.013	-1007.303	3849.554	**
Fsiz	-410.952	220.017	-1.87	.030	-822.535	40.632	**
Prof	22.43	4.626	4.85	0	13.356	31.503	***
Hcap	-275.556	168.935	-1.63	.05	-356.937	305.826	**
sal	235.498	211.941	1.11	.267	-180.244	651.24	
ATR	78.294	52.434	1.49	.068	-28.56	177.147	*
AGE	-202.378	489.279	-0.41	.679	-1162.145	757.388	
FG	.942	.536	1.76	.040	-.91	1.194	**
Constant	1489.293	2014.538	0.74	.46	-2462.407	5440.994	
Mean dependent var		-788.712	SD dependent var			1100.589	
Overall r-squared		0.815	Number of obs			5780	
Chi-square		21.656	Prob > chi2			0.010	
R-squared within		0.785	R-squared between			0.742	

***$p < .01$, **$p < .05$, *$p < .1$
Source: Author compilation

Hence we accept the hypothesis H(a)

Tangibility as denoted by the portion of fixed assets in the overall assets is positively significant with the CCC. Fixed assets proportion in the Firm size is negatively significant with CCC. From this we can infer that as the size of the firm increases it is very hard to manage the overall assets as they are having varieties of the task to be performed whereas the small firms have limited operational work and hence they can utilise their assets in more effective way which will indirectly lead to efficient working capital. This view is also supported by prior research(Chauhan & Banerjee, 2018; Kasozi, 2017).

Profitability of the firm affect the CCC in a positive way, one way of firm to be profitable is that there income should be more than the expenses. In case of MSME's sectors as the firms are having limited resources and very few sources of financing and their growth depend more upon the profitability of the company. Furthermore, majority of affairs are manged by short term financing hence the firm need to reduce the receivable and inventory period to generate more revenues in said period of time which in turn enhances the intensity of profitability in firm. The study (Enqvist et al., 2014) found negative association between CCC and profitability of the firm. Human capital is negatively correlated with efficiency of CCC, as the MSME's are resource constraint firm they cannot invest more on training and development expenses of the employees when compared with the large firms. If the firm is investing more on training having less working capital , it will affect negatively the CCC of the firm. When compared to prior work(Kieschnick et al., 2006) the current research gives the conflicting results Asset turnover ratio is found be positively significant at 0.1 level , this suggest that linear relationship among

ATR and CCC. Firm with high ATR are more liquid and are able to use more external financing for enhancing firm short term efficiency. Also they can avail longer credit line from its vendors due to better ATR.

Growth of the firm positively affects the CCC. Growing firms always feel positive about the affairs of the business. They can make more purchases in credit and avail deferral payment conditions from its suppliers which enhances the WCME. This is also supported by previous studies (Seth, Sharma, Ruparel, et al., 2020).

6. Conclusion

From the above discussion we identified that determinants which can affects working capital of MSME's of India. We used two models for the same by taking various exogenous variables. In the first model where CCC was the dependent variables we found that Tangibility(tang), Profitability(Prof), Asset turnover Ratio(ATR), Firm Growth(FG) were found to be positively contributing to the CCC where as leverage(lever), Firm size(Fsiz), Human Capital(Hcap) were negatively related with the CCC. Few variables like Firms Age (AGE) and Salary (sal) were insignificant with the CCC.

The finding from the study provides a insights of the determining factors for working capital management in India MSME's hence it will add to literature of working capital efficiency management of Small businesses. The study provides understandings for the practitioner and decision makers to take better decision making and formulate concrete plans.

The study is important for effectively analysing the core factors affecting of day to day requirements of firms (working capital) and effectively managing them.

Additionally study can help the MSME's owners and top executives to enhance the productivity of the firms by inculcating the above findings.

7. Limitations and Future Directions

The study only took data from MSME's sector in India. Further more we analysed only those variables for which the data were readily available. Future research can study the same sets of variables in other developing regions level. Also other sets of variables can be incorporated as a mediating effect in analysis of results and may give other dimensions to the study. On methodological aspect we can explore other techniques standing with the data sets and may give different results.

REFERENCES

1. Abbadi, S. M., & Abbadi, R. T. (2012). The Determinants of Working Capital Requirements in Palestinian Industrial Corporations. *International Journal of Economics and Finance*, *5*(1), p65. https://doi.org/10.5539/IJEF.V5N1P65
2. Akinlo, O. O. (2012). Determinants of Working Capital Requirements in Selected Quoted Companies in Nigeria. *Journal of African Business*, *13*(1), 40–50. https://doi.org/10.1080/1522891 6.2012.657951

3. Aktas, N., Croci, E., & Petmezas, D. (2015). Is working capital management value-enhancing? Evidence from firm performance and investments. *Journal of Corporate Finance*, *30*(1), 98–113. https://doi.org/10.1016/J.JCORPFIN.2014.12.008

4. Arunkumar, O. N., & Sonwaney, V. (2019). Enhancing operational efficiency by optimizing working capital management of manufacturing firms. *International Journal of Recent Technology and Engineering*, *8*(3), 2695–2705. https://doi.org/10.35940/ijrte.C4953.098319

5. Baños-Caballero, S., García-Teruel, P. J., & Martínez-Solano, P. (2010). Working capital management in SMEs. In *Accounting and Finance* (Vol. 50, Issue 3). https://doi.org/10.1111/J.1467-629X.2009.00331.X

6. Baños-Caballero, S., García-Teruel, P. J., & Martínez-Solano, P. (2013). The speed of adjustment in working capital requirement. *Http://Dx.Doi.Org/10.1080/1351847X.2012.691889*, *19*(10), 978–992. https://doi.org/10.1080/1351847X.2012.691889

7. Baños-Caballero, S., García-Teruel, P. J., & Martínez-Solano, P. (2016). Financing of working capital requirement, financial flexibility and SME performance. *Journal of Business Economics and Management*, *17*(6), 1189–1204. https://doi.org/10.3846/16111699.2015.1081272

8. Chauhan, G. S., & Banerjee, P. (2018). Financial constraints and optimal working capital – evidence from an emerging market. *International Journal of Managerial Finance*, *14*(1), 37–53. https://doi.org/10.1108/IJMF-07-2016-0131/FULL/PDF

9. Dalci, I., Tanova, C., Ozyapici, H., & Bein, M. A. (2019). The moderating impact of firm size on the relationship between working capital management and profitability. *Prague Economic Papers*, *28*(3), 296–312. https://doi.org/10.18267/J.PEP.681

10. Elbadry, A. (2018). The Determinants of Working Capital Management in the Egyptian SMEs. *Accounting and Finance Research*, *7*(2), 155. https://doi.org/10.5430/afr.v7n2p155

11. Enqvist, J., Graham, M., & Nikkinen, J. (2014). The impact of working capital management on firm profitability in different business cycles: Evidence from Finland. *Research in International Business and Finance*, *32*, 36–49. https://doi.org/10.1016/J.RIBAF.2014.03.005

12. Filbeck, G., Zhao, X., & Knoll, R. (2017). An analysis of working capital efficiency and shareholder return. *Review of Quantitative Finance and Accounting*, *48*(1), 265–288. https://doi.org/10.1007/s11156-015-0550-0

13. Habib, A. M., & Kayani, U. N. (2022). Does the efficiency of working capital management affect a firm's financial distress? Evidence from UAE. *Corporate Governance (Bingley)*. https://doi.org/10.1108/CG-12-2021-0440

14. Habib, A. M., & Mourad, N. (2022). Analyzing the Efficiency of Working Capital Management: a New Approach Based on DEA-Malmquist Technology. *Operations Research Forum*, *3*(3), 32. https://doi.org/10.1007/S43069-022-00155-7

15. Hill, M. D., Kelly, G. W., & Highfield, M. J. (2010). Net Operating Working Capital Behavior: A First Look. *Financial Management*, *39*(2), 783–805. https://doi.org/10.1111/J.1755-053X.2010.01092.X

16. Jaworski, J., & Czerwonka, L. (2022). Which Determinants Matter for Working Capital Management in Energy Industry? The Case of European Union Economy. *Energies*, *15*(9). https://doi.org/10.3390/en15093030

17. Kasozi, J. (2017). The effect of working capital management on profitability: A case of listed manufacturing firms in South Africa. *Investment Management and Financial Innovations*, *14*(2), 336–346. https://doi.org/10.21511/IMFI.14(2-2).2017.05

18. Kieschnick, R., LaPlante, M., & Moussawi, R. (2006). Corporate working capital management: Determinants and Consequences. *International Journal of Managerial Finance*, *3*(2), 164–177.

19. Kieschnick, R., & Moussawi, R. (2006). Corporate working capital management: Determinants and Consequences. *International Journal of Managerial Finance*, *3*(2), 164–177. https://www. researchgate.net/publication/242506805

20. Kindermann, B., Schmidt, C. V. H., Pulm, J., & Strese, S. (2022). The Double-Edged Sword of Entrepreneurial Orientation: A Configurational Perspective on Failure in Newly Public Firms. *Entrepreneurship Theory and Practice*, 104225872211117. https://doi. org/10.1177/10422587221111724

21. Liu, H., Pan, J. X., Yuan, H. Q., Li, H. L., Wang, J., Wang, J. J., & Song, X. H. (2021). Research on Evaluation of Working Capital Management Efficiency of Electric Power Listed Companies. *E3S Web of Conferences*, *251*. https://doi.org/10.1051/e3sconf/202125101095

22. Moussa, A. A. (2019). Determinants of working capital behavior: evidence from Egypt. *International Journal of Managerial Finance*, *15*(1), 39–61. https://doi.org/10.1108/IJMF-09-2017-0219/FULL/ PDF

23. Mutua Mathuva, D. (2014). An empirical analysis of the determinants of the cash conversion cycle in Kenyan listed non-financial firms. *Journal of Accounting in Emerging Economies*, *4*(2), 175– 196. https://doi.org/10.1108/JAEE-10-2011-0045

24. Niskanen, J., & Niskanen, M. (2006). The Determinants of Corporate Trade Credit Policies in a Bank-dominated Financial Environment: the Case of Finnish Small Firms. *European Financial Management*, *12*(1), 81–102. https://doi.org/10.1111/J.1354-7798.2006.00311.X

25. Nunn, K. P. (1981). THE STRATEGIC DETERMINANTS OF WORKING CAPITAL: A PRODUCT-LINE PERSPECTIVE. *Journal of Financial Research*, *4*(3), 207–219. https://doi. org/10.1111/J.1475-6803.1981.TB00604.X

26. Nyeadi, J. D., Sare, Y. A., & Aawaar, G. (2019). Determinants of working capital requirement in listed firms: Empirical evidence using a dynamic system GMM. *Http://Www.Editorialmanager. Com/Cogentecon*, *6*(1), 1–14. https://doi.org/10.1080/23322039.2018.1558713

27. Prasad, P., Sivasankaran, N., Paul, S., & Kannadhasan, M. (2019). Measuring impact of working capital efficiency on financial performance of a firm: An alternative approach. *Journal of Indian Business Research*. https://doi.org/10.1108/JIBR-02-2018-0056/FULL/PDF

28. Rao, P., Kumar, S., Chavan, M., & Lim, W. M. (2021). A systematic literature review on SME financing: Trends and future directions. *Journal of Small Business Management*. https://doi.org/10 .1080/00472778.2021.1955123

29. Salawu, R. O., & Alao, J. A. (2014). Determinants of Working Capital Management: Case of Nigerian Manufacturing Firms. In *Journal of Economics and Sustainable Development www.iiste. org ISSN* (Vol. 5, Issue 14). www.iiste.org

30. Seth, H., Chadha, S., & Sharma, S. (2020). Redesigning the efficiency process analysis for working capital models: Evidences from the determinants. *Journal of Global Operations and Strategic Sourcing*, *13*(1), 38–55. https://doi.org/10.1108/JGOSS-04-2019-0029/FULL/XML

31. Seth, H., Sharma, S., & Chadha, S. (2020). Benchmarking the efficiency model for working capital management: data envelopment analysis approach Working Capital Management-An Empirical evidence from Indian Manufacturing Sector. *International Journal of Productivity and Performance Management*. https://doi.org/10.1108/IJPPM-10-2019-0484

32. Seth, H., Sharma, S., Ruparel, N., Chadha, S., & Sharma, S. K. (2020). Exploring predictors of working capital management efficiency and their influence on firm performance: an integrated DEA-SEM approach. *Benchmarking An International Journal*. https://doi.org/10.1108/BIJ-05-2020-0251

33. Sharma, R. K., Bakshi, A., & Chhabra, S. (2020). Determinants of behaviour of working capital requirements of BSE listed companies: An empirical study using co-integration techniques and

generalised method of moments. *Http://Www.Editorialmanager.Com/Cogentecon*, 8(1). https://doi.org/10.1080/23322039.2020.1720893

34. Singh, H. P., & Kumar, S. (2017). Working capital requirements of manufacturing SMEs: evidence from emerging economy. *Review of International Business and Strategy*, 27(3), 369–385. https://doi.org/10.1108/RIBS-03-2017-0027

35. ur Rehman, A., Wang, M., & Kabiraj, S. (2017). Working capital management in Chinese firms: An empirical investigation of determinants & adjustment towards a target level using dynamic panel data model Working capital management in Chinese firms: an empirical investigation of determinants and adjustment towards a target level using dynamic panel data model. *Afro-Asian J. Finance and Accounting*, 7(1), 84–105. https://doi.org/10.1504/AAJFA.2017.082930

36. Yousaf, M., Bris, P., & Haider, I. (2021). Working capital management and firm's profitability: Evidence from Czech certified firms from the EFQM excellence model. *Cogent Economics and Finance*, 9(1). https://doi.org/10.1080/23322039.2021.1954318

Chapter

Financial Inclusion and Pradhan Mantri Jan Dhan Yojana: Evidence From Durg District

Ankita Tripathi*

Department of Commerce,
Hemchand Yadav Vishwavidyalaya, Durg (C.G)

Ravish Kumar Soni[1]

Department of Commerce,
Kalyan Post Graduate College , Bhilai (C.G.)

Rajkumar[2]

Department of Management,
Birla institute of Technology and Science, Pilani, Pilani Camplus, India

ABSTRACT: Purpose – This research seeks to critically evaluate one of the financial inclusion policies "Pradhan Mantri Jan Dhan Yojana" announced by the Indian government in 2014.

Design/methodology/approach – This research examines PMJDY, a financial inclusion effort of the Goi, and its performance in the different districts of Chhattisgarh. The volume of new saving bank accounts opened (remote, urban, and aggregate) in line with the policy, the total money among these accounts, and the overall amount of debit cards distributed through October 2021 were chosen as the criterion. The macroeconomic factors, infrastructural facilities, education, and workforce participation have been used as indices.

Findings –Durg block emerged as the leading block index for Financial Inclusion underneath the PMJDY programme, trailed by Patan and Dhamdha block. The condition of infrastructure (such as the quantity of roadways) was shown to be the most influential factor. Other influences were employment, poverty, and geographical disparities.

Originality/value – This article is unusual in that financial inclusion policy has been evaluated in terms of both its accessibility and its predictions. This investigation initially considers the three Chhattisgarh blocks.

KEYWORDS: India, Financial inclusion, Durg, Patan, Dhamdha.

*Corresponding Author: Ankita.Tripathi@pilani.bits-pilani.ac.in
[1]soni.ravish27@gmail.com, [2]p20210038@pilani.bits-pilani.ac.in

DOI: 10.4324/9781003415725-8

1. Introduction

Individuals and businesses must have access to affordable financial products and services that meet their needs, such as transactions, transfer of funds, savings, borrowing, and insurance that are ethically and sustainably supplied. Financial inclusion aims to assist individuals in meeting their necessities, such as meals, water, shelter, education, including medical services. Customers will have more constant and fair accessibility, while this also benefits the companies providing them. Every nation must have a financial system that is accessible to everyone. Financial inclusion alone might eliminate poverty, but it can help individuals construct better lives. It may assist people in launching enterprises and help small firms expand. Small farmers may be integrated into the official economic system with the assistance of financial products, allowing for a two-way transmission of data and money. The World Bank includes financial inclusion a crucial factor in reducing excessive poverty and enhancing economic stability. (www.worldbank.org). In countries that are majorly Government owned, even if customers pay a lower fee, they face difficulties in terms of compliance and paperwork thus, becoming a barrier to financial inclusion (Throston 2006). Schemes of financial inclusion will show a positive effect in states with a lower literacy level (Reddy, 2017). It is essential to consider the variations in the cross-country drivers and effects of financial intermediation on economic inequality across socioeconomic groups when selecting the proper policies for attaining inclusive growth at various phases of development(Park & Mercado, 2018). In Long-term, financial inclusion reduces the metropolitan income gap, but short-term inclusion exacerbates it. Two plausible causes for the short-term growth are the rapid spread of banking systems and the discrepancy in education amongst rural and urban regions (Huang & Zhang, 2020). There exists a favourable and lasting correlation among both financial inclusion as well as economic expansion. Todays modern banking clients have access, via a number of channels, sets of potent tools that enable them to perform analyses, make choices, and complete financial transactions while working remotely, from office, or anywhere (Hoehle et al., 2012). Community cohesion, ideological inclusion, economic inclusion, as well as financial inclusion are almost all facets of inclusion. There is potential for financial inclusion to fill up the gaps and assist economic inclusion to a somewhat degree. Financial inclusion challenges are country-specific; hence, there can be no worldwide norm (Reddy, 2017). Due to cumbersome papers, processes, and other formalities, the majority of poor people shun banks. This straightforward structure and methods will increase bank savings (Aggarwal, 2014).

2. The Pradhan Mantri Jan Dhan Yojana: A Programme Towards Financial Inclusion

The PMJDY was created with the intention of providing access to a wide range of financial products, including as bank accounts, need-based financing, remittance facility, pensions, and coverage, to poor groups and disadvantaged segments of the population. With the use of technology, cost was anticipated to be reasonable. The strategy aims for each family to have minimum one deposit account . In addition to providing financially excluded individuals with a basic savings account, the government also provides them with accidental insurance coverage of Rs. 1 Lakh, that has been enhanced to Rs. 2 Lakh as of February 28, 2018. Thus, in addition to advancing Financial Inclusion Consequently, financial security is taken good care of. It has been shown, however, that many individuals do not like establishing a bank account due to their lack of money. In addition to eliminating the minimum balance requirement, this impediment has been eliminated. A Rs 10,000 overdraft facility is made available to those in need, therefore addressing the issue of a lack of finances in situations when it is of the highest importance. The government encourages savings by offering account holders interest on the amount saved. This is an incentive for unbanked individuals to establish the habit of saving. Regarding money withdrawals and other online activities, account users have been provided Rupay cards for their convenience. Since the program's beginning, the number of PMJDY savings accounts has grown steadily, although the number of inactive accounts has also increased. A report provided by the government towards the end of the fifth year of the plan reveals that a total of 1096.4 million saving accounts have indeed been established with deposits exceeding 220 billion dollars. In roughly 69 percent of situations, Aadhaar has always been the main document. Initially, 76% of accounts in the system had zero balances, but that number has decreased to 46% during the last year. Banks have organised numerous financial education courses to increase awareness of the plan and its advantages.

The research explored the viability of PMJDY, a financial programme of the Indian government, in each block of Durg district in the state of Chhattisgarh. As a result, each block presents a distinct cross section for research, and it is intriguing to observe whether the national initiatives on financial inclusion are having the same effects. Importantly, this district is one of the growing region having a complete and trustworthy data set, hence the analysed data may be used to illustrate other regions with comparable characteristics.

Prior evidence in the literature demonstrate the clear relation between financial consolidation and economic expansion (Srivastava, 2004; Barajas et al., 2012). It has been discovered that income, wealth, as well as education play crucial roles in establishing financial access (Claessen, 2006). Through his cross examination of seven African countries, Porteous (2006) determined that employment, age, education, gender, and poverty are significant factors for financial exclusion.

In his research of India, Kumar (2005) observed that the level, wealth, education, and gender were significant determinants, and yet there were also significant variations in availability by region and also by suburb within province, with main distinctions between those living in legal and illegal settlements and in relation to housing quality. Women many of whom are paid less than comparable male peers have a greater cost of accessibility, which is exacerbated by a poor social position.

3. Data and Variables

We utilise Provincial Panel data and the number of saving bank accounts established (remote and metropolitan) during PMJDY for our research (data extracted till October 21, 2021). We chose this time to evaluate the effectiveness of PMJDY throughout Chhattisgarh states territories. The outcome variable in the multiple regression analyses are the overall number of savings bank accounts opened, the total amount of saving bank accounts opened in rural areas , the overall amount of saving bank accounts opened in urban areas , the cumulative amount in bank accounts (in INR crores), as well as the amount of RuPay cards provided. We gradually include these predictors into the different estimation models to determine the influence of provincial variables on the PMJDY's outreach. The data were obtained from the PMJDY status report. All other data were acquired from different RBI and Indian government studies.

4. Result and Discussion

4.1 Estimating the Amount of Rural PMJDY Saving Bank Accounts

Table 8.1 illustrates the regression results of pooled data by applying fixed effect model. In the table we have taken Rural Accounts under PMJDY as dependent variable whereas Bank deposits (BankDep), literacy of female (Fliteracy), Rural roads infrastructure(RuralRds), Rural loans (Rcredits), taken as independent variable. Fixed effect model indicated that the accumulated rural bank deposits previous to Jan dhan yojana and also the quantity of rural highways are strong positive predictors of the overall rural PMJDY account holders, while the overall sum of credit lines before to Pradhan mantri jan dhan yojana and Fliteracy percentage are substantial negative signifiers. The analysis also showed that the amount of rural PMJDY account in the central part is much larger than elsewhere regions. Model R-square is 0.885, adjusted R-square is 0.822.

Table 8.1 Amount of rural PMJDY saving bank accounts

PMJDYRAcc	Coef.	St.Err.	t-value	p-value	[95% Conf	Interval]	Sig
BankDep	120.799	24.654	4.90	.012	-26.17	-214.92	**
Fliteracy	-14241.125	6237.149	-2.28	.033	-17.303	3849.554	**
RuralRds	13.52	6.017	2.24	.030	82.535	40.632	**
Rcredits	-2.43	.626	4.85	0	3.356	31.503	***
CR, CR=1	17325.556	12368.985	-1.63	.05	766.937	305.826	**
Constant	15889.23	12014.538	0.74	.46	242.407	5440.994	
Mean dependent var		71278.12	SD dependent var			1320.589	
Overall r-squared		0.875	Number of obs			2140	
Chi-square		11.32	Prob > chi2			0.021	
R-squared within		0.885	R-squared between			0.822	
***p < .01, **p < .05, *p < .1							

Source: Authors own calculation

4.2 Estimating the Overall Amount of PMJDY Saving Bank Accounts

Table 8.2 illustrates the regression results of pooled data by applying fixed effect model. In the table we have taken Total Bank Accounts both rural as well as urban under PMJDY as dependent variable whereas Roads infrastructure in urban areas(UrbanRds), Workforce participation male(M_labourp), Rural roads infrastructure(RuralRds), taken as independent variable. Different region such Western, Eastern and Central are taken as dummy variables. Fixed effect model indicated that the accumulated overall bank saving accounts before Jan dhan yojana and also the quantity of rural highways are strong positive predictors of the overall rural PMJDY account holders whereas the quantity of urban roads is strong negative predictor. The analysis also showed that the amount of rural PMJDY account in the central, western as well as eastern part , is much larger than elsewhere regions. Model R-square is 0.935, adjusted R-square is 0.916.

Table 8.2   Overall amount of PMJDY saving bank accounts

PMJDYTAcc	Coef.	St.Err.	t-value	p-value	[95% Conf	Interval]	Sig
UrbanRds	10.519	4.994	2.13	.022	276.117	-214.92	**
WR, WR = 1	69.176	32.12	2.15	.031	28.592	12.362	**
RuralRds	1421.125	637.989	2.23	.013	207.303	3849.554	**
M_labourp	-410.952	220.17	-1.86	.030	22.535	40.632	**
ER, ER = 1	2562.13	1464.615	1.75	0	13.356	31.503	***
CR, CR = 1	48275.556	18758.935	2.57	.05	56.937	305.826	**
Constant	163489.293	28544.538	5.72	.046	2462.407	5440.994	**
Mean dependent var		17568.712	SD dependent var			120.847	
Overall r-squared		0.945	Number of obs			2140	
Chi-square		21.656	Prob > chi2			0.010	
R-squared within		0.935	R-squared between			0.916	
***p < .01, **p < .05, *p < .1							

Source: Authors own calculation

4.3 Estimating Aggregate Saving Account Balance in PMJDY Accounts

Table 8.3 illustrates the regression results of pooled data by applying fixed effect model. In the table we have taken Total Bank Accounts balance both rural as well as urban under PMJDY as dependent variable whereas Roads infrastructure in urban areas (UrbanRds), literacy of Women(Fliteracy), Rural roads infrastructure(RuralRds), taken as independent variable. Southern part is taken as dummy variables. Fixed effect model indicated that also the quantity of urban highways are strong negative predictors of the aggregate saving bank account balance under PMJDY(PM_TBAB) whereas the quantity of urban roads(UrbanRds) is strong positive predictor. The analysis also showed that the southern part is significant predictor of PM_TBAB.

4.4 Estimating Aggregate Numbers of Debit Rupay Cards Issued Under PMJDY

Table 8.4 illustrates the regression results of pooled data by applying fixed effect model. In the table we have taken Aggregate nymbers of Rupay cards issued under PMJD scheme

Table 8.3 Aggregate saving Account balance in PMJDY accounts

PM_TBAB	Coef.	St.Err.	t-value	p-value	[95% Conf	Interval]	Sig
UrbanRds	4.316	1.004	4.10	.022	-2706.117	-214.92	**
Fliteracy	-11.125	7.989	-1.13	.013	-1007.303	3849.554	**
SR , SR=1	-2715.556	1268.935	-1.63	.05	-356.937	305.826	**
Constant	14479.293	2104.538	6.88	.46	-2462.407	5440.994	
Mean dependent var		378.712	SD dependent var			59.512	
Overall r-squared		0.718	Number of obs			2140	
Chi-square		11.656	Prob > chi2			0.010	
R-squared within		0.675	R-squared between			0.654	
***p < .01, **p < .05, *p < .1							

Source: Authors own calculation

Table 8.4 Aggregate numbers of debit Rupay cards issued under PMJDY

RDebitCard	Coef.	St.Err.	t-value	p-value	[95% Conf	Interval]	Sig
UrbanRds	106.106	23.399	4.37	.79	-.889	.677	
CR, CR=1	17853.045	3271.003	5.48	0	.04	.051	***
RuralRds	12.68	4.079	2.83	.045	-2.174	.878	**
M_labourp	-21657.25	12856.138	-1.51	.071	-.021	.521	*
ER, ER=1	12893.038	4321.106	2.85	.724	-.246	.171	
WR, WR=1	4328.006	1543.033	2.64	.866	-.07	.059	
UBPL	-21355.139	3276.133	-6.54	.296	-.4	.122	
Constant	15747.901	1679.267	9.32	.477	-3.384	1.583	
Mean dependent var		.303	SD dependent var			1.636	
Overall r-squared		0.769	Number of obs			2140	
Chi-square		297.951	Prob > chi2			0.000	
R-squared within		0.751	R-squared between			0.726	
***p < .01, **p < .05, *p < .1							

Source: Authors own calculation

as dependent variable whereas Roads infrastructure in urban areas (UrbanRds), Workforce participation Male (M_labourp), Rural roads infrastructure(RuralRds), Proportion of Population under poverty line(UBPL), Central Part(CR), Eastern part (ER), Central Part (CR) taken as independent variable. Fixed effect model indicated that the both Rural (Rural Rds) and Urban(UrbanRds) positively affects the Dependent Variable whereas Proportion of Population under poverty line(UBPL) is negative predictors of the Aggregate numbers of debit Rupay cards issued under PMJDY(RdebitCard). The analysis also reveal that Rupay cards usage in eastern, central and central part is comparatively high in numbers compared to other regions. Model R-square is 0.885, adjusted R-square is 0.822.

5. Discussion

Researchers have seen that infrastructure improvements, such as the construction of roads, increases connectivity to banking institutions, and is crucial for every financial inclusion project in both rural and urban settings. In rural area, banks with greater depositors, that can be an evidence of possibly wealthier districts , have been far more effective in their objective to provide Pradhan mantri jan dhan yojana accounts, although banks with substantially greater credit had less requests for Jan dhan yojana accounts. Regions with more female workforce participation in urban areas have reduced PMJDY account usage. This may be due to the fact that employment increases economic independence and autonomy. There's a likelihood that these female already possess bank accounts, resulting in fewer requests for Pradhan mantri jan dhan yojana accounts. Prior research concurs that female's engagement in the labour force results in improved wellness, literacy, as well as other indicators of empowering women. Similar regions with more male rural participation rate had lesser Pradhan mantri jan dhan account requirements. With a greater total female education level, the Pradhan mantri jan dhan yojana account balances are lower. This might be because educated women have greater incomes and could have previously established alternative bank accounts prior to the launch of Pradhan mantri jan dhan yojana. Research have also asserted that education influences investing decisions. In regions with a greater proportion of residents living in extreme poverty, usage for Pradhan mantri jan dhan debit cards is less. There were significant regional variances in respect of Financial Inclusion via Pradhan mantri jan dhan yojana, with the central region ranking higher in the majority of Pradhan mantri jan dhan penetration metrics. One explanation is that the core region of Chhattisgarh does have some of the largest and most populous provinces.

6. Conclusion

This research makes a concerted attempt to determine the scope of Pradhan mantri jan dhan yojana in Chhattisgarh. In accordance with the prior study of financial inclusion as well as the purpose of Pradhan mantri jan dhan yojana to link the economically disenfranchised to the mainstream banking system, we measured the accessibility of PMJDY based on the number of PMJDY savings accounts established and bank account amounts throughout this program. Utilising panel data of multiple districts in Chhattisgarh spanning the first stage of PMJDY, we further explored the variables that determine access to financial services and effectiveness of Pradhan mantri jan dhan yojana.

The research employs multivariate regression analysis, and indeed the findings demonstrate geographical differences in the PMJDY's impact, particularly in central area of the state as well as the economic criteria and position of the each region. This might be due to the central region's infrastructural availability and financial institution concentration. It also suggested less financial accessibility. As demonstrated by its greater reach in the centre zone, the implementation of Pradhan mantri jan dhan yojana may have enhanced bank accessibility.

In respect of rural as well as overall accounts, the multiple regression results indicate that Pradhan mantri jan dhan yojana reach is greatest in the less economically developed and rural regions of India. In urban regions, the access to banks is greater, and the majority of the population is engaged in industry or services. It is more likely that account-opening-required documentation exists. Therefore, it is anticipated that the engaged portion of the population will already have savings accounts. Reach-wise, PMJDY was unable to differentiate significantly across lower and higher economic classes. Rural regions, but at the other hand, have a mostly agrarian economy and are distant from banks. Due to the lack of essential documentation for establishing banking and the lack of access of financial institutions in terms of location, poor and marginal landowners relied on non - institutional sources such as lending for Private money lenders. Institutions were only available to affluent farmers who have the necessary documentation and the economic means to maintain the minimum bank balance. Our data demonstrates that Pradhan mantri jan dhan yojana has made banks reachable to low-income populations in rural regions.

Corresponding with the initiatives of legislators in India and throughout the world who are determinedly pursuing inclusive development, the results support the importance of shared prosperity. The accomplishment of Pradhan mantri jan dhan yojana, a legislators' financial inclusion effort, demonstrates this idea. Consequently, the Indian economy will need comparable measures and creative ideas in the future to maintain the big population within the boundaries of equitable development.

REFERENCES

1. Aggarwal, R (2014). Financial inclusion in India: Challenges and opportunities. International Journal of Research, 1(4), 557–567.
2. Barajas, A., Chami, R. and Yousefi, S.R. (2012), "The finance and growth nexus re-examined: do all countries benefit equally?", Working Paper IMF.
3. Beck, Thorsten; Demirguc-Kunt, Asli; Martinez Peria, Maria Soledad. (2006). Banking Services for Everyone? Barriers to Bank Access and Use around the World. Policy Research Working Paper; No. 4079. World Bank, Washington, DC. © World Bank. https://openknowledge.worldbank.org/handle/10986/8833 License: CC BY 3.0 IGO."
4. Claessens, S. (2006), "Access to financial services: a review of the issues and public policy objectives", WorldBank Research Observer, Vol. 21 No. 2, pp. 207–240.
5. Hoehle, H., Scornavacca, E., & Huff, S. (2012). Three decades of research on consumer adoption and utilization of electronic banking channels: A literature analysis. Decision Support System, 54, 122–132.
6. Banerjee, A., Chandrasekhar, A., Duflo, E., & Jackson, M. O. (2013). The diffusion of microfinance. Science Magazine, 341(6144), 1–48.
7. Huang, Y., & Zhang, Y. (2020). Financial inclusion and urban–rural income inequality: Long-run and short-run relationships.Emerging Markets Finance and Trade, 56(2), 457–471.
8. Kumar, A. (2005), Access to Financial Services in Brazil: A Study, World Bank, Washington DC.
9. Park, C.-Y. & Mercado, R. (2018). Financial inclusion, poverty, and income inequality. The Singapore Economic Review, 63(01),185–206.
10. Porteous, D. (2006), "The enabling environment for mobile banking in Africa", Report to DFID, May.

11. Reddy, Y.V. (2017). Financial policy for the poor: Financial inclusion and micro-debt. 11th UNCTAD Debt Management Conference, Geneva.
12. Sarma, M. (2008), Index of Financial Inclusion, Indian Council for Research on International Economics Relations: New Delhi.
13. Sethi, D., & Acharya, D. (2018). Financial inclusion and economic growth linkage: Some cross country evidence. Journal of Financial Economic Policy, 10(3), 369–385.

Handbook of Evidence Based Management Practices in Business – Satyendra Kumar Sharma et al. (eds)
© 2023 Taylor & Francis Group, London, ISBN 978-1-032-54216-4

Chapter

9

Comparative Analysis of the Financial Structures of Germany and Japan

Nikkita Gupta*

Centre for the Study of Regional Development (CSRD),
Jawaharlal Nehru University (JNU), New Delhi, India

ABSTRACT: The paper aims to make a comparative analysis of the similarities and differences in the financial structures of Germany and Japan in terms of variables such as nature of banks, interest rates, saving rates, aspects of corporate growth, gross domestic product, exports, high investment, individual bank or systemic failures, stability, inflation and exchange rates. The changing environment and changes in their financial structures and policies since the 1970's are also analyzed empirically with an aim to throw light on strengths and weaknesses of their financial system, so as to get insights for critical policy implications for the Indian financial system.

The paper concludes that what is essentially required is a system such as the three-tiered system in Germany (consisting of big private corporate banks, publicly owned savings and Landesbanken banks, and cooperative banks) which would ensure growth as well as inclusiveness. Germany sustained through merger of big banks as an effective policy change. Besides, the deregulation should be accompanied by an appropriate re-regulation. For instance, a big fault made by Japan is implementation of monetary policy for too long with low interest rates which led to inherent risk in the system. Finally, there is a need for regulatory authorities to ensure not only effective implementation of macro-prudential regulations, but also to take active steps in response to financial innovations such as securitization and cryptocurrency so that regulatory power may not implicitly get diluted.

KEYWORDS: Financial systems, Germany, Japan, Macro-prudential regulations

*nikkita44n@gmail.com

DOI: 10.4324/9781003415725-9

1. Introduction

Germany and Japan are late industrializing countries (Germany being industrialized earlier than Japan) both of which emerged as an "economic miracle" during the 1950's and 60's, post-WWII. Even Japan had a great performance with a GDP of around ten percent post world war II. The difference is that while Germany sustained its financial system much well for the whole 20th century, the problems started emerging just in the recent era during the Financial Crisis, 2008. However, Japan could sustain high growth only till 1970's, after which it started suffering problems, as much as the lost decade of 1990's and has not come back to its high growth pace yet. The paper is set as follows: (1) The similarities and differences in the two financial structures are explained; (2) The changing environment and changes in their financial structures and policies since 1970's is explained with an aim to throw light on strengths and weaknesses of their financial system which led to such results.

2. Financial Structures in Germany and Japan (Post WW II till 1970's)

Both Germany and Japan chose 'bank-based financial system', in contrast to the 'market-based system' where market players predominantly decide the level of interest rates and prices of various securities. Thus, a lot of capital for industrialization is mobilized through the banks. The significant aspect is that both have separate tiers/set of parallel banking institutions for dealing with different aims as follows:

Table 9.1 Types of banks in Germany

		Number of Banks: (1995)	Assets Holding (1995)	Aim
Germany (3-pillar system)	Private big commercial banks (motivated by profit-making)	331 banks (9.1%)	Holding 12% assets	For dealing with fragility under High corporate growth
	Publicly owned saving and Landesbanken banks	637 (17%)	Holding 37.7% assets	For dealing with Inclusiveness
	Cooperative banks	Around 2585 banks (69%)	Holding 14.2% assets	For dealing with Inclusiveness

Source: Professor CPC lecture series, winter semester, CESP, JNU 2019

The private commercial banks in Germany and city banks in Japan used to serve as Universal banks conducting all sorts of banking functions ranging from accepting deposits and lending loans to agency, insurance, investment etc. Here, more than the number, what is more significant is the concentration aspect. Starting from the early 1950's, the level of concentration (asset share for city banks and local and regional banks collectively was around 76.5 per cent (56.1+20.4) in 1953, which decreased to 60 per cent in 1963 and later to 53 per cent in 1973 (Chandrashekar 2019). Kazuo Ueda uses the word 'Implicit Subsidies' to address how competition is restricted in Japan (Veda 1994). In the case of Japan, there were city banks (for providing loans to big corporations, short-term loans in nature), regional banks (for providing loans to the MSME sector), trust banks and other banks. There is no evidence of existence of such non-competition in the case in Germany, whose big banks have to compete with even with the saving banks to attract household savings although only limited investments could be taken by the saving banks as their strong mandates depict. Hein et al. (2016) also mentions the low Merger and Acquisition activities in Germany till the 1990s, which increased afterwards due to its unification with the EU. Japan, on the other hand, encouraged mergers, especially of weak banks with stronger banks. As a whole, while Germany has fully addressed the inclusion aspect, without compromising growth in agriculture and MSME sector, the other banks in Japan also considered granting loans to agriculture and MSME, although a certain degree of exclusion [2] was here especially in the starting of industrialization which seems justifiable if short-term.

Firstly, if we see the corporate growth aspect, although both Germany and Japan used to have close relations between the banks and the industries, their approaches to such relationships varied significantly. The continental banking system[1] that exists in Germany whereby Detzer et al. (2017) points out a very powerful position is maintained by big German banks through increasing shareholding and monitoring by big banks, and the increasing takeover of small banks by them. Even since before World War II, banks in Germany used to provide long term loans to commercial banks, but not directly but by rolling over of short-term loans, and in case of financial difficulties, they took advantage by converting loans into shareholding to join the board. For instance: Feldenkirchen cites that in case of financial difficulty faced by Krupp, its short-term loan was converted into a 9-year long term one, along with the condition to allow them to join the company board for monitoring purposes. This is the reason why Detzer et al. (2017) even argue that some corporations such as Siemens preferred to restrict their growth rather than losing independence of the board to get external finance.

In contrast to this, Japan was not even allowed to invest more than 5% in equity of the corporate, although the artificially-set low interest rates (set mainly through informal administrative guidelines and moral suasion)[2], restrictions on the number of branches as well as the stringent control on flow of funds in capital market/ restrictions on direct financing (through controlling of bond market) provided a very suitable the non-competitive environment to these banks that big corporate firms prefer to take more loans from these main banks rather than from securities market. There was also a separation of banking vs. securities industries, short-term vs. long-term banking, and ordinary vs. trust banking till the 1990s.

---

[1]Continental banking system is the system where the role of banks is to coordinate various interest groups and they are expected to act as a "coordinating vehicle" among different groups such as firms, in order to fulfill national aims of economy at a larger level.

[2]It is a very peculiar feature of Japanese banks where huge flexibility and degree of discretion is provided to bank regulators because of the belief that forceful enforcement by law must be the last option.

Even though interest rate ceilings did not exist in Germany explicitly, Fig. 9.2 shows that they generally kept their interest rates below Japan's interest rates[3]. This is because of the competitive nature and low mergers of large banks in Germany. The public savings banks didn't compete with each other, but used to compete with the private commercial banks. Since interest rate ceilings existed in Japan but not in Germany, Fig. 9.1 shows that the interest rate in Japan is systematically getting lower and lower post WWII till 1970's, while Germany's interest rate is showing a lot more fluctuations. Moreover, there is a very informal environment where the companies use to approach banks in case of any trouble.

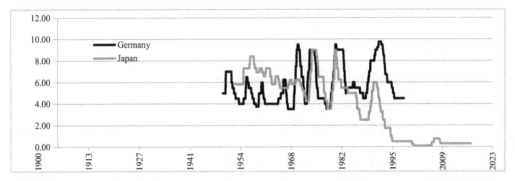

Fig. 9. 1   Interest rates, discount rate, percent per annum, monthly, not seasonally adjusted

Source: FRED

Fig. 9.2   Saving rate (saving as a percent of GDP)

Source: FRED

Now, besides the non-competition and restrictions in the bond market which exist only in Japan, the regulators of two countries provide a protectionist environment to banks so as to address the liquidity management and fragility issues arising due to high amounts of lending and high gearing ratio. Both countries are backed up by supportive central banks which assume risk themselves without letting the private corporate banks/main banks to get failed.

---

[3] It is required to be noted that Allen B. Frankel and John D. Montgomery argue empirically that although Germany has comparatively low concentration, there is still higher concentration of assets by the 5 largest banks in both Germany and Japan than UK and Britain.

In Germany, these central banks function as 'Note-issuing' to address any shortage of funds in such big banks, while in Japan, central bank played dual role: note-issuing as well as by the concept known as over-borrowing and over-lending (Chandrashekhar 2019), whereby a BOJ lending would be provided to the troubled banks, or in more serious cases were merged by the healthier banks. Moreover, the presence of foreign banks in both the countries has been quite limited (Behr et al. 2015).

Coming to the savings rate, as the Figure shows, in order to pursue the aim of high growth with industrialization, Japan has been saving more and more since post-world war 2 and has an amazingly higher saving rate of 35-40% even. During the 'lost decade of 1990's', it started decreasing although. Germany's saving rate is relatively much more stable during the whole period since WWII.

3. Performance and Assessment of the Two Banking Systems

Having studied the similarities and differences in the two countries, if we look how they performed respectively post WWII, we find that empirically, both the countries have performed quite well since post world war till 1970's in terms of GDP, exports, high investment, minimal individual bank or systemic failures and no instability even when there was too high debt-to-GDP ratio in both countries owing to their bank-based and highly protected financial structures by the regulators. Even the Japanese economy grew around 10 per cent per annum till 1973 when the first oil shock took place. Evidence shows that after sustaining the oil price shock quite well, the downfall of Japanese economy started in late 1970's (as shown in Fig. 9.3) and even led to a full lost decade of 1990's, the 1997 crisis, the 2007-08 crisis and has still not picked up that grip as was till the 1970's. Although Germany didn't have a very high growth level, it still sustained its financial structure even after 1970's. Unfortunately, it also faced a real-estate problem that will be discussed in paper later. The paper further proceeds to look at reasons for such performances, especially the significant ramifications described above in the case of Japan.

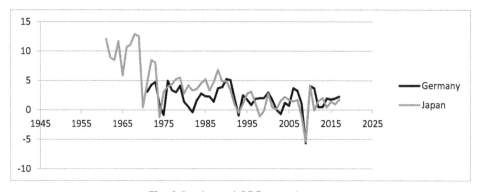

Fig. 9.3 Annual GDP growth rates

Source: World Bank data

There arises the question that if Japan was having risky over-lending, and also, pertaining to high levels of growth during the 1960s [1], there is a risk of inflation too. Figure 9.4 shows the CPI inflation rates in Germany and Japan were rising both in Germany and Japan, which may account to the lax in note-issue by the central bank on funds requirement by the big banks.

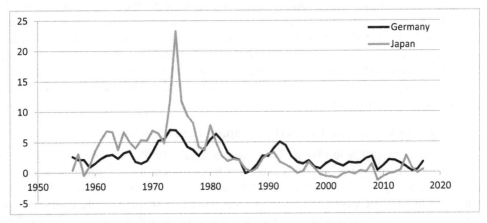

Fig. 9.4   CPI Inflation for Germany and Japan

Source: FRED (CPI)

Assessing both the financial structures so as to find reasons for their relative performances, we proceed as follows:

3.1 Inherent Risk in the Japanese System

Since Japan is conscious not to resort to high fiscal deficit, and thus used to adopt conservative fiscal policy and used to tightly control the financial market (bonds market using interest rate as its primary tool). The inherent unstable structure, as Edward D. Lincoln [6] argued, is due to **over-lending** by the BOJ makes the system so vulnerable that it could have broken any time since 1950's only.

3.2 Was Oil Shock of 1973 the Reason for Japan's Bank Failure

As the oil shock brought a huge trade surplus in Japan (Marius Ioan Mihut and Decean Liviu Daniel [7]) having a very high savings rate of 30-40% found itself with ex-ante excess savings, so to balance out the excess savings to equal zero, the government had to carry out the fiscal deficit. There immediately comes the problem of financing the deficit which the government could necessarily do through the issue of government bonds carrying an attractive high interest rate.

The change in policies via deregulation and liberalization (and thus, the change in financial structure) needs to be noted here. Firstly, there were interest rate controls earlier in order to protect the banks, but now, increased interest rates on government bonds, and subsequently on other interest rates meant no longer protection to the banks. Secondly, earlier interest rate regulation let just a few banks (mainly the main banks and city banks) buy government bonds, but now high interest rates let markets enjoy the high returns and hence, banks had to start trying their fate into real and overseas sectors in search of a new market for loans. Thirdly, The Ministry of Finance deregulated to compensate for the above unfavorable changes in policies for the corporate sector as well as due to constant pressures from the US to liberalize on whom Japan is highly export-dependent. As a result, 'non-bank subsidiaries' were encouraged for investment by banks in the real estate sector and some ratifications in "Foreign Exchange Control Law, 1980" including liberalization of FDI between Japan and other nations was done. So, it seems that it was not the change in oil shock which Japan still sustained (with trade surplus at that time), but the inherent unstable structure where low growth which necessitated deregulation followed by inappropriate regulations such as liberalization which are more likely to be the reasons for Japan's bad luck.

3.3 Can Plaza Accord be blamed for Japan's Lost Decade

Due to pressures from US to play a "level-playing field", the Plaza accord was signed on 22nd September 1985 by US and its counterparts in G-5 countries, including Germany and Japan, leading to depreciation of US currency[4] (with the fiscal and monetary tools of Mundell-Fleming model) at the expense of all other signed nations. Note that both the countries were export-driven, as opposed to domestic-demand driven or debt-led consumption boom. They were able to accumulate huge trade surpluses in the fixed exchange rate till 1971 when the flexible exchange regime came up.

There is a huge debate concerning whether the downfall of Japan is due to the Plaza accord or not. While Conspiracy theory advocates that US used this weapon (Plaza accord) to price the manufactured goods in Japan out of the global market, Jaffrey Frankel [9] points that the reason for Japanese recession in 1990's was result of bubble years, rather than due to dollar depreciation both of which came at a similar time. Further literature points towards that during the bubble years, the purchase of dollars led to vast increase in the money supply and huge price rise in real sector assets and in equities, bursting of which led to the recession. Lincoln [6] raised a very nice argument that to counter the possibility of recession which occurred due to yen appreciation, the regulators used expansionary money supply[5] as a tool to face up the situation leading to asset price bubbles.

Empirically, there wasn't any severe recession due to plaza accord in Japan, and instead of collapse in exports as was predicted, the exports actually increased in all five years after ratification of Plaza accord. Moreover, even if we take appreciation due to plaza accord to be one of the major reasons for downfall of Japanese economy in 1980s and 1990s to compare it with the case in Germany, then as the figure shows, there was currency appreciation (Fig. 9.5) as well as a mild recession for Germany too (not as much as in Japan's case) but its cautious

---

[4]The justification for the Plaza accord is to reduce the current account deficit in the US (which had reached 3.5% of GDP) as well as to help the US deal with its recession of the 1980s. Although the G-5 countries were not in favor of such an agreement, the US pressures let them accept the proposal, especially when there is dependence of the military on the US.

[5]As a policy response, the discount rates were lowered from 5% in 1985 to 3% and further to 2.5% by 1987 (shown in Graph 1) and the Government undertook investments in 'infrastructural projects'.

Fig. 9.5 Exchange rate for Germany

Source: FRED

Fig. 9.6 Exchange rate for Japan

Source: FRED

monetary as well as fiscal policies after learning from Weimar Republic hyperinflation case led to more economic stability. So, it chose a little recession and chose not to opt for 'policy easing', which avoided the creation of bubble. So, in this sense, we can say that Japan's over-reacted policy response caused the lost decade, rather than the 'Plaza accord' per se.

3.4 The Germany's Success

Moreover, the secret behind Germany's success during 1980s and 1990s lies in its discriminatory liberalization (Richard E. Badwin [8]) shelter provided by the European Union. Keeping aside the view that "The one who pays the piper is picking the tune" (meaning the dominance of Germany as they do a high level of hard-work and high payment by them to EU), Germany keeps a huge trade surplus with EU, which benefited largely. Some people even argue that had EU not been there, they could have easily faced the appreciation of Deutschemark leading exports to become non-competitive. It is to be noted that although EU was formed in 1993, but the integration process [10] started much earlier in 1960s and 70s only with the formation of EU-6 including Germany as a founding member.

3.5 The Argument on Real-estate

Some arguments on Japan about this point are discussed above already. The financial deregulation helped in expanding lending in housing sector and the parallel increase in public spending (on rail, roads, infrastructure etc.) all led to nominal appreciation of land value much more the real one leading to creation of boom, which got busted with the huge lost decade and left a huge bad debt problem (as large as around 77 Trillion Yen by 1997) (Lincoln et al. 1998), which further exaggerated the problem through more severe credit crunch in the economy and balance sheet weakness in banks. Again, as Japan had started liberalizing, they started moving into real estate and equity markets in South-East Asia also, due to which it was much more severely affected by the Asian crisis, 1997 than Germany which didn't invest the same in Asian markets.

One of the reasons why Moreover, the real-estate market in Germany is much more stable in general (Hein et al. 2016) owing to 'Specific institutional structures' as Government intervention has led to sufficient supply in housing market, which is demanded by people to purchase their own house only and no appreciation really occurs as a result. Moreover, real estate here carries a relatively conservative system unattractive for international investors relatively, the high taxation and lack of transparency.

However, we need to be careful about the problems occurred in Germany later with the law passed aim to revive East Germany known as 'Fördergebietsgesetz' from 1990 to 1998, which offered really generous tax incentives to the property investors, whereby the entire cost of building or renovating in East Germany could be written off from taxable income over the next 10 years. This led to huge increase in housing demand and the housing prices rose by around 70%. Although tax break got over, but this policy had led to a creation of huge bubble and its bursting at the end of 1990s turned investors' exuberance into gloom and turned housing market into a slump. This is the reason why Germany didn't face further boom in housing prices which had led to Global Financial Crisis of 2008. Germany's housing prices actually fell between 1998 and 2003, as against the international trend at that time, afterwards which the prices still started to rise a bit. Besides this, during 2000's, Germany faced recession in 2001 because of dot-com bubble too.

The 2008 crisis actually reflected the complexity of German financial structure in which a hidden bubble was getting formed since late 20th century only and got burst during that crisis. As opposed to Japan which was investing its surplus in real-estate sector and equity in its own country, Germany was investing overseas, especially in US market as a part of Capital outflows and thus, the bubble was getting formed. The key change in financial structure was the introduction of new financial instruments in form of securitized bonds, which helped banks to convert their individual risk into market risk through collective bunch of securitize bonds. This is essentially the separation of creator and holder of risk, which even the Basel II regulations couldn't predict at that time (as that was a new financial innovation essentially) and later Basel III came to try to counter this shortcoming.

4. Conclusion

We may conclude following desirable and undesirable properties in the above two financial structures:

4.1 Is Bank-based System Good?

A bank-based system is a system in which government intervention becomes easiest through regulation of banking sector so as to gain a typical high growth. However, it may imply a high-debt equity ratio, as well as wide interconnected financial system and hence, downfall of the big corporates increase the chances of bank failures too for which cushion of an institution (such as central bank) is utmost required. What is essentially required is a system such as three-tiered system in Germany which would ensure growth as well as inclusiveness. Besides, there are different studies on whether government intervention is actually good or not, where La Porta, Sapiena and others (Behr et al. 2015, La Porta et al. 2002) point that government owned banks are performing badly with inefficient credit allocation, fraud, corruption, agency problems and political influence; while Stiglitz, Burgress and Pande and others [13] documents its positive role on development and social welfare.

Old wisdom reviews monitoring (Chandershekhar 2019) as positive step towards growth, be it explicit monitoring as in Germany's case (where bank managers find themselves sitting on the boards) or implicit monitoring as in Japan's case (where instead of any physical controls such as licensing, but the relationship between banks and industries ensure compliance); while the new conventional wisdom given by Fisher argues that external finance is the main and monitoring is just fake, with the view further developed by Schmidt. But as a whole, if not good, monitoring is not bad at least, so should be pursued by the countries.

4.2 Deregulation, Not Accompanied by Appropriate Re-regulation

Fiscal vs. monitory policies

Japan carried a big mistake here, firstly by implementing monetary policy for too long with low interest rates, thus leading to inherent risk in the system, and secondly, by being so cautious about having high fiscal deficit since the post-war. Even when they deregulated the interest rates and introduced a 'fiscal stimulus package' later during the wrong time of appreciation of yen so over-activity/ overheating further leading to inflation in housing prices, boomed and burst afterwards.

Liberalization

If we look at different economies, we find that a country mostly liberalised when it faces problem, or faces problem when it liberalizes [2] as we have seen in case of Germany and Japan too. The macroeconomic policies which are required to be changed accordingly with the change in environment was made wrongly in Japan too through overheating of economy by them. Germany sustained through merger of big banks as an effective policy change.

Even after the burst of bubble, then also they BOJ regulated bad loans very badly, which greatly delayed restructuring, leading to a lot of finance wasted in Zombie firms.

4.3 Basel Prudential Regulations

Since the financial crisis exposed many weaknesses of financial structure, the main one being the nature of finance to keep on bringing new financial innovations in form of financial instruments (such as securitized assets) and financial institutions. This essentially highlighted the need for macro-prudential regulations, besides just the micro-prudential ones i.e. Conversion of risks of individual banks into market risk and hence, increasing the interconnectedness and fragility of financial system (where risk can now be transferred from creator to another holder). This directly brings into literature that now the bank-based systems such as Germany and Japan are essentially getting converted implicitly into market-based/Anglo-Saxen kind of the system, where regulatory power is implicitly getting diluted day-by-day as finance is exerting its power. Although efforts are made now to counter the systemic and market risks in various ways, but such prudential regulations are surely not sufficient till such financial innovations keep dominating the structures.

REFERENCES

1. Detzer Daniel, Nina Dodig and others (2017). The Historical Development of the German Financial System. *Part of the Financial and Monetary Policy Studies book series* (FMPS, volume 45)
2. Professor CPC lecture series (2019), winter semester, CESP, JNU.
3. Veda, K. (1994). Institutional and Regulatory Frameworks for the Main Bank System/Aoki M. and Patrik H. (ed.). The Japanese Main Bank System: Its Relevance for Developing and Transforming Economics.
4. Hein, E., Detzer, D., & Dodig, N. (Eds.). (2016). *Financialisation and the financial and economic crises: country studies*. Edward Elgar Publishing.
5. Behr, P., & Schmidt, R. H. (2015). *The German banking system: Characteristics and challenges* (No. 32). White Paper Series.
6. Lincoln, E. J., & Friedman, B. M. (1998). Japan's financial problems. *Brookings Papers on Economic Activity, 1998*(2), 347–385.
7. Mihut Ioan Marius and Decean Liviu Daniel (2012),'First oil shock impact on the Japanese economy', Procedia Economics and Finance.
8. Baldwin, R. E. (2004). Stepping stones or building blocs? Regional and multilateral integration. *Institute of International Studies, Geneva.*
9. Frankel, J. (2015). *The Plaza Accord, 30 Years Later* (No. w21813). National Bureau of Economic Research.
10. Agur, I., Dorrucci, E., & Mongelli, F. P. (2007). How did European institutional integration and intra-European trade interact?. *Economie internationale*, (1), 107–146
11. Behr, P., & Schmidt, R. H. (2015). *The German banking system: Characteristics and challenges* (No. 32). White Paper Series.
12. La Porta, R., F. Lopez-de-Silanes, A. Shleifer. (2002) 'Government ownership of banks', *Journal of Finance* 57, 265–301.
13. Stiglitz, J.E. (1993) 'The role of the state in financial markets', Proceedings of the World Bank Annual Conference on Economic Development, Washington DC, International Bank for Reconstruction and Development/World Bank, 19–56.
14. Nakaso, H. (2001). The financial crisis in Japan during the 1990s: How the Bank of Japan responded and the lessons learnt. BIS Papers No 6, Basel.

15. Detzer, D., Dodig, N., Evans, T., Hein, E., Herr, H., & Prante, F. J. (2017). *The German financial system and the financial and economic crisis* (Vol. 45). Springer.
16. Patrick, H. T. (1988). *Explaining the Japanese financial system: A review of the Bank of Japan's recent volume.*
17. Baba, N., & Hisada, T. (2002). *Japan's financial system: Its perspective and the authorities' roles in redesigning and administering the system.* Institute for Monetary and Economic Studies, Bank of Japan.
18. Baums, T. (1994). *The German banking system and its impacts on corporate finance and governance* (No. 94). Washington, DC: Economic Development Institute of the World Bank.
19. Kahn, R. B., & Meade, E. E. (2018). 17. International aspects of central banking: diplomacy and coordination. *Research Handbook on Central Banking*, 333.

Handbook of Evidence Based Management Practices in Business – Satyendra Kumar Sharma et al. (eds)
© 2023 Taylor & Francis Group, London, ISBN 978-1-032-54216-4

Chapter

Effects of Digitisation on Banknote Durability

Arunima Asthana[1], Tanmoy Kr. Banerjee[2]
Department of Management,
Birla Institute of Technology, Mesra, Ranchi, India
Shubhamoy Dey[3]
Indian Institute of Management, Indore, India

ABSTRACT: Throughout the course of the evolution of monetary philosophy, economists have, for the most part, concentrated their attention on the function of money as a medium of exchange as well as the inherent characteristics of money that make it the most marketable and dependable store of value. However, the social institution of money is always adapting to new technological developments. It is important to note that the adoption of digital payment methods has experienced a meteoric surge in the recent past. As a direct result of this we tend to reconsider the fundamental phenomenology of money. The immaterial role of money as a standard of value and social technology of account is brought to the forefront by digitisation, and as a result, this function is gradually being absorbed by its function as a medium of trade. During the demonetisation period there was a significant decrease in the availability of cash, which in some way had an impact on the long-term sustainability of currency. In this paper, we are going to investigate the durability of banknotes during pre- and post-demonetisation period in relation to their withdrawal for circulation in order to satisfy fundamental requirements.

KEYWORDS: Digitisation, Durability, Banknote

1. Introduction

A banknote's lifespan might be anything from one year to five years. The amount of time it lasts depends on how people keep it; in wallets or in their pockets. Banknotes go through a lot throughout their lifetime: being handed about, being processed by machines, being distributed

[1]aruasthana27@gmail.com, [2]tanmoykumar@rediffmail.com, [3]shubhamoy@iimidr.ac.in

DOI: 10.4324/9781003415725-10

by ATMs, and so on.[1] Over the past five years, the number of currencies in circulation has increased by an annualised rate of 5-7%.[9] More than 576 billion banknotes are now in circulation across the world, and their typical lifespan might be ranging from one year to several years. [2] More than 150 billion new banknotes are printed annually to replace the ones that are retired from circulation due to wear and tear. Banknotes are high-value commodities that come with a wide range of security features and several layers of protection these days.[3] Central banks consider these elements while designing and producing new banknotes. These include: Banknotes must meet certain conditions before being reissued. The currency of India has been the subject of much recent academic study and political debate.[10] In November 2016, large denomination Indian rupee notes (INR500 and INR1000) were retired from circulation and replaced by a new series of INR500 notes and a new denomination of INR2000 notes.[4] The policy was implemented by the Reserve Bank of India (RBI), which is India's central bank and is responsible for managing the country's currency supply.[11] Demonetisation in India was implemented with the hopes of reducing the use of counterfeit money, eliminating the cash-only nature of the parallel economy, and encouraging the government to phase out its reliance on cash (Chen et. al 2020). As a result, non-cash payment options including mobile banking, e-wallets, and credit/debit cards saw huge growth. Little is known, however, regarding the actual reality of the factors thought to effect the demand for cash in the context of economic policies like demonetisation in India. The demand for India's currency has been the subject of some estimated models in the past (Minguez et al. 2020), but these studies generally fail to take into account all of the elements that are expected to effect currency demand in India (in part due to lack of data). New information from the payment system has given researchers a chance to re-evaluate the problem and its policy ramifications. Investigating the cultural and sociological variables that are driving demand for India's currency might be illuminating as well (Bangnall 2014). Data on India's reserves, courtesy of the Reserve Bank (RBI) If we choose 2 as an approximation, then somewhere between 75% and 80% of the total money supply is in circulation at this time. Thus, a study of currency demand can shed light on the bulk of reserve funds. When narrow money is compared to currency, however, we find that 58% of all narrow money is kept in currency (Reserve Bank of India 2017). Depending on the current system, fluctuations in currency demand might influence the transmission of monetary policy (Schuh et al. 2016). Finally, the experimental validation of novel features linked with currency usage might enhance our knowledge of the micro-foundations upon which monetary policy rests (Jonker et al. 2020). This study analyses first-hand information to conjecture on how the popularity of electronic payment systems could influence the long-term viability of paper currency.

2. Literature Review

The income elasticity of spending and the opportunity costs of saving are two of the factors typically studied by money demand models (which go beyond currency demand) (usually proxied by rates of returns on other assets).[5] However, following theories have claimed that the fixed cost of keeping cash implies income elasticities lower than one, contradicting classical theory's premise that money demand rises at the same proportion as incomes. Because of this, (Beijnen 1952) and others proposed the "inventory" theory of money demand, which posited that people primarily utilise money to make transactions (Thakor 2020). Income levels (typically measured by GDP), interest rates on a set of alternative assets (the opportunity cost of holding currency), and financial innovations in transactions that potentially substitute for use of cash (e.g. debit/credit cards) are the three overarching factors hypothesised to predict currency demand (Minguez et al., 2020). The need for hard currency is shown to be greatly reduced with lower levels of industrialisation. The creation of the European Union and the subsequent replacement of European currencies like the Deutsch Mark, the Swiss Franc, and others with the Euro are major drivers of estimates of currency demand in Europe.[6] Prior to the transition, researchers (Stavins et al. 2001) examined the function of foreign currency usage in shaping currency demand. (Moro et al., 2020) conducted research for India and found that demand for money varied significantly among denominations; however, they were unable to account for the scale of the shadow economy due to a lack of information. In a study spanning the years 1999–2007, they used the currency demand technique to calculate shadow economy metrics for 151 nations, including India. The parallel economy in India contributed an average of 24% to GDP, placing the country in the centre of the league[7]. The authors contended that this was because of the widespread use of informal labour practices in sectors outside of agriculture. A decline in cash transactions is expected as the usage of credit and debit card technologies increases (Davis et al. 1989). Despite the fact that some research has identified a favourable effect of debit cards on cash, demand remains strong for a number of reasons (Restoy et al. 2020). According to (Van K., et al. 2014), one of the main reasons why people choose cash over alternative payment methods is that it allows them to maintain control over their liquidity. This article presents a cross-country examination of the demand for small denominations (particularly coins) in OECD countries between 1988 and 2003 (Amromin et al., 2009). Increases in debit card use were shown to reduce demand for tiny bills, whereas demand for larger bills remained unaffected. In light of the recent financial crisis, several research have examined the effects of this phenomenon on the demand for various currencies (Chakravorti et al. 2007). Payment diaries are commonly used in research as a way to analyse a basic household or individual-level decision of payment option and to circumvent aggregation problems (Bagnall et al. 2014). Many other countries and cultures have conducted research along these lines, but comparable micro data for India is still lacking.[8]

3. Methodology

Our research methodology focuses at and explains the methods we used to collect and analyse the data for this study. Any research article will only be as good as its methods. It explains our methods and our results, so that others may evaluate our study's credibility and validity.

I. **Research Design:** The initial stage of every research is to create a research plan. It gives us a complete structure within which to organise and sequence the various parts of the research. In our study, we have chosen to employ a Descriptive Research Design. The nature of our inquiry necessitated the adoption of this design. Our study focuses on the payment habits of a variety of demographic groups, including students, businesspeople, professionals, and retirees; therefore, this research design is most appropriate for our investigation.

II. Data Collection: Our research is completely based on primary data. The primary instrument that we are employing for the collection of data is the Questionnaire Method of collecting data.

(a) **Method used:** We developed a questionnaire containing inquiries about the payment practices of the respondents and how frequently they utilise paper money. We acquire data through the use of the questionnaire utilising three distinct methodologies:

1. We are explaining the questionnaire to the responder face-to-face and subsequently collecting their responses.

2. We are physically disseminating the questionnaire and then requesting their responses.

3. We are distributing the questionnaire online using a Google Drive link and requesting responses through the linked form.

4. The questionnaire has been created in both English and Hindi. The Hindi version of the questionnaire was created to target those from lower socioeconomic classes who did not comprehend English.

(b) **Validation of Questionnaire:** Our questionnaire was validated with the assistance of distributing the questionnaire to the industry professionals and academicians. This helped us check the accuracy of the questions. Convenience sampling method was used to choose a total of eight individuals from these two categories.

   A. Validation of English Questionnaire:

   (a) Our English Questionnaire was validated in order to assess the intelligibility of the questionnaire's contents. The English Questionnaire was delivered to eight individuals.

   (b) **Sampling used:** The samples of these eight people were selected using the Convenience Sampling technique. We have then stratified the individuals into 3 sub-strata's'. Four of the eight selections are recognised bank Branch Managers. Two are from the corporate sector, and the remaining two have academic posts at a prestigious university.

   B. Validation of Hindi Questionnaire: Considering that Hindi is one of the official languages of our nation and that individuals from lower socioeconomic classes have trouble comprehending English, we have validated our Hindi questionnaire with the help of two interpreters.

   (a) **Sampling used:** The sampling method used to choose two interpreters is convenience sampling. We have chosen both the interpreters with the help of Convenience Sampling again. One of them is a part of the Judiciary, while the other is an acclaimed institution's former dean. We requested each of them translate the questionnaire back into English, which verifies the accuracy of the Hindi questionnaire. The findings of the translation may be seen in the annexure that we have provided.

III. Respondent's Sampling: We have stratified our samples depending on demographic groupings such as age, occupation, annual income, and education level of respondents.

Using the Convenience Sampling Method, we plan to choose about 800 respondents from all societal sectors. The study focuses on the Eastern, Western, Northern, and Southern regions of the nation. We have begun collecting replies from each of these four areas and have so far accumulated 400 responses. As stated, we are now gathering further replies, after which we will analyse them for future considerations.

IV. **Removing Biasedness:** Several measures have been taken to eliminate bias from our research. To eliminate the risk of respondent-oriented bias, we have picked a large sample size. Second, we have presented clear, unambiguous questions that have been validated by reliable persons. Thirdly, we allow respondents to submit feedback in their own environment, resulting in unbiased responses. Fourth, we have not generated any hypotheses in our research that would rule out any bias in our findings.

4. Limitations and Future Work

This study is being conducted as part of ongoing research effort that is yet to be finished. Due to the limited amount of time available, we have been able to gather 400 responses thus far and are in the process of collecting responses from all regions of the country. The collected replies will be analysed in the near future. We will persist with our work for future endeavours and continue to gather replies in order to demonstrate the impact that digitisation has had on the durability of the Indian currency. This will allow us to prove that digitisation has increased the currency's endurance.

REFERENCES

1. Amromin, A., Yassine, B., David B., Martina, E., and Lola, H. (2009). Cash remains top-of-wallet! International evidence from payment diaries. Economic Modelling. 69: 38–48.
2. Bech, M., Umar, F., Frederik, O., and Cristina, P. (2018). Payments are changing' but cash still rules. BIS Quarterly Review, (March): 67–80.
3. Beinjan, Walter, C., and M.M.G, F. (1952). The Way We Pay with Money. Journal of Business & Economic Statistics. 7(3): 319–326.
4. Chakravorti, Sujit, and Ted T. (2007). A theory of credit cards. International Journal of Industrial Organisation. 25(3): 583–595.
5. Chen, H., Walter, E., Kim, P., Huychonh, G., Nicholls, Mitchell W.N., and Julia S. (2020). Cash and COVID-19: The impact of the pandemic on the demand for and use of cash. Bank of Canada Staff Discussion Paper:6.
6. Davis, Fred, D. (1989). Perceived usefulness, perceived ease of use, and user acceptance of information technology. MIS Quarterly. 13(3): 319–340. https://doi.org/10.2307/249008.
7. Jonker, N., Carin van der, C., Michiel, B., and Wilko, B., (2020). Pandemic payment patterns. DNB Working Paper: 701.
8. Mínguez, José, G., Alberto, U., and Miguel Péres García de, M., (2020). Consumption in Spain during the state of alert: An analysis based on payment card spending. Banco de España Economic Bulletin: 3.
9. Moro, A., Daniela, M., Matthias, F., Annalisa, F., and Claudio, P., (2020). Spillover effects of government initiatives fostering entrepreneurship on the access to bank credit for entrepreneurial firms in Europe. Journal of Corporate Finance. 62: 101603.

10. Restoy, F. (2020). Central banks and financial stability: A reflection after the Covid-19 outbreak. FSI Occasional Paper: 16.
11. Schuh, S., and Joanna, S. (2016). How do speed and security influence consumers' payment behavior?. Contemporary Economic Policy. 34(4): 595–613. 10.1111/coep.12163.
12. Stavins, J. (2001). Effect of consumer characteristics on the use of payment instruments. New England Economic Review. (3): 19–31.
13. Thakor, Anjan, V. (2020). Fintech and banking: What do we know?. Journal of Financial Intermediation. 41: 100833. 10.1016/j.jfi.2019.100833.
14. Pal, R. and Sanjay, K. B. (2020). Cash, currency and COVID-19. Postgraduate Medical Journal. 96(1137): 427–428. 10.1136/postgradmedj-2020-138006.
15. Reserve Bank of India, Annual Report (2017), https://rbidocs.rbi.org.in/rdocs/AnnualReport/PDFs/0ANREPORT201718077745EC9A874DB38C991F580ED14242.PDF (accessed on 24 Dec, 2022).
16. Runnemark, E., Jonas, H., and Xiao. (2015). Do consumers pay more using debit cards than cash?. Electronic Commerce Research and Applications.14(5): 285–291.
17. Van der, C., Carin, and Frank van der, H. (2019). Cash or Card? Unravelling the Role of Socio-Psychological Factors. De Economist. 167(2): 45–175.
18. Shang, Y., Gaiyan, S., Liuling, L., Tania De, R., and Heiko, S. (2019). Retail payments and the real economy. Journal of Financial Stability. 44: 1010690.

Chapter **11**

Assessing Investment Attractiveness— Developing Economies Perspective

Leena Ajit Kaushal*

Economics & Public Policy,
Management Development Institute Gurgaon, Gurugram, India

ABSTRACT: Asian economies have been an important part of globalisation since the mid-1970s, particularly in global supply chains. China has been a clear leader in this process, becoming the hub of global supply chains. However, trade war threats, the Russia-Ukraine war, COVID-19 pandemic and China's "zero COVID" policy have all disrupted global supply chain management in recent years. Nations around the world are considering diversifying their reliance on China, a strategy known as "China Plus One." The study attempts to rank the major emerging Asian economies as potential destinations for the "plus one" country. According to the findings of the aggregate ranking methodology, India is the most appealing destination for outgoing MNCs.

KEYWORDS: COVID-19, China plus one policy, Developing, Investment attractiveness, Global supply chains

1. Introduction

Supply chains across international boundaries have been instrumental in bolstering globalization's driving forces (Findlay and Hoekman, 2021). Global trade has become the driving force of global economic progress owing to falling transportation costs and tariffs and China's entry into the World Trade Organization in 2001 (Gu, 2019).

Manufacturing and production have long been cantered in China. Numerous international businesses have established operations in China because of the country's large domestic market, cheap labour, advanced infrastructure, and business-friendly government (Depoux, 2022). As

---

*leena.kaushal@mdi.ac.in

DOI: 10.4324/9781003415725-11

a result, foreign direct investment (FDI) has been funnelled into China, totalling billions of dollars. However, the COVID-19 pandemic that has inflicted disorder globally has somewhat disrupted the status quo. China's reputation abroad has taken a hit because it has been made to look like the country where the virus originated (Sharma, 2021; Nguyen and Pham, 2020). Deglobalization and the ongoing trade war between the US and Chinese economies only worsen over time. Therefore, it is essential to consider whether or not China can continue to be the only country attracting FDI in the foreseeable future. Many businesses are considering a "China plus one" strategy to diversify beyond China's borders to take advantage of the high growth potential and similar benefits of several emerging Asian countries.

With the China Plus One strategy, companies and MNCs keen to relocate in a second location abroad while keeping their headquarters in China (Liu et al., 2022). This allows them to keep their longstanding presence in China while exploring opportunities in other attractive economies. MNCs are wisely working on their diversification strategy rather than concentrating on one nation (Zhu et al., 2020). They are spreading production between China and other Asian nations such as Vietnam, Thailand, and Indonesia (Shih, 2020).

While thirty Asian economies are considered "emerging and developing," the study focuses exclusively on eight of these nations compared to China: India, Singapore, Saudi Arabia, Indonesia, Vietnam, the Philippines, Bangladesh, Thailand, and Malaysia. The question of how these nations are compared is fascinating and multifaceted, requiring familiarity with Porter's Model.

Porter's (1990) diamond model, based on reliable national indicators, has been widely used to examine the competitiveness of various nations. Porter's Diamond model comprises four interrelated components: factor conditions, demand conditions, related and supporting industries, firm strategy, structure, rivalry, and two exogenous constraints, government and chance.

One of the most important contributions of Porter's (1990) model is that a country's global competitiveness depends on the interaction between these four components. Therefore, a nation's competitiveness could be assessed as a consequence of these proposed components. China's notoriety as the "factory of the world" (Zhang, 2006) has been seriously impacted by the dreaded coronavirus outbreak in Wuhan (Zhu et al., 2020), the trade war with the USA, and strained China-Taiwan relations (Keegan and Churchman, 2022). Several MNCs have thus moved away from China, and many others are contemplating the move in the near future. The regulatory uncertainties and reputational risk have exceeded the benefits for multinational corporations to remain in the enormous market (TOI, 2021).

The present study employs Porter's diamond model to investigate the relative global competitiveness of the eight Asian economies that could be the future destinations for these outgoing MNCs from China. The study also incorporates—the governance factor—along with *demand conditions, factor conditions, related industries, and business context,* with various sub-factors underneath them for consideration and appropriate ranking. Using the rank aggregation method, the study generates a solitary grand ranking that clusters and integrates all of the individual rankings. The ranking of these eight countries, based on their FDI attractiveness, reveals the relative attractiveness of each economy, which may assist firms if they adopt a China-plus-one model.

2. Data and Methodology

The study focuses on the pool of eight nations comprising of Singapore, India, Saudi Arabia, Indonesia, Vietnam, the Philippines, Bangladesh, Thailand, and Malaysia. The study ranks these nations based on the data spreading across 2010 to 2019. The ranking methodology employed in the study is explained as follows:

2.1 Choosing Indicators for the Ranking

Following Porter's diamond model, we decided to choose indicators based on five broad criteria, namely:

Factor conditions:

The natural, human, and capital resources of a country that are needed for production are called its "factor conditions". The factor conditions are further divided into basic factors inherited by the country (such as climate, natural resources, and unskilled labour, among others) and require no investment. Advanced factors created by the country through cycles of reinvestments may include skilled labour, and investment-related capital, among others. For this study, we have used eight variables, four as basic factors and the rest as advanced factors (Table 11.1).

Table 11.1 Factor conditions

Variable Name	Type	Source
Arable land per person	Basic	World Bank
Labour Force	Basic	ILO
Total Weekly hours of employed person	Basic	ILO
Total natural resources rent	Basic	World Bank
Total Patent applications	Advance	World Bank
Scientific and technical Journals	Advance	World Bank
Percentage employed in Service sector	Advance	World Bank
Percentage employed in manufacturing sector	Advance	World Bank

Source: Author's compilation

Demand Conditions

According to Porter, a nation's home demand is one of the critical determinants of its competitive advantage over the other. Home demand, according to porter, *"shapes the rate and character of improvement and innovation by a nation's firm"*. For this analysis, we have considered two attributes of home demand: (a) The nature of demand (or the types of needs of the consumers) and (b) the size of demand.

The nature of demand is essential because if the domestic buyers are more sophisticated and demanding, then the firms of that nation are in a better position than the others. Sophisticated and demanding buyers nudge the firms to produce higher quality products with more features, regular innovative upgrades, and higher standards. Nature of demand makes the firms plan their way to either innovate (if the degree of sophistication is high) to create new and technologically advanced products, which often leads to collaborative agreements within domestic firms resulting in the rising competitive advantage of the nation and thus Porter argues that demand sophistication is equally as important as demand size, if not more.

Various economists have given conflicting theories relating to demand size and competitive advantage. Some economists consider a large market a necessary strength as it facilitates economies of scale, whereas others consider a large market a weakness. According to them, a smaller market increases pressure on domestic companies to export to international markets, thus helping with the competitive advantage. Porter claims that the nature of demand is essential to explain how the demand size will impact competitive advantage. Each country faces certain local climatic, political, and demographic conditions, which can affect the size of demand. Thus, given the constant demand composition, the demand size still reinforces the national advantage.

However, one can observe that it is common for multinational firms to set up a manufacturing unit in a country and not produce for the domestic market (platform FDI), which questions the relevance of the demand size. Porter argues that demand size is most important to the industries indulged in hefty R&D, which require economies of scale for production, giant technological leaps or high risks. For such industries, a market with large home demand size helps the firms in undertaking risky decisions. The present study considers eight indicators. Six of these indicators use complex data (directly sourced from publicly available databases of international agencies such as the World Bank and the United Nations). For the rest of the two indicators are sourced from the Global Competitiveness Index survey-based dataset.

Following Table 11.2 represents the indicators representing the Demand Criteria.

Table 11.2   Demand conditions

Name of Indicator	Type	Source
Population	Demand Size	World Bank
Gross Domestic Product	Demand Size	World Bank
Per Capita Income	Nature of Demand	World Bank
Exports	Demand Size	World Bank
Imports	Demand Size	World Bank
GDP Growth Rate	Demand Size	World Bank
Degree of Customer Orientation	Nature of Demand	Global Competitiveness Index
Buyer Sophistication	Nature of Demand	Global Competitiveness Index

Source: Author's compilation

Related Industries

"Related industries" is the third vital criterion. Related industries are the supporting industries that allow local industry to thrive. For this study, the related and supporting industries have been divided into industry infrastructure and living environment.

For an industry-wide analysis, it was essential to choose related and supporting industries that are related to all major industries in the considered nations. The variables considered under "industry infrastructure" criterion represent all the transportation and digital infrastructure available in a country. Each firm, whether related to manufacturing, providing services, or agriculture, uses transportation infrastructure to move employees and products and connect with other related and supporting industries. Similarly, digital infrastructure is required to maintain a digital channel to facilitate a fast flow of information between industries and other units of the economy. Hence, industry infrastructure is one of the focus points considered for this analysis.

Like industry infrastructure, the living environment for humans is a crucial sub-criterion. Each industry is supported by the humans working in it. If an economy's working capital is unhealthy and susceptible to an early death before retirement, there are bound to be negative repercussions on the output produced. Thus, the living environment is a necessary sub-criterion to map out the health and living conditions of the workforce of the targeted economies. The variables considered under related and supporting industry are presented in the Table 11.3 below.

Table 11.3   Related industry conditions

Name of Indicator	Type	Source
Broadband subscriptions	Industry Infrastructure	World Bank
Cell subscriptions	Industry Infrastructure	World Bank
Air transport passengers	Industry Infrastructure	World Bank
Liner shipping connectivity	Industry Infrastructure	World Bank
Individuals using internet	Industry Infrastructure	World Bank
Education Index	Industry Infrastructure	World Bank
Access to electricity	Industry Infrastructure	World Bank
Servers per million	Industry Infrastructure	World Bank
Quality of roads	Industry Infrastructure	World Bank
Human development index	Living environment	World Bank
Life expectancy	Living environment	World Bank
health expenditure	Living environment	World Bank

Source: Author's compilation

Business Context

Business context relates to the nation's condition regarding management strategy, organisational structure, and the competitive nature of the firms (Porter, 1990). Hence, the index is constructed based on the following variables in Table 11.4.

Table 11.4 Business context factors

Name of Indicator	Type	Source
Local Competition Intensity	Competition	www.doingbusiness.org
Intellectual Property rights	Competition	www.doingbusiness.org
Ethical Practices of Firms	Strategy	www.doingbusiness.org
Strength of auditing and reporting standards	Strategy	www.doingbusiness.org
Labour Freedom	Organisational structure	Freedom Index

Source: Author's compilation

Governance Quality

"Governance is composed of a country's traditions and institutions. It includes the process by which governments are elected, controlled, and forced to abdicate; the government's ability to effectively formulate and implement sound policies; and citizens and the state's respect for the institutions that govern economic and social interactions between them" (https://info. worldbank.org/governance/wgi/). The six governance factors are proxies for the government's role that may positively or adversely impact the four determinants of Porter's diamond model. Besides the nation's effective policies, the government's capability to implement such policies is equally accountable for the country's economic progress.

The World Bank's six governance parameters are employed to gauge the governance quality of the respective nations under study (Table 11.5).

Table 11.5 Governance factors

Name of Indicator	Type	Source
Rule of law	Governance quality	World Governance Index, World Bank
Control of corruption	Governance quality	World Governance Index, World Bank
Voice & accountability	Governance quality	World Governance Index, World Bank
Democracy	Governance quality	World Governance Index, World Bank
Government Efficiency	Governance quality	World Governance Index, World Bank
Regulatory Quality	Governance quality	World Governance Index, World Bank

Source: Author's compilation

1. Data validation

It was critical to ensure that the dataset created was complete before compiling the ranking list. There were no gaps in the set, implying that all variables contain values for each country and year. Apart from completeness, the dataset had to be consistent; thus, the respective indicators had to be retrieved from the same source for all countries. The following are the methodologies used to ensure completion and consistency:

(a) Completeness

Various mathematical techniques, such as averages and linear regression prediction, were employed to ensure completeness. Following are the three methods explaining how data completion was ensured.

Case 1: When the last term of the time series is missing

For Bangladesh, the indicator representing scientific and technical journal articles does not have data for 2019; thus, using the data for 2010–2018, we created a linear regression model to estimate a value for 2019.

Case 2: When the middle term of time series is missing

For Indonesia, the total number of patents data was missing for the year 2012. To complete this series mathematical average of values under the year 2013 and 2011 were employed.

Case 3: When the beginning terms of time series is missing.

On such occasions as in the case of indicator representing ease of resolving insolvency, it is assumed that the average of the missing number and the subsequent two terms in the time series is equal to the second term of these three numbers and was calculated using the formula:

$$x_1 = 2 * x_2 - x_3$$

Where is the missing term and x_2, x_3 are terms following x_1.

(b) Ensuring Consistency

Like completeness, consistency across datasets is also a highly desirable quality of a dataset to create a ranking list, as in this paper. The various datasets were referred to and dropped throughout the analysis to ensure consistency. The ranking list originally contained one extra country, Taiwan, which was later dropped owing to a lack of publicly available data. The methodologies adopted for completing the data were the same for all the countries. The indicators for which the data was sourced from the ease of doing business index, such as the "ease of doing business score" data for every year, were calculated using the same corresponding methodology.

(c) Scoring

For obtaining the ranking, each country has been subjected to the same scoring methodology to obtain a standardized score out of 100 points for easy comparison. The collected data was organised in a panel of over ten years and x indicators.

Step 1: The first step in scoring was to obtain a yearly score for every country across each indicator. The standard deviation method (SDM) was used to calculate the standardized scores for all indicators.

The calculation method has been explained through the following example: For example, to calculate the scores for the population parameter of the demand criteria for the year 2010, the array of data for all the countries in focus was separated, and for each country, the following formula was used to calculate the scores for the population parameter:

$$\frac{\text{Country population} - \text{Minimum population in the sample}}{\text{Sample Maximum} - \text{Sample Minimum}} * 100$$

For some indicators for which a rise in the indicator's value has a negative effect on competitiveness, as in the case of taxes (the rise in taxes makes the industry less attractive for new businesses), the following formula was used.

$$100 - \frac{\text{Country population} - \text{Minimum population in the sample}}{\text{Sample Maximum} - \text{Sample Minimum}} * 100$$

Step 2: After calculating country-wise scores for each indicator throughout the considered timeline, the scoring process moved to the second step, which involved calculating the weighted average. Each indicator under every sub-criterion was allotted equal weights and was averaged to calculate the score of the sub-criteria. This exercise was undertaken for all the countries and all the sub-criteria. The subsequently obtained scores for each sub-criterion within their respecting criterion were then allotted an equal weightage to calculate further the average which was allotted to the criteria to calculate the score of each criterion further. Each country's final score is calculated by averaging the scores of each criterion. The ranking is then generated for each year based on the final scores.

3. Findings and Discussion

Findings reveal the relative rankings of the eight countries based on Porter's model in Table 11.6. Among the eight Asian economies considered in the study, India scores first on the related industry, infrastructure, and governance fronts and second regarding demand factors. Though its factors and business context are not very strong (sixth rank), it is the most competitive destination for MNCs among the other studied nations.

Table 11.6 Ranking of eight Asian nations based on 5 indices

Countries	Demand score	Factor Score	Related Industry Score	Governance Score	Business Context Score	RANK Investment attractiveness
India	2	6	1	1	5	1
Bangladesh	1	1	2	3	1	2
Vietnam	3	3	3	2	6	3
Saudi Arabia	4	2	4	4	7	4
Philippines	5	4	7	5	2	5
Indonesia	8	5	5	7	4	6
Thailand	6	7	6	6	8	7
Malaysia	7	8	8	8	3	8

Source: Author's compilation

Since businesses worldwide want to move their headquarters out of China, India may be a good option. India may need to fix its preferential market access, logistics costs, transportation infrastructure, tariff and non-tariff barriers, and supply chain architecture to become a competitive place for global supply chain operations Sudan and Taggar, 2021). Lately, the Indian government has implemented the *"Atmanirbhar Bharat initiative"* (self-reliant India), an effort to promote India as a manufacturing hub, with the slogan "create for the world" (TOI, 2020). However, reforms and regulations supporting faster environmental clearances, simplified labour restrictions, prospective tax benefits, and greater technological competence through automation are urgently required to enable competitive and convenient local manufacturing.

In the recent past, Vietnam too has negotiated multiple worldwide trade deals, invested heavily in industrial infrastructure, and increased textile and garment production. Cheaper labour costs (relative to China) are another advantage for Vietnam. Philippine lawmakers, too, are proposing revisions to lower and simplify the existing tax structure and incentivize MNCs to operate in their special economic zones. Export-reliant Malaysia is also working hard to attract investments and promote high-value manufacturing. It has permitted 100% FDI in various sectors, including healthcare, retail, and education. It also offers tax breaks and other incentives for investments, particularly in modern equipment, green technologies, and medical equipment. Thailand's "Thailand 4.0" development program also encourages investment in value-added, innovation-driven, and service-based industries. Automobiles, electronics, high-value hospitality and health tourism, automation and robotics, and digital technology are among the ten industries targeted by this initiative. Bangladesh and Vietnam witnessed unprecedented growth as textile and apparel exporters due to the "China Plus One" policy adopted by the major manufacturers operating in China, which decided to set up additional manufacturing operations outside of China.

Findings reveal that the appropriate legal framework, adequate infrastructure investments, business-friendly legislation, and highly skilled English-speaking cheap labour force in India, followed by Bangladesh and Vietnam, are the most preferred destinations for global manufacturers seeking "China-Plus-One" destinations (Fig. 11.1).

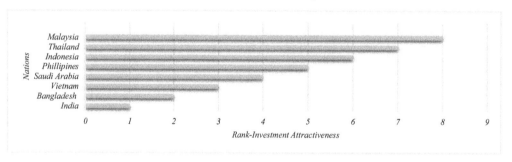

Fig. 11.1 Investment attractiveness ranking of eight Asian nations

Source: Author's compilation

4. Conclusion

To keep MNEs' Asian operations going, businesses may look to other developing Asian countries outside of China, where India appears to hold a very prominent place, based on our analysis. Even though it is currently impossible to predict how the future will unfold, it is unlikely that Asian companies and nations will play a secondary role in the post-pandemic world. For this reason, we agree with Summers (2020) that "if the 21st century turns out to be an Asian century as the 20th was an American one, the pandemic may well be remembered as the turning point".

REFERENCES

1. Depoux, D. 2022. Can Chinese Giants Become Multinational Companies? In *Transition and Opportunity* (pp. 147–158). Springer, Singapore.
2. Findlay, C., and Hoekman, B. 2021. Value chain approaches to reducing policy spillovers on international business. *Journal of International Business Policy*, *4*(3), 390–409.
3. Gu, C. 2019. Urbanization: Processes and driving forces. *Science China Earth Sciences*, *62*(9), 1351–1360.
4. Keegan, D. J., and Churchman, K. 2022. Taiwan and China seek lessons from Ukraine as Taiwan's International position strengthens. *Comparative Connections: A Triannual E-Journal on East Asian Bilateral Relations*, *24*(1).
5. Liu, R., Zhang, J. J., and Vortherms, S. A. 2022. In the Middle: American Multinationals in China and Trade War Politics. *Business and Politics*, 1–29.
6. Nguyen, T. T. M. and Pham, T. P. 2020. Production Relocation of Multinational Companies from China and Chances for Vietnam. *VNU Journal of Economics and Business*, *36*(5E).
7. Sharma, B. 2021. Covid-19 and recalibration of FDI regimes: convergence or divergence? *Transnational Corporations Review*, *13*(1), 62–73.
8. Shih, W. C. 2020. Global supply chains in a post-pandemic world. *Harvard Business Review*, *98*(5), 82–89.
9. Sudan, T. and Taggar, R. 2021. Recovering supply chain disruptions in post-COVID-19 pandemic through transport intelligence and logistics systems: India's experiences and policy options. *Frontiers in Future Transportation*, *2*, 660116.
10. Summers L. 2020. Covid-19 looks like a hinge in history, *Financial Times*, available at: https://www.ft.com/content/de643ae8-9527-11ea-899a-f62a20d54625
11. TOI, 2020. PM Modi pushes for self-reliant India with 'Make for World', available at: https://timesofindia.indiatimes.com/india/pm-modi-pushes-for-self-reliant-india-with-make-for-world-call/articleshow/77568558.cms#:~:text=NEW%20DELHI%3A%20Prime%20Minister%20Narendra%20Modi%20made%20the,and%20raw%20materials%20and%20importer%20of%20finished%20products.
12. TOI, 2021. Explainer: Why are foreign tech firms pulling out of China? available at: https://timesofindia.indiatimes.com/business/international-business/explainer-why-are-foreign-tech-firms-pulling-out-of-china/articleshow/87538043.cms
13. Zhang, K. H. 2006. Is China the world factory? In *China as the world factory* (pp. 279–295). Routledge.
14. Zhu, G., Chou, M. C. and Tsai, C. W. 2020. Lessons learned from the COVID-19 pandemic exposing the shortcomings of current supply chain operations: a long-term prescriptive offering. *Sustainability*, *12*(14), 5858.
15. Zhu, H., Wei, L. and Niu, P. 2020. The novel coronavirus outbreak in Wuhan, China. *Global health research and policy*, *5*(1), 1–3.

Handbook of Evidence Based Management Practices in Business – Satyendra Kumar Sharma et al. (eds)
© 2023 Taylor & Francis Group, London, ISBN 978-1-032-54216-4

Chapter

Sustainable FDI Inflows in Emerging Economies-Indian Perspective

Leena Ajit Kaushal*

Economics & Public Policy,
Management Development Institute Gurgaon, India

Abstract: Green business investment is critical for the long-term sustainable development of a country. To develop a green investment strategy for sustainable development, it is crucial to determine factors influencing sustainable investments. The study aims to investigate sustainable FDI inflows in India, employing an augmented gravity framework in the panel data set from 2011 to 2020. Empirical findings suggest that GDP, economic and social stability, EPU, good governance, and sustainable energy consumption significantly and positively attract FDI in India from the top 15 FDI origins. India has the potential to further attract sustainable FDI by increasing green energy consumption and enhancing trade agreements with developed nations, the major investors in India.

KEYWORDS: Sustainable investment, India, FMOLS, DOLS, Gravity framework

1. Introduction

Foreign direct investment (FDI) is a significant source of capital and a powerful tool for economic growth and development for many countries (Adeniyi, 2020). However, it is critical to ensure that FDI is long-term to significantly contribute to the host country's economic development. Sustainable FDI is a responsibly managed investment that benefits both the host country and the investor. A long-term commitment to the host country is required for sustainable FDI. Numerous academics (Odugbesan et al., 2022; Ling et al., 2020) have addressed the issue of sustainable foreign direct investment (FDI). Researchers believe sustainable FDI is a crucial driver of countries' sustainable economic growth by successfully achieving sustainable development goals (SDGs), which are a blueprint for the planet's long-term future.

*leena.kaushal@mdi.ac.in

DOI: 10.4324/9781003415725-12

By investing in green enterprises, sustainable FDI can assist firms in becoming more environmentally friendly. On the other hand, countries must establish credible institutional infrastructure to achieve consistent economic development while protecting the environment (Chen et al., 2022).

Sustainable investments benefit the host country's social, environmental, and economic growth. The fact that FDI was resilient in Asia during the COVID-19 economic downturn motivated this research, focusing on India. Furthermore, the Alliance of Small Island States highlighted at the recent climate summit in Egypt that immensely polluting emerging economies such as India and China must pay to a climate compensation fund to assist nations in rebuilding after climate change-related disasters. The association referred to India and China as "major polluters (Staff, 2022).

The study emphasizes that attracting sustainable FDI is one of the most critical steps in addressing such issues. The study employs gravity theory and a panel data approach to examine India's sustainable inward FDI pattern from its top 15 FDI partners from 2011 to 2020. Examining inward FDI patterns in India can provide policymakers with valuable insights into improving the nation's long-term foreign investment trends. The study intends to investigate the most critical factors attracting FDI into India, such as political, governance, and social factors, globalization through trade agreements, sustainable energy consumption, and geographical distance.

2. Indian Background

FDI contributes significantly to the economic growth of any nation and satisfies the investment needs of a capital-deficit economy by closing the savings-investment gap. Any country's FDI flow is acknowledged as a significant indicator of its economic potential and strength. Since implementing the liberalisation strategy in 1991, India witnessed a shift in the size and direction of FDI. During 1992–2010, India became one of the fastest-growing, developing FDI beneficiaries, with a significant 7 per cent annual FDI growth (Ghosh and Parab, 2021).

The fundamental benefit of FDI is that it increases the amount of domestic capital available without increasing the national debt. Since liberalization in 1991, our balance of payments situation has improved. The value of the Indian rupee relative to other world currencies has strengthened due to a steady and continuous inflow of foreign capital. FDI is widely acknowledged to advance technology, trade expansion, employment opportunities, and market integration. In recent years, the Indian government has made significant efforts, such as eliminating the requirement for receiving FDI approvals at various stages from the government or other regulatory bodies and easing FDI regulations in a variety of industries, including defence, public sector oil refineries, the telecom sector, and stock exchanges, among others. The "Make in India" program is also a significant step in this direction. Make in India is a robust and inspiring offer to potential investors worldwide to enable India to become a global design and manufacturing centre. Recently, India has become a popular destination for multinational enterprises (MNEs) seeking manufacturing investments. The Indian manufacturing sector reported a significant surge of 76 per cent in FDI inflows from USD 12.09 billion in 2020–21 to USD 21.34 billion in 2021–22 (Ministry of Commerce & Industry). FDI has contributed significantly to the overall expansion of the Indian economy in recent years.

"Sustainable investments can play an important role in delivering the 2030 agenda for sustainable development by bringing capital, employment, export opportunities, greater consumer choice, advanced technologies, managerial know-how, and overall economic growth" (World Economic Forum Report, 2022). There has been growing global support for sustainable investment cooperation. Over 110 economies, representing two-thirds of WTO members, are discussing a multilateral framework on investment facilitation for development.

The COVID-19 pandemic (2019–2020) destroyed the global economic infrastructure and disrupted trade and commerce (Yu et al., 2022). The pandemic resulted in a sharp decline in FDI in 2020 (World Investment Report, 2021). According to the report, global FDI reported a significant 35% decline in 2019 ($1 trillion) vis-a-vis global financial crisis in 2009 ($1.5 trillion). Because of strong flows in Asia, FDI in developing economies fell by a relatively moderate 8%. Two-thirds of FDI went to developing nations, up from under half in 2019. FDI inflows in India in 2020–21 plunged to $54,927 million from $56,006 million in 2019–20 (Ministry of Commerce & Industry). Mergers and acquisitions (M&A) activities contributed increased FDI flows to India. According to current trends in FDI flows across nations, India has generally drawn increased FDI flows and has remained one of the most desirable locations for foreign investors (RBI bulletin, 2022). FDI inflows in India were reported to be significantly high ($83.57 billion) during 2021–22. Since 2003–04, FDI inflows (4.3 billion) in India have surged 20 folds ($83.57 billion) (Ministry of Commerce & Industry). The computer software & hardware sector has been the leading sector attracting FDI (25 cent share), followed by services (12 per cent) and the automobile sector (12%), respectively (Ministry of Commerce & Industry Report, 2020–21).

3. Theoretical Framework and Methodology

The study employs popular Tinbergen's (1962) gravity hypothesis to assess the sustainable FDI pattern of India. The gravity model postulates that trade between nations is encouraged by their respective economic sizes but discouraged by the geographical distances between them.

Besides gravity variables, based on the extant literature (Zander, 2021; Saif et al., 2021; Wang and Lahiri, 2022; Kobilov, 2020), the study identifies the crucial FDI determinants influencing FDI inflows, exhibited in the equation below:

$$FDI_{ijt} = \alpha + \alpha_1(GDP) + \alpha_2(Eindex_{ijt}) + \alpha_3(Gindex_{ijt}) + \alpha_4(Sindex_{ijt}) + \alpha_5(SEC_{ijt}) + \alpha_6(D_{ijt}) + \alpha_7(FTA_{ijt}) + \alpha_8(EPU) + \varepsilon_{it}$$

The study employs Principal component analysis technique to construct economic, social and governance indexes. The variables are sourced from World Bank.

where, FDI_{ijt} represents FDI inflows (current USD million) into nation i from host nation j for the period 2011-2020.

GDP represents gross domestic product of India

Eindex represents economic index (unemployment, Inflation & bilateral exchange rate).

Gindex represents governance index (regulatory quality *(RQ),* control of corruption *(CC),* political instability *(PS)*and rule of law *(RL).*

Sindex represents social index (Urban population growth (annual %), ration of age dependency, school enrolment, tertiary (% gross).

SEC represents sustainable energy consumption (total consumptions of solar, wind, water and nuclear energy)

EPU represent economic policy uncertainty

D_{ij} represents distance between the capitals of countries.

FTA is a dummy variable exhibits a free trade agreement between nations

Contig is a dummy variable showing that there is common border between two nations

i is the country India, *j* is the partner country and *t* is the time indicator (annual).

GDP is a proxy for economic growth. It exhibits the size and condition of a country's economy. Higher economic growth makes the country more attractive to FDI (Zhao et al., 2021). FTA refers to an agreement in which two or more nations have a trade consensus on various issues, including investor protections, intellectual property rights (IPRs), and other requirements involving products and services trade. Hence, it represents trade openness, which may promote sustainable investments. India has negotiated 13 free trade agreements (FTAs) with its trading partners, and a couple of them are in the negotiation stage, for instance, with the UK, EU, and Australia. Numerous studies reveal that FTAs influence FDI inflows favourably (Singh et al., 2022; Trung et al., 2018). Distance is assumed to influence FDI negatively (Gao, 2021).

Sustainable energy consumption has been crucial in preventing environmental degradation caused by rapid economic growth (Kang et al., 2021). This issue requires further attention from policymakers and researchers. Sustainable energy consumption (SEC), consisting of the total consumption of solar, nuclear, wind, and hydropower, is used as a proxy for a green economy (Quang et al., 2021). Studies indicate that rise in economic policy uncertainty (EPU) has a negative influence on foreign investors (Qamruzzaman ,2022; Cheng, 2017). The study employs the principal component analysis technique to compile economic, governance, and social indices. The economic index includes factors like inflation, bilateral exchange, and unemployment rate. The governance index comprises factors like CC, RL, RQ and GE. The social index includes urban population growth, tertiary school enrolment rate, and age dependency ratio.

The study employs fully modified ordinary least square (FMOLS) and dynamic ordinary least square (DOLS) techniques to investigate the short-run and long-run relationship between FDI inflows and the green economy (sustainable energy consumption), and among other determinants. FMOLS, proposed by Phillips and Hansen (1990), is widely used to estimate co-integrating regression equations optimally. However, the study employs Pedroni's (2001) heterogeneous FMOLS technique to overcome issues related to endogeneity and serial correlation (Khan et al., 2019).

4. Empirical Findings and Discussion

The panel unit root test findings indicate the presence of first difference stationary among all determinants in the model (Table 12.1). Most cointegration test results (Kao, Pedroni) further confirm (Table 12.2) the presence of a long-run relationship between the determinants. Post the cointegration test; the study employed FMOLS results reported in Table 12.3. To confirm the robustness of the findings, the study further employs the DOLS estimation technique proposed by several researchers.

Table 12.1   Panel unit root test

	LLC	Im-Pesaran-shin
GDP	-5.31 (0.00)	-9.73(0.00)
EIndex	-9.69 (0.00)	-3.26(0.00)
GIndex	-9.45(0.00)	-5.48(0.00)
SIndex	-2.78 (0.00)	-7.18(0.00)
SEC	-7.54*(0.00)	-2.78(0.00)
EPU	-2.29(0.05)	-6.14(0.000)

Source: Author's compilation

Table 12.2   Cointegration test

Pedroni test for cointegration	Statistic	p-value
Modified Phillips-Perron *t*	5.023	0.000
Phillips-Perron *t*	-32.970	0.000
Augmented Dickey-Fuller *t*	-24.102	0.000
Kao test for cointegration	Statistic	p-value
Modified Dickey-Fuller *t*	-0.341	0.366
Dickey-Fuller *t*	-2.541	0.006
Augmented Dickey-Fuller *t*	0.198	0.421
Unadjusted modified Dickey Fuller *t*	-5.315	0.000
Unadjusted Dickey-Fuller *t*	-5.409	0.000

Source: Author's compilation

FMOLS findings in Table 12.3 suggest that *GDP,* indicating economic growth, has a significant positive impact ($\beta = 0.468$, *p-value 0.000*) in attracting investments. The economic index, represented by unemployment, inflation, and the bilateral exchange rate *($\beta = 0.053$, p-value 0.000),* positively and significantly influence FDI inflows. The findings concur with results reported by Sadiq et al. (2022). *The governance index* represented by CC, RL, RQ and GE has a significant positive impact *($\beta = 0.451$, p-value 0.000).* Findings are concurrent with results reported by Kapuria and Singh (2019*). A social index* representing urban population growth, tertiary school enrolment rate and age dependency ratio also depicts a significant positive impact *($\beta = 0.342$, p-value 0.046).* Similar findings are reported by Tolliver et al. (2021).

Findings further indicate that FTA has a positive ($\beta = 0.090$, p-value 0.107) but insignificant impact on FDI inflows. Sustainable energy consumption too exhibits a positive influence ($\beta = 0.198$, p-value 0.000) on FDI inflows. Globally, India ranks third for renewable energy investments and deployments (https://www.makeinindia.com/sector/renewable-energy). However, the geographical distance between India and the host nation exhibits a significant negative association ($\beta = 0.073$, p-value 0.199). EPU also exhibits a positive impact on FDI inflows, similar to findings reported by Chen et al. (2021).

DOLS estimations confirm the significance of determinants with coefficients and signs similar to the estimated FMOLS coefficients.

Table 12.3   DOLS & FMOLS estimations

	FMOLS	DOLS
GDP$_{sum}$	0.468(0.248) ***	0.513(0.781) ***
E$_{Index}$	0.053(0.0027) ***	0.097(0.035) ***
G$_{Index}$	0.451(0.373) ***	0.535(0.321) ***
S$_{Index}$	0.342(0.241) **	0.485 (0.263) **
Discap	-0.073(0.58) ***	-0.097(0.48) ***
GEC	0.198 (0.318) ***	0.241(0331) **
FTA	0.090 (0.521)	0.073(0.91)
EPU	0.009(0.002) ***	0.003(0.001) **

Note: The symbols ***, **, and * indicate the significance of the coefficient at 1%, 5%, and 10%, respectively. Standard errors are noted in parenthesis.
Source: Author's compilation

Under the automatic method, 100% FDI is permitted in the renewable energy business without government approval. Foreign investments in this industry has risen significantly in recent years, from $414.25 million in 2013-14 to $1.6 billion in 2021-22. In India's renewable energy sector, about $70 billion has been invested over the last eight years. The Indian government's "Make in India" initiative aims to encourage investments in India's manufacturing sector, increase foreign partnerships, and improve Indians' skills and employment prospects. According to data, *'Make in India'* has benefited the renewable sector. FDI in India's coal sector has been near zero since 2013-14, indicating a preference for power sector investment.

International cooperation, including rules and incentives to make business easier for independent power generators and regional players, is at an all-time high. The Ministry of New and Renewable Energy (MNRE) has signed a partnership deal with the International Renewable Energy Agency for 2022. Under this agreement, both sides will facilitate knowledge sharing and skill building to support cost-effective decarbonization and a local green hydrogen economy. India is negotiating with the International Energy Agencies of EU, Italy, US and ASEAN regions to establish international alliances for sustainable energy. India recently signed an agreement with Egypt for $8 billion in green hydrogen infrastructure (www.investindia.gov.in). According to the findings, increasing sustainable energy consumption and allowing 100 per cent FDI in India's renewable sector have significantly attracted sustainable

FDI. A few MNEs in these sectors are Enercon (Germany), Enel (Italy), and Vestas (Denmark), among several others (https://www.makeinindia.com/sector/renewable-energy).

5. Conclusion

The empirical findings revealed that GDP, economic and social stability, good governance, EPU and sustainable energy consumption positively promote FDI in India from the top 15 FDI origins. Investments are negatively impacted by geographic distance, which are regarded of as a proxy for the expense of transportation. Moreover, a free trade agreement (FTA) between India and the host country has a significant but positive influence on FDI inflows. Sustainable energy consuming has become increasingly important in the fight against environmental deterioration driven by rapid economic development. It is also a crucial factor attracting sustainable investments in India. According to the study, policymakers should implement appropriate incentive policies to attract FDIs into the renewable energy sector. The spread of technology via FDI raises the level of technology in the renewable energy industry by introducing new production techniques, ideas, and technology. To attract sustainable or greener FDI, India should strengthen its existing trade agreements, renewable investments, and governance quality.

REFERENCES

1. Adeniyi, F. O. 2020. Impact of foreign direct investment and inflation on economic growth of five randomly selected Countries in Africa. *Journal of Economics and International Finance, 12*(2), 65–73.
2. Ahmed, Z., Cary, M., Shahbaz, M., and Vo, X. V. 2021. Asymmetric nexus between economic policy uncertainty, renewable energy technology budgets, and environmental sustainability: evidence from the United States. *Journal of Cleaner Production, 313*, 127723.
3. Chen, Q., Ning, B., Pan, Y., and Xiao, J. 2022. Green finance and outward foreign direct investment: evidence from a quasi-natural experiment of green insurance in China. *Asia Pacific Journal of Management, 39*(3), 899–924.
4. Chen, Y., Shen, X., and Wang, L. 2021. The heterogeneity research of the impact of EPU on environmental pollution: empirical evidence based on 15 countries. *Sustainability, 13*(8), 4166.
5. Cheng, C. H. J. 2017. Effects of foreign and domestic economic policy uncertainty shocks on South Korea. *Journal of Asian Economics, 51*, 1–11.
6. Gao, X. 2021. The impact of density, distance and division on intellectual property rights protection: the case of Huaihai Economic Zone, China. *International Journal of Urban Sciences, 25*(2), 208–232.
7. Ghosh, T., and Parab, P. M. 2021. Assessing India's productivity trends and endogenous growth: New evidence from technology, human capital and foreign direct investment. *Economic Modelling, 97*, 182–195.
8. Kang, X., Khan, F. U., Ullah, R., Arif, M., Rehman, S. U., & Ullah, F. (2021). Does foreign direct investment influence renewable energy consumption? empirical evidence from south Asian countries. *Energies, 14*(12), 3470.
9. Kapuria, C., and Singh, N. 2019. Determinants of sustainable FDI: A panel data investigation. *Management Decision.*

10. Khan, S. A. R., Sharif, A., Golpîra, H., and Kumar, A. 2019. A green ideology in Asian emerging economies: From environmental policy and sustainable development. *Sustainable development*, *27*(6), 1063–1075.

11. Ling, P. S., Lim, M. K., and Tseng, M. L. 2020. Assessing sustainable foreign direct investment performance in Malaysia: A comparison on policy makers and investor perceptions. *Sustainability*, *12*(20), 8749.

12. Ministry of Commerce and Industry, 2022, available at: https://pib.gov.in/PressReleasePage.aspx?PRID=1845719#:~:text=economies%20for%202021.,India%20is%20rapidly%20emerging%20as%20a%20preferred%20country%20for%20foreign,21%20(USD%2012.09%20billion

13. Ministry of Commerce and Industry Report, 2020–21, available at: https://commerce.gov.in/publications-reports/annual-report-2020-21/

14. Pedroni, P. (2001). Fully modified OLS for heterogeneous cointegrated panels. In *Nonstationary panels, panel cointegration, and dynamic panels*. Emerald Group Publishing Limited.

15. Phillips, P.C.B. and Hansen, B.E. 1990. Statistical Inference in Instrumental Variables Regression with I (1) Processes. *Review of Economic Studies*,57 (1), 99–125

16. Qamruzzaman, M. 2022. Nexus between Economic Policy Uncertainty and Institutional Quality: Evidence from India and Pakistan. *Macroeconomics and Finance in Emerging Market Economies*, 1–20.

17. Odugbesan, J. A., Ike, G., Olowu, G., and Adeleye, B. N. 2022. Investigating the causality between financial inclusion, financial development and sustainable development in Sub-Saharan Africa economies: The mediating role of foreign direct investment. *Journal of Public Affairs*, *22*(3).

18. Sadiq, M., Ou, J. P., Duong, K. D., Van, L., Ngo, T. Q. and Bui, T. X. 2022. The influence of economic factors on the sustainable energy consumption: evidence from China. *Economic Research-Ekonomska Istraživanja*, 1–23.

19. Singh, J., Shreeti, V., & Urdhwareshe, P. 2022. The impact of bilateral investment treaties on FDI inflows into India: Some empirical results. *Foreign Trade Review*, *57*(3), 310–323.

20. Staff S. 2022. COP27: Small island nations want India, China to pay for climate compensation fund, available at: https://scroll.in/latest/1037068/cop27-small-island-nations-want-india-china-to-pay-for-climate-compensation-fund

21. Tinbergen, J. 1962. Shaping the World Economy: Suggestions for an International Economic Policy. The Twentieth Century Fund, New York.

22. Tolliver, C., Fujii, H., Keeley, A. R. and Managi, S. 2021. Green innovation and finance in Asia. *Asian Economic Policy Review*, *16*(1), 67–87.

23. Trung, N. X., Hung, N. D., & Hien, N. T. 2018. Exploiting the trade potential from integration: analysing the impact of free trade agreements between ASEAN and India and China. *China Report*, *54*(4), 442–466.

24. World Economic Forum Report, 2022. Boosting capital for development- Here's how to advance sustainable Foreign Direct Investment, available at: https://www.weforum.org/impact/sustainable-investment/.

25. World Investment Report, 2021. Available at: https://unctad.org/webflyer/world-investment-report-2021

26. Yu, Z., Razzaq, A., Rehman, A., Shah, A., Jameel, K., & Mor, R. S. (2022). Disruption in global supply chain and socio-economic shocks: a lesson from COVID-19 for sustainable production and consumption. *Operations Management Research*, *15*(1), 233–248.

27. Zhao, L., Zhang, Y., Sadiq, M., Hieu, V. M., and Ngo, T. Q. 2021. Testing green fiscal policies for green investment, innovation and green productivity amid theCOVID-19 era. Economic Change and Restructuring

Handbook of Evidence Based Management Practices in Business – Satyendra Kumar Sharma et al. (eds)
© 2023 Taylor & Francis Group, London, ISBN 978-1-032-54216-4

Chapter

A Descriptive Study of the Role of Microfinance in Sustainable Development and its Challenges

Kalpana*

Research Scholar, Department of Banking and Business Economics,
University College of Commerce & Management Studies,
Mohanlal Sukhadia University, Udaipur, Rajasthan, India

ABSTRACT: Role of microfinance is emerging as fruitful tool for poverty alleviation, women empowerment and sustainable development but the present study has only focused on sustainable development and its problems. Microfinance means to provide finance to the rural and vulnerable groups of the society. It helps people to take appropriate small business loans safely, and in a manner which is compatible with moral lending practices. Sustainable development is development in a holistic manner that meets the necessities of the present generations without compromising the ability of future generations to meet their own demand. Scope of the study is that the role of microfinance in sustainable development is to balance the social, economic and ecological objectives of the present generations without affecting for allowing prosperity of future generations. Sustainable development is based on three fundamental pillars: social, economic and environmental. Methodology of the study has based on descriptive research and used secondary data for the analysis of the data. The study found that there is a positive as well as negative role of microfinance in sustainable development and found some major challenges. There should be constant observance in terms of end use and retrieval for the sustainable progress of microfinance. Main conclusion of the study is the microfinance institutions can be a life saver for underprivileged and financially poor stratas of the society. It helps low-income households in stabilizing their income and saving for the future needs. Microfinance institutions allow independence from subsidies and provide an opportunity to financially poor societies with unmet needs to reach sustainable development. Hence, the present research study performance of microfinance in sustainable development brings out stability in the social, economic and environmental and challenges faced by them.

KEYWORDS: Challenges, Microfinance institutions, Performance, Sustainable development

*Corresponding Author: phd22_kalpana@mlsu.ac.in

DOI: 10.4324/9781003415725-13

1. Introduction

The statement given by Pierre Omidyar *"Microfinance has already shown that enabling the poor to empower themselves economically can be a good business."*

The statement given by Ela ben Bhatt *"It is women who are leaders in change and without their participation poverty can never be removed."*

The term microfinance was first time introduced by Muhammad Yunus in the form of "Grameen Page 380 Bank". After that NABARD was taken this term and start new concept of micro finance in India. In layman language microfinance is a small loans provider to poor and low-income group of the society.

In context of India micro finance is a providing of frugality, credit to very small amount to the vulnerable section of the society.

The term sustainable development was introduced by Barbara Ward (Lady Jackson) in 1970s. It is a change that takes place to meet present-day requirements without compromising the capacity of future generations to meet their own needs. Human sustainability, social sustainability, economic sustainability, and environmental sustainability are its four pillars. It is accomplished by carefully balancing the three fundamental components of environmental protection, social inclusion, and economic growth.

1.1 Relationship between Microfinance and Sustainable Development

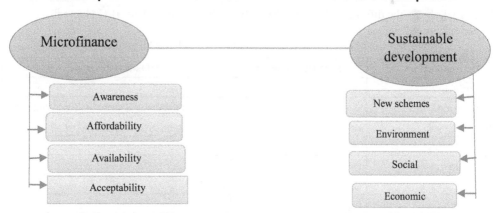

Fig. 13.1 Relationship between microfinance and sustainable development

Source: Author's compilation

The above Fig. 13.1 shows that the relationship between microfinance and sustainable development. In this involves four sub terms in both of them such as awareness is related to new schemes development, affordability is related to environmental development, availability is related to social development, acceptability is related to economic development.

1.2 Role of Microfinance in Sustainable Development

Microfinance is vital for the growth of economies. It is also executing growth in a sustainable development way remain a challenge. The term "sustainable development", it is meant maintaining environmental, social and stable long term financial performance. In 1987 UN World Commission Report gave a definition of sustainable development, it refers to a pattern of resource use that "meets the needs of the present without compromising the ability of future generations to meet their own needs"

Microfinance as an instrument for reaching sustainable development with regards to diverse activities taken by several organizations. It offers a wide range of financial services to those from low-income groups who are unable to get aid in the form of food and other services. Microfinance is "the provision of financial services to low-income poor and very poor self-employed people" Otero (1999, p.8). The main objective of microfinance is to outreach the poor, making positive impact and maintaining financial sustainability for vulnerable society in India. It is a model specially designed for serving the vulnerable society.

1.3 Microfinance Institutions in India

Small business owners and entrepreneurs in India's undeveloped regions can access loans, credit, insurance, savings accounts, and money transfers through microfinance. Those who lack access to these conventional financial resources are the recipients of microfinance. There are three types of microfinance products which includes micro-loans, micro-savings, micro-insurance. Microfinance in India operates through two channels which is Self-help Groups-Bank Linkage Programme (SHG-BLP) and another is Microfinance Institutions-Joint Liability Group (MFIs-JLG).

Table 13.1 shows the difference between SHG-BLP channel and MFIs-JLG channel

Table 13.1   Difference between SHG-BLP channel and MFIs-JLG channel

Parameters	SHG-BLP channel	MFIs-JLG channel
Financial focus	Based on savings	Based on credit
Control and Ownership	With members	With the encouraging microfinance institution
Measurements	Builds inner capacity	Be contingent on external capacity
Efficient focus	Poverty	Finance
Decentralization	High	Low
Cost	Low	High
Elasticity	High	Low

Source: NABARD report 2019-20

2. Review of Literature

Literature review for gaining the existing knowledge about microfinance and it will further connect with sustainable development for the accomplishing purpose of the study and review stated according to the period and chronologically below:

Boro, J., & Goswami, K. C. (2022), the study has focused on, "Microfinance and its social acceptability: A case study among the villeges under dhekiajuli block, Sonitpur, Assam", the research study has aim to ascertain the socioeconomic effects of microloans on the recipients.

Researchers came to the conclusion that village residents were becoming increasingly engaged with MFIs. MFIs themselves visit customers at their homes to provide service and keep minimal formality during the lending process. Hassan M. & Islam M. (2019), in the study, "The socio-economic impact of microfinance in the Poor Family: A study from Bangladesh", the study has examined the role of microfinance in extermination of poverty from Bangladesh. The study found that in some encompass people around the Bangladesh have upgraded their living style and getting triumph. Huma Rehman et al. (2015), the study has based on, "Role of microfinance institutions in women empowerment: A case study of Akhuwat, Pakistan", aim of the effectiveness of MFIs in empowering women politically, socially, economically, and in terms of their beneficiaries' health and education must be evaluated in the study. Both the qualitative and case study approaches have been used in research technique. According to the survey, women are more competent than males when it comes to family management and purchasing household products, and after receiving interest-free loans from MFIs, women see changes in their life. The research paper's conclusion states that microfinance has significantly aided in the empowerment of women in society and that general economic standing has improved. Sarma & Borbora (2015), the study has based on, "Estimation of microfinance demand and supply: With special reference to Assam", Objective of the study has to estimate the imbalance between microfinance supply and demand in Assam and throughout India. According to the survey, both India and Assam have seen an increase in the demand for microloans. Microfinance is not widely available in India as a whole, making up only 0.70 percent of the country's GDP. According to the study's findings, there is a significant disparity between the supply and demand for microloans across all of India's regions when taking the mix-market average loan size into account. Reddy and Sandeep Manak (2005), the study has conducted on, "Self-Help Groups: A keystone of microfinance in India-women empowerment and social security", the study has focused on self-help group that works with NABARD to aid people with their financial and non-financial concerns. According to the study's findings, the management of borrowed micro funds must be properly supervised in order to reduce poverty.

Research Gap: It has been reviewed lots of research papers are to find out the women empowerment through microfinance and socio-economic impact of microfinance in poor families etc. In this study emphasis has been taken on role of microfinance in sustainable development and in role of microfinance includes positive role as well as negative role in sustainable development.

Statement of the problem: Microfinance's contribution to and difficulties with sustainable development in India due to the country's vulnerable population. They lack access to fundamental financial services that are necessary to manage assets and generate revenue. One way to end poverty in India is through this. Poor individuals can understand their need for small loans and protect their funds through microfinance institutions like non-governmental organisations, commercial banks, and even credit unions.

Significance of the study: The study has emphasis on role of microfinance in sustainable development. Researcher carried out an exploratory as well as descriptive research study to get insight into the matter of microfinance. At present time we can use minimum resources for maximum utilization of services and develop new services for reaching to the vulnerable society and it will also help in future generation.

Objective of the study: The main objective of the study is to analyse the role of microfinance in sustainable development and its challenges in India. The study following sub-objectives have been set:

- Role of Microfinance in India
- Role of microfinance in sustainable development
- Challenges faced by the microfinance institutions

3. Research Methodology

The present study has based on descriptive research. The study has mainly based on secondary data. Secondary data has collected from various sources like journals, magazines, newspapers and reports. This study has an exploratory and descriptive in nature to achieve the objective of the study. For analysis of data, period taken from 2018-19 to 2020-21.

4. Analysis and Interpretation

For analysis of data, period has taken for three years which is from 218-19 to 2020-21. Data has taken from Annual report on microfinance in India. Throughout the report NABARD has taken steps for sustainable development in microfinance. The largest microfinance programme in the world, the Self-Help Group-Bank Linkage Programme, which NABARD is proud to say currently reaches 13.8 crore households through more than 112 lakh SHGs and has deposits of over Rs. 37,477 crores, annual loan offtake of more than Rs. 58000 crores, and loan outstanding of more than Rs. 1,03,289 crore, is proudly supported by NABARD.

- *SHG-Bank Linkage Programme:* The SHG-BLP programme has indeed become an example of success of a microfinance programme globally with an outreach to 13.87 crore families, providing social, economic and financial empowerment to the rural poor, especially women. The year wise progress (2018-19 to 2020-21) in savings and credit linkage of SHGs under the SHG-BLP.

- *Microfinance Institutions:* Microfinance industry in India is diverse with several types of players delivering financial services – credit, insurance and pension- to the low-income households. Their legal and operating environment differs and hence, over the years, regulation has become a vital topic for the microfinance industry. Progress of MFIs for two years which is from 2019-20 to 2020-21. As compared to 2019-20 (141 lenders) there were 209 lenders during 2020- 21 which included 87 NBFC-MFIs, 58 NBFCs, 39 Non-profit MFIs, 17 Banks and 8 SFBs. The total industry loan outstanding as on 31 March 2021 is estimated at 247839 crores with 1028 lakh active borrowers, an overall growth of 17% and 12% respectively over the previous financial year. In 2020-21 the SFBs and NBFCs have registered a negative growth in active loans and outstanding portfolio.

- *MFIs' NPA status as of the 31st of March 2020 and 2021:* It is clear that the impact of Covid-19 on microfinance customers' and clients' enterprises, employment losses, reverse migration to communities, and a lack of fresh prospects present issues. Across all ageing categories, on-time recoveries have decreased and PAR numbers have dramatically increased. The microfinance sector's PAR 30 is 9.12%, PAR 90 is 4.15%, and PAR 180 is 6.70% as of March 31, 2021.

5. Challenges Faced by Microfinance in Sustainable Development

Not all poor people experience poverty on a daily basis. Millions of people can escape poverty by successfully implementing new farming techniques, investing in fresh company ideas, or finding new jobs. Due to monetary setbacks, medical challenges, and other shocks, many people face a return to poverty at the same time. There are so many challenges faced by vulnerable section of the society in India which is given below:

High-Interest Rate: MFIs charge exorbitant interest rates that the poor find challenging.

Neglect of Urban Poor: It has been highlighted that MFIs primarily overlook the urban poor in favour of rural communities. Only six of India's more than 800 MFIs are currently concentrating on the urban poor.

Client Retention: A problem with client retention prevents MFIs from expanding. In MFIs, client retention is around 28%.

Loan Default: Because MFIs experience loan default rates of over 73%, this problem hinders the organization's ability to grow and expand.

Low Education Degree: The clientele has a low level of education. Because it makes up over 70% of MFIs, it hinders the organization's ability to grow and expand.

Language Barrier: Since there is a language barrier in communicating with clients (both verbally and in writing) in about 54% of MFIs, this issue hinders the growth and expansion of the organization.

Late Payments: Because MFIs experience a 70% rate of late payments, this problem hinders the organization's ability to grow and expand.

Geographic Factors: Geographical considerations might hinder an organization's ability to grow and expand since they make it challenging to engage with clients in remote locations. The country's BPL population is intended to be assisted by MFIs, however getting to them is challenging due to the lack of infrastructure in such areas.

Debt Management: There is a dearth of client education regarding debt management. 70% of clients at MFIs have no idea how to handle their debt.

7. Conclusion

All segments of the population, including farmers, rural microentrepreneurs, and the poor, should have easy access to sustainable financial services like savings, credit, and insurance provided by self-reliant, sustainable financial institutions in a supportive macroeconomic policy environment and development of MFIs in order to achieve sustainable development. Still there are many challenges to overcome for provide microfinance services in sustainable development. Challenges includes digital literacy in rural areas, lack of technical know-how, lack of awareness in rural people about new schemes and initiatives taken by micro-finance institutions. People must be able to meet all of their demands, both financial and non-financial, in the best possible way. Financial adequacy depends on having access to financial services that can effectively meet the demands of all socioeconomic categories. It is a straightforward kind of lending and offers more services to the next generation to keep it moving forward on the path of sustainable development, microfinance has established itself as the best form of financing for low-income groups.

8. Acknowledgment

I would like to express profound gratitude to Prof. P. K. Singh (Dean & Chairman of UCCMS) and Dr. Mahavir Prasad (Assistant Professor of Govt. PG Law College, Sikar) for his valuable support, encouragement, supervision and useful suggestions throughout this work also. My Parents also gave me moral support and continuous guidance enabled us to complete this work successfully.

REFERENCES

1. Boro, J., & Goswami, K. C. (2022). Microfinance and its social acceptability: a case study among the villeges under dhekiajuli block, Sonitpur, Assam. *Journal of Positive School Psychology, 6*(2), 5330–5351.
2. Hassan, S. M., & Islam, M. M. (2018). The Socio-Economic Impact of Microfinance on the Poor Family: A Study from Bangladesh. *Journal of Asian and African Studies, 00*(0), 1–17.
3. Huma, R., Amani, M., & Nighat, A. (2015). Role of Microfinance Institutions in Women Empowerment: A Case Study of Akhuwat, Pakistan. *Journal of South Asian Studies, 30*(1), 107–125.
4. Sarma, G. K., & Borbora, S. (2015). Estimation of microfinance demand and supply: with special reference to assam. *International Journal Social Science Management, 2*(4), 308–314.
5. Reddy CS & Manak Sndeep (2005). Self Help-Group: A keystone of microfinance in India women empowerment & social security, 1–19.

Chapter

The Impact of Cryptocurrency on the Growth Prospect of Indian Economy

V. Rithul[1]
Student, Christ University, Delhi, India
Varnita Srivastava[2]
Assistant Professor, Amrita Vishwa Vidyapeetham, Bengaluru, India

ABSTRACT: The purpose of this study is to investigate the degree to which people invest in cryptocurrencies and to study their impact on the economy. It identifies the factors that dominate the investment behavior of the individuals in cryptocurrencies, especially during the current economic environment in India. It aims to study how cryptocurrencies have become a preferred tool for investment.

Primary data has been collected using survey method from 300 respondents. Further, using factor analysis variables are categorized in four factors. Karl Pearson's correlation analysis has been done to investigate the degree of correlation existing between the factors affecting the mass adoption of cryptocurrency, factors important for the mass adoption of cryptocurrency, purpose of using cryptocurrency and the economic factors. Finally, using regression analysis the impact of the above-mentioned parameters on macroeconomic variables like the rate of inflation, unemployment rate, consumption rate and taxation structure has been analyzed.

This study finds that only 16% of the total respondents prefer investing in the cryptocurrencies, whereas majority of the respondents prefer investing in stock market, small savings, and conventional investment techniques. This shows the lack of awareness about investing in cryptocurrencies. The regression analysis suggests that there exists significant relationship between the economic factors and independent variables. But their relationship was Low positively correlated, which means no drastic impact can be found in the economic factors due to the factors and purpose of using cryptocurrencies.

This study adds to the current literature on cryptocurrency, and it resulted in a representation of the scale of cryptocurrency use. The results provide with an initial picture of cryptocurrency's use, growth, trustworthiness, and future expectations. The research looked at cryptocurrency

[1]vrithul9@gmail.com, [2]Varnitasrivastava1990@gmail.com

DOI: 10.4324/9781003415725-14

platforms and discovered a slew of difficulties and roadblocks that put the financial system at risk. This study finds that the lack of legislations has exposed the cryptocurrency market to a great deal of risk which discourages the investors. Bringing the right set of regulations in place, can help boost investment in cryptocurrencies.

KEYWORDS: Cryptocurrency, Behavioral finance, Fintech, Bitcoin, Indian economy

1. Introduction

Crypto investing has gained traction around the world recently, and India was no exception. The rapid rise of various cryptographic currencies like Ether, Bitcoin and Litecoin has been clear. Digital currency was relatively new in the country until 2019, and only by the beginning of January 2020 did it begin to make an impact on the Indian economy (Pitta & Julie, 2017). In recent years, digital currency has reached new heights in India, with a growth rate of more than 500% *(Lee, 2021)*. People in India had to make a rational decision to invest in cryptocurrencies to ensure their financial security as this investment sector lack legal assurance in the current scenario *(Kumar, 2022)*. It is not just about cryptocurrencies, but it is about people's mindsets in seeking an alternative investment idea. The cryptocurrency market in India has seen many changes and challenges over the last few years, and this pandemic has added icing to the cake. The rise of cryptocurrency can be traced back to 2008, when the first peer-to-peer electronic cash system, bitcoin, was published (ETtech, 2021). This period also sees the proliferation of digital currency exchanges in India, including Zebpay, Coinsecure, Unocoin, Koinex, and Pocket Bits. The cryptocurrency boom that followed demonetization in 2016 was a highly damaging side effect of that experiment. The emphasis on digital payments prompted clients to look for alternatives to traditional online banking, leading them to bitcoin exchanges. Everything changed in 2018. The RBI issued a circular prohibiting business and cooperative banks, payment banks, small finance banks, NBFCs, and others from managing in virtual monetary forms, and - Offering various types of support to all companies that manage them. The government of India implemented the following regulatory and tax implications in the most recent Union Budget. Around 30% taxation in addition to surcharge and cess at 4% would be payable on capital gains from the crypto assets. Gifts in the virtual digital assets would likewise be burdened in the possession of the recipient. The finance minister likewise proposed to accommodate TDS on payments made corresponding to exchange of digital assets at the rate of 1% of such thought over a financial edge.

This study aims to investigate the extent to which the cryptocurrency has reached the investors' portfolios in India and the degree to which people invest in them and how they impact the economy in a positive manner. This study will aid in comprehending the factors that dominated the investment nature of the individuals in the investment sector especially during the current scenario in India. It explores how cryptocurrencies have become an exceptional tool for the investment purpose and the preference of individuals in choosing cryptocurrencies as the upcoming best investment opportunities. By far, a few Indian researchers have studied the topic, but it still needs further investigation. However, this topic necessitates extensive investigation and advanced analysis, both of which were carried out in this work by utilizing several essential factors and variables. It aims to illustrate the impact that cryptocurrencies can have on the performance of an economy. It also gives useful ideas to modify the regulations to encourage cryptocurrency's impact more effectively on the Indian economy and growth.

2. Theoretical Background and Hypothesis Development

Given that cryptocurrency adoption has only been around for about ten years, it is understandable that there isn't much academic research on it, particularly in the Indian context.

Gupta & Bagga (2017) concluded that cryptocurrency is still in its early stages and has yet to gain a significant user base in India. Nagpal (2018) concluded that cryptocurrency still needs to be adequately regulated, and that one must understand the unpredictable nature of cryptocurrencies, which leads to volatility in trading, scams, the risk of sudden collapse, and total loss. Basu, Saha, & Maity (2018) concluded that 2018 witnessed new opportunities in the cryptocurrency industry. To capitalize on the opportunities in this new digital currency era, the crypto business must address issues such as finance, legal, customer protection, and security risks. Nikam (2018) found that there is an opportunity to improve the efficiency and inclusiveness of India's financial system. Crypto market facilitates the creation of a digitally empowered society, the digital India program and a knowledge economy. Given researchers' recent interest in studying the cause-and-effect relationship between cryptocurrency adoption and the Indian economy, this study attempts to investigate how factors important for cryptocurrency adoption can impact the economy. To investigate this relationship, the following hypothesis was developed:

H1: Factors important for the adoption of cryptocurrency brings a positive impact on the Indian Economy.

Rahman & Dawood (2019) gave a more futuristic account of cryptocurrency by analyzing the few predicative statements regarding the future of bitcoin such (I) the development of portion of advanced buys, (II) client acknowledgment for blockchain development in electronic repayments, payments and banking framework, (III) the rise of bitcoin and furthermore different other cryptographic forms of money as specialty money, and (IV) the ramifications of bitcoin or some other cryptographic money as a particular specialty cash in countries with explicitly frail cash, and (V) the conceivable outcomes of regulative risks of bitcoin utilization in these countries. The primary goal of the research is to organize the various boundaries in Bitcoin selections and provide appropriate clarifications to the issues encountered by Bitcoin clients in India (Javed, Hasan, & Khan, 2020). Based on that, this study assumes that the impact on the economy is associated with the factors influencing cryptocurrency mass adoption. Based on these findings, this study proposes another hypothesis:

H2: Factors affecting the mass adoption of cryptocurrency brings a negative impact on the economy.

Bhat, Nagarkar, & Singh (2021) examined various countries' positions on the regulation and acceptance of digital currencies as part of their legal and financial systems. Rastogi &

Kanoujiya (2022) investigated the volatility spillover impact of digital currencies (Bitcoin, Ethereum, and Litecoin) on India's expansion unpredictability. Finally, these recent studies produced new findings on how the purpose of cryptocurrency can have an impact on the economy. The following hypotheses are proposed in this study:

H3: Purpose of cryptocurrency can bring a positive impact on the economy.

3. Methodology

The respondents include people who have invested in cryptocurrency and those are willing to invest in cryptocurrencies. Their awareness of the research subject has been investigated via a series of screening questions. A survey was carried out to collect primary data from people across the country. The respondent range between 18 to 50 years and above. Sample size is 300. The survey was performed using a five-point Likert scale. The questionnaire was divided into five sections such as Investment preference, cryptocurrency preference, Factors important for the adoption of cryptocurrency, Purpose of using cryptocurrencies and positive impact on the economy. SPSS, Tableau and Excel have been used for data analysis.

Factor analysis has been conducted to reduce variables into a small bunch of conceivable underlying factors. Kaiser-Meyer-Olin (KMO) measure has been used for defining the sampling adequacy.

Factor Analysis reduces countless variables into a small bunch of conceivable underlying factors. It distinguishes the connection between each of the variables included in a dataset, Karl Pearson's Correlation Analysis is used to describe the strength and direction of the linear relationship between two variables and Regression Analysis which is used to evaluate the strength of a relationship between one dependent and independent variables. Regression analysis helps in anticipating how much variance is being accounted in a solitary response by a bunch of independent variables.

4. Data Analysis and Interpretation

Out of 300 respondents, majority respondents were aged less than 25 years. 39% of the respondents invest their money in stock market, followed by 24% invest their money in small savings, then 21% invest in conventional investment techniques and finally the 16% invest in cryptocurrency market. Out of the 300 respondents, 110 believe that cryptocurrency will possibly surpass the other investment options. Majority of the respondents think that the ongoing purchases and sales of cryptocurrencies to pay for goods and services should be regulated in India by the Central Government of India. Around 35% of respondents were satisfied with the recent government policies bought up on cryptocurrencies during the union budget of 2022-23

The KMO test value is 0.899 which is more than 0.5, can be considered acceptable and valid to conduct data reduction technique (Field, 2013).

Factor Analysis reduces countless variables into a small bunch of conceivable underlying factors. It distinguishes the connection between each of the variables included in a dataset.

Table 14.1 Factor analysis

Name	Variables Description	Rotated Loading	% of Variance	Eigen Value
Factors important for the adoption of cryptocurrency	Acceptance of cryptocurrency sale by major banks	0.757	45.51%	8.192
	Steadier cryptocurrency price	0.745		
	Improved government regulations	0.725		
	Openness to website with cryptocurrency at checkout	0.676		
	Secured Storage method of cryptocurrency	0.608		
Purpose of using cryptocurrency	Trading and Investing	0.539	8.62%	1.552
	Selling goods and services	0.827		
	Making purchases	0.725		
	Transferring funds nationally and internationally	0.639		
	Wealth maximization	0.612		
Impact on the economy	Consumption rate	0.804	7.01%	1.261
	Unemployment rate	0.762		
	Inflation rate	0.741		
	Taxation structure	0.679		
Factors affecting the mass adoption of cryptocurrency	Security risk in case of loss	0.753	5.75%	1.035
	Irreversible nature of payment	0.713		
	Market fluctuations	0.675		
	Hidden nature of cryptocurrency transactions	0.496		

Source: Author's compilation

Karl Pearson's Correlation Analysis is used to describe the strength and direction of the linear relationship between two variables.

Pearson correlation of factors affecting the mass adoption of cryptocurrency and the economic factors was found to be Low positively correlated and statistically significant ($p < 0.05$). This shows that increase in the factors affecting the mass adoption of cryptocurrency would lead to increase in unemployment, inflation rate, consumption rate and taxation structure but in a weak or unreliable manner. For the factors important for the mass adoption of cryptocurrency and the economic factors was found to be Low positively correlated and statistically significant ($p < 0.05$). This shows that increase in the factors important for the mass adoption of cryptocurrency would lead to increase in unemployment, inflation rate, consumption rate and taxation structure but in a weak or unreliable manner. For factors important for the purpose of using cryptocurrency and the economic factors was found to be Low positively correlated and statistically significant ($p < 0.05$). This shows that increase in the factors important for the mass adoption of cryptocurrency would lead to increase in unemployment, inflation rate, consumption rate and taxation structure but in a weak or unreliable manner.

Regression Analysis which is used to evaluate the strength of a relationship between one dependent and independent variables. Regression analysis helps in anticipating how much variance is being accounted in a solitary response by a bunch of independent variables.

For Model 1, it was found that the $R^2 = 0.205$. The Hidden nature of cryptocurrency transaction (*coeff = .235, p value = .021*) has been found to be statistically significant and it predicts the unemployment rate. For Model 2, it was found that the $R^2 = 0.205$. The trading and investing (*coeff = .174, p value = .022*), Wealth maximization (*coeff = -.207, p value = .005*), Market Fluctuations (*coeff = .174, p value = .011*) and Steadier cryptocurrency price (*coeff = .206, p value = .008*) has been found to be statistically significant and it predicts the inflation rate. For Model 3, it was found that the $R^2 = 0.326$. Transferring funds nationally and internationally

Table 14.2 Regression analysis

Variables	Unemployment Rate	Inflation Rate	Consumption Rate	Taxation Structure
Trading and investing	0.082	0.174	0.014	-0.244
Selling Goods and Services	0.027	0.041	-0.038	0.026
Wealth Maximization	-0.47	-0.207	0.083	0.044
Transferring funds nationally and internationally	0.102	0.101	0.146	-0.061
Making purchases	-0.052	0.085	0.066	0.122
Hidden nature of cryptocurrency transaction	0.235	0.112	0.281	0.262
Irreversible nature of payment	0.126	0.101	-0.132	0.005
Security risk in case of loss	-0.153	-0.022	-0.184	0.003
Market Fluctuations	-0.051	0.174	0.258	0.067
Improved Government Regulations	0.165	0.164	0.16	0.082
Acceptance of cryptocurrency sale by major banks	0.017	-0.15	-0.11	0.075
Openness to websites with cryptocurrency at checkout	0.12	0.074	-0.012	0.06
Steadier cryptocurrency price	-0.053	0.206	0.177	-0.02
Secured storage methods of cryptocurrencies	-0.05	-0.086	-0.029	0.149
R Square	0.205	0.35	0.326	0.251
Adjusted R square	0.166	0.318	0.293	0.214
* Bold numbers shows the coefficient value * Significant at the 0.05 level				

Source: Author's compilation

(coeff = .146, p value = .027), Hidden nature of cryptocurrency price *(coeff = .281, p value = .003)*, Market fluctuations *(coeff = .258, p value = .000)*, Steadier cryptocurrency price *(coeff = .177, p value = .026)* and Security risk in case of loss *(coeff = -.184, p value = .014)* has been found to be statistically significant and it predicts the consumption rate. For Model 4, it was found that the R^2 = 0.251. Trading and Investing *(coeff = -.244, p value = .003)* and Hidden nature of cryptocurrency transactions *(coeff = .262, p value = .008)* has been found to be statistically significant and it predicts the Taxation structure.

5. Discussion

The findings of regression analysis regarding the second hypothesis suggest that only Hidden nature of cryptocurrency transactions have a positive impact on the Unemployment Rate. This satisfies the second hypothesis of my study which states factors affecting the mass adoption of cryptocurrency brings a negative impact on the economy. However, Trading and investing, Market fluctuations and steadier cryptocurrency prices have a positive impact on the Inflation Rate whereas Wealth maximisation have a negative impact. This satisfies the second hypothesis again, whereas my third hypothesis may vary depending on the purpose of cryptocurrency you choose as Trading and investing gives a positive impact, but wealth maximisation can have a negative impact. Consumption rate in my studies is positively impacted by Transferring funds nationally and internationally, Hidden nature of cryptocurrency transactions, Market fluctuations and steadier cryptocurrency price but at the same time it is negatively impacted by Security risk in case of loss. This satisfies all my three hypothesis. Finally, Taxation structure may have negative impact through Trading and investing but positive impact through Hidden nature of cryptocurrency. This satisfies my second hypothesis.

These results are also supported by Nagpal (2018) clearly proves in his studies that the unpredictable nature of cryptocurrencies will lead to volatility in trading, scams, the risk of collapse, and total loss. Researchers like Rahman & Dawood (2019) who believes that cryptocurrencies will have more benefits for the economy but as per my results unemployment rate, inflation rate and taxation structures will affect our economy more.

6. Conclusions

To forecast the future of the Indian economy, we must delve into several fields that are on the verge of taking over as a key tool in effecting our economy in the near future. Cryptocurrencies are one such new instrument. People are still hesitant to invest in cryptocurrency due to its unpredictable nature. It is not just about cryptocurrencies, but it is about people's mindsets in seeking an alternative investment idea. The cryptocurrency market in India has seen many changes and challenges over the last few years. The purpose of this study is to investigate the degree to which people invest in cryptocurrencies and to study their impact on the economy. It identifies the factors that dominate the investment behavior of the individuals in cryptocurrencies, especially during the current economic environment in India. It aims to study how cryptocurrencies have become a preferred tool for investment.

This study adds to the current literature on cryptocurrency, and it resulted in a representation of the scale of cryptocurrency use. The results provide with an initial picture of cryptocurrency's use, growth, trustworthiness, and future expectations. The research looked at cryptocurrency platforms and discovered a slew of difficulties and roadblocks that put the financial system at risk. This study finds that the lack of legislations has exposed the cryptocurrency market to a great deal of risk which discourages the investors. Bringing the right set of regulations in place, can help boost investment in cryptocurrencies.

In future, both researchers and policy makers must come forward to make people believe that cryptocurrencies are more efficient in every possible way, to make this a success, the government, the people, fin-tech savvys have to go hand in hand.

7. Acknowledgment

Rithul and Varnita sincerely thanks all the students, financial advisors, accountants, and investors who were very much instrumental in conducting this research. Their time and valuable conversations was extremely helpful in providing the required information in order to carry out this study. Finally, we would like to thank our parents and friends for their constant help and support. Their motivation and advice were very helpful in enabling me to conduct the research and bring it to completion.

REFERENCES

1. Pitta, Julie. *Requiem for a Bright Idea.* Forbes, 2017. https://www.forbes.com/forbes/1999/1101/6411390a.html?sh=f3b763d715f6.
2. Lee, Anna Grace. "The History of Cryptocurrency: Bitcoin's Long, Strange Trip to Best-Performing Asset of the Decade." Esquire, May 19, 2021. https://www.esquire.com/lifestyle/money/g36290032/history-of-cryptocurrency/.
3. Kumar, Rajeev. "Financialexpress." Cryptocurrency Tax News Budget 2022 Highlights: 30% Tax, TDS on Crypto, Virtual Digital Assets Explained | The Financial Express, February 2, 2022. https://www.financialexpress.com/budget/cryptocurrency-tax-news-budget-2022-live-updates-tds-rules-crypto-income-taxation-regulation-for-investors-2421636/.
4. ETtech. "Cryptocurrency in India: The Past, Present and Uncertain Future." The Economic Times, December 31, 2022. https://economictimes.indiatimes.com/tech/trendspotting/cryptocurrency-in-india-the-past-present-and-uncertain-future/articleshow/81410792.cms.
5. Gupta, Mukund, and Teena Bagga. "International Research Journal of Management Science and Technology." *STUDY OF CONSUMER AWARENESS ON CRYPTOCURRENCY IN INDIA* 8, no. 10 (2017): 144–50. https://doi.org/10.32804/irjmst.
6. Nagpal, Dr. Sushant. "Cryptocurrency: The Revolutionary Future Money." *SSRN Electronic Journal*, 2017. https://doi.org/10.2139/ssrn.3090813.
7. Basu, Snigdha, Tapash Ranjan Saha, and Swapan Kumar Malty. "IMPLICATIONS OF CRYPTOCURRENCY: A NEW BUSINESS PROPOSITION OF TODAY'S ENTREPRENEURIAL HORIZO." *International Journal on Recent Trends in Business and Tourism* 2, no. 3 (July 2018): 64–70.
8. Nikam, Rahul J. "Model Draft Regulation on Cryptocurrency in India." *Hasanuddin Law Review* 4, no. 2 (2018): 146. https://doi.org/10.20956/halrev.v4i2.1466.
9. Rahman, Afzalur, and Ayub Khan Dawood. "Bitcoin and Future of Cryptocurrency." *Ushus - Journal of Business Management* 18, no. 1 (2019): 61–66. https://doi.org/10.12725/ujbm.46.5.

10. Yousuf Javed, Mohd, Mohammad Hasan, and Ruzaina Khan. "Future of Bitcoin in India: Issues and Challenges." *Journal of Statistics and Management Systems* 23, no. 2 (2020): 207–14. https://doi.org/10.1080/09720510.2020.1724621.
11. Bhat, Viraja, Jeevan Nagarkar, and Ayushi Singh. "Prospects of Digital Currency in India - a Way Forward." *Revista Gestão Inovação e Tecnologias* 11, no. 4 (2021): 5247–66. https://doi.org/10.47059/revistageintec.v11i4.2560.
12. Rastogi, Shailesh, and Jagjeevan Kanoujiya. "Impact of Cryptos on the Inflation Volatility in India: An Application of Bivariate Bekk-Garch Models." *Journal of Economic and Administrative Sciences*, 2022. https://doi.org/10.1108/jeas-08-2021-0167.
13. Field, Andy. *Discovering Statistics Using IBM SPSS Statistics*. Fourthed. s.l., UK: SAGE Publications Ltd, 2013.

Handbook of Evidence Based Management Practices in Business – Satyendra Kumar Sharma et al. (eds)
© 2023 Taylor & Francis Group, London, ISBN 978-1-032-54216-4

Chapter

Economic Burden of Non-Communicable Diseases and Challenges of Health Insurance Coverage: Insights from Primary Survey

Varsha Shukla[1]
Ph.D Scholar,
Birla Institute of Technology and Sciences, Pilani, India

Rahul Arora[2]
Assistant Professor,
Birla Institute of Technology and Sciences, Pilani, India

ABSTRACT: India's health system ranks as one of the world's most heavily dependent on out-of-pocket expenditures (OOPE). According to WHO (2018), roughly 63 percent of health expenditure in India is out-of-pocket. As per the National Sample Survey-75th round of the health survey, approximately 80 percent of the population is without any health insurance coverage. India has witnessed a sharp increase in the share of NCDs in the total disease burden from 30 percent in 1990 to 56 percent in 2016, also percentage of death due to NCDs in India has increased from 37 percent in 1991 to 61 percent during the same period. The rising burden of disease has increased the total share of out-of-pocket expenditure on health, consequently leading to catastrophic health expenditure, impoverishment, and distress financing. The extent of poverty is deeper than the estimated national figure due to high OOPE and negligible health insurance coverage in the era of rising disease burden. Against this backdrop, this study examines the association between health insurance on healthcare utilization and the burden of OOPE among people with reported NCDs. The findings of the study are based on the primary data analysis collected through a web-based survey. Through descriptive and regression analyses, the study presents evidence on awareness, and decision-making process in the insurance uptake, therefore, providing a behavioral approach for policy design to expand insurance coverage.

KEYWORDS: Health insurance, Health seeking behavior, NCDs, OOPE

[1]p20200454@pilani.bits-pilani.ac.in, [2]rahul.arora@pilani.bits-pilani.ac.in

DOI: 10.4324/9781003415725-15

1. Introduction

The rising burden of NCDs has resulted in higher proportion of income on healthcare expenditure, resulting in catastrophic healthcare expenditure (CHE), impoverishment, and distress financing (Yadav et al., 2021). As per the literature, one of the ways of reducing this OOP expenditure is improving the system of health insurance in India, which as per the 2017 estimates covers only 34% of the population of the country. The rising double burden of disease without proper quality and quantity of adequate government initiative, the OOPE will continue to rise leaving behind heavy economic implications (Keane & Thakur, 2018). Policy makers have highlighted expansion of public funded health insurance is the key to achieve Universal Health Care. Despite the successful public health strengthening schemes such as National Rural Health Mission, the health sector remains highly privatized serving 80% of outpatient care and up to 60% of inpatient care in the nation (Azam, 2018). Study conducted by Dave et al., (2021), for evaluating facilitators, barriers, and perception to participation of the private sector health facilities in Health Insurance & government-led schemes, found that only 30% of hospitals were offering cashless private health insurance facility while only 26% of hospitals were offering government health schemes. Administrative problem, heavy patient load, low and delayed reimbursement and fraudulent activity were the common reasons sought for nonenrolment to government health schemes. The plausible reason for the low utilisation despite the high enrolment reported in multiple studies might be due to, first, the asymmetric information; As per the 2014 healthcare use survey, only 1.3% of privately insured households obtained reimbursement for their medical expenditures and second, the restriction in insurance benefits to hospital care; clearly ineffective strategy given evidence that frequent spending on outpatient care accounts for most health-related impoverishment in India. Total current health expenditure in India 35.3% is on inpatient curative care services, the rest being on prescribed medicines (26.8%), outpatient curative care (17.1%), preventive care (6.8%), etc. whereas scheme such as PMJAY only covers hospitalization expenses and up to 3 days of prehospitalization and 15 days post. Therefore, most out-of-pocket health expenses does not fall under the purview of the PMJAY or similar state health insurance schemes (Sinha, 2020).

Against this background, this study aims first, to examine the association between health insurance on health care utilization and the burden of OOPE among people with reported NCDs. Secondly, it assesses the role of perceived susceptibility and severity of health problems for household enrolment in health insurance.

2. Data and Methodology

The study is based on data from a web-based survey, conducted during November-December 2022. The inclusion criteria included anyone above the age of 18. A systematic web questionnaire was designed, including question about socio-economic-demographic profile of the individual in part I, i.e., age, gender, education, occupation etc. In part II, the questions were asked regarding the prevalence of NCDs and medical expenditure/reimbursement received associated with the prevalent NCDs.

The last part of the questionnaire dealt with perception regarding person's own health and awareness/expectation from insurance scheme. Health Belief Model was used to assess the perceived behaviour. Health Belief Model (HBM) is one of the earliest theories in the field of health behaviour. It was created in the 1950s by a team of social psychologists from the U.S. Public Health Service who wanted to understand limited participation in campaigns to prevent and detect disease (Glanz, 1997). For the study purpose, a minimum sample of 200 is targeted which is achieved after deleting few outliers. Descriptive statistics and correlation method will be used to analyse the result of the study. All the analyses were conducted using Microsoft excel.

3. Results

3.1 Socioeconomic and Demographic Profile

The socioeconomic and demographic characteristics of the people participated in the webbased survey is presented in Table 15.1.

Of the total sample population, half of the respondents were between the age bracket of 18-30 years. The percentage of respondent above the age of 50 years were 16 percent and whereas the middle age respondents were around 30 percent. The proportion of male and female respondents was approximately the same. More than 90 percent of the respondents had graduation and above level of education. Most respondents were employed in private sector/organized job, whereas approximately similar percentage of respondents were in government and temporarily salaried job.

3.2 Prevalence of NCDs and Out of Pocket Expenditure

Out of the total respondents approximately 23 percent reported illness due to NCDs. The highest prevalence

Table 15.1 Socio-economic and demographic characteristics

Socio-economic and demographic characteristics	Proportion
Age group:	
18-30	54%
31-45	30%
45 & above	16%
Gender:	
Female Male	47%
	53%
Size of the household:	
1-3	33%
4-6	59%
7-10	7%
Marital Status:	
Married	45%
Unmarried	53%
Widow	1%
Separated	1%
Education:	
No formal Education	1%
Primary Education (till 8th)	3%
10+2	4%
Graduation	26%
Post Graduation	37%
Post Graduation & above	28%
Occupation:	
Government Job	17% 7%
Homemaker	42% 3%
Private Sector/ Organized Job	10%
Retired	21%
Temporary Salaried Job	
Unemployed	
Monthly HH Income:	
Less than 30000	16%
INR 60000-1 lakh	18%
INR 30000-60000	19%
INR 1-3 Lakh	25%
Above 3 Lakh	21%

Source: Author's compilation

was reported for hypertension/hypotension i.e., high/low blood pressure related health issues. Second most report disease was Diabetes and anxiety disorder. 50 percent of the respondents with reported NCDs were in the age bracket of 45 and above. The most prevalent disease in this age bracket was diabetes (Endocrine, metabolic, nutritional) and hypertension/hypotension (cardio-vascular).

Table 15.2 Disease prevalence across age group and gender

Category*	Cardio-Vascular	Endocrine, Metabolic, Nutritional	Psychiatric & Neurological	Respiratory	All NCDs
Age Group					
18-30	11%	22%	60%	33%	32%
31-45	11%	11%	30%	15%	16%
45 above	78 %	67 %	10 %	52 %	52 %
Gender					
Female	56%	67%	40%	34%	51%
Male	44%	33%	60%	67%	49 %
Total	30%	30%	33%	7%	

*Disease categories are matched as per National Sample Survey 75 in schedule 25.2[th] round nature of ailment list
Source: Author's compilation

Anxiety (psychiatric and neurological) was the highest reported disease in the age bracket of 18-30 years. The highest prevalent disease in reported in females was hypertension/hypotension, whereas in the male counterpart the most prevalent disease was asthma (respiratory disorders).

3.3 Mean Medical Expenditure due to IPD, OPD and Diagnosis

The average medical expenditure medical expenditure per hospitalisation episode (IPD) was highest for the age group above 45, and cardiovascular disease. The average medical expenditure for Outpatient visits to the doctor's clinic was highest for the age group of 18-30. The average expenditure for IPD/OPD/diagnosis was higher for private health facilities compared to the public health facilities.

Table 15.3 Average Medical Expenditure

Category	IPD	OPD	Diagnosis (X-Ray, CT Scan, MRI etc.)
Age Group			
18-30		5356	7564
31-45	10000	4126	4384
45 above	295000	1949	3558
Disease category			
Cardio-Vascular	450000	4787	8626
Endocrine, Metabolic, Nutritional	140000	1968	4000
Psychiatric & Neurological	10000	2904	2378
Respiratory		5500	2125

Category	IPD	OPD	Diagnosis (X-Ray, CT Scan, MRI etc.)
Type of facility			
Private Hospital	225000	1300	9500
Public/Government Hospital	150000	3944	3384
Monthly HH Income			
Less than 30000	300000	11255	20005
INR 30000-60000	600000	1383	4542
INR 60000-1 lakh	30000	1654	3500
INR 1-3 Lakh	125000	4595	3953
Above 3 Lakh	20000	3900	1875

Source: Author's compilation

The lowest income quintile reported the highest OPD expenditure, as well as high IPD expenditure compared to the household income. The results are like the studies Keane et al., reporting the increased level of impoverishment due to medical expenses.

3.4 Insurance Uptake, Utilisation, and Reimbursement

Approximately, 67 percent respondents with hospitalisation due NCD were covered under some insurance scheme. And out of this 80 percent were reimbursed for their expenses. About 79% of the total respondents were covered under the private health insurance scheme.

Table 15.4 Insurance uptake across socio-economic-demographic characteristics

Socio-economic-demographic Characteristics	No Insurance	Insurance
Age		
18-30	22.7%	30.5%
31-45	12.1%	18.4%
45 above	7.8%	8.5%
Gender		
Female	22.0%	25.5%
Male	20.6%	31.9%
Marital status		
Married	18.4%	27.0%
Unmarried	24.1%	29.1%
Widow/Separated	0.0%	1.0%

Socio-economic-demographic Characteristics	No Insurance	Insurance
Education		
No formal education	0.7%	0.0%
Primary Education (till 8th)	2.8%	0.0%
10+2	2.8%	1.4%
Graduation	12.1%	14.2%
Post-Graduation	13.5%	23.4%
Post-Graduation and above	10.6%	18.4%
Monthly HH Income		
Less than 30000	11%	5%
INR 30000-60000	10%	10%
INR 60000-1 lakh	6%	11%
INR 1-3 Lakh	9%	16%
Above 3 Lakh	6%	15%

Source: Author's compilation

The statics of the person acquiring health insurance are in line with the existing literature. The highest percentage of people taking health insurance lies in the age bracket of 1830. Within gender, higher proportion of male have acquired health insurance compared to their female counterpart. The uptake of health insurance has positive correlation with the years of education. The percentage of respondents having health insurance increases with the higher level of education. Similarly, the acquiring health insurance have a positive correlation with level of income ($p < 0.05$). The households with the higher level of income have higher probability of taking health insurance than households with lower income.

3.5 Perceived Behaviour

The findings from the study using HBM, identified several factors influencing uptake of health insurance. Financial reasons such as lack of finances and uncertainty of future income remained the major impediment. The correlation between the perception regarding susceptibility (i.e., risk of developing chronic disease), severity (aware of the seriousness/ long run financial consequences of developing the chronic disease) and health insurance uptake were positive and significant. The preferred feature of health insurance reported by the respondents were covering of OPD services, less cumbersome paperwork, and higher upper cap for total claim Most projects focus on in-patient hospital costs, not the larger burden of out-patient cost (Ahlin et al., 2016). Several reviewed studies have documented that public awareness of health insurance in India is poor (Reshmi et al. 2007; Ahmed 2016). Hence the low reimbursed amount discourages people to uptake insurance in future.

4. Conclusion

The empirical evidence in the study indicate variation in healthcare burden across socioeconomic group. The highest burden of NCDs was observed in the age bracket of 45 and above year of population, more population towards ageing hence associated with a higher risk of NCDs (Prabhakaran et al 2018). The highest prevalent disease were CVDs, diabetes, and respiratory disorder, similar to the finding in existing literature (Taylor & Cim, 2010). The expenditure was high across all income quintile however the poor section bears the higher healthcare burden. Also, the healthcare burden was higher for the treatment in private facilities (Menon et al., 2022).

Health insurance programs have the potential to protect individuals in from catastrophic health expenses, hardship financing and reduce their vulnerability to poverty. (James and Acharya, 2022). The HBM model shows the opportunity to reduce disparities in coverage by focusing on the barriers across various socio-economic-demographic population groups. (Khan et al. 2021). As per the literature assessing the efficacy of educational interventions to bridge knowledge gaps using the HBM concluded that educational interventions were effective in raising the awareness of disease severity, and susceptibility also benefits and subsequently lowering perceptions of barriers, which led to higher participation in health promotion activities (Moodi et al., 2011; Shojaeizadeh et al., 2011 Ghaffari et al., 2012; Pirzadeh et al., 2012). Hence, the study advocates further research in understanding various factors involved in willingness to participate and purchase health insurance, therefore providing evidence based policy suggestion to increase health insurance uptake and utilisation.

REFERENCES

1. Ahlin, Tanja, Mark Nichter, and Gopukrishnan Pillai. "Health insurance in India: what do we know and why is ethnographic research needed." *Anthropology & medicine* 23, no. 1 (2016): 102–124.
2. Ahmed, Sayem, Mohammad Enamul Hoque, Abdur Razzaque Sarker, Marufa Sultana, Ziaul Islam, Rukhsana Gazi, and Jahangir AM Khan. "Willingness-to-pay for community-based health insurance among informal workers in urban Bangladesh." *PloS one* 11, no. 2 (2016): e0148211.
3. Azam, Mehtabul. "Does social health insurance reduce financial burden? Panel data evidence from India." *World Development* 102 (2018): 1–17.
4. Barnes, Andrew J., Yaniv Hanoch, Thomas Rice, and Sharon K. Long. "Moving beyond blind men and elephants: providing total estimated annual costs improves health insurance decision making." *Medical care research and review* 74, no. 5 (2017): 625–635.
5. Dave, Harsh S., Jay R. Patwa, and Niraj B. Pandit. "Facilitators and barriers to participation of the private sector health facilities in health insurance & government-led schemes in India." *Clinical Epidemiology and Global Health* 10 (2021): 100699.
6. Ghaffari, Mohtasham, Elaheh Tavassoli, Ahmad Esmaillzadeh, and Akbar Hassanzadeh. "Effect of Health Belief Model based intervention on promoting nutritional behaviors about osteoporosis prevention among students of female middle schools in Isfahan, Iran." *Journal of education and health promotion* 1 (2012).
7. Glanz, Karen. *Theory at a glance: A guide for health promotion practice*. No. 97. US Department of Health and Human Services, Public Health Service, National Institutes of Health, National Cancer Institute, 1997.
9. James, Nigel, and Yubraj Acharya. "Increasing Health Insurance Enrollment in Low-and Middle-Income Countries: What Works, What Does Not, and Research Gaps: A Scoping Review." *INQUIRY: The Journal of Health Care Organization, Provision, and Financing* 59 (2022): 00469580221090396.
10. Keane, Michael, and Ramna Thakur. "Health care spending and hidden poverty in India." *Research in Economics* 72, no. 4 (2018): 435–451.
11. Khan, Pijush Kanti, Jessica M. Perkins, Rockli Kim, Sanjay K. Mohanty, and Sankaran V. Subramanian. "Multilevel population and socioeconomic variation in health insurance coverage in India." *Tropical Medicine & International Health* 26, no. 10 (2021): 1285–1295.
12. Kusuma, Yadlapalli S., Manisha Pal, and Bontha V. Babu. "Health insurance: awareness, utilization, and its determinants among the urban poor in Delhi, India." *Journal of epidemiology and global health* 8, no. 1–2 (2018): 69.
13. Loewenstein, George, Joelle Y. Friedman, Barbara McGill, Sarah Ahmad, Suzanne Linck, Stacey Sinkula, John Beshears et al. "Consumers' misunderstanding of health insurance." *Journal of Health Economics* 32, no. 5 (2013): 850–862.
14. Menon, Geetha R., Jeetendra Yadav, and Denny John. "Burden of non-communicable diseases and its associated economic costs in India." *Social Sciences & Humanities Open* 5, no. 1 (2022): 100256.
15. Moodi, Mitra, MOOD MAHDI BALALI, Gholam Reza Sharifirad, Hossein Shahnazi, and Gholamreza Sharifzadeh. "Evaluation of breast self-examination program using Health Belief Model in female students." (2011): 316–322.

16. Prabhakaran, Dorairaj, Panniyammakal Jeemon, Meenakshi Sharma, Gregory A. Roth, Catherine Johnson, Sivadasanpillai Harikrishnan, Rajeev Gupta et al. "The changing patterns of cardiovascular diseases and their risk factors in the states of India: the Global Burden of Disease Study 1990–2016." *The Lancet Global Health* 6, no. 12 (2018): e1339–e1351.
17. Puri, Raghav, and Changqing Sun. "Increasing utilization of public health insurance programs: Evidence from an experiment in India." *World Development* 139 (2021): 105321.
18. Reshmi, B., N. Sreekumaran Nair, K. M. Sabu, and B. Unnikrishan. "Awareness of health insurance in a south Indian population: A community based study." *Health Popul Perspect Issues* 30, no. 3 (2007): 177–88.
19. Samami, Elahe, Seyed Jalil Seyedi-Andi, Beyrambibi Bayat, Davoud Shojaeizadeh, and Neda Ahmadzadeh Tori. "The effect of educational intervention based on the health belief model on knowledge, attitude, and function of women about Pap smear test at Iranian health centers: a randomized controlled clinical trial." *Journal of Education and Health Promotion* 10 (2021).
20. Shojaeizadeh, Davoud, Seyedeh Zeinab Hashemi, Babak Moeini, and Jalal Poorolajal. "The effect of educational program on increasing cervical cancer screening behavior among women in Hamadan, Iran: Applying health belief model." (2011): 20–25.
21. Sinha, Dipa. "Pradhan Mantri Jan Arogya Yojana–A socio-economic perspective." *Current Medicine Research and Practice* 10, no. 4 (2020): 183–185.
22. Spranca, Mark, David E. Kanouse, Marc Elliott, Pamela Farley Short, Donna O. Farley, and Ron D. Hays. "Do consumer reports of health plan quality affect health plan selection?." *Health services research* 35, no. 5 Pt 1 (2000): 933.
23. Taylor, D. Wayne. *The burden of non-communicable diseases in India*. Cameron Institute, 2010.
24. Yadav, Jeetendra, Shaziya Allarakha, Geetha R. Menon, Denny John, and Saritha Nair. "Socioeconomic impact of hospitalization expenditure for treatment of noncommunicable diseases in India: a repeated cross-sectional analysis of national sample survey data, 2004 to 2018." *Value in Health Regional Issues* 24 (2021): 199–213.

Handbook of Evidence Based Management Practices in Business – Satyendra Kumar Sharma et al. (eds)
© 2023 Taylor & Francis Group, London, ISBN 978-1-032-54216-4

Chapter

Interconnectedness Between Foreign Portfolio Investors and Market Returns: Evidence from Asymmetric Exponential GARCH Model

Faisal Usmani[1]

Department of Commerce, VIT University, Vellore, Tamil Nadu, India.

Imlak Shaikh[2]

Management Development Institute (MDI), Gurgaon, Gurugram, Haryana, India

ABSTRACT: The study attempted to investigate interconnectedness between foreign portfolio investors and Indian market returns using EGARCH model. The results of GARCH (1,1) model show that FPIs do not increase volatility in the Indian markets. However, the results of EGARCH (1,1) show that FPIs increases the volatility significantly. Additionally, leverage effect is also found which suggests markets respond to negative news more severely than positive news. It has been claimed that foreign portfolio investments increase volatility, especially the short-term flows. Hence, it has been suggested that countries should follow policies that would encourage long-term flows. India has to equip well to compete with the world economic giants and present itself as globally competitive open economy.

KEYWORDS: Market returns, GARCH, EGARCH, Foreign portfolio investors

1. Introduction

The increased presence of foreign portfolio investors (FPIs) has major implications for domestic economies for they have volatile nature. India also receives significant amount of FPIs. Consequently, it impacts Indian markets too. There are so many discussions regarding

[1]Faisal.usmani@vit.ac.in, [2]Imlak.shaikh@mdi.ac.in

DOI: 10.4324/9781003415725-16

influence of FPIs on conditional volatility and price movements of capital markets across emerging economies. Large quantum of FPIs investment has created a strong interest in researcher and policy makers across the emerging economies to investigate the impact of FPIs on market returns volatility (Vinh Vo, 2015). During the last few decades, many countries including emerging markets have liberalized their capital markets to take advantage of foreign equity flows and international diversification (Umutlu et al., 2010). The existing literature on FPIs and stock market return volatility is still low in developing economies in comparison with developed economies (Vo Vinh, 2017). Owing to their large trading value of the asset under management and sophisticated trading behavior, they are capable of making a sizeable impact on emerging economies. The gradual removal of barriers for foreign investors has resulted in a huge surge of investments from overseas (Garg & Dua, 2014). The prospects of growth are better in developing economies. They exhibit superior risk-return benefits for international diversification with the scope of further deregulations in domestic market (Batten & Vo, 2015).

2. Review of Literature

Jaleel and Samarakoon (2009) have assessed the influence of FIIs on the Sri Lankan stock market return volatility with reference to liberalization. Using GARCH and TGARCH models of volatility and sixteen-year data on a weekly basis, they found that market opening has a significant role in increasing the volatility of the returns. Furthermore, they found no leverage effect on market returns. The amplified volatility could be attributed to additional information and investing behavior of investors. Chen et al. (2013) revealed that firm-level stock returns volatility has increased with increase in FIIs ownership. Conversely, the findings also revealed that individual foreign shareholdings ease volatility. Umutlu et al. (2013) observed that the most important aspect of FIIs is that they intensify the volatility of returns in emerging markets. Findings of the study revealed total average volatility and net FIIs flows have a positive relationship.Tseng and Lai (2014) found that FIIs results in massive outflow during crisis period than domestic investors. Umutlu and Shackleton (2015) found that irrespective of sale and purchase between individual and institutional investors, volatility had reduced when trade took place. Furthermore, the study found a positive relationship between foreign net outflow and conditional volatility of returns. It implies that foreign investors increase market volatility rather than decreasing. Vo (2015) suggests that foreign investors exert stabilizing effect in developing stock markets. This can be considered as an important reason for rising exposure of the local stock market to foreign investments.

3. Research Method and Data

BSE Sensex returns and Nifty 50 returns are computed by taking its natural log. Most of the studies based on time series data have calculated log-returns of the variables (i.e., Naik and Padhi, 2014). The study is conducted in two parts i.e Whole sample and Subsample. This study has modified the EGARCH model to incorporate the foreign flow variables and dummy variables as per the need of the study.

$$\ln(\sigma_t^2) = \omega + \beta \ln(\sigma_{t-1}^2 + \gamma \frac{u_{t-1}}{\sqrt{\sigma_{t-1}^2}} + \alpha \left[\frac{[u_{t-1}]}{\sqrt{\sigma_{t-1}^2}} - \sqrt{\frac{2}{\pi}} \right] + \psi \text{FII flow} + \phi \text{Dummy\_crisis} \quad (8)$$

In the above equation, this study has included a foreign flow variable and dummy for the financial crisis of 2008.

$$\ln(\sigma_t^2) = \omega + \beta \ln(\sigma_{t-1}^2 + \gamma \frac{u_{t-1}}{\sqrt{\sigma_{t-1}^2}} + \alpha \left[\frac{[u_{t-1}]}{\sqrt{\sigma_{t-1}^2}} - \sqrt{\frac{2}{\pi}} \right] + \psi \text{FII flow} \quad (9)$$

However, in the subsample study, the same equation is written with the only foreign flow as exogenous variables.

4. Results and Discussion

The result asymmetric EGARCH (1,1) model shows the value of FIIN is statistically significant at 5% level of significance. It implies that inflow of FPIs increases the volatility of the BSE Sensex returns and Nifty 50 returns significantly. The asymmetric effect represented by the leverage term in EGARCH model is negative and statistically significant at 1% level. In the presence of negative leverage term, positive shocks have less effect on the conditional variance compared to the negative shocks (Banumathy & Azhagaiah, 2015). Dummy of global financial crisis is significant that implies positive impact on market returns volatility. The coefficient of dummy variable that is used for global financial crises is also positive and significant at 1% level. The leverage effect is statistically significant and negative that indicates an asymmetric effect. Furthermore, the result shows that bad news increases the conditional volatility more than the good news of equal size. Presence of negative leverage effect shows that investors are more cautious of bad news than good news (Asteriou and Hall, 2015). The study of Banerjee and Sarkar (2006) asserts that negative and significant coefficient of leverage in EGARCH confirms the leverage effect. The results are similar in sub sample analysis also.

5. Conclusion and Findings

Literature review chapter pointed out that flow and impact of FPIs has differed from country to country. The study of Nikmanesh (2016) found that market volatility has negative relationship with trade openness in Thailand and positively related to Indonesia and Malaysia. The important finding of GARCH (1,1) model is that the foreign investors have significantly reduced the market volatility. This finding would clarify the situation and quell the fear of uncertainty regarding FPIs flows, in the minds of market regulators (Banerjee & Sarkar, 2006). The study of Anshuman et al. (2016) has reported that FPIs reduces volatility while DIIs increases volatility in the market. This finding is consistent with the findings of Patnaik et.al, (2013), where the researcher has revealed that FPIs exacerbate the distress situation and leave at the first sign of crises. The variations in FPIs purchases and sales have produced contemporaneous volatility in the Indian capital market returns during crises period (Lakshmi & Thenmozhi, 2018). Findings of the study are consistent with findings of Dhingra et al. (2016). Additionally, the study also concluded that FPIs destabilizes Indian capital market through withdrawals. Lai et al. (2008) have also found that FPIs have increased conditional volatility of Taiwanese market returns. In this study, the dummy variable for crisis has a significant positive impact on market volatility, which is in line with the findings of Tseng and Lai (2014). FIIs sales triggered additional volatility of stock exchange during the crisis in Taiwan. They further asserted that FIIs sell more actively than individual investors in the time of distress. The findings of this study will empower the decision-making abilities of the investors and firm managers.

REFERENCES

1. Anshuman, V. R., Chakrabarti, R., & Kumar, K. K. (2016). FII Trading Activity and Intraday Volatility. *Economic & Political Weekly*, *51*(12), 133.
2. Asteriou, D., & Hall, S. G. (2015). *Applied econometrics*. Macmillan International Higher Education.
3. Banerjee, Ashok and Sarkar, Sahadeb (2006), Modeling Daily Volatility of the Indian Stock Market using Intra-day Data, Working Paper, Indian Institute of Management, Calcutta, WPS No. 588/March.
4. Banumathy, K., & Azhagaiah, R. (2015). Modelling Stock Market Volatility: Evidence from India. *Managing Global Transitions: International Research Journal*, *13*(1).
5. Batten, J. A., & Vo, X. V. (2015). Foreign ownership in emerging stock markets. *Journal of Multinational Financial Management*, *32*, 15–24.
6. Chen, Z., Du, J., Li, D., & Ouyang, R. (2013). Does foreign institutional ownership increase return volatility? Evidence from China. *Journal of Banking & Finance*, *37*(2), 660–669.
7. Dhingra, V. S., Gandhi, S., & Bulsara, H. P. (2016). Foreign institutional investments in India: An empirical analysis of dynamic interactions with stock market return and volatility. *IIMB Management Review*, *28*(4), 212–224.
8. Garg, R., & Dua, P. (2014). Foreign portfolio investment flows to India: determinants and analysis. *World development*, *59*, 16–28.
9. Holmes, P., & Wong, M. W. (2001). Foreign investment, regulation and price volatility in Southeast Asian stock markets. *Emerging Markets Review*, *2*(4), 371–386.
10. Jaleel, F. M., & Samarakoon, L. P. (2009). Stock market liberalization and return volatility: Evidence from the emerging market of Sri Lanka. *Journal of Multinational Financial Management*, *19*(5), 409–423.
11. Lai, C. J., Lou, K. R., & Shiu, C. Y. (2008). Foreigner investors and stock volatility: Evidence from Taiwan. *International Journal of Information and Management Sciences*, *19*(2), 315–328.
12. Lakshmi, P., & Thenmozhi, M. (2018). Impact of foreign institutional investor trades in Indian equity and debt market: a three-dimensional analysis. *DECISION*, 1–9.
13. Mukhopadhyay, D., & Sarkar, N. (2003). Stock return and macroeconomic fundamentals in model-specification framework: Evidence from Indian stock market. *Indian Statistical Institute, Economic Research Unit, ERU*, *5*, 1–28.
14. Naik, P. K., & Padhi, P. (2014). Equity Trading Volume and its Relationship with Market Volatility: Evidence from Indian Equity Market. *Journal of Asian Business Strategy*, *4*(9), 108.
15. Nikmanesh, L. 2016. Trade openness and stock market volatility in the ASEAN-5 countries: New evidence using SUR. Investment Analysts Journal. Doi:10.1080/10293523.2016.1172806

16. Pattnaik, R. K., & Kumar, S. S. (2011). Foreign Institutional Investor (Fii) Flows: Some Indian Perspectives. *Foreign Trade Review*, *46*(1), 3–23.
17. Tseng, T. C., & Lai, H. C. (2014). The role of institutional investors in market volatility during the subprime mortgage crisis. *Applied Financial Economics*, *24*(23), 1529–1536.
18. Umutlu, M., Akdeniz, L., & Altay-Salih, A. (2010). The degree of financial liberalization and aggregated stock-return volatility in emerging markets. *Journal of banking & finance*, *34*(3), 509–521.
19. Umutlu, M., Akdeniz, L., & Altay-Salih, A. (2013). Foreign Equity Trading and Average Stock-return Volatility. *The World Economy*, *36*(9), 1209–1228.
20. Umutlu, M., & Shackleton, M. B. (2015). Stock-return volatility and daily equity trading by investor groups in Korea. *Pacific-Basin Finance Journal*, *34*, 43–70.
21. Vo, X. Vinh. (2015). Foreign ownership and stock return volatility–Evidence from Vietnam. *Journal of Multinational Financial Management*, *30*, 101–109.
22. Vo, X. Vinh. (2017). Trading of foreign investors and stock returns in an emerging market-Evidence from Vietnam. *International Review of Financial Analysis*, *52*, 88–93.

Handbook of Evidence Based Management Practices in Business – Satyendra Kumar Sharma et al. (eds)
© 2023 Taylor & Francis Group, London, ISBN 978-1-032-54216-4

Chapter

Impact of Bitcoin Price on the Energy Consumption and Further Estimating its Carbon Footprint

Nishant Sapra[1], Imlak Shaikh[2]

Management Development Institute Gurgaon, Gurugram, India

ABSTRACT: Because of the large amount of energy, they require to run, the Proof-of-Work (PoW) blockchain applications are currently a source of worry due to their carbon footprint. The current study investigates how the price of bitcoin, which is a Proof-of-Work application, affects the amount of energy that is required to mine bitcoin. Because the use of energy results in carbon emission that is dependent on the kind of resource that is used for the generation of energy, we make an effort to estimate the carbon footprint that such an influence has. For the purpose of this study, monthly data from the Bloomberg database were collected and used starting in August 2017 and continuing through July 2022. In order to determine the link that exists between the variables, we employed the ARDL approach. We had sixty observations at our disposal, and the variables came from a range of integration orders. According to the findings, an increase in the price of bitcoin leads to an increase in the amount of energy that is consumed when mining bitcoin, which further increases the amount of carbon emissions. This study helps to illustrate how an increase in the market-driven price of bitcoin as a crypto asset may result in a larger carbon footprint from bitcoin mining.

KEYWORDS: Carbon emission, Cryptocurrency, Environment, Global warming, Proof of work

1. Introduction

The first successful implementation of blockchain technology was cryptocurrency, which can serve as the primary fuel for the worldwide money transmission network.(Hashemi Joo et al.,

[1]Fpm20nishant_s@mdi.ac.in, [2]imlak.shaikh@mdi.ac.in

DOI: 10.4324/9781003415725-17

2020). Out of the all the cryptocurrencies, the most prominent is the virtual currency known as Bitcoin was first introduced to the world in 2008 by an author (or group of authors) going by the pseudonym Satoshi Nakamoto. At the beginning of 2009, the distributed, open, peer-to-peer Bitcoin network subsequently went live (Nakamoto, 2008). Anyone can join this network and provide their computer hardware, such as CPUs, GPUs, or specialized application-specific integrated circuits, to help build fresh blocks of transactions for the blockchain of Bitcoin. The network offers an incentive for adding a new block to the Blockchain network. The Bitcoin system makes it computationally difficult to create a block, which encourages network users to act honestly. To produce blocks that meet certain criteria, participants must spend resources, such as time and electricity for running their hardware. The entire proof-of-work system's process of adding new blocks is referred to as "mining."

The explored literature established that Cryptocurrency using the Proof of Work mining uses significant amount of energy. This in turn has recently given pollution a new impetus. While studying the relationship between carbon credits and the price of bitcoin, it has been established that spillovers from Bitcoin have a greater effect on the carbon market. (Di Febo et al., 2021). In simpler words, Cryptocurrencies using proof-of-work give rise to pollution and have strong impact on carbon market.

Concerns have been raised concerning Bitcoin's contribution to climate change because of the unusual blockchain networks based on the Proof of Work (POW) protocol and the associated "mining" activities, both of which have a growing carbon footprint (Mora et al., 2018). To understand the relationship between cryptocurrencies and energy consumption leading to carbon footprint, we used ARDL method. The findings suggest there is a positive relationship between Bitcoin based electricity consumption (CBECI) and Bitcoin price & Bitcoin trading volume.

2. Literature Review

The cryptocurrency market has significantly grown in the recent years. At the time of drafting this paper, it is estimated to be around US $ 859 billion with 13,159 different cryptocurrencies tracked across 608 exchanges (CoinGecko, 2022). Out of all the cryptocurrencies, many work on the Proof-of-Work (PoW) Protocol of blockchain. It is seen that generally bitcoin is positively impacted by cryptocurrencies like Ethereum, Litecoin, Zcash, Monero, Dash, and Ripple (Hossain and Ismail, 2021). This is possibly due to similar market sentiment towards all cryptocurrencies as an asset. Another quick observation is the common consensus mechanism shared by the cryptos mentioned above. They all work on the Proof-of-Work consensus mechanism. For understanding the relationship between cryptos and bitcoin based energy consumption, we may use Bloomberg Galaxy Crypto Index (BGCI) which reflects the performance of crypto market in totality (Umar and Gubareva, 2020)

Because cryptocurrency mining uses a significant amount of energy, it has recently given pollution a new impetus. According to research, spillovers from Bitcoin have a greater effect on the carbon market (Di Febo et al., 2021). Concerns have been raised concerning Bitcoin's contribution to climate change because to the unusual blockchain networks based on the Proof of Work (POW) protocol and the associated "mining" activities, both of which have a growing carbon footprint (Mora et al., 2018). For understanding the relationship between the bitcoin price and energy consumption, we use the index called The Cambridge Bitcoin Electricity Consumption Index (CBECI), a new resource for daily estimates of the electricity used by the Bitcoin network, added by the University of Cambridge. This offered a replacement for the currently available Bitcoin Energy Consumption Index (BECI) (De Vries, 2020)

3. Data and Methodology

The variables such as Monthly consumption as per CBECI, Bitcoin historical price, Bitcoin Volume and Bitcoins mined were studied using the simple regression technique. We use monthly data from Aug 2017 to July 2022 (60 observations) obtained from the following Bloomberg and CBECI (Cambridge Bitcoin Electricity Consumption Index). The first in our methodology was to check the stationarity of the variables under consideration. We used Augmented Dickey Fuller Test, Philips Perron Test and KPSS test to check the stationarity and they indicated that BMC is integrated of order I(0) and all other variables are integrated of order I(1). The problem of a distinct order of integration is intractable by conventional econometric techniques like the Vector Autoregression (VAR) model or co-integration treatments. In contrast to earlier works that employed VAR or cointegration techniques, we selected an autoregressive distributed lag (ARDL) model and Bounds testing approach based on the seminal work of (Pesaran et al., 2001). The ability to handle data with various orders of integration, which are frequently present when a structural breaks problem arises, is a significant advantage of the ARDL model. Endogeneity, or the situation in which the error term and the explanatory variable are correlated, is another significant problem. In a broad sense, endogeneity might be caused by unobserved heterogeneity or omitted factors.

For trustworthy results, it's crucial to effectively address endogeneity issues and use suitable estimating approaches (Ullah et al., 2021). According to (Pesaran & Shin, 1999), endogeneity is less of an issue if the ARDL model is free of residual correlation. Our diagnostic test findings and LM statistics show no evidence of autocorrelation in the error term and are shown in the Table 17.1 and 17.2.

Table 17.1 Stationarity results from ADF and PP test

	Augmented Dickey Fuller (ADF) Test				Philips Perron (PP) Test			
	Level		First Difference (LNR)		Level		First Difference (LNR)	
Variables	T-Statistics	P-value	T-Statistics	P-value	T-Statistics	P-value	T-Statistics	P-value
LN_BMC	-3.705950	0.0299	-6.700499	0.0000	-3.527582	0.0456	-6.691049	0.0000
LN_BITCOIN	-1.912210	0.6354	-6.894130	0.0000	-1.929503	0.6266	-6.894130	0.0000
LN_BITCOIN_VOL	-3.804795	0.0231	-7.341440	0.0000	-3.463576	0.0529	-18.21381	0.0000
LN_BITCOIN_MINED	-2.446634	0.3527	-10.04914	0.0000	-2.336971	0.4079	-10.05892	0.0000
LN_BGCI	-1.729116	0.7258	-6.823680	0.0000	-1.805944	0.6894	-6.781819	0.0000

Source: Authors calculation

Tables 17.1 and 17.2 depicts the stationarity achieved using the *T*-test values and *p*-values as per ADF, PP and KPSS test. All variables became stationary after the first difference except the BMC.

Table 17.2   KPSS test

Variables	Level LM-Statistics	LM-Statistics First Difference (LNR)	Significance Level	Level	First Difference	Second Difference
LN_BMC	0.083568	0.244872	1%	0.21600	0.73900	0.73900
LN_BITCOIN	0.144692	0.099784	5%	0.14600	0.46300	0.46300
LN_BITCOIN_VOL	0.102206	0.500000	10%	0.11900	0.34700	0.34700
LN_BTCASH	0.117418	0.083783				
LN_BGCI	0.159299	0.099355				

Source: Authors calculation

Table 17.3   Multicollinearity test

	LN_BMC	LN_BITCOIN_ VOL	LN_BITCOIN_ PRICE	LN_BITCOIN_ MINED	LN_BGCI
LN_BMC	1.00	0.12	0.79	-0.70	0.65
LN_BITCOIN_VOL	0.12	1.00	-0.14	0.10	-0.18
LN_BITCOIN_PRICE	0.79	-0.14	1.00	-0.81	0.94
LN_BITCOIN_MINED	-0.70	0.10	-0.81	1.00	-0.70
LN_BGCI	0.65	-0.18	0.94	-0.70	1.00

Source: Authors calculation

4. Results and Interpretation

Out of the variables used, BGCI index and Ethereum price had the correlations higher than 90%. We dropped these variables from the analysis to avoid the multicollinearity problem. We apply the autoregressive distributed lag (ARDL)model with a Bound test approach in the estimate to address co-integration in a mixture of stationary and non-stationary time series. We performed the Auto Regressive Distributed Lag Model (ARDL). When the variables are stationary at I(0) or integrated of order I, the ARDL model is considered to be the most effective econometric method (1). Based on the goals of the study, this model is better than others at capturing both the short-term and long-term effects of independent variables. (Pesaran et al., 2001).

The model is fine with f statistic being 0.000 i.e., less than 0.05. Also, the explanatory power of the model is good enough with adjusted R^2 being 93.384% While creating the model, all the variables were checked for correlation as evident from the Table 17.3 where multicollinearity is accounted for in the table. All the variables with a correlation higher than 90% have been dropped while analysing the impact of independent variables on dependent variables. The

Table 17.4   ARDL results

"Dependent Variable: LN_BMC				
Method- ARDL				
Variable	Coefficient	Std. Error	t-Statistic	Prob.*
LN_BMC(-1)	0.78017	0.048055968	16.23451118	0.000000
LN_BITCOIN_PRICE	0.18087	0.034706269	5.211432852	0.000003
LN_BITCOIN_MINED	0.23059	0.08184052	2.817607447	0.006709
C	-3.77478	1.117152964	-3.378927552	0.001343
"R squared	0.93726	Mean dependent var		1.68130
Adjusted R squared	0.93384	S.D. dependent var		0.48408
F-statistic	273.90093	Durbin-Watson stat"		2.03090
Prob(F-statistic)	0.00000			

Source: Authors calculation

absence of any autocorrelation issue is reflected by the Durbin-Watson stat which is 2.03090. The acceptable criteria being the stat ranging between 1.5 to 2.5 (Durbin & Watson, 1950). Analysing the results obtained, we may infer that bitcoin price and bitcoins mined have a positive impact on Bitcoin based monthly energy consumption with 0.18087 and 0.23059 coefficients respectively. Both the variables are identified to be significant 1% level. The monthly bitcoin-based energy consumption is also affected by its own lagged value (-1).

5. Conclusion

The paper identifies the relationship between the change in price of bitcoin and its impact on energy consumption. The findings supports the zero economic theory or perfect competition theory that indicates the use of excessive energy for mining when it is profitable to do it (Derks et al., 2018). In other words, when the price of bitcoin increases, it lures more miners into the network with more hash power and subsequently more energy consumption. With rise in prices, the miners can spend huge money for more energy in mining, because it becomes feasible for them to incur such expenses. On the other hand, when the price goes down, it becomes unfeasible for the miners to sustain the current costs for mining. Only the efficient miners can sustain this fall in bitcoin price. The entire process is in line with the theory of production where one needs to at least recover the variable cost for mining from the market price of the bitcoin. The recent fall in price of bitcoin in 2022 also backs the findings of this study. In 2022, with plunging crypto prices, Miners' electricity bills are surging. Virtually no one is interested in purchasing their new mining equipment. The marked decrease in 2022 has particularly severe consequences for the miners that took out loans to finance the acquisition of their machinery the previous year. These miners were forced to sell some of their mining rigs and bitcoin holdings as the price of bitcoin continued its downward trend. Otherwise, they would have run out of cash. On the other hand, very few people are interested in purchasing the machines on the secondary market, which drives the price of mining machines even down. (Ostroff, 2022).

Therefore, it is important to understand the relationship between bitcoin price and its energy consumption. With more energy consumption, the carbon emissions are bound to increase as this energy is most of the time powered through non-renewable resources like coal, natural gas etc. Many previous studies show that electricity consumption has a direct and positive relationship with CO_2 emissions (De Vries et al., 2022; Goodkind et al., 2020; Howson & De Vries, 2022; Krause & Tolaymat, 2018). To drive the agenda of sustainability, it is important to gauge and understand the dynamics of market determined bitcoin price and the carbon emissions as a by product of mining the energy intensive cryptos like bitcoin, Ethereum etc.

REFERENCES

1. CoinGecko. (2022). *Crypto Market Cap Charts*. https://www.coingecko.com/en/global-charts
2. de Vries, A. (2020). Bitcoin's energy consumption is underestimated: A market dynamics approach. *Energy Research and Social Science, 70*. https://doi.org/10.1016/j.erss.2020.101721
3. de Vries, A., Gallersdörfer, U., Klaaßen, L., & Stoll, C. (2022). Revisiting Bitcoin's carbon footprint. *Joule, 6*(3), 498–502. https://doi.org/10.1016/j.joule.2022.02.005
4. Derks, J., Gordijn, J., & Siegmann, A. (2018). From chaining blocks to breaking even: A study on the profitability of bitcoin mining from 2012 to 2016. *Electronic Markets, 28*(3), 321–338. https://doi.org/10.1007/s12525-018-0308-3
5. Di Febo, E., Ortolano, A., Foglia, M., Leone, M., & Angelini, E. (2021). From Bitcoin to carbon allowances: An asymmetric extreme risk spillover. *Journal of Environmental Management, 298*. https://doi.org/10.1016/j.jenvman.2021.113384
6. Durbin, J., & Watson, G. S. (1950). Testing for serial correlation in least squares regression. I. *Biometrika, 37*(3–4), 409–428. https://doi.org/10.1093/biomet/37.3-4.409
7. Goodkind, A. L., Jones, B. A., & Berrens, R. P. (2020). Cryptodamages: Monetary value estimates of the air pollution and human health impacts of cryptocurrency mining. *Energy Research and Social Science, 59*. https://doi.org/10.1016/j.erss.2019.101281
8. Hashemi Joo, M., Nishikawa, Y., & Dandapani, K. (2020). Cryptocurrency, a successful application of blockchain technology. *Managerial Finance, 46*(6), 715–733. https://doi.org/10.1108/MF-09-2018-0451
9. Hossain, M. J., & Ismail, M. T. (2021). Is there any influence of other cryptocurrencies on bitcoin? *Asian Academy of Management Journal of Accounting and Finance, 17*(1), 125–152. https://doi.org/10.21315/aamjaf2021.17.1.5
10. Howson, P., & de Vries, A. (2022). Preying on the poor? Opportunities and challenges for tackling the social and environmental threats of cryptocurrencies for vulnerable and low-income communities. *Energy Research and Social Science, 84*. https://doi.org/10.1016/j.erss.2021.102394
11. Krause, M. J., & Tolaymat, T. (2018). Quantification of energy and carbon costs for mining cryptocurrencies. *Nature Sustainability, 1*(11), 711–718. https://doi.org/10.1038/s41893-018-0152-7
12. Mora, C., Rollins, R. L., Taladay, K., Kantar, M. B., Chock, M. K., Shimada, M., & Franklin, E. C. (2018). Bitcoin emissions alone could push global warming above 2°C. *Nature Climate Change, 8*(11), 931–933. https://doi.org/10.1038/s41558-018-0321-8
13. Nakamoto, S. (2008). Bitcoin: A Peer-to-Peer Electronic Cash System. *Cryptography Mailing List at Https://Metzdowd.Com*.
14. Ostroff, C. (2022). *A Bad Year for Crypto Is a Really Bad One for Crypto Miners - WSJ*. https://www.wsj.com/articles/a-bad-year-for-crypto-is-a-really-bad-one-for-crypto-miners-11662970197?mod=e2tw

15. Pesaran, M. H., & Shin, Y. (1999). An Autoregressive Distributed-Lag Modelling Approach to Cointegration Analysis. In S. Strøm (Ed.), *Econometrics and Economic Theory in the 20th Century: The Ragnar Frisch Centennial Symposium* (pp. 371–413). Cambridge University Press. https://doi.org/DOI: 10.1017/CCOL521633230.011
16. Pesaran, M. H., Shin, Y., & Smith, R. J. (2001). Bounds testing approaches to the analysis of level relationships. *Journal of Applied Econometrics, 16*(3), 289–326. https://doi.org/10.1002/jae.616
17. Ullah, S., Zaefarian, G., & Ullah, F. (2021). How to use instrumental variables in addressing endogeneity? A step-by-step procedure for non-specialists. *Industrial Marketing Management, 96*(March 2020), A1–A6. https://doi.org/10.1016/j.indmarman.2020.03.006
18. Umar, Z., & Gubareva, M. (2020). A time–frequency analysis of the impact of the Covid-19 induced panic on the volatility of currency and cryptocurrency markets. *Journal of Behavioral and Experimental Finance, 28.* https://doi.org/10.1016/j.jbef.2020.100404

Chapter

Causality between Defense Expenditure and Economic Growth in India

Prashant Ishwarlal Vadikar[1]

Assist. Professor, The Maharaja Sayajirao University of Baroda,
Vadodara, India

Imlak Shaikh[2]

Associate Professor, Management Development Institute Gurgaon,
Gurugram, Haryana, India

ABSTRACT: The study has analysed the causality between defense spending and Economic growth in India, from 1981 to 2018. The study used the VAR-VECM model to identify the relationship between variables. The study has applied the unit root test, lag order selection criteria, Johnson cointegration test, and various diagnostic tests. All series are auto-regressive effect is witnessed. The study does not find a significant long-run relationship between defense spending and economic growth, but in the short run, there is a uni-direction relationship between defense spending and economic growth.

KEYWORDS: GDP, Military spending, Economic growth, Ganger causality

1. Introduction

The amount of money a nation spends on military expenditure takes away goods and services from civilians, and there is a trade-off. It is a different debate whether the spending on arms increases growth or decreases it. Szymanski (1973) observed that global spending on defense has increased by 51% from 2001 to 2012. One group believes that spending on arms and ammunition leads to growth, and there is an opposite view. Magdoff (1967) reviewed the book "Monopoly Capital" written by Barran and Sweegy (1966) and, analytically remarked the prosperity after the world-war II is the result of defense spending. After this many researchers including Handerson (1998) and Aziz & Asadullah (2017) have come to the conclusion that

---

[1]Prashant-be@msubaroda.ac.in, [2]imlak.shaikh@mdi.ac.in

DOI: 10.4324/9781003415725-18

defense spending stimulates economic growth. Haseeb et al. (2014) noted defense spending negatively affects economic development and economic growth.

1.1 Research Problem

The debate, either the defense spending positively affects or negatively, intended the study to initiate research either what kind of relationship exist in case of India. This study is intended to find a function relationship between defense spending and economic growth. The research problem of study is the defense spending affects economic growth or not, and either the relationship is direct or inverse in nature. The rationality behind time period of study is, the period of 1951 to 1980 the Indian economy achieved traditional growth, which is known as "Hindu growth" by prof. Raj Krishnan. During this period Indian growth rate has constrain, and after 1981 the Indian economy has quite steady economic growth.

2. Review of Literature

Baran & Sweezy (1966) initiated the research on eighteen capitalistic nation's defense spending and economic growth. The research was found that after world war II, the defense spending has brought economic prosperity. Henderson (1998) empirically analysed the relationship between defense spending and poverty with GLS model in USD from 1959 to 19992, and found during peace-time the defense spending has direct relationship with poverty, and in war-time it is inverse. Pradhan (2010) has used error correction model to analyse relationship between defense spending and economic growth for China, India, Pakistan and Nepal during 1988 to 2007. There is long run relationship between economic growth and defense spending in four Asian nations. Tiwari & Tiwari (2010) used VECM to find causality between military spending and economic growth in India and there is presence of bi-directional causality between economic growth and defense spending. Aziz & Asadullah (2017) used panel data of 70 nations to analyse relationship between defense spending and economic growth during 1990 to 2013. The study found there is uni-directional negative relationship between two variables, and it is negative. Haseeb et al. (2014) analysed by applying ARDL model to find relationship between defense spending and economic growth during 1980 to 2013 in Pakistan, it realised the defense spending negatively affects economic growth in long run. Johnson Kennedy et al. (2018) have worked on production function model known as the Feder-Ram model to analyse the relationship between defense spending and economic growth. The Feder-Ram model was criticised for generating quite common simulative effects, and the model found to be static. Abdel-Khalek et al. (2020) have applied VECM model to find cointegrstion relationship between military spending and economic growth in India from 1980 to 2016. The study has used trade openness, Military spending ratio to GDP, and ratio of economic aid to GDP as independent variables in the model. The study found the defense spending promotes economic growth, there is need to develop defense industry to take advantage.

3. Research Methodology

The research methodology part is quite crucial in study, and is framed with the consideration of objectives of study, the kind of data, and some of the primary test to the data.

3.1 Source of Data

There are different secondary sources, including Macrotrends.net, Stockholm International Peace Research Institute (SIPRI), Arms Arm Control and Disarmament Agency (ACDA) which have provided data of nations' defense expenditure, import of defense goods, GDP are published by different. The time period data is 1981 to 2018, it was selected as per the convenience to the objective of the study.

3.2 Basic econometrics Model and Tools for Analysis

The study has used following basic econometrics model.

$$G_t = \alpha + \beta_1\, DE_t + \beta_2\, G_{t-1} + \beta_3\, M_t + \beta_4\, CR + \varepsilon$$

Here, G = Economic Growth, DE = Defense expenditure, M = Defense Import, CR = Exchange rate, indicates external value of currency that reflects in dollar

The $\beta_1, \beta_2, \beta_3$ and β_4 are different co-efficient of respectively G_{t-1}, DE_t, M_t, and CR.

4. Data Analysis and Findings

4.1 Summary of Statistics

Table 18.1 Summary of statistics

Variable/ Parameters	GDP	DE	CR	M
Mean	23.27444	1999.5	868.1998	190.2397
Median	14.09154	1999.5	463.6077	63.21939
SD	18.7499	11.11306	773.866	215.2261
Minimum	5.879007	1981	193.4906	16.34349
Maximum	66.2578	2018	2702.93	640.3008
GDP = Real Gross Domestic Product, DE = Defense spending, CR = Currency value in dollar , M = Import (in Billion $) Time Period: 1981 to 2018				

Source: SIPRI and ACDA

The Table 18.1 represents a summary of statistics that are used in the econometrics model.

4.2 Unit Root Test

This study has used the Augmented Dickey-Fuller (ADF) test for assessing the stationarity of all variables. All time series are found to be stationarity at level one. Based on this outcome presented in Table 18.2, it is decided to go with the VAR-VECM model to find short-run and long-run relationships in the model.

4.3 Econometric Analysis

The Table 18.3 presents various Var Lag order selection criteria, it is found that the optimum lag criteria is 2, on the basis of the majority rule. In the table the LR test statistics (LR), Final prediction error (FPE), Akaike information criterion (AIC), and Hannan-Quinn information

Table 18.2 Result of unit root test

| Variable | At Level | | 1st Degree | | Order of Integration |
	Intercept	Trend & Intercept	Intercept	Trend & Intercept	
LnIND_GDP	-3.63	-4.23	-3.63*	-4.23*	I(1)
LnIND_DE	-3.63	-4.23	-3.63*	-4.23*	I(1)
LnM	-3.62	-4.23	-3.63*	-4.23*	I(1)
LnCR	-3.62	-4.23	-3.63*	-4.23*	I(1)

Source: Author's compilation

Table 18.3 Result display of var lag selection criteria

Lag	LogL	LR	FPE	AIC	SC	HQ
0	7.79	NA	9.40e-06	-0.04	-0.04	-0.16
1	205.00	336.40	2.23e-10	-10.88	**-9. 98***	-10.58
2	232.70	**40.75***	**1.17e-10***	**-11.57***	-9.25	**-11.02***
3	244.36	14.40	1.69e-10	-11.31	-8.98	-10.52
4	259.77	15.41	2.20e-10	-11.28	-8.23	-10.24

Source: Author's compilation

criterion (HQ) indicates lag criteria 2. However, the Schwarz information (SC) criteria indicates lag order at level 1.

The Table 18.4 indicates the null hypothesis of no cointegration between dependent (GDP) and independent variables (Defense spending, Import volume, and external value of Indian currency, is rejected at 1% level of significance and there is a long run relationship between the variables. The result indicates there is at least one cointegrating equations. Since variables are cointegrated, it becomes valid to perform the VECM test further to examine the long run relationship in the model.

Table 18.4 Result of Johnson cointegration test

Unrestricted Cointegration Rank Test (Trace)			
Hypothesized of CE	Trace Statistics	Critical Value at 5%	P-Value
None*	74.43	55.25	**0.0004**
At Most 1	27.54	35.01	0.2507
At Most 2	8.87	18.40	0.5932
At Most 3	1.34	3.84	0.2468
Unrestricted Cointegration Rank Test (Maximum Eigenvalue)			
Hypothesized of CE	Trace Statistics	Critical Value at 5%	P-Value
None*	46.8904	30.8151	**0.0003**
At Most 1	18.6642	24.2520	0.2307
At Most 2	7.5299	17.1477	0.6548
At Most 3	1.3415	3.8415	0.2468
*Denotes rejection of null-hypothesis (H_o:There is no co-integration) at 1%, 5% and 10% significant level **denotes MacKinnon-Haug-Michelis (1999) p-values			

Source: Author's compilation

The outcome in Table 18.5 for VECM model gives mixed result as it revealed the GDP has positive but insignificant relationship with defense spending and Import volume. The outcome also estimates negative and significant relationship between GDP and external value of currency. The defense spending affects positively to GDP but it is insignificant.

Table 18.5 VECM result for long-run relationship

Cointegration Equations:	CointeEq 1		
		Standard Error ()	t-Statistics []
Ln_GDP(-1)	1.0000		
Ln_DE(-1)	-0.103114	(0.07195)	[-1.43311]
Ln_M(-1)	-0.011666	(0.03103)	[-0.37594]
Ln_CR(-1)	0.578684	(0.08635)	**[6.64386]***
C	-6.108273		

Source: Author's compilation

Table 18.6 VECM result for short-run relationship

Cointegration Equations:	Equ:1 ΔLnGDP	Equ: 2 ΔLnDE	Equ: 3 ΔLnM	Equ: 4 ΔLnCR
ECT$_{t-1}$	-1.544088 (0.28420) **[-5.43305]***	-0.746104 (0.41073) [-1.81655]	-2.809632 (0.40451) **[-6.94582]***	1.155097 (0.24365) **[4.74076]***
ΔLnGDP$_{t-1}$	2.043968 (0.50608) **[5.03882]***	1.547970 (0.73138) **[2.11651]***	3.951571 (0.72031) **[5.48596]***	-1.760034 (0.43387) **[-4.05657]***
ΔLnGDP$_{t-2}$	1.139116 (0.41754) **[2.72813]***	0.258086 (0.60343) [0.42770]	2.209913 (0.59429) **[3.71856]***	-0.560019 (0.35797) [-1.56444]
ΔLnDE$_{t-1}$	0.333857 (0.18023) [1.85242]	0.577038 (0.26046) **[2.21545]***	0.012080 (0.25652) [0.04709]	-0.200515 (0.15451) [-1.29773]
ΔLnDE$_{t-2}$	0.159036 (0.19569) [0.81271]	-0.296283 (0.28280) [-1.04766]	0.311235 (0.27852) [1.11745]	-0.107813 (0.16777) [-0.64264]
ΔLnCR$_{t-1}$	2.304690 (0.51431) **[4.48111]***	1.421224 (0.74328) [1.91211]	3.331260 (0.73202) **[4.55077]***	-1.477248 (0.44093) **[-3.35031]***
ΔLnCR$_{t-2}$	0.288133 (0.39005) [0.73870]	-0.670087 (0.16889) [-0.78978]	1.040396 (0.55516) [1.87404]	-0.011825 (0.33440) [-0.03536]
ΔLnM$_{t-1}$	-0.355591 (0.14358) **[-2.47663]***	-0.377767 (0.20750) [-1.82059]	-0.553730 (0.20436) **[-2.70964]***	0.371430 (0.12309) **[3.01748]***
ΔLnM$_{t-2}$	-0.263264 (0.13897) [-1.89441]	-0.148425 (0.20084) [-0.73904]	-0.416301 (0.19779) **[-2.10472]***	0.184850 (0.11914) [1.55154]
C	-0.318020 (0.09670) **[-3.28864]***	-0.074988 (0.13975) [-0.53658]	-0.525688 (0.13764) **[-3.81938]***	0.310530 (0.08290) **[3.74562]***
TREND	0.002194 (0.00113) [1.93831]	0.000111 (0.00164) [0.06771]	0.000630 (0.00161) [0.39123]	-0.001988 (0.00097) **[-2.04827]***
R²	0.67	0.45	0.73	0.69

Source: Author's compilation

The outcome of Table 18.6 shows; The GDP has significant relationship with its own lag, external value of currency, and import volume. It does not have significant short-run relationship with defense spending. The Defense spending has significant short-run relationship with its own lag and the GDP. The import volume has significant relationship with its own lag, GDP, and the external value of currency. The external value of currency has significant relationship with its own lag, import volume, and GDP. The ECT indicates the pace of error correction with exogenous shocks to its state of equilibrium in the long run. There is significant presence of ECT in the equation of GDP, Import volume, and External value of currency. The study has sound R^2 which is quite acceptable.

Diagnostic Test

The diagnostic test in the equation is checked with various residual test and the outcome in Table 18.7 suggest there is no issue of autocorrelation, heteroscedasticity, and normality in the model; and the model is found to be fit.

Table 18.7   Outcome of diagnostic test

Diagnostic Test		
Test	Statistics	P-Value
X^2_{Auto} (2)	78.66968	0.4581
X^2_{Hetro} (2)	1036.927	0.9073
X^2_{Norm} (2)	1527.731	0.7614

Source: Author's compilation

5. Discussion

The defense spending does not significantly impact on GDP in short run or long run, the outcome match with the Mintz & Stevenson (1995) and there is uni-directional relationship (Aziz & Asadullah, 2017) as economic growth affects defense spending. The study finds significant long run causal relationship between economic growth and Exchange rate (Pramanik, 2022) in short run (Shaik & Gona, 2021) and long run (Gowland, 2020). The import volume has bi-directional relationship with economic growth (Guntukula, 2018) in short run and long run. In the series of all variables GDP, defense spending, import volume and exchange rate there is auto-regressive element.

6. Conclusion

The study revealed uni-directional causality between economic growth and defense spending, bi-directional relationship between economic growth and volume of imports, and economic growth and exchange rate in short run. It is quite evident that the import volume generates positive impact and exchange rate generates negatively impact economic growth.

REFERENCES

1. Abdel-Khalek, G., Mazloum, M. G., & El Zeiny, M. R. M. (2020). Military expenditure and economic growth: the case of India. *Review of Economics and Political Science*, 5(2), 116–135. https://doi.org/10.1108/reps-03-2019-0025
2. Aziz, N., & Asadullah, M. N. (2017). Military spending, armed conflict and economic growth in developing countries in the post-Cold War era. *Journal of Economic Studies*, 44(1), 47–68. https://doi.org/10.1108/JES-01-2015-0021
3. Gowland, D. (2020). the Exchange Rate and Economic Policy. *International Economics (Routledge Revivals), October*, 108–118. https://doi.org/10.4324/9780203830185-13
4. Guntukula, R. (2018). Exports, imports and economic growth in India: Evidence from cointegration and causality analysis. *Theoretical and Applied Economics*, 25(2), 221–230. https://www.researchgate.net/publication/326232970
5. Haseeb, M., Aznin Abu Bakar, N., Azam, M., Hassan, S., & Hariyatie Hartani, N. (2014). The macroeconomic impact of defense expenditure on economic growth of Pakistan: An econometric approach. *Asian Social Science*, 10(4), 203–213. https://doi.org/10.5539/ass.v10n4p203
6. Henderson, E. A. (1998). *Military Spending and Poverty Author (s): Errol Anthony Henderson Published by: The University of Chicago Press on behalf of the Southern Political Science Association Stable URL: https://www.jstor.org/stable/2647920 Military Spending and Poverty*. 60(2), 503–520.
7. Johnson Kennedy, P. S., Tobing, S. J. L., Lumbantoruan, R., Tampubolon, E., & Heatubun, A. B. (2018). Mathematical Model: The Long-Term Effects of Defense Expenditure on Economic Growth and the Criticism. *Journal of Physics: Conference Series*, 1114(1). https://doi.org/10.1088/1742-6596/1114/1/012118
8. Magdoff, H. (1967). *Review Reviewed Work (s): Monopoly Capital by Paul A . Baran and Paul M . Sweezy Review by: Harry Magdoff Source: Economic Development and Cultural Change , Oct ., 1967 , Vol . 16 , No . 1 (Oct ., Published by: The University of Chicago Press Stable. 16*(1), 145–150.
9. Mintz, A., & Stevenson, R. T. (1995). Defense Expenditures, Economic Growth, and The "Peace Dividend": A Longitudinal Analysis of 103 Countries. *Journal of Conflict Resolution*, 39(2), 283–305. https://doi.org/10.1177/0022002795039002004
10. Pradhan, R. P. (2010). Defense Spending and Economic Growth in China, India, Nepal and Pakistan: Evidence from Cointegrated Panel Analysis. *International Journal of Economics and Finance*, 2(4), 65–74. https://doi.org/10.5539/ijef.v2n4p65
11. Pramanik, S. (2022). Exchange rate and Economic Growth - a comparative analysis of the possible relationship between them. *Mpra Wp/111504/01/2022,1-6, 111504*, 1–16.
12. Shaik, K., & Gona, B. R. (2021). Exchange rate and the economic growth in India: An empirical analysis. *Journal of Public Affairs*, 21(2). https://doi.org/10.1002/pa.2177
13. Szymanski, A. (1973). *Military Spending and Economic Stagnation Author (s): Albert Szymanski Published by: The University of Chicago Press Stable URL: https://www.jstor.org/stable/2776707. 79*(1), 1–14.
14. Tiwari, A. K., & Tiwari, a P. (2010). Defence Expenditure and Economic Growth: Evidence from India Abstract: *Journal of Cambridge Studies*, 5(January 2010), 117–131. https://doi.org/10.17863/CAM.1363

Handbook of Evidence Based Management Practices in Business – Satyendra Kumar Sharma et al. (eds)
© 2023 Taylor & Francis Group, London, ISBN 978-1-032-54216-4

Chapter

A Study on Financial Literacy amongst the Rural and Urban Area of Surat District

Vijaykumar Gondaliya[1]
Associate Professor, B. V. Patel Institute of Management,
Uka Tarsadia University, Bardoli, Gujarat, India

Nisarg Shah[2]
Research Scholar, Faculty of Commerce and Management,
Uka Tarsadia University, Bardoli, Gujarat, India

ABSTRACT: Financial literacy is the ability to know and application of different financial skills, including management of personal financial, planning for investing and financing various requirements. Government is also promoting financial literacy program in the rural areas. This study measuring financial literacy and its relation with familiarity of investment avenues amongst the household of rural and urban area of Surat district. This study assesses financial literacy using a financial literacy model used by OECD. It has been modified in accordance with local condition.

Scope: The present study focus on level of financial literacy amongst people of Rural and Urban area of Surat District, further research can be applied in different district of Gujarat State.

Methodology: Financial literacy is assessed by asking five basic and five advance multi choice and true/false question. Primary data is collected from the Surat district through structured questionnaire. Total 426 sample is collected through non- probability convenience sampling method. Sampling unit is person involved in financial decision making in household.

Results: It is found that there has been a fair financial literacy among the household of rural and urban area of Surat district. Respondent is well familiar with all investment avenues except derivative. Overall from the study it is found that financial literacy is important for investment decision.

KEYWORDS: Financial literacy, Familiarity, Investment avenue, Rural, Surat, Urban

[1]vijay.gondaliya@utu.ac.in, [2]nisargshah1489@yahoo.com

DOI: 10.4324/9781003415725-19

1. Introduction

Financial literacy is important for providing personal finance management for various financing and investment decision-making as increasing financial responsibility. Today individuals are more responsible about their financial planning as source of income is limited and application of funds is unlimited. Hence, financial planning will help them clarify their goals and ensure that spending, financing, and investing decisions are aligned with those goals.

The topic of financial literacy seems to have gained attention in recent years among the policy makers, businesses, government organisations, and community organisations. Consumers who are knowledgeable about finances should be able to make appropriate choices for their families, enhancing their financial stability and well-being. Secure families are better equipped to support vibrant, thriving communities, which promotes local economic growth. As a result, financial literacy is crucial for communities as well as for each household and family.

People must gain a sophisticated grasp of the financial industry in order to make decisions that are best suited to their financial requirements and aspirations in a world where the variety and complexity of financial products are constantly expanding. Inadequate financial literacy is reported in research from around the world, which rises major questions about people's capacity ti protect their financial well-being. There is evidence that people frequently owe money, under save, and make poor investment (Mitchell, 2011). For emerging economies in particular, financial literacy is important. Enhancing financial literacy would aid in improving the economical well-being of their families with the help of financial appropriate decision making as it improves the financial status of their families by enhancing financial well-being through appropriate financial planning with proper asset mix.

The Organisation for Economic Co-operation and Development (OECD) has defined financial literacy as "a combination of awareness, knowledge, skill, attitude and behaviour necessary to make sound financial decisions and ultimately achieve individual well-being". Therefore, it is important to evaluate or analyse individual's financial attitude and behaviours in addition to their knowledge and awareness about individuals' of financial literacy. It is important to understand the relationship with different aspects of financial literacy and also, investigate association between financial attitudes, behaviour and knowledge.

2. Literature Review

The majority of research has employed an objective test approach to gauge the financial literacy of respondents. In order to quantify financial literacy, many scholars have developed objective test. Some researchers have just used basic financial literacy principle to gauge financial literacy. Other researchers have only evaluated financial literacy using one aspect of personal finance. Survey on financial literacy for health and retirement was done by (Lusardi & Mitchell, 2006). Financial literacy test developed with three different categories of questions to assess peoples' knowledge and understanding about of compound interest, inflation, and risk diversification. Lusardi and Mitchell test for financial literacy became very popular for assessing financial literacy among the many researchers. (Cole, Sampson, & Zia, 2008) applied model of financial literacy developed by Lusardi and Mitchell to assess financial literacy among Indians and Indonesian. These questions were also applied to assess financial literacy level among the Sweden individuals by (Almenberg, J. & Save-Soderberg, J., 2011). (Klapper, L. & Panos, G.A., 2011) used three questions developed by Lusardi and Mitchell to assess the level of financial literacy among the Russian population. To assess the financial literacy among Ducthes people (Alessie, Lusardi, & Rooij, 2008) surveyed to DNB Households. Many researchers, including (Mandell L. , 2004) and (Mandell L. & Linda, 2007) have used the Jump Start Coalition's questions. In USA, the Jump Start Coalition done the survey on Personal Financial Literacy for high school students twice a year. In the survey includes multiple-choice questions on income, investment, management of money, expenses, and credit. Another researcher like (Chen & Volpe) assessed the financial literacy of American college students by administering exams that were meant to gauge their understanding of insurance, investment, financing, and savings. Research has also attempted to measure the people's present position on financial literacy (Hilgert, Hogarth, & Beverly, 2003), as well as the success of financial education initiatives (Hira & Loibl, 2005). Globally, there are unacceptable levels of financial literacy, according to the overall findings of past studies. Low levels of financial literacy have been found among populations when financial literacy has been measured through surveys in different countries (Chen & Volpe, 1998) (H.A.H & A.A.B, 2009).

3. Objectives

To measure the financial literacy amongst residents of rural and urban area of Surat district.

To study the familiarity of financial product amongst resident of rural and urban area of Surat district.

4. Research Design

In this study, descriptive research design was used. The Surat district is chosen as the study region for this research study. The population of this study includes every household member in the Surat district who makes significant financial decision for the home. Multistage sampling has been used to acquire the data for the purpose of the study. In the Surat district, there are nine Talukas altogether. Out of these nine Talukas namely Kamrej, Choryasi, Palsana, Bardoli, and Mahuva were chosen at random from among this nine. A small number of cities, villages and towns are randomly chosen in each of the Talukas.

5. Data Collection

A comprehensive performance test and questionnaire were created, and personal interviews with respondents were conducted in the rural and urban area of Surat district. The personal survey method was administered to collect data, in which close- ended questions were asked with structured self-administered questionnaire. In the present study, 426 samples were collected from the rural and urban area of Surat district. Any person over the age of 18 who participates in household financial decisions can be sampling unit for the study.

6. Variable Under Study

The dependent variables are financial literacy and familiarity for investment decision and independent variables are demographic variables viz., age, gender, income, qualification, family type, marital status, residential area etc.

7. Overview of Questionnaire

The questionnaire had three sections. In the first section, it was to assess individuals' level of financial literacy. Second section related to assess respondents' familiarity towards different financial options by using five-point Likert scale. And in the final section of the questionnaire is related with the respondents' demographic profile. Fundamental questions about financial decisions were posed to the respondents in order to measure financial literacy level. The respondents have to select one of the available options as the proper response. Five of the questions are about basic financial literacy and five are about advanced financial literacy. Literacy questions were modified as per the demographic requirements. Financial literacy question was created using the (Lusardi & Mitchell, 2006).

7.1 Reliability Test

Reliability is the extent to which a survey, test, observation, or other measurement technique consistently yields the same result across time. The Cronbach Alpha test is determined whether a questionnaire is reliable or not. According to different studies, an Alpha value of greater than 0.7 is acceptable. All Likert scale items underwent a reliability test using SPSS 21. The Cronbach Alpha score for the question about familiarity of investment avenues was 0.883. As a result, it is regarded as a trustworthy tool for gathering data.

8. Data Analysis and Interpretation

Financial literacy is divided into two categories in this study: basic financial literacy and advanced financial literacy. The respondents were quizzed on the topics including division, simple interest, compound interest, time value of money, and inflation in order to determine their basic financial literacy. Questions about investment in long term asset, the relation between risk and return, diversification, relationship between bond value and interest rate were asked to the respondents to gauge their advanced financial literacy level. The questions combine multiple choice and true and false statements. The frequency of each financial literacy question being true or false is listed in Table 19.1.

From the Table 19.1, it is found that respondents had a decent understanding of most financial concept, with a few exceptions. Low financial literacy was demonstrated by variables including the long-term return on financial asset and relationship between Interest rate and bond value.

(Gupta, 2017) suggested that the level of financial literacy is determined by the median of percentage of sample respondents, which is then broken down into two subgroups. High financial literacy refers to respondents who outperformed the median, while low financial literacy refers to those who scored below the median. The median score was 6. High financial

Table 19.1   Financial literacy - overall summary

Levels	Sr. No	Parameters used to measure Literacy	Freq. (%)
Basic Financial Literacy	1	Division	91.5
	2	Simple Interest	70.9
	3	Compounding Interest	58.7
	4	Time Value of Money	65.5
	5	Inflation	84.7
Advanced Financial Literacy	6	Long Term Return from Financial Asset	51.2
	7	Diversification	67.8
	8	Financial Decision Making	52.3
	9	Relationship between Risk and Return	61.5
	10	Relationship between Bond Value and Interest Rate	30.3

Source: Authors calculation

literacy is defined as having a score of 6 or more, while low financial literacy defined as having a score of less than 6.

Table 19.2   Respondents' financial literacy

Level of Financial Literacy	Frequency	%
Low Financial Literacy	144	33.8
High Financial Literacy	282	66.2
Total	426	100.0

Source: Authors calculation

From Table 19.2, it can be interpret that 33.8% respondents possess low financial literacy and 66.2% respondents possess high level financial literacy. So, it can be said that overall respondents possess high level of financial literacy.

8.1 Non-Parametric - Chi-Square Test

To determine the relationship between various demographic characteristics and level of financial literacy, the chi-square test was used and hypotheses were formulated as below.

H_{01}: **There is no significant association between demographic profile and financial literacy of the respondents**

In Table 19.3, it shows the result of Chi-Square test of Association between demographic profile and financial literacy was tested.

Table 19.3 shows the test statistics. In the above table P value of education is .001 and occupation is .017, which is less than 0.05. So, the null hypothesis is rejected for education and occupation of the respondents. Therefore, it can be interpreted that there is an association

Table 19.3 Chi- square test – demographic profile and financial literacy of the respondents

	Value	df	Asymp. Sig. (2-sided)	Cramer's V
a. Gender	1.611[a]	1	.204	-
b. Age	3.155[b]	3	.368	-
c. Education	17.796[c]	4	.001	.204
d. Occupation	16.998[d]	7	.017	.200
e. Residential Area	1.025[e]	1	.311	-

Source: Authors calculation

between education and occupation with the financial literacy of the respondents. Furthermore, the association looks weak in both the cases, as the value of Cramer's V is less than 0.5, i.e., .204 and .200 respectively. P value of gender, age, and residential area of the respondents is higher than 0.05, therefore null hypothesis is not able to accept. So, it can be interpreted that there is no association between gender, age, and residential area with financial literacy of the respondents.

Table 19.4 Familiarity of various investment avenues

	% of response	Mean value
Saving Account	88.5	4.45
Fixed Deposit Account	86.4	4.36
Equity Share	62.5	3.66
Govt. Bond	45.1	3.2
Derivatives	29.1	2.7
Mutual Fund	63.9	3.64
PPF	56.6	3.53
NPS	51	3.36
Post Office Product	54	3.43
Life Insurance	82.2	4.24
Money Market	45.4	3.11
Real Estate	65.9	3.76
Gold	86.6	4.39
Non-Conventional Avenues	46.5	3.23

Source: Authors calculation

From the above Table 19.4, it is found that familiarity for saving bank account and fixed deposit account is very high as mean value is more than 4. Familiarity for derivative product is very low as mean value is 2.70. And for the rest of investment avenues respondents are quite familiar.

9. Findings

- There is a fair financial literacy level among the respondents in Surat district.
- There is no association found between
  - Gender and financial literacy of the respondent.
  - Age and financial literacy of the respondent.
  - Residential area and financial literacy of the respondent.
  - Education and financial literacy of the respondent.
  - Occupation and financial literacy of the respondent.
- Females are less familiar with post office product, real estate, NCA than men.
- All investment potions dose not significantly differ with gender of the respondent.
- Familiarity of Saving account, fixed deposit account, real estate, and gold does not significantly differ with education. Familiarity of equity share, Govt. bond/ debenture, derivative, mutual fund, PPF, NPS, Post office product, life insurance, money market, and non-conventional avenues does differ with education.
- Other similar observation through the analysis was familiarity of Public Provident Fund and National Pension Scheme does differ with occupation. Familiarity of other investment options like saving bank account, fixed deposit account, equity share, debenture, mutual fund, derivatives, post office product, life insurance, money market, real estate, gold, and non-conventional options does not differ with the occupation of the respondent.

10. Conclusion

In India, many study carried out to assess financial literacy but few studies carried out to examine financial literacy and its relation with familiarity towards different financial avenues. The survey included 385 household, those who are active in household financial decision making. Overall, there is a fair financial literacy amongst the rural and urban area of Surat district. It is found that there is a relation between familiarity of investment avenues and education of the respondents. Familiarity of investment avenues and occupation is not so related with each other. There is a relation found between familiarity of the investment avenues and age of the respondents.

Financial literacy is important for financial well-being of the household individual for increasing familiarity towards financial avenues. So, it helps investors to choose financial avenues for investment and getting better returns in the future.

REFERENCES

1. Alessie, R., Lusardi, A., & Rooij, M. (2008). Financial literacy, retirement planning, and household wealth. *NBER Working Paper No. 15350.*
2. Almenberg, J., & Save-Soderberg, J. (2011). Financial literacy and retirement planning in Sweden. *CeRP Working Paper No. 112.*

3. Atkinson, A., & Messy, F. (2012). Measuring Financial Literacy: Results of the OECD / International Network on Financial Education (INFE) Pilot Study", OECD Working Papers on Finance, Insurance and Private Pensions, No. 15. *OECD*. Paris.

4. Chen, H., & Volpe, R. (1998). Analysis of personal financial literacy among college students. *Financial Services Review, 7*, 107–128.

5. Cole, S., Sampson, T., & Zia, B. (2008). Money or Knowledge? What drives the demand for financial services in developing countries.

6. Gupta, S. (2017). To Study the Relationship of Financial Literacy and Investment Behaviour of Salaried Class Individuals of Delhi. *International Education & Research Journal, 3*(5), 187–190.

7. Hilgert, M., Hogarth, J., & Beverly, S. (2003, July). Household financial management: The connection between knowledge and behavior. *Federal Reserve Bulletin, 89*, 309–322.

8. Hira, T., & Loibl, C. (2005). Understanding the impact of employer-provided financial education on workplace satisfaction. *Journal of Consumer Affairs, 39*, 173–194.

9. Klapper, L., & Panos, G.A. (2011). Financial literacy and retirement planning in view of a growing youth demographic: The Russian case. *CeRP Working Paper No. 114/11.*

10. Lusardi, & Annamaria. (2012). Numeracy, Financial Literacy, and Financial Decision-Making," Numeracy. *Scholar Commons*, 1–12.

11. Lusardi, A., & Mitchell, O. (2006). Financial literacy and planning: Implications for retirement wellbeing. *MRRC Working Paper No. 2006-144.*

12. Mandell, L. (2004). *Financial Literacy: Are we improving?* Jump$tart Coalition for Personal Financial Literacy.

13. Mandell, L., & L. S. (2007). Motivation and financial literacy. *Financial Services Review*, 105–116.

14. Mitchell, O. S. (2011). Managing risks in defined contribution plans: What does the future hold? Growing Old: Paying for Retirement and Institutional Money Management After the Financial Crisis.

15. Volpe, R. P., Chen, H., & Pavlicko, J.J. (1996). Personal investment literacy among college students: A survey. *Financial Practice & Education, 6*, 86–94.

16. Volpe, R.P., Kotel, J.E., & Chen H. (2002). A survey of investment literacy among online investors. *Financial Counseling and Planning, 13*, 1–16.

Handbook of Evidence Based Management Practices in Business – Satyendra Kumar Sharma et al. (eds)
© 2023 Taylor & Francis Group, London, ISBN 978-1-032-54216-4

Chapter

Portfolio Management Using OPM% Based Dynamic Allocation Strategy

Deepak Sharma*

Birla Institute of Technology and Science,
Pilani (BITS Pilani), Rajasthan, India

ABSTRACT: The performance of an investment portfolio is based on the underlying asset. How an asset behaves shows the potential return of that asset and asset class. The equity asset class has been proven to be the best asset class for an aggressive investor with an optimized risk-to-reward ratio. Here in this study, we have looked at two equity investment schemes for creating an investment portfolio. In this study, we have analyzed the effects of operating profit margin on stock prices. Operating Profit Margin (OPM), the precursor of the Price-to-Earnings (P/E) ratio, can also act as an investment rationale. Businesses with good enough OPM% were screened to be potential investments. We have analyzed that investments based on meticulously chosen high OPM businesses perform better than random selection of OPM screened investments in terms of Compound Annual Growth Rate (CAGR). Our research also studied whether an investment strategy based on an equal-weighted portfolio performs better than dynamic allocation based on OPM%-weighted portfolios. Our research shows that the dynamic allocation strategy based upon OPM-dependent weightage to selected companies generates better returns than the equal-weighted investment strategy.

KEYWORDS: Investment rationale, Portfolio management, Operating profit margin, Dynamic allocation, Equal-weighted allocation

1. Introduction

Investment management is a tedious process as it carries much effort in stock screening and continuous monitoring of risk-adjusted returns. Certain restrictions, such as diversification,

---

*sharma.deepak@pilani.bits-pilani.ac.in

DOI: 10.4324/9781003415725-20

risk-to-reward ratio, and investment tracking limits, make portfolio management arduous. It is therefore suggested that portfolios are never created to beat the benchmark indices and can only be optimized with specific rules. Several such investment strategies are available that famous institutional investors and fund houses popularly use. Value investing and growth investing all focus on a particular part of a company's performance to judge its performance. The allocation of money in a specific business also affects the diversification aspect of investment. It is, therefore, essential to know which investment strategy suits best for a long-term aggressive investor. Generally, an investment horizon of more than ten years is enough to check a portfolio's performance in terms of investment strategy.

The amount of money invested also creates a massive difference in the generation of good returns; on the other hand, it must maintain the risk of concentrating on a few stocks. Therefore, the optimized allocation for a selected stock in an investment portfolio must be known. Diversifying the portfolio is a problem as over-diversification generates average returns, and under-diversification creates the risk of exposure to unseen events, which may erode the portfolio value. It has also been seen that only a few seasoned professionals avoid the rule of diversification as they are well-informed about market dynamics and their investments (Goetzmann et al., 2008). The over-diversification creates the risk of not generating returns better than benchmark indices. It is found that generally under-diversified portfolios are primarily owned by less-educated, low-income, and young individuals. Over-confidence and biases in investment decisions generally cause the choices for such under-diversified portfolios. Therefore it is required that an individual investor must have an investment rationale.

Value investing is one such investment strategy that requires investors to look for potentially undervalued stocks in order to get more potential to generate hefty returns. The price-to-earnings ratio is one measure that is generally utilized by value investors, which is defined as the price paid to generate one unit of earnings. The formula of Price to Earnings ratio (P/E) is obtained by dividing the share's current market price by per-share earnings (Truong, C. 2009). The earnings-per-share is primarily derived from revenues generated by a company subtracting the expenses incurred for a quarter or financial year, also known as the operating profit margin. The operating profit margin% shows the operating profit percentage obtained from revenues. Since the government enforces different taxes on some industries and companies, operating profit margin % or earnings before interest and taxes is a better measure of a company's performance. The operating profit margin (OPM%) positively and significantly affects stock prices (Mahruzal etal., 2012).

Operating profit margin (OPM%), therefore, provides the proxy to a business's success and, therefore, can act as an investment rationale and be used as a strategy for long-term equity investment. It has been proposed that dynamic allocation of funds in equity investments yields better results (Al Janabi, 2011); here in this study, we have analyzed a company's stock prices and the OPM% of the underlying business. We have examined whether OPM% alone can act as an investment rationale for a long-term investment horizon considered 11 years in our study. In this study, we have tested Operating Profit Margin (OPM) to measure a company's performance.

2. Materials and Methods

2.1 Data Curation and Processing

The data curation was the first task, which was accomplished using a web scraping method. We used in-house R script to fetch Profit & loss statements of stocks listed in the NIFTY 500 universe. The curation step downloads raw statements with unnecessary information in uneven formats. These 500 raw profit and loss statements were then cleaned, and stocks for which OPM% data was unavailable from 2011 to 2022 were removed from the OPM data list. All the companies whose OPM% data was available for this duration merged and created a data table (size 11×254) for eleven years for 254 companies. The stock prices for these companies were later fetched from the Yahoo finance website using an in-house python based web scraping script. An investment portfolio can now be created using OPM% to measure potential return-generating business. Out of these companies for which stock prices and OPM% are available for filtration and to get realistic results, we only considered companies for which the OPM% never went below 20% even during the 2020-21 covid period and was never above 80% as that is not sustainable over the years. We created two investment portfolio schemes (Fig. 20.1).

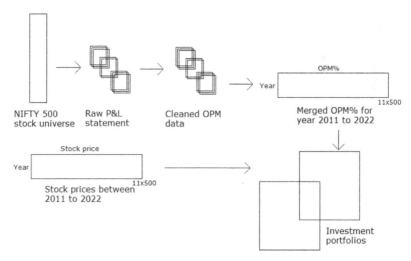

Fig. 20.1   Investment portfolio management through OPM% based optimized fund allocation
Source: Author's compilation

2.2 Portfolio Creation

The number of companies is taken to be ten as it creates diversification and avoids over-diversification. We created a total of 4 portfolio schemes and performed 50 such iterations of each portfolio scheme. In the first scheme, we created a portfolio with equal weights to each randomly chosen company called RE10 (Random & equal-weighted ten stock portfolio). In the other portfolio, randomly chosen but dynamically allocated based on OPM% were used, and this scheme is called RD10. The third portfolio scheme consists of high OPM% stocks but with equal weights given to each stock and is called OE10. In the fourth scheme, the investment amount in each stock was based upon the OPM% of that company, termed OD10 (OPM%-based dynamic portfolio). We performed 50 such portfolios of the four portfolios as mentioned above schemes for the creation and comparisons of 10 stock equal-weighted and dynamic allocation-weighted portfolios (Fig. 20.1).

3. Results

Based on our analysis, we have obtained several findings. We obtained that the correlation between investment duration and OPM% was insignificant (Fig. 20.2). It was observed that over the years, a company's OPM% might increase or decrease (Fig. 20.3). It was shown that there is a good correlation between OPM% and returns generated by the stock in a particular time (Fig. 20.4). The correlation between OPM% and stock prices was statistically significant at $p < 0.05$ with a correlation coefficient of 0.281. It can be seen that it is highly likely to find a stock with a high correlation coefficient between the stock's OPM% and returns generated by this stock (Fig. 20.5). It is also more likely to find a stock whose OPM% is increasing, and its stock price return is increasing over the years.

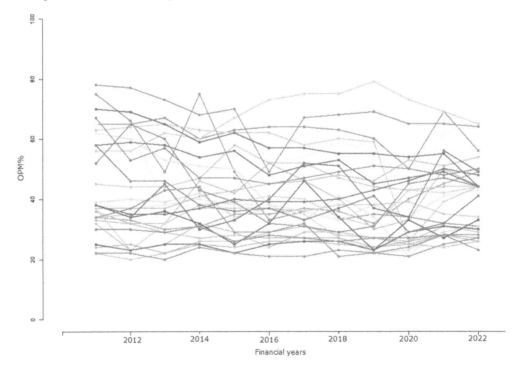

Fig. 20.2   Relation of OPM% and investment duration

Source: Author's compilation

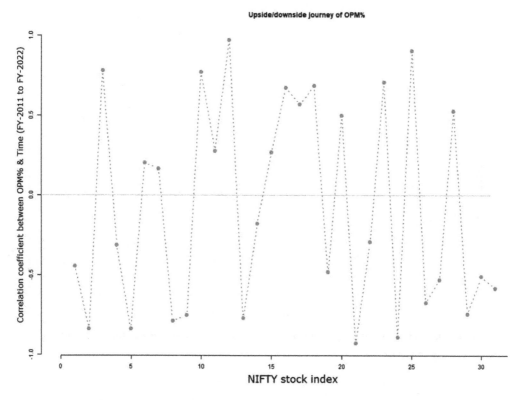

Fig. 20.3 Correlation between OPM% and investment duration

Source: Author's compilation

4. Conclusion

The investment based on OPM% needs to be reevaluated after the business declares its OPM% changes as it may increase or decrease (Fig. 20.2, Fig. 20.3). As evident from the high correlation between a stock's OPM% and stock price, it is suggested that a business' OPM% can be used as an investment rationale as it positively correlates with stock prices (Fig. 20.4, Fig. 20.5). OPM%-based investments have shown better performance than randomly chosen stocks; these findings show that investment rationale is crucial before investing. It also shows that OPM% can act as an investment rationale or be used at least as a screening measure (Table 20.1).

The study also proves that randomly chosen investments did not perform as well as carefully selected investments based on OPM% criteria. Though carefully selected investments perform marginally better, with a long-term investment horizon, a little difference creates a massive difference in wealth generation. Therefore, an investment horizon of more than ten years based upon simple investment rationale, such as a high OPM % with dynamic allocation proportional to their OPM %, can help investors to create wealth in the long term.

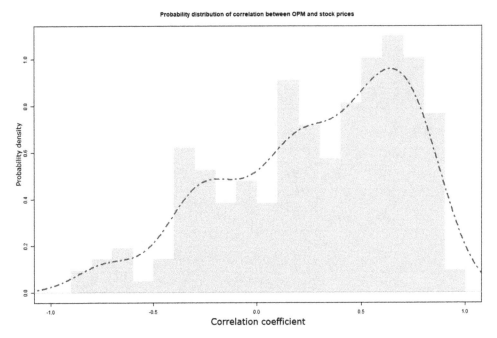

Fig. 20.4   High probability of positive correlation between OPM% and stock prices

Source: Author's compilation

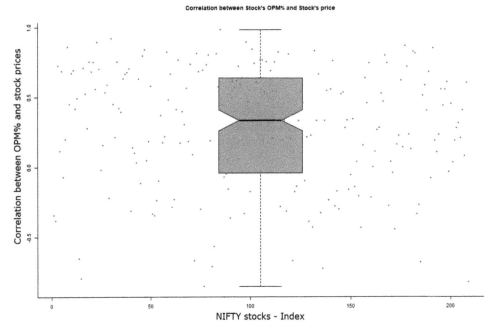

Fig. 20.5   High correlation of Stock prices and OPM%

Source: Author's compilation

Table 20.1 Portfolio schemes and average returns of 50 such equity investment portfolios

Portfolio scheme	Average CAGR
Random equal-weighted 10 stock (RE10)	15.23%
Random OPM based dynamically allocated 10 stocks (RD10)	18.54%
High OPM based equal-weighted 10 stocks (OE10)	20.21%
High OPM based dynamically allocated 10 stocks (OD10)	21.32%

Source: Author's compilation

REFERENCES

1. William N. Goetzmann, Alok Kumar. Equity Portfolio Diversification, Review of Finance, Volume 12, Issue 3, 2008, pp. 433–463. DOI: https://doi.org/10.1093/rof/rfn005
2. Truong, C. (2009). Value Investing using Price Earnings Ratio in New Zealand. University of Auckland Business Review, 11(1), [26]–[32]. DOI: https://search.informit.org/doi/10.3316/informit.036322328786386
3. Mahruzal Mahdi, Muammar Khaddafi. The Influence of Gross Profit Margin, Operating Profit Margin and Net Profit Margin on the Stock Price of Consumer Good Industry in the Indonesia Stock Exchange on 2012-2014 DOI: https://doi.org/10.46336/ijbesd.v1i3.53
4. Al Janabi, M. Dynamic equity asset allocation with liquidity-adjusted market risk criterion: Appraisal of efficient and coherent portfolios. J Asset Manag 12, 378–394 (2011). DOI: https://doi.org/10.1057/jam.2010.28

Chapter

A Brief Appraisal on Tourism Finance Corporation of India

Kurma Sankara Rao*

M.A (P.S), M.A (Tourism), M.T.M, M.Phil (Tourism), Ph.D (Tourism),
Guest Faculty, Department of Tourism and Hospitality Management,
Acharya Nagarjuna University, Guntur Dt., Andhra Pradesh, India

ABSTRACT: Tourism Finance Corporation of India Ltd. It is an Indian financial institution that supports the development of the tourism and hospitality industry in India. Over the past three decades, TFCI has played a catalytic role in the development of infrastructure in the hospitality industry. In addition, TFCI has allowed many companies to redirect their investments into different sectors and regions related to tourism. TFCI has also served as an advisor to the federal government, many state governments, and related organizations. He has contributed to the development of tourism master plans, marketing campaigns, market potential analysis, tourist traffic surveys, market feasibility studies, etc.

This study outlines the overview, vision and mission of TFCI and provides capital for new projects through term loans, structured finance, investment banking and MSME finance.

KEYWORDS: Hospitality, Investments, Projects, TFCI, Tourism

1. Introduction

On January 27, 1989, India Tourism Finance Company Limited was incorporated as a limited liability company. After receiving the certificate of incorporation from the Registrar of Companies, the company commenced operations on 1 February 1989. Together with other financial/investment institutions across India and other institutions nationalized bank, IFCI Ltd. push business. On the advice of the National Tourism Board, the company was established as a specialized financial institution across India to manage the financial needs of the tourism

*kurmasankararao@gmail.com

DOI: 10.4324/9781003415725-21

industry. In 1994, the company issued 1,70,000,000 shares at Rs 10 per share in a public offering with a premium of Rs 20 per share. The company invested in establishing non-traditional tourism projects in 1999, including restaurants, roadside facilities, travel agencies, amusement parks, dolphin tanks, ski lifts, services car rentals, river transport ferries, airport support centers, facilities training centers for hotel staff, etc. The company merged with India Travel Advisory Financial Services Ltd in 2000. Under the Securities and Financial Assets Reconstruction and Security Enforcement Act (SRFAESI), the company acquired ownership of three hotels in the cities of Mukundgarh, Bikaner and Jaisalmer during the 2008-2009 financial year. The company started financing infrastructure projects in 2009-2010, including roads, bridges, power ports and airports. This will encourage tourism and hospitality related initiatives. The company has actively pursued consulting missions to various state governments to draft tourism policy and other tourism/tourism development projects etc. in addition to expanding facilities for existing hotels to renovate, upgrade and set up new projects to expand its portfolio.

2. Objective of the Study

To become a strong financial support for the Indian tourism and hospitality industry to be a new tourism project for the state government

To be financial support for other central and state government agencies

3. Literature Review

Text of research articles from Tourism Finance Corporation of India Ltd, (TFCI). Investor Disclosure, Annual Report, Investor Presentation 2022-23, Q1

4. Research Methods

This research paper is based entirely on conceptual data. Mainly secondary data was collected from various journals, Ministry of Tourism documents and other data was collected from Tourism Finance Corporation of India (TFCI).

4.1 Overview

Indian government companies include Tourism Finance Corporation of India Ltd. The corporation finances tourism-related projects as part of its operations. They offer financial support to businesses so they can establish and/or expand tourism-related facilities and services like hotels, restaurants, vacation resorts, amusement parks, multiplexes, entertainment centres, educational and sporting facilities, safari parks, ropeways, cultural centres, convention centres, transport, travel and tour operating agencies, air services, tourism emporia and sports facilities. The types of financial assistance include rupee loans, guarantees for deferred payments and credit raised abroad, underwriting of public issues of shares and debentures, direct subscription to such securities, equipment financing, leasing assistance under suppliers credit, working-capital financing, takeover financing and advances against credit card receivables. Additionally, the business offers top-notch research and consulting services to the travel and tourism sector in general and to investors in the sector in particular. Accordingly, TFCI has been offering consulting services to various central and state agencies by taking on broad-based assignments to cover macro and micro level tourism-related studies and exercises to make it easier to identify, conceptualise, promote and implement specific tourism-related projects as well as for making policy-level decisions regarding investment and infrastructure expansion, among other things.

TFCI provides many clients with specialized services related to projects. In addition, he has evaluated specific projects for various government organizations and private clients. To meet the diverse needs of the industry, the company has developed and launched several products including the first water theme park in Mumbai. Devigarh Palace in Udaipurs has renovated Umaid Bhawan Palace into a resort hotel, Palace on Wheels, a popular spa, the first water sports resort in Goa, Ananda in the Himalayas and resorts other maintenance is restored heritage.

For more than three decades of existence, TFCI has served as a catalyst in the development of infrastructure in the hospitality industry. In addition, TFCI has allowed many companies to redirect their investments into different sectors and regions related to tourism. A group of government organizations, including IFCI, LIC, OIC, SBI, BOI, Canara Bank, and more, have established TFCI, which has played a key role in developing many of the firsts in the hospitality industry. Including Essel World, the Palace on Wheels for the Indian Railways, the Himalayan spa/wellness resort Ananda and others.

To date, TFCI has provided support for a third of total branded hotel occupancy in India. Major domestic and international hotel brands such as ITC, Leela, Taj, Lalit, Lemon Tree, Hyatt, Marriott, Hilton, Radisson, Holiday Inn, Ramada, etc. are all connected to it. To increase visitor numbers, TFCI has also served as an advisor to the federal government, multi-state governments and affiliated organizations. He has contributed to the development of tourism master plans, marketing campaigns, market potential analysis, tourist traffic surveys, market feasibility studies, etc. It is affiliated with the Government of Gujarat, the Gujarat State Tourism Development Corporation, the Tamil Nadu Tourism Development Corporation, the Himachal Pradesh Government, the Ministry of Environment and Forests (GoI) and the Gujarat Government, the Corporation. Jharkhand Tourism Development, Madhya Pradesh State Tourism Development Corporation Ltd., Delhi Tourist Transport Development Corporation. TFCI has also advised the Ministry of Railways on how to start and operate premium train services across India.

In 2017, the major shareholder, Industrial Finance Corporation of India (IFCI), sold its stake in an open market transaction. India Chances III Pte Ltd., Tamaka Capital (Mauritius) Ltd., LIC of India, Oriental Insurance Company and Mr. Sajeeve Thomas are promoters and shareholders of TFCI (an experienced banker) promoter group professional experience). While continuing to be the No. 1 bank in terms of lending to the hospitality industry, TFCI focuses on lending and investing in a variety of industries, including healthcare, pharmaceuticals, education, and manufacturing. TFCI has also engaged in investment banking activities such as asset buying/selling advice, debt syndication, special situations financing and private equity arrangements. It also maintains an industry leadership position in the hospitality sector and is involved in a wide range of financial activities, including corporate, project, acquisition, and working capital financing. TFCI is also committed to supporting the MSME sector, which is the foundation of our economy.

4.2 Vision

To realize the aspirations of our customers, especially in the MSME segment and deliver excellent value to stakeholders, while maintaining the highest standards of business ethics, transparency and integrity. To be the most highly regarded financial services model and provider in the hospitality, tourism, infrastructure, healthcare, education, manufacturing and other sustainability sectors.

4.3 Mission

To be a technology-driven, financially stable organization and secure a prominent place in the financial services industry through growth and productivity. By achieving leadership positions in designated business segments, we are able to contribute to the development of countries' social and hospitality infrastructures and help leverage their potential. These sectors as an engine of economic growth.

5. Corporate Social Responsibility (CSR)

Total CSR Spending for FY 2021-2022

Education Rs. 80, 06, 700

Malnutrition R. 7, 80, 000 Rs

Sports Rs 3,97,000

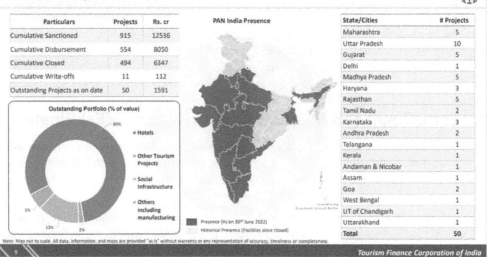

Fig. 21.1   1.7 - Q1FY23 Investor presentation

Source: Tourism Finance Corporation of India Ltd.

6. Term Loans

TFCI leads the market by providing customers with financing assistance in the form of term loans. She is a pioneer in travel-related sponsorship initiatives. With its knowledge and over 30 years of experience, TFCI is able to shape the peculiarities of many funding modalities.

Its main objective is to provide affordable financial solutions to borrowers working in sectors such as tourism, healthcare, education, logistics and pharmaceuticals. It offers term loans in rupees, project loans, corporate loans, stock loans, bridging loans, financing, equity/debit subscriptions, and more. Along with a team of experts with in-depth product knowledge and industry dynamics.

TFCI provides support for new construction projects as well as expansion, diversification and modernization projects. It offers both variable rate loans (linked to our benchmark rate) and fixed rate loans depending on customer needs. In addition, it registers on a case-by-case basis to share and invest in the NCDs of rated companies.

7. Structured Finance

Corporate clients receive tailored structured solutions from TFCI, which is also capable of complex transactions. Customers can use our experience to create innovative solutions that meet their needs. It provides solutions that complement the traditional lending channels offered to customers while keeping up with the ever-changing dynamics of financial markets. Depending on the needs of each customer, it is possible to invest in bonds and non-convertible stocks. Depending on cash flow, asset range and general market conditions, these products are designed for long and short term maturities.

To manage leverage and strengthen capital structure, it also provides consulting/investment solutions to clients using a variety of products such as convertible preferred shares, mezzanine loans, venture capital debt. Convertible bonds, etc. Compared to standard term/project debt, there can be more flexibility in terms of allowable end uses. It responds to consumers' desire for growth by financing existing assets and investments without selling them. Experienced structured finance professionals provide specialized solutions for a wide variety of asset classes and categories. In addition, our clients can contact investors and banks which is an advantage.

8. Micro, Small and Medium Enterprises (MSMEs) Finance

TFCI aims to meet the capital needs of small and medium enterprises operating in areas such as tourism, healthcare, education, pharmaceuticals, logistics, etc with differentiated and personalized products. We have plenty of possible funding opportunities due to the inherent mismatch between supply and demand in these areas.

According to TFCI, the MSME sector will continue to be the foundation of our economy and will be essential to our nation's future growth. His skills and experience in funding these projects will help the players in the segment grow their operations. The company strives to develop a strong SME finance platform based on specialized knowledge and unique solutions.

By emphasizing the development of social infrastructure, which will be supported by the right application of data and technology, TFCI believes that value can be created for all actors in our society. We. With his knowledge of the intricacies of regulatory frameworks, consulting skills and the ability to collaborate with a wide range of government agencies, he will be able to bring significant value to our clients.

9. Investment Banking

To provide its clients with specialized IB solutions, TFCI established a dedicated Investment Banking office in 2019. This office seeks to leverage NBFC industry relationships and more than 30 years of experience. Its strength comes from its relationships with local and international companies, banks, investors in Southeast Asia, Europe and the Americas. In order to provide the most effective solution, help us understand the psychology of investors and customers.

Professionals with extensive experience in all areas of investment banking, such as Private Equity, Venture Capital, Special Situations, M&A, etc. Managing IB activities. By providing tailored advice to customers to maximize value, TFCI believes it can add value to their purchases. His team relationship with a number of investors and agents around the world helps clients gain a good view of their business and understand the current state of the market. Through this desk, TFCI currently provides services in structured finance, private equity investments, mergers and acquisitions, project and infrastructure financing, debt syndication and restructuring debt structure.

10. Consulting Services

Since its establishment, TFCI has provided the tourism industry in general and investors in this field in particular with high-quality research and consulting services. With this in mind, TFCI has provided consulting services to many central and state agencies by undertaking large-scale tasks including macro-micro-research/exercises related to tourism to facilitate the identification, conceptualization, promotion and implementation of specific tourism-related activities. Project as well as decision-making at the political level regarding investment and infrastructure enhancement, among other issues.

TFCI provides project-specific services to a wide range of private sector clients. In addition, he has evaluated specific projects for various government organizations and private clients. TFCI has also effectively managed projects including creating multi-use amusement park complexes, developing viable project concepts around lakes and other bodies of water, and more.

11. Conclusion

Many projects and actions of different states of India, term loans, structured finance, MSME finance, investment banking and consulting services are all covered in this article. More money will be spent on tourism and hospitality industry of India in coming days with support.

REFERENCES

1. HYPERLINK https://www.baou.edu.in
2. HYPERLINK https://www.business-standard.com
3. HYPERLINK http://www.dokumen.pub
4. HYPERLINK http://www.economictimes.indiatimes.com
5. HYPERLINK http://www.gujarati.moneycontrol.com
6. HYPERLINK http://www.icsi.edu
7. HYPERLINK https://www.iittm.ac.in
8. HYPERLINK https://www.incredibleindia.org
9. SUPER LINK http://www.jetir.orgwww.jetir.org
10. HYPERLINK http:// www.outlookindia.com
11. SUPER LINK http://www.reuters.comwww.reuters.com
12. HYPERLINK https://www.tfciltd.com
13. SUPER LINK https//tourism.gov.in
14. HYPERLINKhttp://www.ukessays.comwww.ukessays.com/WpNsL7M,HbEK1@.
58EpMbEIovPma_dE8O(08xgavPTR6xa)28/DPgBBadL0Dk)Dg TYmG_BP3y,emYQvhOA0D0
(/XY.2Z6(i,J9dmaHYb5tVwQhKyiEUPUhKEUqipX7JPx)yrUqOVkkE.FONPFITkHr
f5k(WldrPhGzFYO0uWH(dLeUSSrlIKjy)-lG)L9WN3EE,U91Rdx_NoEOF@0m5H_
KfvVz2Pq/rOzSg(G2w04SJXpCUajWlLj/-)c7LPN6IG3T8)D2ZCT/Kb2ANzLPaokSgNDk/
Mb8SuqK1qqrvD.gH39VHqTW(@LmAu7A/DZ_NjYXIRVN5YKKzCeXs-2cICCxc_h0-
JjGM2TK__he_mOSR9SW-8jH5f9tgR55ySh@ibFVpdMCX8M35v-M4Azd9GEE.WKsC).
DigidlmNQSNlSdaoWjhEmtn63p2-z1URnbYZYPAnY7q)ySTBXx(mxjt.x9hUw4((U@
QDJipWy@bg.OBa@i10v5nATZT8KnEQB51mxm9iz)BeAbEmCmcaYFO@_2Q36gnRfFD)
TdlYJ6B)jVVbAsgZ6wjSJoQSl77Y,dXiJ(x(I_TS1EZBmU/xYy5g/GMGeD3Vqq8K)
fw9xrxwrTZaGy8IjbRcXIu3KGnD1NIBsRuKV.ELM2fiVvlu8zH(W)6-rCSjidDAIqbJx6kASht(
QpmcaSlXP1Mh9MVdDAa VBfJP8 AVf 6Q

Chapter

22

Bibliometric Analysis of Behavioral Finance with VOSviewer: Last Twenty-Five Year

Girish Garg[1], Seema Thakur[2]

Assistant Professor, School of Finance & Commerce, Galgotias University, Greater Noida, UP

ABSTRACT: Scope of the Paper: The entire area of finance has been able to feel the effects of a boom in behavioral finance during the past twenty-five years. Many professionals in the academic world are now willing to evaluate the implications of the irrational characteristics of human judgment as significant for the particular application being discussed. This tendency is most notable for mistakes made by individual market participants; a heated discussion is still ongoing regarding the extent to which psychological bias drives price determination in large and liquid marketplaces. However, current knowledge of finance demands a basis in analytical procedures and psychological approaches. This is in addition to a grounding in analytical techniques. Today, many of the most influential theories covering such fundamental topics as investor behavior, the cross-section of returns, corporate investment, and money management are based on psychological variables. This is because psychological variables can be measured and analyzed.

Methodology: Bibliometric analysis was used to compile a summary of the scientific research that has been done on behavioral finance. In this literature review, the Scopus database was utilized. Using the clusters as a starting point, we analyzed 1052 papers using the VOSviewer software to identify the research gaps and suggest new study ideas.

Conclusion: It was concluded that the author Kudryavtsev A. has the maximum number of research publications on behavioral finance. However, the number of citations that Hirshleifer D. has is 1352. These well-known authors make it possible for the researchers to improve their comprehension of the author's points of view and fill in any information gaps they had previously missed in their continuing research by allowing them to learn more about the author's perspective. According to our findings, the United States of America is the most influential country in terms of the number of papers written with contributions from other nations. In addition, the United States is the oldest country researching behavioral finance, and

---

[1]girish.garg@galgotiasuniversity.edu.in, [2]seema.thakur@galgotiasuniversity.edu.in

DOI: 10.4324/9781003415725-22

this research is being conducted in the country. When we looked at the keyword network, we noticed a lot of potential and research gaps for further studies on experimental economics and heuristics, personal finance, financial literacy, the financial market, and heuristics, personal finance, financial literacy, the financial market, and overreaction.

KEYWORDS: Behavioral finance, Bibliometric analysis, Biases, Psychology, Sociology and VOSviewer

1. Introduction

Financial market anomalies show that markets are not as efficient as imagined during the last century but are influenced by many biases that show their imperfection, creating a new theory called Behavioral Finance. Von Neumann and Morgenstern's (1944) notion of anticipated utility has helped create various financial market models. Modern Finance, founded on the idea that market equilibrium may be described in terms of expected returns, dominated the 20th century (Malkiel and Fama, 1970). one of the most influential modern finance authors defined an *efficient market* as one in which prices constantly reflect available information. Investor rationality and financial market pricing efficiency have been heavily challenged. Simon (1956) was one of the first to argue that learning theories explain observed behavior better than economic and statistical explanations of rational behavior. He found that humans can adjust to meet their needs but not maximize the utility function. However, Tversky and Kahneman (1974) had a more substantial impact on defending investors' irrational behavior, advocating a better understanding of heuristics and biases to improve judgments and decisions in uncertain situations. Kahneman and Tversky (1979) also questioned the expected utility hypothesis. Individual preferences violate this theory's assumptions, leading to prospect theory. Statman and Caldwell (1987) called Behavioral Finance a descriptive theory of choice under uncertainty. It includes psychology and sociology (Shiller, 2003). Behavioral Finance holds that "irrational expectations or non-standard preferences affect asset prices" (Campbell, 2000); therefore, price-value discrepancies depend on investors' psychological motivations. We created a bibliometric analysis of Behavioral Finance to describe its performance, productivity, topics, and condition. To broaden Behavioral Finance, we used VOSviewer software for citation analysis. This helped us identify the research area's most essential themes and classify them by development and importance. This work is structured as follows: In the next section, the literature review used in this study will be presented. In the third section, we will explain the objectives. The fourth section presents the research methodology. The fifth section is the analysis and interpretation of the results. The sixth conclusion was drawn from this study. In the last section, we will highlight the limitations we had to face in this work.

2. Literature Review

Slovic (1972) looked at the impact of psychological research on human decision-making in the investment world. According to the research, a comprehensive understanding of human limitations will ultimately help the decision-maker more than immature mental faith. Tversky and Kahneman (1972) reasoned that heuristic assistance to anticipate the future worth, before making a gauge; we need reference esteem as a wellspring of information, that number will influence the anticipated. Anchoring and adjustment bias is a manner of expressing judgments in the face of uncertainty that is influenced by substantial and predictable forecast errors. This heuristic is defined as a method for determining whether or not a given quantity is suspicious. We aim to find an incentive for the occasion, which is the location where the change is completed, by judging whether it is extremely high or excessively low and gradually adjusting the gauge by "moving it" cognitively from the anchor, based on the data provided. According to studies based on this heuristic, the change interaction is lacking since the evaluations for the value of the event are altered by the value of the security and do not allow for a significant change. Kahneman and Tversky (1979) published a paper titled "Prospect theory: A study of risky decisions." This study is minestrone in the field of behavioral finance. This theory examines how investors make decisions based on the likelihood of outcomes, as well as how these probabilities of outcomes are expressed. They've also demonstrated that investors are risk averse when it comes to rewards, but risk seekers when it comes to losses. Thaler (1980) developed an alternate descriptive theory to describe the prospect theory. Instead of seeing investors as cold and unreasonable, he contends that they are influenced by behavioral biases, which sometimes contribute to suboptimal decisions. Several researchers have occasionally questioned the theory and assumptions of conventional finance and modern finance. Behavioral finance theories, on the other hand, have been the subject of a variety of issues and difficulties. Tversky and Kahneman (1981) found that Investors avoid risk in order to assure profits when information is provided in a positive frame; yet, when the same information is presented in a negative frame, investors are prepared to take the risk in order to prevent losses. As a result, the same information can be provided to investors in either of two ways to persuade them to change their minds. Thaler & Shefrin (1981) conducted research on various economic theories of self-control. According to the report, investors prefer to prevent losses and protect their investments. According to the study, investors should always have some level of tolerance and should work on their self-control. Kahneman and Tversky (1982), "The degree of regret changes with the availability of counterfactual alternatives, and it is dependent on choice- or behavior-focused counterfactual thoughts." Statmin and Shefrin (1985) Investors prefer to sell superior stock to realize early profits, and losing stocks tend to postpone the losses for a very long time. There is far greater a tendency to prevent losses than the will to make profits. Investor final decisions should not depend on the losses perceived, but on the benefits perceived. Thaler (1985) He has put forward the mental accounting theory, which means that investors are divided into a variety of mental groups into different portfolios. Following that, they segregate investing methods for each mental account, such that each mental account has a distinct goal, with the goal of maximizing returns while minimizing risk. This could lead to the selection of profitable portfolios that also satisfy the emotions of investors. De Bondt et al., (1985) investigated the question, "Does the Stock Market Overreact?" They claimed that people frequently overreact to sudden and dramatic news, resulting in major stock market form inefficiencies. Individuals and households use mental accounting to organize, analyze, and keep track of their financial activities. " To investigate the influence of disposition, the researchers utilized a paradigm that included mental accounting, regret aversion, self-control, and tax consideration. According to the study, the impact of dispositions should be smaller at the end of the year since investors may manage themselves more intelligently at that time, knowing that realizing losses might be beneficial for tax purposes. He rejects tax issues irrationally because he is motivated by the pleasurable feelings that come with monetary benefits. As the end-of-the-tax-year deadline approaches, investors find it simpler to sell losing stocks. Kahneman et al., (1990) People emphasize so much what they hold at the moment and don't want to change their position. This makes them forget the most profitable prospects for investment. This makes the prices of some of the highly lucrative securities at an extremely low level; the money is therefore on the market, but suffers from people's ignorance. Kahneman et al., (1991) the endowment effect has been identified as a behavioral element influencing investment decisions. The endowment effect is defined as a situation in which an individual appreciates something they already own more than something they do not own, according to the study. This bias is also known as divestiture aversion, which occurs when an investor keeps to a particular asset due to familiarity and comfort. Shiller (2010) demonstrates that one of the main reasons people imitate others, or engage in "herd behavior," is that they believe the others have information that justifies their actions. Benartzi and Thaler (1995) Loss aversion bias is a theory that has been proposed. It happens because people react to some losses and certain profits in various ways. When presented with certain gains, they are unwilling to take any risks, yet when there is a chance of losses, they are willing to take more risks. This indicates they place a higher priority on loss certainty than loss uncertainty. Kahneman and Riepe (1998) The eventual consequence is unknown with certainty when a decision is made amongst numerous options. While probabilities are assigned to these choices, the individual's prejudices and aspirations are factored in, which can lead to inaccuracies such as optimism bias. Optimism bias is a psychological tendency common among investors in which they exaggerate their capacity to manage events and overestimate their market knowledge. This bias is emotional in nature and can influence financial decisions because investment decisions are dependent on intuition. Olsen (1998) "The study and prediction of the systematic financial market consequences of psychological decision processes" is how behavioral finance is defined. Fama (1998) Market efficiency, long-term returns, and behavioral finance have all been studied. According to the study, market anomalies are consistent with market efficiency since they cause information overreaction or under reaction. Most long-term return aberrations, according to the study, vanish with appropriate changes.

3. Objectives

1. To find out the most influential authors in the Behavioral Finance.
2. To find out which country does the most research in the Behavioral Finance?
3. To find out the gaps in Behavioral Finance Domain.

4. Research Methodology

4.1 Data Collection

Data were extracted from the Scopus database between the years 1998 and 2022. A total of 1052 research publications were taken into consideration for this investigation. It was discovered that the Behavioral Finance would gain momentum beginning in 2007, and much effort will be done until then.

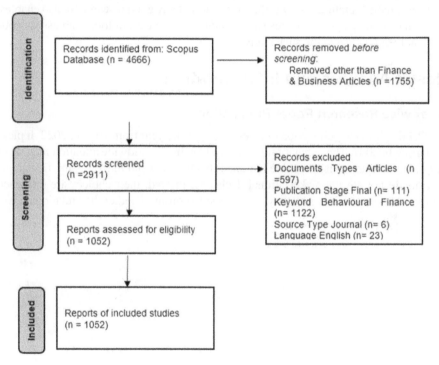

Fig. 22.1 PRISMA Network

Source: Author

Figure 22.1 shows the PRISMA network, which stands for Prevention and Recovery Information System for Monitoring and Analysis, helps us define how we have identified the research documents and what parameters are included for screening and how we limit the articles. At the end, documents are considered for study. We have found a total of 4666 research documents from the Scopus database, which we have included various parameters for excluding, like Subject, publication stage, source types and language.

4.2 Methodology

This study employed a bibliometric approach using VOSviewer software. To develop bibliometric networks, all units of analysis might form distinct associations. This study used a co-occurrence relationship (Callon, Courtial, Turner, & Bauin, 1983). Two items co-occur in a document. This examination reveals a scientific field's conceptual and cognitive themes. We ought to normalize the bibliometric network in order to get useful information about the area from the analysis. We can relativize the relationships between two analysis units by normalizing the network. Association strength was employed as the normalization metric in this study (Van Eck and Waltman, 2010). It will help us determine who the most influential author is on a certain subject, and it will also assist scholars in identifying knowledge gaps. Over the past five years, the bibliometric approach has gained popularity. It can be used to conduct systematic literature reviews, the foundation of any good research. It also enables us to determine the country-by-country research conducted on a certain topic and assists countries that have not yet conducted the such study.

5. Result Analysis and Interpretation

5.1 Year wise Research Paper Publication

Figure 22.2 displays the publication of research papers by year from 1998 to 2022. It picked up steam starting in 2007. The behavioral finance field gained worldwide attention in 2008 during the subprime mortgage crisis because it argued that the financial market is inefficient and that participants do not always make rational decisions. Instead, their choices are influenced by heuristics or biases, which is why they are regarded as ordinary rather than relational investors.

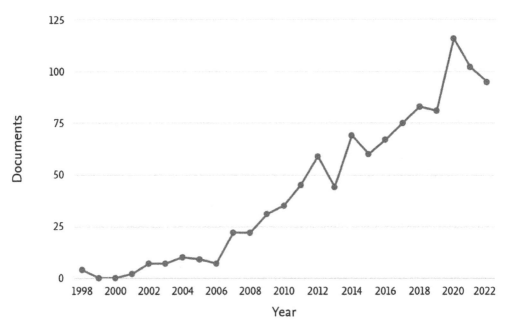

Fig. 22.2 Research paper publication

Source: Author

Shiller (2013) attributes the subprime crisis to overconfidence and demonstrates how these bubbles overextended credit, leading to global credit crunches, write-offs, foreclosures, and bankruptcies. To address the subprime crisis, policymakers will need to restructure the financial system by putting in place a comprehensive set of initiatives, including better financial information, streamlined legal agreements and regulations, expanded markets for risk management, home equity insurance policies, income-linked mortgages, and new safeguards for consumers against unintended inflationary effects.

The publishing of the study paper is broken down by its many sources in Fig. 22.3. It was discovered that the Journal of Economic Behavior and Organization is the most established publication, while the Journal of Behavioral and Experimental Finance is the most recent one. The highest number of research papers ever published in the Journal of Behavioral Finance was 54.

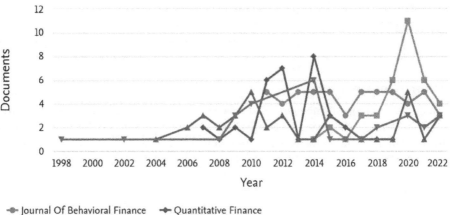

Fig. 22.3 Research paper by source

Source: Author

5.2 Prominent Authors

Table 22.1 show the prominent writers' information according to the number of research papers they have published and the number of citations they have received. We have listed the top 10 authors in this article based on the number of documents and the number of citations they have received. It was discovered that the author Kudryavtsev a. has the highest number of research papers on behavioral finance in the Scopus database, while the number of citations that Hirshleifer d. has is 1352. These well-known authors allow the researchers to gain a better understanding of the author's points of view and fill in any gaps in knowledge that they had previously overlooked in their ongoing research.

Table 22.1 Prominent authors details

Author	Total number of documents	Author	Total Number of Citations
Kudryavtsev a.	11	Hirshleifer d.	1352
Yang c.	9	Teoh s.h.	1161
Hirshleifer d.	8	Jacobs h.	148
Teoh s.h.	8	Blasco n.	146
Ahmad z.	7	Corredor p.	146
Durand r.b.	7	Oehler a.	120
Hens t.	7	Durand r.b.	90
Muga l.	7	Lo a.w.	84
Feldman t.	6	Chang c.-h.	78
Kliger d.	6	Breuer w.	74

Source: Author

5.3 Prominent Country

The country co-authorship network is displayed in Fig. 22.4. By looking at the overlay visualization in the VOSviewer, we concluded that the United States of America is the most significant country in terms of country co-authorship. In addition, the United States is the oldest country that is doing a study on behavioral finance. It was found that there was a total of

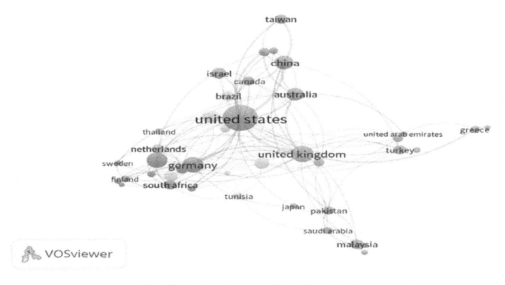

Fig. 22.4 Country co-authorship network

Source: Author

six clusters by looking at the network diagram, which was represented in a variety of colors: cluster 1 was shown in the color red, cluster 2 was shown in the color green, cluster 3 was shown in the color blue, cluster 4 was shown in the color yellow, cluster 5 was shown in the color purple, and cluster 6 was shown in the color sky blue. Recent developments in the field of behavioral finance have been made in India, Pakistan, Hong Kong, and Indonesia. There is a significant amount of untapped potential in behavioral finance for additional research in both underdeveloped countries and developing nations. It was discovered that during the COVID-19 pandemic, there was unprecedented growth in the opening of Demat accounts, and now young people are curious to participate in the stock market to earn a higher rate of return. Since only 2–3% of people in India invest in the stock market, there is plenty of room for behavioral finance. In addition, it was found that lots of space are available for behavioral finance.

5.4 Keyword

The co-occurrence author keywork network is displayed here in Fig. 22.5. The keyword "behavioral finance" appears many times throughout all of the research articles from around the world. The work of Daniel Kahneman and Amos Tversky in behavioral finance began to gain traction around 1970. Both cast doubt on the EMH hypothesis, which was previously thought of as the cornerstone of modern financial theory. They both place a strong emphasis on taking psychology and sociology into account before making any financial decision, and they carry out a large number of experimental studies to prove, in the end, that the interaction of these two fields influences investor decisions. As a result of market anomalies and biases, investor decisions are also influenced by these two fields. When we looked at the keyword network, we noticed a lot of potential and research gaps for further studies on experimental economics and experimental finance, heuristics, personal finance, financial literacy, the financial market, and heuristics, personal finance, financial literacy, the financial market, and overreaction.

Fig. 22.5 Co-occurrence author keywork network

Source: Author

6. Conclusion

Studies have discovered that bibliometric analysis helps them become more knowledgeable about the authors, countries, and keywords most frequently cited with a particular subject. In their current research, researchers are using each of these elements. In the past ten years, there has been a substantial rise in the popularity of bibliometric analysis, and numerous studies have been published in this area of research. It will help with comprehending essential aspects of any particular research topic you choose. In the Scopus database, it was discovered that the author Kudryavtsev A. has the maximum number of research publications on behavioral finance. However, the number of citations that Hirshleifer D. has is 1352. These well-known authors make it possible for the researchers to improve their comprehension of the author's points of view and fill in any information gaps they had previously missed in their continuing research by allowing them to learn more about the author's perspective. According to our findings, the United States of America is the most influential country in terms of the number of papers written with contributions from other nations. In addition, the United States is the oldest country researching behavioral finance, and this research is being conducted in the country. When we looked at the keyword network, we noticed a lot of potential and research gaps for further studies on experimental economics and heuristics, personal finance, financial literacy, the financial market, and heuristics, personal finance, financial literacy, the financial market, and overreaction.

7. Limitations

Since the material for this study article came from the Scopus database, it did not investigate any other reputable journals that were not included in the Scopus database. The research era spanned from 1998 to 2022. However, before that year, a significant amount of work had been done on behavioural finance. However, the relevant journals or research papers were not included in the Scopus journal database. For the sake of this study, we restricted ourselves to using only research papers written in English, which is a constraint given the abundance of high-quality publications written in other languages. In addition to the Scopus database, additional databases are accessible that contain a more significant number of documents; however, we have not considered these databases.

8. Acknowledgement

Special thanks go to Dr Seema Thakur, my colleague who assisted me in data collection and analysis. I also acknowledge Galgotias University for its financial support that facilitated the success of my research. Lastly, I want to thank my parents and wife for their unending support throughout my study.

REFERENCES

1. Benartzi, Shlomo, and Richard H. Thaler. "Myopic Loss Aversion and the Equity Premium Puzzle*." OUP Academic, February 1, 1995. https://academic.oup.com/qje/article/110/1/73/1894013.

2. Callon, Michel, Jean-Pierre Courtial, William A. Turner, and Serge Bauin. "From Translations to Problematic Networks: An Introduction to Co-Word Analysis." *Social Science Information* 22, no. 2 (March 1983): 191–235. https://doi.org/10.1177/053901883022002003.
3. Campbell, John Y. "Asset Pricing at the Millennium." *The Journal of Finance* 55, no. 4 (August 2000): 1515–67. https://doi.org/10.1111/0022-1082.00260.
4. De Bondt, Werner F. M., and Richard Thaler. "Does the Stock Market Overreact?" *The Journal of Finance* 40, no. 3 (July 1985): 793–805. https://doi.org/10.1111/j.1540-6261.1985.tb05004.x.
5. Fama, Eugene F. "Market Efficiency, Long-Term Returns, and Behavioral finance1The Comments of Brad Barber, David Hirshleifer, S.P. Kothari, Owen Lamont, Mark Mitchell, Hersh Shefrin, Robert Shiller, Rex Sinquefield, Richard Thaler, Theo Vermaelen, Robert Vishny, Ivo Welch, and a Referee Have Been Helpful. Kenneth French and Jay Ritter Get Special Thanks.1." *Journal of Financial Economics* 49, no. 3 (September 1998): 283–306. https://doi.org/10.1016/s0304-405x(98)00026-9.
6. Kahneman, Daniel, and Mark W. Riepe. "Aspects of Investor Psychology." *The Journal of Portfolio Management* 24, no. 4 (July 31, 1998): 52–65. https://doi.org/10.3905/jpm.1998.409643.
7. Kahneman, Daniel, and Amos Tversky. "Subjective Probability: A Judgment of Representativeness." *Cognitive Psychology* 3, no. 3 (July 1972): 430–54. https://doi.org/10.1016/0010-0285(72)90016-3.
8. Kahneman, Daniel, and Amos Tversky. "Prospect theory: An analysis of decision under risk". Econometrics, 47, no. 3 (Feb 1979): 263–292. https://doi.org/0012-9682(197903)47:2%3C263:PT AAOD%3E2.0.CO;2-3
9. Kahneman, Daniel, and Amos Tversky. "On the Study of Statistical Intuitions." *Cognition* 11, no. 2 (March 1982): 123–41. https://doi.org/10.1016/0010-0277(82)90022-1.
10. Kahneman, Daniel, Jack L. Knetsch, and Richard H. Thaler. "Experimental Tests of the Endowment Effect and the Coase Theorem." *Journal of Political Economy* 98, no. 6 (December 1990): 1325–48. https://doi.org/10.1086/261737.
11. Kahneman, Daniel, Jack L. Knetsch, and Richard H. Thaler. "Experimental Tests of the Endowment Effect and the Coase Theorem." *Journal of Political Economy* 98, no. 6 (December 1990): 1325–48. https://doi.org/10.1086/261737.
12. Malkiel, Burton G., and Eugene F. Fama. "Efficient Capital Markets: A Review of Theory and Empirical Work*." *The Journal of Finance* 25, no. 2 (May 1970): 383–417. https://doi.org/10.1111/j.1540-6261.1970.tb00518.x.
13. Olsen, Robert A. "Behavioral Finance and Its Implications for Stock-Price Volatility." *Financial Analysts Journal* 54, no. 2 (March 1998): 10–18. https://doi.org/10.2469/faj.v54.n2.2161.
14. Shefrin, Hersh, and Meir Statman. "The Disposition to Sell Winners Too Early and Ride Losers Too Long: Theory and Evidence." *The Journal of Finance* 40, no. 3 (July 1985): 777–90. https://doi.org/10.1111/j.1540-6261.1985.tb05002.x.
15. Shiller, Robert J. "From Efficient Markets Theory to Behavioral Finance." *Journal of Economic Perspectives* 17, no. 1 (February 1, 2003): 83–104. https://doi.org/10.1257/089533003321164967.
16. Shiller, Robert J. "Hedging Inflation and Income Risks." *The Manchester School* 63, no. S1 (September 21, 2010): 1–21. https://doi.org/10.1111/j.1467-9957.1995.tb01445.x.
17. Shiller, Robert J. "The Subprime Solution," January 1, 2013. https://doi.org/10.1515/9781400844999.
18. Simon, H. A. "Rational Choice and the Structure of the Environment." *Psychological Review* 63, no. 2 (1956): 129–38. https://doi.org/10.1037/h0042769.
19. Slovic, Paul. "Psychological Study of Human Judgment: Implications for Investment Decision Making." *The Journal of Finance* 27, no. 4 (September 1972): 779–99. https://doi.org/10.1111/j.1540-6261.1972.tb01311.x.

20. Statman, Meir, and David Caldwell. "Applying Behavioral Finance to Capital Budgeting: Project Terminations." *Financial Management* 16, no. 4 (1987): 7. https://doi.org/10.2307/3666103.
21. Thaler, Richard. "Toward a Positive Theory of Consumer Choice." *Journal of Economic Behavior & Organization* 1, no. 1 (March 1980): 39–60. https://doi.org/10.1016/0167-2681(80)90051-7.
22. Thaler, Richard. "Mental Accounting and Consumer Choice." *Marketing Science* 4, no. 3 (August 1985): 199–214. https://doi.org/10.1287/mksc.4.3.199.
23. Thaler, R. H, and Shefrin, H. M. "An Economic Theory of Self-Control". *Journal of Political Economy, 89 no.* 2 (January 1981): 392–406. http://www.jstor.org/stable/1833317
24. Tversky, Amos, and Daniel Kahneman. "Judgment under Uncertainty: Heuristics and Biases." *Science* 185, no. 4157 (September 27, 1974): 1124–31. https://doi.org/10.1126/science.185.4157.1124.
25. Tversky, Amos, and Daniel Kahneman. "The Framing of Decisions and the Psychology of Choice." *Science* 211, no. 4481 (January 30, 1981): 453–58. https://doi.org/10.1126/science.7455683.
26. Eck, Nees Jan van, and Ludo Waltman. "Software Survey: VOSviewer, a Computer Program for Bibliometric Mapping." *Scientometrics* 84, no. 2 (December 31, 2009): 523–38. https://doi.org/10.1007/s11192-009-0146-3.
27. Von Neumann, J, and Morgenstern, O. "Theory of games and economic behavior". Princeton: Princeton, 1944, University Press.

PART

EVIDENCE BASED
HUMAN RESOURCE MANAGEMENT

Handbook of Evidence Based Management Practices in Business – Satyendra Kumar Sharma et al. (eds)
© 2023 Taylor & Francis Group, London, ISBN 978-1-032-54216-4

Chapter

Changing Paradigms in Training Methods: A Bibliometric Review

A. Naga Ramani[1]
Research Scholar, Department of Management, BITS Pilani,
Pilani Campus, Rajasthan, India

Jayashree Mahesh[2]
Assistant Professor, Department of Management, BITS Pilani,
Pilani Campus, Rajasthan, India

ABSTRACT: Purpose: The study aims to understand changing paradigm in training methods from traditional to modern. 713 articles were retrieved from the Scopus database and a bibliometric analysis of the training methods was conducted. Further, this study also seeks to analyze the outcomes of various training methods. The main objective of the study is to understand the most relevant training techniques in this current volatile, uncertain, complex, and ambiguous (VUCA) work environment.

Design/methodology/approach: The study uses bibliometric data and VOSviewer user interfaces to perform several types of analyses on the data taken from the Scopus database (the largest interdisciplinary database in social sciences). Based on journal citations, well-known authors, popular search terms, and publications in many industries, we chose 713 articles.

Findings: From the content analysis, it has been observed that the pandemic has caused a significant shift in training methods across the majority of sectors. Many industries are adopting modern training approaches including simulation, e-learning, virtual training, blended learning, etc. because of their favorable effects on employee engagement, performance, and knowledge acquisition.

Contribution of the Study: Our study identifies the most effective training methods that can be implemented in various sectors. Further, the study emphasizes the various benefits of different training methods so that practitioners can choose the best training technique which fulfills their organizational objectives.

[1]p20210442@pilani.bits-pilani.ac.in, [2]jmahesh@pilani.bits-pilani.ac.in

DOI: 10.4324/9781003415725-23

Originality/value: Based on the extensive literature review, this is one of the few papers on training methods for the past 10 years that has indicated the shift in training methods from traditional to modern in different sectors. In addition to being relevant for the practitioners, it will also set the agenda for future research.

KEYWORDS: Training methods, Traditional training, Modern training, VUCA, VOSviewer, Bibliometric analysis

1. Introduction

The management of human resources in modern businesses is crucial for their success. The training policy and methods adopted by the organization play a crucial role in the effective management of human resources as they lead to the development of required competencies in their employees. Due to intense competition, the most recent training and development methods are in high demand (Faridi et al., 2017). Globalization has caused changes in training practices (Faridi & Baloch, 2018). As a result, many industries today have altered their strategies by implementing new techniques and laws, particularly in developed nations (Bloom & Van Reenen, 2007; Noe & Peacock, 2008) for their status and place in the market.

According to Kulkarni (2013), training increases employees' capacity to do their tasks to the highest standard which raises employee retention and encourages organizational development. It's interesting to note that various training and development methods help people operate more effectively, have professional attitudes, be engaged and loyal at work, and have higher morale (Faridi et al., 2017; Faridi & Baloch, 2018).

There has been a significant shift in business practices functioning, and operations as a result of competition, the introduction of new market trends, and the development and advancement of cutting-edge technologies (Gusdorf 2009), therefore it's also crucial that staff members develop their knowledge and abilities in a supportive environment (Faridi et al., 2017).

Training and development (T&D) programs are effective in encouraging the highest levels of creativity and innovation among professionals through a supportive environment, skilled instructors, and the most modern methodology. Due to intense competition, innovative training and development methods are in demand (Faridi et al., 2017). Globalization has caused changes in training practices (Faridi & Baloch, 2018). Nowadays different sectors like education, banking, medical have started using modern training methods to educate their workforces. In many firms, conventional training techniques and procedures are no longer effective (Noe & Peacock, 2008). In comparison to firms that use contemporary techniques of training, those who are still employing traditional ways of training are falling behind (Adnan Faridi & Akhtar Baloch,2019).

Despite new methods, some of the traditional methods of training are still used which include lectures, seminars and workshops are more prevalent in emerging economies (Zehra, 2016). However, there is a paradigm change underway, particularly in the private sector. The rising economies are utilizing computer-based training (CBT) and online methodologies (Faridi & Baloch, 2018; Faizan & Zehra, 2016).

The purpose of the study is to know the effectiveness of contemporary methods in comparison to traditional methods. This study accomplishes by looking at the articles that have been published in the Scopus journal using bibliometric approaches. We seek to discover the change in the paradigm of training methods in various sectors and, which shapes the current foundation for the issue.

2. Review of the Literature on Bibliometric

Bibliometrics is a field of study that analyses publication trends using statistical and mathematical techniques, used by academicians as a tool to analyze the published data. It is a suite of resources that researchers can use to examine publicly available data. (McCain, 1996). These methods include bibliometric mapping, citation and co-citation analysis, and co-word analysis. In this study, we have used a co-word analysis of keywords as its purpose is to map and comprehend the dynamics of science (He, 1999). Co-word analysis has been utilized in this work to map the results of conventional and contemporary training methods employed in different sectors. Moreover, to observe how training paradigms in many sectors have shifted from traditional to modern.

For many years, there has been a growth in the use of bibliometric methodologies for the mapping and analysis of the body of knowledge published in numerous fields. These methods have already been applied to the study of several topics in the management field, such as management (Tahai & Meyer, 1999), strategic management (Nerur, Rasheed, & Natarajan, 2008; Ramos-Rodriguez & RuizNavarro, 2004), finance (Alexander & Mabry, 1994; Merigó, Yang, & Xu, 2015), and operations management (Pilkington & Liston-Heyes, 1999; Pilkington & Meredith, 2009), Human resources management and organizational behavior are some more areas of emphasis (Markoulli, Lee, Byington, & Felps, 2017; Fernandez-Alles & Ramos-Rodrguez, 2009).

3. Methodology

713 articles that had been published and were in the field of both conventional and contemporary training methods made up the sample data for this study. Through a series of steps, the data were gathered. The Scopus database from Elsevier was first chosen as the data source. One of the largest multidisciplinary scientific literature databases in the world, Scopus (Bar-Ilan, 2008), has been extensively used as a data source in research illustrating the dynamics of science and technology Gupta & Dhawan, 2009). Second, given the goal of the study, "traditional training" or "conventional training" or "off the job training" or "on the job training" were developed as the entry terms for the search criteria for traditional training, while "modern training" or "virtual training" or "blended training" or "E-learning" were developed for modern training methods. The database was searched using the following built-in search term: Title-ABS-KEY (training) and Title-ABS-KEY (learning) alternatively, Title-ABS-KEY (traditional) or Title-

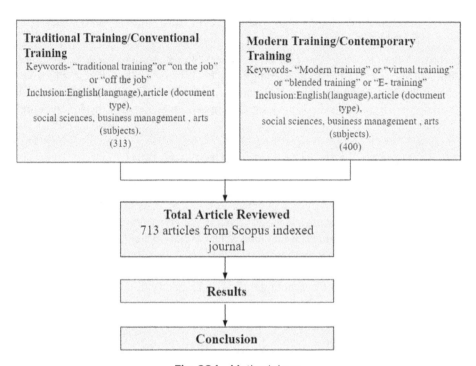

Fig. 23.1 Methodology

Source: Author's compilation

ABS-KEY (modern)) The sample literature's year range was established as 2013 to 2023. The source type was restricted to journal papers written in English.

4. Results and Analysis

To review the literature on training methods in different sectors and their outcomes, we used the selection criteria to search the Scopus main collection database, completed the aforementioned data preparation processes, and found 713 articles. This study used a bibliometric analytic approach. Utilizing co-word analysis, the investigation sought to identify groups of research areas among the articles.

4.1. Co-word Analysis of Keyword

The co-word analysis seeks to map and comprehend the dynamics of science by making use of patterns of co-occurrence of keyword pairs that stand for the various subjects within a subject (He, 1999). Every term that appears in an article is taken to be connected, related, or at the very least vaguely equivalent to every other term therein. This approach involves classifying keywords based on the strength of the links between the terms as evaluated by co-occurrence frequencies derived from the domain literature, using statistical techniques like cluster analysis or factor analysis. Following that, graph-drawing strategies are employed to demonstrate the connections between the keyword groups. The group's keyword placement and correlations can be used to identify the main study topics (Ding, Chowdhury, & Foo, 2001).

4.2 Cluster 1: Traditional Training Methods

Based on keyword analysis, a cluster diagram was developed, represented in Fig. 23.2.

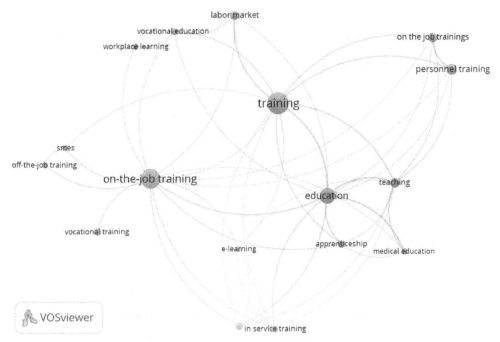

Fig. 23.2   Cluster 1: Traditional training methods

Source: Author's compilation

According to Fig. 23.2 in this cluster, keywords relating to on-the-job training are highly centralized, and the cluster includes terms for in-service training, apprenticeships, vocational education, and personnel training and SMEs typically employ off-the-job training is also evident. Additionally, the clusters collocate show that its main concentration is on unorganized sectors, health care, and education. The two main issues of this cluster are healthcare and education, to put it succinctly.

4.3 Cluster 2: Modern Training Methods

Based on keyword analysis, a cluster diagram was developed, represented in Fig. 23.3.

According to Fig. 23.3, keywords relating to E-learning training are highly centralized, and the cluster includes terms for e-training, distance learning, simulation training, serious games, and blended training. We can see from the diagram that since the pandemic began, e-learning has evolved into many forms. Additionally, the clusters collocate show that its main concentration is on the health care and education sectors. The two main issues of this cluster are healthcare and education, to put it succinctly.

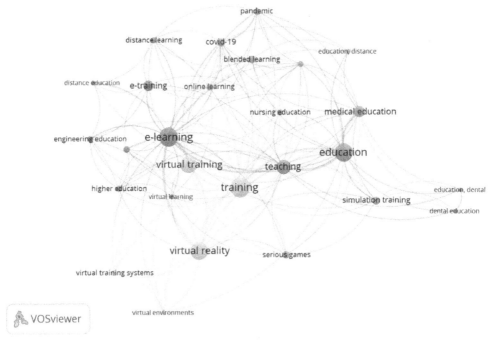

Fig. 23.3 Cluster 2: Modern training methods

Source: Author's compilation

4.4 Cluster 3: Outcomes of Traditional and Modern Training Methods

Based on keyword analysis, a cluster diagram was developed, represented in Fig. 23.4.

Fig. 23.4 Cluster 3: Outcomes of traditional and modern training methods

Source: Author's compilation

According to Fig. 23.4, the keywords display the results of traditional and modern training techniques. From this diagram, we can deduce that regardless of whether training is traditional or modern, results have remained the same, and results of training have enhanced in contemporary. Due to the VUCA environment, using modern training is essential, and it is successful in helping modern organizations remain competitive.

5. Findings

Table 23.1 Findings of training methods

Traditional Training Methods On-The-Job Training	Sectors	Modern Training Methods E-Learning	Sectors	Outcomes
• Apprenticeship • Vocational • Personnel • E-learning	• Health care • Education • Unorganized	• Distance learning • Blended learning • Virtual training • Serious games • E – training • Simulation training	• Healthcare • Education	• Decision making • Performance • Skill • Motivation • Satisfaction • Retention • Leadership • Self-efficacy • Professional development • Professional learning • Professional competence • Knowledge management
Off-The-Job Training	SMEs			

Source: Author's compilation

6. Conclusion and Limitations

This study shows how training techniques are addressed in the literature on business and management, which is a well-established but challenging topic. We examined the articles that were published between 2013 and 2023., and it appears there has been a rapid shift in training methods from traditional to modern training. In our study, we found that the major paradigm change occurred during and after the post-covid-19 era. The sectors which saw a huge shift are the medical and education sector. According to this analysis, e-learning has always been a part of traditional methods, but since the pandemic, it has assumed a new form that includes serious games, virtual reality, and blended training.

Our study has certain limitations. Firstly, Bibliometric analysis is regarded as a trusted technique for analyzing but analysis may vary depending on keywords chosen by researchers. Second, the sample of papers used for the literature study was only drawn from the Elsevier Scopus database. Future research that incorporates articles in other languages and inquiries into different contexts would be fascinating to see. Given that training methods are a common topic. Finally, we believe that our work offers a solid base for creating meta-analyses on this subject.

REFERENCES

1. Bar-Ilan, Judit. "Which h-index? —A comparison of WoS, Scopus, and Google Scholar." *Scientometrics* 74, no. 2 (2008): 257–271.

2. Ding, Ying, Gobinda G. Chowdhury, and Schubert Foo. "Bibliometric cartography of information retrieval research by using co-word analysis." *Information processing & management* 37, no. 6 (2001): 817–842.

3. Faridi, Adnan, and Akhtar Baloch. "The moderating role of modern training and development methods in private banks and work performance: Evidence from contractual employees working in Pakistan banking sector." *Business & Management Studies: An International Journal* 6, no. 3 (2018): 204–215.

4. Faridi, Adnan, and Akhtar Baloch. "Training and development methods affecting professionalism and empowerment of banking sector employees." *Journal of Management Sciences* 6, no. 2 (2019): 75–92.

5. Fernandez-Alles, Mariluz, and Antonio Ramos-Rodríguez. "Intellectual structure of human resources management research: A bibliometric analysis of the journal Human Resource Management, 1985–2005." *Journal of the American Society for Information Science and Technology* 60, no. 1 (2009): 161–175.

6. Gusdorf, Myrna L. "Training design, development and implementation." *Society for Human Resource Management* (2009): 1–38.

7. Gupta, Brij Mohan, and S. M. Dhawan. "Status of India in science and technology as reflected in its publication output in the Scopus international database, 1996–2006." *Scientometrics* 80, no. 2 (2009): 473–490.

8. He, Qin. "Knowledge discovery through co-word analysis." (1999).

9. Merigó, José M., Jian-Bo Yang, and Dong-Ling Xu. "A bibliometric overview of financial studies." In *Scientific Methods for the Treatment of Uncertainty in Social Sciences*, pp. 245–254. Springer, Cham, 2015.

10. McCain, Katherine W. "Dictionary of bibliometrics." (1996): 716–717A.

11. Nerur, Sridhar P., Abdul A. Rasheed, and Vivek Natarajan. "The intellectual structure of the strategic management field: An author co-citation analysis." *Strategic Management Journal* 29, no. 3 (2008): 319–336.

12. Pilkington, Alan, and Jack Meredith. "The evolution of the intellectual structure of operations management—1980–2006: A citation/co-citation analysis." *Journal of operations management* 27, no. 3 (2009): 185–202.

13. Pilkington, Alan, and Catherine Liston-Heyes. "Is production and operations management a discipline? A citation/co-citation study." *International Journal of Operations & Production Management* (1999).

14. Tahai, Alireza, and Michael J. Meyer. "A revealed preference study of management journals' direct influences." *Strategic Management Journal* 20, no. 3 (1999): 279–296.

15. Zehra, Nasreen. "Training & development barometer for effective transformation of organizational commitment and overall performance in banking sectors of KPK, Pakistan: Qualitative study of the workforce of the bank of Khyber." *Training & Development Barometer for Effective Transformation of Organizational Commitment and Overall Performance in Banking Sectors of KPK, Pakistan: Qualitative Study of Workforce of Bank of Khyber. International Journal of Academic Research in Business and Social Science* 6, no. 6 (2016).

Chapter

How Emotions Experienced at Home Impact Employee's Stress at Work: A Study on Indian Working Professionals Working in India

Shridhar Gokhale[1]

OB&HRM, Indian Institute of Management Indore, Indore, India

Raina Chhajer[2]

Humanities and Social Sciences,
Indian Institute of Management Indore, Indore, India

ABSTRACT: We all recognize importance of emotions in our human life. Our emotions are powerful and they influence all aspects of our life. Literature is available on how emotions at workplace influence family life which is known as spill-over effect. However, limited literature is available on reverse effect. We have tried to study this reverse spill-over effect for Indian working professionals working in India. With help of positive and negative affect schedule (PANAS-GEN) and PSS-4 scale we tried to measure how emotions experienced at home impact employee's perceived stress at workplace.

65 Indian working professional working in India have participated in online survey circulated through email and social media. The participation in survey was anonymous and voluntary. At the beginning, 9 general questions were asked to record consent and demography. 10 questions captured positive motions experienced at home and 10 question negative emotions. Last 4 questions captured perceived stress at workplace. The valid responses of 65 participants were analysed using statistical tool. Cronbach alpha for negative emotions is 0.892 and for positive emotions is 0.868 which indicates reliability of the scale is good. However, Cronbach alpha for perceived stress scale is 0.532. Results showed significant correlation between positive or negative emotion experienced at home and perceived stress at work. 19.8 percent of variance (R-square = 0.198) in perceived stress could be explained by negative emotions at home whereas 12 percent of variance (R-square = 0.12) in perceived stress level could be explained by positive emotions.

---

[1]ef21shridharg@iimidr.ac.in, [2]rainac@iimidr.ac.in

DOI: 10.4324/9781003415725-24

The study helped to reiterate existence of reverse spill-over effect which generally people try to suppress. This will help HR professionals in India to design positive psychological intervention to reduce perceived stress at workplace and induce positivity. The findings can be extended to develop a tool to assess stressful condition of employee at initial stage to prevent enhancement of perceived stress level.

KEYWORDS: Emotions experienced at home, Perceived stress at workplace, Positive psychological intervention, Well-being

1. Introduction

Emotions experienced in our daily life exert significant influence on all aspects of our life. Emotions experienced in one domain of life are capable to influence our behaviour in another domain. With growing world economy, majority of workforce have dual responsibility of home and office. Therefore, it is inevitable that family issues have impact on employee, family, and organisations (Lieke L. ten Brummelhuis, Arnold B. Bakker 2012). In work-family life, positive experiences in one role, have enriching effect on another role and improve the quality-of-life (Greenhaus, J. H., & Powell, G. N. 2006). Similarly, we like it or not, negative emotions experienced at home too impact our emotional state at our professional life. To ascertain how and to what extent emotions experienced at home impacts employee's stress level at work for Indian working professional working in India.

2. Review of Literature

Experiences at family domain and work and are reciprocal effect. Our behaviour in one domain have influence of our experience in another domain. Men are more likely to bring emotions from work to home whereas women are more prone to take with them family demands and feelings to the workplace. Those who are deeply involved in family matters, it may be difficult for them to put aside family related thoughts and feelings (Williams, K. J., & Alliger, G. M. 1994).

Demands at family front create repetitive thoughts or negative emotions about an issue in to person's mind and therefore individual is not able to perform optimally at workplace. Daily rumination or thinking about previous day's incident affect effective utilisation of resources available at workplace. The hassles faced by an individual at home on any day also have mediating effect on next day's daily rumination and there is affective and cognitive spill over from family to work (Danyang Du, Daantje Derks, and Arnold B. Bakker, 2018). As indicated in work-home resource model, family life impacts professional life negatively when family domain consumes personal resources or capabilities. In family-work interference results in to psychological preoccupation about home hassles while physically present at workplace. (Carlson, Dawn S, and Michael R. Frone 2003).

In a published paper in 1984, titled as *'Spill over from family to work: The neglected side of the work-family interface'*, A. C. Crouter argued that while work impacts family, it is generally ignored that what way experience at family front too influence the workplace performance. In the study conducted through survey of 55 individuals, author established that family lives do influence them at work. Authors found that women with young children are more likely to have this negative spill over as compared to men and women with older children. Family and work life and closely interlinked and therefore family hassles not just affect family life but also interfere with individual's emotions and performance at workplace (Lambert, 1990).

It is established fact that experiencing emotions and managing them at work & family are not wholly negative but they do have positive aspect too when it comes to protecting desired relationships (Speights, S. L., Bochantin, J. E., & Cowan, R. L. 2020) In the same study, it was found that frustration is the most experienced emotion due to family issues. Hostility is the second and guilt is the third most experienced emotion. In the same study, one more thing came out that in family domain, emotions are supressed to maintain harmony whereas, at work place, emotions are supressed as strategic step for conflict free working. It is revealed that emotions experienced at home and workplace domain are not equivalent.

3. Methodology

3.1 Sample Population and Sampling Criteria

Survey was conducted among the adult working professionals who are born in year 2000 or before, working in India and render their services to organisations or people outside their home premise. Participation in this survey was voluntary. Responses were collected between 23rd August 2022 to 6th September 2022. This online survey was conducted among working professionals, excluding entrepreneurs. Following scales are used.

3.2 Emotions at Home

To measure emotions at home, we used Positive and Negative Affect Schedule (PANAS-GEN). This scale is self-report measure of affect. This consist of 20 emotions which we are likely to experience at home and it is scored from 1 to 5. There are 10 positive emotions and 10 are negative emotions. Both set of answers are added separately. For both sets, total score ranges from 10 to 50. The higher positive score indicates a positive effect and vice versa.

3.3 Perceived Stress at Work

PSS-4 scale is used to measure perceived stress at work. This scale comprises of 4 questions with multiple answers to choose from have score from 0 to 4. Question 1 and 4 negatively structured questions whereas 2 and 3 are positively structured questions. Score of all 4 questions is added which can be between 0 to 16. Higher score is corelated with higher stress.

The participants were asked to provide information about those factors which generally influence emotions while at home i. e. age, gender, marital status, no. of children. Information on emotions experienced by them at home was collected through structured scale on 20 emotions. Score of positive and negative emotion calculated separately. Perceived stress level at work was mapped though 4 structed questions. These scores of emotions and stress level at work analysed statistically using Jamovi software.

4. Analysis

Through online survey 66 responses were received. Out of 66, one was not considered as respondent has declared of not working from past 3 years. Finally, there were 65 valid data points. Following is some information about the participants:

1. Out of 65, 16 are women (24.6%) and 49 are male (75.4%).
2. Though age ranges from 22 years to 67 years, majority participants are from age group of Baby boomers (47 nos. 72.3%) and Millennials (17 nos. 26.1%).
3. 62 participants (95.4%) are married, 2 (3.1%) are yet to be married and 1 (1.5%) participant is from 'other' category.
4. Majority participants (59 nos. or 91%) have 1 or more children whereas 6 (9%) do not have any child.

The reliability of scale was checked by measuring Cronback's Alfa. For negative emotions it is 0.892 (Table 24.1) and for positive emotions it is 0.868 (Table 24.2) which falls in category of good reliability of the scale. However, for perceived stress level Cronback's alpha value is 0.532 (Table 24.3).

Table 24.1	**Table 24.2**	**Table 24.3**
Cronbach's alpha values to check reliability of scales		
Scale Reliability Statistics	Scale Reliability Statistics	Scale Reliability Statistics
	Cronbach's α		Cronbach's α		Cronbach's α
scale	0.892	scale	0.868	scale	0.532

Source: Author's compilation

With help of Jamovi statistical software, following corelation factors have been worked out between Age, no. of children, Geder, Positive emotions score, Negative emotions score and Stress level score.

Table 24.4   Correlation matrix

		Age in years	No of children	Gender index	Total score for +ve items	Total score for -ve items	Stress level score
Age in years	Pearson's r	---					
	p-value	---					
No of children	Pearson's r	0.376**	---				
	p-value	0.002	---				
Gender index	Pearson's r	-0.070	0.177	---			
	p-value	0.581	0.157	---			
Total score for +ve items	Pearson's r	-0.030	-0.141	-0.007	---		
	p-value	0.812	0.261	0.953	---		
Total score for -ve items	Pearson's r	-0.210	0.151	0.027	-0.299*	---	
	p-value	0.093	0.230	0.831	0.016	---	
Stress level score	Pearson's r	-0.090	0.203	0.153	-0.347**	0.445***	---
	p-value	0.474	0.105	0.222	0.005	< .001	---

Note. * p < .05, ** p < .01, *** p < .001

Source: Author's compilation

In Table 24.4, some significant corelations are highlighted (where p value is < 0.01) with blue loop. These factors are naturally corelated i. e. age with no. of children, therefore these corelations are not relevant to this study. Score of positive and negative emotions at home are significantly corelated with stress level at work are highlighted with red loop and are important to this study. The Pearson's corelation coefficient for negative emotions and perceived stress level score is 0.445. As it is > 0.30, we can say it is moderately positively related. However, Pearson's coefficient for positive emotions score at home and stress level at work has value of − (0.347) which indicates somewhat less negative affect to perceived stress level as compared to negative emotions have positive affect on stress level.

With linear regression analysis, we get following table on screen for negative emotion score as independent variable and perceived stress level as dependent variable:

Table 24.5 Linear regression for negative emotion score and perceived stress level

Model Fit Measures

				Overall Model Test			
Model	R	R^2	Adjusted R^2	F	df1	df2	p
1	0.445	0.198	0.185	15.6	1	63	< .001

Model Coefficients - Stress level score

Predictor	Estimate	SE	t	p	Stand. Estimate
Intercept	3.218	0.6388	5.04	< .001	
Total score for -ve items	0.138	0.0351	3.94	< .001	0.445

Source: Author's compilation

In Table 24.5, key values are encircled with red line and we can infer following:

1. The p value is < 0.001 for negative emotion score is significant. It means negative emotions experienced at home are significant indicator of perceived stress level at work place with 95% confidence level.
2. R-square = 0.198 which means 19.8% of the variance in perceived stress at work can be explained by negative home emotions at home.
3. Intercept value means $c = 3.218$ and $b = 0.138$ which means if negative emotions score changes by 1, the corresponding change in stress level at work will be 13.8%.

We get following table on screen for positive emotion score as independent variable and perceived stress level as dependent variable:

From the key values encircled with red line in Table 24.6, we can infer following:

The p value is 0.005 for positive emotion score is significant as it is lower than 0.05. It means positive emotions experienced at home are significant indicator of perceived stress level at work place with 95% confidence level.

R-square = 0.120 which means that 12% of the variance in perceived stress at work can be explained by positive emotions experienced at home.

Table 24.6 Linear regression for positive emotion score and perceived stress level

Model Fit Measures

Model	R	R^2	Adjusted R^2	Overall Model Test			
				F	df1	df2	p
1	0.347	0.120	0.106	8.62	1	63	0.005

Model Coefficients - Stress level score

Predictor	Estimate	SE	t	p	Stand. Estimate
Intercept	9.832	1.4651	6.71	< .001	
Total score for +ve items	-0.115	0.0392	-2.94	0.005	-0.347

Source: Author's compilation

Intercept value means $c = 9.832$ and $b = -0.115$ (value with negative sign) which means if positive emotions score changes by 1, the corresponding change in stress level at work will change by 11.5% in opposite direction i. e. perceived stress level at work will reduce with increased positive emotions score.

5. Conclusion

With above analysis, we can conclude that age, gender, no. of children etc. do not have any significant corelation with perceived stress level at work place. Instead, this survey established that for Indian working professional working in India, positive and negative emotions experienced at home have significant corelation with perceived stress at work place. Positive emotions experienced at home are negatively related to perceived stress level at work whereas negative emotions are positively corelated with perceived stress level at work place. Statistically it is found that 19.8% of the variance in perceived stress at work can be explained by negative home emotions at home whereas positive emotions experienced at home can explain 12% of the variance in perceived stress at work.

The study shown that there is significant reverse spill-over effect present in life of Indian working professional. Organizations and HR professionals need to address this which could be useful to improve workplace performance of the professionals. A tool can be developed and made part of periodic performance appraisal process to understand causes for those employees who have shown slacked performance in recent past. Further to it, a well designed positive psychological intervention model can be used as possible solution to limit the perceived stress at workplace, if not total elimination. This combination of diagnostics and remedy will be a useful solution to safeguard employee's wellbeing and performance from unwanted stresses experienced outside the professional working ecosystem.

REFERENCE

1. Du, Danyang, Daantje Derks, and Arnold B. Bakker. "Daily spillover from family to work: A test of the work–home resources model." *Journal of occupational health psychology* 23, no. 2 (2018): 237.
2. Lambert, Susan J. "Processes linking work and family: A critical review and research agenda." *Human relations* 43, no. 3 (1990): 239–257.
3. Crouter, Ann C. "Spillover from family to work: The neglected side of the work-family interface." *Human relations* 37, no. 6 (1984): 425–441.
4. Carlson, Dawn S., and Michael R. Frone. "Relation of behavioral and psychological involvement to a new four-factor conceptualization of work-family interference." *Journal of business and psychology* 17, no. 4 (2003): 515–535.
5. Ten Brummelhuis, Lieke L., and Arnold B. Bakker. "A resource perspective on the work–home interface: The work–home resources model." *American psychologist* 67, no. 7 (2012): 545.
6. Greenhaus, Jeffrey H., and Gary N. Powell. "When work and family are allies: A theory of work-family enrichment." *Academy of management review* 31, no. 1 (2006): 72–92.
7. Speights, Sabrina L., Jaime E. Bochantin, and Renee L. Cowan. "Feeling, expressing, and managing emotions in work-family conflict." *Journal of Business and Psychology* 35, no. 3 (2020): 363–380.
8. Williams, Kevin J., and George M. Alliger. "Role stressors, mood spillover, and perceptions of work-family conflict in employed parents." *Academy of Management Journal* 37, no. 4 (1994): 837–868.
9. Self report measure of affect (PANAS-GEN) - https://www.brandeis.edu/roybal/docs/PANAS-GEN_website_PDF.pdf (Accessed in September 2022)
10. Perceived stress scale 4 (PSS-4) https://ohnurses.org/wp-content/uploads/2015/05/Perceived-Stress-Scale-4.pdf (Accessed in September 2022)
11. Dimock, Michael. "Defining generations: Where Millennials end and Generation Z begins." *Pew Research Center* 17, no. 1 (2019): 1–7.
12. Jamovi free version 2.2.5.0 (Accessed in September 2022)

Chapter

Unwrap the Roles of Green Human Resource Management Practices with the Mediating Role of Green Innovation

Jyoti Kamboj[1] and Eronimus A.[2]
Department of Financial Administration, School of Management,
Central University of Punjab, Bathinda

ABSTRACT: Going green is becoming a status symbol for companies that are concerned about the environment. The eco-initiatives taken by organizations can contribute to green sustainability. Organizations must adopt green practices due to the rising concern over environmental issues. The future of green HRM as a cutting-edge method seems positive for all stakeholders in the organization. Therefore, the firms should develop and strictly follow environmental strategies and integrate them with green innovation to reduce adverse environmental effects. The objective of this research is to ascertain whether green human resource management practices can foster green innovation among employees and to identify the factors that mediate the relationship between green innovation and green HRM. The study uses primary data, which is collected from various sectors using an online questionnaire and analysed using the structural equation modeling (SEM) technique through SmartPLS4. This study leads to the conclusion that GR and GT have an insignificant impact on EP, whereas GR and GT have a significant impact on GI, and GI has a significant impact on EP. The study also examined the mediation role of green innovation, demonstrating the significant mediating role of GI between GR and EP as well as between GT and EP. The outcomes reveal the necessity of green innovation and environmental strategy to improve environmental performance through appropriate policies and procedures and employees' willingness to participate in sustainable activities.

KEYWORDS: Employee engagement, Environmental performance, Green HRM, Green innovation, Sustainability

[1]jyotikamboj21@gmail.com, [2]eronimus.anthonysamy@cup.edu.in

DOI: 10.4324/9781003415725-25

1. Introduction

The idea of managing human resources with a green perspective is becoming more prominent nowadays. The requirement for an organization to implement environmental policies and programs has been shaped by rising concern for the global environment and a higher temperament, as well as by the creation of new standards for environmental management. Due to the transition to a green economy, organizations as well as individuals are now concerned about the effects of our daily activities on the environment. To implement green management practices, organizations increasingly believe that employees need to be motivated, empowered, and environmentally aware. Environmentally conscious businesses have their own organizational structures. Companies that want to implement environmental policies need employees who are concerned about the environment. Organizations have two methods for achieving these goals: The first one focuses on hiring environmentally friendly candidates, and the second one educates current employees on environmental protection. Companies look for candidates who are environmentally conscious during the hiring process and integrate environmental strategy and plans with hiring practices. However, few organizations identify specific ecological ideals in their job ads to attract candidates who wish to work for an eco-friendly company to fill employment positions. Some organizations use their own selection criteria, such as environmental sensitivity, when choosing candidates for job openings. Companies evaluated candidates by asking them environmental-related questions. Compared to generic selection methods that do not take into account the specifics of the job at hand, this form of a selection procedure is appropriate for any firm looking to hire environmentally friendly individuals. As a core component of GHRM practices, training and development strategies should emphasize the improvement of staff members' abilities, understanding, and attitudes toward environmentally friendly behaviour (Ridhi 2015). This includes training employees in working practices that reduce waste, conserve energy, raise environmental awareness within the company, and provide opportunities for teamwork and environmental problem-solving. Furthermore, it improves workers' capacity for accepting change and helps them to adopt a proactive outlook on aspects of sustainable development. Green HRM practices facilitate innovation and offer the organization a set of guidelines to help in achieving its environmental goals, better managing environmental influences, and reducing pollution.

Environmental issues and resource imbalances are affecting how organizations manage their environments. The operations of today's businesses should be concerned with incorporating sustainable and innovative environmental management practices that result in innovations and improved environmental performance. The HR function can support green innovation practices that increase resource productivity, reduce pollution, and promote environmentally sustainable development. In the environmental era, businesses have used green innovation as a key green strategy. The study is most relevant to the context of how green HRM practices can propel an organization toward green innovation and how these HRM practices are associated with environmental performance through green innovation (Yong, Yusliza, and Fawehinmi 2020). The goal of the current study is to shed insight into the effects of green recruiting and green training on environmental performance. Moreover, it has been examined how green innovation impacts and acts as a mediator between green HR practices and environmental performance.

2. Literature Review

Organisational sustainability is the major concern nowadays for academics and practitioners Green human resource management practices play a key role in advancing organizational sustainability. Companies are now seeking for green practices to continuously develop their employees so they can handle environmental concerns. The relationship between these practices and environmental effects can be mediated by green psychological empowerment, competence, and self-determination (Rashid & Qaseer 2022). Moreover, for the company's continuous competitive advantage and exceptional performance, GHRM procedures actively identify, inspire, and expand employee behaviour. So, the study of (Awwad Al-Shammari et al. 2022) revealed that sustainable performance of SMEs is positively and significantly influenced by green human resource management practices. Further, the study of (Fang et al. 2022) analysed that Green innovation and green culture effectively and sustainably mediate the relationship between GHRM and environmental performance. Furthermore, Employees' inclinations for green innovation boost their psychological response of enthusiasm, which has a favourable impact on their intent to remain with the organization. (Ubeda-Garcia et al., 2022) described that the literature on organizational behavior and strategic management is paying more attention to green innovation. However, there hasn't been much research done on how employees feel about working for companies that have innovative environmental practices. The study on green ambidexterity acts as a mediator in the relationship between the green high-performance work systems (GPWS) and sustainability practices. The findings show that GHPWS promotes the growth of "green ambidexterity" and that this characteristic helps people perform better for the environment. However, the study of (Hussain et al. 2021). Examined that Green human resource management and environmental performance are not directly correlated. Green innovation, on the other hand, acts as a mediator in the interaction between environmental performance and green human resource management. From the view point of (Arora & Kaul 2020) the most prominent green HRM functions within these firms are green recruitment, green training and development, and green safety and health management, whereas the least common green HRM function is green performance appraisal. The banking and financial industry is the least willing to implement green HRM, whereas the IT services sector uses green HRM the most actively. (Sakharina et al. 2020) analysed that Green training improves employee's awareness regarding environmental issues and to possess in-depth knowledge of complex environmental issues, and to have a clear grasp of how the environment affects their working conditions. It is anticipated that businesses aiming to achieve great environmental performance will hire employees with increased environmental awareness and competences. (Hadjri et al., 2019) described that GRS, GTR, and GCO, which make up the GHRM variables, all had favourable effects on GOC and EP. The findings of this study further demonstrate that GRS and GCO have an indirect influence on EP through GOC; however, GTR does not have an indirect influence on EP through GOC as an intervening variable. (Sinaga and Nawangsari 2019) analysed in their study that employee performance is crucial to a business because it has the potential to impact organizational performance. As a result of this organization's green hiring and training practices have a positive effect on employee performance.

3. Need and Significance of the Study

A growing concern for the environment and the use of green management practices has given the research huge relevance in organizations. Green innovation is a wider concept that is employed in all organizations because it is used to uphold environmentally friendly behaviour within the organizational context to minimize waste and boost efficiency by effectively using resources. Employees having competencies to uphold green practices in the firms are recruited through green human resource techniques. Therefore, the "green" concept is typically vital for managing a company's operations and providing a secure atmosphere for the expansion of an organization.

4. Research Objectives

- To observe the effect of green recruitment on environmental performance.
- To observe the effect of green training on environmental performance.
- To examine the impact of green innovation on environmental performance.
- To examine the mediating effect of green innovation in the relationship between green recruitment, green training, and environmental performance.

5. Research Methodology

In the present study, primary data was gathered using a structured questionnaire that included sections about respondents' social and economic circumstances as well as inquiries about the key variables (green HRM practices, including green hiring and training), green innovation, and environmental performance. The Partial Least Square Structural Equation Modeling (PLS-SEM) method was used in the analysis with Smart PLS-4. A total of 69 responses were received, of which 58 were considered pertinent to the study, for a response rate of 65%. The questionnaire was designed to elicit responses on the four key constructs of our study: GHRM practices (green recruitment and training), green innovation, and environmental performance.

6. Hypothesis Development

Based on the above discussion, the following hypothesis is made for this research:

H1: Green Recruitment has a significant impact on environmental performance.

H2: Green Training has a significant impact on environmental performance.

H3: Green Recruitment has a significant impact on green innovation.

H4: Green Training has a significant impact on green innovation.

H5: Green innovation has a significant impact on environmental performance.

H6: Green innovation mediates the relationship between GHRM practices and environmental performance

7. Data Analysis and Result

7.1 Descriptive Analysis

The demographics of the respondents are examined using frequency and percentage in descriptive analysis. The following table lists the outcomes of the descriptive analysis:

Table 25.1 Profile of respondents

Variable	Category	Frequency	Percentage
Age	18-30	46	79.3
	31-40	10	17.2
	41-50	2	3.4
Gender	Male	36	62.1
	Female	22	37.9
Education	Schooling	1	1.7
	Diploma	4	6.9
	Graduate	20	34.5
	Postgraduate	25	43.1
	Professional course	8	13.8
Designation	Office Assistant	6	10.3
	Support associate	6	10.3
	Clerk	6	10.3
	Educator	21	36.2
	Officer	8	13.8
	Engineer	1	1.7
	Doctor	2	3.4
Sector	Public	26	44.8
	Private	32	55.2
Type of sector	Corporate	12	20.7
	Services	46	79.3
Work experience	Less than 3	24	41.4
	3-5	16	27.6
	6-10	12	20.7
	11-15	4	6.9
	Above 15	2	3.4

Source: Primary survey of respondents

Table 25.1 depicts the demographic information about the organization's staff that was provided by the respondents; 79.3% of respondents were involved between the ages of 18 and 30, and 17.2% were involved between the ages of 31 and 40. About 62.1 percent are male, and the remaining 37.9 percent are female. 43.1 percent are at the postgraduate level, and 34.5 percent are at the graduate level. In addition, 13.8 percent of respondents in this survey were officers whereas 36.2 percent of respondents were educators. About 44.8 percent are from the public sector, 55.2 percent are from the private sector, of which 20.7 percent are from the corporate sector, and 79.3 percent are from the service sector. The majority of respondents (41.4 percent) had less than 3 years of work experience, with just 27.6 percent having between 3-5 years of work experience.

7.2 Measurement Model

The evaluation of the measurement model is used to access the constructs' quality. The analysis of the factor loadings is the first step in the assessment of the quality criteria, which is then followed by determining the construct reliability and validity. Two items (GR3 and GT1) that had low factor loadings (<0.600) were eliminated from the study. The study utilized Cronbach's alpha and composite reliability to evaluate the constructs' reliability (CR). Each construct had a Cronbach's alpha that was higher than the required 0.700. The Average Variance Extracted (AVE) was greater than 0.5, indicating convergent validity acceptable. Table 25.2 and Fig. 25.1 of the measurement model both show the results for the items' factor loadings,

Table 25.2 Loadings, Reliability, and Validity

Construct	Items	Loadings	Cronbach alpha	Composite Reliability	AVE
Environmental Performance	EP1	1.000			
Green Innovation	GI1	0.922	0.813	0.914	0.842
	GI2	0.914			
Green Recruitment	GR1	0.951	0.884	0.945	0.896
	GR2	0.942			
Green Training	GT2	0.956	0.911	0.957	0.918
	GT3	0.960			

Source: Primary survey of respondents

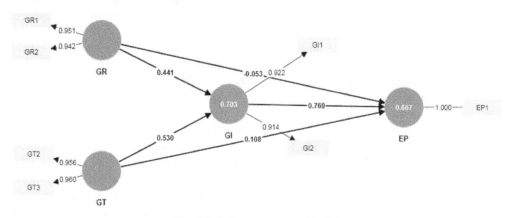

Fig. 25.1 Measurement Model

Source: Author's compilation

reliability and validity. Based on the Fornell-Larcker criterion, which was used to determine the discriminant validity, the square root of the AVE for the construct was higher than the inter-construct correlation, as shown in Table 25.3. The Heterotrait-Monotrait ratios of correlations with values below the criterion of 0.90 were used to evaluate the discriminant validity of the data as shown in Table 25.4.

Table 25.3 Fornell-Larcker Criterion

	EP	GI	GR	GT
EP	1.000			
GI	0.813	0.918		
GR	0.538	0.700	0.946	
GT	0.655	0.745	0.489	0.958

Note: Square-root of AVE values are indicated by italics, Here EP = Environmental Performance, GI= Green Innovation, GR= Green Recruitment, GT= Green Training.

Source: Primary survey of respondents

Table 25.4 Heterotrait-Monotrait (HTMT) ratios

	EP	GI	GR	GT
EP				
GI	0.900			
GR	0.571	0.826		
GT	0.687	0.865	0.543	

Source: Primary survey of respondents

7.3 Structural Model

The paths proposed in the research framework are reflected in the structural model. Based on the R2, R2 adjusted, and significance of paths, a structural model is evaluated. The value of R2 for the dependent variable, which should be equal to or over 0.1, determines the strength of each structural path and thus the validity of the model (Falk & Miller, 1992). All of the R2 values in Table 25.5 are over 0.10, which demonstrates the model's strong predictive accuracy. To determine the significance of the relationship, further evaluations of the goodness of fit were undertaken. H1 determines whether GR has a significant impact on EP. The findings showed that GR has an insignificant effect on EP as indicated in Fig. 25.2, ($\beta = -0.053$), $t = 0.428$, $p = 0.669$. Therefore H1 was not supported. H2 evaluates whether GT has a significant impact on EP. The results showed that GT has an insignificant impact on EP. ($\beta = 0.108$, $t = 0.705$, p=0.481. Hence, H2 was not supported. H3 assesses whether GR has a significant impact on GI. The outcomes revealed that GR has a significant impact on GI. ($\beta = 0.441$, $t = 4.046$, p=0.000). So, H3 was supported. H4 analyzes whether GT has a significant impact on GI. The results revealed that GT has a significant impact on GI. ($\beta = 0.530$, $t = 5.048$, $p = 0.000$). So, H4 was supported. H5 evaluates whether GI a significant impact has on EP. The

Table 25.5 Hypothesis testing

Hypothesis	β	SD	T statistics	P values	Results
GR -> EP	-0.053	0.124	0.428	0.669	Not supported
GT -> EP	0.108	0.153	0.705	0.481	Not supported
GR -> GI	0.441	0.109	4.046	0.000	Supported
GT -> GI	0.530	0.105	5.048	0.000	Supported
GI -> EP	0.769	0.147	5.233	0.000	Supported
	R²		R² adjusted		
EP	0.667	EP	0.649		
GI	0.703	GI	0.692		

Note: GR = Green Recruitment, GT = Green Training, GI = Green Innovation, β = Beta Coefficient, SD = Standard Deviation, P values = Probability value.

Source: Primary survey of respondents

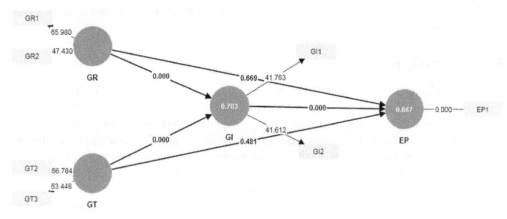

Fig. 25.2 Structural Model

Source: Author's compilation

outcomes revealed that GI has a significant impact on EP. ($\beta = 0.769$, $t = 5.233$, $p = 0.000$). Therefore, H5 was supported.

7.4 Mediation Analysis

Assessment of the mediating role of Green Innovation was done through mediation analysis. The outcomes revealed as shown in Table 25.6 significant ($p < 0.05$) mediating role of GI. (H6a: $\beta = 0.339$, $t = 2.895$, $p = 0.004$) which mediates the relationship between GR and EP whereas, H6b: $\beta = 0.407$, $t = 3.905$, $p = 0.000$) which also mediates the relationship between GT and EP.

Table 25.6 Mediation analysis

	Total Effect	T value	Sig	Direct Effect	Sig		Effect	T statistics	Sig
GR-EP	0.286	2.469	0.014	−0.053	0.669	GR -> GI -> EP	0.339	2.895	0.004
GT-EP	0.515	4.036	0.000	0.108	0.481	GT -> GI -> EP	0.407	3.905	0.000

Source: Primary survey of respondents

8. Implications of the Study

The results of this study may be used to assist firms in setting environmental strategic goals that are associated with GHRM green and innovation activities. Employee involvement in developing environmental policies is therefore likely to be very strong. A company's long-term sustainability may be increased by implementing an environmental management approach. The study also enables managers to concentrate their GHRM initiatives that improve employee motivation and knowledge levels while also enhancing HR advancements. To lessen barriers to GI adoption, which in turn helps firms go green, management should maintain alignment in its human resource processes.

9. Conclusion

The study examined the role of GHRM Practices-Green Recruitment and Green Training in improving Environmental Performance by exploring its direct and mediated effects through Green Innovation. The finding of the study shows that GR and GT have an insignificant impact on EP whereas GR and GT have a significant impact on GI and GI has a significant impact on EP. The research also examined the mediating role of green innovation, which revealed that it had a significant mediating impact between GR and EP as well as between GT and EP, indicating that green human resource management techniques are crucial for enhancing environmental performance by fostering more green innovation in the workplace. This fact may justify why Green Innovation is essential for organisations to improve environmental performance. Organizations may recruit, engage, and maintain Green people for sustainable innovation by implementing GHRM practices. Based on the study's findings, to gain a competitive advantage in the market, the company should employ realistic GHRM tactics and strategies to attract and retain green personnel for green technology. So it is concluded that if firm employees engage themselves in the green human resource management conjecture, they retain great enthusiasm to embrace the green idea.

REFERENCES

1. Arora, Mamta, and Arpita Kaul. 2020. "Green Human Resource Management: An Empirical Study of India." *Visegrad Journal on Bioeconomy and Sustainable Development* 9 (2): 61–66. https://doi.org/10.2478/vjbsd-2020-0012.

2. Awwad Al-Shammari, Awwad Saad, Shaher Alshammrei, Nishad Nawaz, and Muhammad Tayyab. 2022. "Green Human Resource Management and Sustainable Performance With the Mediating Role of Green Innovation: A Perspective of New Technological Era." *Frontiers in Environmental Science* 10 (June): 1–12. https://doi.org/10.3389/fenvs.2022.901235.

3. Fang, Liuyue, Shengxu Shi, Jingzu Gao, and Xiayun Li. 2022. "The Mediating Role of Green Innovation and Green Culture in the Relationship between Green Human Resource Management and Environmental Performance." *PLoS ONE* 17 (9 September): 1–24. https://doi.org/10.1371/journal.pone.0274820.

4. Fazal-e-Hasan, Syed Muhammad, Hormoz Ahmadi, Harjit Sekhon, Gary Mortimer, Mohd Sadiq, Husni Kharouf, and Muhammad Abid. 2022. "The Role of Green Innovation and Hope in Employee Retention." *Business Strategy and the Environment*. https://doi.org/10.1002/bse.3126.

5. Hadjri, Muhammad Ichsan, Badia Perizade, Zunaidah, and Wita Farla. 2019. "Green Human Resource Management, Green Organizational Culture, and Environmental Performance: An Empirical Study" 100 (Icoi): 138–43. https://doi.org/10.2991/icoi-19.2019.25.

6. Hussain, Iftikhar, Mehrab Nazir, Qurrahtulain Khan, Saadullah Shah, and Azad Jammu. 2021. "Linking Green Human Resource Practices and Environmental Performance: The Role of Green Innovation as Mediator and Environmental Strategy as Moderator." *RADS Journal of Business Management* 3 (2): 179–93. https://jbm.juw.edu.pk/index.php/jbm/article/view/68.

7. Management, Magister, Mercu Buana, Magister Management, and Mercu Buana. 2020. "Authentic Happiness As a Mediator of Learning Organization" 2 (1): 112–24. https://doi.org/10.31933/DIJMS.

8. Rashid, S A R, and M A Al Qaseer. 2022. "Testing The Mediating Role Of Green Psychological Empowerment Of Employees In Enhancing The Relationship Between Green Human Resource Management ...." *Journal of Positive School ...* 6 (6): 3138–53. https://journalppw.com/index.php/jpsp/article/view/7815%0Ahttps://journalppw.com/index.php/jpsp/article/download/7815/5107.

9. Ridhi, Sharma. 2015. "An Innovative Approach to Environmental Sustainability." *12th AIMS International Conference on Management*, no. June: 1–15. https://www.academia.edu/download/36500376/K723-final.pdf.

10. Sakharina, Iin Karita, Kadarudin, Farida Patittingi, Muh Hasrul, Birkah Latif, and Sukri Palutturi. 2020. "The Impact of Green Human Resource Practices on Environmental Performance." *Polish Journal of Management Studies* 22 (2): 470–86. https://doi.org/10.17512/pjms.2020.22.2.31.

11. Ubeda-Garcia, Mercedes, Bartolome Marco-Lajara, Patrocinio C. Zaragoza-Sáez, Encarnación Manresa-Marhuenda, and Esther Poveda-Pareja. 2022. "Green Ambidexterity and Environmental Performance: The Role of Green Human Resources." *Corporate Social Responsibility and Environmental Management* 29 (1): 32–45. https://doi.org/10.1002/csr.2171.

12. Yong, Jing Yi, M. Y. Yusliza, and Olawole Olanre Fawehinmi. 2020. "Green Human Resource Management: A Systematic Literature Review from 2007 to 2019." *Benchmarking* 27 (7): 2005–27. https://doi.org/10.1108/BIJ-12-2018-0438.

Handbook of Evidence Based Management Practices in Business – Satyendra Kumar Sharma et al. (eds)
© 2023 Taylor & Francis Group, London, ISBN 978-1-032-54216-4

Chapter

An Integrative Framework of Employees' Flourishing-at-work

Meera Peethambaran[1], Mohammad Faraz Naim[2] and Saurabh Sugha[3]
Department of Management,
Birla Institute of Technology and Science Pilani, Pilani, India

ABSTRACT: Purpose—The main purpose of this paper is to present a conceptual framework, proposing the association among empowering leadership, employee work passion, and flourishing-at-work.

Design/methodology/approach—Based on the extensive literature review and employing conservation of resource theory (COR) and self-determination theory (SDT), this study proposes a conceptual framework connecting empowering leadership, employee work passion, and flourishing-at-work.

Findings—Empowering leaders promoted employee work passion, contributing to employees' well-being (flourishing). The study also demonstrates employee work passion as a crucial link between empowering leadership and employee flourishing.

Research limitations—The proposed framework lacks empirical validation.

Practical implications—Significant contributions have been made to the existing literature on flourishing-at-work by providing new insights into how empowering leadership contributes to employee work passion, resulting in flourishing.

Originality/value—This is the only study to propose the role of employee work passion as a possible conceptual link between empowering leadership and employee flourishing. This paper emphasizes the importance of flourishing-at-work in the current climate of rising mental tensions among employees, which leads to adverse organizational outcomes.

KEYWORDS: Empowering leadership, Employee work passion, Flourishing-at-work, Employee flourishing

[1]P20210037@pilani.bits-pilani.ac.in, [2]mfaraz.naim@pilani.bits-pilani.ac.in, [3]P20210123@pilani.bits-pilani.ac.in

DOI: 10.4324/9781003415725-26

1. Introduction

Irrespective of the time and tide, employee well-being has always attracted considerable attention in a VUCA (Volatile, Uncertain, Complex, and Ambiguous) work environment. In the wake of an unprecedented catastrophe, such as the COVID-19 pandemic, the importance of employee well-being has been boosted to its peak. According to a recent study, the pandemic has accelerated the reported cases of psychological and emotional stress among Indian employees, resulting in a 95% increase in online consultations for mental health issues (Ians, 2021). Similarly, the World Health Organization estimates a global economic loss of $1.03 trillion (between 2012 and 2022) due to the deteriorating mental health of employees (WHO, 2022). Notably, the pandemic has contributed to this sudden shift in employee perspective and expanded the global importance of employee well-being. It is corroborated by research that seven in ten Indians are more likely to prioritize health and well-being over work (Vidya, 2022). Employees now have a new 'worth it' equation where their expectation from work and what they are willing to give in return has changed. All these highlight the importance of employee well-being in an organization.

In accordance with the resource-based view, human capital is regarded as the most crucial factor in determining an organization's competitive edge (Shaw, Park and Kim, 2013). Thus, ensuring employees' emotional, psychological, and social well-being (flourishing) is critical (Naim and Ozyilmaz, 2022). However, addressing employee well-being at the workplace requires supportive leaders. Empowering leadership is one such leadership style to boost positive employee outcomes. Empowering leadership is defined as a set of actions taken by a leader to increase his subordinates' task-related intrinsic motivation and decrease their feelings of powerlessness (Thomas and Velthouse, 1990). Scholars have widely explored the role of empowering leadership on different dimensions of well-being (Mustikarini, Melinda and Octavia, 2022). Despite the scholarly attention given to the link between empowering leadership and well-being, there is still a void in literature identifying the underlying mechanism of the relationship between the two. Therefore, considering this research gap, we have attempted to propose the effect of empowering leadership on flourishing-at-work with employee work passion as the underlying link.

Employee work passion plays a pivotal role in work performance and well-being (Li, Zhang, Shao and Chen, 2019). In addition, work passion positively influences job satisfaction and the well-being of employees (Alam and Shin, 2021). Moreover, passionate employees tend to display several other positive attitudes and behaviors in the workplace. Thus by considering the positive outcomes of employee work passion, we have taken it as the mediating variable in our study. Finally, the study utilized the theoretical support of the conservation of resource theory and self-determination theory to strengthen the propositions further. Therefore, the current study will undoubtedly enhance the literature by providing theoretical and managerial implications that would further nourish the knowledge of the academicians and practitioners. Moreover, the study also provides significant research gaps that must be addressed.

2. Theory and Conceptual Framework

2.1 Empowering Leadership and Employee Work Passion

An empowering leadership style is generally viewed as a compassionate kind of leadership that corresponds more with contemporary HRM approaches than traditional HRM approaches. Empowering leadership is conceptualized as a process in which leaders provide employees with more autonomy and authority to increase employees' motivation at work (Zhang and Bartol, 2010). Generally, empowering leadership behaviors include fostering employee participation in decision-making, granting autonomy from bureaucratic constraints, and expressing confidence in high performance (Na-Nan, Kanthong and Khummueng, 2020).

One of the unique characteristics of empowering leadership is its ability to enhance employees' motivation and sense of autonomy at work (Coun et al., 2022). It seems desirable for empowering leaders to give their employees autonomy to challenge the status quo and make constructive changes that may lead to a passion for work (Liu, Chen and Yao, 2011). In addition, empowering leaders increases employees' obsessive passion by triggering external motivation for one's internalization of work (Hao, He and Long, 2018). As a result, employees reporting to an empowering leader are expected and encouraged to complete their work independently using the power and other resources delegated by empowering leaders (Vecchio, Justin and Pearce, 2010). Moreover, self-determination theory argues that an individual's attitude and investment in an activity are shaped by fulfilling their basic psychological needs like autonomy, competence, and relatedness (Deci and Ryan, 2002). Here empowering leadership provides and satisfies the employee's basic psychological needs and boosts their passion for work (Thibault-Landry et al., 2018). Therefore, the extant scholarship suggests that empowering leadership has a significant positive effect on employee work passion (Appienti and Chen, 2019; Hao, He and Long, 2018). Thus we propose that:

P1: Empowering leadership is positively associated with employee work passion.

2.2 Employee Work Passion and Flourishing-at-work

According to the employee work passion appraisal (EWPA) model, work passion is defined as "an individual's persistent, emotionally positive, meaning-based state of well-being stemming from reoccurring cognitive and affective appraisals of various job and organizational situations that result in consistent, constructive work intentions and behaviors" (Zigarmi et al., 2009, p. 310). Passion for work can be further segregated into harmonious and obsessive passion for work.

Past research has highlighted that passion contributes positively to an individual's well-being, life satisfaction, and happiness (Halonen and Lomas, 2014). Studies reveal that even for academicians, being passionate about their work leads to more happiness and a sense of well-being (Moè, 2016). Likewise, Yukhymenko-Lescroart and Sharma (2019) found that faculties who are passionate about their work and doesn't feel it as a conflict with other parts of their lives (harmonious passion for their work) are more likely to be happy and satisfied with their life. Harmonious passion is not dependent on whether an activity is successful or unsuccessful.

Thus, harmonious passion is a more stable predictor of life satisfaction and consistent well-being.

Another recent study found that harmonious passion is positively associated with positive emotions and results in positive outcomes in the educational domain (complete satisfaction in studies and performance in studies) and also shows vitality, resulting in thriving in one's life (Paquette et al., 2022). Since harmonious and obsessive passion shows significant association with the different domains of well-being and thriving (Feeling and functioning well in the workplace), here in our study, we propose that:

P2: Employee work passion is positively associated with flourishing-at-work.

2.3 Mediating Role of Employee Work Passion

Further, we propose that employee work passion is an emotional, motivational, and behavioral link between empowering leadership and flourishing at work. Firstly, according to self-determination theory, a leader who empowers his or her team members will undoubtedly increase their harmonious and obsessive passion (Deci and Ryan, 2008; Vallerand et al., 2003). Moreover, through the lens of conservation of resource theory empowering leadership practices will initially boost employees' financial, cognitive, and social resources, thereby reducing their stress and fostering their well-being perceptions. Similarly, passion in the workplace can be defined as a consistent sense of well-being and a strong inclination toward one's work (Liu, Chen, and Yao, 2011; Zigarmi et al., 2009). Therefore, this consistently high level of well-being will ultimately result in the flourishing of employees at work. Thus, we propose that-

P3: Employee work passion mediates the positive association between empowering leadership and flourishing-at-work.

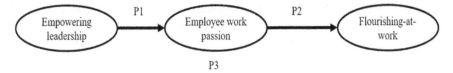

Fig. 26.1 Proposed conceptual framework

Source: Author's compilation

3. Discussion and Implications

This study explores a possible linkage among empowering leadership, employee work passion, and flourishing-at-work. The proposed conceptual framework elucidates the role of empowering leadership in developing employee work passion, leading to a feeling of flourishing-at-work. Interestingly, for this work, we have incorporated employee passion as an underlying mechanism explaining the relationship between empowering leadership and flourishing-at-work. The framework is based on the theoretical underpinnings of COR theory and SDT.

Empowering leadership is considered as one of the most effective leadership styles in times of uncertainty. The study by Coun and colleagues (2021) found that empowering leadership has a significant role in remote work, where employees demand autonomy and motivation. It is also asserted that empowering leadership or employee empowerment increases employees' creativity, motivation, and opportunities to generate, share, and implement novel ideas (Appelbaum et al., 2014). Microsoft is one such company that empowers employees by providing active involvement in decision-making (Alex, 2021). Moreover, studies have found that empowering leaders' ideal level of empowerment can foster the employees' work passion (Appienti and Chen, 2019). Similarly, according to COR theory empowering leadership communicates cognitive, financial, and social resources that spur employees' work passion by providing them with resources to recoup for future use and ensure their well-being (Hobfoll, 2001). Furthermore, SDT suggests that empowering leaders will stimulate the intrinsic and extrinsic motivation of employees and helps them in boosting work passion by providing autonomy, motivation, and a participative environment (Roy, 2022).

The study has provided significant theoretical contributions to the emerging literature on flourishing-at-work by providing new insight into how empowering leadership influences flourishing-at-work via employee work passion. Specifically, the study framework highlights a theoretical linkage between empowering leadership and flourishing-at-work. Another notable aspect is that employee work passion is conceptualized as an underlying link between the two variables. This is one of the first studies of its kind to explore empowering leadership to strengthen employees' flourishing-at-work and link employee work passion with flourishing-at-work.

To elucidate the managerial implication of the proposed framework, its essential to discuss the current well-being scenario of the Indian workforce. Similarly, a study conducted by Assocham (Tech company association) shows that 43% of private sector Indian employees suffer from mental health issues resulting from stress in the workplace. Moreover, according to Microsoft's annual report, 2022 Work Trend Index, 65 percent (62% in 2021) of Indian employees are dissatisfied with their job and are planning to change. Therefore, running a successful business with an Indian workforce will be challenging if management disregards sensitive issues that affect employees' psychological, emotional, and social well-being at the workplace (flourishing-at-work).To gain a competitive advantage and ensure a company's long-term survival in the current global market, it is essential to promote employee flourishing in the workplace (Rothmann, 2013).To an extent, the proposed conceptual framework of our study ensures employees' flourishing-at-work, resulting in a win-win situation for both the employees and the organizations. In this view, empowering leadership behaviors, including providing autonomy, decision-making powers, participative decision-making, and empowerment, contribute to the feeling of being passionate about work, which translates into a sense of holistic well-being (flourishing). Therefore, it is recommended that managers and leaders must display empowering behaviors, and encourage more activities that foster employees' work passion, enabling them to flourish at work.

4. Conclusions and Future Avenues of Research

The present study provides a conceptual framework describing the relationship between empowering leadership and employees' flourishing-at-work, with employee work passion acting as the mediator. Even though the study provides intriguing insights, it has some limitations that can be converted into future research. The article was purely based on an extensive literature review and lacked empirical support. Therefore, the major limitation of this study as a conceptual paper is the lack of empirical validation of the proposed framework. Second, the study has only adopted a single leadership style, i.e., empowering leadership. Therefore, future researchers can conduct the study using other emerging leadership styles like resonant leadership, servant leadership, and other organizational-level variables.

Third, the study lacks potential moderators like trust in leadership, organizational trust, psychological need fulfilment, and psychological capital that can control the degree of relationship between the variables used in the study. Fourth, future research can test the proposed framework using longitudinal data. Finally, to increase the generalizability of the research, we suggest that future researchers conduct the study by collecting samples from multiple industries.

REFERENCE

1. Alam, Mohammad Shahin, and DuckJung Shin. (2021). "A moderated mediation model of employee experienced diversity management: openness to experience, perceived visible diversity discrimination and job satisfaction". *International Journal of Manpower*, 42, no. 5, 733–755.
2. Amundsen, Stein, and Øyvind L. Martinsen. (2015). "Linking empowering leadership to job satisfaction, work effort, and creativity: The role of self-leadership and psychological empowerment". *Journal of leadership & organizational Studies*, 22, no. 3, 304–323.
3. Appienti, William Ansah, and Lu Chen. (2019). "Empowerment, passion and job performance: Implications from Ghana". *International Journal of Manpower*.
4. Appelbaum, Steven H., Robin Karasek, Francis Lapointe, and Kim Quelch. (2014). "Employee empowerment: factors affecting the consequent success or failure – Part I". *Industrial and Commercial Training*, 46, no. 7, 379–386.
5. Birkeland, Ide Katrine, and Robert Buch. (2015). "The dualistic model of passion for work: Discriminate and predictive validity with work engagement and workaholism". *Motivation and Emotion*, 39, no. 3, 392–408.
6. Coun, Martine JH, Robin Edelbroek, Pascale Peters, and Robert J. Blomme. (2021). "Leading innovative work-behavior in times of COVID-19: Relationship between leadership Style, innovative work-behavior, work-related flow, and IT-Enabled presence awareness during the first and second wave of the COVID-19 pandemic". *Frontiers in Psychology*, 4274.
7. Deci, Edward L., and Richard M. Ryan. (2002), "Self-determination research: Reflections and future directions".
8. Halonen, Susanna M., and Tim Lomas. (2014). "A passionate way of being: A qualitative study revealing the passion spiral". *International Journal of Psychological Research*, 7, no. 2, 17–28.
9. Hao, Po, Wei He, and Li-Rong Long. (2018). "Why and when empowering leadership has different effects on employee work performance: The pivotal roles of passion for work and role breadth self-efficacy". *Journal of Leadership & Organizational Studies*, 25, no. 1, 85–100.
10. Hobfoll, Stevan E. (2001). "The influence of culture, community, and the nested-self in the stress process: Advancing conservation of resources theory". *Applied psychology*, 50, no.3, 337–421.
11. Ians, I. A. N. S. (2021) "Nearly 43 per cent of employees in private sector in India suffer from mental health issues at work: Study. *Free Press Journal*. November 23.

12. JH Coun, Martine, Pascale Peters, Robert J. Blomme, and Jaap Schaveling (2022). "To empower or not to empower, that's the question'. Using an empowerment process approach to explain employees' workplace proactivity". *The International Journal of Human Resource Management*, 33, no. 14, 2829–2855.

13. Kim, Daeho, Chul Woo Moon, and Jiseon Shin. (2018). "Linkages between empowering leadership and subjective well-being and work performance via perceived organizational and co-worker support". *Leadership & Organization Development Journal*.

14. Kim, Minseo, and Terry A. Beehr. (2020). "Empowering leadership: leading people to be present through affective organizational commitment?". *The International Journal of Human Resource Management*, 31, no. 16, 2017–2044.

15. Li, Jingjing, Jian Zhang, Bo Shao, and Chunxiao Chen. (2019). "A latent profile analysis of work passion: structure, antecedent, and outcomes". *Personnel Review*, 49, no. 3, 846–863.

16. Liu, Dong, Xiao-Ping Chen, and Xin Yao. (2011). "From autonomy to creativity: a multilevel investigation of the mediating role of harmonious passion". *Journal of Applied Psychology*, 96, no. 2, p. 294.

17. Moe, Angelica. (2016). "Harmonious passion and its relationship with teacher well-being". *Teaching and Teacher Education*, 59, 431–437.

18. Mustikarini, Carolina Novi, Tina Melinda, and Maria Theresia Amadea Octavia. (2022). "The Influence Of Empowering Leadership On Psychological Well-Being And Job Engagement Mediated By Psychological Capital In Family Business Successors: Case Study At Family Business Community Eighth Batch Of Ciputra University". *Journal of Positive School Psychology*, 6, no. 9, 2864–2877.

19. Naim, Mohammad Faraz, and Adnan Ozyilmaz. (2022). "Flourishing-at-work and turnover intentions: does trust in management moderate the relationship?." *Personnel Review* ahead-of-print.

20. Na-Nan, Khahan, Suteeluck N. Kanthong, and Kattikamat Khummueng. (2020). "Development of an empowering leadership scale for salespeople: validation and reliability". *Industrial and Commercial Training*.

21. Paquette, V., Vallerand, R.J., Houlfort, N. and Fredrickson, B.L. (2022). "Thriving through Adversity: The Role of Passion and Emotions in the Resilience Process". *Journal of Personality*.

22. Rothmann, Sebastiaan. (2013). "From happiness to flourishing at work: A Southern African perspective. In Well-being research in South Africa". 123–151. Springer, Dordrecht.

23. S, Vidya. (2022). "Indians most likely to put health ahead of work: Microsoft study". *Business Today*. March 16.

24. Alex (2021). "10 inspiring employee empowerment examples. Matterapp. September 12.

25. Shaw, Jason D., Tae-Youn Park, and Eugene Kim (2013). "A resource-based perspective on human capital losses, HRM investments, and organizational performance". *Strategic management journal*, 34 , no.5, 572–589.

26. Thibault-Landry, Anaïs, Richard Egan, Laurence Crevier-Braud, Lara Manganelli, and Jacques Forest. (2018). " An empirical investigation of the employee work passion appraisal model using self-determination theory". *Advances in Developing Human Resources*, 20, no.2, 148–168.

27. Thomas, Kenneth W., and Betty A. Velthouse. (1990). "Cognitive elements of empowerment: An "interpretive" model of intrinsic task motivation". Academy of management review. 15, no. 4, 666–681.

28. Vallerand, Robert J., and Nathalie Houlfort. "Passion at work". *Emerging perspectives on values in organizations*, 6, no. 8, 175–204.

29. Vecchio, Robert P., Joseph E. Justin, and Craig L. Pearce. (2010), "Empowering leadership: An examination of mediating mechanisms within a hierarchical structure". *The Leadership Quarterly*, 21, no. 3, 530–542.

30. Yukhymenko-Lescroart, Mariya A., and Gitima Sharma. (2019). "The relationship between faculty members' passion for work and well-being". *Journal of Happiness Studies*, 20, no. 3, 863–881.
31. Zhang, Xiaomeng, and Kathryn M. Bartol. (2010), "Linking empowering leadership and employee creativity: The influence of psychological empowerment, intrinsic motivation, and creative process engagement". *Academy of management journal*, 53, no. 1, 107–128.
32. Zigarmi, Drea, Kim Nimon, Dobie Houson, David Witt, and Jim Diehl (2009). "Beyond engagement: Toward a framework and operational definition for employee work passion". *Human Resource Development Review*, 8, no. 3, 300–326.

Chapter

Does Learning Enhance the Psychological Well-Being of Employees at Work? A Pilot Exploration

Anurag Chadha[1]

OB&HR, Indian Institute of Management, Indore, India

Raina Chhajer[2]

OB&HR, Indian Institute of Management, Indore, India

ABSTRACT: Learning is an important facet of employee's productivity, satisfaction and happiness. It's well known that learning improves the job performance as it helps in acquiring new skills. Psychological well-being also leads to better employee satisfaction and enhances the organization performance. Learning can also enhance the psychological well-being of employees. An exploratory study was conducted among 107 working professions to test this correlation. From the analysis it was inferred that learning and psychological well-being have a positive corelation. This has direct implications for employees, leaders and organizations to improve performance.

KEYWORDS: Learning, Organisation performance, Psychological well-being

1. Introduction

Ryff coined the term psychological well-being along with other two attributes which are emotional well-being and social well-being (Ryff 1989). He also defined the psychological well-being as collective of 6 attributes which are Self-acceptance, Personal growth, Purpose in life, Explained Mastery, Autonomy, and Positive relations. Psychological well-being can lead to better employee satisfaction and also enhances the organization performance (Waddell and Pio 2015). Organizations have a need to focus on the psychological well-being.

[1]anurag.chadha@iiml.org, [2]rainac@iimidr.ac.in

DOI: 10.4324/9781003415725-27

Learning is a continuous cycle and the knowledge can be acquired, shared or combined. (Carmeli, Brueller, and Dutton 2009). It helps the employees to grow and to understand the business environment in a better way. Learning is deeply affected by the leadership style (Bhat et al. 2012). Focus on learning should be from the employee's side and leader's side. Proactiveness shown by the employees to learn helps them to perform better. This leads to personal growth over a period of time (Michie and Zumitzavan 2012).

Learning can deeply impact the psychological well-being and there could be a corelation between the two. This need to be empirically tested so an exploratory study was conducted among working professionals. Age and work experience can also impact the psychological well-being. Three hypotheses were formed to test the corelations.

Hypotheses 1: Age does not have a direct corelation with psychological well-being.

Hypotheses 2: Work experience does not have a direct corelation with psychological well-being.

Hypotheses 3: Learning does not have any impact on psychological well-being.

2. Literature Review

Organizations constantly face changing market conditions due to business and technological changes, therefore the employees who actively engage in learning and upgrading become important resources of competitive advantage for the firms (Bezuijen et al. 2010). Besides learning, it is also becoming important for the businesses to consider the well-being of employees for competitive advantage.

Literature review was done on Scopus and WOS across 50 journals to get the details. Post review two key themes emerged. Firstly, Need for employee learning and its impact on organization performance and secondly Importance of employee well-being, and connection between learning and well-being.

2.1 Need for Employee Learning and its Impact on Organisation Performance

Learning activities are discretionary behaviours of employees to master new skills, acquire new knowledge and gain new abilities. Employees learning is becoming an essential prerequisite for organisational competitiveness and adaptability (Bezuijen et al. 2010).

Learning happens through trainings and informally by performing the task itself and by group learning (Green et al. 2015). Learning by individuals depends on the absorptive capacity of employees. Absorptive Capacity can be defined as ability of members to value the new information, assimilate it and then apply it for the commercial ends (Tian and Soo 2018).

Leader Member Theory (LMX) mentions that the relationship between leaders and managers also mediates the learning (Bezuijen et al. 2010). Job designs also influences the learning process for employees because the job characteristics stimulates the process of learning (Holman et al. 2012).

2.2 Importance of Employee Well-being, and Connection Between Learning and Well-being

Wellbeing is affected by both engagement and burnout. Engagement helps in building positive emotions and burnout is negative emotion. Employees who are able to spend leisure time fully detached from work, experience high engagement and well-being at work (Leonardo A. Medrano and Mario A. Trógolo 2018). Well-being is higher for employees who have higher perceived employability as they have control on jobs and can manage situations effectively (Linde Bennie et al. 2015).

The organisation needs to assist employees to learn the ways to manage the ambiguities. Transformational leadership in this plays an important role and has strong influence on well-being of the employees (Rita Berger et al. 2019). Spirituality also supports employee well-being and organisational performance. It improves the quality of life of employees, gives a sense of purpose in work and provides interconnectedness in communities (Karakas 2010).

Learning has been known to improve the employee effectiveness and performance. This productivity increase of the employees assists in their psychological well-being (Watson et al. 2018).

3. Methodology

To understand the relation between learning and psychological well-being, a survey was done among the working professionals. The expectation was to find whether the psychological well-being improves if the learning among the professionals was high.

3.1 Survey and Procedures

The survey was done on Google surveys to get the relevant information. It was circulated to only working professional having working experience of 2 years and above. It was sent to various groups of people ranging from different backgrounds and industries and finally got 107 responses of which 2 were not valid.

Of the total respondents, 67.3% were males and 32.7% were females. The age and working experience were two independent variables along with the questions on learning. The age distribution was nominal and had a good spread. Table 27.1 shows the descriptive analysis for the age and work experience.

Table 27.1 Descriptive analysis of age and work experience

Descriptive Analysis

	Age	Work Exp
N	105	105
Mean	45.2	20.1
Median	45	20
Standard deviation	7.16	7.94
Minimum	24	2
Maximum	66	40

Source: Author's compilation

3.2 Measures

The scale for learning was taken from the learning dimension of thriving given by Porth (Porath et al. 2012). The Likert scale was used on scale of 1 to 7 with 1 being Strongly Disagree and 7 being Strongly Agree (Porath et al. 2012). For the psychological well-being the measurement scale was based on the study done by Ryff and Singer (Ryff and Singer 1996). The Likert scale from 1 to 6 was used where 1 was for Strongly disagree and 6 was Strongly agree (Ryff and Keyes 1995).

3.3 Analysis

Each question was coded appropriately. The learning questions were coded as LDT 1 to LDT 6 and LDT 4 was reverse coded and then mentioned as LDT 4 (R). Similarly, the psychological well-being questions were coded as PWB 1 to PWB 6 and PWB 1, 3, 4 and 6 were reverse coded and were mentioned as PWB 1(R), PWB 3(R), PWB 4(R). PWB 6(R). The mean composite scores for LDT 1, 2, 3, 4(R), 5 was calculated and coded as LDT_MeanComposite score. Similarly, the mean composite score for PWB 1(R), PWB 2, PWB 3 (R), PWB 4 (R), PWB 5, PWB 6 (R) was calculated and coded as PWB_MeanComposite score. To improve the reliability score, the question 3 of PWB was dropped and new mean composite score was coded as PWB_MeanComposite V2.

4. Results

Reliability score was measured through Cornbach's α. The reliability score for all questions on learning was 0.778 which means the survey data is reliable for analysis. The mean for LDT_Meancomposite score is 5.92 and std deviation is 0.841. The reliability score PWB_MeanComposite V2 was 0.548 and was considered reasonable to consider data as reliable. The mean for PWB_Meancomposite score V2 is 4.65 and std deviation is 0.707.

Linear regression for age and PWB_Meancomposite Score V2 did not show encouraging results. The p value was 0.389 which states that there is no significant impact of age on psychological well-being and the hypothesis 1 cannot be rejected. The R^2 was 0.0183 which is very low. The linear regression was done on work experience and PWB_MeanComposite Score V2. The p value was 0.0318 and this shows that the test is not significant and the hypotheses 2 cannot be rejected. The R^2 value is also very low.

Partial correlation was done for LDT_MeanComposite and PWB_MeanComposite V2. The p value was less than 0.001 which shows that the test is significant and Hypothesis 3 is rejected. This means that there is a positive corelation between the learning dimension and psychological well-being based on the pearson r value of 0.424.

Lastly the regression was run for learning and psychological well-being. It was run on LDT_MeanComposite score and PWB_MeanComposite Score V2. The p value was less than 0.001 and it shows that there is a significant relationship between the two scores and also the R^2 value was 0.184 which showed positive dependence. This confirms that there is an impact of learning on psychological well-being.

To validate these results further regression was done considering all three independent variables together. Table 27.2 shows that the results were largely the same and showed that learning impacts the psychological well-being whereas there is no significant impact of age and work experience.

Table 27.2 Multiple regression data with all independent variables

Model Fit Measures

Model	R	R^2	F	df1	df2	p
				Overall Model Test		
1	0.436	0.190	5.88	4	100	< .001

Model Coefficients - PWB_MeanComposite Score V2

Predictor	Estimate	SE	t	p
Intercept [a]	2.8759	0.6908	4.163	< .001
LDT_MeanComposite	0.3489	0.0767	4.551	< .001
Age	-0.0102	0.0174	-0.588	0.558
Work Exp	0.0137	0.0164	0.840	0.403
Gender:				
Male – Female	-0.1550	0.1493	-1.038	0.302

[a] Represents reference level

Source: Author's compilation

5. Discussions and Conclusions

As the hypotheses 1 cannot be rejected, the psychological well-being is not dependent on the age of the employee. Also, the hypotheses 2 cannot be rejected, the psychological well-being is not dependent on work experience of employees.

When we run the regression for learning and psychological well-being then we get very different results. The *p* value in this case is less than 0.001 which signifies that the test is significant and hypothesis 3 can be rejected. When we take all the three independent variables together the R^2 increases to 0.19. Therefor the inference is that focus on learning has a positive corelation on psychological well-being.

These findings are useful to ascertain that when there is focus on learning by the employees then the psychological well-being of the respective employees will be higher. This research has direct implications for the leaders. It is the leader's need to focus on learning of employees. This will also be a great way to enhance the employee performance which can contribute to the organisational performance. It is also imperative that employees should also focus on self-learning which will contribute to the enhanced psychological well-being.

REFERENCES

1. Bezuijen, Xander M., Karen van Dam, Peter van den Berg, and Henk Thierry. 2010. "How Leaders Stimulate Employee Learning: A Leader-Member Exchange Approach." *Journal of Occupational and Organizational Psychology* 83 (3). https://search.ebscohost.com/login. aspx?direct=true&db=edsbig&AN=edsbig.A239955815&site=eds-live&scope=site.
2. Bhat, Aruna B., Neha Verma, S. Rangnekar, and M.k. Barua. 2012. "Leadership Style and Team Processes as Predictors of Organisational Learning." *Team Performance Management: An International Journal* 18 (7/8): 347–69. https://doi.org/10.1108/13527591211281101.

3. Carmeli, Abraham, Daphna Brueller, and Jane E. Dutton. 2009. "Learning Behaviours in the Workplace: The Role of High-Quality Interpersonal Relationships and Psychological Safety." *Systems Research and Behavioral Science* 26 (1). https://search.ebscohost.com/login. aspx?direct=true&db=edsbig&AN=edsbig.A194547953&site=eds-live&scope=site.

4. Green, Francis, Alan Felstead, Duncan Gallie, Ying Zhou, and Hande Inanc. 2015. "Direct Participation and Employee Learning at Work." *Work and Occupations* 42 (4). https://search. ebscohost.com/login.aspx?direct=true&db=edsbig&AN=edsbig.A442449370&site=eds-live&scope=site.

5. Holman, David, Peter Totterdell, Carolyn Axtell, Chris Stride, Rebecca Port, Ruth Svensson, and Lara Zibarras. 2012. "Job Design and the Employee Innovation Process: The Mediating Role of Learning Strategies." *Journal of Business and Psychology* 27 (2): 177–91.

6. Karakas, Fahri. 2010. "Spirituality and Performance in Organizations: A Literature Review." *Journal of Business Ethics* 94 (1): 89–106.

7. Leonardo A. Medrano and Mario A. Trógolo. 2018. "Employee Well-Being and Life Satisfaction in Argentina: The Contribution of Psychological Detachment from Work." *Journal of Work and Organizational Psychology* 34 (June): 069–069. https://doi.org/10.5093/jwop2018a9.

8. Linde Bennie, De Beer Leon, Cockeran Marike, and Van der Vaart Leoni. 2015. "Employee Well-Being, Intention to Leave and Perceived Employability : A Psychological Contract Approach." *South African Journal of Economic and Management Sciences* 18 (1): 32–44. https://doi. org/10.17159/2222-3436/2015/v18n1a3.

9. Michie, Jonathan, and Vissanu Zumitzavan. 2012. "The Impact of 'Learning' and 'Leadership' Management Styles on Organizational Outcomes: A Study of Tyre Firms in Thailand." *Asia Pacific Business Review* 18 (4): 607–30.

10. Porath, Christine, Gretchen Spreitzer, Cristina Gibson, and Flannery G. Garnett. 2012. "Thriving at Work: Toward Its Measurement, Construct Validation, and Theoretical Refinement." *Journal of Organizational Behavior* 33 (2): 250–75. https://doi.org/10.1002/job.756.

11. Rita Berger, Jan Philipp Czakert, Jan-Paul Leuteritz, and David Leiva. 2019. "How and When Do Leaders Influence Employees' Well-Being? Moderated Mediation Models for Job Demands and Resources." *Frontiers in Psychology* 10 (December). https://doi.org/10.3389/fpsyg.2019.02788.

12. Ryff, Carol D. 1989. "Happiness Is Everything, or Is It? Explorations on the Meaning of Psychological Well-Being." *Journal of Personality and Social Psychology* v57 (n6). https://search.ebscohost.com/ login.aspx?direct=true&db=edsbig&AN=edsbig.A8797699&site=eds-live&scope=site.

13. Ryff, Carol D., and Corey Lee M. Keyes. 1995. "The Structure of Psychological Well-Being Revisited." *Journal of Personality and Social Psychology* v69 (n4). https://search.ebscohost.com/ login.aspx?direct=true&db=edsbig&AN=edsbig.A17591434&site=eds-live&scope=site.

14. Ryff, Carol D., and Burton Singer. 1996. "Psychological Well-Being: Meaning, Measurement, and Implications for Psychotherapy Research." *Psychotherapy and Psychosomatics* 65 (1): 14–23.

15. Tian, Amy Wei, and Christine Soo. 2018. "Enriching Individual Absorptive Capacity." *Personnel Review* 47 (5): 1116–32. https://doi.org/10.1108/PR-04-2017-0110.

16. Waddell, Alex, and Edwina Pio. 2015. "The Influence of Senior Leaders on Organisational Learning: Insights from the Employees' Perspective." *MANAGEMENT LEARNING* 46 (4): 461–78. https://doi.org/10.1177/1350507614541201.

17. Watson, David, Olga Tregaskis, Cigdem Gedikli, Oluwafunmilayo Vaughn, and Antonina Semkina. 2018. "Well-Being through Learning: A Systematic Review of Learning Interventions in the Workplace and Their Impact on Well-Being." *EUROPEAN JOURNAL OF WORK AND ORGANIZATIONAL PSYCHOLOGY* 27 (2): 247–68. https://doi.org/10.1080/135943 2X.2018.1435529.

Handbook of Evidence Based Management Practices in Business – Satyendra Kumar Sharma et al. (eds)
© 2023 Taylor & Francis Group, London, ISBN 978-1-032-54216-4

Chapter

Effect of Human Resource Practices on Employees' Behavioral Outcome in Neyveli Lignite Corporation (NIC) India Ltd, Neyveli

R. Ramachandran*

Associate Professor, Department of Commerce, Annamalai University,
Annamalai Nagar, Tamil Nadu, India

ABSTRACT: Introduction—A department inside a corporation responsible for hiring, managing, and leading people is known as human resources. It places a focus on matters relating to pay, performance management, growth of an organization, safety, well-being, benefits, employee motivation, and training. It plays a strategic part in maintaining people in the work environment and circumstances. It may significantly contribute to the company's overall orientation and the accomplishment of its goals and objectives. The human resource management is a strategy created to successfully manage people in order to accomplish desired goals.

Scope of the study—It provides a stronger emphasis on administration that is more accessible, adaptable, and empathetic in order to inspire, develop, and manage staff members so they may give their all to support departmental operational effectiveness. Strong Human Resource Management (HRM) practices support the achievement of departmental goals and the maintenance of company respect.

Goal of the study—The purpose of the current concept is to ascertain how human resource procedures at NLC (Neyveli Lignite Corporation, Neyveli) India Ltd., Neyveli, affect employees' behavioural outcomes.

Methodology—Samples of 600 employees selected on simple random basis were studied. The statistical tools that were used to analyses the collected data are Regression and Path Analysis.

Main conclusions—The results and conclusions of the interpretations produced during the study of analysis to determine the utility of its application and the consequences for implementation plan are the findings and observations. Additionally, it promotes managerial policy development for its efficient operation as well as to uphold excellent ethics and morals.

**profram1968@gmail.com

DOI: 10.4324/9781003415725-28

KEYWORDS: Human resources practices, Organization behavioral outcome, Motivation and employees

1. Introduction

A human resource practice is one that works with enhancing competences, satisfaction, commitment, and culture development. Practices include items like procedures, activities, guidelines, laws, and ways of carrying out tasks. The organization's performance is significantly improved by the appropriate use of human resources. The three C's: Competencies, Commitment, and Culture are enriched by the practices in at least one way. They should be located and cost-effectively executed while being periodically reviewed and modified to improve their effectiveness and applicability.

Human resource management (HRM) in India has a position that is similar to HRM in other nations in a number of ways. They are all affected by the same elements, including corporate culture, awareness of legal requirements and constraints governing HRM activity, and policies and practices relating to skill sets and job competences. The primary goal is to assess and identify the human resource management strategies used by Indian businesses. By fostering a healthy work environment among workers that eliminates costs and waste and makes the best use of available financial resources, human resource management helps an organization effectively achieve its goals.

2. Related Review of Literature

After going through the conceptual components, the research is ready to be conducted to determine the research gap, and as a result, the reviews listed below have been compiled.

Heloíza H. Oliveira (2020) The majority of human resources practices have been found to have a considerable impact on organizational commitment, with affective and normative commitment being most influenced and continuation commitment being affected to a lesser extent. Multiple regressions were used to confirm the survey's developed assumptions, which were tested on 349 employees. The results revealed a higher prevalence of emotional commitment among employees, stronger agreement with the HR practice regarding benefits, and disagreement with career planning for the regulations regulating internal selection, self-development, remuneration policy, and promotion processes.

Timothy C. Bednall, Karin (2021) Our understanding of the connection between HR procedures and outcomes at the employee level has substantially grown as a consequence of research on human resource (HR) strengths. However, there is still a lot of unanswered research regarding the effect of workers' perceptions of HR strength on the connection between HR practises and these results. To address this issue, a meta-analysis of 42 research, 65 samples, and 29,444 different individuals was done. Positive findings are seen in the five worker outcomes—reactions, proactivity, burnout, performance, and perceived organizational productivity, which lend support to the mediation theory. However, employee performance was the only factor that supported the moderating hypothesis.

Manu Sharma, Sunil Luthra (2022) The article's goal is to ascertain the effects of sustainable human resource management (SHRM) and industry 4.0 technology (I4Te) adoption on workers' employability skills (ES). There were 198 valid responses to the survey. The study employed confirmatory factor analysis (CFA) and structural equation modeling (SEM) with SPSS 25.0 and AMOS 25.0 to verify its components and test its hypotheses. I4Te and SHRM practices may help employees develop the skills and competencies that emerging businesses will require.

2.1 Research Gap

The human resource practice plays a vital role between the organization and its employees. The human resource is an area that continuous to debate the practices and its related questions to pursue further attention to bring fulfillment towards organization and its employees. It can be assumed that practices systematically influence employees and their behavioral outcome. Employees' behavioral outcome mainly focuses on job satisfaction work performance and organizational commitment to engage employees in organization. Hence, it is observed that there is a need for potential to examine the factors on situation to influence the human resource practice towards organizational commitment which is core element for organizational up liftment and growth. And, this issue has taken as principle factor with perception of employees in NLC. This study concentrates to address the practices effect the NLC India Limited. In certain situation, the practices will collaborate with employees to meet their needs for their fulfillment. Employee encouragement is particularly important when studying the HR practices and their effect on behavioral outcome.

3. Goals of the Study

The below are the purposes of the present research;

1. To examine the perception and attitude effect of human resource practices among the employees.
2. To analyse how employee commitment to the business is impacted by human resource procedures.

4. Research Method

The descriptive study design has been chosen, and it has been described as a description of the current condition of affairs without any variable control. Descriptive studies are used to characterize a variety of phenomena, a sample population's features, and behavior. It is limited to reporting the organization's historical and present conditions. A strategy used to pick a sample from the population is called sampling design. It is the method the researcher use while choosing the items for the sample. The researcher selected the NLC India Ltd. employees for the current study using the Simple Random Sampling technique. Around 1300 people live in the four departments. The selected respondents are given 700 questions. The respondents returned 600 questionnaires out of a total of 700. Data collection is a methodical approach to collecting and evaluating information from a variety of sources to provide a complete and accurate picture of an area of interest. Primary and secondary data are also used in this study. Regression and Path Analysis are two statistical techniques that were utilized to analyze the data that were gathered.

5. Limitations

The prime limitations are that the study concentrates on supervisors and certain employees of NLC over to examine the perception and influencing factors on behavioral outcome over organizational commitment.

6. Discussion and Results

The data for "Effect of Human Resource Practices on Employees' Behavioral Outcome at Neyveli Lignite Corporation (NLC) India Ltd, Neyveli" are analyzed and interpreted in this article. The current study puts a focus on usage concerns and potential outcomes. The gathered data are analyzed and interpreted using the right methods to produce outcomes that are acceptable for facilitating the organization's finest human resource practices.

Table 28.1   Regression analysis showing impact of hr practices on organizational commitment of employees

Model Summary					
R	R Square	Adjusted R Square	Std. Error of the Estimate	F	p
.873	.762	.757	.49841	170.947	.001

Coefficients						
Sl. No.	HR Practices	Unstandardized Quantities		Standardized Quantities	t	p
		B	Std. Error	Beta		
	Constant	.228	.119		2.316	.048
1	Recruitment Procedures	.133	.041	.123	3.238	.001
2	Training and Development	.254	.051	.193	4.971	.000
3	Employees Motivational Practices	.017	.048	.014	.357	.721
4	Communication	.119	.059	.103	2.014	.044
5	Labor Welfare Facilities	-.047	.046	-.050	-1.028	.305
6	Employee Participation in Management	.069	.035	.070	1.957	.050
7	Grievance Handling	.265	.047	.225	5.582	.000
8	Trade Union Activities	-.071	.042	-.060	-1.681	.093
9	Subordinate Superior Relationship	.125	.048	.104	2.626	.009
10	Compensation	1.039	.041	.918	25.531	.000
11	Performance Appraisal System	-.028	.030	-.026	-.903	.367

Source: Primary data
Dependent Variable: Organizational Commitment

Ho: There is no influence of various HR practices on organizational commitment among employees in NLC.

The impact of HR procedures on organizational commitment is described in Table 28.1. The following factors are all taken into account as independent variables in this study: hiring procedures, training and development opportunities, employee involvement in management, labour welfare resources, grievance handling, union participation, sub - ordinate relationships, remuneration, and performance evaluation systems. The dedication of the organization was regarded as a dependent variable. Multiple linear regressions were also used to test the aforementioned hypothesis. The p ratio was determined to be significant (P = .001) at the one percent level in the model summary, and the null hypothesis was rejected.

The organizational commitment of NLC workers was highly impacted by HR practice characteristics. Additionally, the R square value of 0.762 is found. Independent factors such as employment policies, development and training employee motivational procedures, interaction, labour well-being facilities, employee empowerment in organization, complaint procedures, trade union actions, sub - ordinate superior relationships and systems for remuneration and performance evaluation were inferred to have an influence on organizational commitment at a level of 76.2 percent. The dimensions of HR practices, including hiring practices, training and development, communication, employee involvement in management, grievance handling, subordinate superior relationships, and compensation, are inferred to have a positive impact on organizational commitment based on the standardized beta coefficient and its significant *p* values. Additionally, it is implied that aspects of HR practices like employee motivation practices, labour welfare facilities, trade union activities, and performance appraisal systems do not have an impact on the organizational commitment on the basis of the standardized beta coefficient and the fact that the *p* values are not significant.

Model 1: Path Analysis of Impact HR Practices on Organizational Commitment

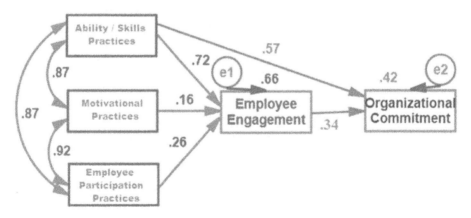

Fig. 28.1 Path analysis of impact HR practices on organizational commitment

Source: Author's compilation

Model Fit Indication

Chi-Square	P	GFI	AGFI	CFI	NFI	RMR	RMSEA Value
14.804	.001	.990	.927	.996	.995	.008	.005

GFI - Goodness of Fit Index   AGFI - Adjusted Goodness of Fit Index
CFI - Common Fit Index   RMR - Root Mean Square Residual
NFI - Normed Fit Indices   RMSEA -Root Mean Square error of approximation

The Chi square value is 14.804 and 0.001 is the p-value. This value is below the cutoff of .05. Good Fit Index is .990 AGF is .927, CFI is .996, and NFI is .995. These readings should all be close to one based on norms. Nearly all of them are one. Thus, this model's fit is suitable. RMR is equal to .008. RMR should have an anticipated norm value of less than 0.08. As a model fit, this is also suitable

Regression Weights

DV		IV	Estimate	S.E.	C.R.	Beta	p
Employee Engagement	<---	Ability/Skill Practices	.863	.062	13.822	.719	***
Employee Engagement	<---	Employee Motivational Practices	.185	.077	2.400	.162	.016
Employee Engagement	<---	Employee Participation Practices	.286	.071	4.012	.261	***
Organizational Commitment	<---	Employee Engagement	.372	.043	5.667	.340	***
Organizational Commitment	<---	Ability/Skill Practices	.567	.052	10.900	.573	***

Ho: Employee engagement among NLC employees is unaffected by ability/skill practices.

The vital ratio, which is determined by regressing the employee engagement mediator variable's weight over the ability/skill practices, is 13.822, and the beta value is .719, or 71.9%. Conclusion: Ho is rejected and H_A is accepted because the mediator variable employee engagement is impacted by ability/skill practices to the degree that it contributes 71.9% and the p value 0.001 is meaningful at the 1% level. This suggests that ability/skill practices have an impact on employee engagement as a mediator variable.

Ho: Employee motivational practices have no impact on NLC workers' engagement in their work.

Employee Motivational Practices' weight in a regression analysis over the mediator variable of employee engagement reveals a crucial ratio of 2.400 and a beta value of .162, or 16.2%, respectively. It can be said that the mediator variable employee engagement is influenced by employee motivational practices to the extent that it contributes 16.2%, and the p value of .016 is significant at the 5% level, causing the rejection of Ho and acceptability of HA. According to this, employee motivational practices have an impact on the mediator variable employee engagement..

Ho: Employee Participation Practices have no impact on NLC workers' levels of engagement.

Employee Participation Practices' weight in a regression analysis over the mediator variable of employee engagement reveals a vital ratio of 4.012 and a beta value of .261, or 26.1%, respectively. It can be said that the mediator variable employee engagement is influenced by employee participation practices to a 26.1% extent, and the p value .001 is significant at the 1% level, leading to the rejection of Ho and acceptance of H_A. This indicates that employee engagement is a mediator variable that is influenced by employee participation practices.

Ho: Employee engagement has no impact on NLC workers' commitment to the organization.

According to a regression analysis of the mediator variable organizational commitment and the outcome variable employee engagement, the vital ratio is 5.667 and the beta value is .340, or 34%. The rejection of Ho and acceptance of H_A may be attributed to the mediator variable employee engagement's effect over the outcome variable organizational commitment, which contributes 34% and has a p value .001 that is significant at a 1% level. This suggests that the outcome variable organizational commitment is influenced by the mediator variable employee engagement.

Ho: Ability/Skill Practices have no impact on NLC workers' engagement to their organisations.

The independent variable Ability/Skill Practices' weight in a regression analysis over the outcome variable Organizational Commitment reveals a vital ratio of 10.900 and a beta value of .573, or 57.3%. It can be said that Ho was rejected and H_A was accepted because to the independent variable Ability/Skill Practices' effect over the outcome variable organizational commitment, which contributes 57.3% and has a significant p value of .001 at the 1% level. The independent variable Ability/Skill Practices can be understood as having an impact on the outcome variable Organizational Commitment..

Covariance's

IV		IV	Estimate	S.E.	C.R.	R	p
Ability/Skill Practices	<-->	Employee Participation Practices	.527	.033	16.018	.866	***
Employee Motivational Practices	<-->	Employee Participation Practices	.589	.036	16.589	.922	***
Ability/Skill Practices	<-->	Employee Motivational Practices	.509	.032	16.113	.875	***

Source: Principal data

Ho: In NLC, there is no correlation between employee motivational practises, employee participation practices, or ability/skill practices toward workers.

The p values are smaller than 0.050, according to the covariance table. As a result, it can be said that there is a strong correlation between employee motivational practices, employee participation practices, and ability/skill practices.

7. Managerial Implications

The present study has identified the most attractive human resource practices for the management to implement and focus on behavioral outcome that influence employees. This study examines the essential features of the employees' behavioral outcome in the NLC and also validates the role of employee engagement and organizational commitment with behavioral outcome to enhance the behaviors of the employees. This study further illustrates certain qualities for the future researchers in analyzing the behavioral outcome of the employees in various aspects of the public sector companies which are searching for their sustainable development.

The research may examine specific actions in determining the determinants that enhance behavioral outcomes and the measures characterized by hiring practices, learning and development, employee empowerment, communication strategies, labour welfare services, employee participation in management, grievance handling, trade union activities, superior-subordinate connections, compensation, performance appraisal system, job involvement, and career progression, among others. Further, the human resource practices factors contributes much to anatomize the existence of behavioral outcome of employees which paves new dimensions to research related to internal dimensional factors of HR practices.

8. Conclusion

The present study aimed to analyze the effect of human resource practices on employees' behavioral outcome in NLC India Ltd. The study has identified the employees who works in the NLC have opinion differences on dimensions of HR practices mediating towards employee engagement on employee behavioral outcome with respect to their demographic variables. Various human resource practices were considered and their opinion about the relevance of these factors were collected as responses and analyzed. It was found that all the HR practices were found to be better during the tenure. Employee engagement is considered as a vital factor for the success of organization. There is a higher need for the studies related to employee engagement and it needs to be frequently examined by the organization because it is considered as a positive attitude of employees towards the organization and its values. The statistical tools are applied in order to answer the research objectives and research hypothesis. The research tools like regression and path analysis were used to identify the significant differences among the variables. The majority of variables are found to be significantly different with the employee behavioral outcome of employees. It is concluded that there is a positive impact between human resource practices and behavioral outcome of employees in NLC India Ltd. Therefore, it is understood that the organization is titled as Navaratna category by Government of India due to the work commitment of the employees and also the organization continuously goes on in maximizing its profit and services.

9. Research for Extension

This research assessed how human resource management practices at NLC India Ltd. influence the employee behavior. The study only covered eleven human resource practices: hiring procedures, learning and development, specific motivational procedures, communicative skills, worker welfare facilities, team work in management, disciplinary procedures, trade union activities, superior-subordinate relationships, remuneration, and performance assessments. As a result, additional human resource management techniques can be investigated and evaluated using employee behavioral outcomes. In the current study, employee engagement has been employed as a mediator between human resource management strategies and employees' behavioral outcomes. For future research, other mediating elements that are pertinent to this can be employed. Only managers and employees of NLC India Ltd, a company in the public sector, were included in the research. The future research may be conducted among the executives of NLC and also with the private organization.

REFERENCES

1. Heloíza H. Oliveira, Luiz C. Honório (2020) Human Resources Practices and Organizational Commitment: Connecting The Constructs In A Public Organization DOI: 10.1590/1678-6971/eRAMG200160.
2. Timothy C. Bednall, Karin Sanders, Huadong Yang (2021) A meta-analysis on employee perceptions of human resource strength: Examining the mediating versus moderating hypotheses First published: 31 May 2021 https://doi.org/10.1002/hrm.22068Citations: 3.
3. Manu Sharma, Sunil Luthra, Sudhanshu Joshi, and Anil Kumar (2022) International Journal of Manpower ISSN: 0143-7720 Article publication date: 14 April 2022 Reprints & Permissions Issue publication analysing the impact of sustainable human resource management practices and industry 4.0 technologies adoption on employability skills date: 24 May 2022.

Handbook of Evidence Based Management Practices in Business – Satyendra Kumar Sharma et al. (eds)
© *2023 Taylor & Francis Group, London, ISBN 978-1-032-54216-4*

Chapter

Dark Tetrad and Work-Life Balance: A Case Study on Married Doctoral Students

Akash Dubey[1], Rajneesh Choubisa[2], Jerin V. Philipose[3]
Department of Humanities and Social Sciences,
BITS Pilani, Rajasthan, India

ABSTRACT: Doctoral education is critical for the enrichment of academic knowledge and the development of society. The significance of scientific progress depends on the work of a doctoral scholar. But how different personality types and behavioural aspects can thwart or improve their work still remains an essential question in the literature. It should be noted that sometimes the actions of the researchers can potentially impact the quality of research and misrepresentation of sensitive data adds to the issues. To check for a potential reason, this study aims to validate the measurement tools of personality and work-life balance in the Indian context and investigate the relationship between the two variables. To achieve this objective, we utilize the Dark Tetrad at Work Scale by Thibault & Kelloway, 2020, and the Work-Life Balance Scale by Brough et al., 2014. Data was collected from married doctoral scholars (n = 102) from a few Indian university campuses. Data analysis was done using regression analysis that further validated the relationship between the variables. Results indicate a significant influence of dark personality on the work-life balance of doctoral students. We conclude our investigation by suggesting extending this working idea to a diverse group of participants.

KEYWORDS: Doctoral scholars, Dark tetrad, Measurement, Personality, Work-life Balance etc.

1. Introduction

We all know that the field of research is a vital element for the development of any society. The work that a researcher undertakes, is significant enough to have either a direct or indirect

[1]p20200478@pilani.bits-pilani.ac.in, [2]rajneesh.choubisa@pilani.bits-pilani.ac.in,
[3]p20200465@pilani.bits-pilani.ac.in

DOI: 10.4324/9781003415725-29

influence over society. The field of academics has a very close connection with research and scholars in the academic setting are its players. The scientific progress of the country depends upon the researchers like research scholars, professors, scientists, etc. Nevertheless, the question as to how factors like the personality of an individual researcher and their ability to balance between work and personal lives influence their approach is yet to be determined.

Doctoral students undergo many roles in their careers while working on their doctoral dissertations, where each role is associated with different contexts, responsibilities, values, and expectations (Kovalcikiene and Buksnyte-Marmiene, 2021, 45). With this, they often develop an identity and personality as a researcher which remains an essential task for doctoral students (Austin and McDaniels, 2006, 51; Grant-Davie et al., 2017; Lamar and Helm, 2017, 2; Mantai 2017, 1; Pipere 2007, 21). Psychological factors like personality traits, thought patterns, values, etc, are considered important factors because peculiarities of personality remain the same. These personality traits determine the propensity to certain activities (Kovalcikiene and Buksnyte-Marmiene, 2021, 47). It is for this reason that turnover intention and other professional behaviours depend on these traits (Steinmayr and Spinath, 2008, 185).

The life of the research scholars can have an overwhelming impact on the overall well-being of an individual. The life of a researcher requires determination and persistence because they face different levels of challenges, which without optimal support and balance can turn into a stressor (Barry et al. 2018; Cotterall 2013, 174). The life of research personnel frequently circles around exploring new ideas and keeping a healthy balance between work and the rest of their life while striving to achieve a pristine scientific record (Rodrigues 2021, 5907). This is one of the major issues in the current scientific system that incites long hours of labour with a high level of competitiveness (Rodrigues 2021, 5909).

The aim of this research is to assess the functioning and validity of the scales related to dark personality tetrad and work-life balance among doctoral scholars in few Indian universities. Even literature suggests that previous studies have left aside the influence of factors of personal lives and aspects of well-being, which can be closely related to personality traits among researchers (McAlpine et al., 2022). This can also include a reduction in well-being, for example, exhaustion and cynicism, a decrease in PhD progress, etc (McAlpine et al., 2022). The major aim of this study is to analyse the existing relationship between the two variables, i.e. dark personality and work-life balance.

2. Review of Literature

Individual personality estimates their integrity and honesty to work. This is represented by personality traits which is related to the stable pattern of thoughts, feelings and behaviour that manifests in an individual (Gouveia et al., 2021). In the field of academics, integrity and honesty are closely related to ethical conduct that is recently lacking on a global level among students (Zhang et al., 2021; Krou et al., 2021). Apart from integrity and honesty, creativity is another significant aspect of a researcher's life. Previous studies have pointed out that personality traits play a significant role in creativity (especially when measured as divergent thinking), which also explains the relationship between creativity and ethical misbehaviour (Jirásek and Sudzina, 2020, 90; Kapoor et al., 2022; Weiss et al., 2021). Dishonesty and ethical misconduct are also important in understanding personality traits (Eshet et al., 2021). Even a study indicates that creative individuals often engage in ethical misconduct, and are smart enough to justify it (Loesche and Francis, 2020, 239). Despite extensive research, there is still a gap in the literature regarding manifestation and preponderance of personality traits (For example, Big Five Personality or Dark Personality, etc.) in academia (Lee et al., 2020).

Work-Life Balance (WLB) is a major concern, which is a consequence of demographic change in the workplace, intensification of work, and equal distribution of time between work and the rest of life (Tan 2013, 185; Chakraborti and Mishra, 2018, 177). In today's workplace context, organizations are expected to have more ethical obligations to help employees achieve WLB (Chakraborti and Mishra, 2018, 178; DeStefano et al., 2018; Heikkinen et al., 2020; Nie et al., 2018; Singhapakdi et al., 2019; Voegtlin et al., 2019; Zhang and Tu, 2018, 1085). According to a study by Hill et al., 2022, the relationship between poor work-life balance and poor mentoring are more common among those with mental health disorders (Hill et al., 2022). Major findings suggest that in academia, work-related stress is closely related to psychological distress (Hill et al., 2022; Anjara et al., 2020; Huppert 2009, 137; Winefield et al., 2003). Apart from these findings, a study has also shown the association between work organization, job content, and work-life balance (Hill et al., 2022).

3. Materials and Methods

The present research is a limited cross-sectional study focusing on doctoral scholars from a few selected residential universities in India. All participants were provided with an informed consent declaration and a socio-demographic form, to which they agreed before being included in the study.

3.1 Participants and Procedure

Data was collected initially from (N = 102) participants, of which omitters and outliers were excluded. The final data included a total of (n = 93) participants (Male = 48.36% and Female = 38.13%), with a response rate of 94.86%. Participants were associated with a public or private university in the position of doctoral scholars of various subject streams. One of the inclusion criteria was the participant's membership to a university as a research scholar, and the second was related to their marital status. Data was collected using an online google form through snowball sampling, which was sent to the participants via online mode.

3.2 Measures

To understand our variables, we selected previously established scales with an excellent level of psychometric properties. With all possible procedures, we tried to keep the length of our scales reasonable. We used the following two scales which were self-report measures for measuring personality traits and work-life balance.

3.3 Dark Tetrad at Work (DTW)

We measured personality traits using the Dark Tetrad at Work scale (DTW) by Thibault and Kelloway (2020). The scale includes 22 items covering the four factors of personality, i.e. Machiavellianism, Narcissism, Psychopathy, and Sadism. Scores are measured with the help of 5 points Likert scale ranging from 1 (Strongly Disagree) to 5 (Strongly Agree). Reliability for this study was calculated with Cronbach's Alpha (α = .85) and McDonald's Omega (ω = .86) which were found to be satisfactory in our case.

3.4 Work-Life Balance (WLB)

We utilized the Work-Life Balance scale (WLB) by Brough et.al. (2014), which is based on Netemeyer, Boles, and McMurrian (1996) Family Work Conflict and Work-Family Conflict scale and Fisher, Bulger, and Smith's (2009) scale. This 5-point Likert scale (1 = Strongly Disagree to 5 = Strongly Agree) contains four items, with one item as reverse coded. The calculated Cronbach's Alpha (α = .88) and McDonald's Omega (ω = .88) were found to be satisfactory for the selected sample.

4. Results

We tested our variables using simple linear regression. Data was also analysed for descriptive analysis and correlation. Independent t-test was used to understand relationship between testing variables and descriptive variables. We used IBM SPSS v27 and R software (v4.2.1), along with Jamovi for analysing our data and looking for estimated relationships. In Table 29.1, the descriptive analysis of our data is shown, with correlation between our datapoints. Our dependent variable, i.e. WLB is showing a moderate level of correlation with Narcissism (r = .30), whereas DTW taken together is showing a low correlation with WLB (r = .16).

Table 29.1 Descriptive statistics and correlations

Variable	Mean	SD	2	3	4	5	6	7
1. Gender	1.44	.49	-	-	-	-	-	-
2. Dark Tetrad at Work (DTW)	52.22	9.23	1	.16	.68	.66	.85	.75
3. Work-Life Balance (WLB)	12.40	3.34	.16	1	.30	.00	.08	.08
4. Narcissism	19.89	3.17	.68	.30	1	.34	.40	.26
5. Machiavellianism	11.95	2.78	.66	.00	.34	1	.42	.26
6. Psychopathy	11.20	3.40	.85	.08	.40	.42	1	.67
7. Sadism	9.17	3.06	.75	.08	.26	.26	.67	1

Source: Author's construction

The second part of our analysis, i.e. regression analysis, is presented in Table 29.2. According to the result, among all sub-scales of dark tetrad at work, narcissism is showing a moderate

Table 29.2 Regression value of predictors of work-life balance

Predictors	Mean	SD	B	F-value	P	R^2	Adjusted R^2
Dark Tetrad at Work	52.22	9.23	.16	2.499	.117	.027	.016
Narcissism*	19.89	3.17	.30	9.208	.003*	.092	.082
Machiavellianism	11.95	2.78	.00	.000	.991	.000	-.011
Psychopathy	11.20	3.40	.08	.624	.432	.007	-.004
Sadism	9.17	3.06	.08	.673	.414	.007	-.004
*p < 0.005							

Source: Author's construction

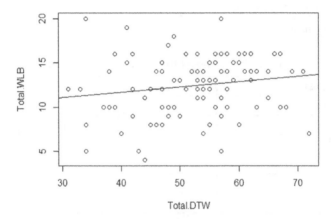

Fig. 29.1 Scatterplot with the regression line

Source: Author's construction

level of significance with WLB (0.003, with $P < 0.005$), with Standardised Beta equivalent to .30 (30% effect) (R^2 = .092 & Adjusted R^2 = .082). Besides, the mean and SD of the narcissism sub-scale is calculated (M = 19.89, SD = 3.17) and the regression line is plotted in Fig. 29.1.

The final analysis includes the Independent sample t-Tests. Table 29.3 highlights an estimation of the type of university and its significance to the given variables. Participants distribution from private and public universities was $n = 69$ and $n = 24$ respectively. The result reflects a level of significance between the type of university and WLB (P-value is .01, $P < 0.05$) (t-Value = –2.35) as well as between the type of university and narcissism (P value is .04, $P < 0.05$) (t Value = –1.70). Table 29.4 estimates the gender differences and their significance with the given variables. The male-to-female ratio was 52:41 and showcases a significant difference among manifestations of dark tetrads. The result shows a level of significance between the gender and psychopathy sub-scale ($t = 1.69$; $p < 0.05$& sadism sub-scale ($t = 1.94$; $p < 0.05$) of the dark tetrads scale.

Table 29.3 Independent Sample *t*-test showing values for mean difference across university types

Variables	t Value	df	P
Dark Tetrad at Work	1.33	91	.09
Work-Life Balance*	2.35	91	.01*
Narcissism	1.70	91	.04*
Machiavellianism	1.39	91	.08
Psychopathy	.14	91	.44
Sadism	.84	91	.20
*P < 0.05 Private University = 69, Public University = 24			

Source: Author's construction

Table 29.4 Independent sample *t*-test showing differences across gender

Variables	t Value	df	P
Dark Tetrad at Work	1.63	91	.05
Work-Life Balance	.39	91	.34
Narcissism	.22	91	.41
Machiavellianism	1.49	91	.06
Psychopathy	1.69	91	.04*
Sadism	1.94	91	.02*
*P < 0.05 Male = 52, Female = 41			

Source: Author's construction

5. Discussion and Conclusion

In the field of academics and research, different personality characteristics manifest diverse thought processes and behaviour. This can influence the quality and integrity of research, as well as, of the researcher. The life of research personnel frequently circles around exploring new ideas, where a healthy balance between work and the rest of their life is significant (Rodrigues 2021, 5912). Our result estimates a moderate relationship between work-life balance and narcissistic personality, where narcissistic personality is a major predictor of work-life balance. Previous research explains the constant struggle of researchers to maintain the focus on their research as well as the remaining parts of their lives (Rodrigues 2021,5907). This is true for nearly all areas of the organization, whether research or non-research field. As indicated in a previous study, a poor level of work-life balance is related to poor mental health status, which explains the resulting creation of a narcissistic personality (Hill et al., 2022). A certain level of narcissism can act as a remedy for work stress, where an individual focus more on him/herself rather than only on work-related concerns.

Differences in the work environment and organizational structure also play a role in maintaining a balance between work and the personal lives of an individual. Our result suggests that the significant difference between work-life balance and the type of university correlates with idea that the satisfaction of employees becomes a significant factor in the different types of organizations (Ivaciuc et al., 2022). Similar is the case with narcissism, which is again significant with the type of university wherein a previous study explains how workplace envy plays a role in such behaviour (Li et al., 2021). The difference in the level of satisfaction depends on the different approaches to management. As a framework of evolutionary psychology, the gender differences in psychopathy and sadism corroborate the fact that a certain level of gender differences exists in the personality of males and females (Lauder et al., 2022).

This working paper is based on a rudimentary idea to understand how personality factors are essential to understand work-related factors, especially in creative careers with research portfolios. The major implication of our study is to provide an understanding of how dark personality traits can help in facilitating creative and research-oriented jobs. We hereby suggest that more extensive investigations must be carried out to improve the work environment in organizations. This study can be considered as a mere starting point in exploring the personality factors and their resultant implications on work-life balance and similar outcome variables.

REFERENCES

1. "The Jamovi Project." 2021. Jamovi. version 2.2 [Computer Software]. https://www.jamovi.org.
2. Anjara, S. G., C. Bonetto, T. Van Bortel, and C. Brayne. 2020. "Using the GHQ-12 to Screen for Mental Health Problems Among Primary Care Patients: Psychometrics and Practical Considerations". IJMHS. International Journal of Mental Health Systems 14, no. 1: 62. https://doi.org/10.1186/s13033-020-00397-0.
3. Austin, A. E., and M. McDaniels. 2006. "Using Doctoral Education to Prepare Faculty to Work Within Boyerís Four Domains of Scholarship." New Directions for Institutional Research 129: 51–65.
4. Barry, K. M., M. Woods, E. Warnecke, C. Stirling, and A. Martin. 2018. "Psychological Health of Doctoral Candidates, Study Related Challenges and Perceived Performance." Higher Education Research & Development 37, no. 3: 468–83. https://doi.org/10.1080/07294360.2018.1425979.
5. Brough, Paula, Carolyn Timms, Michael P. O'Driscoll, Thomas Kalliath, Oi-Ling Siu, Cindy Sit, and Danny Lo. 2014. "Work–Life Balance: a Longitudinal Evaluation of a New Measure Across Australia and New Zealand Workers." International Journal of Human Resource Management 25, no. 19: 2724–44. https://doi.org/10.1080/09585192.2014.899262.
6. Chakraborti, C., and D. Mishra. 2018. "Responsible Business Practices and Some Indian SMEs." Asian Journal of Business Ethics 7, no. 2: 177–203. https://doi.org/10.1007/s13520-017-0083-9.
7. Cotterall, S. 2013. "More than Just a Brain: Emotions and the Doctoral Experience." Higher Education Research & Development 32, no. 2: 174–87. https://doi.org/10.1080/07294360.2012.680017.
8. De Stefano, F., S. Bagdadli, and A. Camuffo. 2018. "The HR Role in Corporate Social Responsibility and Sustainability: a Boundary-Shifting Literature Review." Human Resource Management 57, no. 2: 549–66. https://doi.org/10.1002/hrm.21870.
9. Eshet, Y., P. Steinberger, and K. Grinautsky. 2021. "Relationship Between Statistics Anxiety and Academic Dishonesty: A Comparison Between Learning Environments in Social Sciences." Sustainability 13, no. 3: 1–18. https://doi.org/10.3390/su13031564.

10. Gouveia, V. V., R. C. R. de Araujo, I. C. V. de Oliveira, M. P. Goncalves, T. Milfont, G. L. de Holanda Coelho et al. 2021. "A Short Version of the Big Five Inventory (BFI-20): Evidence on Construct Validity." Revista Internacional de Psicología 55: 1–22. https://doi.org/10.30849/ripijp.v55i1.1312.

11. Grant- Davie et al. (2017). Helping doctoral students establish long-term identities as technical communication scholars. Journal of Technical Writing and Communication, 47(2), 151-171.

12. Heikkinen, S., A. M. Lämsä, and C. Niemistö. 2020. "Work–Family Practices and Complexity of Their Usage: a Discourse Analysis Towards Socially Responsible Human Resource Management." Journal of Business Ethics: 1–17. https://doi.org/10.1007/s10551-020-04458-9.

13. Hill, Nicole T. M., Eleanor Bailey, Ruth Benson, Grace Cully, Olivia J. Kirtley, Rosemary Purcell, Simon Rice, J. Robinson, and Courtney C. Walton. 2022. "Researching the Researchers: Psychological Distress and Psychosocial Stressors According to Career Stage in Mental Health Researchers." BMC Psychology 10, no. 1: 19. https://doi.org/10.1186/s40359-022-00728-5.

14. Huppert, F. A. 2009. "Psychological Well-Being: Evidence Regarding Its Causes and Consequences." Applied Psychology: Health & Well-Being 1, no. 2: 137–64. https://doi.org/10.1111/j.1758-0854.2009.01008.x.

15. Ivasciuc, Ioana Simona, Gheorghe Epuran, Daniela Roxana Vuţă, and Bianca Tescaşiu. 2022. "Telework Implications on Work-Life Balance, Productivity, and Health of Different Generations of Romanian Employees" Sustainability 14, no. 23: 16108. https://doi.org/10.3390/su142316108.

16. Jirásek, M., and F. Sudzina. 2020. "Big Five Personality Traits and Creativity." Quality Innovation Prosperity 24, no. 3: 90–105. https://doi.org/10.12776/qip.v24i3.1509.

17. Kapoor, H., V. Inamdar, and J. C. Kaufman. 2022. "I Didn't Have Time! A Qualitative Exploration of Misbehaviors in Academic Contexts." Journal of Academic Ethics 20, no. 2: 191–208. https://doi.org/10.1007/s10805-021-09407-3.

18. Kovalcikiene, K., and L. Buksnyte-Marmiene. 2021. "Doctoral Students as Future Teachers at Universities: Factors Related to Professional Identity." Journal of Teacher Education for Sustainability 23, no. 2: 45–61. https://doi.org/10.2478/jtes-2021-0016.

19. Krou, M. R., C. J. Fong, and M. A. Hoff. 2021. "Achievement Motivation and Academic Dishonesty: A Meta-Analytic Investigation." Educational Psychology Review 33, no. 2: 427–58. https://doi.org/10.1007/s10648-020-09557-7.

20. Lamar, M. R., and H. M. Helm. 2017. "Understanding the Researcher Identity Development of Counselor Education and Supervision Doctoral Students." Counselor Education & Supervision 56, no. 1: 2–18. https://doi.org/10.1002/ceas.12056.

21. Lauder, Cassandra, and Evita March. 2022. "Catching the Catfish: Exploring Gender and the Dark Tetrad as Predictors of Catfishing Perpetration." Computers in Human Behavior: 107599.

22. Lee, Samuel D., Nathan R. Kuncel, and Jacob Gau. 2020. "Personality, Attitude, and Demographic Correlates of Academic Dishonesty: A Meta-analysis." Psychological Bulletin 146, no. 11: 1042–58. https://doi.org/10.1037/bul0000300.

23. Li, M., X. Xu, and H. K. Kwan. 2021. "The Antecedents and Consequences of Workplace Envy: A Meta-Analytic Review." Asia Pacific Journal of Management. https://doi.org/10.1007/s10490-021-09772-y.

24. Loesche, F., and K. B. Francis. 2020. "Creativity and Destruction." In Encyclopaedia of Creativity, edited by S. Pritzker, and M. A. Runco: 239–45. Oxford: Academic Press.

25. Mantai, L. 2017. "Feeling Like a Researcher: Experiences of Early Doctoral Students in Australia." Studies in Higher Education 42, no. 4: 1–15. https://doi.org/10.1080/03075079.2015.1067603.

26. McAlpine, L., I. Skakni, and K. Pyhältö. 2022. "PhD Experience (and Progress) Is More than Work: Life-Work Relations and Reducing Exhaustion (and Cynicism)." Studies in Higher Education 47, no. 2: 352–66. https://doi.org/10.1080/03075079.2020.1744128.

27. Nie, D., A.-M. Lämsä, and R. Pučėtaitė. 2018. "Effects of Responsible Human Resource Management Practices on Female Employees' Turnover Intentions." Business Ethics: a European Review 27, no. 1: 29–41. https://doi.org/10.1111/beer.12165.

28. Pipere, A. 2007. "Mapping the Researcherís Identity in the University Context: Dimensions of Personal Constructs." Baltic Journal of Psychology 8, no. 1, 2: 21–36.

29. R Core Team. 2022. R: A Language and Environment for Statistical Computing. https://www.R-project.org/. Vienna, Austria: R Foundation for Statistical Computing.

30. Revelle, W. 2019. psych: Procedures for Psychological. "Psychometric, and Personality Research". [R package]. https://cran.r-project.org/package=psych.

31. Rodrigues, Rui S. 2021. "Seizing Balance and Success During Your Ph.D. Experience." European Journal of Neuroscience 54, no. 6: 5907–14. https://doi.org/10.1111/ejn.15410.

32. Singhapakdi, A., D. J. Lee, M. J. Sirgy, H. Roh, K. Senasu, and G. B. Yu. 2019. "Effects of Perceived Organizational CSR Value and Employee Moral Identity on Job Satisfaction: a Study of Business Organizations in Thailand." Asian Journal of Business Ethics 8, no. 1: 53–72. https://doi.org/10.1007/s13520-019-00088-1.

33. Steinmayr, R., and B. Spinath. 2008. "Sex Differences in School Achievement: What Are the Roles of Personality and Achievement Motivation?" European Journal of Personality 22, no. 3: 185–209. https://doi.org/10.1002/per.676.

34. Tan, E. K. B. 2013. "Molding the Nascent Corporate Social Responsibility Agenda in Singapore: of Pragmatism, Soft Regulation, and the Economic Imperative." Asian Journal of Business Ethics 2, no. 2: 185–204. https://doi.org/10.1007/s13520-012-0026-4.

35. Thibault, Tabatha, and E. Kevin Kelloway. 2020. "The Dark Tetrad at Work." Human Performance 33, no. 5: 406–24. https://doi.org/10.1080/08959285.2020.1802728.

36. Voegtlin, C., C. Frisch, A. Walther, and P. Schwab. 2020. "Theoretical Development and Empirical Examination of a Three-Roles Model of Responsible Leadership." Journal of Business Ethics 167, no. 3: 411–31. https://doi.org/10.1007/s10551-019-04155-2.

37. Weiss, S., D. Steger, Y. Kaur, A. Hildebrandt, U. Schroeders, and O. Wilhelm. 2021. "On the Trail of Creativity: Dimensionality of Divergent Thinking and Its Relation with Cognitive Abilities, Personality, and Insight." European Journal of Personality 35, no. 3: 291–314. https://doi.org/10.1002/per.2288.

38. Winefield, A. H., N. Gillespie, C. Stough, J. Dua, J. Hapuarachchi, and C. Boyd. 2003. "Occupational Stress in Australian University Staff: Results from a National Survey." International Journal of Stress Management 10, no. 1: 51–63. https://doi.org/10.1037/1072-5245.10.1.51.

39. Zhang, C., J. Wu, Z. Yang, and G. Perceval. 2022. "How Does Creativity Influence Dishonest Behavior? An Empirical Study of Chinese Students." Ethics & Behavior 32, no. 2: 147–61. https://doi.org/10.1080/10508422.2020.1869552.

40. Zhang, S., and Y. Tu. 2018. "Cross-Domain Effects of Ethical Leadership on Employee Family and Life Satisfaction: The Moderating Role of Family-Supportive Supervisor Behaviors." Journal of Business Ethics 152, no. 4: 1085–97. https://doi.org/10.1007/s10551-016-3306-4.

Chapter

Academic Adjustment and Gratitude in College Students: A First-Hand Evidence from a Psychological Perspective

Jerin V Philipose[1], Akash Dubey[2]
Department of Humanities and Social Sciences,
BITS Pilani, Pilani Campus, Pilani, India

Rajneesh Choubisa[3]
Associate Professor, Department of Humanities and Social Sciences,
BITS Pilani, Pilani Campus, Pilani, India

ABSTRACT: Gratitude is defined as a sense of abundance, the appreciation of little things in life, and the appreciation of what others have done for us. Studies related to gratitude are predominantly related to well-being, happiness, and life satisfaction. A sense of gratitude is helpful for college students in multiple ways, particularly in their academic life, through appreciation from their teachers and friends. However, the mechanism which explains whether academic adjustment leads to the development of gratitude or vice-versa is empirically undiscovered. We attempt to unlock the potential of developing the virtue of gratitude and academic adjustment to see how they influence each other. With the help of the *Gratitude Questionnaire-6* (GQ-6) and *College Adjustment Scale*, we collected data from various college students ($N = 83$). Results utilizing a correlational research design highlight that gratitude helps in academic adjustment or that attaining academic adjustment leads to the development of gratitude among college students. Implications from this research can help implement meaningful interventions that can potentially enhance academic achievement, gratitude, or both depending upon their operational dynamics.

KEYWORDS: Gratitude, Academic adjustment, College students, Correlation, Intervention, etc.

[1]p20200465@pilani.bits-pilani.ac.in, [2]p20200478@pilani.bits-pilani.ac.in,
[3]rajneesh.choubisa@pilani.bits-pilani.ac.in,

DOI: 10.4324/9781003415725-30

1. Introduction

Transitioning from school to university education is transformational for individuals in many ways. During this period, students face various issues in different proportions, primarily associated with adjusting to the academic environment, struggling with frequent examinations and assignments, and managing healthy relationships with peers, seniors, professors, etc. (Sevinc and Gizir, 2014, 1291). In the majority of cases, students can easily find a way out to manage these issues. Nonetheless, these issues can become exorbitant on certain occasions, leading to distress and mental health issues. College students need adequate coping resources to handle college life which can help them succeed (Özgüven 1989). An effective adaptation from secondary to university education increases the chances of student achievement and persistence (Rienties et al., 2012). Therefore, it is worthwhile to understand how to improve students' academic adjustment and explore the factors or underlying dynamics.

2. Academic Adjustment among College Students

An essential component for college students, especially freshers, is managing their socio-psychological and scholarly challenges as they progress to tertiary education. Academic adjustment is the student's positive attitude toward their academic work, goals, and positive valuation of their academic environment (Al-Qaisy 2010, 3). Valuing academic adjustment is pertinent in predicting students' subsequent academic and extracurricular achievements. According to Anderson et al., (2016), there are three concepts related to academic adjustment including; (a) academic lifestyle: which is defined as the "fit between the individual and their temporary role as a student"; (b) academic achievement: associated with "satisfaction with academic progress and performance," and; (c) academic motivation: considered as the "drive for the student to continue and complete their academic sojourn." Unfortunately, there seems to be a dearth in the literature on the impact of coping resources in enhancing academic adjustment. Isik and Tekinalp, (2017, 164), among Turkish undergraduate students, found that the experimental group with gratitude journaling had a higher adjustment to university life compared with controls. Similarly, Liran and Miller, (2017, 51) found psychological capital as a central positive resource for students' academic adjustment. Owing to this dearth, there is a dire need to focus on how students in the Indian context utilize these positive resources for their academic adjustment. Since most studies are restricted to undergraduate students or sophomores, we focus on postgraduates and doctoral scholars in our exploration.

3. Gratitude among College Students

Gratitude is identified both as a state and a trait. Gratitude is the perception of a positive outcome resulting from an intentional act of another person or a moral agent, based on state position (Sun et al., 2014). In contrast, gratitude is conceptualized as a virtue or a characteristic of individuals as a trait (Rash et al., 2011). Previous literature suggests that gratitude predominantly relates to well-being, happiness, and life satisfaction (Tantano and Suparman, 2021, 1048; Hemarajarajeswari and Gupta, 2021). Gratitude is associated with greater hope, happiness, better mood, interpersonal functioning, and lower suicidal risk among college students (Ang et al., 2022). Gratitude also helps students to face stressful events through an approach to the brighter side of life events and managing healthy relationships with others which leads to greater well-being (Qin et al., 2015).

4. The Present Study

The existing literature suggests the role of academic adjustment and gratitude in various facets of college students' mental health (Nawa and Yamagishi, 2021, 2; Zainoodin et al., 2021). Our study tries to analyze the mechanism which explains whether academic adjustment leads to the development of gratitude or vice-versa. We attempt to unlock the potential of developing the virtue of gratitude and academic adjustment to see how they influence each other. Broaden-and-build theory (Fredrickson, 2004, 1453) supports the idea that imbuing gratuitous emotion may act as a positive resource to broaden the thought-action repertoires like other positive emotions and build personal resources by enhancing their physical, intellectual, psychological, and social reservoirs, theretofore enabling people to better cope with life's challenges. Likewise, gratitude helps students to escape the challenges emerging from academic life. Recently, Armenta et al., (2020) found that gratitude motivates students to engage in activities that lead to self-improvement, further helping them to become better and more productive students. Much of the previous research focuses entirely on undergraduate students, which requires clarification on whether postgraduates experience gratitude similarly. It helps to determine whether gratitude predicts academic adjustment or vice versa. Implications from this research can help implement meaningful interventions that can potentially enhance either academic achievement or gratitude, or both.

Based on these assumptions and evidence, we propose the following hypotheses:

H_1: Gratitude would predict academic adjustment among college students.

H_2: Academic adjustment would predict gratitude among college students.

H_3: Gender differences in the manifestation of gratitude and academic adjustment.

5. Method

5.1 Research Design and Sample

We utilized a cross-sectional survey design for the current study and conveniently selected our representative sample through a non-probability method for this working paper. The sample was a heterogeneous mix of students from various universities in different parts of the country, ranging from undergraduate to doctoral students. Insofar as the total participants, 48.2% were males ($n = 40$), and 51.8% ($n = 43$) were females, constituting a total sample of N = 83 participants.

5.2 Data Collection

We utilized Google Forms for collecting data through sharing via various social media platforms. We took informed consent before proceeding with the study measurement tools and informed them that their participation in the study was voluntary and that their identity would be kept anonymous and confidential.

5.3 Measures

Gratitude Questionnaire-6 (GQ-6): Developed by McCullough et al., (2002) and is a self-report 6-item scale based on a 7-point Likert scale ranging from 1- "Strongly disagree" to 7- "Strongly agree". Two items (3 and 6) are reverse scored. Sample items include *"I have so much in life to be thankful."* Internal consistency reliability captured through MacDonald's omega ($\omega = 0.75$) was found to be satisfactory.

Academic Adjustment Scale (AAS): Anderson et al., (2016), developed this scale, a self-report 9-item scale scored on 5- point Likert scale ranging from 1- "Rarely applies to me" to 5- "Always applies to me" where items 2 and 3 are reverse scored. The first three items constitute the Academic lifestyle scale, the next three are based on academic achievement, and the final three contribute to Academic motivation. Sample items include *"I am satisfied with my ability to learn at university."* Reliability values calculated through MacDonald's Omega were ($\omega = 0.69$) close to satisfactory.

6. Data Analysis

Data were analyzed using SPSS version 27. Descriptive statistics were calculated for each scale and subscale consisting of gratitude and academic adjustment, including their subscales. Pearson correlations were run to analyze the strength and direction of relationships between each variable. Linear regression analysis (Stepwise approach) was used to determine whether gratitude predicts academic adjustment or vice versa. We utilized an independent sample *t*-test to analyze the gender differences among variables.

7. Results

Correlational analysis shows (See Table 30.1) no significant correlation between gratitude and academic adjustment ($r = .18$). Linear regression analysis (See Table 30.2) also does not manifest any predictive relationship of gratitude on academic adjustment [$\beta = .17$; $F(1, 81) = 2.58$, $p = .112$] or vice versa. There is no significant gender difference in both gratitude ($t = 1.50$, $df = 81$, $p = .068$) and academic adjustment ($t = 1.58$, $df = 81$, $p = .058$) (See Table 30.3). Since the data collection is still going on, we speculate that these results might

Table 30.1 Descriptive statistics and pearson correlation coefficients for the measurement variables ($N = 83$).

Variables	M	SD	Gratitude	Academic Adjustment
Gratitude	31.30	5.91	1	
Academic Adjustment	34.77	5.44	.18	1

P = Non Significant

Source: Author's compilation

Table 30.2 Linear regression of academic adjustment (AAS) on gratitude

Predictor	β	ΔR^2	ΔF	P
Gratitude	.176	.031	2.58	.112

P = Non-Significant

Source: Author's compilation

Table 30.3 Mean differences of gender on academic adjustment and gratitude

Variables	Male		Female		t (81)	p
	M	SD	M	SD		
Gratitude	30.38	5.46	32.23	6.22	1.50	.068
Academic Adjustment	33.80	5.53	35.67	5.26	1.58	.058

P = Non Significant

Source: Author's compilation

change at a later stage with an increase in sample size. Hence, we have decided to continue our data collection process to check whether our preliminary non-significant results remain valid or not.

8. Discussion

We attempted to understand the mechanism which explains whether academic adjustment leads to the development of gratitude or vice-versa or whether there is a third explanation behind this thesis. We tried to unlock the potential of developing the virtue of gratitude and academic adjustment to see how they influence each other. Contrary to previous studies (Nawa and Yamagishi, 2021,12; Zainoodin et al., 2021), our study couldn't find any significant relationship between gratitude and academic adjustment with the existing sampling frame. Since we are continuing and extending this working paper, it is important to expand the sample and increase the diversity of our sample in the Indian context. As previous studies have highlighted the feasibility of the proposed relationship among undergraduate and first-year students (Ang et al., 2022., Işık and Tekinalp, 2017, 171), we are positive that we might get significant relationships between gratitude and academic adjustment or vice-versa. Establishing the proposed relationship will guide us in developing gratitude-based interventions that can be utilized effectively to foster academic adjustment and tackle mental health issues. Nevertheless, the independent *t*-test showing no gender differences in gratitude and academic adjustment corroborates t that both genders perceive gratitude and academic adjustment in the same way (Jain et al., 2017). Even though the current results are non-significant, there is a tendency for a positive relationship between gratitude and academic adjustment. During further extension of this proposition, we will come to a conclusion whether the hypothesized research direction is plausible or a mere dead-end.

REFERENCES

1. Al-Qaisy, L. M. 2010. "Adjustment of College Freshmen: The Importance of Gender and the Place of Residence." Journal of Educators Online 4, no. 2: 1–14.
2. Anderson, J. R., Y. Guan, and Y. Koc. 2016. "The Academic Adjustment Scale: Measuring the Adjustment of Permanent Resident or Sojourner Students." International Journal of Intercultural Relations 54: 68–76. https://doi.org/10.1016/j.ijintrel.2016.07.006.
3. Ang, J. Y.-Z., V. Monte, and W. Tsai. 2022. "First-Year College Students' Adjustment During the COVID-19 Pandemic: The Protective Roles of Hope and Gratitude." Translational Issues in Psychological Science [Advance online publication]. http://doi.org/10.1037/tps0000320.
4. Armenta, C. N., M. M. Fritz, and S. Lyubomirsky. 2017. "Functions of Positive Emotions: Gratitude as a Motivator of Self-Improvement and Positive Change." Emotion Review 9, no. 3: 183–90. https://doi.org/10.1177/1754073916669596.
5. Fredrickson, B. L. 2004. "The Broaden-and-Build Theory of Positive Emotions." Philosophical Transactions: Biological Sciences 359: 1449–67.
6. Hazan Liran, B., and P. Miller. 2019. "The Role of Psychological Capital in Academic Adjustment Among University Students." Journal of Happiness Studies 20, no. 1: 51–65. https://doi.org/10.1007/s10902-017-9933-3.
7. Hemarajarajeswari, J., and P. K. Gupta. 2021. "Gratitude, Psychological Well-Being, and Happiness Among College Students: A Correlational Study." International Journal of Indian Psychology 9, no. 1: 532–41. https://doi.org/10.25215/0901.053.
8. Işık, Ş., and B. Ergüner-Tekinalp. 2017. "The Effects of Gratitude Journaling on Turkish First Year College Students' College Adjustment, Life Satisfaction and Positive Affect." International Journal for the Advancement of Counselling 39, no. 2: 164–75. https://doi.org/10.1007/s10447-017-9289-8.
9. Jain, D., Tiwari, G. K., and Awasthi, I.D. 2017. "Impact of Metacognitive Awareness on Academic Adjustment and Academic Outcome of the Students." International Journal of Indian Psychology 5, no. 1: 123–38. https://doi.org/10.25215/0501.034.
10. McCullough, Michael E., Robert A. Emmons, and Jo-Ann Tsang. 2002. "The Grateful Disposition: A Conceptual and Empirical Topography." Journal of Personality & Social Psychology 82, no. 1: 112–27. https://doi.org/10.1037//0022-3514.82.1.112.
11. Nawa, Norberto Eiji, and Noriko Yamagishi. 2021. "Enhanced Academic Motivation in University Students Following a 2-Week Online Gratitude Journal Intervention." BMC Psychology 9, no. 1: 71. https://doi.org/10.1186/s40359-021-00559-w.
12. Özgüven, İ. E. 1989. "Üniversite Öğrencilerinin Uyum Sorunları ve Baş Etme Yolları." In Proceedings from I. Üniversite Gençliğinde Uyum Sorunları Sempozyumu, Ankara, Turkey.
13. Qin, Y., S. Qu, J. Yan, and X. Wan. 2015, Aug. "The Role of Life Satisfaction and Coping Style in the Relationship Between Gratitude and School Belonging." In. Advances in Social Science, Education & Humanities Research International Conference on Economy, Management and Education Technology. Atlantis Press 2015: (129–35). https://doi.org/10.2991/icemet-15.2015.29.
14. Rash, J. A., M. K. Matsuba, and K. M. Prkachin. 2011. "Gratitude and Well-Being: Who Benefits Most from a Gratitude Intervention." Applied Psychology: Health & Well-Being 3, no. 3: 350–69. https://doi.org/10.1111/j.1758-0854.2011.01058.x.
15. Rienties, B., S. Beausaert, T. Grohnert, S. Niemantsverdriet, and P. Kommers. 2012. "Understanding Academic Performance of International Students: The Role of Ethnicity, Academic and Social Integration." Higher Education 63, no. 6: 685–700. https://doi.org/10.1007/s10734-011-9468-1.

16. Sevinc, S., ve C. A. Gizir. 2014. "Üniversite Birinci Sınıf Öğrencilerinin Bakış Açılarından Üniversiteye Uyumu Olumsuz Etkileyen Faktörler (Mersin Üniversitesi Örnegi)." Kuram ve Uygulamada Eğitim Bilimleri 14, no. 4: 1285–308. https://doi.org/10.12738/estp.2014.4.2081

17. Sun, R. R., L. Lu, M. Liu, Y. Cao, X. C. Li, H. Liu, … P. Y. Zhang. 2014. "Biomarkers and Heart Disease. European Review for Medical and Pharmacological Sciences" 18: 2927–35.

18. Tantano, E. Y., and M. Y. Suparman. 2021. "The Role of Gratitude Among College Students Who Are" [working undergraduate thesis]. Proceedings of the International Conference on Economics, Business, Social and Humanities. Atlantis Press: (1047–52). https://doi.org/10.2991/assehr.k.210805.164.

19. Zainoodin, N. N., I. J. Hutasuhut, M. A. Abu Bakar, and Nurul Wardhani. 2021. "Gratitude and Its Relationship to Resilience and Academic Performance Among University Students." Journal of Cognitive Sciences & Human Development 7, no. 2: 145–58. https://doi.org/10.33736/jcshd.3808.2021

Handbook of Evidence Based Management Practices in Business – Satyendra Kumar Sharma et al. (eds)
© 2023 Taylor & Francis Group, London, ISBN 978-1-032-54216-4

Chapter

Work Environment: A Review of Established Scales from 50 Years of Literature

Shipra Pandey[1]
Research Scholar, Department of Management,
BITS Pilani, Pilani, Rajasthan, India

Jayashree Mahesh[2]
Assistant Professor, Department of Management,
BITS Pilani, Pilani, Rajasthan, India

ABSTRACT: The physical environment, social dynamics, and work settings significantly impact employees' morale, productivity, well-being, and job satisfaction. Thus, it is crucial to conduct research related to the work environment of the employees and use well-formulated scales to conduct such research. The purpose of this paper is to review the scales related to the work environment domain and identify their significance in the literature. The literature of 149 articles was extracted from the SCOPUS database using the keywords "Work Environment Scales" and analysed through content analysis. It has been observed that the scales of the work environment are widely used in business and other fields such as healthcare, education, etc. According to the literature, no holistic study has been done to compile and present the various validated scales of work environment that have been established and verified. Therefore, this study attempts to provide a glimpse of prominent work environment scales used during 1975-2022. The findings of the study show that similarities and differences in scales depend on the context, industry, and research domain. These findings will help future academicians, practitioners, and managers to determine the suitable scales for their research setting and get insight into the commonalities and differences among various industries. Additionally, corporate organizations can use these insights to improve their context-specific efficiency and effectiveness.

KEYWORDS: Work environment, Work environment scales, Prominent, Review

[1]p20200042@pilani.bits-pilani.ac.in, [2]jmahesh@pilani.bits-pilani.ac.in

DOI: 10.4324/9781003415725-31

1. Introduction

A workplace of the person, or the milieus in which they are surrounded, can be termed as that person's work environment. It is also the social and professional setting around which that person is expected to participate in several different activities. The productivity of employees and their performance is impacted significantly by WE (work environment). The methods, equipment, structure, procedures, and working circumstances that impact the performance of employees favourably or adversely are termed the WE (work environment). it is imperative to maintain a secure and healthy workplace for various reasons. One of those reasons is simply that by offering a supportive and trustworthy workplace, the employees' well-being, and level of trust in the business will increase. Therefore, it is essential to do research on the working conditions of employees, and we require properly developed scales to do so.

According to the literature, Rudolf Moos, a professor in Stanford University, developed the Work Environment Scale in the 1970s. One of nine Social Climate Scales developed by Moos in the 1960s and 1980s, this scale aims to operationalize and quantify the fundamental characteristics of various social contexts. The Work Environment Scale was developed to assess the social climate in the workplace or industrial settings (Moos, 1974). The conceptual theory behind the development of this given measure is "organisational concern for maintaining a healthy working environment," & as a result, there is a necessity to create efficient instruments to accurately analyse the environment. The Work Environment Scale consists of three sets of 90 items of true and false means that reflect 10 dimensions: the Relationship dimension, the System Maintenance and System Change dimensions, and the Personal Growth or Goal Orientation dimensions. It is believed that when utilised properly, the Work Environment Scale can assist a company in assessing employee satisfaction, productivity, and employee expectations, all of which contribute to a productive workplace. There are three ways to administer the Work Environment Scale: Form R, or real, measures how a person feels about their workplace; Form E, or expected, measures an employee's expectations of their working environment, whereas Form I, or ideal, measures the ideal workplace goals and values your employee possesses.

Considering the significance of the work environment, various researchers have proposed work environment scales in different contexts like hospitality, education, public services, etc. However, it is observed from the literature that no study has been done to compile and present the key work environment scales under a single roof. Therefore, by examining and summarising the important work environment scales, this research aims to fill a gap in the literature.

2. Methodology

In this study, literature from the SCOPUS database has been taken from 1975- 2022. The authors performed an electronic search of the SCOPUS database using the keywords "Work Environment Scales." A search result of 151 articles was obtained. Then, after applying the inclusion criteria a total number of 149 articles were used for content analysis. The content analysis resulted in 35 papers on prominent work environment scales. These 35 papers are

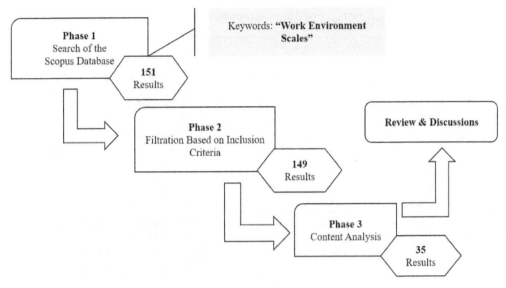

Fig. 31.1 Methodology

Source: Author's compilation

from 1976-2022. In addition, a non-exhaustive review was conducted to get further insights, and the results are reported in the next section of the study.

3. Findings

The authors examined the 35 research publications cited on a few notable scales, highlighting the author(s), study year, nation, application domain, dimensions, and item count of the scales as shown in Table 31.1.

Table 31.1 Work environment scales (1976–2022)

Sr. No.	Author	Year	Country	Domain	Scale, Dimensions, and items
1	Norton R.S., Booth R.F., Webster E.G.	1976	USA	Education	**WE Scale (Work Environment): 10 Dimensions:** Cohesion among peers, autonomy, staff support, clarity, innovation, pressure at work, physical comfort, control, involvement, and task orientation. **90 items**
2	Booth R.F., Webster E.G., Berry N.H., Norton R.S.	1976	USA	Navy	**WE Scale (Work Environment): 10 Dimensions:** Cohesion among peers, autonomy, staff support, clarity, innovation, pressure at work, physical comfort, control, involvement, and task orientation. **90 items**

Sr. No.	Author	Year	Country	Domain	Scale, Dimensions, and items
3	Waters J.E.	1978	Georgia	Law Enforcement Service	**WE Scale (Work Environment): 10 Dimensions:** Cohesion among peers, autonomy, staff support, clarity, innovation, pressure at work, physical comfort, control, involvement, and task orientation. **90 items**
4	Billings A.G., Moos R.H.	1982	USA	Families	**WE Scale (Work Environment): 10 Dimensions:** Cohesion among peers, autonomy, staff support, clarity, innovation, pressure at work, physical comfort, control, involvement, and task orientation. **90 items**
5	Koran L.M., Moos B., Zasslow M., Moos R.H.	1983	USA	Healthcare	**WE Scale (Work Environment): 10 Dimensions:** Cohesion among peers, autonomy, staff support, clarity, innovation, pressure at work, physical comfort, control, involvement, and task orientation. **90 items**
6	Fawzy F.I., Wellisch D.K., Pasnau R.O., Leibowitz B.	1983	USA	Healthcare	**WE Scale (Work Environment): 10 Dimensions:** Cohesion among peers, autonomy, staff support, clarity, innovation, pressure at work, physical comfort, control, involvement, and task orientation. **90 items**
7	Lusk E.J., Geranmayeh A., Neves J., Cormier P., Diserens D.,	1983	USA	Education	**WE Scale (Work Environment): 10 Dimensions:** Cohesion among peers, autonomy, staff support, clarity, innovation, pressure at work, physical comfort, control, involvement, and task orientation. **90 items**
8	Mitchell R.E., Cronkite R.C., Moos R.H.	1983	USA	Healthcare	**WE Scale (Work Environment): 10 Dimensions:** Cohesion among peers, autonomy, staff support, clarity, innovation, pressure at work, physical comfort, control, involvement, and task orientation. **90 items**
9	Fraser B.J.	1988	Australia	Education	**WE Scale (Work Environment): 10 Dimensions:** Cohesion among peers, autonomy, staff support, clarity, innovation, pressure at work, physical comfort, control, involvement, and task orientation. **90 items**
10	Turnipseed D.L.	1990	USA	Healthcare	**WE Scale (Work Environment): 10 Dimensions:** Cohesion among peers, autonomy, staff support, clarity, innovation, pressure at work, physical comfort, control, involvement, and task orientation. **90 items**

Sr. No.	Author	Year	Country	Domain	Scale, Dimensions, and items
11	Maloney J.P., Allanach B.C., Bartz C.	1991	USA	Healthcare	**WE Scale (Work Environment)**: **10 Dimensions:** Cohesion among peers, autonomy, staff support, clarity, innovation, pressure at work, physical comfort, control, involvement, and task orientation. **90 items**
12	Tommasini N.R.	1992	USA	Healthcare	**WE Scale (Work Environment)**: **10 Dimensions:** Cohesion among peers, autonomy, staff support, clarity, innovation, pressure at work, physical comfort, control, involvement, and task orientation. **90 items**
13	Baker G.A., Dewey M., Riley M., Tapper J., Carlisle C.	1992	USA, UK	Healthcare	**WE Scale (Work Environment)**: **10 Dimensions:** Cohesion among peers, autonomy, staff support, clarity, innovation, pressure at work, physical comfort, control, involvement, and task orientation. **90 items**
14	Carlisle C., Baker G.A., Riley M., Dewey M.	1994	UK	Healthcare	**WE Scale (Work Environment)**: **10 Dimensions:** Cohesion among peers, autonomy, staff support, clarity, innovation, pressure at work, physical comfort, control, involvement, and task orientation. **90 items**
15	Long C.G., Hollin C.R., Williams M.,	1995	UK	Healthcare	**WE Scale (Work Environment)**: **10 Dimensions:** Cohesion among peers, autonomy, staff support, clarity, innovation, pressure at work, physical comfort, control, involvement, and task orientation. **90 items**
16	Wilk L.A., Redmon W.K.	1997	USA	Education	**WE Scale (Work Environment)**: **10 Dimensions:** Cohesion among peers, autonomy, staff support, clarity, innovation, pressure at work, physical comfort, control, involvement, and task orientation. **90 items**
17	Waryszak R.Z.	1999	Australia	Hospitality	**WE Scale (Work Environment)**: **10 Dimensions:** Cohesion among peers, autonomy, staff support, clarity, innovation, pressure at work, physical comfort, control, involvement, and task orientation. **90 items**
18	Doughty J., Tong V., May B., Butell S.	2002	USA	Education	**WE Scale (Work Environment)**: **10 Dimensions:** Cohesion among peers, autonomy, staff support, clarity, innovation, pressure at work, physical comfort, control, involvement, and task orientation. **90 items**

Sr. No.	Author	Year	Country	Domain	Scale, Dimensions, and items
19	Borritz M., Mikkelsen O.A., Kristensen T.S., Villadsen E., Bjorner J.B., Rugulies R.	2006	Denmark	Service	**Copenhagen Psychosocial Questionnaire (COPSOQ): 5 Dimensions:** Demands, Active and developmental work, Interpersonal relations at work, Job insecurity, and Job satisfaction. **16 items**
20	Goddard R., Goddard M., O'brien P.	2006	Australia	Education	**WE Scale (Work Environment): 10 Dimensions:** Cohesion among peers, autonomy, staff support, clarity, innovation, pressure at work, physical comfort, control, involvement, and task orientation. **90 items**
21	Cohen J., Stuenkel D., Nguyen Q.	2009	USA	Healthcare	**WE Scale (Work Environment): 10 Dimensions:** Cohesion among peers, autonomy, staff support, clarity, innovation, pressure at work, physical comfort, control, involvement, and task orientation. **90 items**
22	Fletcher T.D., Nusbaum D.N.	2010	Africa, America, and Asia	Education	**Competitive Work Environment Scale: 5 dimensions:** Competition for tangible rewards, Nontangible rewards, Recognition, Status, and Competition influenced by co-workers. **20 items**
23	Ostermann T., Bertram M., Büssing A.	2010	Germany	Healthcare	**Working Environment Scale 10 (WES-10): 4 Dimensions:** Self-realization (SR), Workload, Conflict, and Nervousness. **10 items**
24	Garcia-Garcia I., Ramos Cobos M., Souza A., Serrano J.C., Ramos V.B.	2011	Spain	Healthcare	**WE Scale (Work Environment): 10 Dimensions:** Cohesion among peers, autonomy, staff support, clarity, innovation, pressure at work, physical comfort, control, involvement, and task orientation. **90 items**
25	Olesen K., Carneiro I.G., Flyvholm M.-A., Rugulies Sogaard K., Holtermann A.; Jorgensen M.B., R., Rasmussen C.D.N.	2012	Denmark	Hospitality	**Copenhagen Psychosocial Questionnaire (COPSOQ): 15 Dimensions:** Work Pace, Emotional Demands, Influence, Possibilities for Development, Quality of Leadership, Meaning of Work, Recognition, Role Clarity, Social Support from Colleagues, Job Satisfaction, Trust Regarding Management, Justice, Quantitative Demands, Social Support from Supervisors, Predictability. **40 items**

Sr. No.	Author	Year	Country	Domain	Scale, Dimensions, and items
26	García I.G., Castillo R.F., Santa-Bárbara E.S.	2014	Spain	Healthcare	**WE Scale (Work Environment): 10 Dimensions:** Cohesion among peers, autonomy, staff support, clarity, innovation, pressure at work, physical comfort, control, involvement, and task orientation. **90 items**
27	Von Treuer K., Little G.; Fuller-Tyszkiewicz M.	2014	Australia	Healthcare	**WE Scale (Work Environment): 10 Dimensions:** Cohesion among peers, autonomy, staff support, clarity, innovation, pressure at work, physical comfort, control, involvement, and task orientation. **90 items**
28	Kim J.-K., Yu M., Kim M.J., Kim S.-Y., Lee K.-A.	2014	Korea	Healthcare	**The Korean Scale on Work Environment for Clinical Nurses (KWES-CN): 9 Dimensions:** Manager leadership, Sufficient inventory and supply, supporting environment for nursing work, Hospital's support for the working environment, Patient care environment and professional activities, Violence within the ward, Recognition and respect, Satisfaction with work schedule; and Computer problems. **39 items**
29	Yun S., Kang J., Lee Y.-O., Yi Y.	2014	Korea	Healthcare	**Korean Nursing Work Environment Scale: 4 dimensions:** Institutional support, the leadership of the head nurse, basic work system and interpersonal relationship. **30 items**
30	Verulava T., Jorbenadze R., Dangadz B., Karimi L.	2017	Georgia	Healthcare	**PE Scale (Practice Environment) Scale: 7 dimensions:** participation of nurse in affairs of the hospital; managerial skills of nurse; support & leadership; collegial physician-nurse relations, quality of care; staffing & resource adequacy. **21 items**
31	Pfeiffer B., Brusilovskiy E., Davidson A., Persch A.	2018	USA	Education	**WE Scale (Work Environment): 10 dimensions:** Cohesion among peers, autonomy, staff support, clarity, innovation, pressure at work, physical comfort, control, involvement, and task orientation. **90 items**

Sr. No.	Author	Year	Country	Domain	Scale, Dimensions, and items
32	Dehring T., Von Treuer K., Redley B.	2018	Australia	Healthcare	**WE Scale (Work Environment): 10 dimensions:** Cohesion among peers, autonomy, staff support, clarity, innovation, pressure at work, physical comfort, control, involvement, and task orientation. **90 items**
33	Abbaspour S., Tajik R., Atif K., Eshghi H., Teimori G., Ghodrati-Torbati A., Zandi A.	2020	Iran	Healthcare	**WE Scale (Work Environment): 10 dimensions:** Cohesion among peers, autonomy, staff support, clarity, innovation, pressure at work, physical comfort, control, involvement, and task orientation. **90 items**
34	Sarıköse S., Göktepe N.	2022	Turkey	Healthcare	**(PES-NWI) Practice Work Environment Scale of the Nursing Work Index: 6 dimensions:** Participation of nurses in affairs of the hospital, Nurse-manager ability, Support & Leadership of nurses, collegial nurse-physician relationship, Nursing foundations for care quality, Staffing & Resource adequacy. **31 items**
35	Sousa E., Lin C.-F., Gaspar F., Lucas P.	2022	Portugal	Healthcare	**Quality Nursing Work Environment (IQN-WE): 5 Dimensions:** Professional Development & Team Support; Safe Nursing WE; Team Management & Organization; Information Systems & Risk Control; Welfare & Salary. **65 items**

Source: Author's compilation

4. Discussion and Conclusion

The above articles on 35 work environment scales show that most of the authors have used scales given by Moos. It has also been observed that most of the papers are from western countries like the U.S.A. No study has been found in the Indian context which shows that there is an opportunity for further study to be done in developing nations. Additionally, it has been observed that most of the research was carried out in the healthcare domain. Despite this, there are few prominent studies that have used different scales in different sectors like the service sector and hospitality sector. The analysis also led to the observation that the scale on the work environment given by Moos has the potential to be used in different sectors like hospitals, education, etc. which shows the applicability of the scale in diverse domains.

This review has contributed to the development of a fundamental understanding of the crucial aspects of work environment scales in different contexts of applications. This would make it easier for different academics, professionals, and researchers to locate the appropriate scale in literature for their use and reference.

5. Limitations and Future Scope

The paper aims at providing an overview of various work environment scales used in different domains of application. There are a few limitations observed in this review. First, keywords different from the "Work Environment Scale" can be used to get different results. Second, an exhaustive review can be done in future research by exploring more keywords. Third, the SCOPUS database was used in this study. Future research can be done by using different databases like Web of science, Science Direct, etc.

REFERENCES

1. Abbaspour, S., R. Tajik, K. Atif, H. Eshghi, G. Teimori, A. Ghodrati-Torbati, and A. Zandi. 2020. "Prevalence and Correlates of Mental Health Status among Pre-Hospital Healthcare Staff." *Clinical Practice and Epidemiology in Mental Health* 16 (1): 17–23. doi:10.2174/1745017902016010017.
2. Baker, G. A., C. Carlisle, M. Riley, J. Tapper, and M. Dewey. 1992. "The Work Environment Scale: A Comparison of British and North American Nurses." *Journal of Advanced Nursing* 17 (6): 692–698. doi:10.1111/j.1365-2648. 1992.tb01966. x.
3. Billings, A. G. and R. H. Moos. 1982. "Work Stress and the stress-buffering Roles of Work and Family Resources." *Journal of Organizational Behavior* 3 (3): 215–232. doi:10.1002/job.4030030303.
4. BOOTH, R. F., R. S. NORTON, E. G. WEBSTER, and N. H. BERRY. 1976. "Assessing the Psychosocial Characteristics of Occupational Training Environments." *Journal of Occupational Psychology* 49 (2): 85–92. doi:10.1111/j.2044-8325.1976.tb00333.x.
5. Borritz, M., R. Rugulies, E. Villadsen, O. A. Mikkelsen, T. S. Kristensen, and J. B. Bjorner. 2006. "Burnout among Employees in Human Service Work: Design and Baseline Findings of the PUMA Study." *Scandinavian Journal of Public Health* 34 (1): 49–58. doi:10.1080/14034940510032275.
6. Carlisle, C., G. A. Baker, M. Riley, and M. Dewey. 1994. "Stress in Midwifery: A Comparison of Midwives and Nurses using the Work Environment Scale." *International Journal of Nursing Studies* 31 (1): 13–22. doi:10.1016/0020-7489(94)90003-5.
7. Cohen, J., D. Stuenkel, and Q. Nguyen. 2009. "Providing a Healthy Work Environment for Nurses: The Influence on Retention." *Journal of Nursing Care Quality* 24 (4): 308–315. doi:10.1097/NCQ.0b013e3181a4699a.
8. Dehring, T., K. Von Treuer, and B. Redley. 2018. "The Impact of Shift Work and Organisational Climate on Nurse Health: A Cross-Sectional Study." *BMC Health Services Research* 18 (1). doi:10.1186/s12913-018-3402-5.
9. Doughty, J., B. May, S. Butell, and V. Tong. 2002. "A Profile of the Social Climate of Nursing Faculty in an Academic Setting." *Nursing and Health Care Perspectives* 23 (4): 191–196.
10. Fawzy, F. I., D. K. Wellisch, R. O. Pasnau, and B. Leibowitz. 1983. "Preventing Nursing Burnout: A Challenge for Liaison Psychiatry." *General Hospital Psychiatry* 5 (2): 141–149. doi:10.1016/0163-8343(83)90114-7.
11. Fletcher, T. D. and D. N. Nusbaum. 2010. "Development of the Competitive Work Environment Scale: A Multidimensional Climate Construct." *Educational and Psychological Measurement* 70 (1): 105–124. doi:10.1177/0013164409344492.

12. Fraser, B. J. 1988. "Assessing and Improving School Climate." *Evaluation & Research in Education* 2 (3): 109–122. doi:10.1080/09500798809533248.

13. García, I. G., R. F. Castillo, and E. S. Santa-Bárbara. 2014. "Nursing Organizational Climates in Public and Private Hospitals." *Nursing Ethics* 21 (4): 437–446. doi:10.1177/0969733013503680.

14. Garcia-Garcia, I., V. B. Ramos, J. C. Serrano, M. Ramos Cobos, and A. Souza. 2011. "Nursing Personnel's Perceptions of the Organizational Climate in Public and Private Hospitals in Spain." *International Nursing Review* 58 (2): 234–241. doi:10.1111/j.1466-7657.2010.00871.x.

15. Goddard, R., P. O'Brien, and M. Goddard. 2006. "Work Environment Predictors of Beginning Teacher Burnout." *British Educational Research Journal* 32 (6): 857–874. doi:10.1080/01411920600989511.

16. Kim, J. -K, S. -Y Kim, M. Yu, M. J. Kim, and K. -A Lee. 2014. "Korean Work Environment Scales for Clinical Nurses." *Japan Journal of Nursing Science* 12 (1): 54–68. doi:10.1111/jjns.12048.

17. Koran, L. M., R. H. Moos, B. Moos, and M. Zasslow. 1983. "Changing Hospital Work Environments: An Example of a Burn Unit." *General Hospital Psychiatry* 5 (1): 7–13. doi:10.1016/0163-8343(83)90037-3.

18. Long, C. G., M. Williams, and C. R. Hollin. 1995. "Staff Perceptions of Organization Change of Treatment Delivery on an Addiction Unit." *Journal of Advanced Nursing* 21 (4): 759–765. doi:10.1046/j.1365-2648.1995.21040759.x.

19. Lusk, E. J., D. Diserens, P. Cormier, A. Geranmayeh, and J. Neves. 1983. "The Work Environment Scale: Baseline Data for Dental Schools." *Psychological Reports* 53 (3 Pt 2): 1160–1162. doi:10.2466/pr0.1983.53.3f.1160.

20. Maloney, J. P., C. Bartz, and B. C. Allanach. 1991. "Staff Perceptions of their Work Environment before and Six Months After an Organizational Change." *Military Medicine* 156 (2): 86–92. doi:10.1093/milmed/156.2.86.

21. Mitchell, R. E., R. C. Cronkite, and R. H. Moos. 1983. "Stress, Coping, and Depression among Married Couples." *Journal of Abnormal Psychology* 92 (4): 433–448. doi:10.1037/0021-843X.92.4.433.

22. Moos, R. H. 1974. "Family environment scale." Palo Alto, CA: Consulting Psychologists Press.

23. Norton, R. S., R. F. Booth, and E. G. Webster. 1976. "Correlates and Implications of Continued Participation in a Longitudinal Survey." *Journal of Psychology: Interdisciplinary and Applied* 93 (1): 61–69. doi:10.1080/00223980.1976.9921374.

24. Olesen, K., I. G. Carneiro, M. B. Jorgensen, M. -A Flyvholm, R. Rugulies, C. D. N. Rasmussen, K. Sogaard, and A. Holtermann. 2012. "Psychosocial Work Environment among Immigrant and Danish Cleaners." *International Archives of Occupational and Environmental Health* 85 (1): 89–95. doi:10.1007/s00420-011-0642-7.

25. Ostermann, T., M. Bertram, and A. Büssing. 2010. "A Pilot Study on the Effects of a Team Building Process on the Perception of Work Environment in an Integrative Hospital for Neurological Rehabilitation." *BMC Complementary and Alternative Medicine* 10. doi:10.1186/1472-6882-10-10.

26. Pfeiffer, B., E. Brusilovskiy, A. Davidson, and A. Persch. 2018. "Impact of Person-Environment Fit on Job Satisfaction for Working Adults with Autism Spectrum Disorders." *Journal of Vocational Rehabilitation* 48 (1): 49–57. doi:10.3233/JVR-170915.

27. Sarıköse, S. and N. Göktepe. 2022. "Effects of Nurses' Individual, Professional and Work Environment Characteristics on Job Performance." *Journal of Clinical Nursing* 31 (5-6): 633–641. doi:10.1111/jocn.15921.

28. Sousa, E., C. -F Lin, F. Gaspar, and P. Lucas. 2022. "Translation and Validation of the Indicators of Quality Nursing Work Environments in the Portuguese Cultural Context." *International Journal of Environmental Research and Public Health* 19 (19). doi:10.3390/ijerph191912313.

29. Tommasini, N. R. 1992. "The Impact of a Staff Support Group on the Work Environment of a Specialty Unit." *Archives of Psychiatric Nursing* 6 (1): 40–47. doi:10.1016/0883-9417(92)90053-L.
30. Turnipseed, D. L. 1990. "Evaluation of Health Care Work Environments Via a Social Climate Scale: Results of a Field Study." *Hospital and Health Services Administration* 35 (2): 245–261.
31. Verulava, T., R. Jorbenadze, B. Dangadz, and L. Karimi. 2017. "Nurses' Work Environment Characteristics and Job Satisfaction: Evidence from Georgia." *Gazi Medical Journal* 29 (1): 12–16. doi:10.12996/gmj.2018.04.
32. von Treuer, K., M. Fuller-Tyszkiewicz, and G. Little. 2014. "The Impact of Shift Work and Organizational Work Climate on Health Outcomes in Nurses." *Journal of Occupational Health Psychology* 19 (4): 453–461. doi:10.1037/a0037680.
33. Waryszak, R. Z. 1999. "Students' Expectations from their Cooperative Education Placements in the Hospitality Industry: An International Perspective." *Education + Training* 41 (1): 33–40. doi:10.1108/00400919910255924.
34. Waters, J. E. 1978. "Evaluating Organizational Environments in Law Enforcement Agencies: A Social Climate Perspective." *Criminal Justice Review* 3 (2): 1-6. doi:10.1177/073401687800300202.
35. Wilk, L. A. and W. K. Redmon. 1997. "The Effects of Feedback and Goal Setting on the Productivity and Satisfaction of University Admissions Staff." *Journal of Organizational Behavior Management* 18 (1): 45–68. doi:10.1300/J075v18n01_04.
36. Yun, S., J. Kang, Y. -O Lee, and Y. Yi. 2014. "Work Environment and Workplace Bullying among Korean Intensive Care Unit Nurses." *Asian Nursing Research* 8 (3): 219–225. doi:10.1016/j.anr.2014.07.002.

Handbook of Evidence Based Management Practices in Business – Satyendra Kumar Sharma et al. (eds)
© 2023 Taylor & Francis Group, London, ISBN 978-1-032-54216-4

Chapter

Role Stressors and Burnout: Examining the Mediating Role of Rumination

Nidhi S. Bisht[1]

Organization Behaviour and Human Resource Management,
Management Development Institute, Gurgaon, India

Arun Kumar Tripathy[2]

Strategy and General Management,
Management Development Institute, Gurgaon, India

ABSTRACT: For many decades' burnout has been a grave concern for researchers and practitioners due to its personal and organizational repercussions. In this study, we collect data from Indian higher education institutions in India *and* hypothesize that role stressors - role ambiguity and role conflict are positively related to burnout. Drawing on the transactional theory, we also study the mediating role rumination in the relationship between role conflict, role ambiguity and burnout. The results obtained through structural equation modelling supported the proposed hypotheses. Both job stressors *were positively related to burnout,* and the faculty's tendency to ruminate mediated the relationship between job stressors and burnout. Implications of the result and future research directions are discussed.

KEYWORDS: Job stressors, Role conflict, Role ambiguity, Rumination, Burnout, Higher education

1. Introduction

Higher education faculty create their career through teaching, research and service (Numann and Terosky, 2007), with services covering a plethora of activities like curriculum design (Trowler and Knight, 2000); institutional governance (Jones, 2011). Nonetheless, there is a growing trend of faculty being rewarded and promoted based on the research conducted (McCune,

---
[1]nidhi.bisht@mdi.ac.in, [2]arun.tripathy@mdi.ac.in

DOI: 10.4324/9781003415725-32

2019); making research a significant source of burnout (Singh et al., 1998; Xu, 2019). Burnout has been pointed out as a serious problem in higher education faculty (Rothmann et al., 2008; Singh et al., 1998; Xu, 2019). Some of the reasons identified for burnout in higher education faculty include the relationship with students, staff and administration (Blix et al., 1994); the number of students taught, multiple student evaluations, time invested in various activities (Lackritz, 2004); and academic research (Singh et al., 1998). Few empirical studies even point out how escalation in faculty burnout makes academic careers less attractive (Singh et al., 1998; Rothmann et al., 2008).

In this study, we investigate the relationship between role stressors-role conflict, ambiguity and burnout in higher education faculty in India. *Recognizing the interplay between individual characteristics and environment* (Fernet, Guay, and Senécal, 2004;), *we* also study the mediating role of rumination in the relationship between role ambiguity, role conflict and burnout. It is crucial because, in the academic context, burnout can have severe consequences for individuals and organizations (Talbot, 2000), including low mental and physical well-being (Barkhuizen *et al.* 2004), a slump in teaching and research performance (Singh *et al.* 1998) and increased absenteeism (Blix *et al.* 1994) amongst others. Overall, our study contributes to the literature in two ways. First, adding to the limited body of literature on higher education in India (Sen, 2011), our study provides evidence for higher education faculty in India experiencing burnout due to role conflict and role ambiguity. Second, given the centrality of the interplay between situational and individual factors (Hobfoll, 1989), our study supports rumination partially *mediating the relationship between role ambiguity, role conflict and burnout.*

2. Theoretical Framework and Hypotheses Formulation

Evidence shows that employees perceiving role conflict and role ambiguity at the workplace may be unable to meet the role expectations due to discrepancies between perceived and expected behaviour. Though t*hese roles-related constructs have been viewed as twin problems, these are discrete constructs with different antecedents (Bauer and Spencer, 2003).* While role conflict is defined as the incongruence in expectations, so compliance with one makes it difficult to comply with the other (Rizzo et al., 1970). On the other hand, role ambiguity is the lack of clear and necessary information to perform a role effectively; or when the role player needs clarification about which aspect of the job is more critical (Kahn et al., 1964; Keller, 1975). The literature contains evidence that role conflict and role ambiguity are positively related to various individual and dysfunctional organizational outcomes like low job satisfaction, tension, absenteeism, low satisfaction; low job involvement, low job performance ratings and intent to leave (Rizzo et al., 1970; Schuler et al., 1977).

When an employee is expected to perform multiple roles, it leads to inter-role conflict because of the inability to do justice to the different roles assumed. It may be due to time constraints or the requirements of incompatible behaviour among the roles (Kahn et al., 1964). Also, a lack of necessary information and incompatible expectations associated with one or multiple roles triggers an adverse emotional reaction and make employees uncomfortable (Schaubroeck et al., 1989). *Past research has identified* role conflict and role ambiguity as antecedents to burnout in a different population of workers (see Barber and Iwai, 1996; Yürür and Sarikaya,

2012; Papastylianou and Polychronopoulos, 2009; Capel et al., 1987). Based on past related research, it was expected that role conflict, and role ambiguity would lead to burnout in higher education faculty. Hence, we postulated the following hypotheses:

Hypothesis 1: *Perceived role conflict is positively related to burnout.*

Hypothesis 2: *Perceived role ambiguity is positively related to burnout.*

We draw on transactional theory (Lazarus and Folkman, 1984) to understand the mediating role of rumination in the relationship between role ambiguity, role conflict and burnout. The transactional theory states that stress is a relational concept determined by subjective judgement- that is, an outcome of the interaction between the external stimulation and the individual (Lazarus and Folkman, 1984). In line with the transactional theory, we argue that when people face role ambiguity and role conflict at work, they may have to expend physical or mental energy to cope with the demands (Cropley and Millward, 2009). Rumination about their role-related demands beyond regular working hours could be one such way of coping (Cropley and Zijlstra, 2011). Rumination typically involves repetitive thoughts about past events, present mood states, or lack of progress towards attaining goals (Martin and Tesser,1989). Rumination as an extension of demands experienced at the workplace makes it difficult to mentally switch off after work (Querstret and Cropley, 2012), consequently draining energy by being engrossed in work-related issues (Donahue et al., 2012). People may ruminate retrospectively or prospectively by thinking about issues that have occurred in the past or anticipatively engross in problems and expectations that may arise at work (Cropley and Zijlstra, 2011; Querstret and Cropley, 2012).

Due to rumination, employees may experience physiological arousal even after work (Kuper and Marmot, 2003), which may overwhelm available coping resources (Lazarus and Folkman, 1984) and may not allow employees to derive benefits from off-job time. Draining resources without replenishment may not ameliorate the impact of chronic role stressors facilitating the occurrence of burnout (Hobfoll, 1989). Therefore, rumination about one's role stressors may represent a potential mediator in the relationship between role ambiguity, role conflict and burnout. Thus, we propose the following hypotheses:

Hypothesis 3: *Rumination during off-job partially mediates the relationship between role conflict and burnout.*

Hypothesis 4: *Rumination during off-job partially mediates the relationship between role ambiguity and burnout.*

3. Method

3.1 Sample and Procedure

The data were collected by means of an online questionnaire. The first part of the questionnaire requested demographic information such as age, gender, tenure and total work experience and the second part comprised of scales used in the study. The questionnaire was distributed to a total of 580 higher education faculty of private business schools and engineering colleges of North India with a brief introduction to the survey, describing the purpose of the study. Participation was voluntary, and confidentiality of the data was assured to the participants. With a response rate was 42 %, the final sample comprised of 246 higher education faculty (140 men, 106 women).

4. Measures

4.1 Role Conflict and Ambiguity

The role conflict and ambiguity scales developed by Rizzo, House, and Lirtzman (1970) were used to measure the levels of role conflict and role ambiguity. These measures of role constructs developed by Rizzo et al. (1970) have been *widely used in psychological research* (Role conflict is an eight-item scale with a sample item "I have to do things that should be done differently". Role ambiguity is a six-item scale with a sample item, "I know exactly what is expected of me". Respondents reported their answers on a 7-point Likert scale with anchors ranging from (1) "strongly disagree" to (7) "strongly agree". The internal consistency of the role conflict and ambiguity scale was good (Cronbach's α = .77 and .82, respectively).

4.2 Rumination

The tendency of faculty to ruminate about work was measured using an adapted version of a 13-item Rumination on Sadness scale (RSS) developed by Conway *et al.* (2000). The items were adapted according to the purpose of the study and rumination about "one's sadness" was changed to "one's work". *A sample item was, "In general, I have difficulty getting myself to stop thinking about my work". Items were scored on a 5-point Likert scale ranging from (1) "not at all" to (5) "very much".* The adapted scale version showed high internal consistency (α = .84).

4.3 Burnout

We used emotional exhaustion and depersonalization from the Maslach Burnout Inventory-Human Services Survey (MBI-HSS: Maslach, Jackson, and Leiter, 1996) to measure burnout that constitutes the core dimensions of burnout (Maslach, 1981; and Green, Walkey, and Taylor, 1991). Emotional exhaustion was assessed using eight items subscale (e.g., "I feel like my work is breaking me down"), and depersonalization was assessed using five items subscale (e.g., I really don't care what happens to some of my clients). Items were scored on a 7-point scale ranging from (0) "never" to (6) "every day". The Cronbach's α value for burnout was 0.80.

4.4 Control Variables

Past research suggests that age or years of experience in a position and gender (Pretty, McCarthy, and Catano, 1992) are differently related to burnout. Therefore, we included these control variables (gender, marital status, job tenure and total experience) in the study. Age, total experience, and tenure were measured in years, and gender was a nominal category variable.

5. Preliminary Analyses

The means, standard deviations, Cronbach's alphas and bivariate correlations between control variables, role conflict, role ambiguity, rumination, psychological detachment and burnout are presented in Table 32.1. *Age is positively correlated to total experience and tenure in the organization. Role conflict is positively correlated to rumination and burnout. Likewise, role ambiguity is positively related to rumination and burnout.*

Table 32.1 Means, standard deviations, and correlations between the model variables

	Mean	SD	1	2	3	4	5	6	7	8
Age	42.98	10.34								
Total experience	12.53	9.63	.88**							
Tenure	6.68	5.1	.66**	.61**						
Role conflict	4.10	1.12	-.18*	-.12	-.03	(.77)				
Role ambiguity	3.42	1.14	.07	.07	.05	-.21	(.82)			
Rumination	2.42	0.82	-.09	-.04	-.01	.35**	.16*	(.84)		
Burnout	3.06	1.29	-.25**	-.27**	-.10	.45**	.25**	.65**	-.26**	(.80)

Note: n = 246, *p < .05; **p < .01. Reliability coefficients are on the diagonal.
Source: Author's compilation

6. Analyses

Structural equation modelling (SEM) techniques using AMOS 20 software package (Arbuckle, 2007) was used to analyze the data. Since the data providing measure of the predictor and criterion variable has been provided by the same person, the constructs were tested for any possible standard method variance. Items of the scales were also examined for potential common method variance using the Harman single-factor test (Hair et al., 2006). Before testing the structural model, the measurement models were fitted to the data to identify the best-fitting model. This was done to ensure that the unobserved variables adequately represent the observed variables, as a measurement model defines the relationship between the observed and the unobserved variables. Maximum likelihood estimation methods were used to analyze the covariance matrix of the items. The goodness-of-fit of alternate models was empirically contrasted to identify the best-fitting model. Model fit was assessed using multiple fit indices suggested by Kelloway (1995) like χ^2 goodness-of-fit statistic, Goodness-of-Fit Index (GFI), Adjusted Goodness-of-Fit Index (AGFI); Root Mean Square Error of Approximation (RMSEA) as well as the Comparative Fit Index (CFI) as recommended by Bentler (1990).

7. Results

A four-factor model was estimated where role conflict and role ambiguity items were loaded onto two factors, and rumination and burnout items were loaded onto their respective two factors. Analyses showed that the fit of the hypothesized four-factor structure to the data

(χ^2 = 175.19, df = 109, p < .001; GFI = .94; AGFI = .91; RMSEA = .05; CFI = .98) was superior to that of an alternative one-factor model (χ^2 = 617.55, df = 119, p < .001; GFI= .619; AGFI = .51; CFI = .427; RMSEA = .17) where all items loaded onto one factor, suggesting that these four variables were indeed distinct from each other.

Thereafter, a structural model representing the hypothesized relationships was tested. The model *is composed of two exogenous variables (role ambiguity and role conflict); and two endogenous variables (rumination and burnout)*. Overall, the hypothesized model provided a good fit to the data (χ^2 = 159.68, df = 108, p < .001; GFI = .88; AGFI = .83; RMSEA = .05; CFI = .94). Thereafter, a comparison was made between the hypothesized model and the structural null model where all the paths were specifying the relationship between the constructs were set to zero (χ^2 = 374.23, df = 180, p < .001; GFI = .79; AGFI = .74; RMSEA = .09; CFI = .82). The difference in the chi-square was significant ($\Delta \chi^2$ = 214.55; Δdf = 72) indicating that the proposed model was a better fit to the data.

In order to establish whether there is mediation or not, there should be a direct effect which can be mediated. As predicted in hypothesis 1, results showed that role conflict was positively related to burnout (β = .45, p < .001); hence hypothesis 1 was supported. Similarly, as predicted in hypothesis 2, role ambiguity also had a significant positive relationship with burnout (β = .22, p < .01), thereby supporting hypothesis 2. To further check hypotheses 3 and 4, the significance of the association between the predictor and the mediator and the mediator and the outcome was checked for the whole mediation sequence with bootstrapping (Preacher and Hayes, 2008). Bootstrapping is a non-parametric test which does not violate the assumptions of normality and is recommended for a smaller sample size. Bootstrapping was chosen over the Sobel test of mediation, as it is considered more powerful for testing the effects of mediating variables (MacKinnon et al., 2004). Bootstrapping was done for all the relationships to check two-tailed significance with the bias-corrected percentile method.

Table 32.2 Mediation analysis

Relationship/hypothesis	Direct beta without mediator	Direct beta with mediator	Indirect beta	Mediation type observed
RC Rum Burnout	.45***	.32**	.15**	Partial mediation
RA Rum Burnout	.22**	19*	.10*	Partial mediation

Note: *p < .05; **p < .01; ***p < .001
RC, role conflict; RA, role ambiguity; Mediator, Rum, rumination
Source: Author's compilation

Previous analyses showed that the path between role ambiguity and burnout; and between role conflict and burnout were significant. The significant value of the indirect effect (β =.15, p < .01) and direct effect (β = .32, p < .01) indicates that the rumination partially mediates the relationship between role conflict and burnout. Hence, hypothesis 3 is supported, which states *that rumination during off-job time partially mediates the relationship between role conflict and burnout.* Similarly, the significant value of the indirect effect (β = .10, p < .05) and direct effect (β = .19, p < .05) indicates that rumination partially mediates the relationship between role ambiguity and burnout, supporting hypothesis 4.

8. Discussion

Addressing the paucity of literature on conditions and experiences of burnout for faculty in higher education (Hogan and McKnight, 2007), the present study adds to the body of literature by providing evidence of burnout faced by higher education faculty in India. Firstly, findings revealed that *role conflict and role ambiguity are antecedents to burnout in higher education faculty.* Role conflict and role ambiguity are two significant role-related constructs which are helpful in understanding dysfunctional behaviour leading to human suffering and inefficiency (Ghorpade et al. 2011). Some possible reasons for faculty facing role conflict and role ambiguity could be an ambiguous job description, non-availability of explicit directions from management and disguised/unclear appraisal procedures. The findings lent empirical support for the proposed hypotheses. It was found that the higher education faculty's perception of role conflict and role ambiguity at the workplace promotes the occurrence of burnout. In addition, role conflict was found to be a stronger predictor of burnout than role ambiguity (β = .29, $p < .001$; β = .22, $p < .01$, respectively). These findings are in congruence with the findings reported by Ghorpade et al., 2011. In their study, they found that the higher education faculty perceiving higher levels of role conflict and role ambiguity at the workplace reported higher levels of burnout, with role conflict being a stronger predictor than role ambiguity for burnout.

Burnout is triggered by increased job demands and a scarcity of job resources (Cordes and Dougherty, 1993); and is often perpetuated by ineffective coping strategies and frustrated intentions (Coetzee and Rothman, 2005). The paper provided empirical evidence for the mediating role of rumination in the relationship between role ambiguity, role conflict and burnout. To do this, the significance of the association between the predictor and the mediator and that of the mediator and the outcome was checked with bootstrapping. The results supported the hypothesis that rumination during off-job time positively mediated the relationship between role conflict, role ambiguity and burnout. Secondly, it was also found that ruminative thoughts beyond working hours positively influence the occurrence of burnout. When faculty face conflicting and ambiguous demands at the workplace, they might tend to ruminate beyond normal working hours, due to which individuals cannot detach psychologically from work and derive benefits of unwinding from work. Thus, a lack of psychological detachment does not help ameliorate the impact of role stressors (Sonnentag et al., 2010) and facilitate recovery (Sonnentag, 2003).

This falls in line with the findings of Donahue et al. (2012), who have argued that ruminative thoughts about work during evening hours and weekends may not allow individuals to benefit from their time off work, contributing to burnout. Due to unclear expectations and demands and lack of information at the workplace, faculty may need help understanding which aspect of the job is more important, making it difficult to justify multiple roles assumed, thereby experiencing a lack of progress towards the attainment of goals. This perception of lack of progress toward the attainment of goals may increase the likely hood of ruminative thoughts about the same (Martin and Tesser, 1996), leading to depletion of resources, thus making it difficult to detach psychologically from work beyond regular working hours.

9. Implications for Practice

Several implications can be drawn from this research study. The study results have implications for the management and faculty of higher educational institutions. Given the impact that role ambiguity and role conflict have on burnout, the management of the institutions should figure out the reasons responsible for role conflict and role ambiguity in higher education institutions; and then take remedial actions relating to policies, practices and communication to reduce role conflict and role ambiguity.

Identification and elaboration of reasons responsible for role conflict and role ambiguity can trigger commitment to implement reforms with planned interventions and follow-up to reduce role conflict and ambiguity and its possible negative consequences. At the same time, employees should try to avoid ruminative thoughts, as ruminative thoughts beyond working hours facilitate the occurrence of burnout. This is important as burnout has been recognized by researchers and practitioners as a social problem which requires attention for alleviation (Schaufeli et al., 2009) with various detrimental effects for both organization and employees, ranging from depression, anxiety (Greenglass et al., 1990); negative attitude towards their work (Demerouti et al., 2007); sickness absence (Peterson et al., 2008); sickness presence and over time (Peterson et al. 2008); implying high cost at the individual and organizational level.

10. Limitations and Future Research Directions

A few limitations should be taken into consideration before generalizing the results of the present study. The study included only emotional exhaustion and depersonalization to study burnout. In future, researchers may include reduced personal accomplishment along with emotional exhaustion and depersonalization to study burnout. In addition, future research could examine worry, along with rumination, as a mediator in the relationship between role ambiguity, role conflict and burnout. Worrying may also act as a partial mediator, as both rumination and worry have been found to increase the negative effect and decrease the positive effect (McLaughlin, Borkovec, and Sibrava, 2007).

Future research may also study the moderating role of psychological detachment in protecting faculty from burnout. Importantly, stress encountered due to role ambiguity, and role conflict at the workplace potentially threatens these resources leading to reduced well-being. As a result, the individual strives to gain resources like energy and a positive mood for restoring threatened resources. Research has demonstrated that when the role incumbent perceives role conflict and role ambiguity at the workplace, he/she may attempt to adapt behaviour to solve role-related problems to avoid anxiety, stress and dissatisfaction with the role (Kahn, Wolfe, Quinn, and Snoek, 1964). Here, detaching psychologically and stopping thinking about work-related demands could be a possible solution to regain internal resources such as energy and a positive mood. Though job stressors make psychological detachment difficult after work, mentally 'switching off' from work may facilitate recovery and enhance psychological well-being (Cropley and Millward, 2009; Sonnentag et al., 2010).

REFERENCES

1. Arbuckle, James L. "Amos™ 16.0 User's Guide." *Chicago: SPSS* (1995).
2. Bentler, Peter M. "Comparative fit indexes in structural models." *Psychological bulletin* 107, no. 2 (1990): 238.
3. Blix, Arlene Gray, Robert J. Cruise, Bridgit McBeth Mitchell, and Glen G. Blix. "Occupational stress among university teachers." *Educational research* 36, no. 2 (1994): 157–169.
4. Coetzee, S. E., and Sebastian Rothmann. "Occupational stress, organisational commitment and ill-health of employees at a higher education institution in South Africa." *SA Journal of Industrial Psychology* 31, no. 1 (2005): 47–54.
5. Cordes, Cynthia L., and Thomas W. Dougherty. "A review and an integration of research on job burnout." *Academy of management review* 18, no. 4 (1993): 621–656.
6. Cropley, Mark, and Lynne J. Millward. "How do individuals 'switch-off' from work during leisure? A qualitative description of the unwinding process in high and low ruminators." *Leisure Studies* 28, no. 3 (2009): 333–347.
7. Cropley, Mark, and Fred RH Zijlstra. "Work and rumination." *Handbook of stress in the occupations* 487 (2011): 503.
8. Demerouti, Evangelia, Toon W. Taris, and Arnold B. Bakker. "Need for recovery, home–work interference and performance: Is lack of concentration the link?." *Journal of Vocational Behavior* 71, no. 2 (2007): 204–220.
9. Donahue, Eric G., Jacques Forest, Robert J. Vallerand, Pierre-Nicolas Lemyre, Laurence Crevier-Braud, and Éliane Bergeron. "Passion for work and emotional exhaustion: The mediating role of rumination and recovery." *Applied Psychology: Health and Well-Being* 4, no. 3 (2012): 341–368.
10. Fernet, Claude, Frédéric Guay, and Caroline Senécal. "Adjusting to job demands: The role of work self-determination and job control in predicting burnout." *Journal of vocational behavior* 65, no. 1 (2004): 39–56.
11. Ghorpade, J., Lackritz, J., and Singh, G. (2011). Personality as a moderator of the relationship between role conflict, role ambiguity, and burnout. *Journal of Applied Social Psychology*, *41*(6), 1275–1298.
12. Greenglass, Esther R., Ronald J. Burke, and Mirka Ondrack. "A gender-role perspective of coping and burnout." *Applied Psychology* 39, no. 1 (1990): 5–27.
13. Hair, J. F. "Anderson, RE/Tatham, RL/Black, WC (1998): Multivariate data analysis." *PrenticeYHall, Upper saddle river, NJ* (2005).
14. Hobfoll, Stevan E. "Conservation of resources: A new attempt at conceptualizing stress." *American psychologist* 44, no. 3 (1989): 513.
15. Jones, Willis A. "Faculty involvement in institutional governance: A literature review." *Journal of the Professoriate* 6, no. 1 (2011): 118–135.
16. Kahn, Robert L., Donald M. Wolfe, Robert P. Quinn, J. Diedrick Snoek, and Robert A. Rosenthal. "Organizational stress: Studies in role conflict and ambiguity." (1964).
17. Keller, Robert T. "Role conflict and ambiguity: Correlates with job satisfaction and values." *Personnel Psychology* 28, no. 1 (1975): 57–64.
18. Kelloway, E. Kevin. "Structural equation modelling in perspective." *Journal of Organizational Behavior* 16, no. 3 (1995): 215–224.
19. Kuper, Hannah, and Michael Marmot. "Job strain, job demands, decision latitude, and risk of coronary heart disease within the Whitehall II study." *Journal of Epidemiology and Community Health* 57, no. 2 (2003): 147–153.

20. Lazarus, Richard S., and Susan Folkman. *Stress, appraisal, and coping*. Springer publishing company, 1984.
21. Lackritz, James R. "Exploring burnout among university faculty: Incidence, performance, and demographic issues." *Teaching and teacher education* 20, no. 7 (2004): 713–729.
22. Lyubomirsky, Sonja, and Susan Nolen-Hoeksema. "Self-perpetuating properties of dysphoric rumination." *Journal of personality and social psychology* 65, no. 2 (1993): 339.
23. MacKinnon, D. P., Lockwood, C. M., and Williams, J. (2004). Confidence limits for the indirect effect: Distribution of the product and resampling methods. *Multivariate behavioral research*, *39*(1), 99–128.
24. Martin, Leonard L., and Abraham Tesser. "Toward a motivational and structural theory of ruminative thought." (1989).
25. Martin, Leonard L., and Abraham Tesser. "Some ruminative thoughts." *Ruminative thoughts* 9 (1996): 1–47.
26. Maslach, Christina, and Susan E. Jackson. "MBI: Maslach Burnout Inventory; manual research edition." *University of California, Palo Alto, CA* (1986).
27. Maslach, Christina, Wilmar B. Schaufeli, and Michael P. Leiter. "Job burnout." *Annual review of psychology* 52, no. 1 (2001): 397–422.
28. McCune, Velda. "Academic identities in contemporary higher education: sustaining identities that value teaching." *Teaching in Higher Education* (2019).
29. McLaughlin, Katie A., Thomas D. Borkovec, and Nicholas J. Sibrava. "The effects of worry and rumination on affect states and cognitive activity." *Behavior Therapy* 38, no. 1 (2007): 23–38.
30. Nolen-Hoeksema, Susan, Louise E. Parker, and Judith Larson. "Ruminative coping with depressed mood following loss." *Journal of personality and social psychology* 67, no. 1 (1994): 92.
31. Neumann, Anna, and Aimee LaPointe Terosky. "To give and to receive: Recently tenured professors' experiences of service in major research universities." *The Journal of Higher Education* 78, no. 3 (2007): 282–310.
32. Peterson, Ulla, Evangelia Demerouti, Gunnar Bergström, Mats Samuelsson, Marie Åsberg, and Åke Nygren. "Burnout and physical and mental health among Swedish healthcare workers." *Journal of advanced nursing* 62, no. 1 (2008): 84–95.
33. Querstret, Dawn, and Mark Cropley. "Exploring the relationship between work-related rumination, sleep quality, and work-related fatigue." *Journal of occupational health psychology* 17, no. 3 (2012): 341.
34. Rizzo, John R., Robert J. House, and Sidney I. Lirtzman. "Role conflict and ambiguity in complex organizations." *Administrative science quarterly* (1970): 150–163.
35. Rothmann, Sebastiaan, N. Barkhuizen, and M. Y. Tytherleigh. "Model of work-related ill health of academic staff in a South African higher education institution." *South African journal of higher education* 22, no. 2 (2008): 404–422.
36. Schaubroeck, John, John L. Cotton, and Kenneth R. Jennings. "Antecedents and consequences of role stress: A covariance structure analysis." *Journal of Organizational Behavior* 10, no. 1 (1989): 35–58.
37. Schaufeli, Wilmar B., Michael P. Leiter, and Christina Maslach. "Burnout: 35 years of research and practice." *Career development international* 14, no. 3 (2009): 204–220.
38. Sen, Chiranjib. "A framework for analyzing demand and supply of faculty and the quality of higher education." *IIM Bangalore Research Paper* 350 (2011).
39. Singh, Surendra N., Sanjay Mishra, and Dongwook Kim. "related burnout among faculty in higher education." *Psychological Reports* 83, no. 2 (1998): 463–473.

40. Sonnentag, Sabine. "Recovery, work engagement, and proactive behavior: a new look at the interface between nonwork and work." *Journal of applied psychology* 88, no. 3 (2003): 518.

41. Sonnentag, Sabine, Carmen Binnewies, and Eva J. Mojza. "Staying well and engaged when demands are high: the role of psychological detachment." *Journal of Applied Psychology* 95, no. 5 (2010): 965.

42. Talbot, Laura A. "Burnout and humor usage among community college nursing faculty members." *Community College Journal of Research and Practice* 24, no. 5 (2000): 359–373.

43. Trowler, Paul, and Peter T. Knight. "Coming to know in higher education: Theorising faculty entry to new work contexts." *Higher education research and development* 19, no. 1 (2000): 27–42.

44. Xu, Linna. "Teacher–researcher role conflict and burnout among Chinese university teachers: a job demand-resources model perspective." *Studies in Higher Education* 44, no. 6 (2019): 903–919.

PART

EVIDENCE BASED
MARKETING MANAGEMENT

Chapter

Performance Prediction of Amazon Ad Campaigns Through Past Performance Data Using Machine Learning

Pratyut Sharma*

Department of Computer Science and Information Systems,
BITS-Pilani, Rajasthan, India

ABSTRACT: In the last decade internet connectivity penetration have seen a vast expansion. Therefore, to which, Ecommerce now plays a vital role in our daily lives. It is redefining commercial activities around the world be it selling, buying, or advertising. Amazon among with few other has emerged as major key players on the e-Commerce horizon. We aim to identify and explain the changes of user-controlled variable for a given advertising campaign on its output evaluative parameters (Profits, Impressions, CTR). This got further focused towards developing a prediction model system, that given a set of ad-campaign input specifics (particularly: Bid, Budget) can predict end-measure 'profit' of the campaign in terms of multi-class manner. We propose a multi-staged prediction system whose objective parameter is supposed to pivot around performance of advertisement, keeping comprehensive predictions about an ad in focus. Considering Marketing Funnel, we tried machine learning models at each stage in order to identify KPIs and thus implement profitability measurements. The Model Proposed by author, gives a holistic approach to break down KPIs for each level of the funnel and uses Amazon Ads' calculation methods and thus calculates the expected profitability accordingly. This system invites explorations around WHATIF analysis between actions and their output measures for more redundancy

KEYWORDS: Amazon Ads, Marketing funnel, Machine learning, Decision tree, Marketing KPI, Random forest

*h20210261@pilani.bits-pilani.ac.in

DOI: 10.4324/9781003415725-33

1. Introduction

Ecommerce now plays a vital role in our daily lives. It is redefining commercial activities around the world be it selling, buying, or advertising. Over the years, eCommerce sponsored activities has evolved in profound ways.

In order to make sellers advertise their products to the customer base, amazon provides a real-time bidding-based display advertising arrangement. This bidding environment enables advertisers to buy individual ad impressions via an auction in real-time and facilitates the presentation and the bidding of individual impressions across multiple advertisers. A Pay-per-click (PPC) model is followed here. These are second-price auctions, wherein the winner of bid does not bill according to their bid, but it's supposed to second-highest bid plus $0.01, hence the name.

PPC advertising includes various formats (e.g., search, contextual, social) with a total investment of more than 200 billion USD per year worldwide. Regards to aforementioned facts, the decision-making & selection process around the keywords bidding (which follows PPC) in the advertisement becomes a concerned drivers for generating profits.

Amazon ads acts as the one marketplace (search engine) for such adverting solely targeted at Amazon.com. The search engine operates the marketplace by setting a number of auction parameters, which play an important part in determining the outcome of the auction. An example of an auction parameter is reserve prices; only ads that clear the reserve price participate in the auction.

1.1 Related Business Knowledge—Amazon Advertisement

The knowledge around business logic and other know how's around advertising were primarily gained from amazon ads learning console. This included proprietary courses and information about practices in current times from customers and information about various frequently used key performance indicators (KPIs) for an advertisement.

Various categories of advertisement artifacts have been introduced from Amazon namely being Amazon Sponsored Products, Sponsored Brands, Amazon Sponsored Display Ads. Sponsored products comprise of an individual product (identified by *ASIN identifier)* mapped to various targeted keywords with the bid-value against each mapping. Sponsored brands is a curated collection of various products a seller arranges to be advertised a single entity of their search page. Unlike other 2 categories the Sponsored Display Ads are exclusive to vendors at Amazon. They primarily are placed on the product details page on the right pane, end of search results page, in middle of comments section. All of the above are found to be seen on desktop, mobile and mobile applications.

1.2 Metrics on Amazon Advertisement

We discuss few of the popular metrics about an advertisement in Amazon Ads. These are used to quantify and measure performance of a individual ads. We termed them as 'performance measure' for an individual ad. Some these metrics are:

- *Impression:* whenever a shopper sees an ad that means there was an impression occurred for ad. So, when an ad appears it means 1 impression.
- *Click:* when an individual clicks the ad, like on the ad at search result, details page or else.
- *Conversion:* a conversion happens when someone clicks the advertiser's ad and then takes an action that the advertiser has defined as valuable to his business, such as an online purchase or a call to the advertiser's business.
- *Click-through rate (CTR):* the number of clicks that the advertiser's ad receives divided by the number of times his ad is shown expressed as a percentage (clicks/impressions = CTR). A high CTR is a good indication that users find the advertiser's ads helpful and relevant.
- *CPC (Cost per Click):* it is the average cost of ads for which it has performed in its lifetime the advertiser sets to determine the highest amount that he is willing to pay for a click on his ad. If someone clicks the advertiser's ad, that click won't cost him more than the maximum CPC bid that
- *ACoS (Advertising Cost of Sale):* this talks about for each dollar earned how much amount was spent on advertising.

For a profitable affair, ACoS shall be well below 100%. Though it should also encompass industry margins into consideration.

$$ACoS = (Ad\ Spend/Ad\ Revenue) *100$$

2. Related Work

Cetină et al. [1] attributed various factors that influence the buying decision of customers on e-commerce portals. Eg: Demographical, Economical, Marketing factors, Web-experience, online perception to is name a few. Bala et al. [2] tried to understand internet marketing & its techniques with the objective of how internet marketing can be used more efficiently to induce more audience and new developments in the field of tech that help it.

D Gunawan et al. [3] discussed classifying web-documents based on naïve Bayes classifier and using fast text-based similarity to deduce similarity amongst documents, used cosine similarity based on frequency of words.

Khandelwal et al. [4] considered various bidding strategies for Amazon-EC2 based spot instances. They considered several requirements such as hardware, latency, deadline, and budget constraints. It highlights the objectives of each strategy and provides the suitability of each of the proposed bidding strategies based on the type of application.

Song et al. [5] gave a mechanism that depends on a repeated uniform price auction. It also included bidding adjustment model. They show that uniform price auction achieves optimal efficiency outperforming current amazon-spot market avg-revenue by 14%.

Shi et al. [6], identified the input features that potentially affect the CTR for any advertisement. They also formulated the profit calculations considering revenue and cost per clicks (CPC & RPC). For their analysis, they used 3 models: Linear Regression, Random-Forest, Gradient

Boosting. The Random-Forest approach gave best results among its peers, based on Mean-Square-Error on predicted CTR as measure of accuracy.

3. Methodology

In this section we set out to discuss the outline for our analysis for deducing outcomes specifically related to Amazon advertising environment.

3.1 Data

For our analysis we have arranged the set of anonymised sample retail data of mixed brands, that contains performance of sponsored products of mixed brands. The aim for mixed brands was to prosper the generality in the study. This also brought the anonymity in the observed dataset, hence safekeeping from any trackback to actual source of the data.

3.2 Staged Life Cycle of an Amazon Ad

Here we entail the motivation from the classic marketing funnel, that the marketing funnel shape corresponds with the idea of journey that a shopper goes through, while making purchase from platform. It also points about the customer traffic that reduces through each subsequent stage. Eventually the marketing funnel is a helpful framework for connecting and engaging with customers along their journey. Also, it acts as a ground about how Amazon Ads can help marketers maximize results with a full-funnel advertising approach.

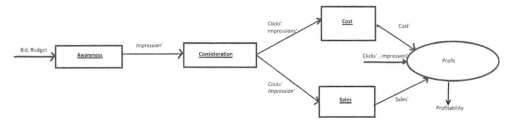

Fig. 33.1 A multi-staged lifecycle of amazon ad from inception to generating profits

Source: Author's Compilation

3.3 Profit Class Classification Problem

The authors here have formulated this prediction problem into a profit class prediction problem, where it divides the continuous ACoS value into 4 classed profits namely: highly lossy, lossy, profitable, highly profitable. Where ACoS varies from <50%, to 50-100%, to 100-150%, to >150% in the respective classes.

For this the author have used regressor based model. To fit in this these classes of model the authors have experimented with Decision-Trees, Random Forest, and also Neural Nets with Relu. Adam optimizer was also incorporated with similar neural network for the comparison of the prediction.

3.4 Models Used

For the mutli-class prediction problem we have employed several models into work. A brief information about them is provided in following section.

1. *Decision Trees:* As a supervised learning approach, decision trees can be used to solve both classification and regression issues. Data is partitioned into subsets whose values are determined by the input features; each partition is represented by a node in the tree, and the final decision is reached by traversing the tree from its root to its leaf nodes. Each node in a decision tree represents a question, and each branch in the tree indicates a possible course of action. In addition, decision trees can process numeric and categorical data, deal with missing information, and account for non-linear correlations between input features and the outcome variable. The risk of overfitting increases as the tree depth and complexity increase; however, this can be mitigated through several methods like as pruning, capping the tree depth, or including a regularization factor in the cost function. The usage of decision trees, which have found widespread application in areas such as finance, healthcare, and customer management, has allowed them to be adapted for use in feature selection.

2. *Random Forest:* Overfitting in decision trees is an issue that can be fixed with the use of a machine learning technique called Random Forest. For its efficiency and simplicity, it is among the best automated machine learning algorithms. In order to achieve high prediction accuracy with less effort spent on data preparation, it collects data that contains the variables to be forecasted or explained along with the essential predictors. It's a sort of ensemble learning that uses the output of many decision trees constructed during training to perform a variety of tasks, including classification and regression. The data's structure can be deduced with its aid. Since the training set is constructed by a sample with replacement strategy, some information may be lost in the process. The unbiased estimate of the classification error is revised to account for this previously unnoticed information as new trees are added to the forest.

3. *Neural Networks:* The idea behind neural networks in deep learning is that machine learning algorithms can also take inspiration from biological neural networks. Layers of nodes, or artificial neurons, communicate with one another. An individual neuron takes in data, processes it, and then outputs the results.

   Numerous applications exist for neural networks, including image classification, NLP, and time series forecasting. They shine when confronted with massive amounts of data and complex input features.

   Neural learning (also known as backpropagation) is the method by which a neural network is trained by exposing it to a dataset. During training, the weights and biases of the artificial neurons are tweaked to achieve a minimum of prediction error.

   Neural networks come in a variety of forms, including the feedforward network, the recurrent network. Each neural network architecture has its own strengths and weaknesses and can perform better than others on a limited set of problems. The authors have limited themselves to feed-forward propagation neural networks only.

3.5 Error Analysis

For regressor prediction, we have used mean absolute percentage error.

$$M = \frac{1}{n}\sum_{t=1}^{n}\left|\frac{A_t - F_t}{A_t}\right|$$

MAPE = (abs(predicted value/actual value − 1) *100)/number of samples

- n is the number of fitted points,
- At is the actual value,
- Ft is the forecast value.

By this, we make sure that we be able to get a relative scale for errors. This also, protects against large delta that is originated from of difference relatively large values.

Also, it awards the case, where error is small, relative to actual values:

(0.5/99) case.

4. Observations

The following observations were made while examining the performance of various machine learning models. The dataset used for all of these was kept same, this gave a level field for analysis of different models which in turn were introduced to solve different business problems.

The impression classification model was implemented with Decision tree, Random Forest, Neural Networks. 4-class classification problem with output being different CTR classes. Input tuple to model was (keyword bid, search type, search rank).

The neural networks were used with different configurations of hidden layers, the authors have documented mainly the results from two of such instances where a neural network with same configuration (hidden layers) was used with different activation functions and optimizers. These were namely Rectified Linear Unit as Activation function and Adam being the optimizer in one of the cases.

The results are tabulated in Table 33.1.

Table 33.1 Performance of Models

Model	Accuracy
Decision Tree	54.6
Random Forest	57.6
Neural Network- ReLU	58.2
Neural Network- Adam	59.4

Source: Author's compilation from Python

5. Conclusions

In the aforementioned study, the authors have made an attempt to solve the profitability prediction problem. Post the pre-processing and wrangling of the relevant input dataset, the business knowledge was put into the practice to join appropriate data between different granularities. Following which, various ML models were applied to predict Accuracy for the prediction of ACOS classes (inferred as profitability in our problem statement).

Based on the observation and comparison studies between various models the Random Forest came out to be giving most efficient results in our aimed business case.

REFERENCES

1. Cetină, I., Munthiu, M. C., & Rădulescu, V. (2012). Psychological and social factors that influence online consumer behavior. Procedia-Social and Behavioral Sciences, 62, 184–188.
2. Bala, M., & Verma, D. (2018). A critical review of digital marketing. M. Bala, D. Verma (2018). A Critical Review of Digital Marketing. International Journal of Management, IT & Engineering, 8(10), 321–339.
3. Gunawan, D., Sembiring, C. A., & Budiman, M. A. (2018, March). The implementation of cosine similarity to calculate text relevance between two documents. In Journal of physics: conference series (Vol. 978, No. 1, p. 012120). IOP Publishing.
4. Khandelwal, V., Chaturvedi, A. K., & Gupta, C. P. (2018, August). Bidding strategies for Amazon EC2 Spot Instances-A comprehensive review. In 2018 Fourth International Conference on Computing Communication Control and Automation (ICCUBEA) (pp. 1–5). IEEE.
5. Song, K., Yao, Y., & Golubchik, L. (2013, August). Improving the revenue, efficiency and reliability in data center spot market: A truthful mechanism. In 2013 IEEE 21st International Symposium on Modelling, Analysis and Simulation of Computer and Telecommunication Systems (pp. 222–231). IEEE.
6. Shi, L., & Li, B. (2016). Predict the click-through rate and average cost per click for keywords using machine learning methodologies. In Proceedings of the International Conference on Industrial Engineering and Operations Management Detroit, Michigan, USA.

Chapter

Social Media Influencer as a Winning Strategy for Influencing Purchasing Decision of Teenage Segment

Nidhi[1]
Research Scholar (Ph.D.), Department of Management,
Maharaja Agrasen University, Baddi (H.P), India

Preeti Thakur[2]
Assistant Professor, Department of Management Studies,
Madanapalle Institute of Technology & Science (MITS), Madanapalle (A.P), India

Rakesh Kumar Gupta[3]
Professor, Department of Management,
Maharaja Agrasen University, Baddi (H.P), India

ABSTRACT: In the competitive era, where the companies are struggling for adapting the effective digital advertising strategy for their product promotion, the new concept of influencer marketing has come up in recent years. Globally, the market size of influencer marketing industry was only $1.7 billion in 2016 and is expected to reach up to $16.4 billion in 2022. Similarly, in Indian context also this industry stood at INR 9 billion in 2021 and is further expected to rise by 25% CAGR in upcoming five years. The reason behind such growing penetration of influencer marketing is aggressive adaptation of social media in Indian settings. Furthermore, teenagers have shown their immense presence on social media platforms than ever before. The surprised change has been noticed in 2018 in the context of US teenager who were only 34% involved in the social media consumption in 2012 has risen to 70% in a day, even out of which 16% and 27% are using the same on constant and hourly basis respectively. Thus, increasing pattern of social media usage results positively significant to influencer marketing. These social media influencers (SMIs) are considered as most trustworthy, transparent and authentic in comparison with traditional celebrities. In consequences, contain more power to influence teenage purchasing decision more effectively among other digital advertising strategy. Thus, it would not be surprised if we say that social media influencers

[1]nidhi4596@yahoo.com, [2]thakurpreeti43@gmail.com, [3]rakeshusol@gmail.com

DOI: 10.4324/9781003415725-34

(SMIs) are the effective phenomenon for the companies to be taken into consideration for their promotional activities. Hence, this conceptual paper is an attempt to discuss the role and importance of SMIs on a specific group (teenage). Thus, this study will provide meaningful insights for marketers and practitioners in respect to the use of marketing influencers as brand promotional strategies.

KEYWORDS: Influencer marketing, Purchasing decision, Social media, Teenagers

1. Introduction

In today's era, companies are continuously putting efforts in findings the new innovative ideas for their product promotion, where the concept of digital advertisement is paved the way. The concept of digital advertisement is more effective than the other traditional advertisement methods. It is evident that the digital advertising spending which was only 521.02 billion dollar in 2021 worldwide would probably enhance by approximate 355 billion dollar in next five year (statista.com). Considering the various channel in digital advertisement such as pop-up ads, company websites, E-WOM, email marketing, the new emerging trend of influencer marketing cannot be ignored. Figure 34.1 shows the market size of influencer marketing worldwide which represents the increase up to $13.8 billion from 2016 to 2021. It is further expected to reach up to 16.4 billion US dollar in 2022 (statista.com). Similarly, in Indian settings also the trend of influencer marketing is increasing rapidly. As shown in Fig. 34.2 the market size of influencer marketing which was $1.7 billion in 2016 is going to increase up to $8.3 billion in next four year (entrackr.com). The increasing pattern of social media usage results positively significant to influencer marketing. Social media influencer is the individual who contains the ability to build and change the customer perception regarding the product through his informative content by using the social media platforms. (Saima and Khan 2020).

Tiers of social media influencer

Social-media influencers are further bifurcated into the various categories as shown in Fig. 34.3. These influencers are categorized on the basis of their number of followers available on social media. As depicted in the Fig. 34.3. Nano influencers are those influencers who are having their followers in the range of 1,000-10,000 and penetrated newly on social media platforms. These are the influencers who are in stage of developing trust with brands and followers even some Nano-influencers promote the brands without charging any fee. These influencers are considered quite cost-effective for product promotion especially suitable for the brands having very limited resources. Micro-influencers are those influencers who are having their followers in the range of 10,000-50,000 and create the effective engagement with their followers. The product promotion of these influencers depend upon their area of interest and also due to having less number of followers they contain the ability to engage the followers personally.

Mid-tier influencers are the influencers having the followers range in between 50,000 - 5,00,000. These influencers are considered more experienced than Nano & Micro influencers.

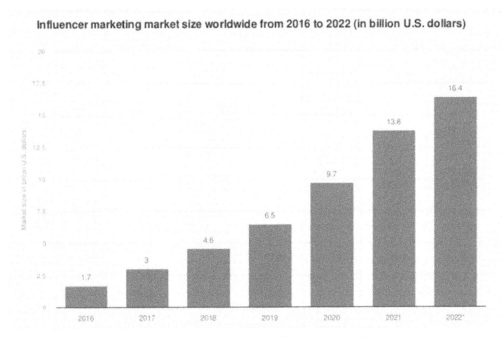

Fig. 34.1 Global trends of influencer marketing

Source: Statista.com

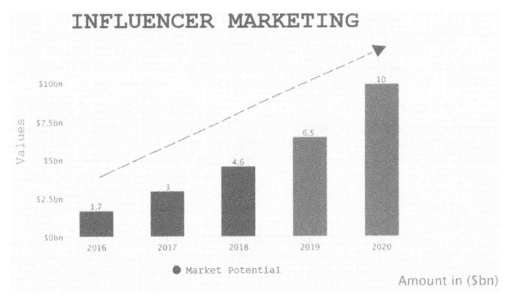

Fig. 34.2 Trends of influencer marketing in India

Source: entrackr.com

The Tiers of Influencers

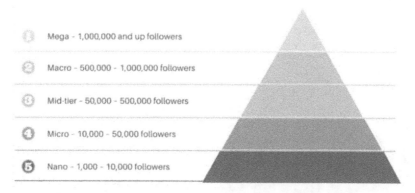

- Mega - 1,000,000 and up followers
- Macro - 500,000 - 1,000,000 followers
- Mid-tier - 50,000 - 500,000 followers
- Micro - 10,000 - 50,000 followers
- Nano - 1,000 - 10,000 followers

Fig. 34.3 Tiers of social media influencer

Source: signalytics.ai

Macro-influencers are the influencers who are having their follower range in between 5,00,000 – 10,00,000 contains the good reputation in the market. These are generally the T.V personalities, athletes and celebrities having low engagement rate with their followers and charge high prices from the brands for their product promotion. Thus, these influencers select product/brand for promotion very cautiously that would not hamper their reputation in the market. Whereas the mega-influencers are the influencers who are having their followers more than 1 million but having very low engagement rate. It has also been found that as level of engagement rate decreases, the number of influencer's increases. These are the influencers who remain active on social media platforms and enjoy the celebrity status on the social media platform.

Teenagers presence on Social media platforms

The increasing fondness of teenagers towards the smartphones is indirectly creating awareness about social networking applications among them. The global teenagers spend average 2.5 hours on social media in a day similarly in India 2.4 hours devotion has been found on the same context. These social media platforms are the entertainment sources for their ideal time. On the other hand, it is the place where Influencers get the opportunity to enhance their popularity and number of followers as well. These Influencers entice the teenagers through their dressing & communicating style, purchasing habits and also provide the product knowledge by their entertaining attitude. Even these SMIs influence the purchasing decision of their followers while using for entertainment purposes (Reilly and Oreilly 2022). The drastic change have been found with the survey conduct on U.S teenagers which resulted that 70% of teens are engaged with social media more than once a day. Moreover, out of which 16% of teens are using the same on constant basis and 27 % on hourly basis (statista.com). On the other hand, the trend has gone when 17% teenagers used to spend time on these platforms as the percentage has reduced to 4% in 2018.

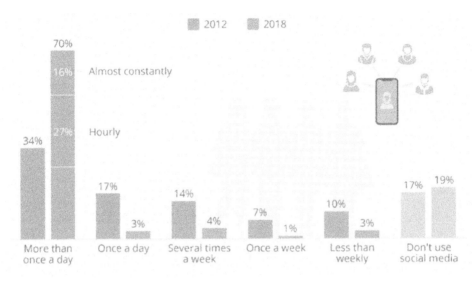

Fig. 34.4 Drastic increase in social media usage among teenagers

Source: statista.com

2. Objectives of the Study

- To discuss the role and importance of social media influencers (SMIs) in market scenario.
- To explore various attributes of the social media influencers (SMIs) with respect to teenage segment.

3. Discussions

The influencer marketing is increasing rapidly in the market due to its authenticity, trustworthiness & reliability. The direct significant relation of credibility has been found with trustworthiness, information quality and entertainment value (Koay et al. 2022). The study has also found the significant indirect relation of credibility with purchase intention. SMIs promote the brands by using their popularity level on social media. In order to create awareness among followers, marketers may find suitable SMIs which are quite relatable and having some effective personality traits to influence their followers (Reilly and Oreilly 2022). As shown in Fig. 34.5 "Komal Pandey" who is a big fashion influencer. She started her YouTube channel in the year 2017 with the video titled "back on YouTube". Even in the year 2015 she was also hired by POPxo due her fashion and comedy vides.

In 2018 she had received the fashion influencer award and two cosmopolitan awards for fashion and beauty in the year 2019. Currently she is having 132 videos related to fashion trends and her life journey which is playing the key role for influencing her followers. These influencers due to authenticity and reliability recommend the brand to their followers. Teenagers (followers) found these influencers more similar and get influenced by them very easily in comparison

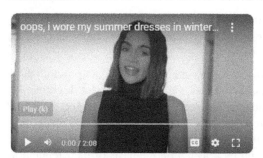

Komal Pandey
@komalpandey3894
1.26M subscribers

| HOME | VIDEOS | SHORTS | LIVE | PLAYLISTS | COMMUNITY | CHANNELS |

oops, i wore my summer dresses in winter & didn't feel cold.

396,350 views · 1 year ago

HI MY CHICKENS!
SO LONG.
i decided to style a couple of my summer dresses the winter and
i swear i didnt feel cold.

i also wanna take a moment and thank you guys for
EVERYTHING, for loving me for who i am, for pulling me up and...
READ MORE

Fig. 34.5 Social media influencer I

Source: youtube.com

from traditional celebrity. Another SMI taken under this study is the "Poonam Devnani" who penetrated on social media platform for providing various easy food recipes. The reason of her unpredictable success on social media platform is that she targeted the people who take the cooking as a challenge and providing many easy tricks for their daily life in the same phenomenon. Currenty she is having more than 5 million subscribers and 1 billion+ views on the channel. Hence, the kitchen appliances companies target these influencers as they are alerady liked by their followers and probability of purchasing become more high by the consumer if the product is promoted by their favourite individual. The teenagers availability on such platform is increasing rapidly year by year. The US teenagers devote 37% of their dialy video consumption on YouTube platform. These influencers consider the difficulty level of their followers and thus considered more reliable and trustworthy by them. Hence, these

Masala Kitchen ⊘
@MasalaKitchenbyPoonam
5.53M subscribers

Fig. 34.6 Social media influencer II

Source: youtube.com

influencer contains more ability to influence the purchasing decision of the teenage segement due to having more transparency, credibility and reliability than the other traditional advertising platforms.

4. Suggestions

The companies should recognize the power of these influencers. These social media influencing marketing is cost effective phenomenon and even more reliable in comparison with celebrity endorsement for the companies.

The engagement rate of SMIs with their followers is only the key for product promotion. As some influencers' such as mega and macro is having less engagement rate but high number of followers. On the other hand, Nano and micro influencers are having the high engagement but less number of followers. Companies are required to take the selection of SMIs more cautiously otherwise may not provide the positive results. As all the category of influencers are not suitable for all type of product. SMIs should be selected on the basis of their reputation, views and their reliability on followers.

On the other side, Influencers are required to remain careful while opting the product category for promotion which should be related with their expertise otherwise this may lead to decrease in their reliability on social platform. For example, promotion of sport brand or fitness product may not be suitable for beauty SMIs (Koay et al. 2022).

The SMIs contains the efficiency to influence their followers more effectively than the traditional celebrities. Thus, companies should give more emphasize on environment friendly products which would definitely be more accepted by the followers if they found the same promoted by their role model (SMIs). This would also lead to the achievement of SDG-13 as per 2030 climate action agenda (Reilly and Oreilly 2022).

5. Acknowledgment

We would like thanks to our Institutes (Maharaja Agrasen University and Madanapalle Institute of Technology & Science) for encouraging us towards research and publication. We express our sincere gratitude to the Management of Institutes for giving us financial support in academic and research growth. We would also like to thank Birla Institute of Technology & Science (BITS) to give us an opportunity to share our work among various academicians across country. Last but not least we express our gratitude to God for always taking care in all the difficulties.

REFERENCES

1. Published by Statista Research Department, and Oct 18. "Global Influencer Market Size 2022." Statista, October 18, 2022. https://www.statista.com/statistics/1092819/global-influencer-market-size/.
2. Published by Statista Research Department, and Jul 27. "Digital Ad Spend Worldwide 2026." Statista, July 27, 2022. https://www.statista.com/statistics/237974/online-advertising-spending-worldwide/

3. Statista. "Digital Ad Spend Worldwide 2026 | Statista." Accessed December 19, 2022. https://www.statista.com/statistics/237974/online-advertising-spending-worldwide/.

4. Howard. "Maximizing Influencer Marketing: Engagement Rate vs. Follower Count." Signalytics, November 10, 2022. https://www.signalytics.ai/influencer-engagement-rate/.

5. Yanogya, Tyagi &. "HYPE SELLS: 'eye-Catching' Growth of Influencer Marketing in India." Entrackr, May 14, 2019. https://entrackr.com/2019/05/influnecer-marketing-india/.

6. Richter, Felix. "Infographic: Teens' Social Media Usage Is Drastically Increasing." Statista Infographics, October 9, 2018. https://www.statista.com/chart/15720/frequency-of-teenagers-social-media-use/.

7. Koay, Kian Yeik, Man Lai Cheung, Patrick Chin Hooi Soh, and Chai Wen Teoh. 2022. "Social Media Influencer Marketing: The Moderating Role of Materialism." European Business Review 34 (2): 224–43. https://doi.org/10.1108/EBR-02-2021-0032.

8. Reilly, Isobel O, and Isobel Oreilly. 2022. "The Role of Influencers in Adolescents ' Consumer Decision-Making Process: A Sustainability Approach Critical Letters in Economics & Finance The Role of Influencers in Adolescents ' Consumer Decision- Making Process: A Sustainability Approach Technologi," no. February. https://doi.org/10.21427/azb6-zn63.

9. Saima, and M. Altaf Khan. 2020. "Effect of Social Media Influencer Marketing on Consumers' Purchase Intention and the Mediating Role of Credibility." Journal of Promotion Management 27 (4): 503–23. https://doi.org/10.1080/10496491.2020.1851847.

10. "Komal Pandey." YouTube. YouTube. Accessed December 14, 2022. https://www.youtube.com/@komalpandey3894.

11. "Masala Kitchen." YouTube. YouTube. Accessed December 14, 2022. https://www.youtube.com/@MasalaKitchenbyPoonam.

Chapter

Interaction Behavior of Customers in Viral Marketing: An Analysis of its Impact on Customer Opinions

Amrit Kaur[1]
Research Scholar, Department of Business Management,
IKG Punjab Technical University, Jalandhar, India

Harmeen Soch[2]
Professor, Department of Business Management,
IKG Punjab Technical University, Jalandhar, India

Sunpreet Kaur[3]
Associate Professor, Department of Business Management,
IKG Punjab Technical University, Jalandhar, India

ABSTRACT: With the advent of the internet, technology-aided marketing is mushrooming fast. One such marketing technique is viral marketing. Viral marketing refers to the phenomenon of marketing communication where the marketing content is shared by the customers themselves, driving exponential growth in the popularity of product/service through online generated buzz and e-WOM. Being cost-effective and exponentially spread, viral marketing is getting the limelight nowadays. This virality is customer-driven, so marketers must understand the customer decision-making process behind virality. The current study aims at understanding the interaction behavior (the behavior exhibited by customers while interacting with content i.e. liking, sharing, commenting, and reposting the content) of customers concerning viral content and its impact on customers' opinions towards content. Besides this, the study also aims at investigating the factors that influence interaction behavior. This research is based on primary data collected from 200 respondents using standardized questionnaires through a convenience sampling technique. The data analysis is done through SPSS using correlation and regression. The findings revealed that content characteristics and source credibility are the major factors driving the virality of content. Further, there is a strong association between interaction behavior and customer opinions. Besides this, the research sheds light on strategies

[1]amritkaur15150@gmail.com, [2]harmeensoch@ptu.ac.in, [3]sunpreetkaursahni@gmail.com

DOI: 10.4324/9781003415725-35

that companies can use to improve the virality of their content. Therefore, this research is fundamental in developing evidence-based marketing strategies for better decision-making.

KEYWORDS: Interaction behavior, Social media, Social engagement behavior, Virality, Viral marketing

1. Introduction

With the advent of the internet, the life of today's generation has undergone a sea change. This emergence of social media has developed a web of networks among people, providing them with opportunities to interact with each other (Abedniya & Sabbaghi, 2010; Feroz Khan & Vong, 2014). Globally, the social media penetration rate is currently 54 percent and is rising at a rapid pace (Statista, 2022). India ranks among the top internet users in the world. Social media in India has grown by leaps and bounds over the past few years, with more users logging on every day to share their experiences and thoughts with the world, build their brands, and learn about others through content shared with them. With the advent of 4G technology, India is crossing 900 million active users. A report by the Institute of Governance, Policies & Politics on Patterns of internet usage among youth in India revealed that over 85 percent of young kids have a smartphone of their own. An average youngster in India spends nearly 5 hours scrolling on social media which accounts for nearly 20 percent of social media. The companies are targeting these social media users to market their products and services through online marketing, e-word-of-mouth marketing, and social media marketing. And the most popular among these is viral marketing. The concept of viral marketing was first mentioned by Rayport in 1996, in his article "The Virus of Marketing". Viral marketing refers to marketing efforts either directed by the company or self-generated by the customers that stimulate electronic word-of-mouth and motivate customers to interact with the content and share it with their immediate peer group. The term viral used for this symbolizes its exponential spread caused by rapid sharing (Rollins et al., 2014). Nowadays, it is one of the most strategic ways to target a large segment of customers cost-effectively. Moreover, the two-way communication and sharing of messages between social groups through trusted group members develop authenticity (Rollins et al., 2014); and increases the trustworthiness of shared message (Chiu et al., 2014).

2. Rationale of Study

The current study is undertaken to identify and understand those factors that a company should focus on while developing and delivering viral content on social media so that it can fetch maximum interactions and eventually influence the users' opinions in general. As viral marketing is customer-driven, therefore the current study is undertaken to record and analyze the responses of customers directly. Also, the previous literature has revealed that virality is instrumental in shaping positive opinions about the brand which is a strong predictor of buying intentions. Therefore, the current study is fundamental in answering the following questions per se;

- Do message characteristics impact the interaction behavior of customers in viral marketing?
- Do source characteristics impact the interaction behavior of customers in viral marketing?
- Does perceived behavioral control impacts the interaction behavior of customers in viral marketing?
- Does interaction behavior influence customer opinions?

3. Theoretical Framework

3.1 Interaction Behavior

Interaction behavior refers to the behavior exhibited by the customer while deciding on interacting with the content. For instance, liking, commenting, sharing, reposting, etc. content which increases the virality of the content (Khan & Vong, 2019; Rechstein and Brusch, 2019; Usmani et. al, 2019; Simmunds, Campbell & Hasley, 2021; Kulkarni, Karlo & Dinesh, 2021; Lee, Lazer & Riedl, 2022). Certain researchers have studied only sharing as a part of the interaction (Yang & Zhou, 2011; De Bruyn & Lilien, 2008; Camarero & Jose, 201, Palka, Pousttchi & Weildmann, 2009; Pescher, Reichhart & Spann, 2013). While with the advent of new modes of interaction, virality was extended from sharing and forwarding to liking, commenting (Kabadayi and Price, 2014; Maiz and Arranz, 2014), and participation in viral campaigns (Tiago, Borges-Tiago and Cosme, 2018). Therefore, the current study aims at understanding the interaction behavior of customers from all these perspectives in viral marketing.

3.2 Factors influencing Interaction Behavior

Message characteristics

Message or content characteristics refer to the quality and nature of content delivered by companies through social media. The different appeals used to make the message interesting also formed part of the message's characteristics. For instance, message characteristics such as emotional and rational appeals influence e-word-of-mouth (Wu & Wang, 2011) and sharing rate (Berger, 2011; Milkman & Berger, 2014; Tsugawa & Ohsaki, 2015). These emotions are mostly positive (Berger & Milkman, 2012; Kohen, 2014) and include humor as major emotion (Golen & Zaidner, 2008). While negative emotions with surprise increase sharing intentions (Berger & Milkman, 2012; Cohen, 2014). Similarly, Yang & Zhou (2011) revealed that entertaining and useful messages increase the intention to share. Similarly, interesting and valuable content also influences interactions with the content (Akpinar & Berger, 2017). Though these message characteristics are well-researched, however, they have been researched only from sharing perspective. Therefore, these message characteristics need to be tested on Interaction behavior which is much wider than sharing and forwarding.

H$_1$: Message characteristics significantly impact the interaction behavior of customers in viral marketing.

Source characteristics

Source refers to the person or the company/ brand that is posting and sharing viral content. The characteristics of the source influence the individual's decision to interact. These characteristics may include the credibility of the source (Gunawan and Huarng, 2015), and a close relationship with the source. For instance, a close relationship with the source increases the probability to accept the viral content (Camarero and San Jose; 2011), impacts the positive evaluation of received content (Gunawan & Huarng, 2015), and increases willingness to share the content (Ketelaar et al., 2016) leading to virality. The source also acts as a major determinant in developing trust in the viral message (Arun & Arul, 2020). Wu & Wang (2011) studied message source credibility as a factor influencing e-WOM which is one of the important components of viral marketing. The prevalence of influencer marketing on social media with loyal followers influences the decision to interact (Hinz et al., 2015; Zhang & Huang, 2021). Companies nowadays focus more on these influencers as they have more customer reach and drive loyalty. Therefore, it is necessary to understand the importance that users give to the credibility and trustworthiness of such sources play while interacting with the content they share.

H$_2$: Source characteristics significantly impact the interaction behavior of customers in viral marketing.

Perceived Behavioral control and ease

As per the theory of planned behavior (TPB), a customer's intentions to perform a behavior can be predicted with high accuracy by understanding his attitudes and perceived behavioral control. Apart from the content and source characteristics, individual perception also influences the decision to interact with the content. This mainly includes perceived behavioral control that denotes a subjective degree of control over the performance of a behavior and can also describe as perceived control over the performance of a behavior (Yang & Zhou, 2011; Yang, 2013). For the current study, perceived behavioral control comes from a consumer's sense of being in control of liking/sharing/commenting/reposting, and forwarding viral messages. Prior literature reveals that consumers are more inclined to embrace forwarding or sharing in viral behavior if they feel unrestrained. However, this is yet to be tested on another form of interaction such as liking/commenting/reposting, etc.

H$_3$: Perceived Behavioral control and ease significantly impact the interaction behavior of customers in viral marketing.

Customer Opinion/Attitude towards content

Customer attitude or opinion refers to overall persistent evaluation towards people, things, or goods that a person encounters; which includes favorable or unfavorable evaluations and behavioral tendencies. The main objective of viral advertising is to develop a positive image or positive opinion about the brand which in turn is dependent on a positive attitude towards the content shared or posted by that brand. However, the influence of interactions on the opinions of individuals is yet to be researched. Or in other words, does it mean that if people interact or do not interact with the content would mean that they are influenced by it, or does more interaction would mean that people have a positive opinion of the content that the company shares? These questions are fundamental in answering the prediction of virality and positive attitude towards the company to which that content belongs. Generally, it is believed that more forwarding or sharing would mean a positive attitude toward the content. However, today with more avenues of interaction, people casually interact with the content without taking many conscious decisions. Reason being, ease of use and ease of interaction. Thus, it is quite necessary to revisit this hypothesis that more interactions would mean a positive attitude or opinion about the content.

H_4: Interactions have a positive impact on customer opinions.

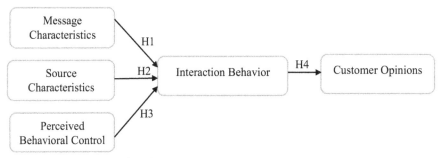

Fig. 35.1 Proposed theoretical model

Source: Author's compilation

4. Research Methodology

The current study has a descriptive and diagnostics design where the impact of one variable over the other. The sampling unit includes social media users across all demographics. The study follows convenience sampling under non-probability sampling. The sample size chosen for the current study is 200 respondents.

Instrument Design: A questionnaire was designed was circulated across social media platforms to collect responses. The scales to measure various constructs were taken from previous literature and were modulated as per the requirement of the study. For instance, the five-point rating scale to measure content characteristics perceived behavioral control, and customer attitude was taken from the research study by Yang and Zhou (2015). Similarly, a scale to measure source characteristics (bi-polar scale) was adapted from the scale used by Wu and Wang (2011). While scaling on interaction behavior which is an eight-point rating scale was adapted from the research study of Achen (2019).

Table 35.1 Reliability testing

Scales	Cronbach's Alpha	Number of Items
Message Characteristics	.905	7
Perceived Behavioral Control	.811	3
Source Characteristics	.927	10
Interaction Behavior	.837	5
Attitude Scale	.709	3

Source: Author's compilation

In Table 35.1, Cronbach's alpha of all the scales came out to be above 0.6 and thus demonstrates high reliability.

Data Analysis: The statistical analysis was performed by calculating descriptive statistics, correlation, and linear regression through SPSS.

5. Analysis and Results

5.2 Descriptive Statistics

From the descriptive, it is revealed that youngsters (especially generation Z) are more inclined towards social media usage (62 percent) and social media usage frequency is quite high (4-5 times a day or more). The most preferably used social media applications are Instagram, WhatsApp, YouTube, Snapchat, and Telegram. The most frequent way of interaction on social media is liking (Mean = 3.65) the content which is followed by simply watching it and then commenting on it. This finding is in line with research studies conducted by Kabadayi and Price (2014); Maiz and Arranz (2014); Achen (2019) and Arun and Arul (2020). In terms of content characteristics, it was found that people prefer to interact with the content which is useful for them (Mean = 3.7). This result is in line with the results of research studies by Wu and Wang (2011) and Apnikar and Berger (2017). Also, the peer group influence on individual interaction behavior is quite less (Mean = 3.33) as compared to previous studies which revealed that sharing content is fundamentally affected by the perception of benefit derived by the person with whom we are sharing that content. The source characteristics revealed that a trustworthy (Mean = 3.41), and expert (Mean = 3.32) source of content or message derives more interactions. These findings are in line with research studies of Wu and Wang (2011); Chui et al., (2014); Maiz and Arranz (2014); Achen (2019); Tiago et al. (2018); and Arun and Arul (2020). While, in terms of perceived behavioral control, respondents feel neutral to agree with this as strongly agreeable responses were almost missing. The findings are in line with the research studies of Yang and Zhou (2011); and Yang (2013).

The customer opinions revealed that customer opinions about the viral content are positive (Mean = 3.42) which indicates that the virality of content drives positive brand value and positive opinions. This indicates that positive opinions can be predicted from the number of interactions with content posted by the company or brand. This finding is in line with the finding of Gunawan and Huarng (2015), Ketellar et al. (2016), and Rao et al. (2022).

5.2 Hypothesis Testing and Inferential Statistics

Based on the hypothesis formulated, correlation and linear regression analysis were applied after testing all the assumptions for linear regression. The results of correlation and simple linear regression are mentioned below:

H_2: *Message characteristics significantly impact the interaction behavior of customers in viral marketing*

The analysis in Table 35.2 revealed a moderate positive correlation exists between interaction behavior and message characteristics. The R square value is 0.252 which indicates that 25 percent of the total variation in interaction behavior can be explained by message characteristics. The results of the regression are significant as the p-value is below 0.05 indicating that, the regression model significantly predicts the interaction variable (i.e., it is a good fit for the data). Therefore, the null hypothesis claiming that there is no significant impact of message characteristics on the interaction behavior is rejected at a 0.05 level of significance. This indicates that message characteristics significantly influence the interaction behavior of respondents.

Table 35.2 Regression analysis

Model	R	R Square	Adjusted R Square	Std. Error of Estimate	F	Sig.
	.502	.252	.248	1.06408	66.633	.000

Source: Author's compilation

Table 35.3 Coefficients table

Model		Unstandardized Coefficients		Standardized Coefficients	t	Sig.
		B	Std. Error	Beta		
1	(Constant)	.613	.307		1.993	.048
	Message Characteristics	.695	.085	.502	8.163	.000

Source: Author's compilation

In Table 35.3, the Beta coefficient indicates that for 0.69 units change in message characteristics, the interactions will change by one unit. The value of t-statistics also shows a significant relationship between message characteristics and interaction behavior ($p < 0.05$). The equation can be written as follows:

$$X = 0.613 + 0.695 \ Y$$

Where X indicates interactions and Y indicates message characteristics.

H_2: *Source characteristics significantly impact the interaction behavior of customers in viral marketing.*

The analysis of Table 35.4 revealed a high positive correlation between interaction behavior and source characteristics. The R square value is 0.594 indicating that 59 percent of the total variation in interaction behavior can be explained by the characteristics of the source. The results of the regression are significant at 0.05 indicating that the source characteristics significantly predict the interaction variable. Therefore, the null hypothesis claiming that there is no significant impact of source characteristics on the interaction behavior is rejected at a 0.05 level of significance. This indicates that source characteristics significantly influence the interaction behavior of respondents.

Table 35.4 Regression analysis

Model	R	R Square	Adjusted R Square	Std. Error of Estimate	F	Sig.
	.771	.594	.592	.78392	289.587	.000

Source: Author's compilation

Table 35.5 Coefficients table

Model		Unstandardized Coefficients		Standardized Coefficients	t	Sig.
		B	Std. Error	Beta		
1	(Constant)	.116	.181		.642	.521
	Source Characteristics	.974	.057	.771	17.01	.000

Source: Author's compilation

In Table 35.5, the Beta coefficient is 0.974 which indicates that for 0.974 units change in source characteristics, the interactions will change by one unit. The value of t-statistics also shows a significant relationship between source characteristics and interaction behavior ($p <$ .05). The equation can be written as:

$$X = 0.116 + 0.974\,Z$$

Where X indicates interactions and Z indicates source characteristics.

H_3: *Perceived Behavioral control and ease significantly impact the interaction behavior of customers in viral marketing.*

The analysis of Table 35.6 revealed a moderate positive correlation between interaction behavior and perceived behavioral control (PBC). The R square value is 0.243 which indicates that 24 percent of the total variation in interaction behavior can be explained by PBC. The results of the regression are significant as the p-value is 0.003 ($p <$ .05) indicating that the regression model significantly predicts the interaction variable (i.e., it is a good fit for the data). Therefore, the null hypothesis claiming that there is no significant impact of perceived behavioral control on the interaction behavior is rejected at 0.05 level of significance. This indicates that perceived behavioral control significantly influences the interaction behavior of respondents.

Table 35.6 Regression analysis

Model	R	R Square	Adjusted R Square	Std. Error of Estimate	F	Sig.
PBC	.408	.243	.039	1.20315	9.991	.003

Source: Author's compilation

Table 35.7 Coefficient table

Model	Unstandardized Coefficients		Standardized Coefficients	t	Sig.
	B	Std. Error	Beta		
(Constant)	2.057	.340		6.045	.000
PBC	.278	.093	.208	2.999	.003

Source: Author's compilation

In Table 35.7, the Beta coefficient is 0.278 which indicates that for 0.274 units of change in perceived behavioral control and ease, the interactions will change by one unit. The value of t-statistics also shows a significant relationship between perceived behavioral control and ease, and interaction behavior with a significance level below 0.05. The equation can be written as follows:

$$X = 2.057 + 0.278\,A$$

Where X indicates interactions and A indicates perceived behavioral control.

H_4: *Interaction Behavior has a positive impact on customer opinions.*

The analysis of Table 35.8 revealed that there is a high positive correlation between interaction behavior and customer opinions. The R square value for the relationship under study is 0.627 which indicates that 63 percent of the total variation in customer opinions can be explained by interaction behavior. This result indicates that interaction behavior is a strong predictor of customer opinions. The results of the regression are significant as the p-value is 0.003 ($p < 0.05$) indicating that the regression model significantly predicts the customer opinions (i.e., it is a good fit for the data). Therefore, the null hypothesis claiming that there is no significant impact of interaction behavior on customer opinions is rejected at a 0.05 level of significance. This indicates that interaction behavior significantly influences the opinions of respondents.

Table 35.8 Regression model

Model	R	R Square	Adjusted R Square	Std. Error of the Estimate	F	Sig.
	.792	.627	.625	.56642	333.032	0.000

Source: Author's compilation

Table 35.9 Coefficients table

Model	Unstandardized Coefficients		Standardized Coefficients	t	Sig.
	B	Std. Error	Beta		
(Constant)	1.560	.107		14.527	.000
Interaction Behaviour	.597	.033	.792	18.249	.000

Source: Author's compilation

In Table 35.9, the Beta coefficient is 0.59 which indicates that for a 0.59 unit change in interaction behavior, the customer opinion will change by one unit. The value of t-statistics also shows a significant relationship between interaction behavior and customer opinions ($p < .05$). The equation can be written as follows:

$$B = 1.560 + 0.597\,X$$

Where X indicates interactions and B indicates customer opinions.

6. Strategic Implications for Marketing

The research has several implications in marketing. For instance, the study shed light on the nature of content i.e. message characteristics that fetch more interactions. Based on the findings, it is recommended that companies need to develop useful content rather than entertaining or humorous content only. A better way will be to develop content that is a combination of usefulness, emotions, and interest. The study also highlighted that the earlier focus on developing shareable marketing content is no more relevant nowadays as people have numerous other options to interact and all types of interactions lead to virality. Therefore, marketing content creators need to redesign their content development strategy by focusing more on useful and interesting content.

The study also highlighted the importance of the trustworthiness of source sharing/ forwarding/ posting the content. This indicates that earlier methods of putting content through celebrities are no more suitable nowadays. Thus, there is a need for a paradigm shift from celebrity endorsement to influencer marketing. Therefore, marketing managers need to realign their marketing strategies using social media influencers. Based on the finding of interaction behavior, it is recommended that all social media platforms should include all modes of interactions in predicting the virality of content. Though certain platforms such as Instagram, YouTube, etc. follow this, all. This needs to be incorporated into all social media platforms. Also, interaction behavior has a strong impact on customer opinions. Therefore, companies can use it in two ways. One, they can predict customer opinions based on several interactions. Second, the companies can focus on increasing interactions as it is a strong predictor of positive customer opinions.

7. Conclusion

To conclude, the current study is fundamental in answering the research gaps in the viral marketing domain. Based on the data analysis the study found that interaction behavior is significantly impacted by the predictor variables. While, source characteristics explained the maximum variation in the interaction behavior, followed by message characteristics. On the other hand, the perceived behavioral control and use predicted the least variation. In terms of the relationship between interaction behavior and customer opinions, it was found that interactions have a significant impact on customer opinions. Overall, all the null hypotheses in the model were rejected at 0.05 level of significance, which implies that all the variables in the model were significantly related and all the independent variables are predictors of variations in the dependent variable.

8. Future Directions

The current research included only three factors that influence interaction behavior. However, many other factors can influence interactions such as personality traits, self-efficacy, social media characteristics, etc. Future research can include these factors for the research. Further, the scales used for the current research were adapted from the previous studies focusing on sharing behavior. While interactions are wider than sharing. Therefore, separate research is needed to develop validated scales for the variables in light of interaction behavior.

Apart from this, the model ends at customer opinions only due to the paucity of time. This model can be further extended to include the impact of customer opinions on a brand image or purchase intentions. Also, the model studies interactions only. While there is another category of people who watch and personally like the content but do not interact with it through formal interaction methods. They certainly hold a certain opinion about viral content. Therefore, this non-interaction behavior also needs to be studied. Further, research can be conducted to understand the impact of influencers on the virality of content as influencer marketing is an emerging field of marketing with limited academic research.

REFERENCES

1. Abedniya, A., and S. Sabbaghi. 2010. The Impact of Social Networking Websites to Facilitate the Effectiveness of Viral Marketing. *International Journal of Advanced Computer Science and Applications* 1, no. 6. http://thesai.org/Publications/ViewPaper?Volume=1&Issue=6&Code=IJACSA&SerialNo= 21.
2. Achen, R.M. 2019. Re-Examining a Model for Measuring Facebook Interaction and Relationship Quality. *Sport, Business and Management: An International Journal* 9, no. 3 (July 8): 255–272. https://www.emerald.com/insight/content/doi/10.1108/SBM-10-2018-0082/full/html.
3. Akpinar, E., and J. Berger. 2017. Valuable Virality. *Journal of Marketing Research* 54, no. 2 (April): 318–330. http://journals.sagepub.com/doi/10.1509/jmr.13.0350.
4. Anon. 2022. Number of Worldwide Social Network Users 2027. *Statista*. Accessed December 31. https://www.statista.com/statistics/278414/number-of-worldwide-social-network-users/.
5. Arul, and Arun. 2020. Trust on Viral Advertising Messages and Its Impact on Consumers Attitude. *Annamalai International Journal of Business Studies and Research* 12, no. 1 (November 30). https://annamalaiuniversity.ac.in/download/journals/AIJBSR%202020%20Vol%2012%20Issue%20 01%20Doc%2006.pdf.
6. Berger, J. 2014. Word of Mouth and Interpersonal Communication: A Review and Directions for Future Research. *Journal of Consumer Psychology* 24, no. 4 (October): 586–607. https://onlinelibrary.wiley.com/doi/10.1016/j.jcps.2014.05.002.
7. Berger, J., and K.L. Milkman. 2013. Emotion and Virality: What Makes Online Content Go Viral? *GfK Marketing Intelligence Review* 5, no. 1 (May 1): 18–23. https://content.sciendo.com/ doi/10.2478/gfkmir-2014-0022.
8. Borges-Tiago, M.T., F. Tiago, and C. Cosme. 2019. Exploring Users' Motivations to Participate in Viral Communication on Social Media. *Journal of Business Research* 101 (August): 574–582. https://linkinghub.elsevier.com/retrieve/pii/S0148296318305630.
9. Camarero, C., and R. San José. 2011. Social and Attitudinal Determinants of Viral Marketing Dynamics. *Computers in Human Behavior* 27, no. 6 (November): 2292–2300. https://linkinghub. elsevier.com/retrieve/pii/S0747563211001464.
10. Chiu, H.-C., A. Pant, Y.-C. Hsieh, M. Lee, Y.-T. Hsioa, and J. Roan. 2014. Snowball to Avalanche: Understanding the Different Predictors of the Intention to Propagate Online Marketing Messages. *European Journal of Marketing* 48, no. 7/8 (July 8): 1255–1273. https://www.emerald.com/insight/ content/doi/10.1108/EJM-05-2012-0329/full/html.
11. Cohen, E.L. 2014. What Makes Good Games Go Viral? The Role of Technology Use, Efficacy, Emotion and Enjoyment in Players' Decision to Share a Prosocial Digital Game. *Computers in Human Behavior* 33 (April): 321–329. https://linkinghub.elsevier.com/retrieve/pii/S0747563213002513.
12. De Bruyn, A., and G.L. Lilien. 2008. A Multi-Stage Model of Word-of-Mouth Influence through Viral Marketing. *International Journal of Research in Marketing* 25, no. 3 (September): 151–163. https://linkinghub.elsevier.com/retrieve/pii/S0167811608000414.

13. Feroz Khan, G., and S. Vong. 2014. Virality over YouTube: An Empirical Analysis. *Internet Research* 24, no. 5 (September 30): 629–647. https://www.emerald.com/insight/content/doi/10.1108/IntR-05-2013-0085/full/html.

14. Golan, G.J., and L. Zaidner. 2008. Creative Strategies in Viral Advertising: An Application of Taylor's Six-Segment Message Strategy Wheel. *Journal of Computer-Mediated Communication* 13, no. 4 (July): 959–972. https://academic.oup.com/jcmc/article/13/4/959-972/4583540.

15. Gunawan, D.D., and K.-H. Huarng. 2015. Viral Effects of Social Network and Media on Consumers' Purchase Intention. *Journal of Business Research* 68, no. 11 (November): 2237–2241. https://linkinghub.elsevier.com/retrieve/pii/S0148296315002325.

16. Hinz, O., B. Skiera, C. Barrot, and J.U. Becker. 2011. Seeding Strategies for Viral Marketing: An Empirical Comparison. *Journal of Marketing* 75, no. 6 (November): 55–71. http://journals.sagepub.com/doi/10.1509/jm.10.0088.

17. Kabadayi, S., and K. Price. 2014. Consumer – Brand Engagement on Facebook: Liking and Commenting Behaviors. Ed. Dr Angela Hausman. *Journal of Research in Interactive Marketing* 8, no. 3 (August 11): 203–223. https://www.emerald.com/insight/content/doi/10.1108/JRIM-12-2013-0081/full/html.

18. Ketelaar, P.E., L. Janssen, M. Vergeer, E.A. van Reijmersdal, R. Crutzen, and J. van 't Riet. 2016. The Success of Viral Ads: Social and Attitudinal Predictors of Consumer Pass-on Behavior on Social Network Sites. *Journal of Business Research* 69, no. 7 (July 1): 2603–2613. https://www.sciencedirect.com/science/article/pii/S0148296315005925.

19. Kulkarni, K.K., A.D. Kalro, and D. Sharma. 2019. Sharing of Branded Viral Advertisements by Young Consumers: The Interplay between Personality Traits and Ad Appeal. *Journal of Consumer Marketing* 36, no. 6 (September 9): 846–857. https://www.emerald.com/insight/content/doi/10.1108/JCM-11-2017-2428/full/html.

20. Lee, J., D. Lazer, and C. Riedl. 2022. Complex Contagion in Viral Marketing: Causal Evidence and Embeddedness Effects from a Country-Scale Field Experiment. SSRN Scholarly Paper. Rochester, NY. https://papers.ssrn.com/abstract=4092057.

21. Maiz, A., N. Arranz, and J.C. Fdez. de Arroyabe. 2016. Factors Affecting Social Interaction on Social Network Sites: The Facebook Case. *Journal of Enterprise Information Management* 29, no. 5 (January 1): 630–649. https://doi.org/10.1108/JEIM-10-2014-0105.

22. Palka, W., K. Pousttchi, and D.G. Wiedemann. 2009. Mobile Word-of-Mouth – A Grounded Theory of Mobile Viral Marketing. *Journal of Information Technology* 24, no. 2 (June 1): 172–185. https://doi.org/10.1057/jit.2008.37.

23. Pescher, C., P. Reichhart, and M. Spann. 2014. Consumer Decision-Making Processes in Mobile Viral Marketing Campaigns. *Journal of Interactive Marketing* 28, no. 1 (February): 43–54. https://journals.sagepub.com/doi/full/10.1016/j.intmar.2013.08.001.

24. Rayport, J. 1996. The Virus of Marketing. *Fast Company*. https://www.fastcompany.com/27701/virus-marketing.

25. Rao et al., 2022. Customer Attitude towards Digital Marketing: A Structural Snapshot on Viral Marketing. *Academy of Marketing Studies Journal* 26, no. 3: 1–8.

26. Reichstein, T., and I. Brusch. 2019. The Decision-making Process in Viral Marketing—A Review and Suggestions for Further Research. *Psychology & Marketing* 36, no. 11 (November): 1062–1081. https://onlinelibrary.wiley.com/doi/10.1002/mar.21256.

27. Rollins, Anitsal, and M. .Anitsal. 2014. Viral Marketing Techniques. *Entrepreneurial Executive*. https://www.researchgate.net/publication/283234049.

28. Siddiqui, D.K.A. 2022. Public Opinion towards Advertising: Factor Analytic Findings From Pakistan. *European Journal of Business and Management*. Accessed December 31. https://www.academia.edu/19873287/Public_Opinion_towards_Advertising_Factor_Analytic_Findings_From_Pakistan.

29. Simmonds, D.M., K. Campbell, and J. Hasley. 2021. Viral Diffusion of Technology Products: A Comprehensive Stage Framework. *Information Systems and E-Business Management* 19, no. 2 (June): 597–619. https://link.springer.com/10.1007/s10257-021-00518-3.

30. Tsugawa, S., and H. Ohsaki. 2015. Negative Messages Spread Rapidly and Widely on Social Media. In *Proceedings of the 2015 ACM on Conference on Online Social Networks*, 151–160. Palo Alto California USA: ACM. https://dl.acm.org/doi/10.1145/2817946.2817962.

31. Usmani, S., S.F. Ali, K. Imtiaz, and H.G. Khan. 2019. The Experimental Study On the Effectiveness of Social Media Ad Campaign: Like, Comment, Share. *International Journal of Experiential Learning & Case Studies* 4, no. 1 (June 30): 116–130. https://journals.iobmresearch.com/index.php/JELCS/article/view/2620/535.

32. Wu, S.-I., and W.-H. Wang. 2014. Impact of CSR Perception on Brand Image, Brand Attitude and Buying Willingness: A Study of a Global Café. *International Journal of Marketing Studies* 6, no. 6 (November 24): p43. https://ccsenet.org/journal/index.php/ijms/article/view/42558.

33. Yang, H. 2013. Market Mavens in Social Media: Examining Young Chinese Consumers' Viral Marketing Attitude, EWOM Motive, and Behavior. *Journal of Asia-Pacific Business* 14, no. 2 (April): 154–178. http://www.tandfonline.com/doi/abs/10.1080/10599231.2013.756337.

34. Yang, H. (Chris), and L. Zhou. 2011. Extending TPB and TAM to Mobile Viral Marketing: An Exploratory Study on American Young Consumers' Mobile Viral Marketing Attitude, Intent and Behavior. *Journal of Targeting, Measurement and Analysis for Marketing* 19, no. 2 (June 1): 85–98. https://doi.org/10.1057/jt.2011.11.

35. Zhang, T., and X. Huang. 2022. Viral Marketing: Influencer Marketing Pivots in Tourism – a Case Study of Meme Influencer Instigated Travel Interest Surge. *Current Issues in Tourism* 25, no. 4 (February 16): 508–515. https://www.tandfonline.com/doi/full/10.1080/13683500.2021.1910214.

Handbook of Evidence Based Management Practices in Business – Satyendra Kumar Sharma et al. (eds)
© 2023 Taylor & Francis Group, London, ISBN 978-1-032-54216-4

Chapter

Talking the Walk: Conceptualizing Antecedents and Consequences of Greenhushing

Anand Thakur[1]

Associate Professor and Dean, School of Management,
Central University of Punjab, Bathinda, India

Kavita Singla[2], Kamini Singla[3]

Research Scholar (UGC-JRF), School of Management,
Central University of Punjab, Bathinda, India

ABSTRACT: As the environmental consciousness is getting momentum these days, disclosure of eco-practices by companies is becoming imperative. In order to gain publicity and visibility, companies are racing to fabricate the sustainability of their green efforts (known as Greenwashing). Many companies, on the other hand, are disclosing their sustainable practices insufficiently. Greenhushing is an emerging concept in which companies deliberately do not publicize their sustainable initiatives or achievements beyond the minimum or prescribed goals. To extend the conceptual understanding of greenhushing practice, this study on the basis of an extensive literature review, aims to postulate the antecedents and consequences of greenhushing.

The focus of this study is to critically examine the role of green perceived risk (functional risk, financial risk, hedonic risk, and self-image risk), perceived consumer scepticism, fear of greenwashing, pure altruism, and environmental certification in the greenhushing practice. The findings reveal that green trust, word of mouth, green satisfaction, green loyalty, and green consumer confusion are significantly influenced by the greenhushing practice. The proposed conceptual model provides significant theoretical implications for scholars and practitioners to develop effective green strategies and practices. This study proposes useful insights for managers, marketers, and policymakers to determine sustainable business operations and effective green communication to enhance the trust and loyalty of their consumers.

KEYWORDS: Altruism, Greenhushing, Green loyalty, Green perceived risk, Green trust, Greenwashing

[1]athakur29s0891@gmail.com, [2]kvsingla11@gmail.com, [3]kaminisingla213@gmail.com

DOI: 10.4324/9781003415725-36

1. Introduction

'Green Marketing Communications' have gathered researchers' interest in the recent past (Grimmer and Woolley, 2014; Bailey et al., 2018; Taufique 2022). Corporations employ green reporting to address the expectations of various stakeholders including consumers, regulators, investors, communities, etc. Over compliance has also been a menace among organisations leading to increased costs of stricter regulations (Denicolò, 2008). Hence, it is disconcerting to observe the practice of being timid regarding a company's sustainable environmental efforts and achievements (Alice et al., 2021). Font et al. (2017) have termed it as 'greenhushing' or 'green blushing.'

'Greenhushing' is believed to overpower the infamous strategy of 'greenwashing' (Simpson, 2016). Greenwashing is understood as the junction of two firm behaviors: low green performance and an exaggerated communication of green efforts (Delmas, 2011). In contrast, greenhushing implies under reporting of green endeavours to keep corporate philanthropy silent (Wang et al., 2021). The moral muteness emerging from greenhushing is, generally, a consequence of an attempt to avoid detrimental effect of perceived lower compliance (Font et al., 2017). The hotel and lodging industry seems to be spearheading the adoption of greenhushing by explicitly choosing to remain silent on their green initiatives (Heras-Saizarbitoria et al., 2020). Suit is followed by winemakers producing certified organic wine (Delmas and Grant, 2014) and printer manufacturers such as Hewlett and Packard using green components (Gunther, 2012) but being discreet about these achievements.

With the increased prevalence of greenhushing, it becomes imperative to extend the conceptual understanding of its antecedents and consequences and to propose a theoretical framework, based on the extant literature, on the areas of 'green marketing communications', 'green washing', 'green blushing' and 'greenhushing'. The antecedents of greenhushing are expected to provide a better view of the reasons behind increased cases of muted green communications. Similarly, a greater understanding of outcomes will facilitate researchers to address the concerns (regarding greenhushing) of environmental actors, regulatory authorities, corporations and policymakers.

2. Review of Literature

The converse of greenwashing, greenhushing is a marketing strategy of conscious concealment of the eco-practices adopted by an enterprise (Font et al., 2017; Coles et al., 2017). Stifleman (2008) coined the term anecdotally to juxtapose with 'greenwashing'. The question of substance here is: Do firms decide not to communicate green achievements because these are not considered worthy of communication (Lynes and Andrachuk, 2008)?

The motivations underlying the adoption of quiet green communications are manifold. Greenhushing seems to be emerged from the fear of accusation of greenwashing (Vallaster et al., 2012). It has been termed as 'hypocrisy avoidance', that is, choosing silence over allegations of inconsideration towards the environment (Carlos and Lewis, 2018). Another identified reason is green perceived risk consisting of functional risk, financial risk, hedonic risk, and self-image risk (Chen and Chang, 2013). Unethical business practices of altering green marketing communications can also lead to enhanced consumer scepticism towards the authenticity of value delivery by the corporations (TM et al., 2021). Pure altruism (Pinto et al. 2019; Ginder et al., 2021; Falchi and Grolleau, 2022) and lack of environmental certifications (Font et al., 2016; Geerts, 2014; Denicolò, 2008) have also been previously examined in the context of sustainability disclosures. The present study critically examines the above mentioned constructs as antecedents of greenhushing.

Varied ramifications of greenhushing can be identified from the extant literature. Green trust stems from the dependability on a product or service based on the environmental declarations of an organization (Chen, 2010). Shying away from communicating green practices may have a negative impact on green trust (Christis and Wang, 2021) and the resultant word of mouth emerging from uncertainty of products' green orientation (Acuti et al., 2022). Further, it has been certified that green satisfaction is influenced by the perceived impact of ecological practices (Hellmeister and Richins, 2019).This implies that discreet declaration of such practices can accentuate green dissatisfaction. Reduced green loyalty and enhanced green consumer confusion are also resultants of sustainability practices such as 'greenwashing' and 'green blushing'. The present study attempts to analyse 'diluting green trust', 'negative green word of mouth', 'green dissatisfaction', 'degrading green loyalty' and 'green consumer confusion' as outcomes of greenhushing.

Previous studies have postulated the reasons and outcomes of greenhushing in segregation (Font et al., 2017; Alice et al., 2021; Amores-Salvadó et al., 2022) and the present study portrays the integrated framework (Fig. 36.1). This article expects to contribute to the literature of greenhushing by postulating that why companies are willing to 'walk the walk' but shy away from 'talking the walk'.

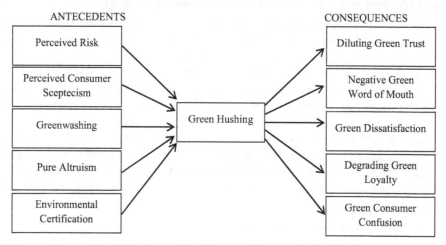

Fig. 36.1 Conceptual framework on greenhushing

Source: Authors' compilation

3. Discussion

3.1 Antecedents of Greenhushing

Association of Perceived Risk with Greenhushing

Four perceived risks namely- functional, financial, hedonic and self-image risk have been elucidated by Chang et al. (2017). Literature reports that corporate green practices evoke green perceived risk among the consumers, especially in the case of luxurious products (Peng and Chen, 2019). For instance Peng and Chen (2019); Line and Hanks (2016) propound that consumers apprehend adopting green practices by luxury hotels as these may reduce the utility and functionality of the services. It originates from perceived functional risk. Consumer hesitation towards green products proliferates due to their perception of low economic value generating perceived financial risk (Ponnapureddy et al., 2017). Wiedmann et al. (2009); Peng and Chen (2019) advocate that luxury products attract the attention of consumers because of an inherent sense of pleasure and self-indulgence whereas Rahman and Chi (2015) point out that companies following green practices evoke the negative consumer attitude as green practices can shrink the pleasure and excitement, stimulating hedonic risk. Luxury products are possessed by customers to express their status and values (Chang and Ko, 2017), but orientation towards sustainable purchase behavior may act as an inhibitor in terms of deteriorating customers' standards (Peng and Chen, 2019; Oliver, 2013). Moreover, Meng and Leary (2019) argue that recycled products are more often condemned by customers and perceived as contaminated, thus, triggering a sense of disgust. Consequently, companies are reluctant to communicate their eco-friendly practices due to the fear of perceived inferiority and diminished brand value (Falchi et al., 2022; Ho et al., 2012; Peng and Chen, 2019).

Perceived Consumers' Scepticism and the Greenhushing Strategy

Consumers' scepticism determines the elaboration of sustainable communication to a large extent (Connors and Matthew, 2017). Many green practices followed by companies result in cost saving and other extrinsic benefits to them. Abstract nature of green initiatives acts as an impediment in consumers' ability to verify the credibility of these practices (Rahman and Chi, 2015). 'Too Loud' communication by firms about their sustainable efforts is not appreciated by public (Morsing et al., 2008). Communication of both intrinsic (cost saving) and extrinsic (environmental protection) motives evokes perceived consumers' scepticism (Falchi et al., 2022; Acuti et al., 2022). Past corporate transgression leads the consumers to believe that green practices claims are just the tactics of companies to reduce the cost and labour (Majeed and Kim, 2022; Chen et al., 2018). This ever increasing consumer scepticism compels the firms to embrace conscientious attitude quietly towards their efficacious green practices (Ginder et al., 2021).

Coping up with Greenwashing Allegations

Fear of being accused of providing deceptive or exaggerated information among the corporate firms is one of the many reasons to embrace the strategy of greenhushing (Byrne, 2022). Risk of loss of reputation due to greenwashing allegation leads companies not to report their genuine sustainable initiatives (Falchi and Grolleau, 2022). Publicising green communication can induce the suspicion of consumers and scrutiny by regulators that renders under-communication of green practices an involuntary activity (Amores-Salvadó et al., 2022). For example, Lindsey (2016) states that despite their remarkable green practices, avoiding the potential litigation and criticism of greenwashing is the leading motive behind Walmart's intent of not disclosing their efforts. Ignoring the fact that market capitalisation of green leadership firms is higher as compared to green quiet firm (Amores-Salvadó et al., 2022), firms engage in greenhushing practices to avoid the litigation of greenwashing (Okazaki et al., 2021).

Greenhushing for Pure Altruism

Sustainable actions are also persuaded by 'true altruism' or 'authentic philanthropy' (Ginder et al., 2021). Despite the fact, consumers with high environmental values respond positively to the altruistic environmental communication (Font et al., 2016), responsible companies induced with pure altruism prefer not to disclose their efforts (Falchi and Grolleau, 2022).

Lack of Environmental Certification and Greenhushing

Lack of authentic information may induce the consumers' mistrust towards green initiatives (Rahman et al., 2015). In order to substantiate the 'green claim' in consumers' perspective, credible environmental certification is necessary (Font et al., 2016). Obtaining environmental certificates from independent and credible agencies not only certifies the sustainable strides of the firms but prove to be a fruitful strategy to avoid any criticism and improve the firm image (Geerts, 2014). Conversely, absence of certification from a credible third party provokes corporations to be quiet about their green initiatives (Falchi and Grolleau, 2022).

3.2 Consequences of Greenhushing

Diluting Green Trust

Degrading environmental conditions are inclining consumers towards eco-friendly choices (Rahman et al., 2015). Up-surging green consumerism demands companies to disclose their sustainable efforts. Companies that are not disclosing their efforts of decarbonisation may face backlash because stakeholders might perceive them as having weak green perspectives (Basiouny, 2022). This strategic silence may lead to increased consumers distrust in the green practices of company (Lindsey 2016; Ginder et al., 2021).

Negative Green Word of Mouth

Publicising the green initiatives of firms can improve their green image (Wang et al., 2018) which can further influence the WoM intention of the consumers (Crane, 2011). As consumers are generally found to be sceptical of CSR initiatives, Connors and Matthew (2017) posit that conveying sustainable activities in elaborative manner can reduce the negative word of mouth intention. Zhang and Lena (2023) postulate that failure to address the on-going participation of firms in green practices is perceived as firm's ineffectiveness in creating environmental value resulting in diminishing consumer's engagement in green behaviour (purchase intention and positive word of mouth). Thus, communicating the sustainable activities adopted by firms directly impacts the green word of mouth among all the stakeholders (Madanaguli et al., 2022; Mele et al., 2019).

Green Dissatisfaction

Chen et al. (2010) have defined green satisfaction as "a pleasurable level of consumption-related fulfillment to satisfy a consumer's environmental desires, sustainable expectations, and green needs". Disseminating green communication improves the green satisfaction of consumers by reducing ambiguity and validating trustworthy claims (Chang, 2014). Moreover, Martínez (2015) suggests companies to adopt integrated marketing communication to effectively promote their green initiatives. Companies embracing greenhushing practices create dissatisfaction among the consumers as they are not able to distinguish the trustworthiness of claim.

Degrading Green Loyalty

Green image of a company plays a significant role in developing green loyalty (Martínez, 2015). Ginder et al. (2021) discover that when companies provide exposure of uniform CSR positioning, consumers perceive this congruent sustainable behaviour as more intrinsically motivated. Consumer's loyalty towards the product or company increases when companies demonstrate responsible sustainable practices (Mele et al., 2019).

Green Consumer Confusion

Consumers are not always familiar with green products (Wang et al., 2018). Unawareness towards substantive environmental benefits creates misperception in the consumer's mind (Tiwari et al., 2011) accentuating backlash regarding green products (Crane, 2011). Green communication educates consumers about the effectiveness of eco-friendly practices and their choice of product (Majeed and Kim, 2022). But, companies practicing greenhushing end up building confusion in the mind of consumers about the greenness of these products, thus, impacting purchase intention negatively (Chen and Chang, 2013). Therefore, instead of adopting greenhushing practices, firms should adopt the 'green knowledge sharing strategy' to disseminate relevant information for substantiating the green claims (Majeed and Kim, 2022).

3.3 Theoretical and Managerial Implications

The present study extends the theoretical understanding of disconcerting strategy of greenhushing by propounding a theoretical framework based on synthesised fragmented fundamentals. Managers may employ the unearthed antecedents and outcomes of greenhushing for designing effective green communication strategies to reconcile the ethical and strategic dilemma faced by companies. The study will facilitate a new beginning towards practices adopted in environmental reporting.

Organisational identity is modelled by its green marketing communications. Raising the standards of green disclosures may fulfil the need to align corporate values with perceived consumers' expectations. The fear of reduced functionality, increased costs, diluted pleasure and self-image may be addressed by educating the consumers about the nugatory effects of green transformations on the conventional qualities of products. Concern of cynicism from consumers and greenwashing litigation can be addressed by transparent disclosures of ecological endeavors. Liberal environmental certifications and uncomplicated procurement procedures can be adopted by policymakers to facilitate increased compliance. Ethical green reporting will allow marketers to keep intact the loyalty and trust of consumers towards green products. As a result, word of mouth can be managed by unwinding the misconceptions that muteness can ensue. It is vital for companies to organise their environmental communications in a manner that the consumers' cognitive processes are not loaded with redundant jargon, and only the pertinent information is shared. It will inhibit the development of green confusion among the consumers. Lastly, it imparts insightful implication for managers to acknowledge the fact that ethicality is not merely confined to 'walking the walk' but motivating the stakeholders for eco practices by 'talking the walk' is imperative.

4. Conclusion

Need of the hour is to wake up to the fake portrayal of green disclosures and redefine the core strategic values of corporate world to adopt a holistic approach towards green marketing communications. The promoters of green transition need to comprehend the phenomenon of greenhushing in a better way. The present study aims to deepen the understanding of this practice by delving into its roots. The green hushing antecedents and outcomes contributed in this study will certainly play a pivotal role in adoption of green practices.

The study can be extended further by diverging from its conceptual nature and collecting quantitative data for empirically testing relationships among the stated constructs. The viewpoints of other stakeholders (such as investors, employees and regulators) regarding silent green efforts may also be studied through qualitative research designs.

REFERENCES

1. Acuti, D., Pizzetti, M., and Dolnicar, S. (2022). When sustainability backfires: A review on the unintended negative side-effects of product and service sustainability on consumer behavior. Psychology & Marketing. 39(10): 1933–1945. https://doi.org/10.1002/mar.21709
2. Amores-Salvadó, J., Martin-de Castro, G., and Albertini, E. (2022). Walking the talk, but above all, talking the walk: Looking green for market stakeholder engagement. Corporate Social Responsibility and Environmental Management. 1–12. https://doi.org/10.1002/csr.2364
3. Bailey, A. A., Mishra, A. S., and Tiamiyu, M. F. (2018). Application of GREEN scale to understanding US consumer response to green marketing communications. Psychology & Marketing. 35(11): 863–875. https://doi.org/10.1002/mar.21140
4. Basioun A. (2022) Greenhushing: Why some firms keep quiet about ESG. Knowledge at Wharton. https://knowledge.wharton.upenn.edu/article/greenhushing-why-some-firms-keep-quiet-about-esg/ (accessed on December 26, 2022)
5. Byrne D. (2022). What is green-hushing? Corporate Governance Institute. https://www.thecorporategovernanceinstitute.com/insights/lexicon/what-is-green-hushing (accessed on December 23, 2022).
6. Carlos, W. C., and Lewis, B. W. (2018). Strategic silence: Withholding certification status as a hypocrisy avoidance tactic. Administrative Science Quarterly. 63(1): 130–169. https://doi.org/10.1177/0001839217695089
7. Chang, Y., and Ko, Y. J. (2017). Consumers' perceived post purchase risk in luxury services. International Journal of Hospitality Management. 61: 94–106. https://doi.org/10.1016/j.ijhm.2016.09.005

8. Chen, H., Bernard, S., and Rahman, I. (2019). Greenwashing in hotels: A structural model of trust and behavioral intentions. Journal of cleaner production. 206: 326–335. https://doi.org/10.1016/j.jclepro.2018.09.168

9. Chen, Y. S., Lin, C. L., and Chang, C. H. (2014). The influence of greenwash on green word-of-mouth (green WOM): The mediation effects of green perceived quality and green satisfaction. Quality & Quantity. 48(5): 2411–2425. https://doi.org/10.1007/s11135-013-9898-1

10. Chen, Y. S. (2010). The drivers of green brand equity: Green brand image, green satisfaction, and green trust. Journal of Business ethics. 93(2): 307–319. https://doi.org/10.1007/s10551-009-0223-9

11. Chen, Y. S., and Chang, C. H. (2013). Towards green trust: The influences of green perceived quality, green perceived risk, and green satisfaction. Management decision. 51(1): 63–82. https://doi.org/10.1108/00251741311291319

12. Christis, J., and Wang, Y. (2021). Communicating environmental CSR towards consumers: the impact of message content, message style and praise tactics. Sustainability. 13(7): 3981. https://doi.org/10.3390/su13073981

13. Coles, T., Warren, N., Borden, D. S., and Dinan, C. (2017). Business models among SMTEs: identifying attitudes to environmental costs and their implications for sustainable tourism. Journal of Sustainable Tourism. 25(4): 471–488. https://doi.org/10.1080/09669582.2016.1221414

14. Connors, S., Anderson-MacDonald, S., and Thomson, M. (2017). Overcoming the 'window dressing' effect: Mitigating the negative effects of inherent skepticism towards corporate social responsibility. Journal of business ethics. 145(3): 599–621. https://doi.org/10.1007/s10551-015-2858-z

15. Crane, A. (2000). Facing the backlash: green marketing and strategic reorientation in the 1990s. Journal of strategic Marketing. 8(3): 277–296. https://doi.org/10.1080/09652540050110011

16. Delmas, M. A., and Burbano, V. C. (2011). The drivers of greenwashing. California management review. 54(1): 64–87. https://doi.org/10.1525/cmr.2011.54.1.64

17. Delmas, M. A., and Grant, L. E. (2014). Eco-labeling strategies and price-premium: the wine industry puzzle. Business & Society. 53(1): 6–44. https://doi.org/10.1177/0007650310362254

18. Denicolò, V. (2008). A signaling model of environmental overcompliance. Journal of Economic Behavior & Organization. 68(1): 293–303. https://doi.org/10.1016/j.jebo.2008.04.009

19. Ettinger, A., Grabner-Kräuter, S., Okazaki, S., and Terlutter, R. (2021). The desirability of CSR communication versus greenhushing in the hospitality industry: The customers' perspective. Journal of Travel Research. 60(3): 618–638. https://doi.org/10.1177/0047287520930087

20. Falchi, A., Grolleau, G., and Mzoughi, N. (2022). Why companies might under-communicate their efforts for sustainable development and what can be done?. Business Strategy and the Environment. 31(5): 1938–1946. https://doi.org/10.1002/bse.2991

21. Font, X., Elgammal, I., and Lamond, I. (2017). Greenhushing: the deliberate under communicating of sustainability practices by tourism businesses. Journal of Sustainable Tourism. 25(7): 1007–1023. https://doi.org/10.1080/09669582.2016.1158829

22. Geerts, W. (2014). Environmental certification schemes: Hotel managers' views and perceptions. International Journal of Hospitality Management. 39: 87–96. https://doi.org/10.1016/j.ijhm.2014.02.007

23. Ginder, W., Suk, W., Sang, K., and Byun, E. (2021). Effects of Internal – External Congruence - Based CSR Positioning: An Attribution Theory Approach. Journal of Business Ethics. 169(2): 355–369. https://doi.org/10.1007/s10551-019-04282-w

24. Grimmer, M., and Woolley, M. (2014). Green marketing messages and consumers' purchase intentions: Promoting personal versus environmental benefits. Journal of Marketing Communications. 20(4): 231–250. https://doi.org/10.1080/13527266.2012.684065

25. Gunther, M. (2012). Greener (brown) toilet paper and the elusive green consumer. GreenBiz. https://www.greenbiz.com/article/greener-brown-toilet-paper-and-elusive-green-consumer. (accessed on December 26, 2022)

26. Hellmeister, A., and Richins, H. (2019). Green to gold: Beneficial impacts of sustainability certification and practice on tour enterprise performance. Sustainability. 11(3): 709. https://doi.org/10.3390/su11030709

27. Heras-Saizarbitoria, I., Boiral, O., Allur, E., and García, M. (2020). Communicating environmental management certification: Signaling without signals?. Business Strategy and the Environment. 29(2): 422–431. https://doi.org/10.1002/bse.2374

28. Ho, K., Stein, L., Yoonjoung, C., and Lee, S. (2012). Consumers ' willingness to pay for green initiatives of the hotel industry. International Journal of Hospitality Management. 31(2): 564–572. https://doi.org/10.1016/j.ijhm.2011.08.001

29. Line, N.D., and Hanks, L. (2016). The effects of environmental and luxury beliefs on intentions to patronize green hotels: the moderating effect of destination image. Journal of Sustainable Tourism. 24(6): 904–925. https://doi.org/10.1080/09669582.2015.1091467

30. Lynes, J. K., and Andrachuk, M. (2008). Motivations for corporate social and environmental responsibility: A case study of Scandinavian Airlines. Journal of International management. 14(4): 377–390. https://doi.org/10.1016/j.intman.2007.09.004

31. Madanaguli, A., Srivastava, S., Ferraris, A., and Dhir, A. (2022). Corporate social responsibility and sustainability in the tourism sector: A systematic literature review and future outlook. Sustainable Development. 30(3): 447–461. https://doi.org/10.1002/sd.2258

32. Majeed, S., and Kim, W. G. (2022). A reflection of greenwashing practices in the hospitality industry: a scoping review. International Journal of Contemporary Hospitality Management, (ahead-of-print). https://doi.org/10.1108/IJCHM-04-2022-0495

33. Martínez, P. (2015). Customer loyalty: Exploring its antecedents from a green marketing perspective. International Journal of Contemporary Hospitality Management. 27(5): 896–917. https://doi.org/10.1108/IJCHM-03-2014-0115

34. Mercade Mele, P., Molina Gomez, J., and Garay, L. (2019). To green or not to green: The influence of green marketing on consumer behaviour in the hotel industry. Sustainability. 11(17): 4623. https://doi.org/10.3390/su11174623

35. Meng, M. D., and Leary, R. B. (2021). It might be ethical, but I won't buy it: Perceived contamination of, and disgust towards, clothing made from recycled plastic bottles. Psychology & Marketing. 38(2): 298–312. https://doi.org/10.1002/mar.21323

36. Morsing, M., Schultz, M., and Nielsen, K. U. (2008). The 'Catch 22'of communicating CSR: Findings from a Danish study. Journal of marketing communications. 14(2): 97–111. https://doi.org/10.1080/13527260701856608

37. Oliver, J. D. (2013). Promoting sustainability by marketing green products to non-adopters. Gestion 2000. 30(3): 77–86. https://doi.org/10.3917/g2000.303.0077

38. Peng, N., and Chen, A. (2019). Luxury hotels going green – the antecedents and consequences of consumer hesitation. Journal of Sustainable Tourism. 27, 2019(9): 1374–1392. https://doi.org/10.1080/09669582.2019.1622710

39. Pinto, D. C., Herter, M. M., Rossi, P., Nique, W. M., and Borges, A. (2019). Recycling cooperation and buying status: Effects of pure and competitive altruism on sustainable behaviors. European Journal of Marketing. 53(5): 944–971. https://doi.org/10.1108/EJM-09-2017-0557

40. Ponnapureddy, S., Priskin, J., Ohnmacht, T., Vinzenz, F., and Wirth, W. (2017). The influence of trust perceptions on German tourists' intention to book a sustainable hotel: A new approach to analysing marketing information. Journal of Sustainable Tourism. 25(7): 970–988. https://doi.org/10.1080/09669582.2016.1270953

41. Rahman, I., Park, J., and Chi, C. G. Q. (2015). Consequences of "greenwashing": Consumers' reactions to hotels' green initiatives. International Journal of Contemporary Hospitality Management. 27(6): 1054–1081. https://doi.org/10.1108/IJCHM-04-2014-0202

42. Simpson, D. (2016). Is 'greenhushing' taking over from 'greenwashing' in the lodging industry?. Green Lodging News. https://www.cabi.org/leisuretourism/news/25345. (accessed December 27, 2022)

43. Taufique, K. M. R. (2022). Integrating environmental values and emotion in green marketing communications inducing sustainable consumer behaviour. Journal of Marketing Communications. 28(3): 272–290. https://doi.org/10.1080/13527266.2020.1866645

44. Tiwari, S., Tripathi, D. M., Srivastava, U., and Yadav, P. K. (2011). Green marketing-emerging dimensions. Journal of Business Excellence. 2(1): 18.

45. TM, A., Kaur, P., Bresciani, S., and Dhir, A. (2021). What drives the adoption and consumption of green hotel products and services? A systematic literature review of past achievement and future promises. Business Strategy and the Environment. 30(5): 2637–2655. https://doi.org/10.1002/bse.2768

46. Vallaster, C., Lindgreen, A., and Maon, F. (2012). Strategically leveraging corporate social responsibility: A corporate branding perspective. California management review. 54(3): 34–60. https://doi.org/10.1525/cmr.2012.54.3.34

47. Wang, H., Jia, M., and Zhang, Z. (2021). Good deeds done in silence: Stakeholder management and quiet giving by Chinese firms. Organization Science. 32(3): 649–674. https://doi.org/10.1287/orsc.2020.1385

48. Wang, J., Wang, S., Xue, H., Wang, Y., and Li, J. (2018). Green image and consumers' word-of-mouth intention in the green hotel industry: The moderating effect of Millennials. Journal of cleaner production. 181: 426–436. https://doi.org/10.1016/j.jclepro.2018.01.250

49. Wiedmann, K. P., Hennigs, N., and Siebels, A. (2009). Value-based segmentation of luxury consumption behavior. Psychology & Marketing. 26(7): 625–651. https://doi.org/10.1002/mar

50. Zhang, X., and Jeong, E. L. (2023). Are co-created green initiatives more appealing than firm-created green initiatives? Investigating the effects of co-created green appeals on restaurant promotion. International Journal of Hospitality Management. 108: 103361. https://doi.org/10.1016/j.ijhm.2022.103361

Chapter

A Bibliometric Review of Greenwashing Research by Using Co-occurrence Analysis and Bibliographic Coupling

Sakshi Goyal[1], Harshika Sondhi[2] and Praveen Goyal[3]
Department of Management,
Birla Institute of Technology and Science, Pilani, India

ABSTRACT: Given the enormous interest in the area of sustainability, greenwashing has gained extensive attention from various researchers. The objective of this paper is to review the existing literature on Greenwashing using Bibliometric Analysis. With the help of keywords co-occurrence and bibliographic coupling, the most prominent and emerging research themes of this domain were identified. Based on the analysis of 393 articles extracted from the Scopus database, one of the most significant themes that have emerged in the literature on greenwashing is Corporate Social Responsibility. Also, the research studies on greenwashing have evolved considerably in the last decade. This review article will guide future scholars in both academia and industry to gain further insights into greenwashing and shed light on the areas for future research and implications for practitioners.

KEYWORDS: Greenwashing, Corporate social responsibility, Bibliometric analysis, Co-occurrence, Bibliographic coupling

1. Introduction

According to UN Global Compact, firms are responsible for being socially and environmentally conscious. Hence, accomplishing the financial objective is not the organization's only concern. They are also responsible for making contributions to society's welfare. The companies are engaged in CSR activities by following a triple-bottom-line approach. According to Slaper and

[1]p20210439@pilani.bits-pilani.ac.in, [2]p20220035@pilani.bits-pilani.ac.in, [3]praveen.goyal@pilani.bits-pilani.ac.in

Hall (2013), the triple bottom line consists of three dimensions: society, environment, and profits. Accordingly, the firms must take into account the environmental, social as well as financial aspects Isil and Hernke (2017). However, to be perceived as socially responsible, companies are making false claims about their green practices and environmental performances. The act of misleading consumers regarding the environmental methods of a company and positive communication about ecological performance is termed Greenwashing TerraChoice (2010). Similarly, it is the selective disclosure of positive information about companies' environmental and social performance without disclosing negative information Lyon and Maxwell (2011). Furthermore, Du (2015) describes Greenwashing as the overcommunication and false advertisement of firms' eco-friendly activities to hide their actual performances. According to Gatti et al. (2019), the gap between socially responsible communication and actual firms' practices is called Greenwashing. It is the phenomenon of companies overemphasizing their environmental activities to be perceived as environmentally significant even though they are not Szabo and Webster (2021). On the whole, greenwashing is the act of falsehood communication about environmental and social performances by which companies tend to act eco-friendly and socially responsible.

Greenwashing is a widely studied topic in the literature on marketing Musgrove et al. (2018); Qayyum et al. (2022), consumer behavior Topal et al. (2020) Jog and Singhal (2020), and CSR Kurpierz et al. (2020); Balluchi et al. (2020). Recently, few researchers have performed bibliometric reviews on Greenwashing Navarro et al. (2021) and Pendse et al. (2022). On the contrary, there is still a need to conduct a widespread study on Greenwashing practices because the previous studies have paid more attention to articles related to the agriculture and food industry and have emphasized greenwashing as an understudied research topic. Since greenwashing is a significant and persistent problem of today's time, the objective of the current study is to conduct a bibliometric analysis of Greenwashing. A bibliometric analysis helps identify trends and patterns and explore specific domains in the existing literature Donthu et al. (2021). This paper is based on co-occurrence analysis and bibliographic coupling technique. The co-occurrence analysis is used to understand the actual content of the publications and to forecast the future research direction Donthu et al.(2021). Furthermore, the bibliographic coupling technique is used to understand the latest developments and current scenarios of the research Donthu et al.(2021). Therefore, this paper highlights the present and future scenarios of greenwashing research.

To do so, the following research questions have been formulated:

RQ1: How the literature on Greenwashing has developed over the last two decades?

RQ2: What are the most prominent research themes in the existing body of knowledge?

RQ3: What is the relationship among citing documents published in the last three years?

RQ4: Which countries have been the most dominant in Greenwashing research?

The overall paper is divided into four sections. Section 2 describes the methodology used to gather data. Section 3 depicts the graphical representation of results obtained from Visualisation of Similarities (VOS) viewer software. The final section describes the significant conclusions drawn, the limitations, and the future implications of the study.

2. Methodology

2.1 Data Collection

This study used "Greenwash OR "Greenwashing" OR Green washing" as a search term to gather data from the Scopus database. The search was performed in November 2022. Therefore, it consists of articles up to November 2022 from 2000. Initially, the search returned 932 publications, further refined based on the subject category. The current study majorly emphasizes the management domain by limiting the subject category to "Business, Management, and Accounting." Eventually, 393 articles were chosen for the review.

2.2 Tools and Techniques

With the assistance of two science mapping techniques such as bibliographic coupling and co-occurrence analysis, the relationships among citing documents, the most dominant countries, and the most prominent keywords are identified. The relationships and network diagram are visually represented through VOS viewer Software.

3. Results

3.1 Development of Greenwashing Literature

To answer RQ1, we have made a bar graph using excel to depict how greenwashing research has developed over the last two decades. Figure 37.1 shows that there has been a considerable increase in the research on greenwashing after 2015. The first reason behind this increase could be the adoption of SDG by 193 member states of the United Nation. Lashitew. (2021). Second, due to extreme pressure from various external stakeholders such as customers, investors, and the government, the firms are making false communication about their environmental practices Marquis et al. (2016)., Netto et al. (2020). Third, investors' increasing interest in those companies involved in green projects and consumers willing to pay premium prices for green products. Pimonenko et al. (2020). Also, we can observe that the research in greenwashing is increasing continuously due to the demand among companies to achieve sustainable development goals by 2030.

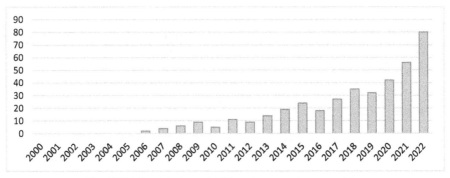

Fig. 37.1 Development of literature on greenwashing

Source: MS Excel

3.2 Most Prominent Themes of Greenwashing

To answer RQ2, we analyzed all the keywords using the co-occurrence technique. With a minimum frequency of 10, Out of a total of 1510 keywords, 16 meet the threshold level. These 16 themes are visually represented through a network diagram (shown in Fig. 37.2) created by VOS Viewer. From Table 37.1, we can observe that after Greenwashing, Corporate social responsibility is one of the most prominent research themes, followed by sustainability and Sustainable development. Moreover, keywords such as Green Marketing, Climate Change, and Environmental performance are some of the emerging themes of Greenwashing.

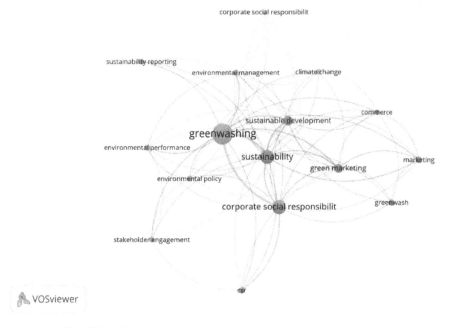

Fig. 37.2 Prominent and emerging themes of greenwashing

Source: VOSviewer

Table 37.1 Co-occurrence of keywords

Keyword	Occurrences	Total Link Strength
Greenwashing	151	146
Corporate social responsibility	71	86
Sustainability	65	87
Sustainable Development	31	47
Green Marketing	28	48
CSR	15	20
Marketing	14	21

Keyword	Occurrences	Total Link Strength
Environmental Performance	13	20
Greenwash	13	11
Corporate Social Responsibility (CSR)	12	10
Environmental Management	12	26
Environmental Policy	12	19
Sustainability Reporting	12	11
Climate Change	11	18
Stakeholder Engagement	11	15
Commerce	10	21

Source: VOSviewer.

3.3 Relationships Among Citing Documents

The RQ3 is answered by applying the bibliographic coupling technique. It is a science mapping technique that divides all publications into thematic clusters based on shared references and similar content Donthu et al. (2021). Figure 37.3. represents the three different clusters formed based on the publications in the last three years.

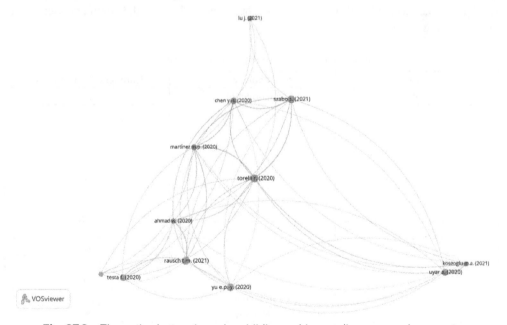

Fig. 37.3 Thematic clusters based on bibliographic coupling among documents

Source: VOSviewer

The red cluster consists of five publications that focus on the effects of greenwashing on customers' perceptions. For instance, Chen, (2020) explains how greenwashing negatively influences the perception of customers toward the brand. Similarly, Torelli, (2020) has shown the effect of greenwashing on the perception of various stakeholders. Consequently, this cluster can be labeled **"Outcomes of perceived greenwashing."** The blue cluster consists of two publications that emphasize the relationship between environmental performance and CSR reporting. For instance, Koseoglu et al. (2020) examine the relationship between CSR performance and CSR reporting by testing the signaling theory and greenwashing tendency. Therefore, this cluster can be called a **"Greenwashing Tendency"** The green cluster consists of five publications that explain how consumers' purchase intentions are influenced by a firm's greenwashing practices. For instance, Ahmad et al. (2020) show that greenwashing activities negatively impact the green buying intentions of consumers. Therefore, it can be labeled as **"Greenwashing affecting purchasing intentions."**

3.4 Most Dominant Countries in Greenwashing Research

Table 37.2 represents the country-wise contribution to greenwashing research. We found that the United States and the United Kingdom are the most dominant countries in Greenwashing research. Probably due to more environmental awareness and strict regulations by authorities in developed countries as compared to developing countries Netto et al. (2020). Moreover, India being a developing country lacks environmental awareness and strict environmental regulations Delmas et al. (2011). Hence, it is not considered one of the dominant countries in Greenwashing research.

Table 37.2 Country-wise research contribution

S.No	Country	Number of Publications
01	United States	98
02	United Kingdom	43
03	China	38
04	France	28
05	Germany	28
06	Italy	25
07	Australia	23
08	Canada	23
09	Netherlands	18
10	Spain	18
11	Brazil	14
12	India	14
13	Switzerland	12
14	Norway	09
15	Turkey	09
16	Sweden	07
17	New Zealand	05
18	Vietnam	05

Source: VOSviewer

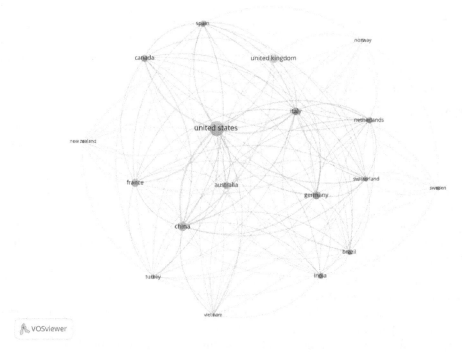

Fig. 37.4 Most dominant countries in greenwashing research

Source: VOSviewer

4. Conclusions

The concern about the environment among stakeholders is rising. Hence, companies are using green marketing as a strategy to be perceived as environmentally and socially responsible by giving false impressions to stakeholders. This is nothing but the concept of greenwashing. Jay Westerveld first described Greenwashing in 1986. Since then, it has gained attention and researchers started studying this topic in depth. The purpose of the current study is to provide an overview of greenwashing research over the last two decades. To do so, the researchers have done a Bibliometric study using VOS Viewer software and Scopus Index. Our review and existing literature show that greenwashing is an emerging and significant research area that requires further investigation. The four research questions mentioned in the first section have been answered throughout the paper. Firstly, the development of greenwashing literature was shown, and it is clearly visible that there has been a substantial increase in the total number of publications in the last decade due to external pressure from stakeholders and the adoption of SDGs by various countries in 2015. Secondly, the most prominent and emerging themes were identified through co-occurrence analysis. From the researchers' analysis, CSR is the most prominent research theme, whereas Green Marketing is one of the emerging themes of Greenwashing. Thirdly, the Bibliographic coupling technique was applied to identify the relationships among the citing documents. As shown in (Fig. 37.3), three significant clusters were formed and can be labeled as "Outcomes of perceived greenwashing," "Greenwashing Tendency," and "Greenwashing affecting purchasing intentions." Finally, the most productive countries in the field of Greenwashing were identified. It was found that due to more environmental awareness and strict green regulations in developed countries, the US and UK are the two most influential and productive countries in greenwashing research.

Despite these significant conclusions, the current study has certain limitations. Firstly, the data was collected using a single database, i.e., Scopus. In the future, it is suggested to use other databases such as Web of Science and Google Scholar or all of them together to increase the generalizability of the study. Secondly, we searched for results using only "greenwashing" as a search term. Hence, the interchangeable keywords, i.e., "greenhushing" and "green sheen," must be used in future studies. Thirdly, we emphasized solely "Business, Management, and Accounting." Thus, it is essential to extend the knowledge in this field by exploring other subject categories in the future. Also, the conclusions drawn in this paper are based on co-occurrence and bibliographic coupling. Therefore, it is suggested to perform co-citation and citation analysis in the future.

However, this paper has both academic and practical implications. From a theoretical perspective, it has provided a conceptual understanding of greenwashing, which further help researchers and academicians by highlighting future research directions. Additionally, from a managerial perspective, it will help managers understand that companies should not further use greenwashing to attract various stakeholders. Since, it deceives and breaks their trust in the companies and further refuses them to consider it a fair corporate practice Pimonenko et al. (2020). Consequently, we recommend that companies must refrain from using greenwashing as a promising marketing strategy.

REFERENCES

1. Slaper, T. F., & Hall, T. J. (2011). The triple bottom line: What is it and how does it work? *Indiana business review*, *86*(1), 4–8.
2. Isil, O., & Hernke, M. T. (2017). The triple bottom line: A critical review from a transdisciplinary perspective. *Business Strategy and the Environment*, *26*(8), 1235–1251.
3. Choice, Terra. "The Sins of Greenwashing: home and family edition." *Underwriters Laboratories* (2010).
4. Lyon, T. P., & Maxwell, J. W. (2011). Greenwash: Corporate environmental disclosure under threat of audit. *Journal of economics & management strategy*, *20*(1), 3–41.
5. Du, X. (2015). How the market values greenwashing? Evidence from China. *Journal of Business Ethics*, *128*(3), 547–574.
6. Pimonenko, T., Bilan, Y., Horák, J., Starchenko, L., & Gajda, W. (2020). Green brand of companies and greenwashing under sustainable development goals. *Sustainability*, *12*(4), 1679.
7. Gatti, L., Seele, P., & Rademacher, L. (2019). Grey zone in–greenwash out. A review of greenwashing research and implications for the voluntary-mandatory transition of CSR. *International Journal of Corporate Social Responsibility*, *4*(1), 1–15.
8. Szabo, S., & Webster, J. (2021). Perceived greenwashing: the effects of green marketing on environmental and product perceptions. *Journal of Business Ethics*, *171*(4), 719–739.

9. Musgrove, C. C. F., Choi, P., & Chris Cox, K. (2018). Consumer perceptions of green marketing claims: An examination of the relationships with type of claim and corporate credibility. *Services Marketing Quarterly, 39*(4), 277–292.

10. Topal, H. F., Hunt, D. V., & Rogers, C. D. (2020). Urban Sustainability and Smartness Understanding (USSU)—Identifying influencing factors: A systematic review. *Sustainability, 12*(11), 4682.

11. Jog, D., & Singhal, D. (2020). Greenwashing understanding among Indian consumers and its impact on their green consumption. *Global Business Review*, 0972150920962933.

12. Kurpierz, J. R., & Smith, K. (2020). The greenwashing triangle: adapting tools from fraud to improve CSR reporting. *Sustainability Accounting, Management and Policy Journal, 11*(6), 1075–1093.

13. Torelli, R., Balluchi, F., & Lazzini, A. (2020). Greenwashing and environmental communication: Effects on stakeholders' perceptions. *Business Strategy and the Environment, 29*(2), 407–421.

14. Montero-Navarro, A., González-Torres, T., Rodríguez-Sánchez, J. L., & Gallego-Losada, R. (2021). A bibliometric analysis of greenwashing research: a closer look at agriculture, food industry and food retail. *British Food Journal*. Vol. 123 No. 13., pp. 547–560.

15. Pendse, M. K., Nerlekar, V. S., & Darda, P. (2022). A comprehensive look at Greenwashing from 1996 to 2021: a bibliometric analysis. *Journal of Indian Business Research*, (ahead-of-print).

16. Donthu, N., Kumar, S., Mukherjee, D., Pandey, N., & Lim, W. M. (2021). How to conduct a bibliometric analysis: An overview and guidelines. *Journal of Business Research, 133*, 285–296.

17. Lashitew, A. A. (2021). Corporate uptake of the Sustainable Development Goals: Mere greenwashing or an advent of institutional change?. *Journal of International Business Policy, 4*(1), 184–200.

18. Marquis, C., Toffel, M. W., & Zhou, Y. (2016). Scrutiny, norms, and selective disclosure: A global study of greenwashing. *Organization Science, 27*(2), 483–504.

19. de Freitas Netto, S. V., Sobral, M. F. F., Ribeiro, A. R. B., & Soares, G. R. D. L. (2020). Concepts and forms of greenwashing: A systematic review. *Environmental Sciences Europe, 32*(1), 1–12.

20. Ahmad, Z., & Esposito, P. (2022, September). THE INFLUENCE OF GREENWASH ON GREEN PURCHACE INTENTIONS; THE MEDIATING ROLE OF GREEN BRAND LOYALTY. In *15th Annual Conference of the EuroMed Academy of Business*.

21. Köseoglu, M. A., Yick, M. Y. Y., & Parnell, J. A. (2021). The dissemination of corporate social responsibility into the intellectual structure of strategic management. *Journal of Cleaner Production, 311*, 127505.

22. Rahman, I., Park, J., & Chi, C. G. Q. (2015). Consequences of "greenwashing": Consumers' reactions to hotels' green initiatives. *International Journal of Contemporary Hospitality Management*.

23. Qayyum, A., Jamil, R. A., & Sehar, A. (2022). Impact of green marketing, greenwashing and green confusion on green brand equity. *Spanish Journal of Marketing-ESIC*, (ahead-of-print).

24. Chen, Y. S., Huang, A. F., Wang, T. Y., & Chen, Y. R. (2020). Greenwash and green purchase behaviour: the mediation of green brand image and green brand loyalty. *Total Quality Management & Business Excellence, 31*(1-2), 194–209.

25. Delmas, M. A., & Burbano, V. C. (2011). The drivers of greenwashing. *California management review, 54*(1), 64–87.

Handbook of Evidence Based Management Practices in Business – Satyendra Kumar Sharma et al. (eds)
© 2023 Taylor & Francis Group, London, ISBN 978-1-032-54216-4

Chapter

Marketing Metrics and Advertisement Campaign Budget: A VECM Approach

Venkat Narasimhan R.[1], Udayan Chanda[2]
Department of Management,
Birla Institute of Technology and Science, Pilani, India

Yashvardhan Sharma[3]
Department of Computer Science and Information Systems,
Birla Institute of Technology and Science, Pilani, India

ABSTRACT: The use of internet advertising as a primary customer acquisition strategy is becoming increasingly common among businesses. Internet companies like Google, Facebook, and Amazon have become platforms for these online advertisements. Standard metrics like impressions, clicks, conversions, click-through rate (CTR), and cost per acquisition (CPA) are used by marketing managers to evaluate the efficiency of advertisements. Managers mainly utilize these indicators to allocate funds to their advertising campaigns, which are then used for bidding on other advertising opportunities. Online advertising is dynamic, and advertising campaigns are susceptible to multiple shocks in demand. Using the data collected from an advertising company that places search ads on e-commerce websites on behalf of consumer-packaged goods companies, we developed a multivariate time series model to investigate the effect of impulse shocks on a specific keyword and its performance. According to the model, we observe the impact of these sudden, impulsive shocks on impressions, clicks, and conversions that define the efficiency of an advertising campaign, a short-run equilibrium among these metrics, and the evolving nature of the keyword in paid search advertisements, and forecast the metrics using the vector error correction estimates. This model can aid managers in their campaign budget allocation decision-making to ensure they can withstand these fluctuations in demand while avoiding either overspending or underspending and longevity of the performance of a keyword.

KEYWORDS: Marketing metrics, Impulse shocks, Vector error correction model (VECM), Online advertising, Co-integration

[1]p20210444@pilani.bits-pilani.ac.in, [2]udayanchanda@pilani.bits-pilani.ac.in, [3]yash@pilani.bits-pilani.ac.in

DOI: 10.4324/9781003415725-38

1. Introduction

Since its inception due to the rise of the internet, online or internet advertising has attracted vast amounts of investment from various organizations attempting to attract consumers. There are different advertising formats, such as search engine and display advertising (Xu, Duan, and Whinston (2014)). Click-through rate (CTR) tracks the efficacy of these advertisements(Drèze et al. 2003). In a dynamic market like search engines and other e-commerce sites, where keywords are auctioned, and there are many competitors, marketing managers use these metrics to decide how much money to spend on an ad campaign and the anticipated bid. Often, they rely on the previous day's metrics as a deciding factor. Of all the metrics, the essential ones that managers use are click-through rate (CTR), and cost per click (CPC). The first two monitor whether the advertisements reach the required number of potential customers, while the latter monitors the ad campaign's return on investment (ROI). However, given the dynamic nature of the market, managers are often forced to change their decisions and need help determining the long-term effects of their ad campaigns.

In their study on understanding the dynamic relationship between search and display ads, they have developed a time series model to investigate the effects of the clicks, their patterns, and the long-term equilibrium of the clicks' performance and its implications on the other online marketing metrics. "Using the persistence modeling technique", they observe a spillover effect of display ad clicks on the search clicks (Pavel et al. 2014). They also apply impulse shocks to these metrics to see their effect on the other marketing metrics. However, their model contributed to the literature on the effectiveness of online advertising and its spillover effects. However, they have applied this model to a particular product type, "bank accounts," which require consumer deliberation before purchasing, such as insurance and investments.

Using a similar principle, in this study, we build a multivariate model to measure the long-term equilibrium at the keyword level of an ad campaign. Keywords are a critical part of online advertising, as consumers use them to search for the product, as a means for the advertiser to reach the consumer, and as the primary revenue source for search engines and websites. Keywords play an essential role in the supply side of decision-making in online advertising, as advertisers must bid for these words on the search engine page (Li and Kannan 2014). Our model explores the longevity of the keyword concerning the performance of marketing metrics. Using the impulse response function, we examine the intermediate impacts of marketing metrics because of sudden shocks to any of these measures and their effects on keyword performance.

2. Data and Methodology and Analysis

To develop our model, we use a dataset from an advertising company that advertises consumer packaged goods on an e-commerce website. The dataset includes metrics like clicks, impressions, cost, CPC, and CTR collected daily for their ad campaigns for 6 months. The primary type of advertisement used by the advertiser is a paid search ad. We have excluded the conversions and sales data from this study, as they are less relevant to this study as our is on

CTR and CPC metrics. This dataset is the aggregate level in nature. The metrics are given in notation in our model as follows:

(i) Cl_t – number of clicks collected in a period t

(ii) Im_t – number of impressions captured in a period t

(iii) Ct_t – expenditure of the advertisement campaign for a period t

(iv) Ctr_t – the click-through rate of an advertisement campaign for a period t

(v) Cpc_t – cost per click of an advertisement campaign for a period t

Online advertising is dynamic; the performance of a campaign is evolving, and so do the metrics that track the performance. To test this hypothesis, we test the stationarity of the variables data using one of the unit root tests, the Augmented Dickey-Fuller (ADF) test. The results of the ADF test on the individual variables revealed that clicks impressions and cost are non-stationary or evolving, and the CTR and CPC are stationary as shown in Table 38.1.

Table 38.1 Augmented Dickey-Fuller (ADF) Test Results

ADF Test/Data	ADF	Lag order	P-value	Results
Impressions	-0.68639	5	0.9704 (>0.05)	Non-Stationary
Clicks	-2.9927	5	0.1597 (>0.05)	Non-Stationary
Cost	-2.5045	5	0.3644 (>0.05)	Non-Stationary
cpc	-4.177	5	0.01 (<0.01)	Stationary
CTR	-3.9792	5	0.01115 (<0.05)	Stationary

Source: Authors' compilation using R studio

From the ADF test results, clicks, impressions, and cost are evolving in nature. Given that CTR and CPC are dependent on the aforementioned variables, they are endogenous in nature, and clicks, impressions, and cost are exogenous nature, as they are dependent on the external variables which are influenced by the consumers. To measure the long-term equilibrium of these variables, we use the Johansens cointegration test on these variables to identify the cointegration relations between them. *"Cointegration means that one or more linear combinations of non-stationary time series are stationary even though individually they are not"*. (Yang and Shahabi, 2005). From Johansen's cointegration test results, we observe that there are 2 co-integration relationships among the variables as shown in Table 38.2.

Table 38.2 Johansen's co-integration test results

Co-integration Relations	Test Value	10pct	5pct	1pct
$r <= 4$	2.49	7.52	9.24	12.97
$r <= 3$	17.42	17.85	19.96	24.60
$r <= 2$	36.36	32.00	34.91	41.07
$r <= 1$	59.59	49.65	53.12	60.16
$r = 0$	92.27	71.86	76.07	84.45

Source: Authors' compilation using R studio

Based on the results of the cointegration test, we introduce an error correction into the results. Through this, we introduce an error term to restore the equilibrium among the variables. The results of the error correction model for a lag value of five. The resulting equation (1) is for a lag time of 1, Where I_t represents the intercept for the multivariate model, Ect and Ecr represent the error correction terms and $\Delta Cpc_{(t-1)}$, $\Delta Ctr_{(t-1)}$, $\Delta Cl_{(t-1)}$, $\Delta Im_{(t-1)}$, $\Delta C_{(t-1)}$ are the coefficients of the variables at lag1 and $x_{11}.....x_{55}$ used to capture the changes in the variables,

$$
\begin{pmatrix} \Delta Cpc_t \\ \Delta Ctr_t \\ \Delta Cl_t \\ \Delta Im_t \\ \Delta Ct_t \end{pmatrix} = \begin{bmatrix} I_{t1} \\ I_{t2} \\ I_{t3} \\ I_{t4} \\ I_{t5} \end{bmatrix} + \begin{bmatrix} x_{11} & x_{12} & x_{13} & x_{14} & x_{15} \\ x_{21} & x_{22} & x_{23} & x_{24} & x_{25} \\ x_{31} & x_{32} & x_{33} & x_{34} & x_{35} \\ x_{41} & x_{42} & x_{43} & x_{44} & x_{45} \\ x_{51} & x_{52} & x_{53} & x_{54} & x_{55} \end{bmatrix} \begin{bmatrix} \Delta Cpc_{t-1} \\ \Delta Ctr_{t-1} \\ \Delta Cl_{t-1} \\ \Delta Im_{t-1} \\ \Delta Ct_{t-1} \end{bmatrix}
$$

$$
+ \begin{bmatrix} Ect_{11} & Ect_{12} & Ect_{13} & Ect_{14} & Ect_{15} \\ Ect_{21} & Ect_{22} & Ect_{23} & Ect_{24} & Ect_{25} \\ Ect_{31} & Ect_{32} & Ect_{33} & Ect_{34} & Ect_{35} \\ Ect_{41} & Ect_{42} & Ect_{43} & Ect_{44} & Ect_{45} \\ Ect_{51} & Ect_{52} & Ect_{53} & Ect_{54} & Ect_{55} \end{bmatrix} \begin{bmatrix} Ecr_{11} & Ecr_{12} & Ecr_{13} & Ecr_{14} & Ecr_{15} \\ Ecr_{21} & Ecr_{22} & Ecr_{23} & Ecr_{24} & Ecr_{25} \\ Ecr_{31} & Ecr_{32} & Ecr_{33} & Ecr_{34} & Ecr_{35} \\ Ecr_{41} & Ecr_{42} & Ecr_{43} & Ecr_{44} & Ecr_{45} \\ Ecr_{51} & Ecr_{52} & Ecr_{53} & Ecr_{54} & Ecr_{55} \end{bmatrix} \begin{bmatrix} 1 \\ \Delta Cpc_{t-1} \\ \Delta Ctr_{t-1} \\ \Delta Cl_{t-1} \\ \Delta Im_{t-1} \\ \Delta Ct_{t-1} \end{bmatrix} + \begin{bmatrix} aCpc_t \\ aCtr_t \\ aCl_t \\ aIm_t \\ aCt_t \end{bmatrix}
$$

$$
\tag{1}
$$

Table 38.3 VEC estimates at Lag 1

	Ect1	Ect2	Intercept	Cpc$_{t-1}$	Ctr$_{t-1}$	Cl$_{t-1}$	Im$_{t-1}$	Ct$_{t-1}$
Cpc$_t$	0.0413	-9.1296	0.0481	-0.2291	5.8824	-0.0048	9.9e-06	0.0033
	(0.0330)	(5.2689)	(0.0149)	(0.0904)	(5.4428)	(0.0062)	(1.9e-05)	(0.0048)
Ctr$_t$	0.0032	-0.5165	0.0009	0.0079	-0.4319	0.0002	-1.3e-06	-4.2e-06
	(0.0007)	(0.1168)	(0.0003)	(0.0020)	(0.1207)	(0.0001)	(4.2e-07)	(0.0001)
Cl$_t$	-0.8336	-27.1793	2.3036	7.7705	143.3258	-0.2632	0.0021	-0.1988
	(2.7353)	(437.1199)	(1.2351)	(7.4982)	(451.5463)	(0.5174)	(0.001)	(0.3941)
Im$_t$	876.5164	-130872.58	158.9332	-689.2098	127033.0586	104.6797	0.2126	-129.7291
	(281.92)	(45052.8)	(127.30)	(772.8194)	(46539.7615)	(53.3233).	(0.1604)	(40.6226)
Ct$_t$	-0.2326	-147.2244	3.0824	11.5584	222.1607	0.3478	0.0036	-0.9011
	(4.3265)	(691.4117)	(1.9536)	(11.8602)	(714.2307)	(0.8183)	(0.0025)	(0.6234)

(level of significance is given within the 'parenthesis')

Source: Authors' compilation using R studio

From Table 38.3, interpreting the vector error correction estimates, the error correction terms Ect1, and Ect2 for CPC is non-negative in Ect1 and negative but not significant in Ect2, thus implying that there is no long-run association. However, Click through rate is significant among all the variables, a long-run association with respect to other variables.

The variables are subjected to impulse shocks to analyze the effects of the variables on each other. In advertising, these shocks can be related to a new promotion campaign, holiday season, etc., which leads to increased impressions and clicks, thus increasing consumer exposure. Since the e-commerce website uses a cost-per-click model to charge the advertiser, advertiser mainly uses CTR and CPC metrics in their budgeting decisions. Here, we apply the impulse shocks to all the impressions, clicks, and costs and measure their sustenance because CTR and CPC are the ratio metrics of these variables. The impulse response figures reiterate that keywords' performance is evolving in nature in online advertising (Skiera et al. 2010).

When impressions are subjected to a shock, there is an impact on the clicks in the short term before sustaining and returning to the equilibrium as shown in Figs 38.1, 38.3, and 38.4. From the Table 38.1, impressions, clicks, and cost are positively correlated, and based on their correlation, we can observe similar effects when they are subjected to an impulse shock as shown in Figs 38.1, 38.3 and 38.4.

Table 38.4 Correlation Analysis for Non-Stationary Variables

Variable	Impressions	Clicks	Cost
Impressions	1		
Clicks	0.7	1	
Cost	0.7	0.9	1

Source: Authors' compilation using Microsoft Excel

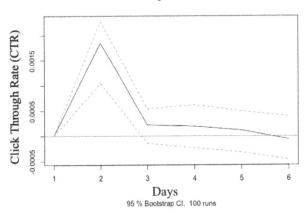

Clicks Impulse on CTR

95 % Bootstrap CI, 100 runs

Fig. 38.1 Impulse shock of Clicks on CTR

Source: Authors' compilation using R studio

The impulse response of CTR when clicks are subjected to the shock like Fig. 38.2 (impressions on clicks), as CTR is a ratio of clicks upon impressions. However, the impulse response of CPC with respect to clicks is different as shown, here we see that CPC is increases with respect to the increase in clicks in evolving pattern before sustaining to equilibrium.

Clicks Impulse on Cost per Click (CPC)

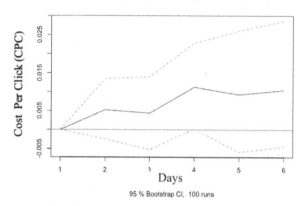

Fig. 38.2 Impulse shock of Clicks on CPC

Source: Authors' compilation using R studio

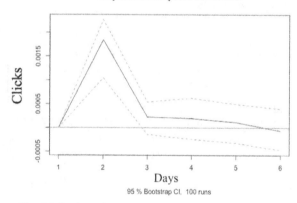

Fig. 38.3 Impulse shock of Impressions on Clicks

Source: Authors' compilation using R studio

Using the vector error correction estimates, Table 38.5 compares the forecasted results for clicks impressions and the cost of the keyword for the seven periods(days). The forecast values of all variables using error correction terms are approximately close to the actual value reported by the firm for the next seven days with a confidence interval of 0.05.

3. Conclusion

Through the results of the VECM model based on our data, we can see the evolving nature of keywords in paid search on other metrics that measure the ad campaign's performance in the dynamic world of online advertising. The presence of equilibrium, albeit in the short run, it generates interest for future researchers. Future researchers can focus on the assorted mix of keywords and their performance, which can aid managers to select the right keyword combination for an ad campaign. One of the major limitations of this study is the online

Clicks Impulse on Cost

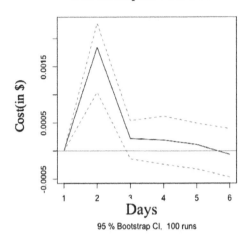

Fig. 38.4 Impulse shock of Clicks on Cost

Source: Authors' compilation using R studio

Table 38.5 Comparison of Forecast vs Actual results of predicted Variables

Days	Forecast (Clicks)	Actual (Clicks)	Forecast (Impressions)	Actual (Impressions)	Forecast (Cost)	Actual (Cost)	Forecast (CTR)	Actual (CTR)	Forecast (CPC)	Actual (CPC)
1	18	21	6291	7816	$32	$37	0.0029	0.003	$2.08	$1.23
2	17	20	6254	6681	$30	$38	0.0027	0.003	$2.27	$1.87
3	19	29	6078	5906	$34	$49	0.0031	0.005	$2.63	$1.32
4	21	30	6185	7435	$38	$49	0.0034	0.004	$2.31	$1.64
5	20	22	6424	2802	$36	$44	0.0032	0.008	$2.17	$2.21
6	18	27	6349	1726	$33	$51	0.0028	0.016	$2.83	$1.63
7	19	27	6321	3861	$34	$51	0.0030	0.007	$2.74	$1.90

Source: Authors' compilation using R studio

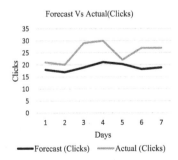

Fig. 38.5 Forecast of Clicks

Source: Authors' compilation using Microsoft Excel

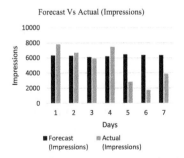

Fig. 38.6 Forecast of Impressions

Source: Authors' compilation using Microsoft Excel

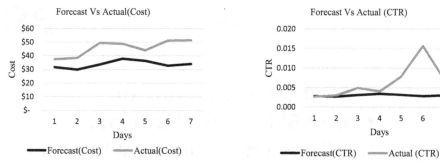

Fig. 38.7   Forecast of Cost

Source: Authors' compilation using Microsoft Excel

Fig. 38.8   Forecast of CTR

Source: Authors' compilation using Microsoft Excel

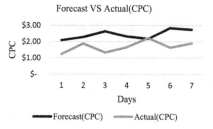

Fig. 38.9   Forecast of CPC

Source: Authors' compilation using Microsoft Excel

advertising type, i.e., paid search ads, as the advertiser only focuses on the paid ads and the time interval of data i.e., 6 months, the future researcher can increase the time period to see the effects of on a long run and also on the metrics such as conversion, which track the number of potential consumers, who convert into purchasers.

REFERENCES

1. Drèze, X., & Hussherr, F.-X. (2003). Internet advertising: Is anybody watching? Journal of Interactive Marketing, 17(4), 8–23.
2. Kireyev, Pavel & Pauwels, Koen & Gupta, Sunil, (2016). "Do display ads influence search? Attribution and dynamics in online advertising," International Journal of Research in Marketing, Elsevier, vol. 33(3), pages 475–490.
3. Kiyoung Yang and Cyrus Shahabi.(2005). On the Stationarity of Multivariate Time Series for Correlation-Based Data Analysis. In Proceedings of the Fifth IEEE International Conference on Data Mining (ICDM '05). IEEE Computer Society, USA, 805–808.
4. Li, H. (Alice), & Kannan, P. K. (2014). Attributing Conversions in a Multichannel Online Marketing Environment: An Empirical Model and a Field Experiment. *Journal of Marketing Research*, *51*(1), 40–56.
5. Skiera, Bernd and Eckert, Jochen and Hinz, Oliver, An Analysis of the Importance of the Long Tail in Search Engine Marketing (2010). Electronic Commerce Research and Applications, Vol. 9, 488–494.
6. Xu, Lizhen, Jason A. Duan, and Andrew Whinston. "Path to Purchase: A Mutually Exciting Point Process Model for Online Advertising and Conversion." *Management Science* 60, no. 6 (2014): 1392–1412.

Chapter

An Analytical Study on Green Skin Care Products: Impact on Consumer Purchase Intention

Anu Grover[1] and Hareesh Kumar T.[2]

Department of Financial Administration, School of Management,
Central University of Punjab, Bathinda, India

ABSTRACT: Increasing environmental awareness and growing global consciousness have spurred people to take a step forward for the protection of the environment by adopting greener ways of living life. Green and natural products not only enhance and preserve human beauty, but also the beauty of nature. In the wide range of green products, this study focuses on skin care cosmetics products. The demand for natural and green cosmetics has increased in recent years due to increased awareness among people regarding the benefits of being "natural". This paper seeks to review the influence of antecedents (health consciousness, price sensitivity, promotional efforts) on the purchase intention of consumers towards green skin care cosmetics products. For serving this purpose, the study uses primary data collected by using an online questionnaire. A total of 100 consumers responded and completed the questionnaire. For the analysis of data Partial Least Squares Structural Equation Modeling (PLS-SEM) was used. The result indicates that there is a positive influence of health consciousness and price sensitivity on the purchase intention of consumers towards green skin care products. However, there is an insignificant relationship between promotional efforts and the purchase intention of green skin care products.

KEYWORDS: Green products, Natural products, Purchase intention

1. Introduction

The cosmetic industry is significantly vital and has become extremely competitive in recent years, as individuals started using cosmetics in their daily lives (Amberg 2019). According to a

[1]groverannu10@gmail.com, [2]hareesh.kumar@cup.edu.in

DOI: 10.4324/9781003415725-39

report the global skin care products market is expected to grow at a compound annual growth rate of 4.6 % from 2022 to 2030. The increment in the market size signifies the consciousness of people for sustaining their outer beauty. People have become more health conscious; therefore they relentlessly take steps for maintaining their inner charm along with the external. Hence, the concept of awareness is not now limited to the food industry but has also extended to the personal beauty industry (Lin, Yang, and Hanifah 2018). The growing concern for health and the environment changed the mindset of individuals to move toward the use of green and natural cosmetics. So, the idea of maintaining one's appearance as well as the need to preserve nature's appearance is becoming imperative among people.

(Hsu et al.2017) indicated that green products are products that are typically durable, non-toxic, and made from naturally driven ingredients (such as herbs, roots, essential oil, and flowers), combined with naturally occurring carrier agents, preservatives, humectants, and emulsifiers. Green and natural products not only enhance and preserve human beauty, but also the beauty of nature. People have become more open to the use of natural cosmetics as they realized the fact that the consequences of using chemical products can be harmful to their skin as well as to the environment (Tengli and Srinivasan 2022). One of the primary reasons for pushing towards natural products is increasing awareness regarding the adverse effect of chemicals. Consequently, a large number of customers have started inclined toward green products for a healthier lifestyle (Amberg, 2019). This inclination towards green products has significantly affected the various decisions of businesses and thus, a new business opportunity has emerged for the firms in the form of a market for green products. But some companies adopt the wrong ways to attract customers by presenting something they do not hold and that is pernicious for customers 'skin. It means that the products barely contain the number of natural ingredients named "natural" however they contain more quantity of synthetic ingredients (Boon and Fern 2020). This deceptive marketing tactic is known as "Greenwashing"(Bernard et al. 2021). Hence, there is a need to dig out into this concept to save the interest of the consumers as well as the environmentalist.

Customers' green purchasing habits can be seen as one of the main factors in maintaining the sustainability of the environment. In order to lessen the harmful effects on the environment, there needs to be a paradigm shift in how consumers think about and act toward green products (Jaini et al. 2020) .Thus, understanding the consumer purchase intention in regard to green cosmetics products is crucial to minimize the impact of high chemical product consumption. Therefore, the present study attempts to investigate the purchase intention of consumers for the green skin care products.

2. Review of Literature

Hsu et al. (2017) opined that increasing consciousness towards the ill effects of chemical cosmetics industries has encouraged customers to adopt eco-friendly products. This research is intended to measure the effect on purchase intention of green skin care products by using the elements of the theory of planned behavior and additional two variables (COO and price sensitivity). They figured out that these variables have a significant impact on the purchase intention of the consumers and the factors such as COO and price sensitivity have a positive effect on the link between purchase intention and its antecedences. The 21st century is evolving into an era of rising digitization and global awareness. In order to compete in today's world, one must constantly adapt to the needs of the surrounding environment. Digitalization has changed the scenario of connecting with people. Businesses and companies repeatedly use social media platforms to connect with or persuade their customers. (Naz, Ramkissoon, and Fekete-farkas 2022) conducted a study to gain insights into understanding the role of social media in influencing customers to purchase green products and examine the green purchase intention of customers. The study has been carried out using the 'Theory of planned Behavior' with additional variables –Green Thinking, Social Media Usage, and, Social Media Marketing and found the positive effect of these variables on the purchase intention of customers. (Chin et al.) conducted an Indonesia-specific study with a sample size of 251 female consumers to evaluate their behavioral intention to buy green skincare products. For the same purpose, they used the PERA model in their study able to describe 62.6% of consumer intention to purchase green skincare products. The result revealed that all five factors of this model have a positive effect on one another and ultimately it persuades consumers to go for green products. The results of the study show the changing attitude of modern customers. The frequent uses of cosmetics by women as well as men have increased the market size for the cosmetic industry. Tengli and Srinivasan (2022) mentioned that the term 'cosmetic' is not only related to women but also to men. In recent years there has been increasing demand for cosmetics among the men's community. This paper used the theory of planned behavior to pinpoint the difference between purchase intention and purchase behavior of male and female consumers. It revealed that there is no difference in the variables influencing the purchase intention of both-male and female consumers toward cosmetics products. Lin et al. (2018) conducted a study to examine consumers' attitudes toward green cosmetics. The growing mindfulness for the environment propels people to go for greener products. The study was conducted with reference to UK markets with a sample size of 30 British women. It ended with the result of a neutral attitude among the women, the reasons for which can be a lack of knowledge and confusing market standards. Pudaruth et al. (2015) focused on identifying the factors influencing the purchasing behavior of women regarding beauty and cosmetics products in Mauritius. The study finds out the eight factors that influence the purchasing pattern of women and it highlights the need for marketers to revise their strategies in order to remain competitive. Wilson Kong et al. (2014) measured the effect of customer perception of green products on their buying intention by using multidimensional variables (green corporate perception, eco-label, green advertising, green packaging, and green product value). (Boon and Fern 2020) described the reasons of why one should choose natural products over chemical products. However, some businesses make claims to be natural when they actually only use a small percentage of natural ingredients, which can make it difficult to gain the trust of consumers. Because consumers are turning away from chemical products and discovering that using natural products is far preferable to using synthetic ones.

3. Need and Significance of the Study

The use of natural and green cosmetics has become more popular as a result of the deteriorating state of the environment and growing cognizance of the negative effects of chemical cosmetics industries. In addition to women, men are now using cosmetics more frequently in their daily lives, which support the growth of the global cosmetics market demand. This trend has made it necessary to recognize the factors influencing their customers' purchase intentions and adjust their business strategies accordingly. The findings of this study would help marketers to better understand their customers' purchase intentions.

4. Objectives of the Study

- To measure the impact of health consciousness on the purchase intention of consumers towards green skin care products.
- To examine the influence of price sensitivity on the purchase intention of consumers towards green skin care products.
- To observe the effect of promotional efforts on the purchase intention of consumers towards green skin care products.

5. Research Methodology

In this study, the data was collected through a self-administrated questionnaire consisting of three main sections: demographical variables, and the measurement of dependent and independent variables. The three independent variables of this study are health consciousness, price sensitivity and promotional efforts and the dependent variable is purchase intention. The Convenience Sampling method was used for this study. The questionnaire was designed to administer the responses on the key constructs of the study. A total number of 100 responses were received. The study applied the Partial Least Square Structural Equation Modeling (PLS-SEM) to assess the hypothesis.

6. Hypothesis Development

H1: There is a significant positive impact of health consciousness on the purchase intention of consumers towards green skin care products.

H2: There is a significant positive impact of promotional efforts on the purchase intention of consumers towards green skin care products.

H3: There is a significant positive impact of price sensitivity on the purchase intention of consumers towards green skin care products.

7. Data Analysis and Interpretation

Table 39.1 summarizes the demographic profile of the respondents. There were 37% of male respondents and 63% of female respondents participated in the survey. This questionnaire categorizes the age into four main categories. The age of 18 to 20 has 15 respondents and the age group of 21 to 25 involved 44% of respondents. Next, the age group of 26 to 30 has 32% of respondents, and last the respondents aged 31 to 35 accounted for 9% of respondents.100 respondents that participated in this study come from different educational backgrounds and

Table 39.1 Profile of respondents

Variable	Category	Frequency	Percentage (%)
Age	18-20	15	15
	21-25	44	44
	26-30	32	32
	31-35	9	9
Gender	Male	37	37
	Female	63	63
Education	Undergraduate	30	30
	Postgraduate	58	58
	Professional	4	4
	Doctorate	8	8
Residential area	Urban	62	62
	Rural	38	38

Source: Primary Survey of Respondents

different residential area.30% of the respondents are undergraduates while the highest number of people (58%) are postgraduates. The respondents who are in professional courses accounted for 4% and 8% are involved under the doctorate level. 62% of the respondents are from urban areas and 38% are from rural areas.

7.1 Measurement Model Assessment

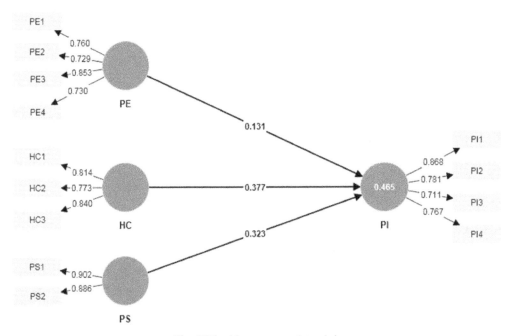

Fig. 39.1 Measurement model

Source: Compiled by Author

Table 39.2 Reliability and validity analysis

Construct	Items	Loadings	Cronbach Alpha	Composite Reliability	AVE (Average Value Extracted)
Health Consciousness (HC)	HC1	0.814	0.738	0.851	0.655
	HC2	0.773			
	HC3	0.840			
Promotional Efforts (PE)	PE1	0.761	0.799	0.853	0.593
	PE2	0.729			
	PE3	0.853			
	PE4	0.730			
Purchase Intention (PI)	PI1	0.866	0.790	0.864	0.615
	PI2	0.787			
	PI3	0.710			
	PI4	0.764			
Price Sensitivity (PS)	PS1	0.903	0.750	0.889	0.800
	PS2	0.886			

Source: Primary Survey of Respondents

Table 39.2 shows the measurement model analysis that was assessed to establish the reliability and validity of the constructs. The study's findings indicate that factor loadings of the entire items in the model range from 0.710 to 0.903 and this signifies that all the items loadings are meeting minimum criteria (Hair et al.2018). Furthermore, the Composite Reliability and Average Variance Extracted values for all the items were higher than 0.700 and 0.500 respectively. (Hair et al. 2018) stated that a strong valid model included factor loadings greater than 0.5, CR values greater than 0.7, and AVE values greater than 0.5. As a result, the findings of this study confirmed that the model constructs fulfilled the convergent validity criteria and internal consistency requirements.

Table 39.3 Fornell and Larcker criterion

	HC	PE	PI	PS
HC	0.809			
PE	0.462	0.770		
PI	0.593	0.453	0.784	
PS	0.478	0.462	0.565	0.894

Source: Primary Survey of Respondents
Note: Values in Italic represent Square-root of AVE, HC: Health Consciousness, PE: Promotional Efforts, PS: Price Sensitivity

Table 39.3 depicts the results of the Discriminant Validity Assessment. Discriminant validity was assessed by the Fornell-Larcker criterion, which shows that the square root of AVE for the construct was greater than the inter-construct correlation.

Table 39.4 HTMT matrix

	HC	**PE**	**PI**	**PS**
HC				
PE	0.543			
PI	0.758	0.466		
PS	0.629	0.573	0.736	

Source: Primary Survey of Respondents
Note: HC: Health Consciousness, PE: Promotional Efforts, PS: Price Sensitivity

Table 39.4 shows the result of the HTMT Matrix for discriminant validity. Discriminant validity was also assessed by the Heterotrait-Monotrait (HTMT) ratio of correlations, with values below the threshold of 0.90. Hence, discriminant validity is established.

7.2 Structural Model Assessment

The structural model reflects the paths hypothesized in the research framework. Following the assessment of the measurement model, the next step is the evaluation of structural path for the evaluation of path coefficients (relationships among study constructs and their statistical significance).

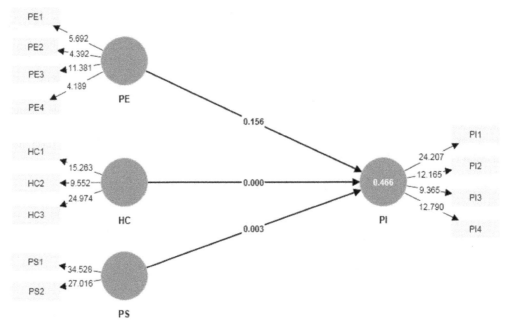

Fig. 39.2 Structural model

Source: Compiled by Author

Table 39.5 Hypothesis testing results

Hypothesis	β = Beta Coefficient	SE = Standard Error	T = t-Statistics,	P = Probability Value
HC -> PI	0.378	0.108	3.489	0.000
PE -> PI	0.128	0.090	1.420	0.156
PS -> PI	0.325	0.111	2.933	0.003
	R^2		R^2 Adjusted	
PI	0.465	PI	0.448	

Source: Primary Survey of Respondents
Note: *Relationships are significant at P< 0.001, HC: Health Consciousness, PE: Promotional Efforts, PS: Price Sensitivity

The summary of the hypothesis testing result is shown in Table 39.4. H1 evaluates whether health consciousness significantly and positively affects purchase intention towards green skin care products. The results revealed that health consciousness has a significant and positive impact on purchase intention (β = .378, t = 3.489, p < 0.001). Hence, H1 was supported.

H2 evaluates whether promotional efforts significantly and positively affect the purchase intention of customers. The results indicate that promotional efforts have an insignificant impact on PI (β = 0.128, t = 1.420, p = 0.156). Hence, H2 was not supported.

H3 evaluates whether price sensitivity significantly and positively affects the purchase intention of customers. The results specify that price sensitivity has a significant impact on PI (β = 0.325, t = 2.933, p = 0.003). Hence, H3 was supported. The strength of each structural path is measured by the R^2 value for the dependent variable, and this value should be greater than 0.1 to indicate the goodness the model. As shown in the above table, the value of R^2 is greater than 0.1.Hence, the predictive validity is established.

8. Conclusion

The market for green cosmetics is expanding globally. This study investigates the direct impact of price sensitivity, health consciousness, and promotional efforts on consumers' intention to buy green skin care products. The results of the study revealed that the majority of consumers keep health consciousness and the price of the products as the important factors while purchasing green and natural cosmetics and the main users are youth. However, the promotional efforts or the claims made by companies have an insignificant impact on the consumer's purchase intention. Therefore, the primary goal of cosmetics companies should be to produce products that have no adverse effects on consumers' health and the environment in order to remain competitive and the secondly, companies should use trustworthy and reliable claims in their advertisement to attract the customers and to win their trust.

REFERENCES

1. Amberg, Nora. 2019. "Green Consumer Behavior in the Cosmetics Market."
2. Authors, For. 2018. "Article Information: When to Use and How to Report the Results of PLS-SEM."

3. Bernard, Authors Manon, Lilana Parker, Manon Bernard, and Lilana Parker. 2021. "The Effect of Conscious Consumerism on Purchasing Behaviors," no. May.

4. Boon, Lim Kah, and Yeo Sook Fern. 2020. "Generation Y ' s Purchase Intention towards Natural Skincare Products: A PLS-SEM Analysis" 12 (1): 61–77.

5. Business, Faculty, Jalan Ums, Kota Kinabalu, Faculty Business, Jalan Ums, Kota Kinabalu, and Jaratin Lily. 2014. "International Journal of Asian Social Science The influence of consumers ' perception of green products Amran Harun Rini Suryati Sulong Contribution / Originality" 4 (8): 924–39.

6. Chin, Jacky, Bernard C Jiang, Ilma Mufidah, Satria Fadil Persada, and Bustanul Arifin Noer. n.d. "The Investigation of Consumers ' Behavior Intention in Using Green Skincare Products: A Pro-Environmental Behavior Model Approach." https://doi.org/10.3390/su10113922.

7. Hsu, Chia-lin, Chi-ya Chang, and Chutinart Yansritakul. 2017. "Crossmark." *Journal of Retailing and Consumer Services* 34 (October 2016): 145–52. https://doi.org/10.1016/j.jretconser.2016.10.006.

8. Lin, Yifeng, Shaohua Yang, and Haniruzila Hanifah. 2018. "Administrative Sciences An Exploratory Study of Consumer Attitudes toward Green Cosmetics in the UK Market." https://doi.org/10.3390/admsci8040071.

9. Naz, Farheen, Haywantee Ramkissoon, and Maria Fekete-farkas. 2022. "Technological Forecasting & Social Change Transforming Consumers ' Intention to Purchase Green Products: Role of Social Media." *Technological Forecasting & Social Change* 185 (October): 122067. https://doi.org/10.1016/j.techfore.2022.122067.

10. Pudaruth, Sharmila, Thanika Devi Juwaheer, Yogini Devi Seewoo, Sharmila Pudaruth, Thanika Devi Juwaheer, and Yogini Devi Seewoo. 2015. "Gender-Based Differences in Understanding the Purchasing Patterns of Eco-Friendly Cosmetics and Beauty Care Products in Mauritius: A Study of Female Customers." https://doi.org/10.1108/SRJ-04-2013-0049.

11. Tengli, Anusha, and Srivatsa Hosur Srinivasan. 2022. "An Exploratory Study to Identify the Gender-Based Purchase Behavior of Consumers of Natural Cosmetics."

Website Reference:

12. https://www.grandviewresearch.com/industry-analysis/natural-skin-care-products-market?msclkid=24f8c174d06811ec9dea7c05092f9145

Handbook of Evidence Based Management Practices in Business – Satyendra Kumar Sharma et al. (eds)
© 2023 Taylor & Francis Group, London, ISBN 978-1-032-54216-4

Chapter

An Analytical Study on the Usage of Debit Card and Credit Card in Indian Economy

Ruchi Gupta*, W. Ramana Rao[1]
Assistant Professor, Faculty of Commerce,
ICFAI University, Raipur (CG), India

Muskan Diwan[2]
Assistant Professor, Faculty of Commerce and Management,
Kalinga University, Naya Raipur (CG), India

ABSTRACT: The banking industry is critical to the financial system's stability. It is critical to the functioning of our country's economy because it ensures that financial resources are allocated effectively to promote economic growth and development.. This study revealed the use of debit cards due to the excess use of credit cards. Debit and credit cards are the two most common types of payment cards used worldwide. Each one has a magnetic stripe on the back, a unique security code, and an integrated microchip on the front that encrypts critical financial and personal data about the cardholder and the account. In this paper, we tried to find out the correlation between the usage of debit cards and credit cards using mean, min, max, standard deviation, correlation, and regression. The result shows that there is a negative correlation between the usage of debit cards and credit cards. Which means there is no impact on the usage of the debit card over the credit card.

KEYWORDS: Banking industry, Credit card, Debit card, Economic growth, Financial system

1. Introduction

An expanding global tendency towards internalization, mergers, takeovers, and consolidation is what distinguishes the banking business worldwide. This industry is become more

*Corresponding Author: my.mail.ruchi@gmail.com
[1]wramanarao@gmail.com, [2]muskandiwan38@gmail.com

DOI: 10.4324/9781003415725-40

tumultuous and cutthroat. By providing alluring financial services and products, non-banking businesses are likewise hopping on the trend of the banking industry. Customers have a variety of options when selecting financial services. With the help of technological advancement, the banking sector tries to increase consumer satisfaction by offering better goods and services and cutting expenses. As a result, the banking sector is advancing through innovation. The most recent breakthrough in online banking, known as E-banking (EB), which has been indicated in a number of empirical investigations, was brought about by the advent of technological advancement, particularly in the domains of telecommunications and information technology (Bielski, 2000; Mia et al., 2007) dedicated to examining the growth and operation of electronic banking. The banking industry is leading the charge to accept the changes throughout the world. The banking sector must be competitive in order to better understand the opportunities and adoption potential of EB and to reap its benefits to the fullest degree possible. EB uses the global computerization network rather than branch offices to carry out its operations. Banks are able to pay greater interest rates than usual because overhead costs are decreased. EB has the opportunity to manage personal finances by finding a mortgage or loan, applying for a loan, applying for credit cards, etc. Some banks provide 24-hour telephone service so that consumers can speak with bank representatives about financial issues. As a result, there is a widespread belief that EB is highly effective and gives banks the ability to offer customers a direct and affordable banking experience. Numerous research has been conducted regarding the reasons for and advantages of EB, particularly with regard to service quality and customer loyalty (Balachandher et al., 2000; Suganthi et al., 2001). It is still in the process of evolving, though. Banking plays a crucial part in the Indian economy among financial services. Indian banking is the largest employer in the country, with a network of 67,000 branches spread out over the nation. Only a few banks in India offer transactional EB, despite almost all of them having websites. Only 10% of clients of big banks have active EB accounts. According to different research, as of March 2005, just 48% of Indian commercial banks were offering EB (Malhotra and Singh, 2007). For a long time, banks have been recognised as one of the major service providers in the Indian economy. It has become essential for banks to offer EB services due to globalization and the liberalization of financial institutions. Competition among banks to provide goods and services grows in India's expanding economy (Ali and Bharadwaj, 2009).

2. Literature Review

Technology advancement added to the obligation of influencing people to choose services that provide convenience, like EB services. According to Pikkarainen et al. (2004), EB is a usable online channel that clients can use for a variety of banking activities, such as investing or paying bills. Different types of banking, including EB, phone banking, and mobile banking activities, are growing in the framework of electronic banking systems (Liao and Cheng, 2002; Chang et al., 2006). Customers are drawn to EB activities because they are simple to use and have quick transaction times (Claessens et al., 2002). In the opinion of Gan et al. (2006), the usage of the internet as a new alternative channel for the financial services distribution and Flavian et al. (2004), cannot be viewed as only a means of attaining competitive advantage, but rather as a competitive necessity. Most banks offer additional services, such as EB, to clients worldwide.

From the perspective of the banks, the main justification for using EB technology is cost savings (Robinson, 2000; Sathye, 1999). According to Pikkarainen et al. (2004), EB is one of the least expensive ways to supply financial products, hence banks should use it. It reduces the chance of making mistakes, saves time, and money. (2000) Jayawardhena and Foley Karjaluoto et al. (2002) provided strong support for EB by claiming that users can easily access their accounts 24 hours a day, wherever in the world. Due to growing competition, banks are increasingly efficiently focusing on various demographic categories to draw in new clients. According to Robinson (2000), EB services help banks build and maintain positive relationships with both current and potential clients. Understanding how relationships affect a person's decision to use electronic banking pays off was encouraged by Kuo et al. (2007). Customers receive a variety of advantages, such as convenient service, reduced transfer costs, and regular account monitoring (Arunachalam and Sivasubramanian, 2007). According to Ravi et al., EB has not yet become well known in India (2007). Malhotra and Singh (2007) discovered through their study that new banks and private banks have implemented EB technology as a consequence of their investigation into factors influencing adoption. The popular advantages of EB are vast, yet there are certain limitations, particularly in terms of system security. According to findings from a recent study by Agarwal et al. (2009), consumers tend to be influenced by the type of account they manage, their age, and their profession, and they give the balance enquiry service among EB services the highest level of usefulness. They cited security and trust as the two most crucial elements influencing consumers' levels of satisfaction and identified poor transaction speeds as one of the most frequent issues encountered when using EB. They identified poor transaction speeds as one of the most frequent problems encountered when using EB and cited security and trust as the two most important factors influencing customers' levels of satisfaction. According to a number of studies, including Jih et al. (2005), consumers' adoption of EB is influenced by their perception of security. The few people who have access to the internet is one of several factors that affects how much demand there is for EB services. Other considerations in this regard include the price and speed of internet connections (Sohail et al., 2003). Customers don't exhibit much confidence in EB transactional and security risks that can arise when online banking, according to Li and Worthington (2004). Stewart thinks that consumers do not yet fully trust the internet (1999). Banks are luring customers with cutting-edge internetofferings. In agreement with the aforementioned viewpoint, Tomiuk et al. (2001) stated that the sound presence of EB will likely have an impact on banks' ability to build a trustworthy relationship between their customers and employees because EB will be a desirable alternative for customers who value efficiency. There are also more ideas that link consumer behaviour to EB uptake and acceptability levels that differ. Perceived security appears to have an impact on user acceptance of EB, according to a number of studies, including Jih et al. (2005). Khalil and Pearson (2007) discovered that trust has a big impact on how you feel about accepting EBs. Khan et al. (2009) presented advice for marketing and researchers to improve many factors in a relatively recent study. Banks must create plans that increase client confidence in the underlying technology to promote EB adoption (Hertzum et al., 2004). The researchers are interested in investigating the factors that influence the speed of EB user acceptance. According to Poon (2008), factors that increase customer happiness include accessibility, convenience, design, and content, whereas factors like privacy and security have the opposite effect.

3. Objective of the Study

1. To study the maximum, minimum, average and Standard deviation of the data set.
2. To study the correlation between debit card and credit card.
3. To find out the usage of credit and debit cards.

4. Research Methodology

The current study relied on secondary data, such as debit and credit card usage. The current research is both analytical and exploratory in nature. As a result, the data used is secondary to the relevant reports, such as the RBI monthly bulletins. Secondary sources for the current study include magazines, newspapers, business dailies, books and journals, E-media, and other literature in this field. The collected data has been organized and thoroughly examined for details pertaining to the RBI site. Descriptive statistics such as mean, Minimum, Maximum and standard deviation, Co-relation are used in the present paper.

Table 40.1 Debit card and credit card statistics from April-2017 to March-22

Year	X credit card	Y Debit card
2017-2018	7810987	8602256374
2018-2019	48193386	56658156684
2019-2020	10041344	8788622251
2020-2021	30783815	355502272
2021-2022	220992212	196770377

Source: www.rbi.co.in

5. Data Interpretation

In the above figure maximum number is 56658156684 in the set of data , minimum number is 7810987 and also average is 7491912970. The standard deviation of the set of data is 17639334786. The Correlation of data set is CORREL (array1, array2) = –0.212164563. According to the study, there is a negative correlation between the credit card and the Debit Card. This strong negative correlation signifies that as the Debit card decreases, the Credit Card increases (and vice versa).

6. Cost of the Current Payment Service

The majority of payment services for retail purchases are offered by banks. Banks impose fees on both consumers and business owners to pay the operating expenses associated with cash, cheques, and credit cards. Banks charge different amounts for these services. They charge a fee in some circumstances for every transaction. A bank may charge a depositor for each check issued, a merchant for each cash deposit, or a depositor for each bundle of checks. Banks may instead charge account fees in other situations rather than transaction fees. Some banks allow depositors to write an unlimited number of free checks while charging a set monthly cost to maintain a deposit account.

The difference between account-based fees and transaction-based costs has significant effects on a consumer's or merchant's willingness to accept a specific payment method.

Customers currently have little motivation to select a payment method based on cost. When making a purchase at a retail location, for instance, a customer normally pays the same price whether cash, a check, or a credit card is used. Each method of payment has a cost, of course, but the cost is only tangentially connected to the frequency of use.

There are two reasons why different payment methods are not priced differently. First, practically all bank costs to customers are account-based rather than transaction-based, partly due to historical factors.

Second, transaction fees levied by banks on merchants are rarely transferred to customers directly. In other words, shops often do not charge customers a varied price dependent on their preferred form of payment (Barron and others). Instead, the price of a retailer's goods and services reflects the cost, which is borne by all customers regardless of the payment method they choose.

Price may play a significant role in a merchant's decision to accept a certain payment method, even though consumers are unlikely to be price sensitive when choosing alternative payment methods.

Due to businesses' increased exposure to transaction-based pricing, this happens.

There are two significant effects of the current payment pricing structure. First, customers have no financial incentive to choose the least expensive payment technology because they do not directly incur the costs of the payments system (Murphy 1977, 1991). In fact, a consumer's decision to pay with cash, a check, or a credit card during a retail transaction is unlikely to be influenced by the perceived cost of the transaction.

Second, because businesses frequently pay transaction-based fees, they are more inclined to consider the relative costs of different payment options when deciding whether to accept or advertise a particular form of payment.

7. Findings on Debit card and Credit card Usage

- Compared to public sector banks, POS transactions were higher in private sector banks and overseas banks than ATM transactions.
- In comparison to public sector banks, credit card transactions were much greater in private sector banks and international banks.
- When comparing the use of credit cards at POS and ATMs, POS transactions outnumbered ATM transactions in all bank groups with the exception of the public sector bank group.

8. Discussions

The findings indicate that there is a negative correlation between the usage of debit cards and credit cards. Which means there is no impact on the usage of the debit card over the credit card. The usage of credit cards does not give any impact on debit cards. Bot cards are used by customers at the time of payment. As more and more significant shared ATM networks encourage the use of debit cards, the recent surge in their use should continue. Debit cards won't likely totally replace current payment methods due to the pricing barrier. Debit cards are most likely to significantly increase their market share in specific situations where consumers value their convenience and businesses see it as a way to save costs or boost revenues. Debit cards may also become a crucial payment option for individuals who have little access to other payment options. Debit's potential future expansion is also expected to be influenced by marketing initiatives, technology advancements, and adjustments to the costs of current payment options.

9. Recommendations

In this paper we only focused on the usage of debit cards and credit cards but we are not focused on the area of E-banking like usage of Paytm, phone pay, and Bharat pay. All these platforms play a important role in today's economy and all are considered as the most convenient payment method.

10. Acknowledgement

Very much thankful to all colleagues, assistants and well-wishers who helpedout the authors to complete this paper.

REFERENCES

1. Bihari, S. C., & Mohaptra, R. (2010). An Analysis of the Shortcomings of Banking Industry Technology Leading to Default & Fraud With Special Focus on State Bank of India. iManager's Journal on Management, 4(4), 70
2. Berger, A. N., R. J. Herring, and G. P. Szegö. (1995). The role of capital in "Financial institutions. Journal of Banking & Finance 19:393–430.
3. Black, L., R. Correa, X. Huang, and H. Zhou. (2016). The systemic risk of European banks during the "Financial and sovereign debt crises. Journal of Banking & Finance 63:107–125.
4. Burns, P., & Stanley, A. (2002). Fraud management in the credit card industry. Federal Reserve Bank of Philla Payment Cards Center Discussion Paper, (02–05).
5. Calvin Fei, Francis Jacobs and J Mark Stockton, (2003), "Method and apparatus for conducting transactions on an ATM", US Patent App., (09), pp 925, 972.
6. Citi Handlowy. RaportRozczny. 2020. Available online: https://www.citibank.pl/poland/homepage/raport_roczny_2020/files /raport_roczny_2020_pl.pdf#zoom=80 (accessed on 13 December 2021).
7. Das, Ashish (2008). Acceptability Standards in Credit Card Industry. November 10, 2008. http://www.math.iitb.ac.in/~ashish/workshop/CreditCard23November10.pdf
8. Diwakar, H., & Naik, A. (2008, July). Investigation of Information Security Management Practices in Indian Pubic Sector Banks. In 2008 IEEE 8th International Conference on Computer and Information Technology Workshops (pp. 276–281). IEEE.
9. de Haan, Jakob, Choudhry Tanveer Shehzad, and Bert Scholtens. 2010. The impact of bank ownership concentration on impaired loans and capital adequacy. Journal of Banking and Finance 34: 399–408.

10. EBF. Consultation Response to the Draft Report of the Platform on Sustainable Finance on a Social Taxonomy; European Banking Federation: Brussels, Belgium, 2021. Available online: https://www.ebf.eu/wp-content/uploads/2021/09/EBF_AdditionalFeed back_SocialTaxonomy.pdf (accessed on 27 September 2021).

11. Emeka E Okafor and Favour N Ezeani, (2012), "Use of ATM among bank customers in Ibadan Metropolis, South Western Nigeria", European Journal of Business and Management, 4, (7), pp. 18–33.

12. European Banking Authority. EBA Publishes Its Report on Management and Supervision of ESG Risks for Credit Institutions and Investment Firms. 2021. Available online: https://www.eba.europa.eu/eba-publishes-its-report-management-and-supervisionesg-risks-credit-institutions-and-investment (accessed on 27 September 2021).

13. Gabor, D. and Brooks, S. (2017). The digital revolution in financial inclusion: international development in the fintech era. New political economy, 22(4): 423–436

14. Hodson, R., Dwyer, R., & Neilson, L. (2014). Credit Card Blues: The Middle Class and the Hidden Costs of Easy Credit. The Sociological quarterly, 55(2), 315–340.

15. Howard A Schechtman and Peter Paradiso, (2008), "Method and system for providing an incentive to use an ATM", US Patent (7) pp. 421, 410.

16. Handriani, Eka, and RobiyantoRobiyanto. 2019. Institutional ownership, independent board, board size, and firm performance: Evidence from Indonesia. Contaduría y Administración 64: 1–16.

17. Kaatz, A., Vogelman, P. N., & Carnes, M. (2013). Are men more likely than women to commit scientific misconduct? Maybe, maybe not. Mbio, 4(2), e00156-13.

18. Kutan, Ali M., Nahla Samargandi, and KaziSohag. 2017. Does institutional quality matter for financial development and growth? Further evidence from MENA countries. Australian Economic Paper 56: 228–48.

19. Jana, D. S., Khedkar, A. E., &Khedkar, C. E. (2021). Digital Banking: The Future of Banking. Vidyabharati International Interdisciplinary Research Journal, 12(2), 281–284. http://www.viirj.org/vol12issue2/45.pdf

20. Kewei, X., Peng, B., Jiang, Y., & Lu, T. (2021, January). A hybrid deep learning model for online fraud detection. In 2021 IEEE International Conference on Consumer Electronics and Computer Engineering (ICCECE) (pp. 431–434). IEEE

21. J. Kummer, T. F., Singh, K., & Best, P. (2015). The effectiveness of fraud detection instruments in not-for-profit organizations. Managerial Auditing Journal.

22. Khanna, J., & Kumari, N. (2017). Cashless Payment: A Behaviourial Change to Economic Growth. International Journal of Scientific Research and Education, 5(7), 6701–6710.

23. Lukman, O. O., & Dauda, O. Y. (2013). Alternative Payment System Implication For Currency Demand and Monetary Policy in Developing Economy: A Case Study of Nigeria. International Journal of Humanities and Social Sciences, 3(20), 253–260.

24. Li, L., P. E. Strahan, and S. Zhang. 2020. Banks as lenders of "rst resort: Evidence from the Covid-19 crisis. The Review of Corporate Finance Studies.

25. Marshall, J. N. (2004). Financial institutions in disadvantaged areas: a comparative analysis of policies encouraging financial inclusion in britain and the united states. Environment and Planning A, 36(2): 241–261.

26. Kaatz, A., Vogelman, P. N., & Carnes, M. (2013). Are men more likely than women to commit scientific misconduct? Maybe, maybe not. Mbio, 4(2), e00156-13.

27. Revathi, P. (2019). Digital banking challenges and opportunities in India. EPRA International Journal of Economic and Business Review, 7(12), 20-23. https://doi.org/10.36713/epra2985.

28. Pavithra, C. B., & Geetha, K. (2021). Factors affecting customers' perception towards Digital Banking Services. Turkish Journal of Computer and Mathematics Education (TURCOMAT), 12(11), 1608-1614. https://www.turcomat.org/index.php/turkbilmat/article/view/6091/5077

29. P. Jayant, Vaishali, D. Sharma, Survey on Credit Card Fraud Detection Techniques, International Journal of Engineering Research & Technology (IJERT), ISSN: 2278–0181, Vol. 3 Issue 3, March – 2014.

30. PricewaterhouseCoopers. Six Key Challenges for Financial Institutions to Deal with ESG Risks. Available online: https://www.pwc.nl/en/insights-and-publications/services-and-industries/financial-sector/six-key-challenges-for-financial-institutions-to-deal-with-ESG-risks.html (accessed on 27 September 2021).

31. Shetty, A. A., & Murthy, K. V. (2022). Investigation of Card Skimming Cases: An Indian Perspective. Journal of Applied Security Research, 1–14

32. Stroud D, Evans C and Weinel M (2020) Innovating for energy efficiency: Digital gamification in the European steel industry. European Journal of Industrial Relations 26(4): 419–437

33. Stuart M and Lucio MM (2008) Employment relations in the UK finance sector: Between globalisation and re-regulation. CERIC Working Papers (1): 1–28.

34. Telikani, A., Tahmassebi, A., Banzhaf, W., &Gandomi, A. H. (2021). Evolutionary machine learning: A survey. ACM Computing Surveys (CSUR), 54(8), 1–35.

35. SegovianoBasurto, M., and C. Goodhart. 2009. Banking stability measures. IMF working papers pp. 1–54.

36. Truong, T., Phan, H., & Tran, M. (2020). A study on customer satisfaction on debit cards: The case of Vietnam. Uncertain Supply Chain Management, 8(2), 241–251

37. Vahdati, S., &Yasini, N. (2015). Factors affecting internet frauds in private sector: A case study in cyberspace surveillance and scam monitoring agency of Iran. Computers in Human Behavior, 51, 180–187.

38. Vinayagamoorthy, A. &Senthilkumar, K. (2012). An Analysis of Growth of Credit card Industry. Indian Journal of Applied Research, 1(5).

39. W. E. Pangesti, R. Suryadithia, M. Faisal, B. A. Wahid and A. S. Putra, "Collaborative Filtering Based Recommender Systems For Marketplace Applications," International Journal of Educational Research & Social Sciences, vol. 2, no. 5, pp. 1201–1209, 2021.

40. Wałowski, T. Zrównowazonefinanse—Czyliwszystko, co najwa ̇ zniejszedlasektorafinansowego. ̇ Głos Bank. Spółdz. 2021, 3, 20–26.

41. Westman, Hanna. 2011. The impact of management and board ownership on profitability in banks with different strategies. Journal of Banking and Finance 35: 3300–18.

42. Uddamari, N., &Ubbana, J. (2021). A Study on Unsupervised Learning Algorithms Analysis in Machine Learning. Turkish Journal of Computer and Mathematics Education (TURCOMAT), 12(14), 1946–1957.

43. Xie, Y., Liu, G., Cao, R., Li, Z., Yan, C., & Jiang, C. (2019, February). A feature extraction method for credit card fraud detection. In 2019 2nd International Conference on Intelligent Autonomous Systems (ICoIAS) (pp. 70–75). IEEE.

44. Ojugo, A. A., & Nwankwo, O. (2021). Spectral-cluster solution for credit-card fraud detection using a genetic algorithm trained modular deep learning neural network. JINAV: Journal of Information and Visualization, 2(1), 15–24.

45. Abdulahi Hasan, A., & Fang, H. (2021, May). Data Mining in Education: Discussing Knowledge Discovery in Database (KDD) with Cluster Associative Study. In 2021 2nd International Conference on Artificial Intelligence and Information Systems (pp. 1–6).

46. Nasim Matar, Ahmed Hassan, Yousef El-Ebiary, Farah, Yasser Tarshany, Yazeed Al Moaiad. (2022). Cyber Attack Detection Using K-means Machine Learning. International Journal of Special Education, 3(37), 6521–6536.

47. Yazeed Al Moaiad, Yasser Mohamed Abdelrahman Tarshany, Nasir Ahmed Algeelani, Wafa Al-Haithami. (2022). Cyber Attack Detection Using Big data analysis. International Journal of Computer Science and Information Technology Research, 3(10), 26–33.

Chapter

Experiential Perspective and Technology Adoption of Digital Educational Ecology Amid Pandemic Context

Virendra Singh Nirban[1], Tanu Shukla[2]
Associate Professor,
Department of Humanities and Social Sciences, BITS, Pilani Campus
Mounika Prashanthi Vavilala[3]
Independent Scholar

ABSTRACT: Technology is all ubiquitous in our endeavors, personal and professional. COVID-19 has dissipated the essential spatial demeanor of the personal and professional contexts. Overnight, homes became schools and devices and the internet became the catalysts to deliver the essential education to millions of students worldwide. This overnight migration required a quick adoption of the digital online educational artifacts. Technology adoption has been seen from individual intrinsic and extrinsic attributes of users. Based on the literature review and various theoretical models, the study identified Accessibility, Affordability and Tech-Entanglement of Digital Educational Ecology as contributing factors explaining technology adoption. A 5 point Likert scale was used to measure the Technology Adoption behavior of students from higher education institutions broadly divided into either rural or urban geography. Other two categories of moderators include gender and family structure, i.e. joint or nuclear family. Independent sample t-Test was used to examine the group differences based on moderating categories and Multiple linear regression to understand the impact of Accessibility, Affordability and Tech-Entanglement on Technology Adoption. Qualitative inputs were taken through interviews of the students. Results of the study indicate that Accessibility and Tech-Entanglement are powerful predictors of Technology Adoption. The results also indicate that there are significant differences among moderating categories with respect to Accessibility, Affordability and Tech-Entanglement of Digital Educational Ecology.

KEYWORDS: Accessibility, Affordability, Digital educational ecology, Technology adoption, Higher education, Pandemic, COVID-19

[1]nirban@pilani.bits-pilani.ac.in, [2]tanushukla8@gmail.com, [3]vmprashanthi@gmail.com

DOI: 10.4324/9781003415725-41

1. Introduction

'Artifacts' of technology have become an indispensable element of the 'Actors' of contemporary networked society. Technology *artifacts* refer to the material components such as the computers, mobile phones, laptops, earphones, internetwork, software and the virtual space, while the *actors* include the users. The entanglements between the two, the artifacts and the actors, has been a topic of interest for researchers in recent decades. More so since the advent of innovative new media digital technologies. And the inquiry of these entanglements makes more sense considering the context of COVID-19 during which technology became the bridge not only to connect people but also to overcome the 'social distancing' through affordances of 'social (media) networking'. The COVID-19 induced technology intervention gave rise to the Digital Educational Ecology where the elements of ecology included devices, internet, users (students, teachers, parents), online platforms for educational delivery, educational technology industry, government agencies etc. All these elements came together to supposedly create an environment to deliver education online.

Education, one of the very critical spheres of modern day social development, bore the immediate brunt of COVID-19. Educational institutions, schools and colleges, were shut down depriving millions of students of learning space. However, technology-enabled online education was largely seen as a viable substitute and was rapidly implemented across the spectrum of educational institutions. Over the period of pandemic, it was realized that technology-enabled online education was not a substitute but a stop-gap arrangement and that it would remain a supplement to physical space based educational ecology.

The roots of this realization lies in the aforementioned entanglements of the artifacts and actors in the digital ecology. These entanglements are referred to as 'Tech-Entanglement' which has been defined as the constitutive entanglement of the social and the material in everyday organizational life [Orlikowski, Barley and Scott, 2007, 2010 and 2008]. Tech-Entanglement derives its basic tenants from *Actor-Network theory* and stipulates that users, space, artifacts and digital ecology are entangled through the threads of language, interactions and practices in the organizations.

A prerequisite for entanglements with technology include technology accessibility and affordability. Accessibility has been operationally defined to connote the degree to which the user (student) is able to utilize the technology according to his or her needs. Similarly, Affordability can be defined as a user's capability to bear the cost of owning or using a technology artifact.

Entanglements are however not enough to completely understand the supplementary nature of technology-enabled online education. It is equally important to investigate the technology adoption behavior of users in educational ecology. The users here refer to students. Despite mobile telephony device penetration of more than 80 percent in India, 50 percent internet penetration in India, the technology adoption behavior remains a complex and social phenomenon. The conventional models of Technology Adoption accounts for intrinsic and extrinsic individual facets, ignoring the issues of accessibility and affordability at larger units (conjoined factors).

The objectives of this study are:

1. To examine the group differences based on gender, place of study and family structure of students on the total scores of technology accessibility, affordability, Tech-Entanglement and technology adoption.
2. To examine the impact of accessibility, affordability and Tech-Entanglement on technology adoption among students.
3. To investigate the various facilitating and limiting factors of technology adoption and transforming institutions as digital ecological space delivering quality of education for all.

2. Literature Review

The domain of technology studies has seen an increase in critical enquiry in terms of materiality of technology (Callon, 1999; e.g., Latour, 2005; Law, 1992). Of late, however, these materiality enquiries have breached the spheres of humanities and social sciences to make more sense of human entanglements with technology in organizational contexts (Packer, 2013; Van Dyke, 2015). Some authors have used the terms materiality and socio-materiality interchangeably (Jones, 2014; Kallinikos, Leonardi and Nardi, 2012).

While it is easy to think of artifacts (technology) and actors (students) as two exclusive entities which play an important role in digital ecology, their entanglements and embeddedness within each other are difficult to visualize. One of the reasons for this is that the digital is a new practice which inherently is different from conventional pedagogical practices which embody conventional artifacts (such as classroom, desks, books, peers, school space, teacher, labs etc). The incongruence of the linear juxtaposition of digital practices and convention practices makes it difficult to see the entanglements. However, it is also true that the contemporary educational context entails certain essential technology enabled practices which are increasingly becoming mainstream. Given the COVID-19 scenario during which the digital became the savior substitute, it is important to understand these entanglements and their impact on the eventual technology adoption. Research has established the significance of technology enabled learning in and outside the classroom. Numerous and innovative digital tools are available to teachers and students for their academic tasks. This is significant in the light of GoI's 'Digital India' program which aims to diffuse digital literacy into the general masses of the country. Therefore, it is important to understand the factors responsible for technology diffusion in society. Technology Adoption behavior of users differs from one segment to another and from one purpose to another. If crucial factors which affect the decision of a user to start using technology can be identified, then educational technology can be designed keeping those factors in mind.

Scott and Rockwell (1997) studied how technology anxiety affects technology usage in education. The results have suggested that computer/technology anxiety puts a negative effect on using a new technology. Similarly, Chang, Yan, and Tseng (2012) measured the use of mobile phone technology for learning English. The authors have argued that convenience is an important factor which motivates a learner to use a technology. Rogers (2003) identified

Relative Advantage, Compatibility, Complexity, Trialability, and Observability as important dimensions of technology diffusion in society.

Davis, Bagozzi and Warshaw (1989) used the Theory of Reasoned action and the Technology Acceptance Model to observe the acceptance behavior of a group of people towards the usage of computers. It was found that the subjective norm does not have a significant relation with the intentions of a person to accept a technology. Whereas, the variable perceived ease of usefulness is a very strong determiner to accept a technology. Venkatesh, Morris, and Ackerman (2000) used the Theory of Planned Behavior to observe the effect of gender in making decisions to accept a new technology. A longitudinal study was conducted and 4 organizations were selected for the purpose and 355 people were observed for 5 months. The results revealed that the variables of the framework come into effect in different ways for both genders. Hartshorne and Ajjan (2009) used the Decomposed Theory of Planned Behavior on 136 participants to observe the adoption behavior of students in adopting web 2.0 tools for learning. They concluded that attitude and perceived behavioral control are the two most significant determiners that affect the person's usage behavior. Nirban and Chasul (2014) noted that performance expectancy and social influence are strong predictors to form an intention to use Learning Management System in a university. Shukla, Dosaya and Nirban (2020) observed that investing in building a learning platform with sufficient resources, trained professionals to effectively integrate technology in education can help in increasing accessibility and usage of online learning platforms for knowledge acquisition, skill development and build their competencies. Also, Dosaya, Shukla and Nirban (2020) in their study figured out that three factors out of the four proposed by the UTAUT Model, i.e. performance expectancy, effort expectancy and social influence account for womens' acceptance or rejection behavior largely, whereas in males, performance expectancy works the best in eliciting a positive response towards accepting a technology. However, there are equally important concerns related to technology interventions in education. Only 4.4% of rural households have computers while the number is 23.4% for urban households. The percent of households having internet connectivity in rural and urban India is 14.9% and 42% respectively. In rural India, for users above five years of age, 9.9% were able to operate computers and the percentage is 32.4% in urban India [NSO, 2019]. It suggests that there is still a long way to go to make technology interventions education a reality in a meaningful sense. The digital gap and divide needs to be bridged. The technology adoption models discussed and used in contemporary research have focused on aspects of usability of technology, self-directed attributes such as self-efficacy and auxiliary characteristics such as social influence and facilitating conditions. We deviate from this conventional framework and have tried to account for larger issues of Accessibility of Digital Artifacts, Affordability of Digital Artifacts and Tech-Entanglement of the Digital Ecology.

3. Methodology

This study used a mixed method approach involving both quantitative and qualitative inputs to address the objectives of the study. The quantitative data were collected from the questionnaires and interviews and focus group discussions were conducted to assess the qualitative data. The variables of the study are technology accessibility, affordability, Tech-Entanglement and technology adoption. Questionnaires were formulated based on the literature review. To establish content validity, questionnaires were shared with expects and items of relevance were retained. The questionnaires were administered on students from different public and private universities using a random sampling method. The internal consistency is measured using Cronbach's alpha and the Cronbach's alpha values were above .80 of all the variables, indicating good reliability. The sample size consists of 89 students, out of which 42.69% are girls and 57.31% are boys. With discourse analysis of incisive interviews, this study was able to assimilate meaningful insights not only into the technology access and use phenomenon but also into the socio-materiality practices phenomenon. The inventory was shared with the identified sample subjects in advance for experiential retrieving before the interviews. The sample subjects for the qualitative input were conducted on twenty-five students from across rural-urban locations.

4. Results

Preliminary analysis was conducted to remove any outliers, normal distribution of data. The results were computed using SPSS 22 version to examine the group differences based on different demographic characteristics against the total scores of technology accessibility, affordability, Tech-Entanglement and technology adoption behavior. Further to investigate the impact of technology accessibility, affordability, Tech-Entanglement on technology adoption behavior using multiple regression. The questionnaires were administered on 89 college students from various public and private universities in Rajasthan. Out of 89, 42.69% were girls and 57.31% were boys. 44.94% of students belong to rural areas and 55.06% were from the urban locality. 43.82% of students live in a joint family set up and 56.18% were from nuclear family set up. Table 41.1 shows the frequency and percentage of students against various demographic categories.

Table 41.1 Demographic characteristics of the respondents (N 89)

Demographic Category	Number of students	Percentage
Females	38	42.69
Males	51	57.31
Rural	40	44.94
Urban	49	55.06
Joint Family	39	43.82
Nuclear Family	50	56.18

Source: Authors compilation

4.1 Accessibility

Results from the independent sample t-test revealed significant group differences on the total score of accessibility at 0.01 significance level. The results from Table 41.2 indicate that boys expressed higher levels of accessibility (M = 15.54, SD = 1.98) as compared to girls (M = 14.68, SD = 2.25), *t* value 2.06, significant at 0.01 level. Students studying in the urban areas expressed higher levels of perceived technology accessibility (M = 15.55, SD = 2.28) as compared to students from rural areas (M = 14.65, SD = 1.94), *t* value 2.01, significant at 0.01 level. Students from the Joint family showed higher accessibility of technology (M = 15.54, SD = 2.26) than students from nuclear family structure (M = 14.61, SD = 1.95), *t* value 2.11, significant at 0.01 level.

Table 41.2 Accessibility mean differences with demographics

	N	Mean	SD	*t*
Female	38	14.68	2.25	2.06**
Male	51	15.54	1.98	
Rural	40	14.65	1.94	2.01**
Urban	49	15.55	2.28	
Nuclear	39	14.61	1.95	2.11**
Joint	50	15.54	2.26	

Source: Authors compilation

4.2 Affordability

Results showed significant group differences on the total score of affordability at 0.01 significance level. The results from Table 41.3 indicate that boys expressed higher levels of affordability (M = 11.52, SD = 0.92) as compared to girls (M = 10.57, SD = 1.53), *t* value 3.32, significant at 0.01 level. Students studying in the urban areas expressed higher levels of technology affordability (M = 11.52, SD = .093) as compared to students from rural areas (M = 10.62, SD = 1.51), *t* value 3.3, significant at 0.01 level. Students from the Joint family showed higher affordability (M = 11.54, SD = 0.96) than students from nuclear family structure (M = 10.58, SD = 1.78), *t* value 3.44, significant at 0.01 level.

Table 41.3 Affordability mean differences with demographics

	N	Mean	SD	*t*
Female	38	10.57	1.53	3.32**
Male	51	11.52	0.92	
Rural	40	10.62	1.51	3.30**
Urban	49	11.52	.93	
Nuclear	39	10.58	1.78	3.44**
Joint	50	11.54	.95	

Source: Authors compilation

4.3 Tech-Entanglement

Independent sample t-test results revealed significant group differences on the total score of Tech-Entanglement at 0.01 significance level. The results from Table 41.4 indicate that boys expressed higher levels of Tech-Entanglement (M = 15.43, SD = 1.7) as compared to girls (M = 14.05, SD = 2.19), *t* value 3.26, significant at 0.01 level. Students studying in the urban areas expressed higher levels of Tech-Entanglement (M = 15.42, SD = 2.23) as compared to students from rural areas (M = 14.12, SD = 1.69), t value 3.12, significant at 0.01 level. Students from the Joint family showed higher Tech-Entanglement (M = 15.44, SD = 2.21) than students from nuclear family structure (M = 14.07, SD = 1.69), t value 3.29, significant at 0.01 level.

Table 41.4 Tech-entanglement mean differences with demographics

	N	Mean	SD	t
Female	38	14.05	2.19	3.26**
Male	51	15.43	1.70	
Rural	40	14.12	1.69	3.12**
Urban	49	15.42	2.23	
Nuclear	39	14.07	1.69	3.29**
Joint	50	15.44	2.21	

Source: Authors compilation

4.4 Regression Analysis

Multiple linear regression was used to examine the amount of variance explained by technology accessibility, affordability and socio materiality on technology adoption. Results from Table 41.5 indicate that accessibility, affordability and Tech-Entanglement (together as a model) explained significant (16.8%) proportion of variance towards technology adoption among the students (R^2 = .168, adjusted R^2 = .138, F(3, 85) = 5.731, p < 0.01). Additionally, Accessibility and Tech-Entanglement were found to contribute significantly in predicting technology adoption but not affordability.

Table 41.5 Multiple regression analysis

Predictors	B	SEB	β
Accessibility	.506	.199	.697
Affordability	.041	.096	.042
Tech-Entanglement	.729	.205	.973
R2	.168		
C	9.09		
F	5.713	p < 0.01	

Note: Dependent variable: Technology Adoption; B = unstandardized beta coefficient,
SEB = standardized error of beta, β = standardized beta coefficient,
Source: Authors compilation

5. Discussion

Adoption of technology is a vital cog in the ever increasing sphere of digital ecology. While COVID-19 ushered a new era of technology enabled education delivery, it remains to be seen whether it is a substitute or a supplement. Following sections discuss the findings from the data analysis with the help of qualitative inputs gathered via interviews.

5.1 Accessibility

Accessibility has been explained in varied ways depending on the subject and object of enquiry. In general terms, accessibility means that a given technology is usable by a wide range of users irrespective of their functional abilities. It has been defined as use of a product (technology) in an efficient and effective way by the users (ISO 9241-171,2008). For differently abled users the term assistive technology is used for the same phenomenon. However, for the purpose of this study, Accessibility has been defined as overlapping with availability of technology and the degree to which the user (student) is able to utilize the technology according to his or her needs. From inferential statistical analysis and qualitative data, it can be inferred that students from rural space and those from joint family setup faced accessibility problems. Moreover, females found themselves as less preferred candidates for gaining access to technology for online education. For rural students, there were two-fold bottlenecks; first, the availability of auxiliary services such as electricity and telecom infrastructure. Non-availability of electricity during school timing leads to complete miss of school. Similarly lack of essential telecom infrastructure such as broadband towers and data charging point of sales resulted in missing the school. If students came from joint family setups, they had to share the resources such as devices and data packs with other students in the family and hence none could not completely utilize the resource or attend online school.

5.2 Affordability

Affordability, in the context of technology, can be defined as a user's capability to bear the cost of owning or using a technology artifact. In the last two decades, following Moore's law, the power and penetration of digital tele-communication technology has increased while the cost has declined. However, over the last three decades, owing to socio-economic and political reasons, the purchasing parity of the large population has remained stagnant. Students from rural and joint family structures opined that due to online education, the routine household expenses had to be adjusted against the new needs of internet connectivity and digital artifact requirements such as purchase of a smart mobile phone and laptops. Due to rural income generation sources, which were mainly concentrated on agriculture and farming, the constraints became severe in the long run of COVID-19. Students in joint family structures compromised on attending the complete university class schedule and activities because the physical devices and internet data resources had to be shared. This eventually led to lower learning outcomes and declined engaged education. Also, the female university students felt that whenever possible it was they who were compromised in the name of rising hold costs because of the expenses on online education.

5.3 Tech-Entanglement

The entanglements of technology and users (students) play an important role in the eventual efficacy of digital ecology to fulfil the objective of meaningfully delivering education. The COVID-19 ushered technology-enabled education overnight on students irrespective of student's readiness for the paradigm shift. Primarily and largely, Mobile phones and desktops/ laptops (to some extent) with the essential component of internet connectivity, were the technology artifacts. Additionally, the digital platform used to deliver education, which varied from Whatsapp, facebook, Google Meet, Microsoft Teams, Learning Management Systems (LMS) such as Moodle, Youtube, to simple Emails, SMS and messaging apps, also became significant digital artifacts. Teachers, on their part, made an effort to replicate the conventional practices such as creating the classroom environment, interacting with the students, facilitating peer learning, encouraging out-of-the-class engagement, activity and role based learning etc. However, from a student perspective, these practices didn't materialize for them. According to the respondents, one aspect is the physicality of the practice. The Google meet never seemed like a classroom. There was no feel. Due to bandwidth issues, they were always told to disable their video and audio functionality. All this had a ripple effect on the other practices such as peer learning and scaffolding. There was no Zone of proximal development. Moreover, students from rural geography faced issues of intermittent audio failures. Another important aspect was the 'artifactness' of the digital ecosystem. Students felt that the issues of screen space (small and big), varied user friendly interface (Whatsapp, LMS, Google Meet, Microsoft Teams), Information Design (how instructional material is presented, students resources are presented, supplementary material is presented, how is information stacked during the coursework), navigation (arrangement of links and hyperlinks), physicality of keypad (physical or virtual) played an important role in eventual acceptance/resistance of the online education.

5.4 Technology Adoption

According to Bohlen and Beal (1957) there are five types of technology users in terms of their adoption behavior, namely: Innovators, Early Adopters, Early Majority, Late Majority and Laggards. These categories are classified based on users age group, education level, socio-economic status, and social influence. However, for the purpose of this study we have considered technology adoption behavior as a cumulative impact of accessibility, affordability and Tech-Entanglement on a user (student) placed in a mandatory condition. It is the degree to which a student is willing to adopt a technology artifact in an enforced digital ecology in higher education context. Students from rural place of education found it less enticing to embrace technology for education. This was largely because of the perceived less accessibility, affordability and Tech-Entanglement of the digital artifacts and partly because of the inefficacy resulting from the same. Female students felt that they were less inclined to adopt the online mode as they had minimal choice in terms of access to the devices and internet services. There was not enough motivation to adopt and experiment with online education. Students from joint families also opined that because of the shared resources of the digital ecology, there wasn't enough motivation to embrace the new form of education. These real experiences with online education led to lower levels of technology adoption behavior among the students in higher education. It can be observed that there is a discernible difference between the technology adoption behavior of student populations coming from discrete and exclusive demographic categories. From regression, it can be concluded that Accessibility and Tech-Entanglement experiences are strong and significant predictors of Technology Adoption behavior.

6. Conclusions

The study considered Tech-Entanglement perspective to gauge the technology adoption behavior of students from higher education context. The Tech-Entanglement perspective included Accessibility, Affordability and Tech-Entanglement of digital ecology of education. Three moderating variables were considered, namely- Gender, Place of Education and Family Structure. Following conclusions can be drawn from the quantitative and qualitative data analysis. Male and Female students had different experiences with respect to Accessibility, Affordability and Tech-Entanglement. Female students found themselves in a disadvantageous position for accessing and affording the cost of online education. Similarly, students from rural places of education were not able to access and afford online education in a meaningful manner as compared to students from urban places of education. Students from joint families found themselves struggling for resources. In terms of Tech-Entanglement, students from urban places felt a higher degree of propinquity with digital ecology as compared to students from rural places owing to better technology infrastructure and access. It can be inferred from the findings that there exists a digital divide within the digital educational ecology. These digital divides give rise to gaps of access and affordance of the digital artifacts. Unless the prerequisites of entanglements with technology are in place, technology adoption and diffusion in larger society would be short of meaningful impact.

REFERENCES

1. Bohlen, Joe M.; Beal, George M. (May 1957). "The Diffusion Process". Special Report No. 18. 1: 56–77
2. Callon, M. (1999). Actor-Network Theory: The Market Test. In J. a. H. Law, J. (Ed.), Actor Network Theory and After (pp. 181–195). Oxford: Blackwell Publishers.
3. Chang, C. C., Yan, C. F., & Tseng, J. S. (2012). Perceived convenience in an extended technology acceptance model: Mobile technology and English learning for college students. Australasian Journal of Educational Technology, 28(5).
4. Davis, F. D., Bagozzi, R. P., & Warshaw, P. R. (1989). User acceptance of computer technology: a comparison of two theoretical models. Management science, 35(8), 982–1003.
5. Dosaya, D., Shukla, Tanu, & Nirban, V. S. (2020). Transformation of Academic Ecology through Information Communication Technology Adoption. International Journal of Information and Education Technology, 10(5), 372377
6. Hartshorne, R., & Ajjan, H. (2009). Examining student decisions to adopt Web 2.0 technologies: theory and empirical tests. Journal of computing in higher education, 21(3), 183.
7. ISO 9241-171. (2008). Ergonomics of human-system interaction — Part 171: Guidance on software accessibility (2008). ISO. Retrieved October 9, 2019, from https://www.iso.org/standard/39080.html.
8. Jones, M. (2014). A Matter of Life and Death: Exploring Conceptualizations of Tech-Entanglement in the Context of Critical Care. Mis Quarterly, 38(3).
9. Kallinikos, J., Leonardi, P. M., & Nardi, B. A. (2012). The Challenge of Materiality: Origins, Scope, and Prospects. In P. Leonardi, B. Nardi, & J. Kallinikos (Eds.), Materiality and organizing: Social interaction in a technological world (pp. 1–22). Oxford: Oxford University Press.

10. Latour, B. (2005). Reassembling the Social: An Introduction to Actor-Network-Theory: Oxford University Press, USA.
11. Law, J. (1992). Notes on the theory of the actor-network: Ordering, strategy, and heterogeneity. Systemic practice, 5(4), 379–393.
12. Leonardi, P. M., & Barley, S. R. (2010). What's under construction here? Social action, materiality, and power in constructivist studies of technology and organizing.
13. Nirban, V.S. and Chasul, (2014). "Learning management system acceptance behaviour of students in higher education", 2014 IEEE International Conference on MOOC, pp. 108–111, 2014.
14. NSO, Survey conducted by National Statistical Office[NSO] titled 'Key Indicators of Household Social Consumption on Education in India', [2019]
15. Orlikowski, W. J. (2007). Sociomaterial Practices: Exploring Technology at Work. Organization Studies (28)9, pp. 1435–1448.
16. Orlikowski, W. J., and Scott, S. V. (2008). Tech-Entanglement: Challenging the Separation of Technology, Work and Organization. The Academy of Management Annals (2)1, pp. 433–474.
17. Packer, J. (2013). Communication matters: Materialist approaches to media, mobility and networks: Routledge.
18. Rogers, E. M. (2003). Diffusion of innovations, edn. Free Pres., New York.
19. Shukla, Tanu, Dosaya, D., Nirban, V. S., & Vavilala, M. P. (2020). Factors Extraction of Effective Teaching-Learning in Online and Conventional Classrooms. International Journal of Information and Education Technology, 10(6), 422–427
20. Scott, C. R., & Rockwell, S. C. (1997). The effect of communication, writing, and technology apprehension on likelihood to use new communication technologies. Communication education, 46(1), 44–62.
21. Van Dyke, R. M. (2015). Materiality in Practice: An Introduction. In R. M. Van Dyke (Ed.), Practicing materiality (pp. 3–32). Tucson: University of Arizona Press.
22. Venkatesh, V., Morris, M. G., & Ackerman, P. L. (2000). A longitudinal field investigation of gender differences in individual technology adoption decision-making processes. Organizational behavior and human decision processes, 83(1), 33–60.

Chapter

Impact of Seed Type and Fertilizer on Pearl Millet Yield: A Descriptive Study in Selected Districts of Rajasthan

Nikita Dhankar[1]

Research scholar, Mechanical Engineering Department,
BITS Pilani Campus, Pilani, India

Srikanta Routroy*

Professor, Mechanical Engineering Department,
BITS Pilani Campus, Pilani, India

Satyendra Kr. Sharma[2]

Associate Professor, Department of Management,
BITS Pilani Campus, Pilani, India

ABSTRACT: Various input factors for cultivation practices are adopted in the upstream supply chain such as seed quality, fertilizer use, rainfall, temperature and farmer awareness play an important role to maximize the pearl millet yield. A survey questionnaire was developed considering these factors and 473 farmer responses were collected from the semi-arid zone of Rajasthan. The adoption of different seed types for pearl millet are 77% (Desi), 22% (Hybrid), and 0.40%(both). Whereas the fertilizers usage is 67.44% (Organic), 5.50% (Inorganic), 19.66% (Both), and 7.40% (Not used). These factors have an impact on the yield of pearl millet. Therefore, there is a need to inform the benefits of hybrid seeds among the farmer through incentive schemes and various stakeholders such as SHGs (Self-Help Groups) for its increased adoption. Also, government should take steps so that marginal farmers can use both organic and inorganic fertilizers depending upon their cultivated land. The findings of the current research will be useful for the policy maker to develop different policies related to pearl millet and Stover yield and will be a valuable addition to the upstream pearl millet supply chain in specific.

KEYWORDS: Upstream supply chain, Descriptive analytics, Pearl millet yield, Stover yield

*Corresponding Author: srikanta@pilani.bits-pilani.ac.in,
[1]p20210001@pilani.bits-pilani.ac.in, [2]satyendrasharma@pilani.bits-pilani.ac.in

DOI: 10.4324/9781003415725-42

1. Introduction

Among other millets, pearl millet is the food crop with the sixth-largest millet species. In the arid lands of the African nations, millet are grown in 30 million hectares, accounting for 50% of the world's millet production (Satyavathi et al., 2021). While in India, pearl millet is farmed on more than 9 million hectares, and ranks 3rd after rice and wheat in the area. It is mainly planted for meals and dry feedstock which is known as Stover (O. P. Yadav et al., 2012). Rajasthan, Gujarat, Haryana, Uttar Pradesh, and Maharashtra are the leading pearl millet-growing states in India, making up approximately 90 percent of the country's overall production. Rajasthan state produces the highest among other states (Tomar et al., 2021). Many studies have emphasized the benefits of pearl millet, noting that it may be produced in regions where other cereals would not flourish due to its resistance to challenging environmental circumstances like famine, extreme heat, and poor soil health (Basavaraj et al., 2010). It is a common diet for 9 million poor people, is highly nutritious, and has plenty of health benefits. It requires minimal resources for procurement, and is essentially immune to biotic stressors (Tomar et al., 2021). The percentage of cultivated land used for pearl millet cultivation is directly proportional to yield of pearl millet and Stover. The pearl millet is cultivated on less fertile soil as well as little ability to retain water in extreme heat and it produces grain and fodder. The production of fodder is either twice or more than the yield of pearl millet grains, and it varies depending on the type of hybrid seeds used to grow this crop (Yadav, Kant and Yadav, 2008). Also it indicates the farmer's motivation for cultivating pearl millet. Basavaraj et al., (2010) made an analysis on the use and availability of land for pearl millet output in India's key growing states. Rajasthan, key pearl millet growing state, suffers from a fodder shortage. Rearing cattle is a potential source of income for farmers. The quality of fodder determines dairy outputs such as milk and meat. Numerous operations including cultivation, irrigation, crop growth, harvesting, threshing, and transportation to the storage houses are considered as upstream supply chain operations (Morales Chavez et al., 2020). These operations, location specific factors those include but not limited to cultivation practices adopted in upstream supply chain, seed quality, fertilizer use, soil characteristics, rain fall, ground water quality and temperature are linked to the yield of both pearl millet and Stover. Also the uncertainties involved with these factors and farmer attitude and awareness play an important role in the yield. The factors such as hindered access to labour, early harvesting by farmers with fewer resources, low soil fertility, inferior soils, diseases, early water stress, ineffective integrated pest management, unstable marketplaces, a lack of needed variety selections, poor availability of credits, yields that suffer from the use of outdated technology, and inaccurate information throughout value chains limit pearl millet yield and farmer income (Fermont et al., 2009 and Hamukwala, 2010). The emerging economic factors in recent years, information visibility, training, credit facilities, seed availability, fertilizer availability and use, irrigation facilities etc. have pushed farmer to boost the overall productivity (Haruna Kaugama and Abba Ahmed, 2020). Unfortunately, limited access to advanced technology such as high- yielding varieties of seeds prevents major efficiency gains (Hamukwala et al., 2010). The seed type impacts both the yield of pearl millet and Stover. Matuschke, Mishra and Qaim (2007) studied on hybrid seeds and reported that despite of the expensive seed prices and frequent requirements for replacing seeds, small-holders benefit from the cultivation of hybrid wheat to a greater extent than their large-scale equivalents. The adoption of hybrid wheat is significantly influenced by income and informational accessibility. The type of fertilizer use (Organic, inorganic and both) has an impact on of pearl millet yield, Stover yield and farmer income. Alemu and Bayu (2005) carried out research to evaluate the effects of farmyard manure alone with coupled inorganic fertilizer on Sorghum crop. The results indicated that applying both in combination does have a positive impact on the sorghum's panicle weight and Stover productivity. Pearl millet is frequently mixed with other crops by farmers in dry and semi-arid areas of Rajasthan to boost productivity per unit area, and may reduce the likelihood of crop failure since legume crops, particularly mung bean is more stable in grain yields in a dry area. Ram and Meena (2014) studied the effectiveness of intercropping methods for mung beans and pearl millet in dry regions of Rajasthan (India). They concluded that intercropping with moonbeams will greatly boost Stover yield for farmers. With the assistance of agricultural specialists and organized bodies, the government should educate farmers about the benefits of intercropping in order to increase their output and overall income. Numerous studies suggest that fertilisers, and seed type, together with other input parameters, have a considerable impact on crop yield. However, there hasn't been any research done on the pearl millet crop in India. From the above discussion, it is obvious that there is a need to carry out a comprehensive study consisting of cultivation environment which includes resources utilization such as fertilizers, type of seed, use of advanced technologies and their functions for enhancing yield of both pearl millet and Stover in the semi-arid zone of India. However, no study has been reported in the literature for comprehensive analysis of upstream supply chain operations of the pearl millet. Therefore, upstream supply chain operations are studied in the semi-arid zone of Rajasthan region and outcomes of the study may be generalized for the semi-arid zone of India. Therefore, current study has carried out in these directions to fill the research gap. The outcomes of this study will definitely assist the policymakers, researchers, and farmer community as a whole to enhance the supply chain performance and it is a step toward doubling the farmer income.

2. Material and Methods

Pearl millet is a popular and major crop for food and feed in arid and semi-arid regions. Because it can endure the harsh climatic circumstances that hinder other crops while being advantageous for this crop's growth. To provide the context and background of the upstream supply chain operations on pearl millet and Stover yield, the study was conducted in the arid and semi-arid regions of Rajasthan such as Jhunjhunu, Churu and Jodhpur districts during the year 2020-21 using primary data from 473 sample households from different villages.

2.1 Study Area

The core of north-eastern India's arid and semi-arid regions are mainly composed of the desert areas of Rajasthan, Gujarat, Punjab, and the Rann of Kutch, make up almost 9,56,750 square kilometres of land of the country. Arid regions consist of less than 25 cm (10 inches) of rainfall yearly whereas, semi-arid regions are those where annual rainfall is between 25 cm and 50 cm (Arid & Semi-Arid Region Platform-National Park Service, 2021). The world-wide arid environments have been among the most ecological systems, which are concentrated even more vulnerable to frequent droughts and they incredibly vary in terms of their geographical shapes, biodiversity, minerals, plants, wind, water, and anthropogenic factors (Goyal et al., 2013).

2.2 Questionnaire Design for the Survey

The initial survey questionnaire was developed on the basis of extensive literature review of the upstream supply chain operations of pearl millet and number of discussions held with various stake holders such as farmers, government officials and field experts including scientists. The literature suggests that factors such as seed type, fertilizer use, and intercropping influences significantly the yield of pearl millet and Stover. The farmers should also be encouraged to employ modern agriculture techniques to increase yields to enhance pearl millet production (Tomar et al., 2021). Parameters including soil quality/health, fertilizer availability and use, environmental conditions including global warming, ground water availability and quality, integrated pest management for disease control and labour availability are crucial for maximizing crop productivity (Yadav, Peterson and Easter, 1997; Alemu and Bayu, 2005; Fermont et al., 2009, Laux et al., 2010 and Sain, 2022). The initial questionnaire was refined in light of feedback received from the pilot study. The final questionnaire was developed both in English and Hindi. The questionnaire consists of respondent farmer's personal details and it includes name, district, village, mobile number, education, available land for cultivation, and cultivated land for pearl millet, information related to factors which have significant impact on yield of pearl millet and Stover such as seed type (desi, hybrid), quantity of seed used, fertilizers type (organic, inorganic or both). In order to get clarity about the yield, the yield information from farmer is captured for one hectare of cultivated land.

2.3 Data Collection and Representative Population

Most of the marginal farmers are not familiar with online mode of survey. Hence, off-line mode was adopted for collecting information. The survey data collected through face-to-face interactions with farmers, telephonic conversation with farmers, meeting with small farmer groups at village level, and meeting the farmers in Krishi Mela held at Krishi Vigyan Kendra (KVK), Sardarshahar, Churu. A sample of 473 respondents was drawn for the survey from the farmers at different villages of selected districts. The geographic location of three selected districts in Rajasthan considered in the study which comes under semi-arid zone are 55.6, 38.27 & 6.13 % of respondent from each district.

2.4 General Characteristics and Distribution of Respondents

The farmer household members participate completely or partially in various upstream pearl millet supply chain operations and the same was also observed in the current study. In the current study, 95 % respondents are found to be literate. The distribution of respondents in three districts (i.e., Jhunjhunu, Churu and Jodhpur). In order to gather information, form the Jhunjhunu, Jodhpur & Churu districts, in-person interviews with farmers were conducted in the communities. The percentage of land cultivated for pearl millet in Jhunjhunu, Churu and Jodhpur districts are 55.6, 38.27, and 6.13 respectively.

2.5 Data Analysis

IBM Statistical Package for the Social Sciences (SPSS) version 25 was used for the analysis of survey data of the current study. The current study adopted the descriptive analytics for analysing the upstream pearl millet supply chain operations. The survey data are both qualitative and quantitative in nature. The data collected from 473 farmers in the semi-arid region of Rajasthan as per the questionnaire. The descriptive analysis was carried out for seed type and fertilizer type. The current practices being used in various villages of Rajasthan region and the usage of input factors such as seed type, fertilizer type are discussed in this Section. The outcomes of this analysis are presented in Fig. 42.1, Fig. 42.2, and Fig. 42.3, and Fig. 42.4.

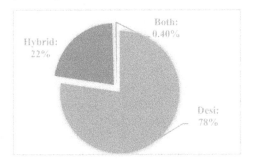

Fig. 42.1 Usage of seed types for pearl millet

Source: Authors compilation

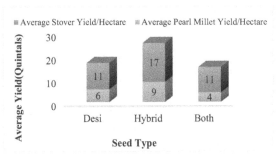

Fig. 42.2 Relationship of seed type with yield

Source: Authors compilation

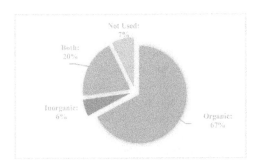

Fig. 42.3 Adoption of fertilizer types for pearl millet

Source: Authors compilation

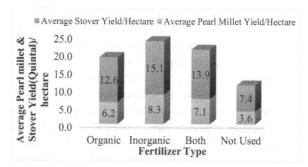

Fig. 42.4   Relationship of fertilizer types with yield

Source: Authors compilation

3. Result and Discussion

This survey provides the explanatory findings. This study describes and demonstrates the important aspects of upstream supply chain operations of pearl millet with respect to yield of both pearl millet and Stover. It was observed that the respondents are less aware of the optimum usage of the seed type, fertilizer type, and intercropping frequency. Therefore, the outcomes of the study will be quite useful for various stake holders in general and farmer in specific. The adoption of different seed types for pearl millet are observed to be desi: 77%, hybrid: 22%, and both: 0.40%. It also reveals that desi seeds are preferred significantly more compared to hybrid seeds due to several reasons such as expensive cost of hybrid seeds. Additionally, although desi seeds can be used for multiple crop seasons but hybrid seeds can be used for only the following harvest. The outcomes of the study (Fig. 42.2) reveal that the hybrid seeds are gives more yield (pearl millet and Stover). There is a need to sensitize the benefits of hybrid seeds among the farmer through incentive schemes and various stakeholders such as SHGs, FIGs and FIOs for its increased adoption. The bifurcation of the percentage usage of different types of fertilizers are observed to be organic: 67.44%, inorganic: 5.50%, both: 19.66%, and not used as 7.40%. It was observed that the farmers are using organic fertilizers as compared to other types because in-house rearing of animals makes inorganic farming makes it inexpensive. It is evident that farmers who choose to use both types of fertilizers in their farm benefits more in terms of yield (Fig. 42.4). Therefore, the government should provide subsidy on inorganic fertilizers to small farmers depending upon their cultivated land so that they may afford to utilize both organic and inorganic fertilizers.

4. Conclusion

The demand of pearl millet exists in Indian and global market whereas the demand for Stover exists locally. However, it is observed that the farmers are not motivated to cultivate pearl millet because of low income in comparison to other agriculture produces. Desi (country side) seed and organic fertilizer is popular among the farmers although it gives low yield for both pearl millet and Stover. There is a need to inform the benefits of hybrid seeds, use of both organic and inorganic fertilizers among the farmer through incentive schemes and various stakeholders such as SHGs. The level of awareness is found to be different in different districts and hence the yield. Therefore, there is a need for Government to provide a platform to exchange the information between the farmers so that the learning and implementation of better practices will be in place. The farmers should understand and carry out various operations and practices such as organic farming, certification, dynamic market price, and quality of inputs (i.e., seed type and fertilizer) adoption. Various stakeholders such as Government and NGOs should create a platform to increase this awareness and its implication on farmer income. The farmers connected to SHGs, and training institutes have earned more in comparison to those farmers who are not connected. The marginal farmers are not able adopt mechanization in various upstream operations due to high investment for ownership and low utilization. But this is feasible if farmers will be linked through SHGs. The famers should be motivated and incentive should be given them for their linkage with SHG. The farmer income considering various upstream supply chain operations and practices have never been examined in such a way before. Government of India has been putting continuous efforts for the implementation of various schemes and programs for enhancing farmer yield & income in general and marginal farmer in specific. The results obtained from the study can be generalized for Rajasthan state and cannot be generalized for other pearl millet producing states in India and countries. However, the current study can be extended in different dimensions to fulfil the research gaps and to make valuable addition to the pearl millet supply chain in specific. Two key input elements (seed type and fertilizer type) that farmers directly control and have a significant impact on the yield are the subject of this study. In order to gain more advantages, a similar study might be conducted while taking into account variables under the control of the environment, such as temperature, rainfall, and farmer affiliation with self-help groups. Additionally, different statistical tools like MANOVA can be employed to determine a relationship between the input parameters and the yield.

5. Acknowledgment

This work is funded by Ministry of Science and Technology, Department of Science and Technology, SEED Division, Government of India, New Delhi and is funded through the project Sanction No: SEED/ASACODER-018/2018(G) dated 25.06.2021 entitled, "Doubling Farm Women's income: Entrepreneurship development through post-harvest processing and technology integration in arid zone".

REFERENCES

1. https://aps.dac.gov.in/APY/Public_Report1.aspx
2. https://www.nps.gov/subjects/geology/arid-landforms.htm
3. Alemu, G., & Bayu, W. (2005). Effects of farmyard manure and combined N and P fertilizer on sorghum and soil characteristics in northeastern Ethiopia. *Journal of Sustainable Agriculture*, 26(2): 23–41. https://doi.org/10.1300/J064v26n02_04.
4. Basavaraj, G., Rao, P. P., Bhagavatula, S., & Ahmed, W. (2010). Availability and utilization of pearl millet in India. *SAT ejournal*, 8: 1–6.

5. Fermont, A. M., van Asten, P. J. A., Tittonell, P., van Wijk, M. T., & Giller, K. E. (2009). Closing the cassava yield gap: An analysis from smallholder farms in East Africa. *Field Crops Research*, 112(1): 24–36. https://doi.org/10.1016/j.fcr.2009.01.009

6. Hair JR, J. F., Black, W. C., Babin, B.J. and Anderson, R.E. (2010), *Multivariate Data Analysis*, Pearson Prentice Hall, Upper Saddle River, New Jersey, Last Accessed-28/12/2022

7. Matuschke, I., Mishra, R. R., & Qaim, M. (2007). Adoption and Impact of Hybrid Wheat in India. *World Development*, 35(8): 1422–1435. https://doi.org/10.1016/j.worlddev.2007.04.005

8. Morales Chavez, M. M., Sarache, W., Costa, Y., & Soto, J. (2020). Multiobjective stochastic scheduling of upstream operations in a sustainable sugarcane supply chain. *Journal of Cleaner Production*, 276. https://doi.org/10.1016/j.jclepro.2020.123305

9. Ram, K., & Meena, R. S. (2014). Evaluation of pearl millet and mungbean intercropping systems in arid region of Rajasthan (India). *Bangladesh Journal of Botany*, 43(3):367–370. https://doi.org/10.3329/bjb.v43i3.21616

10. Satyavathi, C. T., Ambawat, S., Khandelwal, V., & Srivastava, R. K. (2021). Pearl Millet: A Climate-Resilient Nutricereal for Mitigating Hidden Hunger and Provide Nutritional Security. *Frontiers in Plant Science*, 12: 1–18. https://doi.org/10.3389/fpls.2021.659938

11. Tomar, M., Bhardwaj, R., Kumar, M., Pal Singh, S., Krishnan, V., Kansal, R., Verma, R., Yadav, V. K., dahuja, A., Ahlawat, S. P., Rana, J. C., Bollinedi, H., Ranjan Kumar, R., Goswami, S., T, V., Satyavathi, C. T., Praveen, S., & Sachdev, A. (2021). Nutritional composition patterns and application of multivariate analysis to evaluate indigenous Pearl millet ((Pennisetum glaucum (L.) R. Br.) germplasm. *Journal of Food Composition and Analysis*, 103: 104086. https://doi.org/10.1016/j.jfca.2021.104086

12. Yadav, O. P., Rai, K. N., Rajpurohit, B. S., Hash, C. T., Mahala, R. S., Gupta, S. K., Shetty, H. S., Bishnoi, H. R., Rathore, M. S., & Kumar, A. (2012). Twenty-five years of pearl millet improvement in India. All India Coordinated Pearl Millet Improvement Project, 1–122.

13. Yadav, Satya, Willis Peterson, and K. William Easter. 1997. Do Farmers Overuse Nitrogen Fertilizer to the.Pdf. *Environmental and Resource Economics* 9: 323–40.

14. Yadav, Yash Pal, Shashi Kant, and H. P. Yadav. (2021). Correlation and Path Cofficient Analysis of Dry Fodder Yield and Its Attributes in Dual Purpose Pearl Millet (pennisetum glaucum). 9(3): 323–4.

Chapter

Adoption and Usage of the Electronic National Agriculture Market: A Literature Review

Nirankush Dutta[1], Udayan Chanda[2]
Department of Management,
Birla Institute of Technology & Science, Pilani

S. R. Singh[3]
Chaudhary Charan Singh National Institute of Agricultural Marketing

ABSTRACT: Agricultural marketing is one of the lifelines for a sizeable population of India and it contributes 25 percent of the GDP. An effective agricultural marketing system can help farmers market their products at a fair and reasonable price. In recent years due to technological breakthroughs, the Indian agriculture sector is experiencing substantial shifts in irrigation strategies and the result is reflected in the surplus production of crops. Despite record production in crops the visible changes in farmers' earnings are very negligible. The more profitable production of crops emphasizes the importance of agricultural marketing for the inclusive development of the agriculture and welfare of the farmers. *"Thus the government and other organizations are trying to address the key challenges of agriculture in India, including small holdings of farmers, primary and secondary processing, supply chain, the infrastructure supporting the efficient use of resources and marketing, and reducing intermediaries in the market"* (Sharma 2021). The National Agriculture Market (eNAM)- a pan-India electronic trading portal introduced in April 2016 to connect the Agricultural Produce Market Committees (APMC) mandis and to set up an integrated nationwide market for agricultural commodities. *"It unites surplus production regions with deficit regions through an online platform, which may lead to better market competition, and thus better prices for farmers for their produce"* (Venkatesh et al, 2021). This initiative was widely considered to be a game changer for farmers and the overall agricultural marketing sector of India. The present research paper reviews existing literature on the adoption of the e-NAM platform across different Indian states to highlight the status of adoption and acceptance by its various stakeholders.

[1]nirankush.dutta@pilani.bits-pilani.ac.in, [2]udayanchanda@pilani.bits-pilani.ac.in, [3]sattramsingh@gmail.com

DOI: 10.4324/9781003415725-43

KEYWORDS: National agriculture market (eNAM), Adoption and acceptance, Literature review, Online trading

1. Introduction

The Indian agricultural markets are still underdeveloped and flawed and lack both horizontal and vertical integration (Pavithra, et al, 2018). The supply chains for agricultural commodities in India are mostly controlled by several intermediaries causing a significant price spread from the point of production to end-consumption. Chand (2012) established the presence of at least four intermediaries from the farm produce to end-consumers resulting in a reduction in the producers' net income from the overall profit.

Besides the intermediaries, complexities of the agricultural marketing also increase multi-fold due to the multiple taxations and licensing systems, market fees, and increasing transaction costs (Patnaik 2011).

The government of India (GOI) and other organizations are focusing on the key challenges in the agriculture sector and developing policies to improve the economic conditions of the farmers by supporting them in the efficient use of resources and marketing and reducing intermediaries in the market. Vadivelu and Kiran (2013) advocated market reforms besides proper pricing strategy through a regulated market system that can reinforce the agricultural marketing sector of India. Among other measures of reforms in agricultural marketing in India, the authors also suggested starting local outlets at each village where the farmers can sell their produce directly to the consumers/ authorized buyers at fixed prices, and strengthening the public distribution system that can provide realistic prices to the farmers for their produce. The Electronic National Agriculture Market aimed at implementing some of these suggestions.

2. Background of the Electronic National Agriculture Market (e-NAM)

The National Agriculture Market (e-NAM) has been accepted across most of the states and union territories, with Bihar, Ladakh, Sikkim, and North-Eastern states (Arunachal Pradesh, Assam, Meghalaya, Manipur, Mizoram, Nagaland, and Tripura) being the major exceptions. The e-NAM is linked with 1000 markets (APMCs) in 18 states and 2 union territories, with over 50 lakh farmer membership in 18 states.

Pavithra, et al. (2018) suggested that the E-tendering process could be considered the initial phase for accomplishing the objective of market unification. The authors suggested that the e-tendering system could pervade the necessary competition and transparency to reduce the costs of trade in agricultural markets. However, the authors also suggested that for proper implementation of e-NAM, GoI requires building infrastructure in the form of storage, warehousing, banks, grading and assaying facilities, etc. inside the market yard, to encourage the traders to participate in e-tendering.

Nuthalapati, Bhatt, and Beero (2020) pointed out the expected benefits of e-NAM: "*accessibility of farmers to a common agriculture market; real-time price discovery; transparency in the agriculture marketing system; reduction the transaction costs of buyers and sellers; real-time information on prices, market arrivals, etc; bidding on quality parameters of commodities; online bidding for more transparency; online payment system to reduce the payment risk and ensure timely payments to farmers, cleaning, sorting, grading and weighing facilities and additional services such as soil testing laboratories at the e-NAM*".

3. Literature Review

3.1 Studies Conducted in Karnataka

Reddy (2018) studied the experience of e-markets among farmers, traders, commission agents, and market committee members in Karnataka using daily prices and arrivals data from 2007 to 2016. Based on the analysis the author concluded that e-markets intensify competition and eradicate collusion among traders to promote farmers' overall incomes. The author also witnessed modest resistance to e-auction from traders and commission agents as they did not find any benefit of it against the physical auction. Aggarwal, Jain, and Narayanan (2017) considered the case of Karnataka's experience with the implementation of e-NAM and pushing other reforms in the agricultural sector, recommended that "rules of the game", "incentives for agents to participate actively in the market" and "infrastructure" could be three pillars for pushing reforms in the agricultural sector of India.

3.2 Studies Conducted in Uttar Pradesh

Tewari et al. (2017) tried to investigate the farmers' experience towards the modern agricultural marketing system and consumers' perception concerning the modern organized retail system. Based on a survey conducted with 140 farmers, 20 traders, and 20 consumers from three districts of Uttar Pradesh the authors identified that most farmers were not pleased with the marketing practices in regulated markets whereas the consumers were happy with the modern organized retail system. The study also revealed that the major constraints with the adoption of the e-NAM initiative were the lack of infrastructure, computer incompetency, and unified licensing. Katoch and Singh (2021) tried to explore the effect of improving market integration and recent marketing reforms viz. implementation of GST and e-NAM wheat crops. They concluded that prices of wheat crops from different markets of Uttar Pradesh (viz Agra, Aligarh, Prayagraj, Bulandshahr, and Kanpur) moved simultaneously in the positive direction and were well integrated.

3.3 Studies Conducted in Haryana

Sekhar and Bhatt (2018) did systematic research on the functioning of e-NAMs in Haryana keeping five objectives in mind. Based on the analysis they concluded that the sale process via e-NAM could be improved by providing the proper infrastructure for sorting and grading, developing a proper refrigeration facility, and reducing delays in online transactions.

3.4 Studies Conducted in Madhya Pradesh

Mishra and Rathore (2020) examined the proper accessibility of infrastructural facilities and innovative agricultural marketing practices in the adoption of e-NAM in the Bundelkhand Region of Madhya Pradesh. The study revealed that the common hindrances towards the adoption of e-NAM by the farmers were due to *"computer illiteracy, lack of interest, lack of computer facility, lack of time, costly technology, and illiteracy"*.

3.5 Studies Conducted in Kerala

Nair (2021) examined the structural and functional dimensions of the agriculture marketing institutions in Kerala emphasizing the existing marketing infrastructure and identifying the improvement areas by taking the opinion of multi-stakeholders. The author advocated well-organized marketing infrastructure facilities at all stages of the supply chain for the future development of agriculture intending to provide food self-sufficiency and security along with sustainable income generation for farmers.

3.6 Studies Conducted in Andhra Pradesh

Singh and Alagawadi (2021) did a study to explore the awareness of farmers and traders towards the benefit of adopting e-NAM platforms using sample data from three selected mandis in Andhra Pradesh. The authors identified that educational qualification and age are the two important variables that have a strong association with awareness of e-NAM platforms. The authors concluded that creating awareness and familiarization with the benefit of e-NAM can certainly increase the adoption of e-NAM among farmers and traders.

3.6 Studies Conducted in Rajasthan

Jirli and Saini (2021) tried to evaluate the issues related to the difference in price received in the traditional market and e-NAM platform using data from two districts of Rajasthan. The authors concluded that the use of the e-NAM platform could avoid price discrimination among the farmers and the e-NAM platform can provide price trends, arrival, trading activities & forecast online, and levies market fees at a single point. This information can help the framers and the traders to take decisions based on the actual demand & supply of the commodity. Kumar, Pant, and Chandra (2019) in their report made a detailed study on the effect of e-NAM on the price received by the farmers; the perception of operation and execution, and the advantages of e-NAM. Based on the analysis authors suggested sensitization approaches to make different stakeholders aware of e-NAM platforms.

3.7 Other Studies

Kalamkar, Ahir & Bhaiya (2019) in their report suggested some of the important benefits of e-NAM to farmers and *"vis-à-vis agriculture market as real-time price discovery, transparency in the agriculture marketing system, reduction in the transaction costs of buyers and sellers, real-time information on prices, market arrivals, bidding on quality parameters of commodities, online bidding for more transparency, online payment system to reduce the payment, etc"*. Though the authors have discussed several benefits of the e-NAM portal in their report, they also stated that the awareness level among the farmers for the e-NAM portal is very limited. Bhargav (2017) studied the challenges associated with agricultural marketing and the initiatives taken by GoI to overcome these problems to increase the earnings of rural farmers. The author identified that GoI had initiated several schemes and programs to improve agricultural marketing in rural India, viz Pradhan Mantri Krishi Sinchaee Yojana (PMKSY), Grameen Bhandaran Yojana (Rural Godown Scheme), Soil Health Card Scheme, Pradhan Mantri Fasal Bima Yojna, India emergence campaign through village emergence, National Agriculture Market (e-NAM), My Village My Pride, A Scheme for Promotion of Innovation, Rural Industry and Entrepreneurship (ASPIRE), NavKalpana Kosh, etc. However, the author also argued that these schemes would remain ineffective if a proper channel was not devised to move agricultural produce from the farmers to the consumers at a reasonable price and with very less interventions.

Gupta and Badal (2018) discussed challenges in the implementation of eNAM in terms of Infrastructure, Institution, and Information and concluded that responsiveness, inclusiveness, and technology-enabled markets can help to increase the adoption of e-NAM. This will have a positive influence on the livelihood and food security of India. Kathuria, Singh, and Raina (2019) examined whether market reforms could influence the opinion of commission agents and observed that largely the commission agents had a negative or neutral opinion on the current agricultural marketing reforms. The authors concluded that this negative opinion might be built due to a lack of awareness or partial awareness towards the change or reform. Reddy and Mehjabeen (2019) observed that the potential of the e-NAMs platform in different marketplaces was not fully utilized due to issues related to the evaluation of the produce and unfamiliarity on the part of farmers and traders with the usage of the platform. They identified a positive relationship between prices obtained by the farmers and an increase in market arrivals in the e-NAM.

Singh, Pant, and Sathyendra (2020) in their report "Performance Evaluation of e-National Agriculture Market" made an extensive study to assess the status of e-NAM implementation on several dimensions viz technology adoption, operation, and infrastructure creation. They recommended urgent requirements to improve the infrastructure facility related to e-NAM, installation of POS machine facility in different mandis, human resource development in the areas of IT, installation of electronic weighing machine/bridge facility, etc. Chaudhary and Suri (2021a) developed an e-trading adoption framework for agricultural marketing in India using the Neural Network method. Based on the review of the scholarly articles they identified eight constructs viz *"price, transaction cycle, easy to use, infrastructure, customer care, social influence, trust, and cost"* that plays important role in the adoption framework. They concluded that the digital eNAM e-trading platform could be one of the important initiatives by the GoI aimed at doubling the farmers' income.

Levi et al. (2020) tried to assess the influence of the implementation of the Unified Market Platform (UMP) on market prices and farmers' profitability. They argued that the success of UMP in the Indian agricultural market depended on the necessary infrastructure that could integrate remote Agri-markets through systemic supply chain logistics and process design. Kumar et al. (2020) made an extensive study to understand the facilities and awareness of

APMC mandi in adopting the e-NAM. They reported some ambiguities in the effective implementation of e-NAM e.g. skipping of quality testing during peak marketing seasons making the reliability of the grading system highly questionable. Chaudhary and Suri (2021b) ranked *"Trust", "Cost", "Perceived Ease of Use", and "Facilitating Conditions"* respectively are the four important factors that influence e-trading in India and concluded that special emphasis should be given to these four factors to strengthen and increase the adoption of eNAM.

In another study, Chaudhary and Suri (2022) identified *"perceived ease of use, facilitating conditions, social influence, and lower cost"* as the most significant enablers along with trust and perceived usefulness. Based on the analysis the authors recommended that the GoI should give enough importance to these enablers to improve the supply chain of agricultural produce and thereby enhance the adoption of the e-NAM platform.

4. Challenges in the Adoption of the e-NAM

The e-NAM helps farmers to trade directly on their own through the mobile app or registered commission agents. However, the adoption of the e-NAM among farmers is not quite satisfactory. Some reports have suggested that contrary to the claims by the Government, most of the transactions recorded on e-NAM were conducted through the old system. The actual gain to the farmers through the use of this facility is questioned by some researchers. Others have suggested that the e-NAM has not been able to solve issues related to market fragmentation, multi-level taxation, and license issues in APMCs. Vilification of traders and middlemen may have added one more hurdle to the actual wide-scale implementation of the e-NAM. Low digital illiteracy in rural areas and limited internet connections have also increased the challenge to its adoption. Besides these, there are practical issues related to assaying and transportation, despite the government's initiatives to solve these problems (e.g. Kisan Rath). A simple look at the downloads of the e-NAM app across Google Playstore and Apple's Appstore reveals that the numbers are minuscule. A report published in 2019 noted that less than 15% of the farmers were using the e-NAM facility till then (BusinessLine, 2019).

5. Conclusion

Although the e-NAM has a lot of potentials to change the scenario of the agricultural products market in India, the government needs to work on increasing its awareness among farmers, provide uninterrupted and low-cost Internet connectivity in markets, ensure access to computers and mobile devices, develop easy-to-use mobile apps for traders and commission agents, set up help desks through public-private partnership (PPP) mode, skill up-gradation for market functionaries, alleviate the fear of taxation among traders and commission agents and solve conflicts of interest among different stakeholders. Competent authorities should organize capacity-building programs for the farmers and create suitable infrastructure to attract the attention of stakeholders of the agricultural marketing system. The implementation of the e-NAM platform could only achieve its desired goal if GoI identified and provided the solutions to each stakeholder's problems to increase the adoption of e-NAM across all the stakeholders.

6. Acknowledgment

This research is supported by the Ch. Charan Singh National Institute Of Agricultural Marketing (CCSNIAM/Research Project /2021-22).

REFERENCES

1. Aggarwal, N., Jain, S., & Narayanan, S. (2017). The long road to transformation of agricultural markets in India: Lessons from Karnataka. *Economic and Political Weekly*, 52(41), 47–55.
2. Bachaspati S and H Pathak. (2018). Impact of e-NAM on arrival and prices of major commodities: a case study of Bhatapara APMC in Chhattisgarh. Journal of Pharmacognosy and Phytochemistry, 27(4): 3301–3304.
3. Bhargav, S. (2017). Agricultural Marketing in Growth of Rural India. *International Journal of Management, IT & Engineering*, 7(7), 306–319.
4. BusinessLine. (2019,. July 10). Just 14% of farmers registered on eNAM platform. Retrieved from www.thehindubusinessline.com: https://www.thehindubusinessline.com/economy/agribusiness/just-14-of-farmers-registered-on-enam-platform/article28363454.ece
5. Chand, R. (2012). Development policies and agricultural markets. *Economic and Political Weekly*, 47(52), 53–63.
6. Chaudhary, S., & Suri, P. K. (2021b). Ranking the factors influencing e-trading usage in agricultural marketing. Global Journal of Flexible Systems Management, 22(3), 233–249.
7. Chaudhary, S., & Suri, P. K. (2022). Modelling the enablers of e-trading adoption in agricultural marketing: A TISM-based analysis of eNAM. Vision, 26(1), 65–79.
8. Gupta, S., & Badal, P. S. (2018). E-national Agricultural Market (e-NAM) in India: A Review. BHU Management Review, 6(1), 48–57.
9. Jirli, B., & Saini, S. (2021). Can India become Atmanirbhar without e-Mediation in agricultural education. *J. Farm Sci.*, 34(5), 470–475.
10. Kalamkar, S. S., Ahir, K., & Bhaiya, S. R. (2019). Electronic National Agricultural Market (eNAM) in Gujarat: Review of Performance and Prospects (https://www.spuvvn.edu/academic_centres/agro_economic_centre/research_studies/177_Electronic_National_Agricultural_Market_(eNAM)_in_Gujarat.pdf)
11. Kathuria, K., Singh, K., & Raina, K. K. (2019). Agriculture marketing reforms in India, relationship between awareness and attitude of commission agents in APMC Mansa (Punjab). *Journal of Pharmacognosy and Phytochemistry*, 8(5), 93–98.
12. Katoch, S., & Singh, R. (2021). Price dynamics and market integration of wheat markets in Uttar Pradesh. Indian Journal of Agricultural Marketing, 35(1), 196–203.
13. Kumar, A D Sathyendra, Pant, Satish Chandra and Chandra, Ravi Kumar (2019). *Performance of eNAM in Rajasthan –A CASE STUDY*. Published By: CCS National Institute Of Agricultural Marketing.
14. Kumar, R, S Kumar, P C Meena, B G Kumar and N Sivaramane (2020). *Strengthening E-NAM in India: way forward*. ICAR-National Academy of Agricultural Research Management, Hyderabad, India. pp 1–119. https://naarm.org.in/wp-content/uploads/2021/07/2020_eNAM_Report.pdf
15. Levi, R., Rajan, M., Singhvi, S., & Zheng, Y. (2020). The impact of unifying agricultural wholesale markets on prices and farmers' profitability. *Proceedings of the National Academy of Sciences*, 117(5), 2366–2371.
16. Mishra, A., & Rathore, V. K. (2020). Analysis of Impact of eNAM on the stakeholders of Tikamgarh Region, Madhya Pradesh. *JNKVV Research Journal*, 54(1-3), 11–19.

17. Nair, Manju S (2021). A Collaborative Study on Agriculture Marketing Infrastructure In Kerala Centre For Agroecology And Public Health Department Of Economics University Of Kerala. *Nabard Research Study* – 12. (https://www.nabard.org/auth/writereaddata/tender/0906211304NRS-12-Agri-Market%20Infrastructure%20in%20Kerala.pdf)

18. Nuthalapati, C. S. R., Bhatt, Y., & Beero, S. K. (2020). *Electronic National Agricultural Market (e-NAM) A Review of Performance and Prospects*. Research Study Report Submitted to the Ministry of Agriculture and Farmers' Welfare, Government of India, New Delhi.

19. Patnaik, G. (2011, November). Status of agricultural marketing reforms. In workshop on *Policy Options and Investment Priorities for Accelerating Agricultural Productivity and Development in India*, New Delhi, India.

20. Pavithra, S., Gracy, C. P., Saxena, R., & Patil, G. G. (2018). Innovations in agricultural marketing: a case study of e-tendering system in Karnataka, India. *Agricultural Economics Research Review*, 31, 53–64.

21. Reddy, A. A. (2018). Electronic national agricultural markets. *Current Science*, 115(5), 826–837.

22. Reddy, A. A., & Mehjabeen. (2019). Electronic National Agricultural Markets, Impacts, Problems and Way Forward. IIM Kozhikode Society & Management Review, 8(2), 143–155.

23. Sekhar, C. S. C., & Bhatt, Y. (2018). *Electronic national agricultural market (e-NAM): a review of performance and prospects in Haryana*. Agricultural Economics Research Centre, University of Delhi, Delhi. http://du. ac. in/du/uploads/C entre/Report_Final_AERC_Delhi_eNAM-2018. pdf.

24. Singh, N. K., & Alagawadi, M. (2021). Awareness Of Farmers and Traders Towards Benefits Of Electronic National Agriculture Market (E-Nam). *J. Res. ANGRAU* 49 (2) 119–125.

25. Singh, S.R., Pant, Chandra, Satish and Sathyendra, A D (2020). Performance Evaluation of e-National Agriculture Market. Published By: CCS National Institute of Agricultural Marketing.

26. Sharma, M. (2021). *The future of Indian agriculture. Down to earth* (https://www.downtoearth.org.in/blog/agriculture/the-future-of-indian-agriculture-75384).

27. Tewari, H., Singh, R., Singh, O. P., Rani, R., & Agarwal, P. (2017). A Study on Stakeholder's Perception on Present and New Marketing Systems and Price Information in Uttar Pradesh. *Trends in Biosciences* 10(11), 2015–2019.

28. Vadivelu, A., & Kiran, B. R. (2013). Problems and prospects of agricultural marketing in India: An overview. International journal of agricultural and food science, 3(3), 108–118.

29. Venkatesh, P., Singh, D. R., Balasubramian, M., & Jha, G. K. (2021). The changing structure of agricultural marketing in India: a state-level analysis of e-NAM. Agricultural Economics Research Review, 34 (Conference Number), 97–109.

Chapter

Agro-tourism: A Literature Review

Praveen Goyal[1], Saurabh Chadha[2]
Department of Management,
Birla Institute of Technology & Science, Pilani

S. R. Singh[3]
Chaudhary Charan Singh National Institute of Agricultural Marketing

ABSTRACT: For many centuries, the agricultural sector has been considered an important sector of the economy. Over a while, the contribution of this sector to economic growth has declined for various reasons. These reasons include rapid industrialization, migration to the urban areas, more focus on white-collar jobs, and a decline in agricultural land resulting in the downfall in the farmer's income. Governments across the globe, in general, and especially in developing economies, are exploring various ways to increase the income of rural households.

Agro-tourism has emerged as an important way to increase farmers' income globally. Governments are implementing various policies to promote agro-tourism activities. In recent years, this concept has captured the interest of scholars, practitioners, and policymakers and further resulted in the growth of research in this field. This study presents a review of the literature in the field of agro-tourism. The literature for the study was collected from the Scopus database using specific keywords. Research studies published in the last 20 years were collected for the review. The study results show a significant growth in the literature in the field of agro-tourism across the globe.

KEYWORDS: Agro-tourism, Literature review

1. Introduction

In the last few decades, rural tourism has emerged as one of the areas which captured the attention of policymakers, and scholars, which can help in achieving the objective of increasing

[1]praveen.goyal@pilani.bits-pilani.ac.in, [2]saurabh.chadha@pilani.bits-pilani.ac.in, [3]sattramsingh@gmail.com

DOI: 10.4324/9781003415725-44

the income in rural areas. Agro-tourism has emerged as an area to achieve this objective. These activities help farmers by diversifying their business and, on the other hand educating tourists about various farm-related activities (Colton & Bissix, 2005). Agro-tourism is part of rural tourism (Phillip et al., 2010). Agro/Agri tourism is defined as expanding and opening agricultural activities as tourism spots for visitors from different places. It is also considered a diversification of core agricultural work. "In *the agri-tourism sector, diversification is shown through the presence of recreational and cultural services (e.g., hospitality, catering) and the preservation and enhancement of the territory (e.g., direct sales, birdwatching)*" (Giaccio et al., 2018, p. 217).

In recent years, agrotourism has captured the attention of scholars, practitioners, and policymakers. According to Weaver and Fennell (1997), agrotourism includes a tourism component along with regular agricultural activities. Further, Arroyo et al. (2013) proposed the usage of agri-activities for entertainment and education. Flanigan et al. (2010) characterize agri-tourism on three parameters. These parameters are defined as visitor-agriculture interaction, visitor experience on the farm, and realistic functioning agricultural activities. Paul and Patil (2022) study the understanding of sustainable agrotourism by converting traditional agricultural land into a smart tourist destination. Upadhye and Shingare (2021) study various practices Agrotourism farms apply to retain their customers. Trung and Tharu (2021) recognize the significance of promoting and protecting agricultural lifestyle values in agro-tourism activities in the Vietnamese context. Shinde (2021) argues in favor of agrotourism as an essential prospect for farmers' growth in the Pune region of India. Pujiasmanto et al. (2021) explore an opportunity to develop agro-tourism using agricultural resources. The research identifies various supporting factors to promote community-based organic tourism attractions.

There has been a significant growth of literature in the field of agro-tourism across the globe. The following section presents critical studies in the last 20 years to understand the various trends in this field.

Nowers et al. (2002) used a mixed method approach to find modus operandi, problems, and achievements that can help people establish a similar route. Their findings suggest appointing a skilled and knowledgeable PR officer or manager. There is a need to make policies and strategies that are needed to make the linkage between the wine and tourism industries. These two industries complement each other well and can become base of a healthy rural economy.

Loureiro et al. (2005) studied Norway to assess farmers' role in adopting agro-tourist activities. Two types of activities are famous in rural tourism, i.e., license for fishing and rights for hunting; second is renting rooms on the farm and selling food to tourists or travelers. Results show that the farm's size and location play a vital role in deciding agro-tourism activities in a particular farm. Further, social demographics, like the female partner's presence and the age of the primary farm operator, have a crucial role in adopting various tourism activities on the farm.

Marques (2006) discuss the role of agritourism in rural areas as a tool for upliftment by using cultural values and nature. Data was collected through interviews. The findings show that tourism helps people market their products, preserve their heritage, and also helps in developing human and physical capital in rural areas that need to catch up.

Veeck (2006) studied the factors associated with the successful operations of agricultural tourism. The interest in this area has grown. People living in rural and looking for new economic activities and increasing their income through sales. People visit farms for various purposes such as purchase, enjoyment, education, etc.

Mcgehee et al. (2004) again has done a quantitative study to explore the prospective differences in motivations for agritourism entrepreneurship between genders. Data was analysed using statistical tools. Analysis shows that men and women show similar characteristics in agritourism as both want to look for multiple sources of income, make optimum use of available resources, and believe in enhancing the customer's knowledge. The difference is that women show a much higher ranking for all positive motivation than men. The study finds that motivation level of female is high to develop agri-tourism facilities as business ventures than their male counterparts. The study further suggests that to have a better and more generalized understanding; more studies need to be conducted.

Kline et al. (2007) say that people use Agritourism to conserve family farms, increase revenue, teach people about farming life, etc. The farmers should know about the new product, and they should explore, evaluate, and also be educated about the product.

Burrows et al. (2007) discusses the linkage between agricultural enterprise and regional artist and create a mass attraction. This article is the best example of partnership between all stakeholders; it also highlights the issues and steps taken by participants so that there will be continuous development in the state.

Barbieri et al. (2008) investigate the firm's and owner's characteristics' effect on the overall income of agritourism farms. The data for the study was collected using an internet-based survey method, and collected data were further analyzed using different quantitative techniques. The study's findings show that the age of business, the number of workers, and farm estate positively affect farm's performance by increasing the yearly sale.

Carpio et al. (2008) have used quantitative methods to find the factors responsible for American visitors and estimate the rural landscape's economic value. The study found that on average, a person takes 10.3 trips in a year, and the estimated surplus for one trip is 174.82dollar out of which 83.50 dollars is due to the rural landscape. Although there is a need to do scrutiny as something important is happening regarding economic valuation.

Shen et al. (2009) have studied the agro-tourism sustainability from the perspective of rural families. A survey method was used. Data was collected in the year 2003. People's perceptions of sustainability were measured on 4 aspects: economic, social, environmental, and institutional.

Chatzigeorgiou et al. (2009) used emotions, expectations, and satisfaction to study the association between complete customer satisfaction and customer re-purchase. Data were collected using the survey method. The study's findings show that emotions are of two types positive and negative. If a person has positive emotions, then the person's response to the product will also be positive. We cannot generalize the findings of this research as data was collected from only two businesses (inland and mountain). There is a need to do research in other areas and lodgings for a broader perspective.

Srikatanyoo and Campiranon (2010) did a quantitative study to find the need and motivation factors for Agritourism in Thailand. Data was collected from people who stayed in the accommodation.

Phillip et al. (2010) have tried identifying and providing specific and essential characteristics to define agritourism. They have also covered a list of definitions that are mentioned in the literature. The authors have identified five types of agritourism typology based on three discriminators.

Hashimoto and Telfer (2010) discuss the issues of creating sustainable collaborations for agritourism in various agrarian destinations, such as a landscapes exhibition, indigenous tourism resorts, resorts & spas, and each initiative as farm owners' markets. According to continued fieldwork research conducted from 2003, there are substantial obstacles to building lasting partnerships inside and between programs/attractions, such as a lack of cohesion, divergent perspectives on tourism-related initiatives, and different social responsibilities. These must be acknowledged if economic growth should be effectively revitalized and repositioned around Agritourism.

Tew and Barbieri (2011) focus on examining agritourism benefits. A survey of 164 Missouri agritourism properties yielded the following information. Results indicated that Agritourism primarily helps attract new farm consumers, educate the masses about farming, and improve local farmer families' well-being, reflecting financial and nonfinancial advantages. Organized by goal aspects, the results revealed that Agritourism should not always be judged as greater profitability but also as a tool to promote farming activities.

Yang L. (2012) analyzes the influence of Agritourism on an indigenous group and addresses the obstacles encountered by locals wanting to enhance their lives via ecotourism in light of its growing relevance for both industrialized and developing nations. The study used qualitative research methods for a sample of homes, revealing favorable economic and social outcomes. In addition to providing a supplemental income and new job prospects for the rural population, Agritourism, however, has improved environmental preservation and understanding of minority cultures as well as remote livelihood.

Barbieri (2013) evaluated economic, social, and ecological sustainability indices across agritourism fields versus fields with other diversified operations. 873 usable responses that satisfied the study's requirements were collected via an online questionnaire in the last quarter of 2005. The result shows that Agritourism seems much more ecological. Agritourism generated much greater operating profits for the farm, which should explain better family incomes, despite a more significant payroll, than their competitors.

Asciuto et al. (2013) reviewed the agritourism availability in Sicily land endowments and identified the ecological and sustainability elements likely to influence business performance. Evidence gathered via provincial statistics reports was complemented with qualitative data from interactions with a random sample of agritourist businesses operating in various rural regions of Sicily. Finding provides evidence that widespread Agritourism in Italy gives major financial assistance to agricultural businesses and even the tourism industry, moving visitor flows beyond coastal to interior locations.

Ammirato and Felicetti (2014) examined the feasibility of agritourism as a tool for inclusive growth. To achieve this objective, the researcher provides the results of an exploratory survey conducted in 2012 in the Italian area of Calabria on a sample of 52 farms performing agritourism initiatives. The study attempts to determine role of agritourism to the environmental sustainability of a remote town that serves as the core of an "agritourism rural network."

Schilling et al. (2014) examined the impact of agritourism on the net capital revenue of each hectare of New Jersey farms. According to the findings, agritourism has statically meaningful and favorable benefits on farm profitability. In furtherance, Profit implications are greatest with small farmlands run by persons whose primary occupation is farming, while leisure fields see a favorable but lower effect. The impact of farm size on profits was not conclusive.

Choo and Petrick (2013) scrutinize the fundamental resource theory-derived conceptual link between agritourists' social relationships and fulfillment. Additionally, the research investigates agritourists' responses to getting specific vs. broader resources through service providers. The study's findings show that specific resources shared during agritourism interactions add more pleasure than standardized resources. Consequently, agritourism service providers must prioritize resource exchange alongside respective agritourists and clients. Instead of only being incentives, universal resources, such as monetary discounts or special pricing, must be tailored to express personal care and care to each consumer.

Fernández et. al. (2016) segments regional ecotourism in La Palma, Canary Islands, using a cluster analysis. They evaluate the degree of visitors' environmental sentiments as an explanatory variable for customer segmentation. The findings indicate that market categories are pretty heterogeneous and that conventional rural tourism comprises a tiny portion of the entire market. Rural tourism destinations may strengthen their economic health by concentrating on such sectors that attract visitors with the environmental issue and by enacting regulations that boost the sustainability performance among those areas.

Liang A (2017) embraced the notion of service-dominant logic and developed a conceptual framework to aid entrepreneurs in planning agritourism services that would improve the tourists' perspective among four small farm field trials. Findings indicate that rural culture and tourists' reciprocal interaction were essential for agribusiness to incorporate the particular features of internal service delivery. Further author believes that Agritourism programs must assist visitors in gaining agricultural information via a pleasurable and engaging experience, laying the groundwork for value co-creation.

2. Conclusion

The study presents that there is significant evidence of growth in the literature of agro-tourism in different countries. Agro-tourism has emerged as an essential part of tourism, significantly increasing rural households' income. These advantages of agro-tourism have also captured the attention of policymakers in different parts of the globe. The present reviews provide how effectively this concept has been studied in different countries. The findings suggest that ago-tourism is mainly studied in the context of developed economies. The studies in the case of developing economies where a large population depends on agriculture as the primary source of income require more attention. In order to explore the impact of agro-tourism in developing economies more studies need to be conducted in the context of emerging economies. These studies will help different stakeholders to understand the importance of agro-tourism. The farmers will be more interested in agro-tourism activities, and policymakers will make suitable policies to encourage these activities.

3. Acknowledgment

This research is supported by the Ch. Charan Singh National Institute of Agricultural Marketing (CCSNIAM/Research Project /2021-22).

REFERENCES

1. Ammirato, S., & Felicetti, A. M. (2014). The Agritourism as a means of sustainable development for rural communities: a research from the field. *The International Journal of Interdisciplinary Environmental Studies*, 8(1), 17–29.
2. Arroyo, C. G., Barbieri, C., & Rich, S. R. (2013). Defining Agritourism: A comparative study of stakeholders' perceptions in Missouri and North Carolina. *Tourism Management*, 37, 39–47.
3. Asciuto, A., Di Franco, C.P. and Schimmenti, E., 2013. An exploratory study of sustainable rural tourism in Sicily. International Journal of Business and Globalisation, 11(2), pp.149–158
4. Barbieri, C. (2013). Assessing the sustainability of Agritourism in the US: A comparison between Agritourism and other farm entrepreneurial ventures. *Journal of Sustainable Tourism*, 21(2), 252–270
5. Barbieri, C. and Mshenga, P.M., 2008. The role of the firm and owner characteristics on the performance of agritourism farms. *Sociologia ruralis*, 48(2), pp.166–183.
6. Burrows, R., Fennell, A., Redlin, M. and Verschoor, L., 2007. Agri-cultural tourism: linking the arts and humanities with agricultural direct marketers and specialty producers. *Journal of Extension*, 45(6).
7. Carpio, C.E., Wohlgenant, M.K. and Boonsaeng, T., 2008. The demand for agritourism in the United States. *Journal of Agricultural and Resource Economics*, pp. 254–269.
8. Chatzigeorgiou, C., Christou, E., Kassianidis, P. and Sigala, M., 2009. Examining the relationship between emotions, customer satisfaction and future behavioural intentions in agrotourism.
9. Choo, H., & Petrick, J. F. (2013). Resource exchanges for agritourism service encounters. *Journal of Hospitality Marketing & Management*, 22(7), 770–780.
10. Fernández-Hernández, C., Leon, C. J., Arana, J. E., & Díaz-Pére, F. (2016). Market segmentation, activities and environmental behaviour in rural tourism. *Tourism Economics*, 22(5), 1033–1054.
11. Flanigan Hashimoto, A. & Telfer, D. J. (2010) Developing sustainable partnerships in rural tourism: the case of Oita, Japan, Journal of Policy Research in Tourism, Leisure and Events, 2:2, 165–183,
12. Giaccio, V., Giannelli, A., & Mastronardi, L. (2018). Explaining determinants of agri-tourism income: Evidence from Italy. *Tourism Review*.
13. Hashimoto, A., & Telfer, D. J. (2010). Developing sustainable partnerships in rural tourism: The case of Oita, Japan. Journal of Policy Research in Tourism, Leisure and Events, 2(2), 165–183.
14. Henderson, J.C., 2009. Agro-tourism in unlikely destinations: A study of Singapore. *Managing Leisure*, 14(4), pp. 258–268.
15. Kline, C., Cardenas, D., Leung, Y.F. and Sanders, S., 2007. Sustainable farm tourism: Understanding and managing environmental impacts of visitor activities. *Journal of Extension*, 45(2), pp. 1–4.

16. Li Yang (2012) Impacts and Challenges in Agritourism Development in Yunnan, China, Tourism Planning & Development, 9:4, 369–381.
17. Liang, A. R. (2017), Considering the role of agritourism co-creation from a service-dominant logic perspective, Tourism Management, 61 (2017), pp. 354–367
18. Loureiro, M.L. and Jervell, A.M., 2005. Farmers' participation decisions regarding agro-tourism activities in Norway. *Tourism economics*, *11*(3), pp. 453–469.
19. Marques, H., 2006. Searching for complementarities between agriculture and tourism—the demarcated wine-producing regions of northern   Portugal. *Tourism economics*, *12*(1), pp. 147–155.
20. McGehee, N. G., & Kim, K. (2004). Motivation for agri-tourism entrepreneurship. *Journal of travel research*, *43*(2), 161–170.
21. Nowers, R., de Villiers, E. and Myburgh, A., 2002. Agricultural theme routes as a diversification strategy: the Western Cape wine routes case study. *Agrekon*, *41*(2), pp. 195–209
22. Paul, T., & Patil, A. (2022). Sustainable Agro Tourism: A Case Study of "Farm of Happiness". *International Journal of Risk and Contingency Management (IJRCM)*, *11*(1), 1–11.
23. Phillip, S., Hunter, C. and Blackstock, K., 2010. A typology for defining Agritourism. *Tourism management*, *31*(6), pp. 754–758
24. Schilling, Brian J. & Attavanich, Witsanu & Jin, Yanhong, 2014. "Does Agritourism Enhance Farm Profitability?," Journal of Agricultural and Resource Economics, Western Agricultural Economics Association, vol. 39(1), pp. 1–28, April.
25. Shen, F., Cottrell, S.P., Hughey, K.F. and Morrison, K., 2009. Agritourism sustainability in rural mountain areas of China: A community perspective. *International Journal of Business and Globalisation*, *3*(2), pp. 123–145
26. Shinde, R. (2021). Agrotourism: Avenue for Rural Areas with Special Reference To Pune Region. Turkish Journal of Computer and Mathematics Education (TURCOMAT), 12(12), 3558–3565.
27. Srikatanyoo, N., & Campiranon, K. (2010). Agritourist needs and motivations: The Chiang Mai case. *Journal of Travel & Tourism Marketing*, *27*(2), 166–178.
28. Tew, C., & Barbieri, C. (2012). The perceived benefits of agritourism: The provider's perspective. *Tourism management*, *33*(1), 215–224.
29. Upadhye, N., & Shingare, D. (2021). Best Practices implemented by Agro tourism Farms in the Era of pandemic to retain the customers
30. Van Trung, H., & Tharu, D. (2021). Exploitation and Preservation Agricultural Way of Life for Agro-Tourism Development, A Case Study at Tra Que Village, Quang Nam Province, Vietnam
31. Veeck, G., Che, D., & Veeck, A. (2006). America's changing farmscape: A study of agricultural tourism in Michigan. *The professional geographer*, *58*(3), 235–248.
32. Weaver, D. B., & Fennell, D. A. (1997). The vacation farm sector in Saskatchewan: A profile of operations. *Tourism Management*, *18*(6), 357–365.

Chapter

45

Performance of Farmer Producer Organisations in Rajasthan: An Empirical Assessment

Krishna Muniyoor[1]

Associate Professor, Department of Economics and Finance,
BITS Pilani, Pilani Campus, Jhunjhunu, India

Sabhya Yadav*

Research Associate, Department of Economics and Finance,
BITS Pilani, Pilani Campus, Jhunjhunu, India

Rajan Pandey[2]

Assistant Professor, Department of Economics and Finance,
BITS Pilani, Pilani Campus, Jhunjhunu, India.

Satyendra Kumar Sharma[3]

Associate Professor, Department of Management,
BITS Pilani, Pilani Campus, Jhunjhunu, India.

Srikanta Routroy[4]

Professor, Department of Mechanical Engineering,
BITS Pilani, Pilani Campus, Jhunjhunu, India

ABSTRACT: India is predominantly an agrarian economy. According to the recent Economic Survey (2021-22), agriculture and allied sectors continue to be the mainstay of the Indian economy as it is the largest employer of the working population and contributes about 19 to the total gross value added of the country in 2021-22. Unlike the agriculture system in Western Europe, Indian agriculture is dominated mainly by small and marginal farmers, accounting for more than four-fifths of the total landholding size. More recently, due to government intervention, many strategies, including agri-business models, have been developed to tackle

*Corresponding Author: sabhya.yadav@pilani.bits-pilani.ac.in
[1]krishna@pilani.bits-pilani.ac.in, [2]rajanpandey@pilani.bits-pilani.ac.in, [3]satyendrasharma@pilani.bits-pilani.ac.in, [4]srikanta@pilani.bits-pilani.ac.in

DOI: 10.4324/9781003415725-45

the marginalisation of farmers by bringing them under one umbrella. With the recommendation of a committee headed by YK Alagh, the formation of Farmer Producer Organisations (FPOs) has become a reality by incorporating a special provision in part IXA of the Companies Act, 1956. In this context, our attempt in this paper is to evaluate the financial performance of FPOs registered in Rajasthan.

KEYWORDS: Agriculture, FPO, Asset-turnover, Investment, Rajasthan

1. Introduction

India is predominantly an agrarian economy. According to the recent Economic Survey (2021–22), agriculture and allied sectors continue to be the mainstay of the Indian economy as it is the largest employer of the working population and contributes about 19 to the total gross value added of the country in 2021-22. Unlike the agriculture system in Western Europe, Indian agriculture is dominated mainly by small and marginal farmers, accounting for more than four-fifths of the total landholding size. Notably, small and marginal farmer are increasingly being excluded from the benefits of government welfare schemes that inadvertently support and favours large and medium farmers (Singh and Vatta 2019; Verma et al., 2019; Thamban et al., 2020; Rafi, 2020). For instance, we can clearly distinguish between large and small farmers regarding market imperfections, such as access to credit, technological knowledge, and labour resources. As a result of this disparity and the small size of the land holding, the yield per land continues to be lower for small and marginal farmers, who are unlikely to experience economies of scale.

As a step forward, the government initiated forming cooperative societies, which brought about promising avenues in the lives of small and marginal farmers. However, the formation of cooperative societies has increasingly become insufficient because of constraints such as the lack of adequate skills and knowledge of farmers, lack of financial resources, inadequate infrastructure, and lack of awareness. More recently, due to government intervention, many strategies, including agri-business models, have been developed to tackle the marginalisation of farmers by bringing them under one umbrella. With the recommendation of a committee headed by YK Alagh, the formation of Farmer Producer Organisations (FPOs) has become a reality by incorporating a special provision in part IXA of the Companies Act, 1956.

With the special provisions of the Companies Act 1956, India has recorded a movement towards forming FPOs across states, including Rajasthan, the largest state, accounting for 10.5 per cent of the total geographical area of the country. Over the last decade, FPOs have played an instrumental role in enhancing agricultural activities, mainly farm income and output. Moreover, FPOs have gained substantial momentum primarily due to the pecuniary and non-pecuniary support from implanting agencies such as the National Bank for Agriculture and Rural Development (NABARD), Small Farmers' Agri-Business Consortium (SFAC), and other government schemes and institutions. As per the available records, India has over 17000 registered FPOs and more than 250 registered FPOs in Rajasthan. It is estimated that about 1.5 lakh farmers have benefited from functioning FPOs. The main agricultural and business activities undertaken by FPOs include input sales, procurement, marketing, and arranging credit facilities. Besides bringing a wide range of opportunities, the proliferation of FPOs has raised several challenges, including connecting the FPOs to reliable and affordable sources of financing, access to the market, basic infrastructure, and regulatory issues.

Given this backdrop, the main objective of this paper is to examine the performance of FPOs in Rajasthan. Using Data Envelopment Analysis (DEA), we assess the performance of 28 registered FPOs in Rajasthan. The remainder of this paper is structured as follows. Section 2 presents a description of the FPOs in India in General and Rajasthan in particular, followed by a brief literature review. Data sources and methodology is explained in section 4, and the results are presented in the next section. As usual, the last section offers the discussion and concluding remarks.

2. Background

One of the main objectives of forming FPOs is to enhance agricultural output and improve the bargaining power of small and marginal farmers by collectively organising them. The intervention of FPOs is expected to facilitate a lucrative market price, a reduction in the overall cost of cultivation, and sustainable and long-term growth of agriculture (Tagat and Tagat 2016; Manaswi et al., 2018; Kumar et al., 2018). It aids farmers in adopting new technology sources and providing services such as purchasing farm inputs like seed, fertiliser, pesticides and equipments and supplying them to member farmers at a reasonable cost. FPOs also play a fundamental role in aggregating all the produce of member farmers and creating value addition by processing, sorting, cleaning, grading, packaging, and enhancing the scope of exporting agricultural commodities. FPOs are also entrusted with the responsibility of storage and transportation of perishable and non-perishable items. Therefore, looking at the roles and responsibilities of FPOs, it is evident that it plays an essential role in the overall supply chain system of agricultural activities.

3. Literature Review: Nature and Functions of FPOs

Many empirical studies evaluate the performance of FPOs in India (Singh and Vatta 2019; Venkattakumar et al., 2019; Kumar et al., 2019; Shalini 2012; Bishnoi and Kumari 2020). FPOs are supported and promoted by several implementing agencies and institutions such as NABARD, National Cooperative Development Corporation (NCDC), Non-governmental Organisations (NGOs), SFAC, and various government schemes. FPOs may be classified into five categories based on their nature and functions. First, service providers based on the different types of crops, or maybe a few specific crops, or crops that significantly account for the value chain system (Onumah et al. 2007). Second, FPOs that integrate the domestic market with the international market primarily export agricultural commodities, mainly commercial cash crops and rain-fed crops (Singh et al., 2018; Paty and Gummagolnath, 2018). Besides produce, we also find several registered FPOs in allied agriculture sectors. For instance, the

FPOs such as milk producer companies (MPC), non-farm producer companies and women producer companies are active in the state of Rajasthan.

Interestingly, the MPCs account for about 3 per cent of the total registered FPOs in the country. Nonetheless, the non-farm producer companies comprise a negligible share (less than one per cent) of the total FPOs in the country. Third, Women-led FPOs engaged in farm and non-farm activities play an instrumental role in enhancing the well-being of women in the country (Trebbin, 2014; Ramappa and Yashashwini, 2018.).

4. Data Sources and Methodology

4.1 Data Sources

The analysis of this study is mainly based on the primary data collected from the registered FPOs in the state of Rajasthan, which comprise 33 districts. As a first step, we prepared a list of all the registered FPOs in Rajasthan before 2019. In other words, we designed the list of those FPOs completed at least three years after registration. As per the latest data collected from Rajasthan State Agriculture Marketing Board, there are 275 registered FPOs in Rajasthan. Out of the 275 registered FPOs, we randomly selected 40 FPOs registered in different districts of Rajasthan, comprising various business activities and crops. It is important to note that, of the 40 selected FPOs, we found that 12 FPOs are not currently operational, and the remaining 28 FPOs comprise the study's sample size. Figure 45.1 presents the district-wise data on the registered FPOs in Rajasthan. As per the records obtained from the Jaipur district accounts for the highest number of FPOs, followed by Nagaur district.

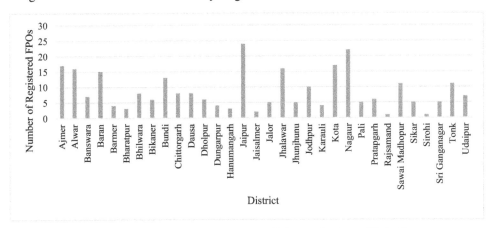

Fig. 45.1 The Number of Registered FPOs by districts of Rajasthan

Source: Compiled by authors from the data collected from

4.2 Method: Data Envelopment Analysis (DEA)

Measuring efficiency is vital to understand the relative performance of business units. In academic terminology, there are several ways of measuring efficiency. Data Envelopment Analysis (DEA), which was formulated by Charnes, Cooper and Rhodes (1978), is generally applied to measure relative efficiency across disciplines. Some studies include Shewell and Migiro (2016), Pyatunin et al. (2016), and Shao et al. (2018). Apart from DEA, other parametric techniques such as Stochastic Frontier Analysis (SFA), Thick Frontier Approach (TFA) and Distribution Free Approach (DFA) are applied to measure efficiency. The main distinction between DEA and SFA is that while the former is a nonparametric method, the latter, which is also referred to as Composed Error Regression, is a parametric method. Among all these techniques, we applied DEA, which is the most appropriate tool to measure the performance efficiency of FPOs, in this study as it identifies efficient performers in a given population. The data analysis performed using DEA involves three significant steps: first, identifying the decision-making units (DMU); second, specifying inputs and outputs for each DMU; and third, the DMUs must belong to homogenous groups. The data analysis was carried out using STATA 15 version.

5. Empirical Results

Asset turnover ratio is one of the most popular financial measures used to assess the company's ability to transform its assets into a turnover. Higher the ratio, the higher the efficiency of the company. The ability of a company to generate revenue from each rupee of the assets determines whether the company will perform in the long run. It shows the amount of income generated per unit of investment in assets. Table 45.1, which presents the sample specifications of efficiency used under the DEA model for seven sample FPOs, shows that FPO 1 generates Rs 0.63 lakh revenue with every one lakh rupee investment in the asset. In the sample specification model, we consider one input and one output. It should be noted that both input and output are measured in lakh rupee. It is worth noting that the revenue generated per unit of asset differs across FPOs, as the FPOs are of different categories.

Table 45.1 Sample specifications of efficiency model with a single input and output

Asset Turnover Ratio	FPO 1	FPO 2	FPO 3	FPO 4	FPO 5	FPO 6	FPO 7
Total Assets (₹ in Lakh)-I	25	17.5	11	31	12	3.5	5.8
Turnover (₹ in Lakhs)-O	32	130	13	45	350	18	35
Output /Input	1.28	7.43	1.18	1.45	29.17	5.14	6.03

Source: Authors' calculation based on the data collected from the respective FPOs in 2022–23

Figure 45.2 presents the turnover on the vertical axis and the asset on the horizontal axis. It can be seen that there are two lines: while the red line is a frontier line, the blue line is a regression line. Fundamentally, there is a distinction between DEA and the regression model. In the DEA model, the efficient frontier must touch at least one FPO, and all other FPOs are on or below the frontier line. Technically speaking, the frontier line envelops the remaining points. The frontier line represents the most efficient FPO, and the deviation of the most efficient FPO reflects the performance of the other FPOs in the sample units.

On the other hand, the regression model is based on the least square principles, considers the mean of the data points, and the deviation from the regression line shows evidence for the degree of efficiency. From a policy perspective, the inefficiency of FPOs reflects that the

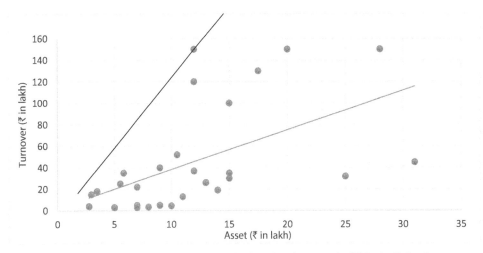

Fig. 45.2 Regression line and frontier line for the sample FPOs in Rajasthan

Source: based on the authors' calculation

intervention by the promoting agencies and government, be it state or central, needs to be strengthened to fulfil the national goals and targets. One of the most critical challenges is how to transform the inefficient FPOs into efficient FPOs without compromising the turnover of the company?

The application of DEA analysis first determines the frontier's DMUs and subsequently estimates the efficiency level of other DMUs in the sample relative to DMUs on the frontier. While running the DEA analysis, it is essential to specify the returns to scale (RTS), which may be constant returns to scale (CRS), variable returns to scale (VRS), decreasing returns to scale (DRS), and non-increasing returns to scale. Two types of DEA analysis can be performed: input-oriented DEA and output-oriented DEA. Table 45.2 presents the output-oriented DEA measures of 28 sample FPOs.

Table 45.2 The output-oriented DEA measures of the sample FPOs

dmu	i_x	o_q	CRS_TE	VRS_TE	SCALE	RTS
1. FPO	25	32	0.10	0.21	0.48	irs
2. FPO	17	130	0.61	0.87	0.71	irs
3. FPO	11	13	0.09	0.09	1.00	-
4. FPO	31	45	0.12	0.30	0.39	irs
5. FPO	12	150	1	1	1	-
6. FPO	3	18	0.48	0.48	1.00	-
7. FPO	5	35	0.56	0.73	0.76	irs
8. FPO	10	52	0.42	0.43	0.97	irs

dmu	i_x	o_q	CRS_TE	VRS_TE	SCALE	RTS
9. FPO	9	5	0.04	0.04	1.00	-
10. FPO	12	37	0.25	0.25	1.00	-
11. FPO	15	100	0.53	0.67	0.80	irs
12. FPO	15	30	0.16	0.20	0.80	irs
13. FPO	7	3	0.03	0.03	1.00	-
14. FPO	7	5	0.06	0.06	1.00	-
15. FPO	5	25	0.40	0.40	1.00	-
16. FPO	3	15	0.40	0.40	1.00	-
17. FPO	5	3	0.05	0.05	1.00	-
18. FPO	20	150	0.60	1.00	0.60	drs
19. FPO	12	120	0.80	0.80	1.00	-
20. FPO	8	3.5	0.04	0.04	1.00	-
21. FPO	9	40	0.36	0.38	0.94	irs
22. FPO	14	19	0.11	0.13	0.86	irs
23. FPO	13	26	0.16	0.17	0.92	irs
24. FPO	10	4.5	0.04	0.04	1.00	-
25. FPO	2	4	0.16	0.16	1.00	-
26. FPO	28	150	0.43	1.00	0.43	drs
27. FPO	7	22	0.25	0.25	1.00	-
28. FPO	15	35	0.19	0.23	0.80	irs

Source: Computed by authors using STATA 15

6. Conclusion and Future Scope

This paper has examined the financial efficiency of FPOs in Rajasthan by selecting 32 sample units across districts. The significance of measuring the performance efficiency of FPOs in India is vital as the functioning and performance of FPOs in India are greatly influenced by the financial support from the promoting institutions and government policies. It is a matter of grave concern as a large number of FPOs underperform without fully utilising the assets possessed by them. Our study indicates that a few FPOs registered in the state does not perform efficiently. Possibly, with adequate investment in infrastructure development and the provision of required skills and knowledge, the functioning of FPOs may be invigorated in the state. The future study may extend our one-input one-output DEA analysis to a model comprising multiple inputs and outputs.

REFERENCES

1. Bishnoi, R. and Kumari, S., 2020. Challenges Faced by FPOs & Strategies to Overcome: A Review. *International Journal of Advances in Agricultural Science and Technology (IJAAST)*, 7(6), pp. 25–33.
2. Kumar, K., 2022. Technical Efficiency of Rice in Telangana, India: Data Envelopment Analysis Farmers (DEA). *Research on World Agricultural Economy*, 3(2455-2022-794), pp. 1–12.
3. Kumar, P., Manaswi, B.H., Prakash, P., Anbukkani, P., Kar, A., Jha, G.K., Rao, D.U.M. and Lenin, V., 2019. Impact of farmer producer organisation on organic chilli production in Telangana, India. *Indian Journal of Traditional Knowledge (IJTK)*, 19(1), pp. 33–43.
4. Paty, B.K. and Gummagolnath, K.C., 2018. Farmer Producer Companies: Issues and Challenges. *Extension Digest*, 1(3), pp. 1–36.
5. Rafi, D., 2020. To assess the technical efficiency of inputs on farmer producer organisations (FPO) and non-farmer producer organisations (non-FPO) farms in Kurnool district of Andhra Pradesh. *Journal of Pharmacognosy and Phytochemistry*, 9(1), pp. 343–351.
6. Ramappa, K.B. and Yashashwini, M.A., 2018. Evolution of Farmer Producer Organisations: Challenges and Opportunities. *Research Journal of Agricultural Sciences*, 9(4), pp. 709–715.
7. Shao, Y., Bi, G., Yang, F. and Xia, Q., 2018. Resource allocation for branch network system with considering heterogeneity based on DEA method. *Central European Journal of Operations Research*, 26(4), pp. 1005–1025.
8. Shewell, P. and Migiro, S., 2016. Data envelopment analysis in performance measurement: A critical analysis of the literature. *Problems and Perspectives in Management*, (14, 3 pp. 705–713.
9. Singh, G., Budhiraja, P. and Vatta, K., 2018. Sustainability of farmer producer organisations under agricultural value networks in India: a case of Punjab and Gujarat. *Indian Journal of Agricultural Economics*, 73(3), pp. 70–85.
10. Singh, G. and Vatta, K., 2019. Assessing the economic impacts of farmer producer organisations: a case study in Gujarat, India. *Agricultural Economics Research Review*, 32(347-2020-1020).
11. Trebbin, A., 2014. Linking small farmers to modern retail through producer organisations–Experiences with producer companies in India. Food policy, 45, pp. 35–44.
12. Kumar, M., Singh, R. and Patel, S., 2018. Economic analysis of mustard production by members of farmer producer organisation in swai Madhopur District of Rajasthan. Editor's Message, p. 68.
13. Manaswi, B.H., Kumar, P., Prakash, P., Anbukkani, P., Kar, A., Jha, G.K. and Rao, D.U.M., 2018. Progress and performance of states in promotion of farmer producer organisations in India. Indian Journal of Extension Education, 54(2), pp. 108–113.
14. Shalini, V., Prajapati, M.R. and Vahoniya, D.R., 2022. A study of farmer producer companies (FPCs) in selected district of Telangana State. The Pharma Innovation Journal, SP-11 (11), pp. 508–511.
15. Singh, G. and Vatta, K., 2019. Assessing the economic impacts of farmer producer organisations: a case study in Gujarat, India. Agricultural Economics Research Review, 32(347-2020-1020).
16. Tagat, V. and Tagat, A., 2016. The potential of farmer producer organisations in India. Available at SSRN 2972488.
17. Thamban, C., Jayasekhar, S., Chandran, K.P. and Rajesh, M.K., 2020. Sustainability of Farmer Producer Organisations-The case of producer organisations involved in the production and marketing of 'neera'in the coconut sector in Kerala, India.
18. Venkattakumar, R., Mysore, S., Venugopalam, R., Narayanaswamy, B., Balakrishna, B., Atheequlla, G., Paripurna, A. and Reddy, T.M., 2019. Performance of Farmers Producers Organizations

(FPOs) and Associated Factors in Karnataka: Producers' Perspectives. Indian Research Journal of Extension Education, 19(2&3), pp. 7–12.

19. Verma, S., Sonkar, V. K., Kumar, A. and Roy, D., 2019. Are farmer producer organisations a boon to farmers? The evidence from Bihar, India. Agricultural Economics Research Review, 32(347-2020-1019).

20. Charnes, A., Cooper, W. W., & Rhodes, E. (1978). Measuring the efficiency of decision making units. *European journal of operational research*, 2(6), 429–444.

21. Onumah, G., Davis, J., Kleih, U., & Proctor, F. (2007). Empowering smallholder farmers in markets: Changing agricultural marketing systems and innovative responses by producer organizations.

Handbook of Evidence Based Management Practices in Business – Satyendra Kumar Sharma et al. (eds)
© 2023 Taylor & Francis Group, London, ISBN 978-1-032-54216-4

Chapter

Greenwash Perception and Sustainable Consumer Purchase Behaviour

Bharti Ramtiyal[1]

Graphic Era Deemed to be University, Dehradun

Paras Garg[2], Gunjan Soni[3]

Malaviya National Institute of Technology, Jaipur

ABSTRACT: Today's production is heavily sustainable. Social media and the internet make sustainability more visible to stakeholders. This article examines how corporate greenwashing and stakeholders' environmental concerns affect sustainable consumer behaviour. This study examines how these two criteria affect sustainable purchase behaviour. This study also examines Green Word of Mouth and Green Brand Loyalty as mediators of Greenwash perception and Sustainable Purchase Behaviour.

KEYWORDS: Perceived customer effectiveness, Greenwash perception, Sustainable purchase behaviour

1. Introduction

Sustainable living has become more popular in recent years. Corporations adopted socially conscious business practises. Today, practically every company is striving to help or claim to benefit a segment of society. Social media has greatly increased this effect. This led to Corporate Social Responsibility, which includes establishing homeless shelters, donating to cancer or AIDS research, offering free school supplies to disadvantaged children, etc (CSR). This study how Greenwash Perception affects Sustainable Purchase behaviour through Green Word of Mouth and Green brand loyalty. This study also examines customer environmental concerns. The average customer is concerned about the environment due to natural disasters and climate change news.

[1]bharti.mnit2022@gmail.com, [2]in.parasgarg@gmail.com, [3]gsoni.mech@mnit.ac.in

DOI: 10.4324/9781003415725-46

2. Literature Review

2.1 Sustainable Purchase Behaviour

Customers' green behaviour is influenced by environmental concerns (Parguel et al., 2015). This changes consumer behaviour, benefiting companies with effective environmental policies (Hameed et al., 2020). Sustainable Consumer Purchase Behaviour (GSCM) is the tendency of consumers to buy or reject green items. "Customer actions around product purchase, consumption, and disposal" are consumer behaviour (Engel et al., 1995). Organizational influence on consumer behaviour has major environmental impacts.

2.2 Factors affecting Sustainable Purchase Behaviour

The following section discusses Sustainable Purchase behaviour and the CSR factors that affect it. These factors can be considered the latent constructs used to determine their effects on GPB. According to the literature, Sustainable purchase behaviour depends on the factors mentioned in Table 46.1

Table 46.1   Factors of sustainable purchase behaviour

Sr No.	Dependent Factors
1	Perceived Greenwash
2	Brand trust
3	Green Brand Loyalty
4	Green Skepticism
5	Innovation
6	Novelty
7	Environmental Concern
8	Perceived risk
9	Perceived Benefit
10	Attitude
11	Green Word of mouth
12	Subjective Norms
13	Behavioural Control
14	Perceived Customer Effectiveness

Source: Authors compilation

From the literature, we can see that Sustainable Purchase Behaviour is studied concerning many factors. Still, it is virtually impossible to include all the elements in the analysis as it will make the model very complex, and the research will become quite rigorous. Hence the following shortlisting criterion (Table 46.2) is adopted to exclude factors.

Table 46.2 Shortlisting criterion

Exclusion Criterion	Excluded Factors
Factors whose measuring variables were not readily available in the literature.	Green Skepticism Innovation Novelty Subjective Norms
Factors which were less popularly revived in the literature.	Perceived risk Perceived Benefit Attitude Behavioural Control
Factors similar to other factors.	Green Brand Trust

Source: Authors compilation

Final List of Selected factors:

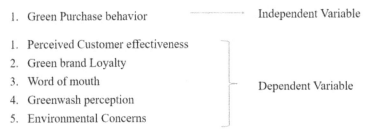

1. Green Purchase behavior — — — — — — Independent Variable

1. Perceived Customer effectiveness
2. Green brand Loyalty
3. Word of mouth — Dependent Variable
4. Greenwash perception
5. Environmental Concerns

3. Construct Relationships

3.1 Greenwash Perception and Green Purchase Behaviour

Greenwash is one of the most influential constructs in this study. Greenwashing is the method corporations use to mislead customers by perpetuating the narrative that their products and services are more sustainable than they are (Parguel et al., 2011). It is a well-known fact that sustainable actions taken by companies affect their economic output (Leonidou & Chari, 2013) and the investors' and consumers' behaviour (Li and Wang, 2017).

The construct relationships are as shown in Fig. 46.2.

4. Research Methodology

The article is based on survey research. The survey was performed in an unbiased way. Without the researcher's intervention, a survey questionnaire (Annexure 2) was given to the respondents, who were mainly customers. All the information obtained was through the primary survey.

Model generation includes defining the objectives and indicator variables and generating the hypotheses. Based on the research questions from the literature review, the following purposes are defined for the analysis of this project:

RO1: To examine the relationship between GWP and GPB.

RO2: To examine the relationship between PCE and GPB.

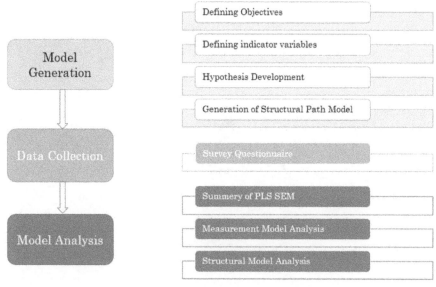

Fig. 46.1 Research Methodology

Source: Authors compilation

RO3: To determine whether PCE mediates the relationship between EC and GPB.

RO4: To determine whether Green WoM mediates the relationship between PGW and GPB.

RO5: To determine whether GBL mediates the relationship between GWP and GPB.

4.1 Scale Development

Indicator variables are used as a measure to define the latent constructs. According to the definition, the latent constructs cannot be measured directly(Hair et al., 2010). The indicators are used to describe a property representing a latent construct—the indicator variables for each construct are given below and are briefly depicted in Table 46.3 (scale development).

Table 46.3 Scale Development

Construct	Scale	No. of items	Reference
Perceived Greenwash	5-point Likert Scale	5	(Chen & Chang, 2012
Word of Mouth	5-point Likert Scale	3	(Molinari, 2008)
Green Purchase Behaviour	5-point Likert Scale	5	(Abdul, 2007), (Goh, 2016)
Green Brand Loyalty	5-point Likert Scale	5	(Hameed, 2021)
Perceived Customer Effectiveness	5-point Likert Scale	5	(Kim & Choi, 2005)
Environmental Concern	5-point Likert Scale	5	(Kim & Choi, 2005)

Source: Authors compilation

From the defined hypotheses, the structural model can be constructed. The Path model is an inner structure of the overall PLS-SEM model that represents the relationship between the study's independent and dependent latent constructs(Becker et al., 2012).

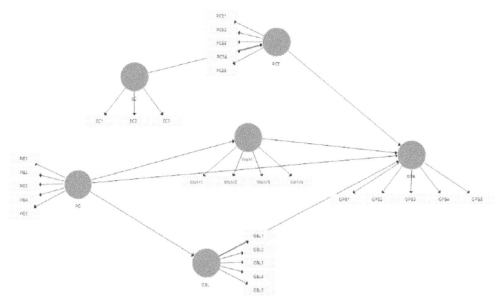

Fig. 46.2 PLS-SEM path Model

Source: Authors compilation

4.2 Data Collection

An initial survey was carried out to get the data. The questionnaire was created based on a one to five Likert scale. One is the statement least agreeable, and five is the most agreeable. The questionnaire was distributed to mostly undergrad and postgrad students of different colleges and universities. Composite reliability also determines the repeatability of the experiment. This means the model should output a consistent result when analyzed multiple times using varying datasets. According to the literature, the model is reliable if the Composite Reliability and Cronbach's alpha are more than 0.7 (hair et.al., 2011). Figure 46.3 (Measurement Model) shows that all the values of Composite reliability and Cronbach's Alpha are greater than 0.7. This indicates that all the constructs are statistically reliable and can be considered further for structural analysis.

Discriminant validity represents the distinction between the constructs(Hair et al., 2011). To what extent do the study's constructs differ from other constructs. The constructs need to be sufficiently distinct for the model to be valid. To evaluate discriminant validity, the square root of the average variance extracted must be greater in value than the correlations of other study constructs(Hair et al., 2011). Table 46.4 (Fornell – Larcker Criterion) represents that when the correlations with all the constructs are compared, the SRAVE has a higher value than other items(Fornell & Bookstein, 1982).

- Heterotrait – Monotrait ratio (HTMT)
- While evaluating the convergent validity, HTMT is one of the newer methods, along with Fornell – Larcker Criterion used for variance–based Structural equation modelling.

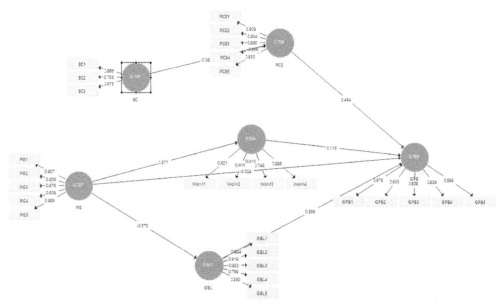

Fig. 46.3   Measurement Model

Source: Authors compilation

Table 46.4   Fornell – Larcker Criterion

	EC	GBL	GPB	PCE	PG	WoM
EC	0.869					
GBL	-0.021	0.769				
GPB	-0.218	0.412	0.894			
PCE	-0.389	0.144	0.492	0.840		
PG	-0.002	-0.570	-0.271	-0.144	0.859	
WoM	0.025	-0.541	-0.194	-0.192	0.377	0.798

Source: Authors compilation

With the above criteria satisfied, we can safely say that the validity of the measurement model has been sufficiently satisfied with the three objects of Convergent and discriminate validity. The measurement model is reliable and valid. Next, we can move on to the assessment of hypotheses using a structural model.

4.3 Structural Model

The structural model represents the relationship's actual extent and direction among various constructs. This is done using Bootstrapping option in SmartPLS 3.0.

4.4 Mediation Analysis

The mediation analysis was tested using the bootstrapping function of SmartPLS. The β value representing the relationship between EC, PCE and GBP was calculated to be –0.11 with a significant *p*-value which indicates that PCE mediates partially mediates the relationship between EC and FPB.

The β value representing the relationship between PG, GBL and GBP was calculated to be -0.226 with a significant *p*-value; this indicates that GBL mediates partially mediates the negative relationship between PG and GPB.

The β value representing the relationship between PG, WoM and GBP was calculated to be 0.044 with a non - significant *p*-value; this indicates that WoM does not mediate the relationship between PG and GPB.

5. Discussion

Greenwash Perception and Sustainable Purchase Behaviour were linked by literature. Hypothesized association was negative. Sustainable buying increases as greenwash perception decreases. The idea validates consumers' advertising defect detection. Perceived Customer Effectiveness and Sustainable Purchase Behaviour were linked by research. Positive. Consumer Perceived Customer Effectiveness enhances sustainable buying behaviour. Customer effectiveness is the customer's view that their environmental efforts are effective. Perceived Customer Effectiveness and Sustainable Purchase Behaviour were linked by research. Positive connection. PCE mediated the association between environmental concerns and sustainable purchase behaviour. Greenwash Perception and Sustainable Purchase Behaviour were linked by literature. Hypothesized association was negative. Green Word of Mouth mediated this interaction. Green WoM partially mediates GWP-GPB. The literature linked perceived greenwash to sustainable purchase behaviour. Hypothesized association was negative.

6. Conclusions

The primary purpose of this study was to study the relationship between Greenwash perception and Environmental Concerns on Sustainable Purchase Behaviour. We found that both factors influence the customer's purchase behaviour. Greenwash perception did not have any direct relationship with Sustainable Purchase behaviour. However, this relationship was also studied using two mediating variables.

REFERENCES

1. Atkinson, L., & Rosenthal, S. (2014). Signalling the Green Sell: The Influence of Eco-Label Source, Argument Specificity, and Product Involvement on Consumer Trust. In Journal of Advertising (Vol. 43, Issue 1, pp. 33–45). Informa UK Limited.
2. Bang, G. (2010). Energy security and climate change concerns: Triggers for energypolicy change in the United States? Energy Policy, 38(4), 1645–1653.
3. Blome, C., Foerstl, K., & Schleper, M. C. (2017). Antecedents of green supplier championing and greenwashing: An empirical study on leadership and ethical incentives. In Journal of Cleaner Production (Vol. 152, pp. 339–350). Elsevier BV.

4. Brunner, M., & SÜβ, H.-M. (2005). Analyzing the Reliability of Multidimensional Measures: An Example from Intelligence Research. In Educational and Psychological Measurement (Vol. 65, Issue 2, pp. 227–240). SAGE Publications.

5. Chen, Y.-S., & Chang, C.-H. (2012). Greenwash and Green Trust: The Mediation Effects of Green Consumer Confusion and Green Perceived Risk. In Journal of Business Ethics (Vol. 114, Issue 3, pp. 489–500). Springer Science and Business Media LLC.

6. Cuganesan, S., Guthrie, J., & Ward, L. (2010). Examining CSR disclosure strategies within the Australian food and beverage industry. In Accounting Forum (Vol. 34, Issues 3–4, pp. 169–183). Informa UK Limited.

7. de Freitas Netto, S. V., Sobral, M. F. F., Ribeiro, A. R. B., & Soares, G. R. da L. (2020). Concepts and forms of greenwashing: a systematic review. In Environmental Sciences Europe (Vol. 32, Issue 1). Springer Science and Business Media LLC.

8. Dixon, L. (2020). Autonowashing: The Greenwashing of Vehicle Automation. In Transportation Research Interdisciplinary Perspectives (Vol. 5, p. 100113). Elsevier BV.

9. Do Pao, A. M. F., & Reis, R. (2012). Factors affecting scepticism toward greenadvertising. Journal of advertising, 41(4), 147–155.

10. Environmental Concern, and PCE", Advances in Consumer Research Volume 32. Association for Consumer Research, Pages: 592–599.

11. F. Hair Jr, J., Sarstedt, M., Hopkins, L., & G. Kuppelwieser, V. (2014). Partial least squares structural equation modeling (PLS-SEM). In European Business Review (Vol. 26, Issue 2, pp. 106–121). Emerald.

12. Gatti, L., Seele, P., & Rademacher, L. (2019). Grey zone in – greenwash out. A review of greenwashing research and implications for the voluntary-mandatory transition of CSR. In International Journal of Corporate Social Responsibility (Vol. 4, Issue 1). Springer Science and Business Media LLC.

13. Goh, S. K., & Balaji, M. S. (2016). Linking green scepticism to green purchasebehaviour. Journal of Cleaner Production, 131, 629–638.

14. Guo, R., Tao, L., Li, C. B., & Wang, T. (2017). A path analysis of greenwashing ina trust crisis among Chinese energy companies: The role of brand legitimacyand brand loyalty. Journal of business ethics, 140(3), 523–536.

15. Hameed, I., Hyder, Z., Imran, M., & Shafiq, K. (2021). Greenwash and green purchase behavior: an environmentally sustainable perspective. In Environment, Development and Sustainability (Vol. 23, Issue 9, pp. 13113–13134). Springer Science and Business Media LLC.

16. Han, H., Hwang, J., Lee, M. J., & Kim, J. (2019). Word-of-mouth, buying, andsacrifice intentions for eco-cruises: Exploring the function of norm activationand value-attitude-behavior. Tourism Management, 70, 430–443.

17. Karlsson, I., Rootzén, J., & Johnsson, F. (2020). Reaching net-zero carbon emissions in construction supply chains – Analysis of a Swedish road construction project. In Renewable and Sustainable Energy Reviews (Vol. 120, p. 109651). Elsevier BV.

18. Katta, R. M. R., & Patro, C. S. (2017). Influence of Perceived Risks on Consumers' Online Purchase Behaviour. In International Journal of Sociotechnology and Knowledge Development (Vol. 9, Issue 3, pp. 17–37). IGI Global.

19. Koseoglu, M. A., Uyar, A., Kilic, M., Kuzey, C., & Karaman, A. S. (2021). Exploring the connections among CSR performance, reporting, and external assurance: Evidence from the hospitality and tourism industry. In International Journal of Hospitality Management (Vol. 94, p. 102819). Elsevier BV.

20. Laufer, W. S. (2003). Social accountability and corporate greenwashing. Journalof business ethics, 43(3), 253–261.
21. Leonidou, L. C., Kvasova, O., Leonidou, C. N., & Chari, S. (2013). Businessunethicality as an impediment to consumer trust: The moderating role of demographic and cultural characteristics. Journal of Business Ethics, 112(3), 397–415.
22. Lyon, T. P., & Montgomery, A. W. (2013). Tweetjacked: The Impact of social media on Corporate Greenwash. In Journal of Business Ethics (Vol. 118, Issue 4, pp. 747–757). Springer Science and Business Media LLC.
23. Lyon, T. P., & Montgomery, A. W. (2015). The Means and End of Greenwash. In Organization & Environment (Vol. 28, Issue 2, pp. 223–249). SAGE Publications.
24. Martínez, M. P., Cremasco, C. P., Gabriel Filho, L. R. A., Braga Junior, S. S., Bednaski, A. V., Quevedo-Silva, F., Correa, C. M., da Silva, D., & Moura-Leite Padgett, R. C. (2020). Fuzzy inference system to study the behavior of the green consumer facing the perception of greenwashing. In Journal of Cleaner Production (Vol. 242, p. 116064). Elsevier BV.
25. Oliver, R. L. (1999). Whence Consumer Loyalty? In Journal of Marketing (Vol. 63, Issue 4, pp. 33–44). SAGE Publications.
26. Parguel, B., Benoit-Moreau, F., & Russell, C. A. (2015). Can evoking nature in advertising mislead consumers? The power of 'executional greenwashing'. In International Journal of Advertising (Vol. 34, Issue 1, pp. 107–134). Informa UK Limited.
27. Paul, J., Modi, A., & Patel, J. (2016). Predicting green product consumptionusing theory of planned behaviour and reasoned action. Journal of retailingand consumer services, 29, 123–134.
28. Rahbar, E., & Abdul Wahid, N. (2011). Investigation of green marketing tools'effect on consumers' purchase behavior. Business strategy series, 12(2), 73–83.
29. Scanlan, S. J. (2017). Framing fracking: scale-shifting and greenwashing risk in the oil and gas industry. In Local Environment (Vol. 22, Issue 11, pp. 1311–1337). Informa UK Limited
30. Schultz, P. W. (2000). New Environmental Theories: Empathizing With Nature: The Effects ofPerspective Taking on Concern for Environmental Issues. In Journal of Social Issues (Vol. 56, Issue 3, pp. 391–406). Wiley.
31. Schultz, P. W. (2000). New Environmental Theories: Empathizing with Nature: The Effects ofPerspective Taking on Concern for Environmental Issues. In Journal of Social Issues (Vol. 56, Issue 3, pp. 391–406). Wiley.
32. Souiden, N., & Pons, F. (2009). Product recall crisis management: the impact on manufacturer's image, consumer loyalty and purchase intention. In Journal of Product & Brand Management (Vol. 18, Issue 2, pp. 106–114). Emerald.
33. Sreen, N., Purbey, S., & Sadarangani, P. (2018). Impact of culture, behavior and gender on green purchase intention. In Journal of Retailing and Consumer Services (Vol. 41, pp. 177–189). Elsevier BV.
34. Thomas P Lyon & John W Maxwell (2011) Greenwash: Corporate Environmental Disclosure under Threat of Audit, Journal of Economics & Management Strategy, Volume 20, Number 1, Spring 2011, 3–41.
35. Yeonshin Kim and Sejung Marina Choi (2005),"Antecedents of Green Purchase Behavior: An Examination of Collectivism,
36. Zhang, X., & Yu, X. (2020). The Impact of Perceived Risk on Consumers' Cross-Platform Buying Behavior. In Frontiers in Psychology (Vol. 11). Frontiers Media SA.
37. Zhu, J., & Wang, C. (2020). Biodegradable plastics: green hope or greenwashing? In Marine Pollution Bulletin (Vol. 161, p. 111774). Elsevier BV.

Handbook of Evidence Based Management Practices in Business – Satyendra Kumar Sharma et al. (eds)
© 2023 Taylor & Francis Group, London, ISBN 978-1-032-54216-4

PART

EVIDENCE BASED
OPERATIONS AND INFORMATION
MANAGEMENT

Handbook of Evidence Based Management Practices in Business – Satyendra Kumar Sharma et al. (eds)
© 2023 Taylor & Francis Group, London, ISBN 978-1-032-54216-4

Chapter

Retailer's Ordering Policy Under Influence of Inflation and Dynamic Potential Market Size in a Supply Chain System

Alok Kumar[1], Jitendra Kumar Das[2]

FORE School of Management, New Delhi, India

Udayan Chanda[3]

Birla Institute of Technology and Science Pilani, Rajasthan, India

ABSTRACT: The retailer's ordering policy and the optimal ordering policy are greatly influenced by the parameters which are consistent with business necessities and the nature of consumers' needs and demands. Thus it is important to formulate the demand function by taking into account the parameters which can represent the business need and requirements. One of the important areas in inventory research in the current market dynamics present is to develop policies for the particularly dynamic market. Therefore, the role of dynamic potential market size is greatly acknowledged. It has also been observed that the impact of inflation affects the demand function and hence the optimal ordering policy is affected therein, therefore, ignoring the impact of inflation is unjustified. In this paper, an inventory model on the retailer's optimal ordering policy has been developed where the impact of dynamic potential market size and the influence of inflation is incorporated.

KEYWORDS: Inflation, Dynamic potential market size, Ordering policy, Supply chain

1. Introduction & Literature Review

In the environment of dynamic potential market size, the formulation of a retailer's optimal ordering policy is a crucial task. Therefore, to maintain the smooth functioning of the supply chain system, the change in the potential market size over time needs to be captured. Aggarwal

[1]alok@fsm.ac.in, [2]j.das@fsm.ac.in, [3]udayanchanda@pilani.bits-pilani.ac.in

DOI: 10.4324/9781003415725-47

et al. (2011) discussed an inventory model for economic order quantity where the demand for the product is influenced by dynamic potential market size. They have used the potential market size which varies with time where two different cases of the potential market size such as potential market size increasing linearly and exponentially with time was considered. Aggarwal and Kumar (2014) developed an economic order quantity model for price-dependent potential market size. Here, they have used the potential market size which decreases exponentially as the price of the item increases with time. Chanda and Kumar (2017) developed a fuzzy EOQ model using dynamic potential market and price-sensitive demand. Kumar and Chanda (2018) developed an EOQ model for a growing potential market and a two-warehouse inventory system using an innovation-driven demand rate. Chanda and Kumar (2019) developed an economic order quantity model for new products for dynamic potential market size under a multi-stage adoption process. Also, it has been experienced that inflation and the time value of money significantly affect the EOQ policy, therefore, it becomes necessary to incorporate its effects while developing the inventory policy. In the beginning, the effect of inflation and the time value of money was considered in the economic order quantity model by Buzacott (1975) and Misra (1975). An EOQ model with inflation under time discounting and deterioration was developed by Bose et al. (1995). Under the effect of the time value of money with a finite replenishment rate and deterioration, an inventory model was developed by Wee and Law (2001). The authors such as Yang et al. (2001), Yang (2004), Hsieh et al. (2008), and Dey et al.(2008) have taken the effect of inflation and the time value of money to develop their inventory model. Chanda and Kumar (2012) developed an inflationary-based economic order quantity model where demand is influenced by the innovation diffusion criterion. Kumar (2019) proposed an inventory model for new products under permissible delay in payments and with the effect of inflation and the time value of money. In this paper, an EOQ is proposed for varying potential market that increases exponentially with time. The effect of the time value of money and inflation is also incorporated into this model.

2. Model Information

2.1 Suppositions
- There is an instantaneous replenishment rate
- Lead time is zero
- Shortages are not approved
- The rate of demand varies with time
- The market potential is dynamic and that varies with time
- The parameter of innovation rate is constant

2.2 Notations
A: Ordering cost per order.

C: Per unit cost.

I: Inventory carrying charge per unit per unit time.

$I(t)$: Inventory level at any time t.

T: Length of the replenishment cycle.

Q: Lot size per cycle.

$PW(T)$: Total present worth of the system per unit time

h: Inflation rate

p: Innovation coefficient

r: Discount rate representing time value of money

$R = r - h$: Net discount rate of inflation

$\dfrac{dN(t)}{dt}$: Demand rate at time t.

g: Coefficient representing the potential market size growth rate

N_0: Initial Potential market size

$N(t)$: Cumulative number of adopters at time t.

3. Model Formulation

Aggarwal et al. (2011) formulated the demand model which is based on the dynamic potential market size as described below:

$$\lambda(t) = \frac{dN(t)}{dt} = p(\bar{N}(t) - N(t)), \bar{N}(t) = N_0 e^{gt}, g > 0 \tag{1}$$

The differential equation for the inventory level $I(t)$ at any time t during the interval $(0, T)$ is given by

$$\frac{dI(t)}{dt} = -\lambda(t), 0 \le t \le T \tag{2}$$

Using equations (1) and (2), the solution of the differential equation (2) after applying the boundary condition $I(T) = 0$ is given as follows:

$$I(t) = \frac{pN_0}{(p+g)}(e^{gT} - e^{gt}) + \frac{pN_0}{(p+g)}(e^{-pt} - e^{-pT}), 0 \le t \le T \tag{3}$$

The lot size Q is given by

$$Q = I(0) = \frac{pN_0}{(p+g)}(e^{gT} - 1) + \frac{pN_0}{(p+g)}(1 - e^{-pT}) \tag{4}$$

The present worth of the ordering cost per unit time, $PW_{oc} = \dfrac{A}{T}$ (5)

The present worth of the Material cost per unit time, $PW_{MC} = \dfrac{CQ}{T}$ (6)

$$\Rightarrow \qquad PW_{MC} = \frac{CpN_0}{T(p+g)}(e^{gT} - 1) + \frac{CpN_0}{T(p+g)}(1 - e^{-pT}) \tag{7}$$

The present worth of the Inventory carrying cost per unit of time, PW_{ICC} is given by

$$PW_{ICC} = \frac{IC}{T}\int_0^T e^{-Rt}I(t)dt \tag{8}$$

$$\Rightarrow \quad PW_{ICC} = \frac{ICpN_0}{T(p+g)}\left(\frac{(1-e^{-(R+p)T})}{(R+p)} + \frac{(1-e^{(g-R)T})}{(g-R)} + \frac{(1-e^{-RT})(e^{gT}-e^{-pT})}{R}\right) \tag{9}$$

Total present worth per unit time, $PW(T)$ is given by

$$PW(T) = PW_{oc} + PW_{MC} + PW_{ICC} \tag{10}$$

$$\Rightarrow \quad PW(T) = \frac{A}{T} + \frac{ICpN_0}{T(p+g)}\left(\frac{(1-e^{-(R+p)T})}{(R+p)} + \frac{(1-e^{(g-R)T})}{(g-R)} + \frac{(1-e^{-RT})(e^{gT}-e^{-pT})}{R}\right)$$

$$+ \frac{CpN_0}{T(p+g)}(e^{gT}-1) + \frac{CpN_0}{T(p+g)}(1-e^{-pT}) \tag{11}$$

The necessary criterion for the present worth $PW(T)$ given in equation (11) to be optimum is

$$\frac{dPW(T)}{dT} = 0 \tag{12}$$

and for $PW(T)$ to be convex, $\dfrac{d^2PW(T)}{dT} > 0$ \hfill (13)

One can get the optimum value of T by using the solution of the equation

$$\frac{dPW(T)}{dT} = 0 \text{ and by satisfying the condition } \frac{d^2PW(T)}{dT} > 0. \tag{14}$$

4. Numerical Examples

We carry out the sensitivity analysis in this section on the parameters of the innovation coefficient, the growth rate of potential market size, the inflation rate, and the discount rate that represents the time value of money has been in the Tables (47.1–47.4) given below. The sensitivity analysis is based on a few parameters that have been used to develop the model. The values of these parameters are given as follows:

A = \$1500/order, C = \$300/unit, I = 0.25/unit time, N_0 = 5000

Table 47.1 Sensitivity analysis with respect to p

g = 0.61, r = 0.15, h = 0.11			
p	**T***	**PW(T*)**	**Q(T*)**
0.005	1.009	13207	34
0.006	0.994	15543	40
0.007	0.983	17873	47
0.008	0.975	20199	53
0.009	0.968	22521	59

Source: Authors compilation

Table 47.2   Sensitivity analysis with respect to g

p = 0.005, *r* = 0.15, *h* = 0.11			
g	*T**	*PW(T**)	*Q(T**)
0.65	0.943	13450	32.49
0.66	0.928	13502	31.97
0.67	0.914	13550	31.47
0.68	0.900	13595	30.98
0.69	0.886	13637	30.51

Source: Authors compilation

Table 47.3   Sensitivity analysis with respect to r

p = 0.005, *g* = 0.61, *h* = 0.11			
r	*T**	*PW(T**)	*Q(T**)
0.16	1.01	13201	35.16
0.17	1.02	13193	35.55
0.18	1.03	13184	35.95
0.19	1.04	13173	36.36
0.20	1.05	13162	36.79

Source: Authors compilation

Table 47.4   Sensitivity analysis with respect to h

p = 0.005, *g* = 0.61, *r* = 0.20			
h	*T**	*PW(T**)	*Q(T**)
0.12	1.04	13173	36.36
0.13	1.03	13184	35.95
0.14	1.02	13193	35.55
0.15	1.01	13201	35.16
0.16	1.00	13207	34.78

Source: Authors compilation

5. Conclusion

The ignorance of parameters that are consistent with reality can not be justified, therefore, it becomes significant to understand the role of such parameters and their effects on inventory policies. Here, the parameters pertaining to the dynamic potential market size, the inflation, and the time value of money play an important role in shaping the optimal inventory policies for retailers. The sensitivity analysis for the parameters as discussed above has been well captured which gives us a kind of relationship based upon which one can take the optimum decisions regarding the optimum lot size, optimum cycle length, and the optimum present worth.

6. Acknowledgment

"The infrastructural support provided by the FORE School of Management, New Delhi, and BITS Pilani in completing this paper is gratefully acknowledged".

REFERENCES

1. Aggarwal, K. K., Jaggi, C. K., & Kumar, A. (2011). Economic order quantity model with innovation diffusion criterion having dynamic potential market size. *International Journal of Applied Decision Sciences, 4*(3), 280–303.
2. Aggarwal, K. K., & Kumar, A. (2014). Economic order quantity model with innovation diffusion criterion under influence of price-dependent potential market size. *International Journal of Innovation and Technology Management, 11*(5), 1450028.
3. Buzacott, J. A. (1975). Economic order quantities with inflation. *Journal of the Operational Research Society, 26*(3), 553–558.
4. Bose, S., Goswami, A., & Chaudhuri, K. S. (1995). An EOQ model for deteriorating items with linear time-dependent demand rate and shortages under inflation and time discounting. *Journal of the Operational Research Society, 46*(6), 771–782.
5. Chanda, U., & Kumar, A. (2012). Economic order quantity model on inflationary conditions with demand influenced by innovation diffusion criterion. *International Journal of Procurement Management, 5*(2), 160–177.
6. Chanda, U., & Kumar, A. (2017). Optimisation of fuzzy EOQ model for advertising and price sensitive demand model under dynamic ceiling on potential adoption. *International Journal of Systems Science: Operations and Logistics, 4*(2), 145–165.
7. Chanda, U., & Kumar, A. (2019). Optimization of EOQ model for new products under multi-stage adoption process. *International Journal of Innovation and Technology Management, 16*(2), 1950015.
8. Dey, J. K., Mondal, S. K., & Maiti, M. (2008). Two storage inventory problem with dynamic demand and interval valued lead-time over finite time horizon under inflation and time-value of money. *European Journal of Operational Research, 185*(1), 170–194.
9. Hsieh, T. P., Dye, C. Y., & Ouyang, L. Y. (2008). Determining optimal lot size for a two-warehouse system with deterioration and shortages using net present value. *European Journal of Operational Research, 191*(1), 182–192.
10. Kumar, A., & Chanda, U. (2018). Two-warehouse inventory model for deteriorating items with demand influenced by innovation criterion in growing technology market. *Journal of Management Analytics, 5*(3), 198–212.
11. Kumar, A. (2019). Trade credit induced inventory model for new products. In *Operations research in development sector* (pp. 1–14). Springer, Singapore.
12. Misra, R. B. (1975). A study of inflationary effects on inventory systems. *Logistics Spectrum, 9*, 51–55.
13. Wee, H. M., & Law, S. T. (2001). Replenishment and pricing policy for deteriorating items taking into account the time-value of money. *International Journal of Production Economics, 71*(1–3), 213–220.
14. Yang, H. L., Teng, J. T., & Chern, M. S. (2001). Deterministic inventory lot-size models under inflation with shortages and deterioration for fluctuating demand. *Naval Research Logistics, 48*(2), 144–158.
15. Yang, H. L. (2004). Two-warehouse inventory models for deteriorating items with shortages under inflation. *European Journal of Operational Research, 157*(2), 344–356.

Handbook of Evidence Based Management Practices in Business – Satyendra Kumar Sharma et al. (eds)
© 2023 Taylor & Francis Group, London, ISBN 978-1-032-54216-4

Chapter

Designing a Robust Supply Chain Model for the Distribution of—'COVAXIN'

Ankur Roy[1]

Assistant Professor, Management Development Institute, Gurgaon

Imlak Sheikh[2]

Associate Professor, Management Development Institute, Gurgaon

Satyendra K. Sharma[3]

Associate Professor, Birla Institute of Technology and Science, Pilani

ABSTRACT: COVID-19 is an international pandemic. It currently has nearly 9.27 million active cases in India alone and nearly 135,000 people have died because of it. A robust and agile supply chain model is required to distribute the vaccine to the huge population of India and the world alike. The distribution system must have fail-safe as well, so that one setback does not hamper the whole supply chain. COVAXIN is an indigenous COVID-19 vaccine developed by Bharat Biotech in collaboration with Indian Council of Medical Research (ICMR) - National Institute of Virology (NIV). The vaccine is currently in phase I & II of human trials.

As this is a novel problem, hence a new supply chain model is to be designed and implemented. Companies such as Amazon and Flipkart are very agile in delivering products to remote locations; on the other hand, firms like VRL Logistics or Mahindra Logistic are capable of handling freight movement to different parts of country and international market.

KEYWORDS: Pandemic disaster, Supply chain, Planning

1. Introduction

On 11 March 2020, World health Origin (WHO) declared Novel Coronavirus Disease (COVID-19) outbreak as a pandemic and reiterated the call for countries to take immediate actions and scale up response to treat, detect and reduce transmission to save people's lives.

[1]ankur.roy@mdi.ac.in, [2]imlak.shaikh@mdi.ac.in, [3]satyendrasharma@pilani.bits-pilani.ac.in

DOI: 10.4324/9781003415725-48

India being the second largest country in terms of population is worst hit. With total cases reaching around 9.27 million and total deaths reaching up to 135000 numbers, India is severely affected. Approximately 15.27% of all the Corona Victims are from India, which are quite a huge number and an alarming bell to us.

India

Total cases	Recovered	Deaths
9.27M	8.68M	135K
+44,489		+524

Worldwide

Total cases	Recovered	Deaths
60.7M	38.9M	1.43M

Fig. 48.1 No. of cases in India and the world

Source: https://www.worldometers.info/coronavirus/country/india

The five major COVID hotspots in India are – Maharashtra, Karnataka, Andhra Pradesh, Tamil Nadu and Delhi. These areas become extremely critical for us when we are designing a supply chain for COVAXIN.

Some other serious concerns for us which becomes crucial for this project are as follows:

- No. of cases
- No. of asymptomatic cases
- Gatherings
- Weather conditions
- Unavailability of vaccine
- No supply chain

Attempts made by Indian companies in developing a vaccine for COVID'19

Many Indian companies have come up with potential vaccines and are in different phases of vaccine development, some of them are mentioned below:

- Covaxin, Bharat Biotech
- AstraZeneca, Serum Institute of India
- ZyCoV-D, Zydus Cadila
- Panacea Biotec

- Indian Immunologicals
- Mynvax
- Biological E

2. Background Work in the Field with Citations

2.1 Logistics of the COVID-19 Vaccine Distribution in India

The COVID-19 crisis has transformed the role of key stakeholders in the medical supply chain. Once focused mainly on regulatory matters and alleviating the social consequences of situations, governments and government agencies are now moving towards a more active role in the supply chain to finance, secure, and provide medical supplies, including PPE, tests, therapeutics, and vaccines. As the challenges of PPE kits and medical equipment have almost been resolved, the next major challenge in front of the government and various other stakeholders in the healthcare sector is handling the production and distribution of the COVID-19 vaccine in India.

2.2 Identifying Pain Points in the Existing Vaccine Supply Chain in India

India will conduct vaccines distribution on such a large scale for the first time. Although the country has previous experience of running large-scale polio vaccination, the subjects were a small subset of its population. The only adult vaccination program in the history of independent India was the tetanus vaccination program. It will be a rigorous task to identify and forecast demand this time, and data analytics capacity is required to be expanded for the same. Presently, India is the largest producer of vaccines globally, but many raw materials are sourced from other countries. Once a vaccine is approved for use, the demand for its APIs will also increase, and the vaccine manufacturers in India need to prepare themselves for such a situation. The concentration of most of the vaccine manufacturing facilities in some areas of the Southern and Western parts of the country will also turn out to be a logistical bottleneck in the supply chain.

Presently, there are around 250 forerunners of the COVID-19 vaccine globally; these vaccines are based upon seven different platforms like novel RNA platform, viral vector platform, etc. A few the leading COVID-19 vaccines under development will need to be kept at temperatures as low as minus 80 degrees Celsius (minus 112 degrees Fahrenheit) from the moment they are bottled to the time they are ready to be injected into patients' arms. Today India has a well-functioning logistics infrastructure. Considering the above temperature requirements, many cold chain logistics providers have said that the existing cold chain logistics is only a small subset of the larger logistics chain and insufficient for vaccine distribution in the whole country

The vaccine administration in a country with a 1.3 billion populations will also require a large healthcare workforce. Most of the vaccines under development will need two doses for complete immunization. The second dose to be administered about a month after the first. They are thus making logistics and distribution even more challenging.

2.3 Characteristics of a Successful Logistics Network Provider

The end-to-end logistics of the vaccine supply chain considers multiple factors to ensure the timely delivery of the vaccine to people in various parts of the country. The most feasible supply chain network consists of the following stages. At the production facility, the vaccines will be stored in the ice boxes containing dry ice, and these iceboxes will be packed in the form of pallets. The pallets from the production facility will be flown to the regional hub through air cargo planes. The pallets will be sorted at the regional hub and sent to the state hub through haul-line trucks or air freight, depending on the distance. These pallets will be stored in the temperature-controlled warehouse at the state hub. The pallets will then be dispatched to the warehouse in the district headquarters in haul line trucks/ delivery trucks. At the district headquarters, the ice boxes will be taken out of the pallet and dispatched to various hospitals and healthcare centers to be administered to the people. It must be kept in mind that once the icebox is taken out of pallets, their life is just 2-3 days, so this step should be carried out before the last mile delivery.

Logistical Equipment For Potential Vaccine Supply Chain

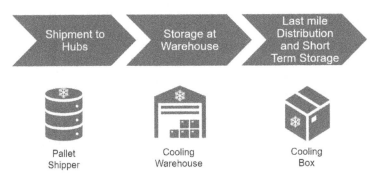

Source: Authors compilation

Considering the above mentioning pain points in mind, it will be highly beneficial for the government to partner with one or multiple logistic service providers throughout the supply chain to get advantage of their integrated logistics planning.

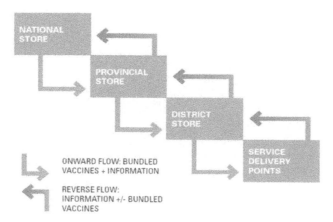

Fig. 48.2 Flow of information in a vaccine supply chain

Source: Authors compilation

Some of the characteristics of an effective logistics network provider are as follow:

1. Access to world class shipping network
2. Extensive local presence
3. Process excellence
4. Crisis Response and Resilience
5. Data driven insights

Devising a supply chain for a vaccine is not easy and that too in a situation of pandemic when the vaccine is long awaited and wanted by all. It becomes very important to understand the current situation and how the information flows in such a supply chain.

2.4 Importance of Effective Supply Chain

An effective supply chain can:

- Ensure that every international or domestic supply of vaccines from a manufacturer reaches its first destination in a country in satisfactory condition.
- Control temperature and it can be ensured that vaccines are distributed within a robust cold-chain system.
- Check transport of vaccine between each level in the supply chain
- Be effective and ensure proper transport contingency plans

The factors we have identified for the same are – operational experience, target population, storage requirement and precautions during transit, transport, stores, service delivery strategy, vaccinator skills, risk of adverse event after immunization.

3. Suggested Supply Chain Model

The suggested supply chain model as per the temperature requirement is quite self-explanatory and can be seen in Fig. 48.5.

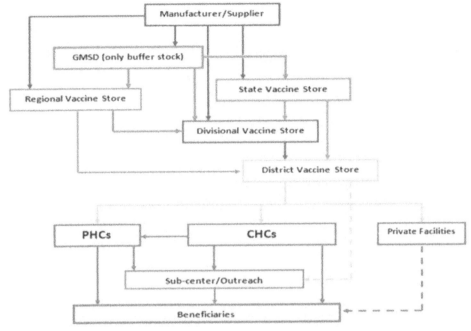

Fig. 48.3 Existing cold supply chain

Source: Authors compilation

Parameter	Polio Vaccine	COVID Vaccine
Operational experience	Extensive experience	Novel condition hence no experience
Target Population	0-5 years children (11.5%)	Whole Population
Storage requirement and precautions during transit	Vaccine vials can be stored until expiry date (usually 2 years) at −20 Degrees or at +2 to +8 Degrees Celsius for a maximum of 6 months. During shipment or in the field, vaccine may be thawed and refrozen.	Expiry date unclear hence will be kept deep frozen at −60 Celsius. Kept at 2-4 Celsius for administration.
Transport	Relies on road and rail network primarily	Need agile system hence will use air transport.
Stores	Vaccines are stored for a long time (nearly 3 months in each level)	Storage is needed for short time (one week at most) as demand is very high
Service delivery strategy	Combination of fixed post and house to house	Fixed post due to temperature constraint.
Vaccinator skills	Volunteers can administer	Skilled staff needed
Risk of Adverse event after Immunization	Extremely low	Data still not sufficient to comment

Fig. 48.4 Comparison between existing and proposed supply chain

Source: Authors compilation

4. Model Building

To build our model we will look in following key factors:

- Products: Information about the product and handling details

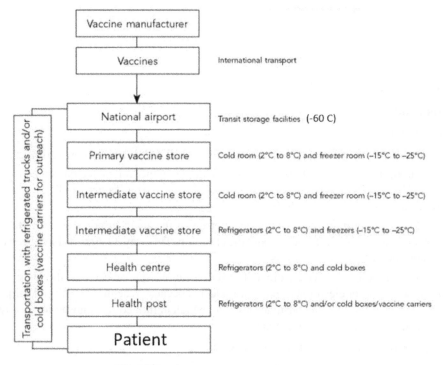

Fig. 48.5 Suggested supply chain model

Source: Authors compilation

- Facilities: Where the product is made and stored, cost associated with it
- Vehicles& routes: The mode used for transportation

4.1 Data Required

We have looked into the primary data of existing logistics and supply chain consulting firms and analyzed their strengths. We have also looked into their failures and analyze their shortcomings so that the gap can be bridged.

(i) Variables Identified

Following variables have been considered to solve covaxin supply chain problem.

Datasets used:

List of airports in India (Source: IATA- International Air Transport Association)

Infection dataset (Source: ICMR- Indian Council of Medical Research)

- State-wise population
- Number of covid-19 infection cases in each state
- Number of covid-19 linked deaths in each state
- Number of covid-19 recoveries in each state

- Airport Name
- Airport latitude
- Airport Longitude
- Airport elevation
- Airport IATA score

(ii) Data Points

Airport Selection

- India has an air network of 355 airports spread over the states and union territories.
- Each airport is assigned an IATA score depending upon the freight and passenger capacity handled by the airport. IATA score increases as freight and passenger handling capacity of airport increases which is desirable.
- To select an airport for each state we referred to the main airports in each state and compared them using IATA scores and the elevation. This way 34 airports have been taken into consideration for the analysis.
- Airports with a higher IATA score and lower elevation were selected as the main airport for the state. Lower elevation airports are selected because reaching low altitude airport is easier for an aircraft and it consumes less fuel which in turn corresponds to lower costs as extra added fuel requirement decreases.

Forming the distance matrix of the airports

- To form the state-wise airport distance matrix we used the following formula to calculate distances using the latitude and longitude of the airport
- Following formula has been used to calculate distance between any two airports based on latitude, longitude data of the respective airport

  Formula=3443.8985 * (ACOS((SIN(F3*PI()/180) * SIN(B5*PI()/180) + COS(F3*PI()/180) * COS(B5*PI()/180) * COS(C5*PI()/180-G3*PI()/180))))

- **Mortality Index**

  State Mortality rate = No. of deaths/No. of infection cases

  Mortality Index = State Mortality rate/$\sum$State Mortality Rates

- **IATA Score Index**

  IATA Score Index = Airport IATA score/$\sum$Airport IATA score

- **Composite Score**

  To incorporate the severity of covid cases in various states in our model, and for hubs to act as efficient vaccine distribution, we formed the composite score. For this the capabilities of airports to handle traffic is taken which can be derived from IATA score index and combined with mortality index to cover highly affected areas first.

  Composite Score = 1/(Mortality index * IATA score index)

(iii) State-wise Proximity Matrix

Setting the hub location radius:

- This was done by performing an EDA i.e. exploratory data analysis on the distance matrix

Measure	Value
Population Average of Airport to Airport Distance	703 Km
Population Standard Deviation of Airport to Airport Distance	345.68 Km
Population Variance	123771.2

- Average State border distance = 351.5 KM
- To calculate the distance so that any state can act as hub, following calculations are done:
- Hub location radius = 351.5 + 0.2 * Population Standard Deviation of Airport to Airport Distance = 420 Km
- A rounded off distance of 400 Km was decided as this would factor in all neighboring states of any state.

State wise proximity matrix:

- 0 – The corresponding state doesn't fall within 400km of the state in question
- 1 – The corresponding state falls within 400km of the state in question

4.2 Model

(i) Designing the model for establishing the supply chain for Covid vaccine

The objective of the problem is to find the hub location such that to minimize the overall time of supplying the vaccine. As assumed, it can be done by minimizing the distance between the hub node airport and other nodes. Since, minimizing distance and time would result in minimization of overall costs and this is the main aim of designing this model.

(ii) Model Assumptions

1. A longer airport to airport distance is directly related with a longer flight duration and that by minimizing this distance factor, the time is minimized.
2. The data from the dataset by ICMR would remain relevant at the time the vaccine is finally developed.
3. The government would allow usage of civil airports for the distribution of the vaccine.

(iii) Objective Function and its Constraints

Objective Function:

Minimize Hub Factor = $\sum$Composite Score$_i$ * H$_i$

Where i = State

H$_i$ -Hub Decision Variable = 0, if state doesn't qualify as hub

= 1, if state qualifies as hub

Constraints:

- For Maharashtra,

    HMaharashtra + HTelangana + HGujarat + HMadhya Pradesh + HGoa >= 1

- For Karnataka,

    HKarnataka + HTamil Nadu + HKerala + HTelangana + HGoa + HPuducherry + HLakshadweep >= 1

- For Tamil Nadu,

    HTamil Nadu + HKarnataka + HAndhra Pradesh + HKerala + HTelangana + HGoa + HPuducherry >= 1

- For Delhi,

    HDelhi + HUttar Pradesh + HRajasthan + HHaryana + HMadhya Pradesh + HPunjab + HJammu & Kashmir & Laddakh + HUttarakhand + HHimachal Pradesh + HChandigarh >= 1

- For West Bengal,

    HWest Bengal + HOrissa + HBihar + HChhattisgarh + HAssam + HJharkhand + HTripura + HManipur + HMeghalaya + HNagaland + HSikkim + HMizoram >= 1

- For Manipur,

    HManipur + HWest Bengal + HAssam + HTripura + HManipur + HArunachal Pradesh + HMeghalaya + HNagaland + HSikkim >= 1

- For Andaman & Nicobar,

    HAndaman & Nicobar + HSikkim >= 1

Similarly, constraints were drawn for all other states, with the basic format

$\sum Hi >= 1$ where i=1, which signifies that the state is within 400kms radius of the state under observation.

5. Data Analysis

Results

As a result of solving the objective problem, we identified seven airports for which hub factor came out to be minimum. Each of the airport spoke node was assigned to single hub node so that all the spoke airports with distance under 400 kms could be assigned (for achieving operational achieving operational efficiency).

Decision Vars	Airport Used as Hub	Composite Score
Maharashtra	1	0.430096319
Karnataka	1	1.673663171
Andhra Pradesh	0	318.4788784

Decision Vars	Airport Used as Hub	Composite Score
Tamil Nadu	1	1.485214781
Kerala	O	298.7921309
Delhi	1	1.393835572
Uttar Pradesh	O	76.27895158
West Bengal	1	54.48914666
Odisha	O	236.0439768
Telangana	O	176.3284679
Rajasthan	O	123.815242
Bihar	O	204.9349814
Chhattisgarh	O	117.7154386
Haryana	O	142.6278596
Assam	O	269.982816
Gujarat	O	56.13091623
Madhya Pradesh	O	72.40135775
Punjab	O	45.60306091
Jharkhand	O	140.7134893
J&K and Ladakh	O	76.79279496
Uttarakhand	O	88.56301419
Goa	O	90.95776633
Puducherry	O	280.2793654
Himachal Pradesh	O	288.7243671
Tripura	O	126.1651843
Manipur	1	123.3840625
Chandigarh	O	91.60155714
Arunachal Pradesh	O	8164.331307
Meghalaya	O	148.8501591
Nagaland	O	255.5826626
Sikkim	O	194948.7751
Andaman and Nicobar	1	109.6565497
Mizoram	O	18446.35581
Lakshadweep	O	11293292.68

Source: Authors compilation

The resulting model was then logically examined, if it made practical sense. We observed that Manipur, Tamil Nadu & Andaman & Nicobar Islands were chosen as hub states due to the radius constraint of 400 km or less. However, with little logical leeway these three states could be eliminated from the model as hubs. States unique to these hubs were compared and assigned to as follows:

State with Discrepancy	Distance from Hubs (in km)				Anomalous State Assigned to Hub
	Maharashtra	Karnataka	New Delhi	West Bengal	
Andaman & Nicobar Islands	1233.8	886.69	1343.3	706.05	Karnataka
Andhra Pradesh	596.26	419.58	734.08	417.19	Karnataka
Goa	229.63	261.05	813.13	937.31	Maharashtra
Madhya Pradesh	273.5	582.7	358.31	701.07	Maharashtra
Arunachal Pradesh	1347.2	1331.6	964.31	495.58	West Bengal

Source: Authors compilation

For these three states, one hub state was assigned among four main hub states (stated below) in accordance with the load they had after considering the distance criteria.

The following airports were finalised to be used as hubs for forwarding vaccines throughout India:

- Chhatrapati Shivaji International Airport, Maharashtra
- Kempegowda International Airport, Karnataka
- Indira Gandhi International Airport, New Delhi
- Netaji Subhash Chandra Bose International Airport, West Bengal

Each of these airports has been selected on the basis of its freight handling capabilities with respect to its neighbour and the severity of covid in the state.

6. Findings and Managerial Implications

(i) Recommended Plan

The following plan must be used to route the vaccines from the identified airport hubs:

Airport Hub	States which the hub must supply to
Maharashtra	Gujarat, Madhya Pradesh, Goa, Maharashtra
Karnataka	Kerala, Telangana, Puducherry, Lakshadweep, Andhra Pradesh, Tamil Nadu, Karnataka, Andaman & Nicobar Islands
New Delhi	Chandigarh, Uttar Pradesh, Rajasthan, Haryana, Punjab, Jammu & Kashmir, Ladakh, Uttarakhand, Himachal Pradesh, New Delhi
West Bengal	Orissa, Bihar, Chhattisgarh, Assam, Jharkhand, Tripura, Manipur, Meghalaya, Nagaland, Sikkim, Mizoram, Arunachal Pradesh, West Bengal

Source: Authors compilation

(ii) Supply Chain Network Diagram

See diagram on next page.

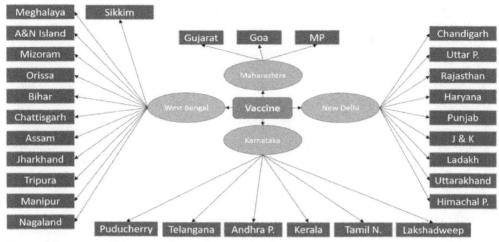

Source: Authors compilation

7. Conclusion

- The number of airport hubs has been brought to 4 upon logical examination
- Maharashtra, Karnataka, New Delhi & West Bengal have been finalised as hubs
- The average distance between any two locations shown in the supply chain network diagram is less than or equal to 400kms
- The average time taken to travel to any endpoint = Time taken to reach hub + Time taken to reach airport from hub = 400/700+400/700 = 1.143 hrs or 68.58 minutes (Considering average speed of aircraft to be 700 km/hr)

On the basis of study conducted on existing supply chain and uncertainties linked with the possible supply chain of Covid vaccine, aforementioned plan has been advised for India.

This model has been designed to achieve seamless and robust supply chain model for the distribution of Covid vaccine in India in minimum time possible.

REFERENCES

1. www.ncbi.nlm.nih.gov/pmc/articles/PMC1802111/
2. inclentrust.org/inclen/wp-content/uploads/Cold-Chain-Full-Report.pdf
3. World Health Organization. Vaccines, immunization and biologicals. The cold chain [cited 2006 Oct 18] URL: http://www.icn.ch/matters_colds.htm
4. UNICEF report on cold chain logistics and vaccine management during polio supplementary immunization activities
5. en.wikipedia.org/wiki/Template: COVID-19_pandemic_data
6. García, L. Y., & Cerda, A. A. (2020). Contingent assessment of the COVID-19 vaccine. *Vaccine*, *38*(34), 5424–5429.

7. Awasthi, R., Guliani, K. K., Bhatt, A., Gill, M. S., Nagori, A., Kumaraguru, P., & Sethi, T. (2020). VacSIM: Learning Effective Strategies for COVID-19 Vaccine Distribution using Reinforcement Learning. *arXiv preprint arXiv:2009.06602*

8. Lane, P. C., Clarke, D., & Hender, P. (2012). On developing robust models for favourability analysis: Model choice, feature sets and imbalanced data. *Decision Support Systems*, *53*(4), 712–718.

9. Caprara, A., Toth, P., & Fischetti, M. (2000). Algorithms for the set covering problem. *Annals of Operations Research*, *98*(1-4), 353–371.

10. ReVelle, C., Toregas, C., & Falkson, L. (1976). Applications of the location set-covering problem. *Geographical analysis*, *8*(1), 65–76.

11. Dsouza, D. D., Quadros, S., Hyderabadwala, Z. J., & Mamun, M. A. (2020). Aggregated COVID-19 suicide incidences in India: Fear of COVID-19 infection is the prominent causative factor. *Psychiatry Research*, 113145.

Handbook of Evidence Based Management Practices in Business – Satyendra Kumar Sharma et al. (eds)
© 2023 Taylor & Francis Group, London, ISBN 978-1-032-54216-4

Chapter

Identification and Extraction of Retailer's Expectations in the Last-Mile Delivery

Krishna Veer Tiwari*, Leela Rani[1], Satyendra Kumar Sharma[2]

Birla Institute of Technology & Science, Pilani, Rajasthan, India

ABSTRACT: In today's competitive environment, as customers generate a high demand for products, retailers/manufacturers face additional pressure to meet the dynamic nature of customer demand in a sustainable manner. Last-mile delivery (LMD) is the last leg of the process and is an essential part of the delivery process. Various techniques in the past decade have come up with innovative solutions to optimize the LMD, like the Internet of Things (IoT), Machine learning (ML), autonomous vehicles, parcel lockers, and drone-based delivery, some of which are currently being implemented in industries to improve existing practices. The study involves an extensive review of literature to identify the evolution of retailer's expectations, including the role of sustainability aspect to meet the Sustainable Development Goals (SDGs) in future delivery models. The literature is synthesized based on the methods adopted, definitions given over the years, and foundational or innovative solutions used. Using keyword cluster analysis and the software VOSviewer, the study highlighted the main enablers of evolving trends in LMD from the standpoint of different stakeholders, such as retailers, and their respective expectations. We compare the results to the present SDGs and group the findings into technology, infrastructure, and society as the three most important drivers. By identifying the research gaps, we propose the future implications for LMD that the focus should be on a specific location-based optimization technique. The value addition of the study is in the form of a comprehensive summary of three decades of literature in LMD from the perspective of the retailer and the investigation of the evolutionary trends.

KEYWORDS: Last-Mile delivery, Supply chain, Distribution center, Omnichannel, Order fulfilment, E-commerce

---
*Corresponding Author: p20200038@pilani.bits-pilani.ac.in
[1]Leela_r@pilani.bits-pilani.ac.in, [2]satyendrasharma@pilani.bits-pilani.ac.in

DOI: 10.4324/9781003415725-49

1. Introduction

The increase in e-commerce growth and penetration of access to the internet in developing economies like India has created a strong upsurge in supply and demand in past few years (Moagar-Poladian, Dumitrescu, and Tanase, 2017; IPC, 2015). Since 2016, e-retail, including e-grocery and online food ordering, accounted for nearly 8.7% of the entire sales in the retail segment worldwide, and is estimated to be around 1.86 trillion U.S. dollars (eMarketer, 2018). In India, the retail segment is estimated to be 779 billion U.S. dollars and is estimated to grow at 9% over 2019-2030 to 1407 billion U.S. dollars, as per Kearney Research (2019). Due to the availability of a vast amount of data and accurate movement of products, manufacturers and retailers can coordinate among themselves and allow the aggregation of goods for profitable delivery movement. As we arrive at the products' final point of the movement: the last mile delivery (LMD), the aggregation of goods becomes difficult due to multiple delivery points. Due to the strong upsurge in internet users, retailers are challenged to reach more customers and expand their distribution channels. However, with the help of technology, they can predict the demand for the products in the short-term and long-term. This has led to optimization in terms of resources, manpower, inventory, and delivery to the customers.

Thus, the LMD becomes the most expensive part of the delivery and supply chain (Gevaers et al., 2011). Due to the emergence of ultra-fast delivery models, aggregation becomes difficult or impossible and creates a rupture in the supply chain as the products travel back and forth from the customer to the retailer. To achieve and remain competitive in the market, retailers seek innovative delivery solutions or outsource their delivery parts (Ghajargar, Zenezini, and Montanaro, 2016; Iwan, Kijewska, and Lemke, 2016). Innovative research solutions include delivery by parcel lockers, drones, and autonomous vehicles (Joerss et al., 2016). Since these are new trends and much of the implementation part is still left unexplored most retailers are in a quandary and wish to see the success of these techniques before making heavy investments.

This leads to a spiral loop of confusion as without test-and-trial with the customers, these techniques cannot be proven worthy, and at the same time, without success, retailers are wary of the investment. Customers opting for e-commerce platforms expect a higher level of service quality and product delivery at a no or marginal increase in cost. E-retailers providing online service further accentuate the competition by providing flexible delivery options, delivery locations, and a delivery time slot to the customers for ease in the collection and return of their products (Michalowska, Kotylak, and Danielak, 2015).

The customer journey theory proposed by Lemon and Verhoef (2016) is determined to be apt for the current research study on expectations being done here. Reports suggest in the coming age of e-commerce, investments in customer products would be redirected to expectations and experience innovations associated with a customer (Gartner, 2015).

1.1 Benefits of LMD in e-grocery

Based on the customer journey theory, Lemon and Verhoef (2016) have suggested four touchpoints influencing the overall customer's expectation: partner-owned, brand-owned, social/external, and customer-owned. These touchpoints constitute the customer journey and expectations. From a customer standpoint, the associated retailer shapes the experience is irrespective of the role of the retailer during product delivery.

Considering the customers' expectations in e-grocery-based LMD gives a holistic perspective of customers, and e-retailers. The level of customers' involvement in the supply chain in taking responsibility and control for the coordination of the activities influences the retailers' control over the customer experience. Based on the literature review, we identify the significant benefits of LMD to the customer provided by the retailer, including economic benefits (rewards like scratch cards, premium service), social benefits, and no-cost delivery.

1.2 Challenges in LMD

Based on the literature review, we identify the significant challenges in LMD encountered by the retailer while serving a customer, including flexibility of payment options, delivery location, time slots for delivery and omnichannel integration (Patricio et al., 2008). In e-grocery, maintaining the freshness of the product is a significant challenge as the weather conditions in India are averse. For new entrants in the market space, integration of omnichannel is quite a difficult task. Providing both online and offline modes of service creates an unpredictable flow of products in the supply chain and mismanages manpower and resources (Laukkanen, 2016; Martin et al., 2016).

2. Extraction of Variables from Review of Literature

An extensive review of literature for this purpose was conducted where, first, all research studies where similar studies (which sought to address understanding different expectations associated with retailers addressed relating to the purchase, service, perception, or satisfaction) were found and studied to identify an exhaustive list of all expectations. These studies are summarized in Table 49.1.

2.1 Quantitative Systematic Review of Literature

In the initial step of quantitative analysis, the foundational articles in the initial years of publication are identified as related to "last mile delivery" AND "retailers' expectations" in Scopus and WoS databases. The first relevant article related to "last mile" AND "retailers' expectations" was published in 2001 (Punakivi M., Yrjölä H., Holmström J, 2001). It evaluated the reception and delivery box concept to reduce the cases of missed deliveries during the delivery of goods to the customers' homes. The first article to appear in the WoS database to include "last mile delivery" was in 2003 (Chan, 2003). The article is based on a survey of the role of major world governments in assuring e-logistics service transactions.

The grouping of the keywords "last mile delivery" AND "retailers' expectations" in the Scopus database resulted in multiple articles published during an expanded timeline, one of which was in 2016 (Lim *et al.*, 2016). The article describes the typology and configurations of a last-mile supply network (LMSN) in omnichannel retailing.

The issues pertaining to the last mile and supply chain, in general, are growing in terms of focus in the field of research and are expected to increase exponentially in the future. The

Table 49.1 Relevant articles from the period of 2006-2021

Author & Year	Title	Journal	Objective	Key Findings
So et al., 2006	Last Mile fulfilment strategy for competitive advantage	International Journal of Logistics Systems and Management	It explains and defines a framework of the Last-Mile benefit from a competitive standpoint.	The advancement in the Last-Mile could not only be limited to the channel of distribution, but also include innovation, product standard, internal operations, supply chain adaptability connections, trusts, and personal contacts, among others, and they require additional research to match diverse business contexts.
Kull et al., 2007	Last-mile supply chain efficiency: an analysis of learning curves in online ordering	International Journal of Operations & Production Management	Concentrating on customer order - to - delivery efficiency improvements through the "interpretability" of websites, given that supply chain efficiency is dependent on the usefulness of the web-based ordering system.	The scientific proof supports a wide range of power-law learning techniques for internet ordering (i.e., the first few orders involve substantial learning). Nonetheless, there are substantial differences among websites, and a fraction of the order processing may be invariant.
Sharon Cullinane 2009	From Bricks to Clicks: The Impact of Online Retailing on Transport and the Environment	Transport Reviews	To describe the multimodal transportation relationships engaged in digital shopping, focusing on the interplay between freight and passenger aspects, and to shed light on the environmental influence of digital shopping.	The impacts of electronic shopping on the climate are not unambiguous; instead, the issue is multifaceted and evolving, involving both social actions and tough market decisions.
Edwards et al., 2010	Comparative analysis of the carbon footprints of conventional and online retailing A "last mile" perspective	International Journal of Physical Distribution & Logistics Management	Concentrate on the co2 emission of "last mile" delivery times (i.e., shipments from local storage facilities to the household) and personalized shopping tours.	The findings indicate that neither household delivery time nor traditional shopping has an outright CO2 benefit; however, household delivery is likely to emit less CO2 than traditional shopping in the majority of cases. However, Emissions of co2 per item for intensive/occasional bus shopping trips could be comparable to online buying/household delivery.

Author & Year	Title	Journal	Objective	Key Findings
Kalyanmoy Deb 2011	Multi-objective Optimization Using Evolutionary Algorithms: An Introduction	Multi-objective Evolutionary Optimization for Product Design and Manufacturing	To define a dynamic scheduling optimization technique with an emphasis on the fuel efficiency of the operation. This article presents a mathematical simulation of last-mile supply disruptions, including routing and assignment issues, following a thorough literature review.	The outcomes include an algorithmic methodology on black hole maximisation, and the efficiency is validated using various test functions. Validation consists of different scenario analysis to evaluate the model and assess its performance in maximizing energy efficiency in the last mile delivery.
Boysen et al., 2015	Vehicle scheduling under the warehouse-on-wheels (WOW) policy	Discrete Applied Mathematics	To explore a routing issue between a standard distribution center and a production plant under the WOW strategy.	The WOW vehicular scheduling algorithm and its subsequent computational burden analysis for various problem variations are performed, and effective exact solution processes are provided.
Gansterer et al., 2017	Collaborative vehicle routing: a survey	European Journal of Operational Research	To identify three major streams of research (1) Centralized collaborative planning, (2) Decentralized planning without auctions, and (3) Auction-based decentralized planning	A structured overview and classification of literature is given along with recent developments and proposed future work directions
Jha et al., 2020	Meta-heuristic algorithms for solving the sustainable agro-food grain supply chain network design problem	Modern Supply Chain Research and Applications	To investigate a problem related to sustainable routing protocol in the setting of a Indian agro - business supply chain	The model reduces the overall transportation expenditure and carbon dioxide emissions tax associated with transporting food grains from food producers to hubs and then warehouses.

Source: Authors compilation

second step involves the quantitative analysis by identifying the articles in databases with the highest number of citations. The most relevant articles on the topic of LMD on retailers' expectations are segregated based on the focus of the variable identified in the studies. The foundational studies referred to the period 1990-2005 since before 2005, the term last mile was under the umbrella term order fulfilment. The trend in articles being published in the area of LMD is shown in Fig. 49.1. It is visible that post-2015, the number of studies incorporating research on "last mile delivery" started to increase tremendously, and each year the number almost doubled.

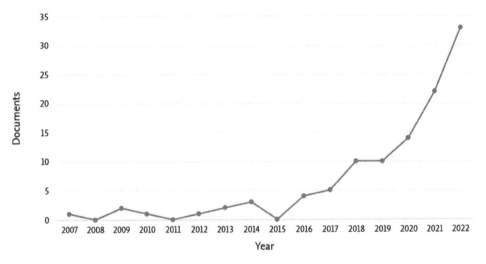

Fig. 49.1 Documents published in Scopus – by year

Source: Authors compilation

3. Existing Gaps and Findings

The review of the studies mentioned in Table 49.2 revealed retailers' expectations in various studies and the associated service levels, perceptions and satisfaction of the customer in LMD. A list of five unique factors was extracted after removing overlapping and similar list obtained from the literature review. In future, we aim to do an exploratory study to identify the performance-related behaviour of the retailers to serve customers in various categories of retail formats in a Tier-II city in India.

The next task was to map the variables of retailers' expectations in grocery last-mile delivery for already identified factors. The future study will be designed to be conducted with a structured yet slightly modified questionnaire developed by the author (Guneri, Yurt and Kaplan, 2008).

The entire process adopted by a retailer is shown in a straightforward manner in Fig. 49.2. and the identified variables are laid out across the supply chain for easy understanding. The process involves the procurement of goods from the manufacturer. In the case of fresh groceries, the manufacturer is the farmer, and the procured products are sent in bulk amounts to the warehouses and cold storage facilities to maintain the freshness of the goods. A minor

Table 49.2 Research studies identifying the list of factors

Variables	References
Product	Jauhar et al. (2022), Schmutz et al. (2009), Kohli et al. (2004), Sun et al. (2014), Pratap et al. (2021), Liu et al. (2008), Nisar and Prabhakar (2017)
Supply & warehousing	Wilson and Christella (2019), Vakulenko et al. (2019), Mishra et al. (2021), Hidayanto et al. (2017),
Distribution	Vakulenko et al. (2019), Murae et al. (2019), Wilson and Christella (2019), Gupta et al. (2019), Mogale et al. (2018), Prajapati et al. (2020)
Logistics Service	Nica (2015), Jauhar and Pant (2016), Jen-Hwa Hu et al. (2017), Oláh et al. (2019), Qin et al. (2021)
Reverse Logistics	Nisar and Prabhakar (2017), Jain et al. (2020), Siltonga et al. (2020), Huang (2011), Zhu et al. (2017), Jen-Hwa Hu et al. (2017), Goswami and Daultani (2021), Mishra et al. (2021), Hidayanto et al. (2017), Riyanto and Renaldi (2018), Arora et al. (2019)

Source: Authors compilation

Fig. 49.2 Movement of goods across the supply chain

Source: Authors compilation

part of the goods is displayed in-store for customers who prefer to shop offline. The customers deploying online and hybrid modes of grocery shopping are served from the in-store inventory or directly from the warehouse.

4. Discussion and Future Scope of Work

To the best of the author's knowledge, the extensive review of literature and the extraction of variables presented systematically is one of the most holistic works. In future, an integrated case study can be done to allow for thorough research in the future in the field of LMD to address current gaps. The factors extracted will be used in future studies to develop a questionnaire to allow empirical validation with the retailers to ensure the factors are relevant in the Indian context. The five variables – product, supply and warehousing, logistics service, distribution, and reverse logistics are spread across the entire supply chain, and each factor pinpoints the challenges faced by the retailer during LMD provided to the customer. These points of challenges are also the points that can be turned into optimization areas for improved customer satisfaction, repeated purchase intention and a profitable delivery model for the retailer.

REFERENCES

1. Boyer, K. K., Frohlich, M. T., & Hult, G. T. M. (2005). *Extending the supply chain: how cutting-edge companies bridge the critical last mile into customers' homes.* New York: American Management Association

2. Chan, F. W. H. (2003). E-logistics: Some legal and policy debates. Conference 8th Conference of the Hong-Kong-Society-for-Transportation-Studies.

3. Deb, K. (2011). Multi-objective Optimization Using Evolutionary Algorithms: An Introduction. *Multi-Objective Evolutionary Optimization for Product Design and Manufacturing*, 3–34. https://doi.org/10.1007/978-0-85729-652-8_1

4. Edwards, J. B., McKinnon, A. C., & Cullinane, S. L. (2010). Comparative analysis of the carbon footprints of conventional and online retailing. International Journal of Physical Distribution & Logistics Management, 40(1/2), 103–123. https://doi.org/10.1108/09600031011018055

5. Gansterer, M., Hartl, R. F., & Salzmann, P. E. H. (2017). Exact solutions for the collaborative pickup and delivery problem. *Central European Journal of Operations Research*, 26(2), 357–371. https://doi.org/10.1007/s10100-017-0503-x

6. Gupta, E. V., Mogale, D. G., & Tiwari, M. K. (2019). Optimal control of production and maintenance operations in smart custom manufacturing systems with multiple machines. IFAC-PapersOnLine, 52(13), 241–246. https://doi.org/10.1016/j.ifacol.2019.11.148

7. Hidayanto, A. N., Ovirza, M., Anggia, P., Budi, N. F. A., & Phusavat, K. (2017). The roles of electronic word of mouth and information searching in the promotion of a new e-commerce strategy: A case of online group buying in Indonesia. Journal of Theoretical and Applied Electronic Commerce Research, 12(3), 69–85. https://doi.org/10.4067/S0718-18762017000300006

8. Jauhar, S. K., & Pant, M. (2016). Sustainable supplier selection: a new differential evolution strategy with automotive industry application. In Recent developments and new direction in soft-computing foundations and applications (pp. 353–371). Springer. https://doi.org/10.1007/978-3-319-32229-2_25

9. Jen-Hwa Hu, P., Han-fen, H., & Xiao, F. (2017). Examining the mediating roles of cognitive load and performance outcomes in user satisfaction with a website: A field quasi-experiment. MIS Quarterly, 41(3), 975–987. https://doi.org/10.25300/MISQ/2017/41.3.14

10. Jauhar, S. K., Raj, P. V. R. P., Kamble, S., Pratap, S., Gupta, S., & Belhadi, A. (2022). A deep learning-based approach for performance assessment and prediction: A case study of pulp and paper industries. Annals of Operations Research, 1–27. https://doi.org/10.1007/s10479-022-04528-3

11. Kohli, R., Devaraj, S., & Mahmood, M. A. (2004). Understanding determinants of online consumer satisfaction: A decision process perspective. Journal of Management Information Systems, 21(1), 115–136. https://doi.org/10.1080/07421222.2004.11045796

12. Kull, T. J., Boyer, K., & Calantone, R. (2007). Last-mile supply chain efficiency: an analysis of learning curves in online ordering. International Journal of Operations & Production Management, 27(4), 409–434. https://doi.org/10.1108/01443570710736985

13. Liu, X., He, M., Gao, F., & Xie, P. (2008). An empirical study of online shopping customer satisfaction in China: A holistic perspective. International Journal of Retail & Distribution Management, 36(11), 919–940. https://doi.org/10.1108/09590550810911683

14. Mogale, D. G., Lahoti, G., Jha, S. B., Shukla, M., Kamath, N., & Tiwari, M. K. (2018). Dual market facility network design under bounded rationality. Algorithms, 11(4), 54. https://doi.org/10.3390/a11040054

15. Nica, E. (2015). Environmentally sustainable transport and e-commerce logistics. Economics, Management, and Financial Markets, 10(1), 86–92.

16. Nisar, T. M., & Prabhakar, G. (2017). What factors determine e-satisfaction and consumer spending in e-commerce retailing? Journal of Retailing and Consumer Services, 39, 135–144. https://doi.org/10.1016/j.jretconser.2017.07.010

17. Oláh, J., Kitukutha, N., Haddad, H., Pakurár, M., Máté, D., & Popp, J. (2019). Achieving sustainable e-commerce in environmental, social and economic dimensions by taking possible trade-offs. Sustainability, 11(1), 89. https://doi.org/10.3390/su11010089

18. Prajapati, D., Harish, A. R., Daultani, Y., Singh, H., & Pratap, S. (2020). A clustering based routing heuristic for last-mile logistics in fresh food Ecommerce. Global Business Review, 0972150919889797. https://doi.org/10.1177/0972150919889797

19. Pratap, S., Daultani, Y., Dwivedi, A., & Zhou, F. (2021). Supplier selection and evaluation in e-commerce enterprises: A data envelopment analysis approach. Benchmarking: An International Journal., 29(1), 325–341. https://doi.org/10.1108/BIJ-10-2020-0556

20. Qin, J., Fu, H., Wang, Z., & Xia, L. (2021). Financing and carbon emission reduction strategies of capital-constrained manufacturers in Ecommerce supply chains. International Journal of Production Economics, 241, 108271. https://doi.org/10.1016/j.ijpe.2021.108271

21. Vakulenko, Y., Shams, P., Hellström, D., & Hjort, K. (2019). Service innovation in e-commerce last mile delivery: Mapping the e-customer journey. Journal of Business Research, 101, 461–468. https://doi.org/10.1016/j.jbusres.2019.01.016

22. Wilson, N., & Christella, R. (2019). An empirical research of factors affecting customer satisfaction: A case of the Indonesian e-commerce industry. DeReMa Jurnal Manajemen, 14(1), 21–44. https://doi.org/10.19166/derema.v14i1.1108

23. Schmutz, P., Heinz, S., Métrailler, Y., & Opwis, K. (2009). Cognitive load in eCommerce applications—Measurement and effects on user satisfaction. Advances in Human-Computer Interaction, 2009, 1–9. https://doi.org/10.1155/2009/121494

24. Silitonga, K., Fakhrorazi, A., & Ikhsan, R. (2020). Drivers of buyer retention in e-commerce: The role of transaction characteristics and trust. Management Science Letters, 10(15), 3485–3494. https://doi.org/10.5267/j.msl.2020.6.046

25. So, H. W., Gunasekaran, A., & Chung, W. W. (2006). Last Mile fulfilment strategy for competitive advantage. International Journal of Logistics Systems and Management, 2(4), 404. https://doi.org/10.1504/ijlsm.2006.010384

26. Sun, Y., Fang, Y., & Lim, K. H. (2014). Understanding knowledge contributors' satisfaction in transactional virtual communities: A cost–benefit trade-off perspective. Information & Management, 51(4), 441–450. https://doi.org/10.1016/j.im.2014.02.008

Handbook of Evidence Based Management Practices in Business – Satyendra Kumar Sharma et al. (eds)
© 2023 Taylor & Francis Group, London, ISBN 978-1-032-54216-4

Chapter

Supply Risk Indicators to Assess Location and Environmental Risk

Ankur Roy[1], Imlak Shaikh[2]

Management Development Institute, Gurgaon, India

Satyendra K. Sharma[3]

Birla Institute of Technology and Science, Pilani, India

ABSTRACT: Over the past decade, supply chain vulnerability has become a popular area of research, because of the recent series of fatal events that have caused disruptions in the economy and supply chain across the Globe. In this study, we concentrated on the supply risk, which is upstream supply chain risk, and can be further bifurcated into multiple categories. The objective of this report is to analyze particularly the supply risk associated with the location using a risk assessment model. Due to the lack of availability of representative statistical data and other complexities, the statistical models fail to analyse the Supply Chain Risk. Therefore, we examined the supply risk using Analytical Hierarchy Process based on the subjective assessment, intuition, and expert statements. The estimated results from the analysis show that the observed supply chain has low total risk with maximum weightage for risk due to operational contingencies and lowest weightage for risk due to Disease Outbreak.

KEYWORDS: Analytical hierarchy process (AHP), Supply risk

1. Introduction

With the rapid growth and technological innovation, the supply chains are also becoming more complex with different factors like information flow coming into play. The literature encompasses multiple definition of supply chain management and the most suitable definition which we have adopted for this study is "The management of upstream and downstream

[1]ankur.roy@mdi.ac.in, [2]imlak.shaikh@mdi.ac.in, [3]satyendrasharma@pilani.bits-pilani.ac.in

DOI: 10.4324/9781003415725-50

relationships with suppliers and customers in order to create enhanced value in the final market place at less cost to the supply chain."[i]

In recent times, the shift towards the leaner supply chain has led to the rise of new vulnerabilities and risks. The objective of cutting the cost by maintaining lower inventory across different stages of the supply chain resulted in very low buffer inventory for interruptions. This amplifies the impact of any disruption on the supply chain.

The risk associated with the supply chain can be divided into four categories–supply risk, demand risk, process risk, and product risk. In this study, we will mainly focus on supply risk, which is upstream supply chain risk. Further, supply risk can be subdivided into disruption risk and operational risk. Disruptions are usually external to a supply chain and are defined as unforeseen events that cause disturbances in the normal flow of goods and materials within a supply chain. These disruptions can be any form of regulatory changes, natural disaster (environmental risk), climate changes, terrorist activities, etc.

The location of a facility in a supply chain affects a wide range of factors, including environmental risk, legal and regulatory risk, availability of qualified workforce, level of connectivity, security from theft, and economic benefits.

2. Literature Review

Many studies have been conducted by researchers to evaluate the various supply risk and their potential impact.

In 2005, Kleindorfer identified operational contingencies, sudden disruption in the supply chain, and Natural Hazards as three major subcategories of the supply chain risk. Here, operational contingencies refer to the failure due to the mistake of an employee or machine failure. Sudden disruption in the supply chain can be caused by labor strikes, scams, shortage of working capital, etc.[ii]

Another set of researchers deduced that disturbance in the supply chain can be defined as random events by constructing the vulnerability map for an organization. However, the probability associated will vary with the type of event. Similarly, probability of a mishap or company failure can be determined using industry data. Although, the likelihood of a premeditated inference is tough to determine because it depends on humans, politics, company and industry, along with a lack of historical data. They also examined how a particular industry or company is more vulnerable to certain types of risk.[iii]

---

[i]CIPS, "Supply Chain Vulnerability," *Chartered Institute of Procuement and Supply Kwowledge Works*, no. January (2013): 1–8.
[ii]Paul R. Kleindorfer and Germaine H. Saad, "Managing Disruption Risks in Supply Chain," *Production And Operations Management Vol. 14, No. 1, Spring 2005, Pp. 53–68* 14, no. 1 (2005): 434–38, https://doi.org/10.1109/ICEMMS.2010.5563408.
[iii]Yossi Sheffi and James B. Rice Jr., "Yossi Sheffi and James B. Rice Jr. (2005," *Zeitschrift Für Untersuchung Der Lebensmittel* 63, no. 1 (2005): 21–30, https://doi.org/10.1007/BF01654241.

JianXin Xu (2008) identified that being resilient to all kinds of disruptions has become one of the most important factors in determining the success of the modern supply chain.[iv]

Extant literature also provides the following list of various types of supply risk arising due to location.

1. *Natural Hazards*—It includes all natural disaster like an earthquake, storms, floods, landslide, the outbreak of a disease, etc. The earthquake caused huge and sudden shortage in the supply at the semi-conductor suppliers across the globe.

2. *Climate and Weather Changes*—Weather changes refer to the midterm weather conditions for which businesses can prepare themselves up to some extent by looking at the forecast. However, climate changes include long-term changes in weather and environment which can cause Natural Hazards.

3. *Operational Contingencies*—It includes equipment malfunction and systematic failure. It is not directly related to location but changes in the location's climate may lead to the equipment malfunction.

4. *Terrorism and political instability*—It encompass political and economic instability including trade wars and terrorist activity in a country which often adversely affect the businesses operating in the region.

5. *Availability of skilled labor*—In the modern supply chain, human capital has become as vital as physical capital. However, growing skilled labor shortages, labor strikes, and an increase in minimum wages have resulted in a less efficient and responsive supply chain. This factor is more evident in developing economies, where the poor infrastructure for higher education led to more unqualified individuals.

6. *Legal and Regulatory Risk*—Border, custom regulation and other legal requirement comprises a significant portion of the cost. Border and custom regulations include tariffs, export subsidiary, and quota and are based on the trade agreement between two countries. Legal requirement considers everything from environment taxes to corporate taxes to safety regulations at workplaces.

7. *Cultural and Moral Values*—It refers to the risk associated with failing to understand the difference in cultural values. Failure of the understanding of the differences in cultural and moral values between different societies by the businesses can lead to huge failure and cost.

8. *Disease Outbreak*—The recent outbreak of COVID-19, has undoubtedly shown us how the outbreak of a disease can disrupt the supply chains at the global as well as local level. The effect of a disease outbreak can vary from country to country depending on the size of the population, implementation of safety policies, general health, etc.

9. *Level of connectivity and Economic benefit*—Transportation and storage cost contributes to the significant portion of the cost. The other economic benefits like subsidiaries by the government, low-cost land, fewer taxes ease of availability of raw materials also help in cutting down the production cost.

[iv]Xu Jianxin, "Managing the Risk of Supply Chain Disruption: Towards a Resilient Approach of Supply Chain Management," *Proceedings - ISECS International Colloquium on Computing, Communication, Control, and Management, CCCM 2008* 3 (2008): 3–7, https://doi.org/10.1109/CCCM.2008.9.

10. *Technological Innovation*—It comprises risk associated with the power of the country's infrastructure in which the company is establishing the plant. Developed countries are more technologically advanced and have better infrastructure than developing countries which provides them with a variety of efficient options for production.

3. Research Objective and Methodology

From the existing literature, we have observed that there are numerous types of risks linked with the modern SC. With increasing complexities and dynamic nature of the supply chains, the management of the supply chain risk plays a vital role in minimizing the associated risks. The objective of this study is to analyze particularly the supply risk associated with the location using a risk assessment model.

A risk map containing individual risk and levels of risk in the supply chain is often used in the industry for the analysis. The map shows the individual risks as points R_1, R_2, ..., R_i, ..., R_n on a graph, with probability of events on the y-axis and the expected outcome on the x-axis (Fig. 50.1).[v]

Here, $R = P * C$

where P = Probability of a non-desired event

C = Expected consequences/ loss

Also, $R_T = \sum_{i=1}^{n} R_i = \sum_{i=1}^{n} P_i * C_i$

where R_T = Total Risk

R_i = Partial Risks

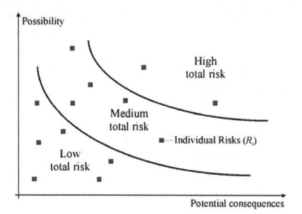

Fig. 50.1   Individual risks and probability of events

Source: Adapted from Radivojević and Gajović (2014)

[v]Gordana Radivojević and Vladimir Gajović, "Supply Chain Risk Modeling by AHP and Fuzzy AHP Methods," *Journal of Risk Research* 17, no. 3 (2014): 337–52, https://doi.org/10.1080/13669877.2013.808689.

However, the provision for the statistical indicators of frequency and the effect of negative historical events are two major issues associated with the risk assessment. Additionally, the huge impact and the level of diversity associated with each risk, absence of correlation in samples, and numerous reoccurrences of the early events which were the cause of risk make the problem more difficult to solve.[vi]

Due to these factors, supply chain risks are not analyzed using standard statistical models but are being examined on the basis of intuition, expertise, and experience. AHP and FAHP are two models frequently used for understanding supply chain risk in the absence of any statistical data. For this report, we only considered the AHP method to analyze the list of the above-mentioned risk.[vii]

Analytic hierarchy process (AHP) is a multicriteria rank method.[viii,ix] This process is based on evaluating a problem in a hierarchal manner. Under this method, a problem is broken down hierarchically and then partial problems are solved. Afterward, the partial solutions are consolidated together to resolve the primary problem.

4. Empirical Analysis and Results

In this study, we have considered 10 different risks, with an assessment of the supply risk as the aim of the model. On the second level, we took 10 subcategories of risk mentioned above, and the third level contains the level of risk which we defined as Low, Medium, and High Total Risk (as per the extant literature). Afterwards, we compared the last two levels of the hierarchy using the elements i and j, and the formation of the matrix, which represent the entry data for the application of the AHP. Also, the elements of the matrix are determined using the existing research papers by the experts and by considering the Saaty scale from 1 to 9.

Table 50.1, 50.2 and 50.3 shows the results computed for the defined hierarchy through AHP via MS excel. The values for the pair-wise comparison matrix are taken from expert estimates. Additionally, the following abbreviations are used while constructing the Table and their meaning has been explained in the literature review section.

OC = Operational Contingencies

CWC = Climate and Weather Changes

NH = Natural Hazards

TPI = Terrorism and Political Instability

ASL = Availability of skilled worker

LRR = Legal and regulatory Risk

[vi]Vladimir Gajović, Marija Kerkez, and Jelena Kočović, "Evaluation of Risk in Logistic Processes by Applying Fuzzy Analytic Hierarchy Process," *Simulation*, 2012.

[vii]Radivojević and Gajović, "Supply Chain Risk Modeling by AHP and Fuzzy AHP Methods."

[viii]T. L Saaty, "The Analytic Hierarchy Process," *Resources Policy*, 1980.

[ix]T. L. Saaty, "A Scaling Method for Priorities in Hierarchical Structures.," *Journal of Mathematical Psychology* 119, no. June (1977).

CMV = Cultural and Moral Values

DO = Disease Outbreak

CEB = Connectivity and Economic Benefit

TI = Technological Innovation

Off-ME = Off Shore in Middle East

Off-As = Off Shore in Asia

OnS = Onshore Location

W = Criteria Weights

Table 50.1 Pairwise comparison matric for risk categories

	OC	CWC	NH	TPI	ASL	LRR	CMV	DO	CEB	TI	W
OC	1	5	5	5	3	3	3	5	1	1	0.208
CWC	0.2	1	1	1	1	0.3	0.5	1	0.2	0.2	0.041
NH	0.2	1	1	1	1	0.3	1	1	0.2	0.2	0.044
TPI	0.2	1	1	1	1	0.5	1	2	0.25	0.25	0.051
ASL	0.3	1	1	1	1	1	1	3	0.3	0.3	0.065
LRR	0.3	3	3	2	1	1	2	3	1	0.3	0.105
CMV	0.3	2	1	1	1	0.5	1	3	0.3	0.3	0.065
DO	0.2	1	1	0.5	0.3	0.3	0.3	1	0.2	0.2	0.033
CEB	1	5	5	4	3	1	3	5	1	1	0.185
TI	1	5	5	4	3	3	3	5	1	1	0.203
λ	10.26414		CI	0.037592		CR	0.02523				

Source: Created by authors

Computed values of 'w' (the priority vector) are shown in Table 50.1 along with the pairwise comparison matrix for different level of risk with values as suggested by the existing literature. Additionally, the Principal Eigenvalue of the matrix (λ), Consistency Index (CI), and consistency ratio (CR = CI/RI) determined through AHP are also presented in Table 50.1. For the calculation of CR, we directly used the values from the Standard Random Index given in the literature for different values of n. Comparison of the calculated CI (3.75%) with the standard value of 10% allow us to accept the computed values of 'w'. From the Table 50.1, we can also observe that the Operational contingencies has the highest weightage of 20.8% and Disease outbreak has lowest weightage of 3.3%.

In Table 50.2, we computed the 'w' and comparison matrix for each level using Analytical Hierarchal Process. Table 50.3 depicts the values of the estimated local and global priority vector for each alternative. The estimated result shows that Low Total Risk is the major risk in the considered supply chain.

Table 50.2 Comparison matrices and local priorities for risk level

OC	Off-ME	Off-As	OnS	w
LTR	1	3	5	0.633
MTR	0.33	1	3	0.26
HTR	0.2	0.33	1	0.106
	CI = 0.002	λ = 3.04	CR = 0.03	

NH	Off-ME	Off-As	OnS	w
LTR	1	3	3	0.6
MTR	0.33	1	1	0.2
HTR	0.33	1	1	0.2
	CI = 0	λ = 3	CR = 0	

CWC	Off-ME	Off-As	OnS	w
LTR	1	3	3	0.6
MTR	0.33	1	1	0.2
HTR	0.33	1	1	0.2
	CI = 0	λ = 3	CR = 0	

TPI	Off-ME	Off-As	OnS	w
LTR	1	2	3	0.54
MTR	0.5	1	2	0.30
HTR	0.33	0.5	1	0.16
	CI = 0.007	λ = 3.00	CR = 0.013	

ASL	Off-ME	Off-As	OnS	w
LTR	1	1	3	0.429
MTR	1	1	3	0.429
HTR	0.33	0.33	1	0.143
	CI = 0	λ = 3	CR = 0	

CMV	Off-ME	Off-As	OnS	w
LTR	1	2	3	0.52
MTR	0.5	1	3	0.33
HTR	0.33	0.33	1	0.14
	CI = 0.04	λ = 3.05	CR = 0.07	

DO	Off-ME	Off-As	OnS	w
LTR	1	2	2	0.48
MTR	0.5	1	3	0.35
HTR	0.5	0.33	1	0.17
	CI = 0.09	λ = 3.14	CR = 0.16	

CEB	Off-ME	Off-As	OnS	w
LTR	1	5	3	0.633
MTR	0.2	1	0.33	0.106
HTR	0.33	3	1	0.26
	CI = 0.002	λ = 3.04	CR = 0.03	

TI	Off-ME	Off-As	OnS	w
LTR	1	3	5	0.633
MTR	0.33	1	3	0.26
HTR	0.2	0.33	1	0.106
	CI = 0.002	λ = 3.04	CR = 0.03	

LRR	Off-ME	Off-As	OnS	w
LTR	1	3	5	0.633
MTR	0.33	1	3	0.26
HTR	0.2	0.33	1	0.106
	CI = 0.002	λ = 3.04	CR = 0.03	

Source: Created by authors

Table 50.3 Priority vector (global and local) via AHP method

	OC	CWC	NH	TPI	ASL	LRR	CMV	DO	CEB	TI	Final Priority Vector W
	0.208	0.041	0.044	0.051	0.065	0.105	0.065	0.033	0.185	0.203	
Off-ME	0.633	0.6	0.6	0.54	0.429	0.633	0.52	0.48	0.633	0.633	**0.600**
Off-As	0.26	0.2	0.2	0.30	0.429	0.26	0.33	0.35	0.106	0.26	**0.247**
OnS	0.106	0.2	0.2	0.16	0.143	0.106	0.14	0.17	0.26	0.106	**0.152**

Source: Created by authors

5. Conclusion

Over the years, supply chains have successfully become more efficient and agile. However, the modern supply chain comes with its own set of risks and vulnerabilities. In this study, we observed that supply risk, process risk, demand risk, and product risk are the main four categories into which supply chain risk can be divided, and deeply examined the supply risk. From the extant literature, we created an exhaustive list of supply risks associated with the location. Further, we analyzed the subcategories of the supply risk associated with a location using the Analytical Hierarchy Process, which includes breaking down of risks in a hierarchal manner. The estimated result indicates that the observed supply chain has a Low Total Risk with the highest weight for Operational Contingencies followed by Technological Innovation.

REFERENCES

1. Gajović, Vladimir, Marija Kerkez, and Jelena Kočović. 2012. "Evaluation of Risk in Logistic Processes by Applying Fuzzy Analytic Hierarchy Process." In Proceedings of the XX International Conference on Material Handling, Constructions and Logistics–MHCL'12, pp. 269–272.
2. Guertler, Benjamin, and Stefan Spinler. 2015. "Supply Risk Interrelationships and the Derivation of Key Supply Risk Indicators." Technological Forecasting and Social Change 92: 224–36.
3. Ivanov, Dmitry, Alexandre Dolgui, and Boris Sokolov. 2019. "The Impact of Digital Technology and Industry 4.0 on the Ripple Effect and Supply Chain Risk Analytics." International Journal of Production Research 57, no.: 829–46.
4. Radivojević, Gordana, and Vladimir Gajović. 2014. "Supply Chain Risk Modeling by AHP and Fuzzy AHP Methods." Journal of Risk Research 17, no. 3: 337–52.
5. Saaty, T. L. 1980. "The Analytic Hierarchy Process." Resources Policy.
6. Wagner, Stephan M., and Christoph Bode. 2008. "An Empirical Examination of Supply Chain Performance Along Several Dimensions of Risk." Journal of Business Logistics 29, no. 1: 307–25.
7. Wilson, Martha C. 2007. "The Impact of Transportation Disruptions on Supply Chain Performance." Transportation Research Part E: Logistics and Transportation Review 43, no. 4: 295–320.

Chapter

An Indian Approach to AI Policy:
A Comparative Study Between Three Sectors

Anand R. Navaratna[1]
Student of Masters, Department of Computer Science & Engineering,
Indian Institute of Technology, Jodhpur, India

Deepak Saxena[2]
Assistant Professor, School of Management & Entrepreneurship,
Indian Institute of Technology, Jodhpur, India

ABSTRACT: Artificial Intelligence (AI) has emerged as the most discussed disruptive technologies that this decade has seen. Many countries around the world have adopted varied policy approaches towards its implementation. Between 2016-2020 countries like the United States of America, United Kingdom, European Union, and China have not only released their AI roadmap but also have started reaping the benefits of AI through institutionalised frameworks, legislations, and regulations. India is also not left behind. Through its first AI for all discussion paper in 2018 a slew of initiatives has been undertaken by various government machineries. India stands at a crucial crossroad to become 'Garage' for developing and emerging economies by leveraging the power of AI. We in this paper will suggest India's policy approach towards AI by deriving lessons from three sectors. These three sectors are in spirit and nature comparable to AI. In this paper, we have analysed India's policy approach towards sectors like Information Technology and Information Technology Enabled Services (IT&ITES), Telecommunications and Biotechnology from their nascent stages through an evidence-based approach. The paper analyses (a) the policy approach the government took towards development of each sector (b) Highlight the cross difference in policy approach between these three sectors and, finally (c) From the historic evidence suggest which route the Indian government can take to build upon policy, legislation and regulation for AI.

KEYWORDS: Artificial intelligence, AI, Public policy, Indian government, Development policy

[1]navaratna.1@iitj.ac.in, [2]saxenad@iitj.ac.in

DOI: 10.4324/9781003415725-51

1. Introduction

Artificial Intelligence (AI) has emerged as one of the most discussed disruptive technologies that this decade has seen. Furthermore, AI is not just disruptive but has the potential to disrupt other technology and human aspects that we are aware of (Chace, 2015; Chen, 2018). Despite the initial slow development and considerable doubt on the applicable scope of AI, the technology today has already made inroads into many applications across industries, public welfare, and government. From developments in speech recognition to autopilot to household robotics, AI is shaping the lives of many (Sclove 1995, 2020). With the advent of large computational power, maturity in machine learning algorithms, availability of large data and economic enthusiasm in investment towards technology, AI has developed at a faster pace than expected.

Financially, some believe that AI will be the driving force towards the realisation of the fourth industrial revolution (Syam & Sharma, 2018). The Artificial Intelligence market is projected to grow from $387.45 billion in 2022 to $1,394.30 billion by 2029, at a CAGR of 20.1% in the forecast period (*Artificial Intelligence [AI] Market Growth, Trends | Forecast, 2029*, 2022). The ability of computers to save data and process was well known. During the advent of computers, it was embraced as a means to reduce the time taken to carry out certain activities compared to a human carrying out the same activity. What has changed is the advent of useful information from large chunks of data (Amani, 2015; Calo et al., 2016). Industry enthusiasm has increased also due to the development of fundamental AI research in the field of automation, robotics, natural language processing, computer vision and Augmented/Virtual Reality (AR/VR). These fundamental verticals of AI have a wide range of applications with the potential to reach a large population worldwide.

With technological progress and financial enthusiasm, the next probable logical step is the institutionalisation of the concept. Public policy and government recognition are desired to drive the development of the AI objectives as deemed fit to the social and economic fabric of each country. The political will and policy foresight towards steering the AI objectives for a country can provide a vision towards the realisation of AI's potential for social good. Countries all around the world are now drawing out broader plans towards the rollout of AI-based objectives and strategies. "The National Artificial Intelligence Research and Development Strategic Plan" was released in 2016 by the National Science & Technology Council in the United States of America. During the same period "Preparing for the Future of Artificial Intelligence" was also released. The United Kingdom on the other hand released a slew of public policies towards the development of AI research and industrial development. "Robotics and Artificial Intelligence" (*House of Commons - Robotics and Artificial Intelligence - Science and Technology Committee*, 2016) and "Growing The Artificial Intelligence Industry In The UK" (Hall et al., 2017) are a few. The European Union through its "Robotics 2020 Multi-Annual Roadmap For Robotics in Europe" (*SPARC*, 2016) provided policy direction towards AI. China through the "New-Generation Artificial Intelligence Development Plan" issued by The State Council of the People's Republic of China in 2017 has steadfast AI development in the country. Similarly, Japan, Saudi Arabia, France and Germany also have evolved in a big way towards the legislation of AI policy or frameworks. India has also embarked on its AI journey that this study seeks to analyse.

2. AI Policy in India

2.1 National AI Strategy

National Strategy for AI or popularly known as #AIforAll issued in 2018 by Indian Policy Think Tank Niti Aayog remains till today by far the most important guiding document towards the development of the AI ecosystem in India. The aim of the discussion paper is threefold, namely (a) To empower and enhance the skills of Indians so as to obtain quality jobs, (b) To achieve social and economic growth and invest in research with sector-specific emphasis, and (c) To thrive to make India a global garage for AI and scale up to the world. The discussion paper emphasises five focus areas for AI intervention namely healthcare, agriculture, education, Smart cities-infrastructure and smart mobility-transportation. Since 2018, numerous activities have taken place to achieve resilience in the AI domain. Many ministries within the Government of India have come out with sector-specific policies, while many other ministries have constituted sub-committees or study groups to suggest measures which can form a strong policy or framework. The Ministry of Electronics and IT constituted 4 committees in 2019 ("Artificial Intelligence Committees Reports | Ministry of Electronics and Information Technology, Government of India" 2022) with an expectation that a policy framework can be derived. The committees were:

Table 51.1 Committees formed to frame policy with specific agenda/task for each vertical

Committee	Agenda/Task
Committee A	Platforms and data on Artificial Intelligence
Committee B	Leveraging AI for identifying national missions in key sectors
Committee C	Mapping technological capabilities, key policy enablers required across sectors, skilling and reskill
Committee D	Cyber security, safety, legal and ethical issues

Source: Author's compilation ("Artificial Intelligence Committees Reports | Ministry of Electronics and Information Technology, Government of India" 2022)

The reports were published in December 2019. Similarly, the Ministry of Commerce and Industry, in 2017 formed an Artificial Intelligence Task Force with a view to 'embed AI in our Economic, Political and Legal thought processes so that there is the systemic capability to support the goal of India becoming one of the leaders of AI-rich economies' ("Report of Task Force on Artificial Intelligence | Department for Promotion of Industry and Internal Trade | MoCI | GoI" 2018).

2.2 Shortcomings and Areas of Improvement

The government of India to date has not issued any official policy framework towards the implementation of AI through legislation. The National AI Strategy is explicit and touches on most of the sectors, R&D, Industry-Academia relations and the setting up of Centers of Excellence. Since 2018, many Ministries at their level have issued guidelines towards instituting or undertaking AI-based projects. However, aspects of policy framework, ethics, security, and privacy are not addressed (Chatterjee, 2020). Similarly, the laws pertaining to AI development and ethics are absent. Moreover, the discussion paper does not provide concrete steps towards regulation and governance. The basic layer for the development of AI is data (Shilton, 2009; Fulgoni, 2013; Verdino, 2013). Data accessibility cannot be isolated from privacy. To provide checks and balances towards ensuring privacy and trust, regulation could be required (Chopra & White, 2011; Kraakman et al., 2017).

The impact of AI in general also is expected to have an impact on all sectors of the country. Yet there does not exist any national level body or means or policy to deal with this. This body can help in avoiding duplication of effort in terms of AI projects between the ministries. Having a national strategy to bolster the economy and ecosystem to invite investment and create jobs is totally different from bringing in a legislation towards security, ethics, privacy, and regulation. The European Union in 2021 has brought in a Proposal for a Regulation Laying Down Harmonised Rules on Artificial Intelligence (Artificial Intelligence Act). The United States has gone a step ahead and has studied the impact of AI in combat and the military through its 2020 published congressional research on AI and National security (Schmidt, 2020). India appears clearly far from regulation, legislation, or offensive use of AI.

3. Evolution of Public Policy in India for Technology-Based Sectors

During the course of the literature review, there did exist many publications which highlighted the evolution of AI in many countries like the United States (*AI Policy Levers: A Review of the U.S. Government's Tools to Shape AI Research, Development, and Deployment*, 2021), United Kingdom (Kazim et al., 2021), or China (Roberts et al., 2021). Moreover, there exists sufficient publications available analysing the AI ecosystem in India (Chatterjee, 2020). While there exist some publications on the impact of the Nation AI Strategy issued by Niti Aayog in India (Chatterjee, 2020), there are not many publications that compare the evolution of technology and associated policy within India.

Nevertheless, conclusions may be drawn from the policy evolution of similar technologies. Hence in this paper, we choose three fields which are comparable in essence to AI. They are (1) Information Technology (IT) and IT-enabled Services (ITES) (2) Telecommunications, and (3) Biotechnology. These fields have evolved in India post 1980. The Indian government through its policy has nurtured these fields so that they evolve in India. To understand the underpinning trend in the evolution of technology and the support provided by the Indian government, three sectors are compared. This is discussed in the next section.

4. Policy Evolution in Other Key Sectors

The objective of this comparison is to study the nature of the evolution of these three fields in India. From the lessons that are derived, we can determine what path the government can take in bringing in a policy framework for AI in India.

4.1 IT/ITES

The development of IT and ITES in India was a direct result of continued hand-holding by policies formulated by the Government from time to time (Dhar & Joseph, 2019). The above timeline indicated in Fig. 51.1 is an indication of the development of three subfields viz., electronics, IT and then ITES. The initial policy that was formulated in 1963 was the Electronics Committee headed by Homi Bhabha, with an intention to build electronic components to fulfil Indian emerging needs (Agarwal, 1985). Consequently, in 1970-71 a separate Department of Electronics(DoE) was formed and Electronic Corporation of India Ltd (ECIL) was brought under DoE from the Dept of Atomic Energy (DAE). ECIL continued to manufacture components but was unable to cope with rising demand while keeping manufacturing costs low. Thus, ECIL's customer base remained with other government organisations (Brunner, 1991; Rajaraman, 2012). It was in 1984, that the government bifurcated Electronics and computer policy which changed the direction of IT and ITES evolution in India. As a support mechanism, a separate clause for software development and satellite link provision was included in Foreign Trade Policy. Numerous policy pushes from 1984-1997 ensured that IT and ITES brought in the revolution thereby creating employment and generating revenue. Building of supercomputer in 1991, setting up of Santa Cruz Electronics Export Processing Zone (SCEEPZ), establishing institutions like Centre for Development of Advanced Computing (C-DAC), Technology Development Council, Centre for Development of Telematics (C-DoT) and setting up of numerous Software Technology Parks resulted in expanding the in-house capabilities in the electronics and computer sector. IT was strengthened by government establishments while ITES was revolutionised by private players (Dhar & Joseph, 2019). Till today ITES has maintained its stead and continues to invite FDIs. From a policy perspective, the electronic hardware sector was conceptualised before computer policy but did not take off the way it was expected. Lack of R&D spending is attributed to be the main reason (Dhar & Joseph, 2019).

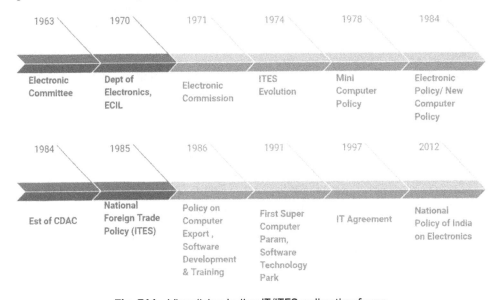

Fig. 51.1 Visualising Indian IT/ITES policy timeframe

Source: Author's compilation

The evolution of IT & ITES is a mixed bag in many ways. Firstly, the consistent push with subtle course correction in policy by the government from time to time resulted in the IT revolution in India. Secondly, the government recognised in the early stages of policymaking that the ITES field requires active participation from private players. Thirdly, Electronics and Computer policy that was started as a self-sustenance initiative for government and government-led institutions was able to scale up to the larger national objective. Finally, IT & ITES continue to be a self-regulated field without much intervention from the government. Thus, this shows the professionalism and maturity of the industry and the sensibility of government's policy approach towards this sector.

4.2 Telecommunication

Telegraphs as it was known were brought under the aegis of the Department of Post and Telegraph in 1980. By 1985, the government realised that the Post and Telegraph were too big to be managed by one department. Thus by 1985, the departments were demerged and the Department of Telecommunications (DoT) was formed. From 1985-1994 the DoT's main task was to provide services across the country through its Department of Telecommunications (DoT), Videsh Sanchar Nigam Limited (VSNL) and Mahanagar Telecom Nigam Limited (MTNL). The first major initiative in terms of policy was only in 1994 through National Telecommunication Policy, where private players were allowed to provide value-added services (VAS). By 1999, due to modern network requirements, the emergence of Wireless-data networks and better voice circuits a New Telecommunication Policy was introduced. The NTP 1999, aimed at attracting investment in the telecommunication segment and bifurcating the operational arm(thus creating Bharat Sanchar Nigam Limited-BSNL in 2000) and licensing arm (DoT). By 2002 VSNL's monopoly in International Communication was ended. This paved

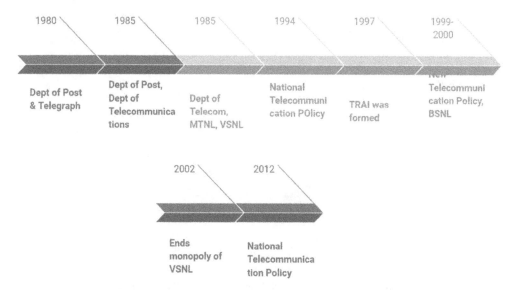

Fig. 51.2 Visualising Indian telecommunication policy timeframe

Source: Author's compilation

the way for the Unified Access Regime (avoiding multiple licensing for each service by the same player). Further, the Government 2022 has issued a draft National Telecommunications Policy. As of 2022, India has achieved a teledensity of 85.12%, with 7,30,750 towers and over 117.281 crore subscribers (*Department of Telecommunication*, 2022). Figure 51.2 provides an indication of policy evolution timeframe for telecommunication sector in India.

Here the fine print that emerges is (a) these Policy initiatives by the government in the initial days helped in the development of telecommunications in India from zero, (b) With the widening of the customer base and type of services offered, there was a need to create many more independent or dependent bodies which aid telecommunication authority. Today we have a Telecom Commission to take care of policymaking, TRAI as a Regulatory body, DoT as licensing body, a Wireless Planning Centre for spectrum allocation & planning and finally Technical Evaluation Committee for evaluation/ approval of communication equipment. Thus, unlike IT & ITES, Telecommunication evolution was aided by government policy from time to time but also has created a slew of sub-verticals of expertise. This has increased transparency in the system as functionality is clearly demarcated (c) The policy did bring in investment and involvement of private players, which otherwise was a totally government-owned and controlled sector.

4.3 Biotechnology

The Indian Government was one of the first in the world to recognise the importance of Biotechnology (BT) and provided for budget allocation towards its development in the 1980-1985 6th Five-year plan. In 1982 a National BT Board (NBTB) was established under the

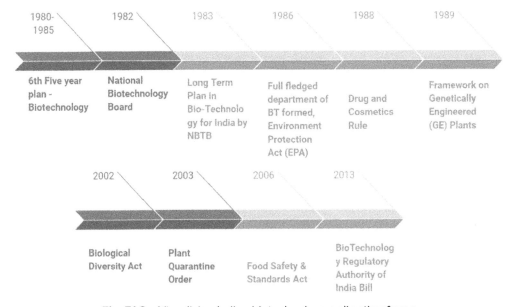

Fig. 51.3 Visualising Indian biotechnology policy timeframe

Source: Author's compilation

chairmanship of the Chairman of the Planning Commission. However, a need was felt in having a full-fledged department under the Ministry of Science and Technology was felt in 1986. It involved members and active funding from the Department of Science and Technology (DST), Department of Biotechnology (DBT), Council of Scientific and Industrial Research (CSIR), Indian Council of Medical Research (ICMR), Indian Council of Agriculture Research (ICAR) and University Grants Commission (UGC), Department of Scientific and Industrial Research (DSIR). The first autonomous institute, the National Institute of Immunology which was set up in 1981 was brought under DBT. It was followed by the National Facility for Animal Tissue and Cell Culture of Pune in 1986 which was later christened by the National Centre for Cell Science. Between 1990-2000 many other institutes like The National Institute for Plant Genome Research (NIPGR), the National Brain Research Centre (NBRC), the Centre for DNA Fingerprinting & Diagnostics, Institute of Bioresources and Sustainable Development and the Institute of Life Sciences took shape. Subsequently, several other prominent institutes like Translational Health Science and Technology Institute (THISTI), Institute for Stem Cell Biology and Regenerative Medicine (INstem), National Agri-Food Biotechnology Institute (NABI) at Mohali, and National Institute of Biomedical Genomics (NIBMG) were established.

The first known policy towards biotechnology in India apart from planning commission's recognition was Long Term Plan in BT issued by NBTB. This was followed by policies directly issued by DBT or other government ministries related to biotechnology. The major ones are Environment Protection Act, Framework on GE plants, Biological Diversity Act, Plant Quarantine Order and finally, BT Regulatory Authority bill. It is pertinent to note that the department has issued various guidelines and policies towards its 19 autonomous bodies and PSUs. As of 2022, DBT has a total of 2607 sanctioned projects, more than 25000 research personnel, 11794 publications and 452 patents filed (*Department of Biotechnology*, 2022). Figure 51.3 indicates evolution of Indian biotechnology policy evolution.

The evolution of Biotechnology in India is unique compared to IT/ITES or Telecommunications. The major takeaways from the comparison are (a) Though the government initiated the initial development of BT in India, it was mostly driven by the autonomous bodies and PSUs already existing or created soon after. These individual institutes are unique in their role and are specialists in their verticals. (b) DBT is a professional body which is mandated towards promoting large scale use of Biotechnology, support R&D and manufacturing in Biology, be responsible for Autonomous Institutions, promote University and Industry Interaction, identify, and set up Centres of Excellence for R&D and serve as the nodal point for the collection and dissemination of information relating to biotechnology (*Mandate*, 2019). (c) There exists a regulatory body for BT. Biotechnology Regulatory Authority of India (BRAI) was set up in 2013 with a specific mandate to regulate the use of genetically modified organisms (GMOs). BRAI was set up in India as India had signed the Cartagena Protocol which mandates the setting up of a Regulatory Body.

4.4 Cross-Comparison

By comparing the evolution of the above-mentioned sectors and their policy few general trends and patterns could be derived. Moreover, a few unique aspects peculiar to the sector can also be observed. The observations can be listed as:

1. All three sectors witnessed the birth of evolution between 1980-1985. Though in the case of IT/ITES, the evolution started back in 1963, a clear policy direction was obtained only in 1984 with the formulation of computer policy.

2. All three sectors were led by a dedicated department under a ministry. For IT, it was the Department of Electronics, for Telecommunications it was DoT while for BT it was DBT. In the case of biotechnology, the department was formed in 1986, while till that time it was led by a dedicated board. This gives financial independence for development under the umbrella of a larger ministry within the Government of India structure.

3. In all three sectors, the policy and roadmap for individual verticals were the precursors to the creation of a department or evolution of the vertical. The usual time frame from policy formulation to the creation of a department is observed to be about 2-6 years.

4. These three sectors were predominantly organic. The government and the environment around the world had the appetite to adopt these technologies for development in India. The policy push subsequently provided for the participation of private players. However, in the field of BT, the policies were more towards nurturing R&D and projects within its umbrella institutes rather than for the private sector. IT and Telecommunication remained a monopoly of the government for a substantially long period of time, while ITES from the start has been driven by private participation.

5. With the evolution of the sector, the shaping of these policies shows interesting trends. IT and ITES sectors themselves showed variance from each other. ITES remains self-regulated and driven by private players, Electronics still lags enthusiasm and remains in hands of the government. The semiconductor mission under Digital India Corporation is the latest initiative towards this. On the other hand, the telecommunications vertical saw active participation from private players since 1994 and there exist many service providers today. However, policy wise the structure of telecommunication authority is composed of various bodies like Telecom Committee, TRAI, DoT, WPC and TEC. Thus, the policy demarcation is clear. The sector also saw the emergence of a regulator to ensure neutrality. Furthermore, the government with the establishment of BSNL exited from the competition and remains a neutral entity. On the other hand, BT by nature since its inception has remained a department of independent institutes and PSUs. The vertical also has a regulator set up in 2013 in accordance with a world treaty under the UN. It's evident that these sectors had different evolutionary histories, the government adopted different policy approaches and had different viewpoints towards the sustenance policy of sectors. Thus, the government's approach to nurturing these verticals post their evolution is flexible and specific to the domain. The government did not impose one size fits all policy to these individual sectors. Today in 2022, these sectors are striving and have made substantial progress since 1980-1985. They are deemed a success story providing service to the country.

5. Conclusion

AI in many ways is next big evolution in technology that has capability to bring in revolution across platform and domain. Like the way IT/ITES, Telecommunication or Biotechnology brought in socio-economic revolution; AI has if not greater can bring in comparable effect. Also in terms of policy adaptation for a technological field, these sectors were relatable sectors. During emergence of these sectors, it would have posed a challenge for policy makers. These were challenging also as the policy makers did not have any relatable field from which lessons could be drawn. We through this paper are emphasising on the fact that, these three fields in particular have valuable lessons for AI policy in India. The broad take away which emerges from each sector were brought out in detail in above segments. Three central aspects that emerges as common factors, which emerges as policy catalyst for development can be listed as time frame for setting up a central agency to empower an emerging domain, the need for a central department/ ministry or nodal agency to enable focused growth of emerging sector and finally aspect of need to have a regulatory authority to keep a check on emerging sector. Deriving the evolutionary lessons from these three sectors to AI in India, we can conclude that,

1. **Time Frame**: The National AI Strategy of 2018 by Niti Aayog does not explicitly speak about setting up any kind of central agency or department for AI development in India. However, as our study indicates, it would be ideal for the government to set up a central national agency or a department for AI by 2024, going by the empirical 2-7years trend. This will also help in the funding of projects and research centrally.

2. **Need for a central department/ ministry or nodal agency to enable focused growth**: IT/ ITES, Telecommunication or biotechnology had a dedicated ministry to enable a focused development in terms of focus of policy and finances. Within acknowledgement of emergence of said technology, a dedicated ministry/board was setup for its focussed development. The discussion paper has proposed two national-level institutes viz. Centres for Research Excellence in Artificial Intelligence (CORE), whose focus is on fundamental research while International Center for Transformational Artificial Intelligence (ICTAI) focuses on product development and deployment. There is also an overarching body - the Center for Studies on Technological Sustainability (CSTS) which looks into the international competition of AI products (Aayog, 2018). Apart from these, the ministry of commerce and industry has set up a national task force and the ministry of defence has set up a DAIPA. Many more vertical-specific or ministry-specific AI bodies may be set up as per their requirement. Thus, as this article is written, there does exist many AI study groups, committees or academic/centre of excellence which are already recognised or proposed to be setup by various ministries/departments. Thus in ethos a 'department of departments' or 'Centre of Centres' approach like loosely observed in case of biotechnology can be seen in horizon for AI. However, in case of biotechnology, there did exist a central department, which as of now does not exist for AI.

3. **Regulatory Authority:** The aspect of privacy and security is envisaged to be addressed by the creation of legal frameworks, CORE and by sectoral regulatory guidelines. Going by our study, in BT and Telecommunication, a central regulatory body was set up much later, though there was no initial plan for the same. Thus, it is suggested that by seeing the cross-sectoral impact AI is going to have a central regulatory body is desired to ensure transparency, privacy and maintain neutrality. Moreover, there is need to have a sector neutral agency whose fundamental agenda will be focussed on legality, do's/ don'ts and compliance of AI framework on all AI projects.

Some limitations of this study are to be noted. The study is limited to timelines of policy specific to each sector and its known impact. The study has not dwelled on the financial impact these policies had on the sectors. The study is limited to three technological sectors. There could be other sectors within technology or otherwise from which interesting policy trends may be analysed. For international benchmarking, Indian approach towards AI can be compared to other (developed as well as developing) countries.

REFERENCES

1. Aayog, NITI. 2018. "National AI Strategy: Discussion Paper." INDIAai. https://indiaai.gov.in/documents/pdf/NationalStrategy-for-AI-Discussion-Paper.pdf.
2. Agarwal, S. M. 1985. "Electronics in India: Strategies and future possibilities." *World Development* 13 (3): 273–292.
3. *AI Policy Levers: A Review of the U.S. Government's Tools to Shape AI Research, Development, and Deployment.* 2021. N.p.: Future of Humanity Institute, University of Oxford.
4. Amani, Z. 2015. "Commitment as a mediator of the relationship between trust and relationship loyalty to retailer." *Journal of Business Studies Quarterly* 6 (3): 144–163.
5. Amani, Z. 2015. "Commitment as a mediator of the relationship between trust and relationship loyalty to retailer." *Journal of Business Studies Quarterly* 6 (3): 144–163.
6. "Artificial Intelligence [AI] Market Growth, Trends I Forecast, 2029." n.d. Fortune Business Insights. Accessed October 16, 2022. https://www.fortunebusinessinsights.com/industry-reports/artificial-intelligence-market-100114.
7. "Artificial Intelligence in Defence." 2022. Department of Defence Production. https://www.ddpmod.gov.in/sites/default/files/ai.pdf.
8. "Artificial Intelligence Market Size & Trends Report [2022-2029]." n.d. Fortune Business Insights. Accessed October 10, 2022. https://www.fortunebusinessinsights.com/industry-reports/artificial-intelligence-market-100114.
9. Barrat, James. 2013. *Our Final Invention: Artificial Intelligence and the End of the Human Era.* N.p.: St. Martin's Press.
10. Brunner, H. P. 1991. "Building technological capacity: A case study of the computer industry in India, 1975–87." *World Development* 19 (12): 1742.
11. Calo, M. R., Michael Froomkin, and Ian R. Kerr, eds. 2016. *Robot Law.* N.p.: Edward Elgar Publishing.
12. Chace, C. 2015. "Surviving AI: The Promise and Peril of Artificial Intelligence." *Three Cs, Bradford.*
13. Chatterjee, Sheshadri. 2020. "AI strategy of India: policy framework, adoption challenges and actions for government." *Transforming Government: People, Process and Policy* 14 (2): 757–775. 10.1108/TG-05-2019-0031.
14. Chen, N. 2018. "Are robots replacing routine jobs?" *Harvard College Thesis, Applied Mathematics Cambridge,MA.*
15. Chopra, K. 2019. "Indian shopper motivation to use artificial intelligence: generating Vroom's expectancy theory of motivation using grounded theory approach." *International Journal of Retail and Distribution Management* 47 (3). 10.1108/IJRDM.
16. Chopra, S., and L. White. 2011. "A Legal Theory for Autonomous Artificial Agents." *The University of MI Press, Ann Arbor.*
17. "Department of Biotechnology." 2022. Department of Biotechnology: Home. https://dbtindia.gov.in/.

18. "Department of Telecommunication." 2022. Home I Department of Telecommunications I Ministry of Communication I Government of India. https://dot.gov.in/.
19. Dhar, Biswajit, and Reji K. Joseph. 2019. "India's Information Technology Industry: A Tale of Two Halves." *Innovation, Economic Development, and Intellectual Property in India and China* ARCIALA Series on Intellectual Assets and Law in Asia. Springer, Singapore. 10.1007/978-981-13-8102-7_5.
20. Fulgoni, G. 2013. "Big data: friend or foe of digital advertising? Five ways marketers should use digital big data to their advantage." *Journal of Advertising Research* 53 (4): 372–376. 10.2501/JAR-53-4-372-376.
21. Greenstone, M. 2022. "The Impacts of Environmental Regulations on Industrial Activity: Evidence from the 1970 and 1977 Clean Air Act Amendments and the Census of Manufactures." *Journal of Political Economy* 110 (6): 1175–1219. 10.1086/342808.
22. Greenstone, M. n.d. "The impacts of environmental regulations on industrial activity: evidence from the 1970 and 1977 clean air act amendments and the census of manufactures." *Journal of Political Economy* 110 (6): 1175–1219. 10.1086/342808.
23. Hall, Vendy, and Pesenti. 2017. "Growing the artificial intelligence industry in the UK." *Department for Digital, Culture, Media & Sport and Department for Business, Energy & Industrial Strategy. Part of the Industrial Strategy UK and the Commonwealth.*
24. "House of Commons - Robotics and artificial intelligence - Science and Technology Committee." 2016. Parliament (publications). https://publications.parliament.uk/pa/cm201617/cmselect/cmsctech/145/14502.htm.
25. Kazim, E., N. Kingsmen, and D. Almeida. 2021. "Innovation and opportunity: review of the UK's national AI strategy." *Discover Artificial Intelligence* 1 (14).
26. Kraakman, R., J. Armour, P. Davies, and L. Enriques. 2017. "The Anatomy of Corporate Law: A Comparative and Functional Approach." *3rd edition Oxford University Press, Oxford.*
27. "Mandate." 2019. Department of Biotechnology. https://dbtindia.gov.in/about-us/mandate.
28. "New-Generation Artificial Intelligence Development Plan." 2017. *The State Council of the People's Republic of China.*
29. Rajaraman, V. 2012. "History of computing in India (1955–2010)." *Bangalore: Supercomputer Education and Research Centre, Indian Institute of Science.*
30. "Report of Task Force on Artificial Intelligence I Department for Promotion of Industry and Internal Trade I MoCI I GoI." 2018. DPIIT. https://dpiit.gov.in/whats-new/report-task-force-artificial-intelligence.
31. Roberts, Huw, Josh Cowls, Jessica Morley, Mariarosaria Taddeo, Vincent Wang, and Luciano Floridi. 2021. "The Chinese approach to artificial intelligence: an analysis of policy, ethics, and regulation." *AI & SOCIETY* 36: 59–77. 10.1007/s00146-020-00992-2.
32. Roland, Alex, and Philip Shiman. 2002. *Strategic Computing: DARPA and the Quest for Machine Intelligence, 1983-1993.* N.p.: MIT Press.
33. Schmidt, Eric. 2020. *THE NATIONAL SECURITY COMMISSION ON ARTIFICIAL INTELLIGENCE.*
34. Sclove, Richard. 1995. *Democracy and Technology.* N.p.: Guilford Publications.
35. Sclove, R. 2020. Democracy and technology: an interview with Richard Sclove from Beth Simone Noveck. *Digital Government: Research and Practice, 1*(1), 1–6.
36. Shilton, K. 2009. "Four billion little brothers? Privacy, mobile phones and ubiquitous data collection." *Communications of the ACM* 52 (11): 48-53. 10.1145/1592761.1592778.
37. Solaiman, S. M. 2016. "Legal personality of robots, corporations, idols and chimpanzees: a quest for legitimacy." *Artificial Intelligence and Law* 25 (2): 155–179. 10.1007/s10506-016-9192-3.
38. *SPARC.* 2016. N.p.: The Partnership for Robotics in Europe.

39. Syam, N., and A. Sharma. 2018. "Waiting for a sales renaissance in the fourth industrial revolution: Machine learning and artificial intelligence in sales research and practice." *Industrial marketing management* 69:135–146.

40. Verdino, G. 2013. "From the crowd to the cloud." *Marketing Insights* 35 (2): 26–30.

41. Yang, Chao, and Cui Huang. 2022. "Quantitative mapping of the evolution of AI policy distribution, targets and focuses over three decades." *Technological Forecasting and Social Change* 174. https://doi.org/10.1016/j.techfore.2021.121188.

Handbook of Evidence Based Management Practices in Business – Satyendra Kumar Sharma et al. (eds)
© 2023 Taylor & Francis Group, London, ISBN 978-1-032-54216-4

Chapter

CTR Prediction: A Bibliometric Review of Scientific Literature

Arti Jha[1], Yashvardhan Sharma[2]
Department of Computer Science and Information Systems,
Birla Institute of Technology and Science, Pilani
Udayan Chanda[3]
Department of Management,
Birla Institute of Technology and Science, Pilani

ABSTRACT: Internet giants like Google, Facebook, and Amazon have relied heavily on revenue from online advertising sales in recent years. The Click-through rate of an advertisement is the percentage of people who clicked it out of those who viewed it. The CTR as a metric represents the performance of their online advertisements. For over two decades now, researchers in academia and industry have paid great attention to getting good CTR prediction accuracy because of the demand it has generated in the digital world. This paper reviews the scholarly literature on CTR prediction during the previous decade by a bibliometric analysis of 1051 publications from journals indexed by Scopus. The goals of this research are to (1) conduct a structured quantitative analysis of the bibliometric data, (2) chart the development of CTR Prediction research, and (3) identify the most recent and relevant research literature and viewpoints in the field. A handful of studies have been conducted on this subject, and they have presented an in-depth analysis of specific methods and learning models being applied for CTR prediction. In addition to the previously submitted studies, this literature review aims to provide an overall bibliometric analysis showing the evolution of techniques employed for CTR prediction in the articles published over the last ten years, using a combination of bibliographic coupling, citation, and co-citation. The outcome of this literature evaluation will aid future researchers in gaining a deeper comprehension of the scientific studies around CTR prediction.

KEYWORDS: Click-through rate, CTR prediction, Online advertising, Bibliometric methods, Literature review, Bibliographic coupling

[1]p20210471@pilani.bits-pilani.ac.in, [2]yash@pilani.bits-pilani.ac.in, [3]udayanchanda@pilani.bits-pilani.ac.in

DOI: 10.4324/9781003415725-52

1. Introduction

The Click-through rate (CTR) is a metric used in the marketing industry that determines how frequently individuals click on a link, an advertisement, or an email. Understanding and maintaining a close watch on CTR is a crucial measure for marketing managers to ensure the success of an online advertisement campaign. Many researchers are focusing on CTR prediction because of its importance and unique challenges in the business and academic worlds. From simple logistic regression (LR) [9,10], factorization machines (FM) [7], and decision trees [1,5], CTR prediction models have progressed to deep neural networks (DNN) [2,3]. Notably, a large number of deep models, such as Wide&Deep [2], DeepFM [4], DCN [11], xDeepFM [8], FiBi-NET [6], DIN [12], etc., have demonstrated considerable performance increases in commercial CTR prediction issues. In addition to the previously presented studies, this literature review aims to provide an overall bibliometric analysis showing the evolution of techniques employed for CTR prediction in the articles published over the last ten years, using a combination of bibliographic coupling, citation, and co-citation.

2. Techniques

2.1 Overview of the Bibliometric Technique Applied

Previous research is essential for academic advancement [14,15]. Literature may be synthesized using qualitative and quantitative literature reviews. Some researchers offer a structural technique for scanning resources, organizing a literature review, constructing a bibliography, recommending research methodologies, and evaluating outcomes. This technique is more impartial and comprehensive than narrative reviews. In accordance with [16], this work evaluates linked papers to identify key thematic topics and interesting research interests. Bibliometric approaches compare geographies, fields, publications, and authors. It maps the findings. Journals [17,18], fields [19,20], institutions, and nations [21] have been analyzed bibliometrically. We attempted to include the following analysis to achieve the aim of our research:

- Citation and co-citation analysis;
- Bibliographic coupling;

2.2 Database

Using the Scopus database, the Click through rate-related research papers were located. The following steps were followed to get the related data from the Scopus database.

1. The keywords used for data collection include " Click-through rate", "CTR prediction", "online advertising", "Bibliometric methods", and "Literature review". Using the search function in the Scopus database.

2. We acquired and archived journal articles (excluding conference papers, books, and their chapters) that matched the specified search keywords.

3. The materials were restricted to Computer Science, Mathematics, Decision Sciences, Psychology, Economics, Econometrics, Finance, Business administration, and accounting.

4. Those publications published during the ten years between 2012 and 2022 were filtered out.

5. From the Scopus database, the CSV (comma-separated values) file was exported, which was then used as input in the VOSviewer tool to generate visualizations for analysis.

VOSviewer is a software tool for constructing and visualizing bibliometric networks. These networks may for instance, include journals, researchers, or individual publications, and they can be constructed based on citation, bibliographic coupling, co-citation, or co-authorship relations.

3. Experiments and Results

3.1 Trends in Publications

Figure 52.1 displays the publishing trends within the CTR Prediction area. The data on research reveals a total of 1051 articles. Table 52.1 supports Fig. 52.1's results. According to Table 52.1, 2021 was the most prolific year with 150 publications. This information demonstrates that CTR Prediction research is gaining momentum.

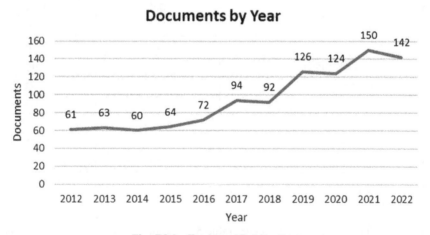

Fig. 52.1 Trends of Publications

Source: Microsoft Excel

3.2 Countries Leading in CTR Prediction Research

Multiple nations are publishing substantial research on CTR Prediction. This section examines the output and impact of the most influential nations from 2012 through 2022. Table 52.2 provides the results of the top ten countries' publications in CTR Prediction research. The position was determined by the number of papers. In the event of a tie, the nation with the

Table 52.1 Trends of Publications

No.	Year	Publications
1	2012	61
2	2013	63
3	2014	60
4	2015	64
5	2016	72
6	2017	94
7	2018	92
8	2019	126
9	2020	124
10	2021	150
11	2022	142

Source: Microsoft Excel

Table 52.2 The most productive countries and regions

Rank	Countries	Documents	Citations
1	China	321	1794
2	United States	312	125
3	India	85	41
4	United Kingdom	70	46
5	South Korea	50	1
6	Spain	45	96
7	Taiwan	42	35
8	Germany	41	722
9	Hong Kong	39	57
10	Australia	38	4472

Source: Microsoft Excel

most number of citations was rated higher. Table 52.2 demonstrates that China was the most prolific nation with 321 publications and 4472 citations. This indicates that Chinese academics are focusing more on the CTR Prediction domain to enhance e-commerce strategy. The United States scored second with 312 articles and 125 citations, followed by India with 85 publications and 592 citations, and the United Kingdom with 70 publications and 46 citations. South Korea follows with 50 publications and 405 references to these works.

Similarly, Spain scored sixth in the CTR Prediction domain with 45 publications and 389 citations, while Taiwan rated sixth with 42 publications and 360 citations. Germany was placed eighth with 41 articles and 844 citations, Hong Kong was ranked ninth with 39 publications and 633 citations, and Australia was ranked tenth with 38 publications and 1794 citations in the CTR Prediction category.

Figure 52.2 depicts the results of the bibliometric relationship. Each ring represents a nation, and its size represents production; the larger the ring, the more productive the nation. China was the nation with the highest rate of bibliographic coupling. It is evident that it would have the most significant bibliometric connections with other nations. Figure 52.3 depicts the connection between co-authorship and nationalities. Remember that with the co-author, we might comprehend the extent of a country's publications and its most important collaborations with other nations. The graphic reflects a distinct hue to illustrate the co-authorship network. China had tight ties with the United States, the United Kingdom, and Hong Kong, whilst India had strong alliances with Japan, Singapore, and the Netherlands, in addition to active nations such as the United States and the United Kingdom. The United Kingdom collaborated closely with Spain.

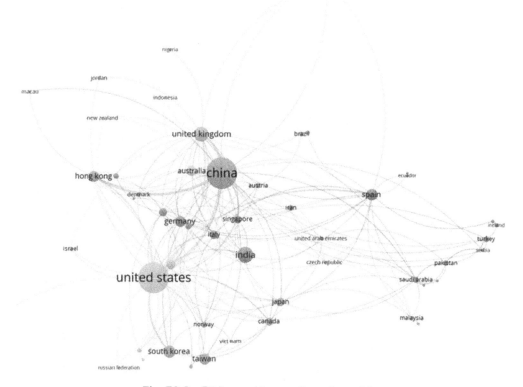

Fig. 52.2 Bibliographic coupling of countries

Source: VOSviewer

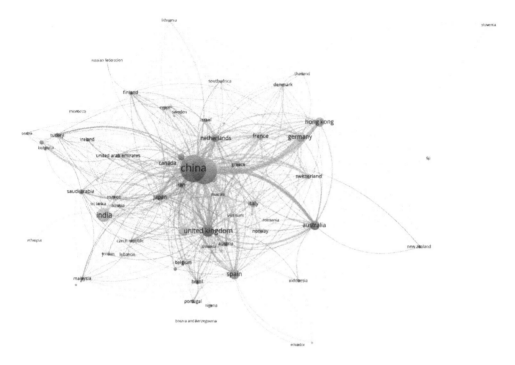

Fig. 52.3 Co-authorship among countries

Source: VOSviewer

3.3 Journals Leading in this Domain

An key component of the bibliometric analysis was to examine the most popular sources (i.e., sources that conducted more CTR Prediction research than others). Table 52.3 lists the top 10 sources of CTR Prediction research publications.

Table 52.3 Top 10 journals with highest citations

Rank	Sources	Publications	Citations
1	IEEE Access	46	380
2	Expert Systems with Applications	21	295
3	Electronic Commerce Research and Applications	19	340
4	IEEE Transactions on Knowledge and Data Engineering	19	304
5	Management Science	17	897
6	ACM Transactions on Information Systems	16	409
7	Decision Support Systems	16	352
8	Computational Intelligence and Neuroscience	14	169
9	Information Processing and Management	14	166
10	Knowledge Based Systems	14	193

Source: Microsoft Excel

Between 2012 and 2022, the journal with the most articles was IEEE Access, with 46 publications and 380 citations.

With 21 articles, Expert Systems with Applications ranked second. Third and fourth were Electronic Commerce Research and Applications and IEEE Transactions on Knowledge and Data Engineering, with 19 articles and 340 and 304 citations, respectively. With 14 publications, Knowledge Based Systems was the least productive source on the list.

3.4 The Most Productive Authors Related to CTR Prediction Research

Refer to Table 52.4, which lists the most prolific CTR Prediction researchers. Liu Y. topped the list with 17 publications and 182 citations, ranking first overall. Wang H. ranked second with 14 articles that received 106 citations, Li Y. ranked third with 14 publications that received 73 citations, Liu Z. ranked fourth with 13 publications that received 66 citations, and Zhang J. ranked fifth with 13 publications that received 79 citations.

Table 52.4 The most productive authors in CTR Prediction

Rank	Author	Publications	Citations
1	Liu Y.	17	182
2	Wang H.	14	106
3	Li Y.	14	73
4	Liu Z.	13	66
5	Zhang J.	13	79
6	Zhang X.	13	132
7	Zhang Y.	13	118
8	Chen Y.	12	164
9	Wang X.	12	216
10	Li X.	11	111

Source: Microsoft Excel

3.5 The Most-Cited Publication in CTR Prediction Research

The publication with the most citations was "Deep Sentence Embedding Using Long Short-Term Memory Networks: Analysis and Application to Information Retrieval" authored by Palangi H. et al. in 2016. Yu J. et al2014 .'s paper earned 444 citations, making it the second-most-cited publication overall. "Social networks, tailored advertising, and privacy restrictions" was the title of the third-most-cited paper, written by C.E. Tucker in 2014, and it earned 393 citations. Lee D.'s 2018 work titled "Advertising content and consumer engagement on social media: Evidence from Facebook" earned 336 citations, making it the fourth-most-cited publication overall. Yu J. et al. produced the fifth-most-cited paper in 2015, which earned 444 citations, followed by "Automated web usage data mining and recommendation system utilizing K-Nearest Neighbor (KNN) classification approach" with 244 citations, and so on. "Deep Multimodal Distance Metric Learning Using Click Constraints for Image Ranking" is

Table 52.5 The most cited publication

Rank	Authors	Citations	Year	Title	Sources
1	Palangi H., Deng L., Shen Y., Gao J., He X., Chen J., Song X., Ward R.	489	2016	Deep Sentence embedding using long short-term memory networks: Analysis and application to information retrieval	IEEE/ACM Transactions on Audio Speech and Language Processing
2	Yu J., Rui Y., Tao D.	444	2014	Click prediction for web image reranking using multimodal sparse coding	IEEE Transactions on Image Processing
3	Tucker C.E.	393	2014	Social networks, personalized advertising, and privacy controls	Journal of Marketing Research
4	Lee D., Hosanagar K., Nair H.S.	336	2018	Advertising content and consumer engagement on social media: Evidence from Facebook	Management Science
5	Yu J., Tao D., Wang M., Rui Y.	327	2015	Learning to Rank Using User Clicks and Visual Features for Image Retrieval	IEEE Transactions on Cybernetics
6	Adeniyi D.A., Wei Z., Yongquan Y.	244	2016	Automated web usage data mining and recommendation system using K-Nearest Neighbor (KNN) classification method	Applied Computing and Informatics
7	Yu J., Yang X., Gao F., Tao D.	242	2017	Deep Multimodal Distance Metric Learning Using Click Constraints for Image Ranking	IEEE Transactions on Cybernetics
8	Kwok L., Yu B.	219	2013	Spreading Social Media Messages on Facebook: An Analysis of Restaurant Business-to-Consumer Communications	Cornell Hospitality Quarterly
9	Chapelle O., Manavoglu E., Rosales R.	200	2014	Simple and scalable response prediction for display advertising	ACM Transactions on Intelligent Systems and Technology
10	Bleier A., Eisenbeiss M.	198	2015	The Importance of Trust for Personalized Online Advertising	Journal of Retailing

Source: Microsoft Excel

the title of the sixth most cited work by Yu J. et al., which has 242 citations. With 219 citations, "Spreading Social Media Messages on Facebook: An Analysis of Restaurant Business-to-Consumer Communications" is the eighth most referenced work, followed by Chapelle O.'s "Simple and Scalable Response Prediction for Display Advertising." In 2015, Bleier A. and Eisenbeiss M. released the tenth most cited paper, which was titled "Advertising content and consumer engagement on social media: Evidence from Facebook." Table 52.5 presents the top 10 most referenced papers with additional information.

4. Conclusions and Future Work

In response to the need for a comprehensive analysis of their scientific performance, the objective of this study was to determine the productivity (number of publications) and degree of influence of publishing organizations. According to the data, the annual publication of papers has increased substantially over time. In tandem with the increase in the number of documents, the number of citations acquired by publications has also increased, proving the acceptance of electronic marketing as a subject of study. With increasing publications and new authors, one of the limitations of this article is that the results continue to evolve over time. As a result, it is prudent to be current on developing trends.

REFERENCES

1. Chen, T., & Guestrin, C. (2016, August). Xgboost: A scalable tree boosting system. In *Proceedings of the 22nd acm sigkdd international conference on knowledge discovery and data mining* (pp. 785–794).
2. Cheng, H. T., Koc, L., Harmsen, J., Shaked, T., Chandra, T., Aradhye, H., ... & Shah, H. (2016, September). Wide & deep learning for recommender systems. In *Proceedings of the 1st workshop on deep learning for recommender systems* (pp. 7–10).
3. Covington, P., Adams, J., & Sargin, E. (2016, September). Deep neural networks for youtube recommendations. In *Proceedings of the 10th ACM conference on recommender systems* (pp. 191–198)..
4. Guo, H., Tang, R., Ye, Y., Li, Z., & He, X. (2017). DeepFM: a factorization-machine based neural network for CTR prediction. *arXiv preprint arXiv:1703.04247*.
5. Huang, T., Zhang, Z., & Zhang, J. (2019, September). FiBiNET: combining feature importance and bilinear feature interaction for click-through rate prediction. In *Proceedings of the 13th ACM Conference on Recommender Systems* (pp. 169–177).
6. Juan, Y., Zhuang, Y., Chin, W. S., & Lin, C. J. (2016, September). Field-aware factorization machines for CTR prediction. In *Proceedings of the 10th ACM conference on recommender systems* (pp. 43–50).
7. Lian, J., Zhou, X., Zhang, F., Chen, Z., Xie, X., & Sun, G. (2018, July). xdeepfm: Combining explicit and implicit feature interactions for recommender systems. In *Proceedings of the 24th ACM SIGKDD international conference on knowledge discovery & data mining* (pp. 1754–1763).
8. McMahan, H. B., Holt, G., Sculley, D., Young, M., Ebner, D., Grady, J., ... & Kubica, J. (2013, August). Ad click prediction: a view from the trenches. In *Proceedings of the 19th ACM SIGKDD international conference on Knowledge discovery and data mining* (pp. 1222–1230).

9. Rendle, S. (2010, December). Factorization machines. In *2010 IEEE International conference on data mining* (pp. 995-1000). IEEE.

10. He, X., Pan, J., Jin, O., Xu, T., Liu, B., Xu, T., ... & Candela, J. Q. (2014, August). Practical lessons from predicting clicks on ads at facebook. In *Proceedings of the eighth international workshop on data mining for online advertising* (pp. 1–9)..

11. Richardson, M., Dominowska, E., & Ragno, R. (2007, May). Predicting clicks: estimating the click-through rate for new ads. In *Proceedings of the 16th international conference on World Wide Web* (pp. 521–530).

12. Wang, R., Fu, B., Fu, G., & Wang, M. (2017). Deep & cross network for ad click predictions. In *Proceedings of the ADKDD'17* (pp. 1–7).

13. Zhou, G., Zhu, X., Song, C., Fan, Y., Zhu, H., Ma, X., ... & Gai, K. (2018, July). Deep interest network for click-through rate prediction. In *Proceedings of the 24th ACM SIGKDD international conference on knowledge discovery & data mining* (pp. 1059–1068).

14. Saura, J. R., Palacios-Marqués, D., & Iturricha-Fernández, A. (2021). Ethical design in social media: Assessing the main performance measurements of user online behavior modification. *Journal of Business Research, 129*, 271–281.

15. Ribeiro-Navarrete, S., Saura, J. R., & Palacios-Marqués, D. (2021). Towards a new era of mass data collection: Assessing pandemic surveillance technologies to preserve user privacy. *Technological Forecasting and Social Change, 167*, 120681.

16. Salton, G., Wong, A., & Yang, C. S. (1975). A vector space model for automatic indexing. *Communications of the ACM, 18*(11), 613–620.

17. Farrukh, M., Shahzad, I. A., Meng, F., Wu, Y., & Raza, A. (2021). Three decades of research in the technology analysis & strategic management: a bibliometrics analysis. *Technology Analysis & Strategic Management, 33*(9), 989–1005.

18. Nawaz, K., Aslam, T., & Saeed, H. A. (2020). A bibliometric analysis of international journal of sports marketing & sponsorship. *International Journal of Business and Psychology, 2*(1), 45–60.

19. Gu, Z., Meng, F., & Farrukh, M. (2021). Mapping the research on knowledge transfer: A scientometrics approach. *IEEE Access, 9*, 34647–34659.

20. Nawaz, K., Saeed, H. A., & Sajeel, T. A. (2020). Covid-19 and the State of Research from the Perspective of Psychology. *Int. J. Bus. Psychol, 2*, 35–44.

21. Cancino, C. A., Merigó, J. M., Urbano, D., & Amorós, J. E. (2020). Evolution of the entrepreneurship and innovation research in Ibero-America between 1986 and 2015. *Journal of Small Business Management*, 1–31.

22. Gao, P., Meng, F., Mata, M. N., Martins, J. M., Iqbal, S., Correia, A. B., ... & Farrukh, M. (2021). Trends and future research in electronic marketing: A bibliometric analysis of twenty years. *Journal of Theoretical and Applied Electronic Commerce Research, 16*(5), 1667–1679.

Handbook of Evidence Based Management Practices in Business – Satyendra Kumar Sharma et al. (eds)
© 2023 Taylor & Francis Group, London, ISBN 978-1-032-54216-4

Chapter

An Investigation into Understanding Consumer Opinion About Adoption of Electric Vehicles Using Machine Learning

Pooja[1], Abhishek Tripathi[2]
Research Scholar, School of Management Studies,
MNNIT-Allahabad, Prayagraj, India

Yatish Joshi[3]
Assistant Professor , School of Management Studies,
MNNIT-Allahabad, Prayagraj, India

ABSTRACT: Increasing environmental issues has alarmed the government across the world to take suitable measures for environmental protection. To contain the environmental pollution and reducing the dependency on traditional non-renewable fuels more and more companies are focusing on production and marketing of electric vehicles. Electric vehicles reduce the dependency on fossil fuels and also diminish the impact of ozone depleting substances. However, the organizations are facing challenges in term of customers' acceptance of these electric vehicles. The primary concern of the present research is the understand the consumer opinion and emotions about adoption of electric vehicles. To do so the research employs data extraction from social media website. In the proposed research data were extracted from twitter, frequency of attribute was generated, and consumer sentiment were analyzed about adopting electric vehicles. The analysis identifies the consumer sentiment about electric vehicles. The result show positive opinions of the customers about electric vehicles, with more and more customers are joyful and happy for this transition.

KEYWORDS: Consumer sentiments, Electric vehicles, Emotions, Twitter

[1]poojayadav2699@gmail.com, [2]abhishektripathie@gmail.com, [3]yatish.joshi24@mnnit.ac.in

DOI: 10.4324/9781003415725-53

1. Introduction

Climatic change caused due to Green House Gas (GHG) emission is an alarming issue for us at the present time. According to EPA (2020), transportation sector is the primary source of GHG emission contributing up to 27% of total U.S. GHG emission. Carbon-dioxide is the major gas emitted from transportation, emanating from combustion of petroleum-based product such as diesel fuel which consequently makes it necessary to supplant traditional non-renewable fuel vehicle with electric vehicle to curb the effect of GHG emission. Electric vehicles comprising Battery Electric Vehicles and Plug-in Hybrid Electric Vehicles are usually renowned as "Green" can substantially reduce GHG emission (Thomas 2015). Over the past few years the governmental policy measures have been increasingly promoting the adoption of electric vehicle across the world (Rietmann and Lieven 2019). Consequently, the sales of electric vehicles are increasing exponentially. According to IEA (2022) electric car attained the highest sales totaling 6.6 million in 2021 which is nearly double as compared to 2020.

Despite being environmentally friendly and having other benefits such as low running and maintenance cost, better performance etc., the manufacturers are facing challenges in terms of customer acceptance. The reason behind such a limited use of electric vehicles is that the mass acceptance of it relies predominantly on the consumers' perception (Rezvani, Jansson, and Bodin 2015). It is very important to understand the public perception about electric vehicles to discover their feeling and emotions regarding new technologies. Consumers' perception and opinion about electric vehicles are subject to numerous factors. Previously many researchers have examined these factors that cause disparity in adoption of electric vehicles. (Huang and Ge 2019) applied Theory of planned behavior to introduce the consumer cognitive status, product perception and incentive policy measure (including monetary and non-monetary) to develop purchase intention influence mechanism model for electric vehicles.

In the light of the above discussion, this study tries to understand the consumer opinion and emotions regarding electric vehicle adoption employing sentiment analysis. In this study we have used one of the leading social media platforms i.e. Twitter for the sentiment analysis. The main aim of the study is:

1. To look into consumer opinion and emotion about adoption of electric vehicle.
2. To provide insights to marketers which will assist in understanding consumer sentiments and mindset while formulating marketing strategies.

The following sections include literature review, research design, data analysis, discussion and implications and conclusion.

2. Literature Review

Electric vehicles are the alternative fuel vehicle that have an electric motor rather than internal combustion engine. Hybrid Electric Vehicle (HEV), Plug-in Hybrid Electric Vehicle (PHEV), Battery Electric Vehicle (BEV) and Extended-Range Battery Electric Vehicle (E-REV) are some of the types of electric vehicles that use different technologies (Rezvani, Jansson, and Bodin 2015). Since electric vehicles use clean energy and are eco-friendly, it is gaining prevalence in the recent times. However, there is a substantial inconsistency in the adoption of electric vehicles. So far, many researchers have studied several factors that affect the adoption of electric vehicles (Egbue and Long 2012; Sierzchula et al. 2014; Huang and Ge 2019). Public opinion and emotions play a vital role in building perception about electric vehicle and hence affect the adoption of the same. Suggested by (Schuitema et al. 2013), the purchase intention of electric vehicle is influenced by anticipated emotions such as pleasure and joy. To boost the sales of electric vehicle, personal and social issues of people must be examined along with improving technical limitation such as battery capacity and weight (Jena 2020).

Sentiment analysis is a Natural Language Processing (NLP) technique that evaluates the written or spoken languages and determines the articulation i.e., whether it is positive, negative or neutral and to what extent. (Alsaeedi and Khan 2019). According to (Taboada, Brooke, and Voll 2011) Sentiment analysis is defined as a extensive technique that is used to bring out subjectivity and polarity from the given text. In the recent times, the use of social media such as Twitter, Facebook, etc. to express opinions has increased exponentially. This in turn assists in knowing the consumer sentiments regarding the product (Jena 2020).

In this study Twitter social media platform has been used for the sentiment analysis. Twitter is a micro-blogging website where people share their real time opinions about trending issues, product experience, complains, etc. which are also used by manufacturer to explore about the consumer sentiments and emotions (Alsaeedi and Khan 2019).

3. Research Design

The study has employed sentiment analysis using R programming language which is used for statistical computing and graphics. The sentiment analysis has been done on the data extracted from twitter using R studio platform. To run the program various packages such as twitteR, rtweet, tm, syuzhet lubridate, etc. were installed. Initially, Application Programming Interface (API) codes were generated to run the codes. Around 5000 tweets were extracted using the key word "Electric Vehicle". The next step involves removing of punctuations, numbers and spaces using word corpus. After that cleanest is used for further cleaning of data by removing irrelevant words and whitespaces. Afterwards, bar plot and word cloud were generated depicting the frequencies of number of tweets of the words related to the keyword "Electric Vehicle" followed by the sentiment score graph exhibiting consumer sentiments (positive and negative) and emotions (anger, anticipation, disgust, fear, joy, sadness, surprise and trust).

4. Data Analysis

In Fig. 53.1, the barplot illustrates that the words related to electric vehicles have high frequencies. The word electric has the highest frequency which means that people are shifting from traditional vehicles to electric vehicles. In word cloud (Fig. 53.2) the bigger and bolder words are more frequently appeared in the sample tweets. "Electric" has appeared 3769 times, "electricvehicle" being appeared for 100 times.

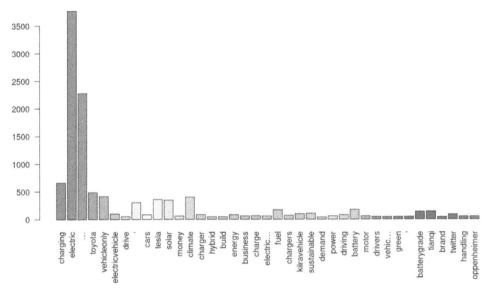

Fig. 53.1 Barplot showing maximum used keywords

Source: Author's compilation

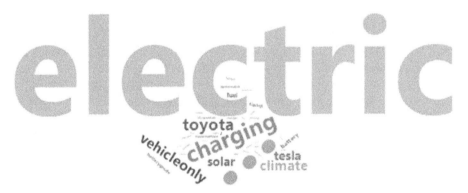

Fig. 53.2 Word cloud for electric vehicle

Source: Author's compilation

Figure 53.3 depicts the sentiment score for 5000 tweets. The sentiment for electric vehicle is positive which signifies that the public opinion about adoption of electric vehicle is positive. Joy and surprise are the predominant emotions which denotes that the consumers feel joy and happiness after the transition.

5. Discussion and Implications

This study applied sentiment analysis to examine the consumer opinions and emotion towards adoption of electric vehicle by extracting opinions from twitter. The results showed that total 5000 tweets were extracted depicting that people discuss and share views about electric vehicle

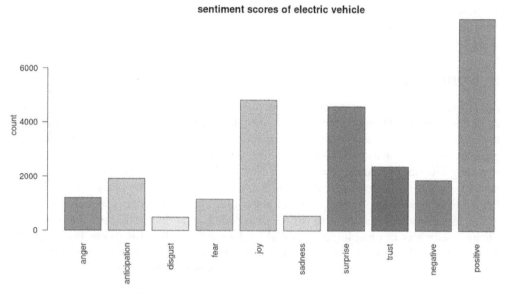

Fig. 53.3   Sentiment score of electric vehicle

Source: Author's compilation

to a great extent. This signifies that the consumers are gaining awareness about the electric vehicle and their usefulness over time. The results of the study also show that people are having high positive sentiments in respect to adoption of electric vehicles. Consumers' positive reviews and opinions lead to the increased sales of electric vehicles (He and Wang 2022). The study also shows that the people are exhibiting high levels of 'Joy' signifying their happiness over the perceived value of electric vehicles and 'Surprise' signifying that the electric vehicle offering is surpassing their expectations. However, electric vehicle market at national level is relatively smaller than overall automobile sales (Sierzchula et al. 2014). This gap can be due to various reasons. For example, the sustainability and environmental benefits of electric vehicles are vital factors that influence the adoption of electric vehicles but still price and performance play the prominent role (Egbue and Long 2012).

This study provides several theoretical implications to academicians. This study contributes to the literature through analyzing consumer sentiments regarding adoption of electric vehicles through sentiment analysis via opinion-mining from Twitter. The results of this study shows positive sentiment towards electric vehicle which reflects that consumers are shifting from conventional vehicle to electric vehicle. Also, the results articulate joy and surprise emotions of the consumer regarding electric vehicles. This study also contributes by employing twitter which is the largest social media platform and provides analysis of real-time consumer opinions.

This study also provides managerial implications. This study provides insights about the consumer emotions and opinions towards adoption of electric vehicles. The managers can use these insights in formulating marketing strategies and policies regarding sales of electric vehicles. Since consumers are having positive sentiments in respect of electric vehicle, the marketers can use this opportunity to create awareness about benefits of electric vehicles and motivate them to switch from conventional transportation to electric vehicle. Marketer by providing high quality customer experiences can elevate the trust emotion towards electric vehicles.

6. Conclusion

Acknowledging the environmental problems, this study focuses on the consumers' opinion and emotion towards adoption of electric vehicle. The study applied sentiment analysis using twitter to ascertain consumers' sentiments. It also contributes significantly towards the literature and provides insights to managers about consumers' opinion. The study indicates positive results regarding adoption of electric vehicle which can be utilized by the marketers while formulating marketing strategies. There are certain limitations to this study. In the first place, the study is limited to only 5000 tweets per corpus of keyword. Future researchers can increase the size of corpus. Secondly, the study is only limited to twitter social media for consumers' opinion. Future researchers can employ other social media platforms like Facebook, Instagram, etc. Thirdly, this study conducts cross-sectional study. Future researchers can apply longitudinal study to understand the change in consumer sentiments and emotion over the course of time.

REFERENCES

1. Alsaeedi, Abdullah, and Mohammad Zubair Khan. 2019. "A Study on Sentiment Analysis Techniques of Twitter Data" 10 (2): 361–74.
2. Egbue, Ona, and Suzanna Long. 2012. "Barriers to Widespread Adoption of Electric Vehicles: An Analysis of Consumer Attitudes and Perceptions." *Energy Policy* 48 (2012): 717–29. https://doi. org/10.1016/j.enpol.2012.06.009.
3. He, Shifan, and Yingming Wang. 2022. "Evaluating New Energy Vehicles by Picture Fuzzy Sets Based on Sentiment Analysis from Online Reviews." *Artificial Intelligence Review*, no. 0123456789. https://doi.org/10.1007/s10462-022-10217-1.
4. Huang, Xiangqian, and Jianping Ge. 2019. "Electric Vehicle Development in Beijing : An Analysis of Consumer Purchase Intention." *Journal of Cleaner Production* 216: 361–72. https://doi. org/10.1016/j.jclepro.2019.01.231.
5. IEA (2022), Electric Vehicles, IEA, Paris https://www.iea.org/reports/electric-vehicles, License: CC BY 4.0
6. Jena, Rabindra. 2020. "An Empirical Case Study on Indian Consumers' Sentiment towards Electric Vehicles: A Big Data Analytics Approach." *Industrial Marketing Management* 90 (December 2019): 605–16. https://doi.org/10.1016/j.indmarman.2019.12.012.
7. Rezvani, Zeinab, Johan Jansson, and Jan Bodin. 2015. "Advances in Consumer Electric Vehicle Adoption Research: A Review and Research Agenda." *Transportation Research Part D: Transport and Environment* 34: 122–36. https://doi.org/10.1016/j.trd.2014.10.010.
8. Rietmann, Nele, and Theo Lieven. 2019. "How Policy Measures Succeeded to Promote Electric Mobility e Worldwide Review and Outlook National Conference of State Legislatures." *Journal of Cleaner Production* 206: 66–75. https://doi.org/10.1016/j.jclepro.2018.09.121.
9. Schuitema, Geertje, Jillian Anable, Stephen Skippon, and Neale Kinnear. 2013. "The Role of Instrumental , Hedonic and Symbolic Attributes in the Intention to Adopt Electric Vehicles." *Transportation Research Part A* 48: 39–49. https://doi.org/10.1016/j.tra.2012.10.004.

10. Sierzchula, William, Sjoerd Bakker, Kees Maat, and Bert Van Wee. 2014. "The Influence of Financial Incentives and Other Socio-Economic Factors on Electric Vehicle Adoption." *Energy Policy* 68: 183–94. https://doi.org/10.1016/j.enpol.2014.01.043.

11. Taboada, Maite, Julian Brooke, and Kimberly Voll. 2011. "Lexicon-Based Methods for Sentiment Analysis," no. September 2010.

12. Thomas, C E Sandy. 2015. "How Green Are Electric Vehicles?" *International Journal of Hydrogen Energy* 37 (7): 6053–62. https://doi.org/10.1016/j.ijhydene.2011.12.118.

Handbook of Evidence Based Management Practices in Business – Satyendra Kumar Sharma et al. (eds)
© 2023 Taylor & Francis Group, London, ISBN 978-1-032-54216-4

Chapter

Click-Through Rate: An Overview of Scientific Research in Management

Venkat Narasimhan R.[1], Udayan Chanda[2]
Department of Management,
Birla Institute of Technology and Science, Pilani, India
Yashvardhan Sharma[3]
Department of Computer Science and Information Systems,
Birla Institute of Technology and Science, Pilani, India

ABSTRACT: Since the introduction of online advertising, an increasing number of advertisers and firms are relying on this ad type to acquire consumers, making it an important revenue source for search engines and other internet giants like Google, Amazon, etc. Clicks are used as a metric in two ways: (i) for advertisers, it is used to measure the effectiveness of an advertisement, and (ii) for internet companies, it is used as a quality metric for their search engine or website. The click-through rate is the ratio of the number of impressions to the number of clicks of an advertisement. Managers are using this metric to allocate the budget for their advertisement campaigns based on their effectiveness. In the last decade, due to the growing industry demand, it has attracted scholars from industry and academia. This literature review article examines click-through rate evolution from an empirical standpoint using the bibliometric methods, reviewing 596 articles from the Scopus index. This review article (i) identifies the most influential articles, authors, and journals, serving as a baseline for future research, and (ii) charts the evolution of the topic over the last decade, assisting managers and future researchers in gaining a performance-based comprehensive view of click-through rate.

KEYWORDS: Bibliometric methods, Citations, Click-through rate, Ctr, Performance analysis

1. Introduction

The introduction of the internet gave rise to a new type of advertising, "Online Advertising," which again gave rise to new subtypes, i.e., paid search, display advertising, video ads, etc.

[1]p20210444@pilani.bits-pilani.ac.in, [2]udayanchanda@pilani.bits-pilani.ac.in, [3]yash@pilani.bits-pilani.ac.in

DOI: 10.4324/9781003415725-54

This new type of advertisement is produced by many internet giants like Google, Amazon, and Facebook, and through which most advertisers and organizations reach out to consumers. Unlike traditional advertising, online advertising provides advertisers with a unique opportunity to deliver marketing messages to consumers through various digital platforms (e.g., search engine portals, social media, e-commerce platforms, etc.) (Yang Y et al. 2017). Online advertising has become a dominant form of advertising and is expected to reach $982.82 billion by 2025 (Yanwu et al., 2021).

In online advertising, impressions, clicks, and click-through rates are used to measure the ad campaign's performance. The impressions are used primarily to measure the ad's exposure to potential consumers in each period, creating awareness about the advertisements (like a billboard ad) among potential consumers, which prompts them to click on the ad to gain more information, leading to a conversion. In other terms, impression is a passive exposure to the advertisement, whereas the click is an active opt-in that leads to further information exposure (Rutz et al., 2011). Hence, clicks are an essential element of online advertising campaigns as they are (i) a reflection of the relevance of advertisements from consumers' perspective (Yanwu et al., 2021), (ii) a significant revenue source for the search engines, (iii) and a practical measurement for advertisers to track the effectiveness of the ad campaign and valuable in decision making.

Click-through rate is a performance gauge used to measure the performance of keywords in an online advertisement campaign. It is the ratio of the number of clicks to the number of impressions (Google Ads). It is beneficial for advertisers to determine the budget allocation for the advertisement campaign based on its performance. In recent years, CTR has attracted scholars and managers from varied backgrounds due to increased industrial needs.

In the past decade, numerous articles have been published on CTR and CTR prediction. Yanwu et al. (2021) have recently centered their literature review article on CTR prediction, focusing on the modeling frameworks using systematic review methodology. However, to our knowledge, there are no literature articles on the business and management aspect of the click-through rate, and future researchers in management and business subjects would be beneficial from a structured study that highlights the

1. Most influential articles and countries in CTR in the management discipline
2. Mapping the evolution of the research trends in CTR in the past decade

This research article analyzes the existing literature on CTR using bibliometric methodologies, thus making a significant contribution not only to the researchers in business and management disciplines but also to marketing managers interested in CTR as a one-stop overview of the evolution of CTR.

2. Methodology

Our article follows the bibliometric methodology and quantitative techniques on bibliometric data (units of publication and citation) (N Donthu et al. 2021). Bibliometric analysis is primarily divided into (i) performance analysis (a measurement of research components, e.g., authors, publications, countries) and (ii) science mapping (explores the relationship among the research components).

We use the performance analysis to determine the total citations and average citations per. A year and the science mapping using bibliometric analytical methods, i.e., citation analysis, co-citation analysis through VOSviewer to map the most influential articles, authors, countries, and science mapping to map research trends in CTR evolution in the past decade.

Citation analysis determines the impact of a publication by the number of citations it receives, which enables it to ascertain the most influential articles in a research field. Co-citation analysis is used to identify the thematic clusters in the research field, using the fundamental idea that two articles cited together frequently are similar. Researchers use it to map past research development. (N. Donthu, 2021).

3. Data

The existing literature collected from the SCOPUS index between 2012-2022 in business, econometrics, and decision sciences. A total of 605 articles were collected from the initial query; after careful consideration and further filtering the criteria by excluding specific research articles not relevant to this study, 596 were used in our bibliometric analysis. The following search terms were used in the initial query "Click through rate," "CTR," "Clicks," "Online Advertising," and "sponsored search."

4. Results

The following sub-sections discuss the results of the bibliometric analysis of the database.

4.1 Performance Analysis

Table 54.1 Total citations and average number of citations in CTR research

Year	Articles per Year	Total Citations (TC)	Average Citations (AC)
2012	36	1374	38
2013	36	1526	42
2014	53	2142	60
2015	47	1727	48
2016	44	928	26
2017	55	1049	29
2018	56	1219	34
2019	64	765	21
2020	74	1017	28
2021	76	380	11
2022	61	57	2

Source: Author's compilation using MS Excel

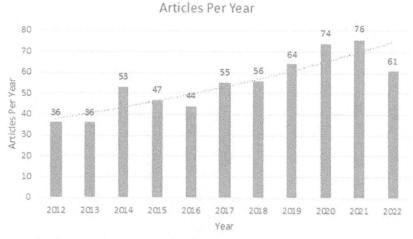

Fig. 54.1 Annual publications of research articles between 2012-2022

Source: Authors' compilations using MS Excel

From Table 54.1, the annual publications in CTR research show a growing trend that peaks in 2021 with a marginal slowdown in 2014, 2015, and 2022. The movement can be attributed to the consumer's purchase behavior shift from brick-mortar stores to online websites. The upward change from 2019 coincides with the COVID-19 era, a period of lockdowns forcing consumers to purchase goods online, thus contributing to increased online advertisements.

4.2 Citation Analysis

Table 54.2 Top 20 most productive countries and sources in CTR

(a)

Country	Documents	Citations
United States	286	7887
China	101	1854
United Kingdom	47	1209
India	36	326
Germany	33	1159
France	30	355
Spain	26	232
Hong Kong	24	621
Canada	22	279

(b)

Sources	Documents	Citations
Management Science	35	1322
Marketing Science	30	999
Electronic Commerce Research And Applications	26	457
Operations Research	21	203
Decision Support Systems	18	559
Information Systems Research	17	450
Journal Of Research In Interactive Marketing	17	301
Information Processing And Management	16	130
Journal Of Retailing And Consumer Services	15	509

Country	Documents	Citations	Sources	Documents	Citations
Netherlands	21	605	ACM Transactions On Information Systems	15	395
Australia	20	301	Information Sciences	15	132
South Korea	20	245	Journal Of Marketing Research	13	1278
Taiwan	17	293	Knowledge-Based Systems	12	119
Belgium	10	76	Electronic Commerce Research	10	135
Israel	10	114	Journal Of The Association For Information Science And Technology	10	93
Italy	9	122	ACM Transactions On Economics And Computation	10	63
Switzerland	9	186	International Journal Of Electronic Commerce	9	108
Turkey	9	109	International Journal Of Industrial Organization	8	144
Iran	8	61	Journal Of Business Research	7	71
Singapore	8	72	European Journal Of Operational Research	6	257
			Mis Quarterly: Management Information Systems	6	212

Source: Authors' compilation using VOSviewer

Using citation analysis through the VOSviewer tool, we find that from 2012 to 2022,1180 organizations from 50 countries contributed to CTR research in business, decision sciences, and econometrics. The United States of America has contributed the highest number (286) of the total publications, followed by China (101), the United Kingdom (47), India (36), and Germany (33), as displayed in Table 2(a). One of the reasons behind the US and China in the top two positions could be their high purchasing power and significant presence of major online websites like Amazon, Alibaba, etc. The highest number of articles were published in Management Science (35), followed by Marketing Science (30), Electronic Commerce Research and Applications (26), Operation Research (21), and Decision Support Systems (19), the top 20 sources and countries are displayed in table 2 and 23. This proves that CTR research is multidisciplinary through analyzing the primary sources publishing the article in our data collection.

Table 54.3 displays the top 10 most cited articles in the CTR research between 2012 and 2022. By analyzing these articles, the researchers have explored various issues about clicks, including information privacy, the context of the advertisements, cross channel purchases, and Click prediction.

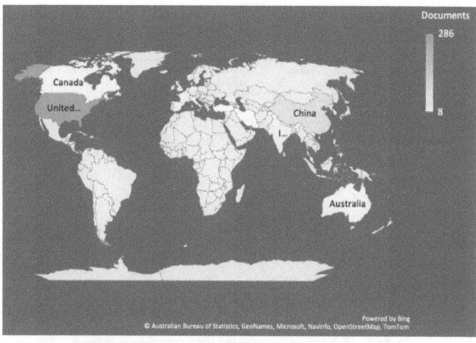

Fig. 54.2 Top 20 most productive countries in CTR research

Source: Author's compilation using Microsoft Excel

Table 54.3 Top 10 most influential articles in CTR research

Article Title	Source	Year	Citations
Social Networks, Personalized Advertising, and Privacy Controls	Journal of Marketing Research	2014	395
Advertising content and consumer engagement on social media: Evidence from Facebook	Management Science	2018	341
Categorization of multiple channel retailing in Multi-, Cross-, and Omni-Channel Retailing for retailers and retailing	Journal of Retailing and Consumer Services	2015	318
Adding bricks to clicks: Predicting the patterns of cross-channel elasticities over time	Journal of Marketing	2012	273
When does retargeting work? Information specificity in online advertising	Journal of Marketing Research	2013	262
Spreading Social Media Messages on Facebook: An Analysis of Restaurant Business-to-Consumer Communications,	Cornell Hospitality Quarterly	2013	221
Attributing conversions in a multichannel online marketing environment: An empirical model and a field experiment	Journal of Marketing Research	2014	211

Article Title	Source	Year	Citations
The Importance of Trust for Personalized Online Advertising	Journal of Retailing	2015	198
Promotional marketing or word-of-mouth? Evidence from online restaurant reviews	Information Systems Research	2013	198
Airbnb: Online targeted advertising, sense of power, and consumer decisions	International Journal of Hospitality Management	2017	176

Source: Authors' compilation using VOSviewer

4.3 Co-citation Analysis

Fig. 54.3 High-impact articles in the co-citation analysis network

Source: VOSviewer

Using co-citation reference analysis, we identify 4 clusters with 28 articles from our dataset. These 4 clusters, displayed in Fig. 54.3, are identified using linkage clustering by VOSviewer.

Early insights into CTR Research

The articles from the analysis in cluster 1 establish the early foundations of the click-through rate as a measure of internet advertising effectiveness (Drèze et al. 2003). Articles in the first cluster provide an early insight (pre-2012) into the clicks, click-through rate, and online advertising with a broad focus, including tracing its origin, empirical model, and effectiveness. Their model results show a positive interdependence between the CTRs of organic and paid search advertising. Bucklin, r.e, et al. (2009) article discuss the nature of the clickstream through a review of the significant development of the clickstream and identifies new opportunities and emerging areas for future researchers. Yang et al. (2009) analyzes the relationship between organic and sponsored search advertising using click-through rates and conversion rates of the respective types of advertisements through a Hierarchical Bayesian modeling framework.

Clicks and CTR from consumers' perspective in Search Engine Marketing

The articles in the second cluster focus on the clicks and CTR in search engine marketing from the consumers' perspective. Ansari et al. (2003) explore the clicking behavior in their optimized online information customization model. Blake. et al. (2015) measure the effectiveness of the paid ads, and their findings show that the loyal consumers of a brand are more likely to click on the paid ads and show that there is no measurable short-term value in keywords brand advertising. Ghose. A et al. (2009) used Bayesian modeling to develop a framework for understanding the relationship between click-through rates, cost per click, conversion rates, and ad ranking. The model analysis shows that the higher click-through rate is not necessarily obtained from the main keywords, are not necessarily the most profitable. Yang et al. (2010) explores if there is any effect on click-through rates of a paid search ad due to the presence of an organic ad for a given firm. Using a Bayesian hierarchical modeling framework, they observe that the click-through rates of the organic ads and the click-through rate of paid ads are positively interdependent.

Clicks, CTR, and Auction

Articles in the third cluster explore internet advertising concerning the auction mechanism used by search engines like Google and Yahoo! and optimizing them. Gopal. R et al. (2011) studied the impact of the ad impression on their channel and cross-channel click rates. They find that ad impressions on search and content channels sync with a decreased CTR and vice versa. However, they also observe that within a channel, The increase in ad impressions on the search channel is related to the decrease in CTR on the same search channel. Yao et al. (2010) develop a dynamic model to explore how the interactions of the searchers(consumers), advertisers, and search engines affect the firm's profits. Their study finds that frequent clickers give importance to the ad's position and that 10% of consumers in their dataset do the 90%of clicks. They also explore the effects of the changes to the search engine policy through various simulations. Edelman B. et al. (2007) focus on the generalized second price (GSP) auction and its properties in sponsored search, in which clicks and CTR are an essential part, to explore the equilibrium of GSP and its differences concerning Vicky-Clarke-Groves'(VCG) auction mechanism.

Clicks, CTR, and Other Online Ad Measures

In the fourth and final cluster, the articles are clustered around the ad measures of online advertising, including CTR, conversions, ranking, and pricing. Ashish A. et al. (2011) evaluate the impact of ad placements on revenues and profits from a sponsored search ad campaign by measuring the effect of ad position on click-through rate and conversion rate through Bayesian hierarchical modeling; their study observes that the CTR decreases with the position, i.e., the higher the position of the ad, the higher the click-through rate. Rutz O. J et al. (2012) developed a modeling approach to evaluate the performance of the individual keywords' conversion rates. Their findings reiterate Ashish et al. (2011) observation that higher positions increase click-through and conversion rates.

5. Conclusion

In the past ten years, we have seen that researchers across different research disciplines have contributed to online advertising and its components such as clicks, keywords, etc., even inside a particular field; researchers have focused on various aspects of the CTR, as displayed by the results of this study. Apart from identifying the leading countries, sources, and influential articles, this study also shows that the performance of the research in CTR in the management domain has been increasing, albeit with occasional drops concerning the previous year. Nevertheless, the overall research trend is growing, as shown in Fig. 54.1.

This study also maps the evolution of the research in the past decade by using co-citation analysis to identify the past research in the CTR. Based on the investigation, the initial years of the research on CTR in management theme focused on establishing CTR as a metric for ad effectiveness, later progressing to exploring its relationship with other ad metrics like conversion rate, etc., and also in the overall performance of an ad campaign from consumer, advertiser and search engine perspective. Thus, our article highlights the salient articles, countries, and sources of CTR research in the management discipline using bibliographic methods and exploring the evolution of the study in the past decade.

This article mainly focuses on the management, and decision science disciplines of CTR research, thus making it a significant limitation to our study; as the computer power increased over the last few years, there has increased focus among researchers on CTR prediction in computer science and information sciences disciplines using various tools like Artificial intelligence and Machine learning, etc., Also, this study focused on the co-citation methodology used to explore the past. Future researchers can use other bibliography methods like Bibliography coupling and keyword co-occurrence which explore the present and the future emerging areas in the research field. Thus, providing a complete overview of the click-through rate.

REFERENCES

1. Ansari, A., & Mela, C. F. (2003). E-Customization. Journal of Marketing Research, 40(2), 131–145.
2. Blake, T., Nosko, C. and Tadelis, S. (2015), Consumer Heterogeneity and Paid Search Effectiveness: A Large-Scale Field Experiment. Econometrica, 83: 155-174.
3. Bucklin, R. E., & Sismeiro, C. (2009). Click Here for Internet Insight: Advances in Clickstream Data Analysis in Marketing. Journal of Interactive Marketing, 23(1), 35–48.
4. Edelman, Benjamin, Michael Ostrovsky, and Michael Schwarz. (2007). "Internet Advertising and the Generalized Second-Price Auction: Selling Billions of Dollars' Worth of Keywords." *American Economic Review*, 97 (1): 242-259.
5. Gopal, Ram, Xinxin Li, and Ramesh Sankaranarayanan. "Online Keyword Based Advertising: Impact of Ad Impressions on Own-Channel and Cross-Channel Click-through Rates." Decision Support Systems 52, no. 1 (2011): 1–8.
6. Ghose, Anindya, and Sha Yang. "An Empirical Analysis of Search Engine Advertising: Sponsored Search in Electronic Markets." *Management Science* 55, no. 10 (2009): 1605–22.
7. Rutz, O. J., Bucklin, R. E., & Sonnier, G. P. (2012). A Latent Instrumental Variables Approach to Modeling Keyword Conversion in Paid Search Advertising. Journal of Marketing Research, 49(3), 306–319.
8. Rutz, O.J. Bucklin, R.E., from generic to branded: a model of spillover in paid search advertising (2011). journal of marketing research, 48 (1), pp. 87-102.
9. Yang, Y., Yang, Y., Jansen, B. J., & Lalmas, M. (2017). Computational advertising: A paradigm shift for advertising and marketing? *IEEE Intelligent Systems, 32*(3), 3-6. [7933928]
10. Yanwu Yang and Panyu Zhai.(2022). Click-through rate prediction in online advertising: A literature review. Inf. Process. Manage. 59, 2.
11. Yang, S., & Ghose, A. (2010). Analyzing the Relationship Between Organic and Sponsored Search Advertising: Positive, Negative, or Zero Interdependence? Marketing Science, 29 (4), 602–623.
12. Yao, Song, and Carl F. Mela. "A Dynamic Model of Sponsored Search Advertising." *Marketing Science* 30, no. 3 (2011): 447–68.

Chapter

Consumer's Safety Concerns on Fire Hazards and Readiness of Electric Vehicle Batteries in India

Vikash Joshi[1]

Ph.D Scholar, IBS, ICFAI University, Jaipur, India

Payal Phulwani[2]

Asst. Professor, IBS, ICFAI University, Jaipur, India

ABSTRACT: Mother Earth is suffering from continuous emission of CO_2 and other Green House gases.

As per WHO report, Air pollution causing 13 deaths per minute worldwide. In India, nearly 5 deaths per minute due to fossil fuels burning.

Unfortunately, approx. 27% of the carbon emission is coming from global transportation system. A developed transportation system is life blood and key pillar of our modern era and a more advanced and sustainable transportation infrastructure ensure smooth & timely mobility of resources at required destinations resulting in better productivity. At the same time carbon emission is crucial as it is increasing global warming to an alarming state, leading to drastic change in the climate and threatening all the lives of our planet.

Battery Electric Vehicles (BEV) has emerged as best possible alternative to the traditional transportation systems as on date, as it has almost zero emission and provides a continuous power generation with concern on marginal and limited impact on our environment.

Objectives: BEV technology has been making rapid progress every single day, but at the same time EV Industry is getting set-backs due to recent incidents of fire and safety concerns in electric vehicle batteries. Such unfortunate incidents are not only creating doubts in the consumer's mind but also hampering the demand of BEVs and thus effecting the whole cycle. This paper is about consumer's concerns on fire hazards and safety readiness of electric vehicles batteries in India to raise awareness regarding the safety challenges of EV batteries

[1]vikashjoshi007@gmail.com, [2]payalphulwani@gmail.com

DOI: 10.4324/9781003415725-55

and solutions to overcome them. This paper also highlights the existing safety concerns and described the way forward for a much safer Electric Vehicle battery ecosystem within the country.

Research Methodologies: This paper is about consumer's concerns on fire hazards and safety preparedness of EV batteries in India to raise consciousness regarding the safety challenges of EV batteries and best possible way out to overcome them. This paper also charted the way forward for a safer EV battery ecosystem in India.

In this paper, we have tried to find out various major concerns of the consumers in terms of capacity and safety of electric vehicle batteries through circulating a questionnaire and conducting semi structured interviews with industry peers and experts.

A detailed literature review has been conducted at regular intervals to get better understanding and deeper knowledge about the factors responsible for the fire incidents in EV Batteries and from what prospect consumers are looking at it.

Major Findings

1. This paper helps us to analyse the important technical factors for consumers while planning to buy an electric vehicle such as
   (a) Battery Capacity and
   (b) Battery Safety ranking
3. Major causes of fire in EV batteries in India are Internal & External short circuits, Overcharging, exposure to high temperature & mechanical deformation & impact.
4. In this paper we have also emphasises on the key measures required to be taken to deal with safety concerns of the EV batteries.

Future scope of Research: Future is unpredictable as researchers across the globe are continuously working hard to invent better and more advanced technology. With unlimited scope and boundless opportunities, extensive research and experiments will be carried on and we would witness a number of newer products to be introduced in coming days.

As research on EV technology is a never-ending process, more and more inventions are bound to happen and thus there would always be a need to conduct more research keeping in view of the safety concerns of the consumers.

KEYWORDS: Consumer safety in EV, Consumer's concerns on fire hazards of EVs, Electric vehicles, EV batteries, Types of EV, Safety readiness of EVs.

1. Introduction

Air pollution kills approx. seven million people worldwide every single year. Data from WHO shows that almost 99% of the global population breathe air that exceeds WHO guideline limits containing high levels of pollutants, with low- and middle-income countries suffering from the highest exposures. WHO is appealing all the countries to address air pollution on priority basis.

It is a matter of great concerns that nine out of the ten most polluted cities are in India. (World Health Organization, 2018). Most of the traditional vehicles have been non-compliant with the current Indian emission standards, releasing various types of highly toxic gases into the atmosphere (Dey and Mehta, 2020). A general consciousness is on rise that conventional vehicles that are running on fossil fuels must gradually be replaced by BEVs, because of their more environment-friendly and energy-efficient quality.

Battery Electric vehicles (BEVs) have successfully positioned themselves as a best possible alternate green and clean technology.

The Global Electric Vehicle market was valued at $ 238 Billion in 2020 and is projected to reach $ 824 Billion by 2030, registering a CAGR of 13.22% from 2021 to 2030.

This paper is about consumer's concerns on fire hazards and safety readiness of electric vehicles batteries in India. A detailed study has been conducted to understand the major concerns of the consumers related to Battery safety and performance. This paper would help in raising the awareness regarding the current safety related challenges of electric vehicle batteries and best possible solutions to overcome the same.

2. Theoretical Background

In this research paper, a brief introduction of different types of Electric Batteries has been given with their pros and cons to understand the nature of each type.

A detailed survey has also been conducted by designing a questionnaire on various factors responsible for creating demand of electric vehicles in India. We have received 180+ online and 200+ offline responses till 31st October'22.

In this research paper, we have tried to explain major causes of fire and challenges associated with electric batteries India.

We have also explained key measures required to be taken to deal with safety concerns of electric batteries in our country.

2.1 Various chemistries of Lithium-ion Batteries

Lithium batteries are getting more and more popular every single day. The battery pack is among most important and beneficial components in an EV, accounting for approx. 30% to 40% of the total cost of the vehicle. Although, all of these electronics devices use lithium-ion batteries but they all are not using the same types of lithium-ion batteries. Below are six main types of lithium batteries:

Types of Lithium Ion Battery:

1. Lithium Cobalt Oxide (LCO)
2. Lithium Iron Phosphate (LPF)
3. Lithium Manganese Oxide (LMO)
4. Lithium Nickel Manganese Cobalt Oxide (NMC)
5. Lithium Nickel Cobalt Aluminium Oxide (NCA)
6. Lithium Titanate (LTO)

3. Response Received and Major Findings

3.1 Major Causes of Fire in Electric Vehicles in India

Challenges Associated with EV Batteries

Reasons behind the fire safety challenges in the Indian EV market are many. A deep and more careful analysis of recent and unfortunate fire incidents which has happened, suggests that most common causes are overcharging of batteries and self-ignition due to short circuit. Few accidents also happened due to failure in detection of the abnormalities at the cell level.

Below are the main categories of above technical faults in Electric Vehicle batteries:

(a) Internal Short Circuit: Main reason for internal short circuit could be due to some manufacturing defect in the cell. (i.e., punctured separators, metal lump, misalignment of electrodes etc.).

(b) External Short Circuit: This could be caused by exposure to an external fire or also due to lose connections during the assembling line of the batteries at manufacturing stage.

(c) Exposure to High Temperature: At usually high temperatures, most of the lithium-ion battery chemistries demonstrate low thermal stability. A strong and efficient thermal management system is highly desirable for LIBs in electric vehicles due to space constraints. Sudden rise in the temperature can also be caused due to manufacturing faults. Another popular cause of fire in electric vehicle batteries is rise of extreme ambient temperature due to increased self-heating.

(d) Overcharging and Over discharging: Overcharging of battery pack could lead to thermal runaway while charging/discharging. Other reasons could be high and unstable current, operating at higher C-rate and discharging the battery below the required minimum voltage levels.

(e) Mechanical Deformation and Impact: During the movement and transportation of batteries, punctures or deformation in the cell can also cause fire. A collation during the movement or a faulty cell may also lead to fire incident in the batteries.

Apart from above mentioned main reasons, there could be some other reasons for recent EV battery fires which are as below:

Compromise in Quality due to costs, Poor battery pack design due to lack of proper research and infrastructure, Limited knowledge among the consumers and service providers to maintain minimum required levels of the safety, Lack of proper skills and extreme operational conditions etc.

Poor quality cells, inadequate protection to counter, overcharging situation and low-efficiency BMSs, are among the major causes for the recent unfortunate fire incidents in India. It is the need of the hour to plan and develop a nationwide policy and framework to understand the safety preparedness of the EV batteries technologies which are currently available in the Indian market and we must proceed towards the best possible design solutions to overcome the current crisis. This would help and support the manufacturers in a great way if we could understand the root cause of above-mentioned incidents to implement best possible preventive measures to minimise the risk factors.

4. Research Findings

Key measures required to be taken to deal with safety concerns:

(a) Battery Design and chemistry to be Tailormade according to Indian Conditions.

(b) Robust Testing and Certification of EV Batteries is required.

(c) Stringent Safety Standards and Regulations should be in place.

(d) Battery Technology upgradation to be done as per Indian Conditions.

(e) Need to promote Innovations Across All Levels of Battery Production Cycle.

(f) Requirement of the Creation of Circular Economy for EV Batteries.

Fig. 55.1 Important key action Points for electric vehicle battery technologies

Source: Compiled by WRI India

5. Conclusions

A well-developed and effective transportation system is the life blood for the development of any economy and really a need of the hour, but unfortunately approx. 27% of global carbon emission is coming from it.

In a quest of finding better alternatives of traditional transportation system depending heavily on ICE (internal combustion engine) vehicles, Battery operated Electric Vehicles has emerged as best possible alternative. BEV or EVs are getting popular at an unexpected pace and we are witnessing more and more companies are investing heavily in EV sector.

Huge demand of EVs is pushing OEMs to increase their production capacity manifold. Thus, creating risk of acquisition of inferior quality raw-materials and producing poor quality products, non-compliance of set SOPs, limited focus on continuous and quality research etc. All of these factors resulting in higher risk of batteries catching fire and putting life safety of the consumers at risk.

5.1 Major Findings

In this paper, we have tried to find out various major concerns of the consumers in terms of capacity and safety of electric batteries through circulating a questionnaire and conducting semi structured interviews with industry peers and experts.

This paper is about consumer's concerns on fire hazards and safety preparedness of EV batteries in the country and also to raise consciousness regarding existing safety challenges of EV batteries and best possible solutions to overcome them.

5.2 Research Contribution

In this research paper, we have addressed the various factors responsible for recent unfortunate fire incidents in Electric vehicle lithium-ion batteries. This paper would create the awareness about various types of Lithium-ion batteries and their pros and cons among the consumers.

This research paper will also help various stakeholders such as OEMs, State & Central Govt. bodies, Distribution Channel partners etc. in deciding the various policies and take corrective measures to ensure a safer EV battery ecosystem in India.

5.3 Limitation of Research

Research is a continuous process, and researchers across the globe are continuously putting in their efforts to find out better solutions in EV industry in term of battery life, capacity, mileage and safety.

We are and will continue to witness newer and more advanced types of batteries coming in and creating its impact in the market. Thus, above research is limited to the types of lithium-ion batteries currently available to us.

5.4 Future scope of Research

Future is unpredictable as researchers across the globe are continuously working hard to invent better and more advanced technology. With unlimited scope and boundless opportunities, extensive research and experiments will be carried on and we would witness a number of newer products to be introduced in coming days.

This research paper will show the path to all future researchers to carry on further study on the subject. As EV technology is never-ending, more and more inventions are bound to happen and thus there would always be a need to conduct more research keeping in view of the safety concerns of the consumers.

REFRENCES

1. Ali, H. A. A., and Z. N. Abdeljawad. 2020. "Thermal Management Technologies of Lithium-Ion Batteries Applied for Stationary Energy Storage Systems: Investigation on the Thermal Behavior of Lithium-Ion Batteries." Sweden: Mälardalen University and Vattenfall Research and Development. https://www.diva-portal.org/smash/get/diva2:1443146/FULLTEXT01.pdf.

2. Bak, S. M., E. Hu, Y. Zhou, X. Yu, S. D. Senanayake, S.-J. Cho, K.-B. Kim, et al. 2014. "Structural Changes and Thermal Stability of Charged LiNi x Mn y Co z O2 Cathode Materials Studied by Combined in Situ Time-Resolved XRD and Mass Spectroscopy." ACS Applied Materials & Interfaces 6 (24): 22594–601. https://www.scinapse.io/papers/1971672415.

3. ET Auto 2022. "Consumer concerns about safety of e-scooters grow 8X in past 6 months." April 01, 2022. https://auto.economictimes.indiatimes.com/news/two-wheelers/scooters-mopeds/ consumer-concerns-about-safety-of-e-scooters-grow-8x-in-past-6-months-report/90587145

4. Casals, L.C., B.A. García, and C. Canal. 2019. "Second Life Batteries Lifespan: Rest of Useful Life and Environmental Analysis." Journal of Environmental Management 232: 354–63. https://pubmed.ncbi. nlm.nih.gov/30496965/.

5. Cohn. 2021. "Second Life Electric Vehicle Batteries: Microgrid Game Changer?" Microgrid Knowledge (blog). December 3, 2021. https://microgridknowledge.com/second-life-electric-vehicle-batteries-microgrid/

6. Contractor, S. 2022. "Ola S1 Pro Electric Scooter Catches Fire In Pune, Company Launches Investigation." Car&bike, March 26, 2022. https://www.carandbike.com/news/ola-s1-pro-electric-scootercatches-fire-in-pune-company-launches-investigation-2845249

7. Department of Science & Technology n.d. "ARCI Develops Indigenous Technology for Synthesizing LTO Anode for Fast Charging Li-Ion Battery Used in EVs." n.d. Accessed August 9, 2022. https://dst.gov.in/arci-develops-indigenous-technology-synthesizing-lto-anode-fast-charging-li-ion-battery-used-evs.

8. Deccan Chronicle. 2022. "Electric Bus of TSRTC Catches Fire; No Injuries," February 22, 2022. https:// www.deccanchronicle.com/nation/in-other-news/220222/electric-bus-of-tsrtc-catches-fire-no-injuries.html.

9. International 28 (6): 653–66. "Temperature effect and thermal impact in lithium-ion batteries: A review", December 2018 https://www.sciencedirect.com/science/article/pii/S1002007118307536.

10. IDTechEx. 2021. "EV Fires: A Disaster for Automakers, But an Opportunity for Material Suppliers, Reveals IDTechEx." PR Newswire, August 10, 2021. https://www.prnewswire.com/news-releases/ev-firesa-disaster-for-automakers-but-an-opportunity-for-material-suppliers-reveals-idtechex-301352114.html.

11. Ma, S., M. Jiang, P. Tao, C. Song, J. Wu, J. Wang, T. Deng, et al. 2018. "Temperature Effect and Thermal Impact in Lithium-Ion Batteries: A Review." Progress in Natural Science: Materials International 28 (6): 653–66.

12. Press Information Bureau Delhi. 2022. "BIS Formulates Performance Standards for Electric Vehicle Batteries." June 24, 2022. https://www.pib.gov.in/www.pib.gov.in/Pressreleaseshare. aspx?PRID=1836787.

13. The Times of India. 2022. "RTC E-Bus Catches Fire during Charging in Secunderabad." The Times of India, February 23, 2022 *https://timesofindia.indiatimes.com/city/hyderabad/rtc-e-bus-catches-fireduring-charging/articleshow/89759325.cms.*

Chapter

Policy Uncertainty and Purchasing Managers' Index

Imlak Shaikh*

Management Development Institute Gurgaon,
Gurugram, Haryana, ndia

ABSTRACT: The Purchasing Manager's Index (PMI) helps in forecasting several vital economic variables and is used widely in the form of an indicator of various economic trends. Employment, Inventories, New orders, Supplier deliveries, and Production, for the manufacturing sector, are the five seasonally adjusted diffusion indices that compose PMI, which is a composite index. There have been several attempts to forecast its direction because of its vast importance. It has been established that Economic Policy Uncertainty and Trade Policy Uncertainty, along with T-bill interest rates are correlated with the GDP. In this research, it has been attempted to predict the PMI of the USA, China, and Japan with the help of a neural network and regression technique. Results indicate that the uncertainties in the Trade Policy and Economic Policy, along with the changes in the T-bill lead and forecast changes in the PMI by an average of 5 months in case of China, and by an average of 10 months in case of Japan and USA. The root mean square error, along with the r squared statistic, has been used for the determination of the effectiveness of the forecasts. It was found that the regression technique gave better results compared to the neural network technique due to the availability of fewer data points.

KEYWORDS: Policy uncertainty, Trade policy, Purchasing manager index, T-bill

1. Introduction

In the year 1980, the Institute for Supply Management (ISM), along with the United States Department of Commerce, led to the introduction of the Purchasing Managers' Index (PMI),

*imlak.shaikh@mdi.ac.in

DOI: 10.4324/9781003415725-56

with the assistance of an economist Theodore Torda. Five seasonally adjusted diffusion indices—Employment, Inventories, New orders, Supplier deliveries, and Production, for the manufacturing sector, lead to the composition of the composite index PMI. These five diffusion indexes are seasonally adjusted from 0 to 100, where 50 has a crucial significance. A PMI score of 50 indicates no change, and growth is indicated by a PMI score higher than 50, whereas a score below 50 forecasts a dawdling manufacturing economy. This index is a valuable and dependable near-term economic activity indicator that is widely recognized by business practitioners and economists and is released on each month's first business day at 10:00 a.m. EST. PMI became popular because it has an early release time as compared to most of the other monthly economic reports like- GDP and employment reports. (Lindsey & Pavur, 2005; Koenig, 2002; Kauffman, 1999; Dasgupta & Lahiri, 1993; and Harris, 1991) showed that the PMI demonstrates an ability to detect changes in economic trends and thereby provides clues in advance on the business cycles' turning points.

Some researchers like (Raedels, 1990; Lindsey & Pavur, 2005; and Larrain, 2007) gave immense importance to gaining perception about the economy's direction in the future by forecasting the PMI accurately. The current paper seeks to contribute with the help of neural networks, to the forecasting research to predict the PMI.

This study attempts to extend the work of (Larrain, 2007) in which the forecasting of PMI is done using neural network models, by utilizing the inverted T-bill interest rate. This research focuses on the effects of Trade Policy Uncertainty and Economic Policy Uncertainty on PMI. It is observed that it is possible to forecast PMI changes. It is inferred from the results that change in the T-bill interest rates, the Uncertainty in both the Trade Policy and the Economic Policy lead and forecast changes in the PMI by an average of five months in case of China; and by an average of ten months in case of Japan and USA.

2. Data and Method

Data on Trade Policy Uncertainty, Economic Policy Uncertainty, T-bill, and PMI of 373 months from August 1985 to August 2016 for the USA, 98 months from July 2008 to August 2016 for Japan and 114 months from September 2007 to December 2016 for China, was taken from Bloomberg mostly and some websites on the internet. The pre-processing of data involved calculating the three-month moving average of the Trade Policy Uncertainty, Economic Policy Uncertainty, T-bill, and PMI, and further calculating the 24-month changes of the three-month moving average of the T-bill and PMI.

As given in (Wang and Traore, 2009), MLPs or the multilayer perceptrons are the most commonly used artificial neural network for time-series predictions. They can be used efficiently for the approximation of any input/output map. When MLPs are extended with local recurrent connections and short-term memory structures, the TLRNs or the time-lagged recurrent networks are obtained. Inputs are delayed by multiple time points at the input layer before being fed to the system. Data changes with time because of which the time structure contains data for most of the data of the real world. TLRNs are very efficient at prediction involving nonlinear time series. It uses the gradient descent technique for the minimization of errors.

3. Results and Discussion

The interest rates, Trade Policy Uncertainty, and Economic Policy Uncertainty are related to and lead the PMI because there is a correlation between GDP and PMI. It is found that the Uncertainty in Trade Policy and Economic Policy, along with the changes in the T-bill predict the changes in the PMI by an average of five months in case of China, and by an average of ten months in the case of the Japan and USA. The average lead of the PMI compared to the independent variables was found out by using the trial and error method.

In both the regression and neural network forecasting models, three independent variables-Trade Policy Uncertainty, Economic Policy Uncertainty and T-bill rate differences are related to one dependent variable- differences in the PMI. A long-range of data of 373 months from August 1985 to August 2016 was tested, and an out of sample forecast was done for 25 months from July 2017 to July 2019. The out of sample forecasts of both the neural network technique and regression technique along with the actual values of twenty-four-month changes of the three-month moving average of PMI, has been plotted in Fig. 56.1.

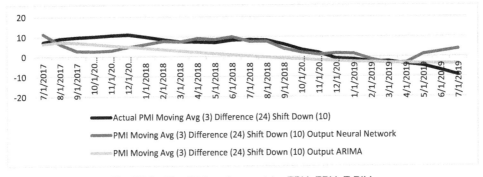

Fig. 56.1 The PMI as forecast by TPU, EPU, T-BILL

Source: Author's compilation

Patterns of the neural network forecast are like that of the actual PMI, but it is slightly off from late 2017 to early 2018, and from May 2019 onwards. The estimates generated by the regression technique is more accurate and can catch the PMI's overall direction in a slightly better way. The RMSE of the forecasts generated by the neural network technique is 4.744, while that of the regression technique is 4.689. R squared values of both methods also suggest that better results are obtained from the regression technique. It is observed that the predicted PMI has a lead of 10 months compared to the independent variables.

A short-range of data of 98 months from July 2008 to August 2016 was tested, and an out of sample forecast was done for 25 months from July 2017 to July 2019. The out of sample forecasts of both the neural network technique and regression technique along with the actual values of twenty-four-month changes of the three-month moving average of PMI. Patterns of the neural network forecast are like that of the actual PMI, but it is slightly off before November 2017, and from September 2018 onwards. The estimates generated by the regression technique is much more accurate and can catch the PMI's overall direction in a much better way. For the neural network technique forecast, RMSE is 14.994, and R squared is 0.594, whereas for the regression technique, the RMSE is 2.9534, and R squared is 0.975. This suggests that better results are obtained from the regression technique. It can be observed that the predicted PMI has a lead of 10 months compared to the independent variables.

When the USA's Economic Policy Uncertainty Index is used instead of Japan's, there is little improvement in the results of the neural network technique but not in the results of the regression technique. For the neural network technique forecast, RMSE is 9.128, and R squared is 0.617, whereas for the regression technique, the RMSE is 3.099, and R squared is 0.9789. Hence, it can be concluded that the USA's Economic Policy Uncertainty Index is not a reliable indicator of Japan's PMI. When the USA's Trade Policy Uncertainty Index is used instead of Japan's, there are slight improvements in the results of both the neural network and regression technique. For the neural network technique forecast, RMSE is 7.782, and R squared is 0.4726, whereas for the regression technique, the RMSE is 2.5258, and R squared is 0.9753. Hence, it can be concluded that the USA's Trade Policy Uncertainty Index is a reliable indicator of Japan's PMI.

When both the USA's Trade Policy Uncertainty Index and Economic Policy Uncertainty Index are used instead of Japan's, there is little improvement in the results of the neural network technique but not in the results of the regression technique as can be seen in Fig. 56.2. For the neural network technique forecast, RMSE is 11.107, and R squared is 0.5198, whereas for the regression technique, the RMSE is 3.2132, and R squared is 0.9760. Hence, it can be concluded that the USA's Trade Policy Uncertainty Index and Economic Policy Uncertainty Index are not reliable indicators of Japan's PMI.

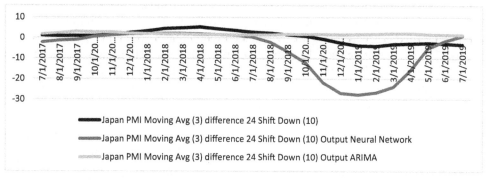

Fig. 56.2 The PMI as forecast by USA EPU, USA TPU & Japan T-BILL

Source: Author's compilation

A short-range of data of 114 months from September 2007 to December 2016 was tested, and an out of sample forecast was done for 25 months from June 2017 to June 2019. The out of sample forecasts of both the neural network technique and regression technique along with the actual values of twenty-four-month changes of the three-month moving average of PMI. Patterns of the regression forecast are like that of the actual PMI, but it is off before September 2018. The estimates generated by the regression technique is much more accurate than the neural network technique and can catch the PMI's overall direction in a much better way. For the neural network technique forecast, RMSE is 21.264, and R squared is 0.5446, whereas for the regression technique, the RMSE is 2.9637, and R squared is 0.54462. This suggests that better results are obtained from the regression technique. It can be observed that the predicted PMI has a lead of 5 months compared to the independent variables. When the USA's Economic Policy Uncertainty Index is used instead of China's, there is little improvement in the results of the regression technique but not in the results of the neural network technique. For the neural network technique forecast, RMSE is 2.1871, and R squared is 0.112, whereas for the regression technique, the RMSE is 2.3589, and R squared is 0.9505. Hence, it can be concluded that the USA's Economic Policy Uncertainty Index is not a reliable indicator of China's PMI. When the USA's Trade Policy Uncertainty Index is used instead of China's, there is little improvement in the results of the regression technique but not in the results of the neural network technique. For the neural network technique forecast, RMSE is 5.5042, and R squared is 0.1722, whereas for the regression technique, the RMSE is 2.842, and R squared is 0.9511. Hence, it can be concluded that the USA's Trade Policy Uncertainty Index is not a reliable indicator of China's PMI. When both the USA's Trade Policy Uncertainty Index and Economic Policy Uncertainty Index are used instead of China's, there are little improvements in the results of both the neural network technique and regression technique. For the neural network technique forecast, RMSE is 3.1304, and R squared is 0.3571, whereas for the regression technique, the RMSE is 2.5516, and R squared is 0.9515. Hence, it can be concluded that the USA's Trade Policy Uncertainty Index and Economic Policy Uncertainty Index are reliable indicators of China's PMI.

4. Implications

In this research, performance measures like the root mean squared error and the r squared statistic were used to determine the relative effectiveness of the regression and the neural network techniques. It was found that due to the availability of fewer data points, the neural network- Time Lagged Recurrent Network could not be trained well due to which it could not perform better than ARIMA regression technique. With the help of the trial and error method, it was determined that the uncertainty in trade policy and economic policy, when clubbed with changes in the T-bill interest rates, are capable of leading and forecasting the changes in the PMI by an average of five months in case of China, and by an average of ten months in the case of Japan and USA. This means that the independent variables of January would help to predict the PMI changes for June for China and for November in the case of Japan and China.

It can also be concluded that the ARIMA results are found to be best for Japan, followed by China and the USA, respectively, in the case when all the independent and dependent variables belong to that same country. When the USA's Trade Policy Uncertainty is used as one of the independent variables, Japan shows better results than China. When the USA's Economic Policy Uncertainty is used as one of the independent variables, China shows better results than Japan. When both the USA's Trade Policy Uncertainty and Economic Policy Uncertainty are used as independent variables, China shows better results than Japan. PMI forecasts allow for future estimation of crucial economic variables- Inflation indicators like Consumer Price Index; Gross Domestic Product, trade flow & export indices, input prices of producer, productivity, durable goods orders factory goods orders, non-farm payrolls or , employment payrolls, profitability, backlogs of capacity or work indicators, service sector output or manufacturing output, delivery times of supplier, inventory indicators, and purchasing activity which would help financial institutions, governments, and corporates in analysing, forecasting, and planning ahead of time. The forecasts would help Supply Chain Managers to forecast and benchmark sales, inventory, and price trends; to monitor supply and demand, and to track supplier's performance. As it is known that it is that the usage of one quantitative approach or technique is rarely suggested for the generation of useful forecasts, so, the estimates of the regression and neural network models should be used in combination with various other models and subjective forecasts. A combination of forecasts is a more efficient procedure.

5. Conclusion and Future Scope

This paper has presented the forecasts of the rate of change of the Purchasing Managers' Index with the help of regression and neural network techniques. The regression forecasts were generally better than the neural network forecasts because of the availability of fewer data points. With the availability of more data points, the training of the neural network would improve further, which would lead to better results obtained from the neural network technique. A slightly higher level of accuracy achieved by the ARIMA forecasts can help in making decisions and doing managerial planning ahead of time. The relationship between the T-bill, the PMI, and the Uncertainty in Trade Policy and the Economic Policy has been explored through this study. This relationship was explored in an intertemporal dimension. It is found that Uncertainty in Trade Policy and the Economic Policy, and changes in the T-bill lead and forecast changes in the PMI by an average of five months in case of China, and by an average of ten months in the case of Japan and USA. In the future, this research can be extended by forecasting changes in PMI for more countries according to the availability of the required dependent and independent variables.

REFERENCES

1. Raedels, A. (1990). Forecasting the NAPM Purchasing Managers' Index. *Journal of Purchasing and Materials Management, 26*(4), 34–39. https://doi.org/10.1111/j.1745-493x.1990.tb00519.x
2. Kamijo, K. ichi, & Tanigawa, T. (1990). *Stock price pattern recognition--A recurrent neural network approach.* 215–221. https://doi.org/10.1109/ijcnn.1990.137572
3. Kimoto, T., Asakawa, K., Yoda, M., & Takeoka, M. (1990). *Stock market prediction system with modular neural networks.* 1–6. https://doi.org/10.1109/ijcnn.1990.137535
4. Harris, E. S. (1991). Tracking the Economy with the Purchasing Managers' Index. *FRBNY Quarterly Review*, 61–69.
5. Dasgupta, S., & Lahiri, K. (1993). On the use of dispersion measures from NAPM surveys in business cycle forecasting. *Journal of Forecasting, 12*(3–4), 239–253. https://doi.org/10.1002/for.3980120306
6. Nicholas Refenes, A., Zapranis, A., & Francis, G. (1994). Stock performance modeling using neural networks: A comparative study with regression models. *Neural Networks, 7*(2), 375–388. https://doi.org/10.1016/0893-6080(94)90030-2
7. Pollack-Johnson, B. (1995). Hybrid structures and improving forecasting and scheduling in project management. *Journal of Operations Management, 12*(2), 101–117. https://doi.org/10.1016/0272-6963(94)00008-3

8. Sanders, N. R., & Ritzman, L. P. (1995). Bringing judgment into combination forecasts. *Journal of Operations Management, 13*(4), 311–321. https://doi.org/10.1016/0272-6963(95)00039-9

9. Freisleben, B., & Ripper, K. (1995). Economic forecasting using neural networks. *IEEE International Conference on Neural Networks - Conference Proceedings, 2*(Fb 12), 833–838. https://doi.org/10.1109/icnn.1995.487526

10. Albertson, K., Aylen, J., Adya, M., Collopy, F., Fojt, M., Benítez, J. M., … Niu, H. (1995). Forecasting the 30-year U . S . Treasury Bond with a System of Neural Networks. *Journal of Supply Chain Management, 12*(2), 162–169. https://doi.org/10.1111/j.1745-493X.2005.tb00182.x

11. Church, K. B., & Curram, S. P. (1996). Forecasting consumers' expenditure: A comparison between econometric and neural network models. *International Journal of Forecasting, 12*(2), 255–267. https://doi.org/10.1016/0169-2070(95)00631-1

12. Cheng, W., Wagner, L., & Lin, C.-H. (1996). Forecasting the 30-year U . S . Treasury Bond with a System of Neural Networks. *Journal of Computational Intelligence in Finance, 4*(1), 10–16. Retrieved from http://citeseerx.ist.psu.edu/viewdoc/download?doi=10.1.1.27.1844&rep=rep1&type=pdf

13. Benítez, J. M., Castro, J. L., & Requena, I. (1997). Are artificial neural networks black boxes? *IEEE Transactions on Neural Networks, 8*(5), 1156–1164. https://doi.org/10.1109/72.623216

14. Adya, M., & Collopy, F. (1998). How effective are neural networks at forecasting and prediction? A review and evaluation. *Journal of Forecasting, 17*(56), 481–495. https://doi.org/10.1002/(sici)1099-131x(1998090)17:5/6<481::aid-for709>3.3.co;2-h

15. Kauffman, R. G. (1999). Indicator Qualities of the NAPM report on business®. *Journal of Supply Chain Management, 35*(1), 29–37. https://doi.org/10.1111/j.1745-493X.1999.tb00234.x

16. Aiken, M. (1999). Using a neural network forecast inflation. *Industrial Management & Data Systems, 99*(7), 296–301. https://doi.org/10.1108/02635577199500001

17. Wolstenholme, E. F. (1999). Qualitative vs quantitative modelling: The evolving balance. *Journal of the Operational Research Society, 50*(4), 422–428. https://doi.org/10.1057/palgrave.jors.2600700

18. Gaafar, L. K., & Choueiki, M. H. (2000). A neural network model for solving the lot-sizing problem. *Omega, 28*(2), 175–184. https://doi.org/10.1016/S0305-0483(99)00035-3

19. Gonzalez, S. (2000). *Neural Networks for Macroeconomic Forecasting.* 5–7.

20. Tkacz, G. (2001). Neural network forecasting of Canadian GDP growth. *International Journal of Forecasting, 17*(1), 57–69. https://doi.org/10.1016/S0169-2070(00)00063-7

21. Goodwin, P. (2002). Integrating management judgment and statistical methods to improve short-term forecasts. *Omega, 30*(2), 127–135. https://doi.org/10.1016/S0305-0483(01)00062-7

22. Koenig, E. F. (2002). Using the Purchasing Managers' Index to Assess the Economy's Strength and the Likely Direction of Monetary Policy. *Economic and Financial Policy Review, 1*(6), 1–14. Retrieved from http://67.208.38.236/assets/documents/research/efpr/v01_n06_a01.pdf%5Cnpapers2://publication/uuid/96BFE0E6-0B0A-4C11-8EB3-5B5085ECC3B1

23. Albertson, K., & Aylen, J. (2003). Forecasting the behaviour of manufacturing inventory. *International Journal of Forecasting, 19*(2), 299–311. https://doi.org/10.1016/S0169-2070(01)00147-9

24. Pelaez, R. (2003). A Reassessment of the Purchasing Managers' Index. *Business Economics, 38*(4), 35.

25. Bowersox, D. J., Calantone, R. J., & Rodrigues, A. M. (2003). Estimation of Global Logistics Expenditures Using Neural Networks. *JOURNAL OF BUSINESS LOGISTICS, 24*(2), 21–36.

26. Lindsey, M. D., & Pavur, R. J. (2005). As the PMI turns: A tool for supply chain managers. *Journal of Supply Chain Management, 41*(1), 30–39. https://doi.org/10.1111/j.1745-493X.2005.tb00182.x

27. Cho, D. I., & Ogwang, T. (2006). Conceptual perspectives on selecting the principal variables in the purchasing managers' index. *Journal of Supply Chain Management, 42*(2), 44–52. https://doi.org/10.1111/j.1745-493X.2006.00011.x

28. Chai, S., & Lim, J. (2007). Economic Turning Point Forecasting Using The Fuzzy Neural Network and Non-Overlap Area Distribution Measurement Method. *Korean Economic Review*, *23*(1), 111–130.

29. Larrain, M. (2007). The PMI, the T-bill and inventories: A comparative analysis of neural network and regression forecasts. *Journal of Supply Chain Management*, *43*(2), 39–51. https://doi.org/10.1111/j.1745-493X.2007.00030.x

30. Cho, D. I., & Ogwang, T. (2007). A conceptual framework for computing U.S. non-manufacturing PMI indexes. *Journal of Supply Chain Management*, *43*(3), 43–52. https://doi.org/10.1111/j.1745-493X.2007.00034.x

31. Cho, D. I., & Ogwang, T. (2008). An objective evaluation of the Ivey Purchasing Managers Index. *Journal of Enterprise Information Management*, *21*(4), 393–408. https://doi.org/10.1108/17410390810888679

32. Maciel, L. S., & Ballini, R. (2008). Design a Neural Network for Time Series Financial Forecasting : Accuracy and Robustness Analysis. *Universidade Estadual de Campinas (UNICAMP)*, (2008), 1–21. https://doi.org/10.1097/PSY.0b013e31819ccd2a

33. Wang, Y. M., & Traore, S. (2009). Time-lagged recurrent network for forecasting episodic event suspended sediment load in typhoon prone area. *International Journal of Physical Sciences*, *4*(9), 519–528.

34. Joseph, A., Larrain, M., & Turner, C. (2011). Forecasting purchasing managers' index with compressed interest rates and past values. *Procedia Computer Science*, *6*, 213–218. https://doi.org/10.1016/j.procs.2011.08.040

35. Charaniya, N. A., & Dudul, S. V. (2013). Time Lag recurrent Neural Network model for rainfall prediction using El Niño indices. *International Journal of Scientific and Research Publications*, *3*(1), 1–5.

36. Dalto, M. (2015). Deep neural networks for time series prediction with applications in ultra-short-term wind forecasting. *Industrial Technology (ICIT), 2015 IEEE International Conference On*, (January), 1657–1663. Retrieved from http://ieeexplore.ieee.org/xpl/articleDetails.jsp?arnumber=7125335

37. Wang, J., Wang, J., Fang, W., & Niu, H. (2016). Financial Time Series Prediction Using Elman Recurrent Random Neural Networks. *Computational Intelligence and Neuroscience*, *2016*. https://doi.org/10.1155/2016/4742515

38. Cui, Z., Chen, W., & Chen, Y. (2016). Multi-Scale Convolutional neural networks for time series classification. *Journal of Systems Engineering and Electronics*, *28*(1), 162–169. https://doi.org/10.21629/JSEE.2017.01.18

39. Granger, C. W. J., & Newbold, P. (2016). *Some comments the evaluation of economic forecasts*. *6846*(June), 37–41. https://doi.org/10.1080/00036847300000003

40. Smalter Hall, A., & Cook, T. R. (2017). Macroeconomic Indicator Forecasting with Deep Neural Networks. *SSRN Electronic Journal*, (September). https://doi.org/10.2139/ssrn.3046657

41. Zhao, B., Lu, H., Chen, S., Liu, J., & Wu, D. (2017). Convolutional neural networks for time series classification. *Journal of Systems Engineering and Electronics*, *28*(1), 162–169. https://doi.org/10.21629/JSEE.2017.01.18

42. Siliverstovs, B. (2018). Dissecting the purchasing managers' index: Are all relevant components included? Are all included components relevant? *Panoeconomicus*, *65*(4), 381–394. https://doi.org/10.2298/PAN150504014S

43. Tran, D. T., Kanniainen, J., Gabbouj, M., & Iosifidis, A. (2019). *Data-driven Neural Architecture Learning For Financial Time-series Forecasting*. 2–5. Retrieved from http://arxiv.org/abs/1903.06751

Chapter

Food Waste Management in BITS Pilani

Ujjwal Aggarwal[1]
Computer Science, Birla Institute of Technology and Science,
Vidya Vihar, Pilani, Rajasthan, India

Arkya Aditya[2]
Electronics and Instrumentation, Birla Institute of Technology and Science,
Vidya Vihar, Pilani, Rajasthan, India

ABSTRACT: The agricultural revolution in Britain in the 18th century led to a gradual transformation of traditional farming practices. There have been numerous revolutions, including the green revolution, which increased global food grain production, especially wheat and rice; the silver revolution, which increased poultry production, and the red revolution, which increased tomato and meat production. Such revolutions contributed to the widespread reduction of poverty and global hunger, raising incomes and thus improving the lifestyle of people. However, food wastage has also increased on a massive scale and it has become a significant societal challenge in the modern era. With the rising population, it has been very difficult to ensure equitable access to healthy food for everyone and rising food wastage has made it even more difficult. Studies have shown that food waste left to decompose in open dumps contributes significantly to global greenhouse emissions. Developing an effective waste management system has always been a major challenge, especially in developing countries where it is not only expensive but also less popular. The paper explores and analyses the food waste management system and its implementation at Birla Institute of Science and Technology (BITS) in Pilani, Rajasthan, a renowned engineering college in India. The paper analyses the viewpoints of managers, staff, and workers in messes and eateries on the issue of food waste management, as well as provides insight into the institute's current food waste management practices. It reviews the challenges in characterising food waste and discusses the opportunities and obstacles in the implementation of food waste management plans. Specifically, the paper highlights the sustainable development goals (SDGs) proposed by the United Nations regarding the management of food waste. A discussion of the current system's efficiency in achieving

[1]f20212427@pilani.bits-pilani.ac.in, [2]f20210276@pilani.bits-pilnai.ac.in

DOI: 10.4324/9781003415725-57

SDG 12.3 is presented. The paper will assist the decision-making body in identifying existing flaws and incorporating necessary changes to improve waste management techniques.

KEYWORDS: BITS Pilani, Food wastage, Global hunger, SDG 12.3, Waste management

1. Introduction

In the modern era, food waste is one of the world's most pressing concerns. Food waste causes hunger, insecurity, rising food prices, and climate change. Despite agricultural revolutions and dramatic increase in global food supply in recent decades, many countries still have malnutrition and undernutrition. A third of all food is lost or wasted worldwide, wasting 25% of human calories. (IFPRI, 2022).

1.1 Measuring Food Waste

Because various organizations define food loss in different ways, their results about food waste differ. According to the United Nations, food loss refers to food that suffers unintentional deterioration in quality or quantity as a result of food spills, spoils, bruising, wilting, or other such damage caused by infrastructure limitations at the production, storage, processing, and distribution stages of the food lifecycle. To analyse food loss across the value chain, two basic estimating approaches have been utilised: a macro approach, using aggregated data from national or local authorities and large companies, and a micro approach, using data regarding specific actors in the different value chain stages (Delgado, Schuster, & Torero). However, very little research is conducted on the amount of food loss. As a result, the governments of these nations are oblivious to the issue and fail to make choices and formulate policies on food waste management.

1.2 Policies on Food Waste Management System

The United Nations Sustainable Development Goal 12.3 aims to "halve per capita global food waste at the retail and consumer levels and eliminate food losses along production and supply chains, including post-harvest losses" by 2030. On September 29, the International Day of Awareness of Food Loss and Waste calls on the public, politicians, governments, and businesses to establish robust food waste management systems and reduce food waste. Many institutes like the International Food Policy Research Institute (IFPRI) undertake global surveys and seek to improve food value chain efficiency and eliminate waste. In India, mega food parks and cold chain projects modernise processing and preservation capacities by increasing processing and value addition, reducing wastage, and strengthening food safety and quality assurance infrastructure (India, Ministry of Food Processing Industries, 2022). Indian organisations like All India Roti Bank Trust, Annashestra, Feeding India, Delhi Langer Seva society, and others provide food safety and security to everyone at low prices and minimal food waste. India's food subsidies helped minimise the impacts of COVID-19 on food and economic insecurity.

The paper consists of six sections: abstract, introduction, literature review, methodology, results and discussion, and conclusion.

2. Review of Literature

The literature review explores different kinds of food waste management techniques that are prevalent around the world. It also discusses some new problems that this paper does not describe and also proposes solutions for those problems. Filimonau & De Coteau, 2019 provided a critical, analytical evaluation of hospitality food waste by examining the challenges associated with its classification, quantification, characterization, and management. The literature review revealed that key definitions remain ambiguous while there is no standardised methodology to assess the volume and value of hospitality food waste due to decreasing research in this area since 1992. There is substantial evidence of successful mitigation being applied by hospitality enterprises across the globe, but no comprehensive inventory of effective business practices has been developed that can be adopted as an all-in-one management framework. The absence of such a framework hampers hospitality enterprises' application of food waste mitigation measures worldwide. The paper also suggested examples of activities that can be undertaken by hospitality managers to minimise food waste occurrence. The suggested methods can be used by any organisation to manage food waste efficiently. Katajajuuri et al., 2014 determined the volume of avoidable food waste and its distribution among all parties involved in the Finnish food supply chain. Only the agricultural phase was excluded from the study. The research was specifically targeted at households, but the food service sector, industry and retail sector were also included in the study. Different types of methodologies were used to measure food waste in different places like households, cafes and restaurants, the retail sector and the industry. The economic value analysis and environmental analysis of household food waste were also presented. Unsurprisingly, the paper found that there was more food wastage in student canteens than in restaurants in Finland. It was also found that items like pork and beef products discarded by households in Finland were among the highest emitters of greenhouse gases than other food waste categories. Garrone et al., 2014 addressed the multifaceted concept of food supply chain sustainability by presenting a model of surplus food generation and management, which encompasses the integrated food supply chain (i.e. business, environmental and social players). This model is called ASRW, which stands for Availability-Surplus-Recoverability-Waste. A bottom-up methodology was used to create the model, which involved 30 exploratory case studies, continuous theory development, and data analysis. To show how the model can be used to identify food waste reduction methods, three confirmatory case studies from various points in the food supply chain are also discussed. The applicability of this model can be tested for BITS Pilani, among the other things discussed.

3. Methodology

This paper evaluates BITS Pilani's food management system and examines managers, restaurant employees, and messes' food waste management practices. The respondents were people in managerial positions, staff, and mess workers, and because the number of such positions is limited, any further generalisations from the data will not be made when the results are extracted. It is assumed that the respondents are truthful and do not try to conceal their irresponsibility. Students were also given a separate questionnaire to better understand their perspectives on food waste management. Qualitative research gives the paper a deeper understanding of themes, relationships, and context. Exploratory case study research is used. After analysing responses on a 1-to-5 Likert scale, the averages were calculated. The institute's food management strategy and small sample size necessitated qualitative research. It evaluates the plan, discusses results, and suggests improvements. Quantitative research was not preferred because it only showed daily food wastage statistics without explaining the reason behind it. Before data collection, a pilot study was undertaken to understand the institute's food management system from raw ingredients to storage, distribution, and waste management. The pilot survey interviewed heads and managers about their roles. The managers assisted the researchers in collecting data by directing them to other managers working in the particular domain. This established the complete flow. This pilot study informed the questionnaire. The fact that not everyone in the sample spoke English fluently necessitated the translation of the questions into their native tongue (Hindi). SSMS workers, mess managers, mess crew, and eatery workers were sampled. Each group had a Likert-scale questionnaire. No external data was found during the research. The mess, SSMS, and eatery managers' offices were visited to ask them the prepared questions in English or Hindi and record their responses.

4. Results and Discussion

4.1 Storage Facilities

When the SSMS members were asked about unnecessary food wastage due to improper storage facilities, they tended to agree (Fig. 57.1). By properly maintaining storage facilities, food wastage can be reduced. Conducting stock audits, using technology to manage the expiry dates of items, and switching to more modern appliances that have been proven to be effective in reducing food spoilage.

How strongly do you feel that current storage facilities lead to unnecessary food wastage?
5 responses

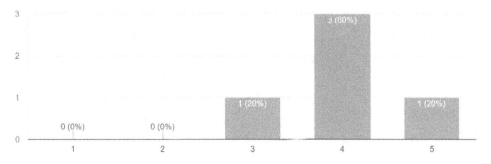

Fig. 57.1 Mean: 4.00

Source: Author's compilation

4.2 Popularity of the Prepared Food

Upon bringing up the question about mess chefs being untrained, the SSMS respondents confidently replied it was false (Fig. 57.2). The chefs were professionals and were selected through interviews. They also received training for performing in the mess kitchen.

How strong is your opinion regarding the statement that "Mess chefs don't know how to cook some of the items properly that are in the SSMS list and this leads to food wastage"?
5 responses

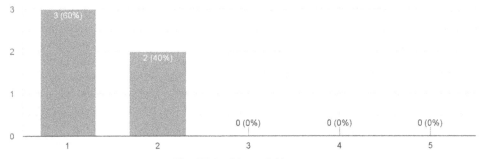

Fig. 57.2 Mean: 1.40

Source: Author's compilation

Upon asking the student community about the food cooked by mess chefs, received the following response.

Do you agree mess chefs are unable to cook certain items and due to this you don't prefer eating it?
190 responses

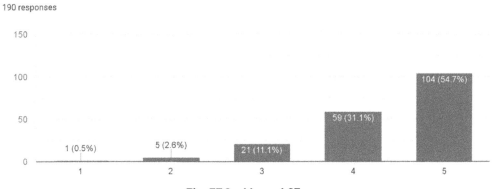

Fig. 57.3 Mean: 4.37

Source: Author's compilation

Clearly, the students do agree that mess chefs are unable to cook certain items and this leads to more food wastage since the students avoid eating it. (Fig. 57.3)

However, when SSMS was asked about some specific dishes citing the example of South Indian dishes, the following response was received.

Most students complain that the chefs are unable to prepare south Indian dishes properly. How strongly do you agree with this that improper food menu decisions lead to food wastage?
9 responses

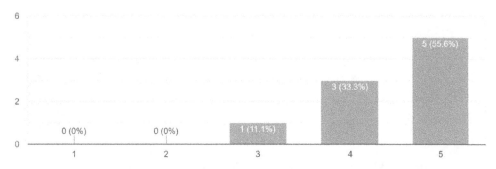

Fig. 57.4 Mean: 4.44

Source: Author's compilation

It was a common opinion that improper food menu decisions have led to food wastage (Fig. 57.4). If students do not like the meal, a lesser amount will be consumed thus generating unnecessary food waste.

Even though the chefs are trained professionals, most of the students do not like the food served. There is a great contradiction in the responses of SSMS and the student community. A solution can be found by establishing a proper feedback system. The students should constantly rate the food, and state what they feel is improper. The policymakers can then take appropriate action. There needs to be a common and convenient mechanism for everyone to give feedback. There need to be more reviews and feedback, and action should be taken based on the results. This would greatly reduce the leftovers.

4.3 Giving Alternatives Other Than the Main Course

"The facility for students to pay for alternative meal results in food wastage", how strongly do you agree with this?
9 responses

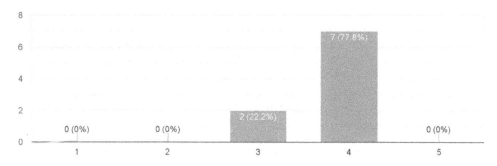

Fig. 57.5 Mean: 3.78

Source: Author's compilation

The respondents tended to agree when asked about food wastage due to the facility of alternative meals. (Fig. 57.5)

Do you prefer ordering food items that are kept as paid alternatives rather than the mess food when you don't like the menu?
190 responses

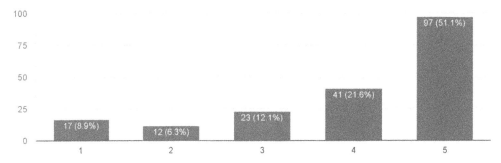

Fig. 57.6   Mean: 3.99

Source: Author's compilation

A vast majority of the students prefer going for buying alternative food items rather than the main course when they did not like the menu (Fig. 57.6). This leads to the generation of unnecessary food waste. The plating skills of kitchen staff can be improved so that no food is wasted due to aesthetic reasons (Charlebois et al., 2015). Keeping the menu short and focussing more on quality and presentation may help reduce such kind of wastage. Presentation of food needs to be focused upon. Asking students if food presentation matters to them the following responses were collected.

Do you feel not to try some some dish only because it does not look good?
190 responses

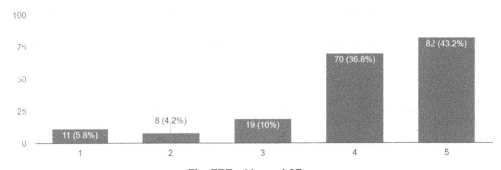

Fig. 57.7   Mean: 4.07

Source: Author's compilation

Thus, students strongly agree that food presentation matters to them. (Fig. 57.7)

5. Conclusion

Food waste is a major problem which may be resolved by collaborative efforts amongst everyone involved in the food chain. Food waste management requires an accurate assessment of food waste, which is hampered by a lack of data. No restaurants or messes could estimate their food waste. As Filimonau and De Coteau (2019) found, food service providers don't keep accurate food wastage records.

The analysis identified several intriguing research avenues. First, mess and restaurant storage facilities need optimised refrigeration with multiple temperature compartments for different food items to extend ingredient shelf life. Second, student food consumption must be analysed by time of day (breakfast, lunch, and supper), weather, and exam periods. Third, changing the menu to reflect student preferences and making better use of leftovers will improve sustainability. The menu-setting body must prioritise statistical forecasting methods. After detailed data analysis, additional variables can be found. Fourth, menus should maximise leftover use by using available resources. Fifth, self-servicing should also be avoided. Sixth, staff and charity centres can receive leftover food. It can improve staff relations. Leftover food can be sold online at last-minute markets. Restaurants should offer takeout boxes for leftovers, and staff should offer them. Technology and ingenuity can automate processes. Clean plates may receive rewards at eateries. It would encourage consumers to eat only what they need. To raise food waste awareness, restaurants and mess halls can display banners and posters.

Managers must have a structure for food waste audits, a list of initiatives at each stage, instructions for internal and external duties, and a quality benchmark compared to other firms. These methods improve waste management. Awareness programmes are the best way to educate people on the latest food waste reduction strategies, technologies, and goals. If India's top chefs led these programmes, they would reach more people and raise food waste awareness. The institute should promote awareness programmes. This study found that consumers generate most food waste. Future research should identify and quantify the main causes of wasteful consumer behaviour in institute messes and eateries. The evaluation of effective food waste mitigation programmes implemented by other institutes in light of their potential relevance to BITS Pilani students is another promising research direction.

REFERENCES

1. Beretta, Claudio, Matthias Stucki, and Stefanie Hellweg. "Environmental Impacts and Hotspots of Food Losses: Value Chain Analysis of Swiss Food Consumption." *Environmental Science & Technology* 51, no. 19 (September 20, 2017): 11165–73. https://doi.org/10.1021/acs.est.6b06179.
2. Willersinn, Christian, Gabriele Mack, Patrik Mouron, Andreas Keiser, and Michael Siegrist. "Quantity and Quality of Food Losses along the Swiss Potato Supply Chain: Stepwise Investigation and the Influence of Quality Standards on Losses." *Waste Management* 46 (December 2015): 120–32. https://doi.org/10.1016/j.wasman.2015.08.033.
3. Beiriger, Angie. "Portland's Restaurants, Breweries, and Bars: From Food Carts to Fine Dining, Get Ready to Eat, Drink, and Be Wowed." *College & Research Libraries News* 76, no. 2 (February 1, 2015): 66–71. https://doi.org/10.5860/crln.76.2.9257.

4. Kim, Hong-seop, and Yufei Shang. "A Study on the Activation Schemes of Cold Chain Logistics System in Incheon Port." *Journal of Korea Port Economic Association* 35, no. 3 (September 30, 2019): 19–40. https://doi.org/10.38121/kpea.2019.09.35.3.19.

5. Lipinski, Brian. "SDG TARGET 12.3 on Food Loss and Waste: 2021 Progress Report." United Nations, September 2021. https://champions123.org/publication/sdg-target-123-food-loss-and-waste-2021-progress-report.

6. Gregory, P. J. "The International Food Policy Research Institute (IFPRI): Three Recent Publications." *Food Security* 7, no. 5 (August 26, 2015): 1091–92. https://doi.org/10.1007/s12571-015-0496-z.

7. Liang, Yangyang, Qingbin Song, Gang Liu, and Jinhui Li. "Uncovering Residents and Restaurants' Attitude and Willingness toward Effective Food Waste Management: A Case Study of Macau." *Waste Management* 130 (July 2021): 107–16. https://doi.org/10.1016/j.wasman.2021.05.021.

8. Silvennoinen, Kirsi, Heikkilä, Lotta, Katajajuuri, Juha, and Anu Reinikainen. "Food waste volume and origin: Case studies in the Finnish food service sector." *Waste Management 46*, (2015): 140–145. Accessed December 31, 2022. https://doi.org/10.1016/j.wasman.2015.09.010.

9. Hwang, Jinsoo, and Chihyung Ok. "The Antecedents and Consequence of Consumer Attitudes toward Restaurant Brands: A Comparative Study between Casual and Fine Dining Restaurants." *International Journal of Hospitality Management* 32 (March 2013): 121–31. https://doi.org/10.1016/j.ijhm.2012.05.002.

10. Cesareo, Massimo. "No Waste by Default: Nudging to Prevent Food Waste in Restaurants." Ergonomics International Journal 3, no. 1 (2019). https://doi.org/10.23880/eoij-16000191.

11. Charlebois, Sylvain, Amy Creedy, and Mike von Massow. "'Back of House' – Focused Study on Food Waste in Fine Dining: The Case of Delish Restaurants." *International Journal of Culture, Tourism and Hospitality Research* 9, no. 3 (August 3, 2015): 278–91. https://doi.org/10.1108/ijcthr-12-2014-0100.

12. Kvitkova, Zuzana. "Language-Specific Differences in Online Reviews: Case of Fine-Dining Prague Restaurants." *Turizam* 23, no. 4 (2019): 100–106. https://doi.org/10.5937/turizam23-21570.

13. Grote, Ulrike. "IFPRI: Global Food Policy Report 2018." *Food Security* 10, no. 6 (September 22, 2018): 1665–67. https://doi.org/10.1007/s12571-018-0844-x.

14. Kennard, Nicole Josiane. 2019. "Food Waste Management." Encyclopedia of the UN Sustainable Development Goals, 1–17. https://doi.org/10.1007/978-3-319-69626-3_86-1.

15. foodnavigator.com. 2021. "Unilever Talks Food Waste: 'Our Mission Is to Inspire Consumers to Be More Resourceful with Food.'" April 1, 2021. https://www.foodnavigator.com/Article/2021/04/01/Unilever-talks-food-waste-Our-mission-is-to-inspire-consumers-to-be-more-resourceful-with-food.

Handbook of Evidence Based Management Practices in Business – Satyendra Kumar Sharma et al. (eds)
© *2023 Taylor & Francis Group, London, ISBN 978-1-032-54216-4*

Chapter

Assessment of EVs Adoption in India Using AHP-BWM Approach

Sudhanshu Ranjan Singh[(i)1], Abhijeet K. Digalwar[(i), (ii)]* and Srikanta Routroy[(i)2]
[(i)]Mechanical Engineering Department,
Birla Institute of Technology and Science Pilani, Pilani-333031, India
[(ii)]Symbiosis Centre for Management Studies (SCMS),
Symbiosis International (Deemed University) (SIU) Nagpur, Maharashtra, India

ABSTRACT: The deployment of electric vehicles (EVs) is considered as one of the potential solutions for addressing the issues like climate change, energy security and air pollution. At present, for most of the people, pollution has become an alarming concern. Pollution free environment is what everyone is aiming for, but the actions are taking apart from the goal of sustainable and environment friendly surroundings. Among various factors for pollution in India, the transportation sector holds a significant share of approximately 21% of CO_2 emissions. While, the pacing numbers of registrations of automobiles in India, needs an immediate direction which must result into sustainable and environmentally friendly modes of transportation. The possible solution to this current dilemma is shifting on EVs. However, EV acceptance is not taking place at a desirable rate, although it is intended to grow in the coming years. This qualitative study incorporates exploration of various factors necessary for the adoption of EVs. Although, a big set of complex factors are tangled when considering the adoption of EVs in a developing country like India. The purpose of this study is to catalyse the adoption of EVs in India by highlighting the crucial factors, and validating them using hybrid multi-criteria decision-making method, including best-worst method (BWM), and analytic hierarchy process (AHP).

KEYWORDS: EVs adoption, MCDM techniques, BWM, AHP, EV sustainability

*Corresponding Author: head_resnagpur@siu.edu.in
[1]p20220047@pilani.bits-pilani.ac.in, [2]srikanta@pilani.bits-pilani.ac.in

DOI: 10.4324/9781003415725-58

1. Introduction

According to the reports of World Health Organization, in the world every nine out of ten people are inhaling polluted air, contributing to the annual global death toll of approximate 7 million people (World Health Organization, 2018). The major share of contribution to this pollution is discharge from automobile vehicles only (World Health Organization, 2019). Globally, it is even more alarming that in the list of most polluted cities, nine out of ten are Indian cities only (World Health Organization, 2018). Irrespective of the Indian emission standards, many conventional vehicles are non-complaint to the defined standards and release various toxic pollutants into the environment(Dey and Mehta 2020). Also, the growing stock of internal combustion engine passenger vehicles is contributed India at a position of country with third highest oil-consumption and greenhouse gas (GHG) emissions worldwide.

To address such upsetting issues, previously the Indian government aimed to have an automotive sector with 100% plug-in electric vehicles (PEVs) by 2030 (IEA, 2020). But, the struggle in implementation and deployment stage of EVs made the government to adjust the aspirational goal, ended up with setting a target to achieve 30% share of EVs out of whole automobile sector (Forbes, 2019). The Indian government is also looking forward for transforming the India into EVs manufacturing hub with global outreach (Ghosh, 2019). These targets of government are backed by introduction of various initiatives which are briefly mentioned in the points (Digalwar et al. 2022).

- Allocation of INR 10,000 crores for promoting EV deployment and charging infrastructure development over the period of three years.
- Guidelines and instructions for establishment of charging stations along the roads and highways.
- Procurement of 10,000 EVs by Energy Efficiency Services Limited (EESL) for different departments of government.
- Launch of National Electric Mobility Mission Plan, 2020 for promoting full and hybrid EVs to elevate the automobile industry's GDP share.
- Incentivising the purchase of EVs by providing subsidies of variable amount depending on the vehicle type under the scheme Faster Adoption and Manufacturing of Hybrid and EV (FAME) Phase-I and Phase-II

With the growth of EVs, which are anyhow eating up the share of internal combustion engine equivalents, the automotive sector is undergoing a major revolution in engineering and technology. With the active participation of automobile industries and support of government initiatives, the EV technology in India has experienced a leap in advancement. Although, the high import duties and lack of charging infrastructure are anchoring the EV sales as compared to what it was supposed to be. In India, the conditions of EV deployment or adoption differs from the other parts of the world due to numerous barriers and restrictions.

Globally, many studies have been done on understanding the role of various factors involved into adoption of EVs. Mainly studied factors include driving distance, EV cost, charging time, battery cost, charging infrastructure availability etc. (Khurana, Kumar, and Sidhpuria 2020). However, few researchers have tried to get to the roots of behaviour of consumer and analysed the root cause for the hesitation in adopting EVs. The hurdles to EVs adoption concluded by (Kumar, Vyas, and Datta 2019) include absence of infrastructure and sustainable credentials, initial costs, and consumer indecisiveness hampers the EV sales in India. Recently, eleven barriers in adoption were listed down by (Panwar, Kumar, and Chakrabarti 2019) that comprise of financial, policy-related, regulatory, technical, and attitudinal barriers.

Prakash et al. (2018) used Interpretive Structural Modelling (ISM) to identify different barriers and inter-relationship among those. However, they missed out to consider the social aspect, which have been an important factor in analysing the extensive acceptance of EVs. Similarly, the study conducted by (Haider, Zhuang, and Ali 2019) commented on the attitude-behaviour gap of the customers of EV and their perceptions on EVs acceptance. Goel et al. (2021) conferred the importance of role of government in actively rolling out policies for infrastructure development and mentioned the future impacts of EVs due to limitations of available technology of batteries.

The findings reported in previous research works are primarily based on the perceptions of experts. Hence, this study is intended to fill the gap by incorporating all the viewpoints. Present study positions to encompass a variety of stakeholders, including manufacturers, potential and existing customers, academicians, suppliers, and government officials. The obtained data is analysed by using a hybrid multi-criteria decision-making method (MCDM) which involves best-worst method (BWM) for determining the weights to different criteria. Then analytic hierarchy process (AHP) is used to compute the relative importance of criteria and options. At last, ranking of some criteria and alternatives is done using Macbeth method. This gives the study more holistic perspective and comprehensive, especially when it comes in context to a developing market like India.

2. Methodology

Initially, a three-step study technique was followed execute an assessment of factors for adoption of EVs in India which includes questionnaire preparation, data collection, relative importance index analysis, assigning weights and alternatives shown in Fig. 58.1. Effective data collection and management was required for proper data analysis which was managed by using Microsoft excel tool and survey responses were coded. Both quantitative and non-quantitative, open-ended replies were recorded for all-embracing analysis.

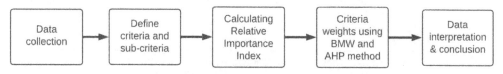

Fig. 58.1 Flow chart of methodology

Source: Author's compilation

The focus of the present study is to find and evaluate the important criteria which are crucial in adoption of EVs in India and rank them from the perspective of manufacturers and suppliers. For the present study 11 reliable and valid factors along with 20 variables have been adopted from the previous study. Due to word limits and page restrictions, details of these factors and variables are not included in the present study. However, researchers and readers can refer Digalwar et al. (2022) for more details of these factors and their variables.

Table 58.1 Details about identified factors, brief details, variables, and their nomenclatures

Factors	Brief details	Variables/Sub-criteria	Nomenclature
Technological	Directly or indirectly relate to electric mobility, battery, charging, material, and electric grid technology	Battery Life	TEC1
		R&D related to EV technology	TEC2
Economic	Considers the cost associated with it such as initial cost, operation & maintenance cost, replacement cost, battery cost, and fuel price	Purchase cost	ECO1
		Operating cost	ECO2
		Maintenance cost	ECO3
		Replacement cost	ECO4
Environmental	Concerns of harmful environment phenomena and its impacts	Photochemical oxidation formation	ENV1
Social	Relate to the part of society which influence the intention to purchase or adopt an EVs	Training	SOC1
		Awareness	SOC2
Sociotechnical	Factors that interrelate the social and technological aspects of society like potential customers, consider top speed, power, comfort, appearance, safety etc.	Power of EV	SOT1
		Safety of EV	SOT2
		Reliability of EV	SOT3
Political	Central and state government policies in the adoption of electric mobility	Free public charging	POL1
		Dedicated lanes for EVs	POL2
Cultural	Cultural values affect customer's decision-making in switching to cleaner technology	Recycling mentality	CUL1
Infrastructural	Supporting infrastructures like charging stations, service, maintenance, and R&D infrastructure	Charging infrastructure for home, workplaces, public places, and highways	INF1
Behavioural	Factors like resistance to change, driving distance and time, parking time, and distance driven per day	Driven distance	BEH1
Geopolitical	Factors that are influenced by the geographical location for example China dominates the lithium-ion production	Lithium-ion reserve	GEP1
		Climate policy	GEP2
Geographical	Factors such as having public charging and cost of charging	Regional difference in electricity price	GEO1

Source: Author's compilation

2.1 Goal and Objectives of Study

The focus of the research is to perform the assessment of EVs adoption in India. The assessment factors will showcase the mindset of consumers and stakeholders' opinions regarding the deployment of EVs. Different variable of segregated genre has been mentioned in the table above on which the assessment is framed and carried on. The nominal clustering technique was used to assess the elements relevance. The nominal grouping approach is a method of grouping data in an organised way that assists in combining individual importance ratings into the group's final weighted priorities.

2.2 Identification of Factors

A comprehensive analysis of the topic has been conducted out to determine the factors such as technological, economic, social and many more. The repeatability and significance evaluation of factors were done using a filtration procedure, the following questionnaire was used for the same –

- Is there a clear indicator in the objective?
- Is the scale consistent and coherent?
- Is there enough information in the indicator?
- Is there a way to collect data on factors?
- Is the indicator considerable in both regional and national levels?

This shortlisted the list of criteria and sub-criteria to a final number 11 and 20 respectively.

2.3 Survey Design

A survey instrument has been designed to assess the significance and the uniformity of the specified factors form viewpoint across India. It was first put to the test by academics and practitioners to see if it was simple and adequate. After that, a survey tool was created online (Google forms) and offline (personal interaction) survey modes. Experts form many academic backgrounds were selected: Engineers, Experts from respective fields, Investors and Non-Governmental Organizations and others. Politicians, social workers, and government servants are examples of 'others' with knowledge. Experts from many sectors were considered for their perspective and suitable evaluation of factors. Experts were given a five-point system of Likert' scale for evaluating their decisions.

1. Not acceptable, 2. Less acceptable, 3. Moderately acceptable, 4. Acceptable, 5. Highly acceptable

2.4 Calculation of Relative Importance Index (RII)

The questionnaire's numerical values offered a gauge to the strength of thinking on the impact of each criterion and sub-criteria on the adoption of EVs. The formula adopted by (Digalwar et al. 2022) is used to convert the obtained numerical values into a relative significance index.

Relative Importance Index (RII) = $\Sigma Wi/AT$

where, T = number of respondents, A = maximum weight, Wi = weight whose values ranges from 1 to 5, given by the respondent

The indices of importance lie between 0 to 100. The relevance of the factors listed in the questionnaire is reflected in these indices. To reflect the respondents' judgements, the importance indices are divided into five groupings:

- Very important: $80 < I \le 100$
- Important: $60 < I \le 80$
- Preferred: $40 < I \le 60$
- Less important: $20 < I \le 40$
- Not important: $0 < I \le 20$

2.5 Assessment of Criteria Weights

In this research, the best worst method (BWM), which is one of the latest MCDM methods, is performed in order to realize the targeted objectives, i.e., weight for different criteria. The prime reason for selecting BWM method is because it requires less pairwise comparison, provides more consistent results, speed, ease, and robustness of computation. The five steps of BWM are shown in the flow chart below, Fig. 58.2 and using that methodology the relative weight values are calculated and ranked, as shown in Table 58.2.

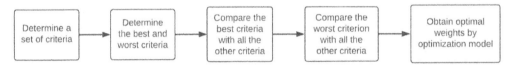

Fig. 58.2   Steps of BWM

Source: Author's compilation

Table 58.2   Relative weight values for all variables using BWM

S. No.	Variables	Weights	Rank	S. No.	Variables	Weights	Rank
1.	TEC1	0.044872	5	11.	TEC2	0.025641	9
2.	INF1	0.046695	4	12.	GEP2	0.012452	15
3.	ECO3	0.012982	14	13.	ECO2	0.01731	13
4.	BEH1	0.055556	1	14.	GEP1	0.030651	8
5.	ECO1	0.038947	7	15.	SOC1	0.04057	6
6.	SOT1	0.053333	2	16.	CUL1	0.02439	10
7.	SOT2	0.021667	11	17.	POL1	0.051205	3
8.	GEO1	0.017682	12	18.	ENV1	0.003992	19
9.	ECO4	0.003709	20	19.	SOT3	0.008333	18
10.	POL2	0.011044	17	20.	SOC2	0.012062	16

Source: Author's compilation

AHP decision making approach is used for calculating the relative importance of criteria and options. It uses pairwise comparisons to simplify preference ratings among choice criteria. The weights obtained from AHP methodology is tabulated below in Table 58.3.

3. Results and Findings

The study elicited 904 responses from different area and specializations, including 741 men and 163 women. The gathered information on respondents includes various levels of education

Table 58.3 Relative weight values for all variables using AHP

S. No.	Variables	Weights	Rank	S. No.	Variables	Weights	Rank
1.	TEC1	0.0577	2	11.	TEC2	0.01072	14
2.	INF1	0.04765	5	12.	GEP2	0.01527	12
3.	EC03	0.00976	15	13.	EC02	0.02194	9
4.	BEH1	0.06393	1	14.	GEP1	0.03745	7
5.	ECO1	0.00976	15	15.	SOC1	0.04696	6
6.	SOT1	0.05592	3	16.	CUL1	0.02913	8
7.	SOT2	0.02029	10	17.	POL1	0.04951	4
8.	GEO1	0.01964	11	18.	ENV1	0.00303	20
9.	ECO4	0.00379	19	19.	SOT3	0.00712	18
10.	POL2	0.00925	17	20.	SOC2	0.01347	13

Source: Author's compilation

in order to better comprehend the relevance of variables ranging from people of different educational backgrounds. The respondents were categorized by age into young adults (18-31 years), middle-aged adults (31-45 years), older years (46-61 years), and elderly people (greater than 61 years). A lot of valuable detail is obtained from the feedback by categorizing the analysis on surveying age ranges. The ranking of the weights obtained using BWM and AHP methods are shown in Fig. 58.3 and 58.4. The criteria

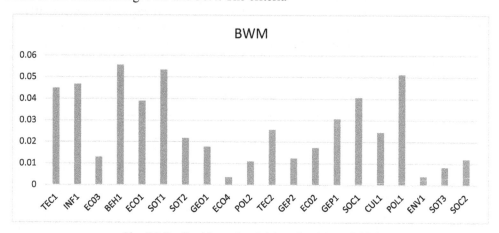

Fig. 58.3 Ranking of weights gained from BWM

Source: Author's compilation

In addition, the responses are ranked based on the respondent's level of competence. Academicians, NGO's the environment, investors, and engineer's expert categories all have their own RII calculation. The economic and sociotechnical category have three factors. Technological, social, political, and geopolitical have two factors. Other categories have only one indicator.

Age range categorized analysis reveals whether there is a substantial link between age and subsequent attitudes and behaviours. It has been noted that young adults have placed the most

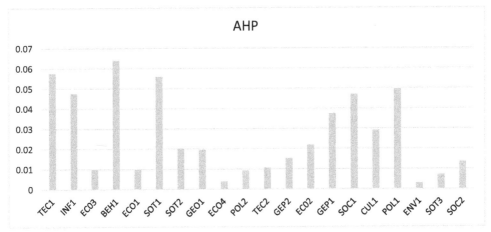

Fig. 58.4 Ranking of weights gained from AHP

Source: Author's compilation

emphasis on the "Charging Infrastructure" (0.873) and "Recycling Mentality" (0.856). While, the least amount of weight has been given to "Power of EV" (0.671) and "R&D related to EV" (0.679). Middle-aged adults also preferred the "Charging Infrastructure" (0.858) and "Recycling Mentality" (0.820). While "Climate Policy" (0.579) was considered as the least important indicator. Similarly, older adults gave the highest preference to "Awareness" (0.816) and "Purchase cost" (0.795), and the least preference was given to "Power of EV". Elderly people also gave priority to the same factor as the former but showed least preference for "Lithium-ion reserves".

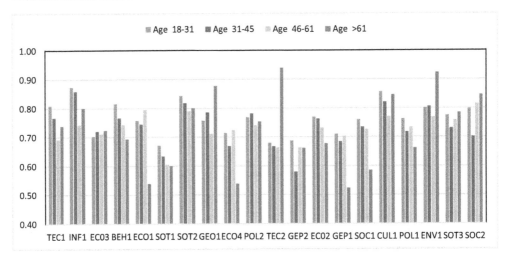

Fig. 58.5 Relative importance Index (RII) data for different age groups

Source: Author's compilation

In social research, gender is an important demographic trait to analyse. The statistics of different variables from gender perspective is given in the Fig. 58.6. which shows that males

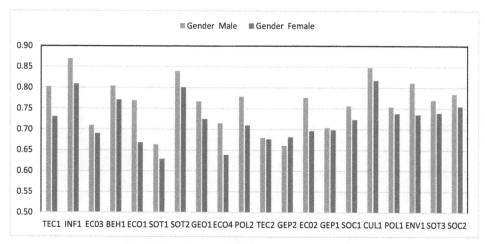

Fig. 58.6 Criteria preference based on gender

Source: Author's compilation

have given more attention towards the "Charging Infrastructure" (0.869) and "Recycling Mentality" (0.848), while the "Climate Policy" (0.661) and "Power of EV" (0.663) got least importance. Females have given the most important priority to "Recycling Mentality" (0.817) and "Charging Infrastructure" (0.809), while minimum importance to "Power of EV" and "Replacement cost" with RII being (0.628) and (0.638) respectively.

In the educational category, the highest RII is given to "Awareness" (0.844) and "Charging infrastructure" (0.770) by the respondents of doctorate level, while least preference was given to "Power of EV". It is observed at the post graduate level, the uppermost priority was delivered to "Recycling mentality" whereas minimum was to "Climate policy". A detailed order of preferences for every educational level is shown by the bar graph chart in Fig. 58.7.

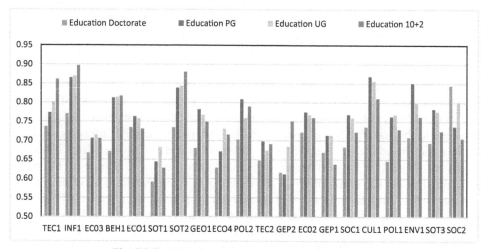

Fig. 58.7 Criteria preference based on education

Source: Author's compilation

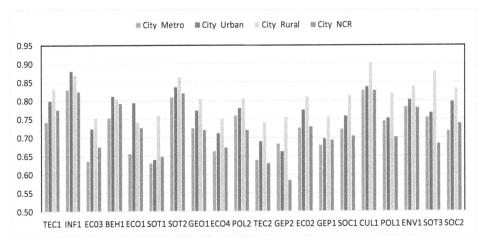

Fig. 58.8 Criteria preference based on geographical location

Source: Author's compilation

In the educational category, the highest RII is given to "Charging Infrastructure" because India lacks in charging infrastructure, whereas location, accessibility, charging time, and power play a major role.

On the basis of city of residence, it was found that metropolitan and urban people have also placed the greatest emphasis on "Charging Infrastructure" only. On the other end rural people choose to give priority to "Recycling Mentality" as respondents are more concerned about the environment and surroundings.

4. Conclusion

The outcome of the study is captured under the factors and variables around drivers of adoption, barriers to adoption and support mechanism required for encouraging the EV adoption. Overall, the study is evocative that India is at the cusp of transformation towards accepting EVs as its prime mode of transport in times to come. However, for this change to be faster and smoother, essential actions are must to be done at multiple levels. A collaboration of industry higher educational institutions and government is crucial at the level of research and development to invest sensibly in technology, innovation, skilling, and capital. The extent of financial incentives per EV currently offered in India would need to be optimized in such a way that it benefits the major portion of population. But also, public charging infrastructure barriers are also critical to address. A significant proportion of potential customers lives in apartment buildings and dwellings with no dedicated parking spaces for home charging. This zeal also gets justified by the RII values of urban and metropolitan people. Out of all variables, a clear focus was on few variables only which illustrates that the penetrative adoption of EV is relying on those few variables only. Those are the only areas in which we need to dedicate more focus on. The results of this study provide the influential strengths of each variable to identify the perspective of manufacturers and suppliers. Along with the infrastructure development and financial support, the government and industry must amplify the awareness about the causes and effects of adopting a conventional internal combustion engine automobile and an EV. Because this will infuse rapid adoption of EV among the people and lead to the goals in the swift timeline.

REFERENCES

1. Alagh, Yoginder K. 2006. "India 2020." *Journal of Quantitative Economics* 4 (1). https://doi.org/10.1007/BF03404634.
2. Dey, S., and N. S. Mehta. 2020. "Automobile Pollution Control Using Catalysis." *Resources, Environment and Sustainability* 2 (November): 100006. https://doi.org/10.1016/j.resenv.2020.100006.
3. Digalwar, Abhijeet K., S. K. Saraswat, Arpit Rastogi, and Rohaan George Thomas. 2022. "A Comprehensive Framework for Analysis and Evaluation of Factors Responsible for Sustainable Growth of Electric Vehicles in India." *Journal of Cleaner Production* 378 (December). https://doi.org/10.1016/j.jclepro.2022.134601.
4. Forbes, 2019. India's Plan to Turn 200 Million Vehicles Electric in Six Years. Available at: https://www.forbes.com/sites/scottcarpenter/2019/12/05/can-india-turn-nearly-200-million-vehicles-electric-in-six-years/#5516b27815db.
5. Ghosh, Malyaban, 2019. Govt steps on the gas to put India's EV mission in fast lane. https://www.livemint.com/budget/news/govt-steps-on-the-gas-to-put-india-s-ev-mission-in-fast-lane-1562350841874.html.
6. Goel, Pooja, Nitika Sharma, K. Mathiyazhagan, and K. E.K. Vimal. 2021. "Government Is Trying but Consumers Are Not Buying: A Barrier Analysis for Electric Vehicle Sales in India." *Sustainable Production and Consumption* 28: 71–90. https://doi.org/10.1016/j.spc.2021.03.029.
7. Haider, Syed Waqar, Guijun Zhuang, and Shahid Ali. 2019. "Identifying and Bridging the Attitude-Behavior Gap in Sustainable Transportation Adoption." *Journal of Ambient Intelligence and Humanized Computing* 10 (9): 3723–38. https://doi.org/10.1007/s12652-019-01405-z.
8. Khurana, Anil, V. V.Ravi Kumar, and Manish Sidhpuria. 2020. "A Study on the Adoption of Electric Vehicles in India: The Mediating Role of Attitude." *Vision* 24 (1): 23–34. https://doi.org/10.1177/0972262919875548.
9. Kumar, Mukesh, Shashank Vyas, and Alekhya Datta. 2019. "A Review on Integration of Electric Vehicles into a Smart Power Grid and Vehicle-to-Grid Impacts." *2019 8th International Conference on Power Systems: Transition towards Sustainable, Smart and Flexible Grids, ICPS 2019*, 3–7. https://doi.org/10.1109/ICPS48983.2019.9067330.
10. Panwar, Umakant, Anil Kumar, and Deepankar Chakrabarti. 2019. "Barriers in Implementation of Electric Vehicles in India." *International Journal of Electric and Hybrid Vehicles* 11 (3): 195–204. https://doi.org/10.1504/IJEHV.2019.101273.
11. Prakash, Surya, Maheshwar Dwivedy, Sameer Sharma Poudel, and Dilesh Raj Shrestha. 2018. "Modelling the Barriers for Mass Adoption of Electric Vehicles in Indian Automotive Sector: An Interpretive Structural Modeling (ISM) Approach." *2018 5th International Conference on Industrial Engineering and Applications, ICIEA 2018*, 458–62. https://doi.org/10.1109/IEA.2018.8387144.
12. WHO, 2018. https://www.ccacoalition.org/en/news/world-health-organization-releases-new-global-air-pollution-data. Last accessed December 19, 2022.
13. WHO, 2019. https://www.who.int/sustainable-development/transport/health-risks/air-pollution/en/. Last accessed December 19, 2022.

Handbook of Evidence Based Management Practices in Business – Satyendra Kumar Sharma et al. (eds)
© 2023 Taylor & Francis Group, London, ISBN 978-1-032-54216-4

Chapter

Identification and Analysis of Health Parameters for the Development of a Mobile App and Sensor Based Wearable Health Band

Mayuri Digalwar[1], Dinesh Tundalwar[2], Rashmi Pandhare[3]
Indian Institute of Information and Technology, Nagpur, India
Abhijeet Digalwar[4]
Birla Institute of Technology and Science, Pilani, India

ABSTRACT: During Covid-19 pandemic, the World has experienced a crisis at a scale that was never witnessed before in history. The entire ecosystem all over the globe has been changed after the pandemic. The life style of each and every community of people changed drastically. Therefore, the health awareness has been increased due to the situations realized by the people during pandemic.

With this in view, the current research makes an attempt to explore various challenges faced by the people in the community during and post Covid and comes up with the study of identification and analysis of health parameters for the design and development of an integrated mobile app and sensor based wearable device. In addition to biological health parameters, we also surveyed and analyzed the mental stress and anxiety issues among the people.

To accomplish this objective, we conducted an online survey among 500 to 600 Indian population to understand the health-related issues of people of different ages. The data collected from the survey is analyzed and based on the analysis, health parameters are identified for building a mobile app integrated with a health cum safety band. The findings of our study show that there is an immense need for the design and development of an interactive mobile app and sensor based wearable device which will help the people to overcome their health-related problems.

KEYWORDS: Stress, Health parameters, Mobile app, Wearable device, Sensor-based health band

[1]mayuri@iiitn.ac.in, [2]dtea21ece001@iiitn.ac.in, [3]rpandhare@iiitn.ac.in, [4]akd@pilani.bits-pilani.ac.in

DOI: 10.4324/9781003415725-59

1. Introduction

In last two to three years, the world has experienced a crisis at a very large scale that is never witnessed before in history due to the spread of Covid-19 and its variants. The exponential spread of the disease was so huge that the World Health Organization (WHO) was imposed to declare an international public health emergency. This sudden global situation led to an enormous reaction from the common citizens of all the affected countries including the people of India.

In spite of the genuine efforts put by the government and other social organizations, there exist some people or community who require a convincing way of communication to help overcome their health-related issues and reduce their anxiety and stress. Apart from the directly affected people, there are so many people who are indirectly but extremely affected and under gone severe depression. Few among such people are the youngsters who have fear of losing jobs or those who have lost the jobs, senior citizens who are living alone, students who are preparing for competitive exams etc. The extreme level of anxiety, stress and paranoid feelings among the people is a serious concern during and post pandemic which needs to be addressed by creating scientific and social awareness through some platform. This awareness platform should result in providing them immediate help to resolve health related matters and reduce their negative reactions, relax them and give them strength to face stressful situations.

This study focusses on the identification and analysis of biological and mental health parameters in order to make a health aid mobile app and wearable smart health band. In order to accomplish the objectives, a questionnaire-based survey instrument has been made and a survey is conducted among different kinds of the people at different ages. Based on the collected data, statistical analysis has been done which helped us to design various features of the mobile app and wearable device.

The paper is organized into the following five sections. The first section introduces the objective and motivation behind the study. The second section justifies the need of the study by presenting thorough literature review. The following third section explains in detail the methodology of the research work in this paper. Then the results and discussion are described in the fourth section followed by the last section on conclusion of the work.

2. Literature Review

This section discusses the review of various existing mental health parameters studied by the researchers during and post Covid-19 pandemic. The review of existing research articles published during Covid- 19 pandemic identifies various mental health parameters of the people around the globe (like US, India, China, Bangladesh etc.) from different communities like college students, working professionals, young people etc. The mental health parameters that are identified in the literature are through the method of online survey by floating questionnaire among the people. All the health parameters are compiled and represented in Table 59.1.

From the review, it is observed that the objective of the existing literature is to analyze the depth of deteriorating mental state of the people during pandemic and resulting lockdown so that the Government and other authorized agencies should take prompt actions to mitigate this falling mental state of the people.

Table 59.1 Literature survey on health parameters

Citation	Objectives	Mental Health Parameters
Srivastava et. al., 2020	To identify the stress among Indian Population during the Covid-19 pandemic	Anxiety, obsession and fear
Rossi et. al., 2020	To evaluate the rate of rise of mental health among Italian population during Covid-19 pandemic	PTSS, depression, anxiety, insomnia, perceived stress, and adjustment disorder symptoms (ADS)
Zurlo et. al., 2020	To develop and validate the questionnaire and to evaluate university students stress during lockdown	Fear of contagion, fear of personal and relational life, fear of isolation
Son et. al., 2020	To evaluate effect of pandemic among American university students	Stress and anxiety, difficulty in sleeping, concentrating, fear of losing loved once, fear of performing bad in academics
Islam et. al., 2020	To perform perception-based study on Covid-19 related stress among the youth of Bangladesh.	Economic Stress, fear of taking medical treatment, fear of losing job, stress for managing food, stress through social media and TV, mental pressure due to chaos in family, suicidal tendency
Xiong et. al., 2020	To evaluate effect of pandemic among general population of China, Spain, Italy, Iran, US, Turkey, Nepal and Denmark	Anxiety, depression, psychological distress, post-traumatic stress dis-order etc.
Wang et. al., 2020	To investigate the mental health of US college students during pandemic	Stress, anxiety, fear of academic performance, physical health concerns, financial concerns, lifestyle related concerns
Roy et. al., 2021	To evaluate effect of pandemic among general population of India	Depression, anxiety, stress, denial, anger, fear, insomnia, panic, suicidal thoughts
Whitehead and Torossian, 2020	To investigate a mixed method analysis of stresses and joy by Older Adults	Perceived stress, negative affect, and positive affect of covid 19. Stressors like restrictions, concern for others and isolation. Sources of Joy/comfort were family/friends' relationship, digital social contacts, hobbies
Chaturvedi et. al., 2021	To evaluate the effect of pandemic on education, social life and mental health of students	Mental health parameters include Stress and anxiety. Other parameter like social media, sleeping habits, fitness routine leading to increasing weight etc.
Rehman et. al., 2021	To explore the psychological distress among the Indian people during pandemic	Depression, anxiety and stress among people who did have sufficient supply of daily needs during lockdown
Gabriele et. al., 2021	To study the Post-Traumatic Stress Symptoms among the Health care workers	Particularly focused on Post-Traumatic Stress Symptoms

Citation	Objectives	Mental Health Parameters
Kar et. al., 2021	To study and evaluate the effect of pandemic on mental health of the common people	Stress, anxiety and depression
Panigrahi et. al., 2021	To evaluate the psychological distress among Indian people due to pandemic	Psychological distress
Green et. al., 2021	To study and examine the worries due to watching the news on social media among the mobile app users of US	Stress and worries
Varma et. al., 2021	To explore the psychological distress among the young people during pandemic	Stress, anxiety and depression

Source: Author's compilation

Keeping the existing work in consideration, we have further extended the survey in order to design and develop a health awareness and assistance mobile app with an integrated wearable health band. The detailed survey instrument and analysis is discussed in the following section.

3. Methodology

3.1 Survey Instrument

Based on the literature review, a tentative list of health parameters has been developed. Then to screen the list, many experts from medical field were approached, most of them were Doctors, Health Consultants, Academician from medical institutes but because of some or the other reasons supports from only ten experts had been obtained. Inputs from the various experts helped to determine appropriateness of the questions. To collect the data, five sets of questionnaires using a five-point Likert scale, where 1 represented strongly disagree and 5 represented strongly agree, was developed. There were two parts to the questionnaire. Part A questionnaire seeks background information related to participants, and Part B requires assessment by participants on statements related to the factors and their variables. Survey was administrated between October to December 2021 and between May to July 2022. Snowball sampling approach was adopted for data collection. Total of 560 responses were received, out of which 10 were rejected due to incomplete data. A usable sample of 550 was used for further analysis.

3.2 Demographic Analysis

The demographic characteristics of the study sample are given in Table 59.2. The category of people who have attempted the survey are working professionals, students, business people and old age people.

3.3 Statistical Analysis

In order to perform the feasibility study of the project work, a survey is conducted to uncover the ground reality and to identify the actual problems faced by different category of people

Table 59.2 Demographic characteristics of the respondents

Sr. No	Category		Characteristics		Out of 550	Percentage (%)
1	Working Professionals	(a)	Age	22-29	141	25.6
				30-44	310	56.4
				45-59	85	15.4
		(b)	Education	SSC/HSC	43	7.7
				Bachelors	198	35.9
				Masters	240	43.6
		(c)	Employment	Full Time	410	74.4
				Self-Employment	71	12.8
				Part Time	71	12.8
2	Students	(a)	Age	20-25	258	46.8
				15-20	229	41.5
				15-20	47	8.5
		(b)	Education	SSC/HSSC	355	64.5
				Bachelors	119	21.5
				Masters	77	14
3	Businessman	(a)	Age	30-44	101	18.2
				45-59	101	18.2
		(b)	Education	SSC/HSSC	151	27.35
				Bachelors	101	18.2
4	Old Age	(a)	Age	55-60	53	9.5
				60-65	79	14.3
				>65	79	14.3
		(b)	Education	SSC/HSC	101	18.2
				Bachelors	251	45.5
				PhD	51	9.1
		(c)	Employment	Full Time	175	31.8
				Self-Employment	101	18.2
				Home maker	75	13.6
				Retired	125	22.7

Source: Author's compilation

during pandemic and the problems they are bound to be faced after the lockdown period. The results and analysis of this survey would act as a basic criterion for the design of awareness and stress relieving contents. Following steps are followed to carry out the survey:

(i) Four categories of people based on age, gender, profession, location etc. are identified. They are: Working professionals, Students, Business people and old age people.

(ii) Separate five-point scale-based questionnaires for each category is designed by having thorough understanding of their behaviour, education, life style, economic background etc.

(iii) Distribution of questionnaires among the people in each category through different electronic media such as emails, whatsapp etc is carried out.

Following are the results of the survey conducted for respective category of people:

COVID-19's impact on Working Professionals:

The following charts in Fig. 59.1 represent the impact of Covid-19 on working professionals. It specifically shows the percentage of people feeling mentally stressed in the range of 5-point scale. It is observed from the following graphical and the tabular representations that the majority of the participants were from the age group of 30 to 40 and belong to urban and sub-urban area. A considerable number of respondents (51.8%) had a feeling of anxiety, depression and nervousness and very few of them (5.6%) thought of suicide during the peak of pandemic. This can be demonstrated with the help of the various questions asked in the survey. The following Table 59.3 and Fig. 59.1 show the results of few important questions from the survey:

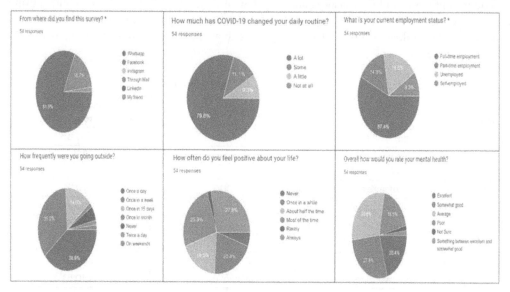

Fig. 59.1 Analytical representation of results on working professionals

Source: Author's compilation

Table 59.3 Survey results of working professionals

Sr. No.	Question	% of people giving positive response to the question
1	Was your daily routine badly affected?	79.6%
2	Not feeling any joy while talking to people other than family members?	25.9%
3	Finding work from home harmful to mental health?	55.6%
4	Worried about getting affected?	59.3%
5	Worried about losing the relationships?	24.1%
6	Finding difficulty in sleeping?	24.1%
7	Worried about utilizing the public transport?	57.4%
8	Worried about financial problems?	51.9%
9	Worried about children education?	46.3%
10	Fear of losing jobs?	50%
11	Worried about future job perspectives?	29.6%

Source: Author's compilation

COVID-19's impact on Students:

Among all participants, majority of the students (50.4%) were of the age between 20 to 25 years and pursuing their graduation (58.8%). Around 55.2% of respondents had a feeling of anxiety, depression and nervousness and very few of them (10.3%) thought of suicide during the peak of pandemic. This can be demonstrated with the help of the various questions asked in the survey. The following Table 59.4 and Fig. 59.2 show the results of few important questions from the survey.

Table 59.4 Survey results of students

Sr. No.	Question	% of people giving positive response to the Question
1	Pandemic made you feel frustrated?	57.8%
2	Did you end up with addictions and bad habits like excessive use of mobile phones	25%
3	Increased use of screen (mobile/ laptop)	70.1%
4	Worried about campus placement?	60.3%
5	Worried about academic performance?	65.5%
6	Worried about practical skills?	45.7%
7	Finding difficulty in concentration?	63.8%
8	Worried about changing nature of exams and evaluation patterns?	40.5%
9	Your intellectual and social development affected?	58.6%
10	Post covid medication issues?	28.4%
11	Did you tend to spirituality?	13.8%

Source: Author's compilation

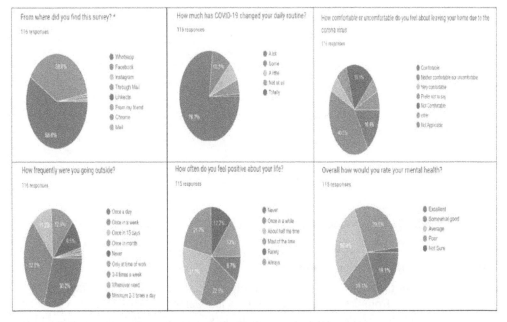

Fig. 59.2 Analytical representation of results on students

Source: Author's compilation

COVID-19's impact on person belonging to Business People:

Among all participants, majority of the people (42.9%) were of the age between 45 to 59 years and belong to urban area (80%). Around 52.3% of respondents had a feeling of anxiety, depression and nervousness and thought of suicide during the peak of pandemic. This can be demonstrated with the help of the various questions asked in the survey. The following Table 59.5 and Fig.59.3 show the result of few important questions from the survey.

Table 59.5 Survey results of business people

Sr. No.	Question	% of people giving positive response
1	Worried about temporary/permanent closure of your business?	28.6%
2	Finding difficulty in sleeping?	47.6%
3	Forced to layoff and reduce working hours?	52.4%
4	Worried about not being able to pay your bank instalments?	57.1%
5	Difficulty in managing education expenses of children?	61.9%
6	Reduction in weekly profits and decline in revenue generation?	52.3%

Source: Author's compilation

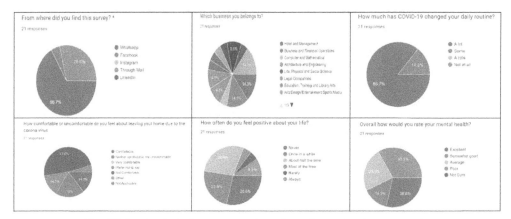

Fig. 59.3 Analytical representation of results on business people

Source: Author's compilation

COVID-19's impact on Older People:

It is observed from the following graphical and tabular representations that the majority of the participants were from the age group of 55 to 65 and belong to urban area. A considerable number of respondents (52.9%) had a feeling of anxiety, depression and nervousness and very few of them (38.9%) thought of suicide during the peak of pandemic. This can be demonstrated with the help of the various questions asked in the survey. The following Table 59.6 and Fig. 59.4 show the results of few important questions from the survey:

Table 59.6 Survey Results of Older People

Sr. No.	Question	% of people giving positive response
1	Experienced boredom, loneliness and negativity.	33.3%
2	Frustration due to lack of freedom	50%
3	Dependency on others for essential needs	50%
4	Accessibility to health care and treatment was difficult.	50%
5	Finding difficulty in sleeping	32%
6	Worried about post Covid medical complications	44.4%
7	Worried about taking the Vaccine	14%

Source: Author's compilation

Need of Wearable Device and Mobile App:

Based on the analysis of the online survey, various issues faced by people are identified. The experts for each category are also identified by contacting various dignitaries who are most suitable for each community. Experts helped us to develop the stress relaxing content for each community. For example, "Spiritual Expert" is a right person to convey the scientific awareness of pandemic to old age people, Professional Counsellor of some company is a right person to address the stress related problems of youngsters. Motivational and scientific awareness content are developed on the basis of the issues identified in the survey and the discussions carried out with the identified experts. Under the guidance of the experts, the development of

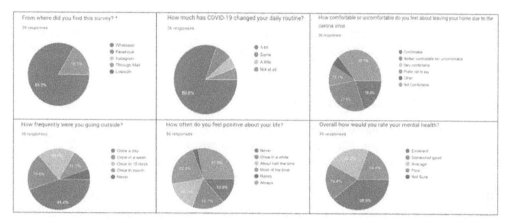

Fig. 59.4 Analytical representation of results on older people

Source: Author's compilation

interactive content in the form of audio and video clips is in process. An android application is designed and developed for proper display of the collected audio and video content. Based on survey results and developed content, the layout of android app is designed.

In addition to an awareness app, a Wearable Health Band is designed which can sense and display the vital health parameters like SPo2, Temperature, Pulse Rate, Heart Rate, Sudden Fall Detection and Body Position of a person wearing this band on Mobile App. This device also provides the real time assistance in terms of getting immediate access to the medical facilities.

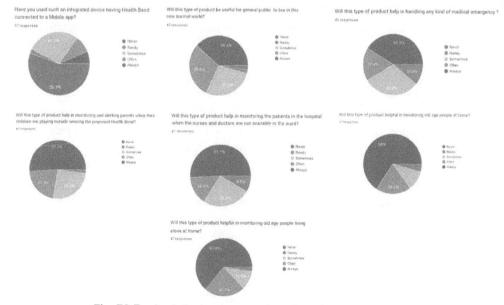

Fig. 59.5 Analytical representation of results on older people

Source: Author's compilation

In order to validate the necessity of the Mobile App and Wearable Health Band, we designed and conducted an online survey whose results are represented in the following pie charts. These pie charts show that there is a vital need of having such an integrated system for human survival in new normal.

4. Results and Discussion

The main objective of this research is to identify the necessity of the proposed integrated system of Wearable Health Band and Mobile App in post Covid new normal life of people. As the focus of Mobile App is on mental health attributes, the data collected through online survey was specific to mental health parameters (like stress, anxiety, depression etc) among different kinds of the people. We considered Working Professions, Students, Older People and Business People.

Among the working professionals, it is observed that majority of the people felt that their daily routine was badly affected as they have to stay at home for the whole day. Their strict schedule of sleep, food and work was completely disturbed. Also, working from home was hectic for around 50% of the people. This can be due to struggle in balancing the household and professional responsibilities.

On the other hand, most of the business people were concerned about the profit in their business as it was difficult for them to pay salaries to their workers, pay the bank instalments etc. Also, their weekly revenue generation was severely reduced which might have affected their family financial needs like children education, medical expenses etc.

The majority of the students who attempted the survey were between the age group of 20 to 25 years and were pursuing their graduation. The analysis shows that due to lockdown and compulsion to stay at home forced this category of people to get frustrated and motivated them towards use of mobile phones and laptops. This led to an increase in screen time and even addictions such as gaming, social media etc. This has severely affected their mental health and resulted in reduced academic performance. Most of the students were also worried about their campus placement as they feel that they are not perfect in their academics and also lack practical skills. The pandemic and resulting lockdown have severely affected the intellectual and social development of the children and the young generation.

The survey shows that the senior citizens have also gone through different kinds of pain during pandemic. They mostly suffered from loneliness, negativity and boredom as they were not free to go outside and even at home, they had lots of restrictions as there were very limited access to the medical facilities.

The results of the survey on the need of proposed system shows that majority of the people belonging to all the categories strongly suggest the need of the proposed system as it contains monitoring and alerting system at the times of medical emergency and also gives lots of motivating content for the people to overcome the negativity.

5. Conclusion

The present study clearly shows that the Covid-19 and resultant lockdown have severely affected the people in various ways such as working from home for working professionals was very challenging, balancing studies and social media/gaming was the big problem with student community, managing self-expenses and worker's salary were the pain points for the moderately established business people and finding motivation in living the remaining life was very difficult for the sensitive old people. The proposed system would help mitigate the stress or depression faced by the people and also help them in their medical emergencies by providing them the immediate medical assistance.

6. Acknowledgment

This research work is funded by Department of Science and Technology, Government of India. The authors thank the funding agency to provide the financial support required to carry out the research.

REFERENCES

1. Chaturvedi, Kunal, Vishwakarma, Dinesh Kumar and Singh, Nidhi. 2021. "COVID-19 and Its Impact on Education, Social Life and Mental Health of Students: A Survey." *Children and Youth Services Review* 121: 105866.
2. d'Ettorre, Gabriele, Giancarlo Ceccarelli, Letizia Santinelli, Paolo Vassalini, Giuseppe pietro Innocenti, Francesco Alessandri, Alexia E Koukopoulos, Alessandro Russo, Gabriella d'Ettorre, and Lorenzo Tarsitani. 2021. "Post-Traumatic Stress Symptoms in Healthcare Workers Dealing with the COVID-19 Pandemic: A Systematic Review." *International Journal of Environmental Research and Public Health* 18 (2): 601.
3. Green, Jennifer, Jennifer Huberty, Megan Puzia, Chad Stecher, 2021. "The Effect of Meditation and Physical Activity on the Mental Health Impact of COVID-19–Related Stress and Attention to News among Mobile App Users in the United States: Cross-Sectional Survey." *JMIR Mental Health* 8 (4): e28479.
4. Islam, S M Didar-Ul, Md Bodrud-Doza, Rafid Mahmud Khan, Md Abidul Haque, and Mohammed A Mamun 2020. "Exploring COVID-19 Stress and Its Factors in Bangladesh: A Perception-Based Study." *Heliyon* 6 (7): e04399.
5. Kar, Nilamadhab, Brajaballav Kar, and Shreyan Kar. 2021. "Stress and Coping during COVID-19 Pandemic: Result of an Online Survey." *Psychiatry Research* 295: 113598.
6. Panigrahi, Sasmita, Sujata Mohapatra, Asha P Shetty, Renju Sussane Baby, and Arvind Kumar Singh. 2021. "The Burden & Contributing Factors of Psychological Distress across India during the COVID Pandemic." *Archives of Psychiatric Nursing* 35 (6): 678–84.
7. Rehman, Usama, Mohammad G Shahnawaz, Neda H Khan, Korsi D Kharshiing, Masrat Khursheed, Kaveri Gupta, Drishti Kashyap, and Ritika Uniyal. 2021. "Depression, Anxiety and Stress among Indians in Times of Covid-19 Lockdown." *Community Mental Health Journal* 57 (1): 42–48.
8. Rossi, Rodolfo, Valentina Socci, Dalila Talevi, Sonia Mensi, Cinzia Niolu, Francesca Pacitti, Antinisca di Marco, Alessandro Rossi, Alberto Siracusano, and Giorgio di Lorenzo. 2020. "COVID-19 Pandemic and Lockdown Measures Impact on Mental Health among the General Population in Italy." *Frontiers in Psychiatry*, 790.

9. Roy, Adrija, Arvind Kumar Singh, Shree Mishra, Aravinda Chinnadurai, Arun Mitra, and Ojaswini Bakshi. 2021. "Mental Health Implications of COVID-19 Pandemic and Its Response in India." *International Journal of Social Psychiatry* 67 (5): 587–600.

10. Son, Changwon, Sudeep Hegde, Alec Smith, Xiaomei Wang, Farzan Sasangohar, and others. 2020. "Effects of COVID-19 on College Students' Mental Health in the United States: Interview Survey Study." *Journal of Medical Internet Research* 22 (9): e21279.

11. Srivastava, Amit, Renu Bala, Anoop K Srivastava, Anuj Mishra, Rafat Shamim, and Prasenjit Sinha. 2020. "Anxiety, Obsession and Fear from Coronavirus in Indian Population: A Web-Based Study Using COVID-19 Specific Scales." *Int J Community Med Public Health* 7 (11): 4570–77.

12. Varma, Prerna, Moira Junge, Hailey Meaklim, and Melinda L Jackson. 2021. "Younger People Are More Vulnerable to Stress, Anxiety and Depression during COVID-19 Pandemic: A Global Cross-Sectional Survey." *Progress in Neuro-Psychopharmacology and Biological Psychiatry* 109: 110236.

13. Wang, Xiaomei, Sudeep Hegde, Changwon Son, Bruce Keller, Alec Smith, Farzan Sasangohar, and others. 2020. "Investigating Mental Health of US College Students during the COVID-19 Pandemic: Cross-Sectional Survey Study." *Journal of Medical Internet Research* 22 (9): e22817.

14. Whitehead, Brenda R, and Emily Torossian. 2021. "Older Adults' Experience of the COVID-19 Pandemic: A Mixed-Methods Analysis of Stresses and Joys." *The Gerontologist* 61 (1): 36–47.

15. Xiong, Jiaqi, Orly Lipsitz, Flora Nasri, Leanna M W Lui, Hartej Gill, Lee Phan, David Chen-Li, et al. 2020. "Impact of COVID-19 Pandemic on Mental Health in the General Population: A Systematic Review." *Journal of Affective Disorders* 277: 55–64.

16. Zurlo, Maria Clelia, Maria Francesca Cattaneo Della Volta, and Federica Vallone. 2020. "COVID-19 Student Stress Questionnaire: Development and Validation of a Questionnaire to Evaluate Students' Stressors Related to the Coronavirus Pandemic Lockdown." *Frontiers in Psychology* 11: 576758.

Handbook of Evidence Based Management Practices in Business – Satyendra Kumar Sharma et al. (eds)
© 2023 Taylor & Francis Group, London, ISBN 978-1-032-54216-4

Chapter

Risk Propagation Modelling for Agri-Food Supply Chain: An Indian Perspective

Khalid Hussain Ansari[1], Srikanta Routroy*
Mechanical Engineering Department,
Birla Institute of Technology and Science Pilani, Jhunjhunu, India

Shailender Singh[2]
Institute of Business Management,
GLA University, Mathura, India

Krishna Muniyoor[3]
Economics and Finance Department,
Birla Institute of Technology and Science Pilani, Jhunjhunu, India

ABSTRACT: The structure of agri-food supply chains (AFSCs) is getting increasingly complicated and therefore, more susceptible to various risks. Therefore, the associated risks with AFSCs must be efficiently managed to improve supply chain performance. In order to understand the risk propagation in the AFSC, a framework based on the identified risk factors is proposed in the current study. Risk assessment studies through the model to predict the impact of risk factors on supply chain performance are limited in previous studies. The goal of the present study is the risk factors identification to create a tool for assessing and determining the risk exposure to AFSC in India. The risk factors are identified through expert interviews and literature reviews. The proposed risk network illustrates the basic framework of associated risk factors in AFSC in India. The supply chain executives can anticipate the likelihood of any potentially disruptive risk factors in AFSC with suggested framework.

KEYWORDS: Supply chain, Agri-food, Bayesian network, Risk identification, Risk propagation

*Corresponding Author: srikanta@pilani.bits-pilani.ac.in
[1]p20210050@pilani.bits-pilani.ac.in, [2]shailendersingh35@gmail.com, [3]krishna@pilani.bits-pilani.ac.in

DOI: 10.4324/9781003415725-60

1. Introduction

Food waste has a variety of causes around the world. The major determinants of these losses are ineffective harvesting, poor storage facilities, along with low quality packaging and manufacturing processes. In developing nations, it is conceivable to state that food waste occurs at or close to the farm level. This substantial variation in loss is due to the fact that a significant portion of food spoils before being consumed or is discarded due to its appearance and flavour. Hence, it might be claimed that developed nations experience food waste nearer to consumers (Beretta et al. 2013). The supply chain can be effective resource and efficient strategy to improve food security (George and McKay 2019), sustainably, fight hunger, reduce the amount of agricultural land needed for production, rural development, and make farmers financially strong by minimising post harvesting losses (Hodges, Buzby, and Bennett 2011). Considering the significance of minimizing post-harvest losses in improving food security, it is crucial to restructure the existing supply chain, particularly in developing country such as India. The AFSC is the process of producing and delivering agricultural goods in a series of processes from production to consumption. A diversified and extensive range of issue in foods not only generate anxiety in the public, but also constitute a severe threat to the existence and development of all food supply chain enterprises. The risk factors that trigger food supply chain problems are often unknown in compared to the broader supply chain. These instances serve as a helpful reminder to organisations about the need of risk management in the food supply chain. In order to address risk in the supply chain, the current study develops models for identifying and evaluating supply chain risks in the food industry. It provides a theoretical framework for managing risks and making decisions. The present study attempted to set the groundwork for risk analysis in agri-food supply networks using BN and to minimize them.

2. Literature Review

Farmers are facing issues such as financial shortages, insufficient raw materials and information exchange. Farmers are also burdened with other issues such as post-harvesting losses, seasonal uncertainty and uncertain land policies, pricing, lack of bargaining power, and physical infrastructure (Gardas et al. 2019). Climate changes, such as below-average rainfall, extreme weather patterns, insects and crop diseases, all have an impact on agricultural production. One the challenging issues for managers dealing with AFSC is predicting, raising awareness for analysing, monitoring, and reducing risks. According to (Ho et al. 2015), Supply chain risk is the probability of unexpected occurrence that have a negative impact on supply chain performance. (Lavastre, Gunasekaran, and Spalanzani 2012), define supply chain risk management as a methodology to identify, comprehend, and evaluate supply chain risk with the goal of reducing it. It is critical to understand the sources of these risks, as well as the techniques to control them. The highly unstructured architecture of Indian agriculture, in particular, makes data collection extremely difficult for researchers and policymakers. As a result, implementing data-driven decision about how to improve the overall supply chain process in the agri-food industry has become extremely challenging. According to (Dani and Deep 2010), variations and mismatches in demand and supply create food supply chain risks. The studies covering BN application in supply chain risk domain exists in the literature significantly. However, these BN-based models in the literature for supply chain covers the manufacturing business, which differs from the agri-food industry in significant manner. Therefore in the current study risk factors are identified that may have an effect on the AFSC and framework to quantify the identified risk factors.

3. Research Methodology

The current study seeks a baseline to analyse the different risks of AFSC. A detailed literature review was carried out to develop the questionnaire for conducting interviews with experts, academicians and supply chain managers to identify risks factors associated with AFSC. The data were collected from experts, academicians, supply chain managers. The risk factors for AFSC are mentioned and detailed in Table 60.1. These risks are interconnected. To create the risk propagation's BN structure, expert opinion and collected data were converted into probabilities and conditional statements.

Table 60.1 Proposed model's node details for BN

Nodes	Description	Reference
Seasonal uncertainty	Production and plan of product changed on a certain seasonal trend	(Osadchiy, Gaur, and Seshadri 2016) (Shi and Wang 2022)
Supply variation	Delays, bottlenecking, changes in product demand and costs.	(Bandaly, Satir, and Shanker 2016; Osadchiy, Gaur, and Seshadri 2016)
Poor raw material quality	Variability in the quality of raw material	(Suryaningrat 2016)
Low yield	Yield uncertainty due to uncontrollable weather factors	(Behzadi et al. 2017; Shi and Wang 2022)
High manufacturing cost	Increase in the cost of production	(Heckmann et al., 2015)
Machine breakdown	Equipment breakdown, production stops, shipment of product delays	(Hosseini and Ivanov 2020; Pournader, Kach, and Talluri 2020)
Unmet demand	When product perceived as ineffective at meeting consumers' needs.	(Behzadi et al. 2017; Heckmann, Comes, and Nickel 2015)
Low product price	Price of product falls down	(Behzadi et al. 2018; Xie et al. 2011)
Delay in delivery of goods	Delivery delays caused by upstream can spread to downstream supply chain, raising customer value risk and operational risk.	(Cao, Bryceson, and Hine 2019)
Payment delay	Payment gets delayed	(Majumdar, Shaw, and Sinha 2020)
Capital return delay	Delay in the total return of capital including profit	(Höhler and Lansink 2020)
High transportation cost	Increase in the cost of transportation	(Raut and Gardas 2018)
Customers disappointment	Suppliers provided all available stock to preferred customers and left others empty handed	(Craighead, Ketchen, and Darby 2020)
Customer switches to rival	Customers move to the other competitor for purchasing	(Craighead, Ketchen, and Darby 2020; Er Kara, Oktay Fırat, and Ghadge 2020)

Source: Author's compilation

4. Results and Discussion

The measured risks rely on the collected data from industrial experts and supply chain managers. The prior probability of each risk event is determine by the value of risk measured. Whenever the parent node and child node are combined, this is referred to be a scenario. Supply chain managers can use BN to understand supply chain risk factors and analyse how those factors affect business profitability. Figure 60.1 shows the BN model, nodes such as seasonal uncertainty and delays in delivery of goods are parent nodes, while others are child nodes.

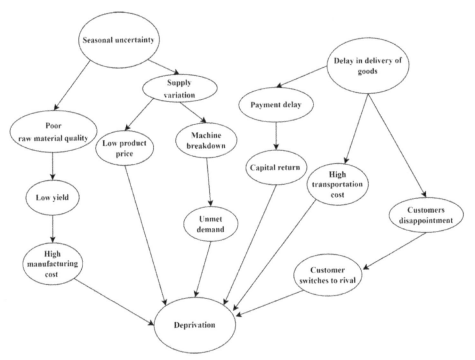

Fig. 60.1 BN risk model for AFSC

Source: Author's compilation

As shown in Fig. 60.1, the major parent nodes, such as seasonal uncertainty and delivery date of goods, are the root cause of risk propagation in the AFSC. Risk further propagates via risk factors such as poor raw material quality and supply chain variation from the seasonal uncertainty parent node. These risks in AFSC further spread in the form of low yield, high manufacturing costs, low product price, machine breakdown, and unmet demand. Similarly, delivery delays of goods spread through payment delays, capital return delays, high transportation costs, customer disappointment, and customer migration to a competitor.

5. Conclusions and Future Perspectives

Identified risk involving seasonal uncertainty and delivery delay are utilised as parent node to develop and illustrate the model for investigation risk propagation in AFSC. Through their causal relationships, the established BN model generally explains how risks propagate in the AFSC. Hence, the outcome of this study illustrates a clear picture of the associated risk factors in different scenarios of AFSC in India. The current study will be useful to SC policymakers and will aid in reducing the risk of AFSC in India. The present study is generic nature but it can be extended to selected agriculture produce in specific location. The risks mentioned may react differently in various agri-food products, depending on factors like seasonal rotation perishable pace and value reduction in warehousing or during the transportation phase.

6. Acknowledgment

This work is funded by Ministry of Science and Technology, Department of Science and Technology, SEED Division, Government of India, New Delhi and is funded through the project Sanction No: SEED/ASACODER-018/2018(G) dated 25.06.2021 entitled, "Doubling Farm Women's income: Entrepreneurship development through post-harvest processing and technology integration in arid zone".

REFERENCES

1. Bandaly, Dia, Ahmet Satir, and Latha Shanker. 2016. "Impact of Lead Time Variability in Supply Chain Risk Management." *International Journal of Production Economics* 180 (October): 88–100. https://doi.org/10.1016/j.ijpe.2016.07.014.
2. Behzadi, Golnar, Michael Justin O'Sullivan, Tava Lennon Olsen, Frank Scrimgeour, and Abraham Zhang. 2017. "Robust and Resilient Strategies for Managing Supply Disruptions in an Agribusiness Supply Chain." *International Journal of Production Economics* 191 (September): 207–20. https://doi.org/10.1016/j.ijpe.2017.06.018.
3. Behzadi, Golnar, Michael Justin O'Sullivan, Tava Lennon Olsen, and Abraham Zhang. 2018. "Agribusiness Supply Chain Risk Management: A Review of Quantitative Decision Models." *Omega (United Kingdom)* 79 (September): 21–42. https://doi.org/10.1016/j.omega.2017.07.005.
4. Beretta, Claudio, Franziska Stoessel, Urs Baier, and Stefanie Hellweg. 2013. "Quantifying Food Losses and the Potential for Reduction in Switzerland." *Waste Management* 33 (3): 764–73. https://doi.org/10.1016/j.wasman.2012.11.007.
5. Cao, Shoufeng, Kim Bryceson, and Damian Hine. 2019. "An Ontology-Based Bayesian Network Modelling for Supply Chain Risk Propagation." *Industrial Management and Data Systems* 119 (8): 1691–1711. https://doi.org/10.1108/IMDS-01-2019-0032.
6. Craighead, Christopher W., David J. Ketchen, and Jessica L. Darby. 2020. "Pandemics and Supply Chain Management Research: Toward a Theoretical Toolbox *." *Decision Sciences* 51 (4): 838–66. https://doi.org/10.1111/deci.12468.
7. Dani, Samir, and Aman Deep. 2010. "Fragile Food Supply Chains: Reacting to Risks." *International Journal of Logistics Research and Applications* 13 (5): 395–410. https://doi.org/10.1080/1367556 7.2010.518564.
8. Er Kara, Merve, Seniye Ümit Oktay Fırat, and Abhijeet Ghadge. 2020. "A Data Mining-Based Framework for Supply Chain Risk Management." *Computers & Industrial Engineering* 139 (January): 105570. https://doi.org/10.1016/j.cie.2018.12.017.

9. Gardas, Bhaskar B., Rakesh D. Raut, Naoufel Cheikhrouhou, and Balkrishna E. Narkhede. 2019. "A Hybrid Decision Support System for Analyzing Challenges of the Agricultural Supply Chain." *Sustainable Production and Consumption* 18 (April): 19–32. https://doi.org/10.1016/j. spc.2018.11.007.

10. George, Neetu Abey, and Fiona H. McKay. 2019. "The Public Distribution System and Food Security in India." *International Journal of Environmental Research and Public Health* 16 (17). https://doi.org/10.3390/ijerph16173221.

11. Heckmann, Iris, Tina Comes, and Stefan Nickel. 2015. "A Critical Review on Supply Chain Risk - Definition, Measure and Modeling." *Omega (United Kingdom)* 52 (April): 119–32. https://doi. org/10.1016/j.omega.2014.10.004.

12. Ho, William, Tian Zheng, Hakan Yildiz, and Srinivas Talluri. 2015. "Supply Chain Risk Management: A Literature Review." *International Journal of Production Research* 53 (16): 5031–69. https://doi.org/10.1080/00207543.2015.1030467.

13. Hodges, R. J., J. C. Buzby, and B. Bennett. 2011. "Postharvest Losses and Waste in Developed and Less Developed Countries: Opportunities to Improve Resource Use." *Journal of Agricultural Science* 149 (S1): 37–45. https://doi.org/10.1017/S0021859610000936.

14. Höhler, Julia, and Alfons Oude Lansink. 2020. "Measuring the Impact of COVID-19 on Stock Prices and Profits in the Food Supply Chain." *Agribusiness Wiley*. https://doi.org/10.1002/agr.21678.

15. Hosseini, Seyedmohsen, and Dmitry Ivanov. 2020. "Bayesian Networks for Supply Chain Risk, Resilience and Ripple Effect Analysis: A Literature Review." *Expert Systems with Applications* 161 (December): 113649. https://doi.org/10.1016/j.eswa.2020.113649.

16. Lavastre, Olivier, Angappa Gunasekaran, and Alain Spalanzani. 2012. "Supply Chain Risk Management in French Companies." *Decision Support Systems* 52 (4): 828–38. https://doi. org/10.1016/j.dss.2011.11.017.

17. Majumdar, Abhijit, Mahesh Shaw, and Sanjib Kumar Sinha. 2020. "COVID-19 Debunks the Myth of Socially Sustainable Supply Chain: A Case of the Clothing Industry in South Asian Countries." *Sustainable Production and Consumption* 24 (October): 150–55. https://doi.org/10.1016/j. spc.2020.07.001.

18. Manuj, Ila, and John T. Mentzer. 2008. "Global Supply Chain Risk Management Strategies." *International Journal of Physical Distribution & Logistics Management* 38 (3): 192–223. https:// doi.org/10.1108/09600030810866986.

19. Osadchiy, Nikolay, Vishal Gaur, and Sridhar Seshadri. 2016. "Systematic Risk in Supply Chain Networks." *Management Science* 62 (6): 1755–77. https://doi.org/10.1287/mnsc.2015.2187.

20. Pournader, Mehrdokht, Andrew Kach, and Srinivas (Sri) Talluri. 2020. "A Review of the Existing and Emerging Topics in the Supply Chain Risk Management Literature." *Decision Sciences* 51 (4): 867–919. https://doi.org/10.1111/deci.12470.

21. Raut, Rakesh, and Bhaskar B. Gardas. 2018. "Sustainable Logistics Barriers of Fruits and Vegetables: An Interpretive Structural Modeling Approach." *Benchmarking* 25 (8): 2589–2610. https://doi.org/10.1108/BIJ-07-2017-0166.

22. Shi, Yan, and Fulin Wang. 2022. "Agricultural Supply Chain Coordination under Weather-Related Uncertain Yield." *Sustainability* 14 (9): 5271. https://doi.org/10.3390/su14095271.

23. Suryaningrat, Ida Bagus. 2016. "Raw Material Procurement on Agroindustrial Supply Chain Management: A Case Survey of Fruit Processing Industries in Indonesia." *Agriculture and Agricultural Science Procedia* 9: 253–57. https://doi.org/10.1016/j.aaspro.2016.02.143.

24. Xie, Gang, Wuyi Yue, Shouyang Wang, and Kin Keung Lai. 2011. "Quality Investment and Price Decision in a Risk-Averse Supply Chain." *European Journal of Operational Research* 214 (2): 403–10. https://doi.org/10.1016/j.ejor.2011.04.036.

Handbook of Evidence Based Management Practices in Business – Satyendra Kumar Sharma et al. (eds)
© 2023 Taylor & Francis Group, London, ISBN 978-1-032-54216-4

Chapter

Impact of External Risk Factors on Indian Road Construction Supply Chain Performance

Anubhav Tiwari[1], Prasanta K. Sahu[2]
Civil Engineering Department,
Birla Institute of Technology and Science Pilani, Hyderabad, Telangana, India

Shailender Singh[3]
Institute of Business Management,
GLA University, Mathura, India

Srikanta Routroy*
Mechanical Engineering Department,
Birla Institute of Technology and Science Pilani, Jhunjhunu, India

ABSTRACT: Integration of supply chains is one of the most important parameters in managing a road construction project. While the concept of 'supply chain' has been around for some time, its specific applications in large projects such as road construction projects are still not well-understood. Although few studies have been carried out on the construction supply chain in India, it is at a nascent stage for Indian road projects. A significant amount of research needs to be carried out in the construction supply chain in India and for road projects along with enablers, impediments, and risks in specific. The sample survey questionnaire for the identification of risks in the construction supply chain for Indian road projects related to various identified potential areas is developed based on a literature review and information collected during focused group discussions with different stakeholders such as suppliers, Government officials, concessionaire, consultants, contractors, and users. Ten risks were identified via a literature review and discussion with fifty experts in the Indian Road Construction Industry. As per the opinion of industry experts and twenty-two years of experience of the author, these risks are further divided into two types, internal risk, and external risk. The objective of this study is to understand the impact of external risk on the performance of construction supply chain management for Indian road projects.

KEYWORDS: Road construction, Supply-chain management, Construction risk, Focus group

*Corresponding Author: srikanta@pilani.bits-pilani.ac.in
[1]p20210050@pilani.bits-pilani.ac.in, [2]krishna@pilani.bits-pilani.ac.in, [3]shailendersingh35@gmail.com

DOI: 10.4324/9781003415725-61

1. Introduction

The Indian road construction industry is a highly complex, interdisciplinary, and dispersed enterprise. Depending on the nature of the job and the scope, each road project has its' own unique characteristics. Therefore, the performance of a road construction project is heavily dependent on effective communication, teamwork, and the integration of numerous departments and skillset (Gustavsson et al. 2012). It is believed that there is a lack of communication and coordination between the organizations involved in India's road construction projects. The conventional supply chain flow for road building contains the delivery of supplies, skilled & semi-skilled labor, plant & machinery, and specialized agencies. For a very long time, this flow of the Indian road construction process has not changed significantly (Client, Investor, Consultant, Designer, Developer, and Subcontractor) (Michalski 2019). The lead author reported that the Indian Construction Industry has received limited exposure to the Road Construction Supply Chain (RCSC) considering his experience in various parts and projects for nearly two decades. Despite the fact that there are some connections between procedures, road construction projects are always unique and contain numerous sources of risk. Road Construction projects are typically intricate and dynamic, with various reaction processes. A multitude of stakeholders, including individuals, groups of individuals, and companies or groups of companies, are actively involved in a road construction project and may be positively or negatively affected by its success. Numerous construction projects entail numerous significant hazards that significantly affect project cost, duration, and work quality. It is acknowledged that risk management is essential for key project stakeholders such as clients, consultants, developers, subcontractors, and suppliers of materials, manpower, and machinery in order to minimize their negative influences on road construction project performance in terms of cost, duration, and quality objectives. Traditionally, practitioners have associated the success of a highway project with these three factors: time, money, and quality (Bankvall et al. 2010). Throughout the several phases of a highway project, from its inception to its completion, there are significant risks involved. It is essential, when searching for alternatives, to minimize the project's cost while preserving the product's excellent quality. As the time, performance, perfection, and cost of a road construction project are influenced by risk (Perera et al., 2009), risk assessment and management are central for mitigating construction hazards. Consequently, the purpose of this research is to investigate the impact of external risk variables on the Indian RCSC. Although few theoretical studies based on interaction or interviews with concerned experts have been documented for the use of RCSC, a substantial amount of research is required for the use of RCSC in India, particularly for high-volume projects such as highway projects along with enablers, impediments, and risks.

2. Literature Review

The construction sector comprises a variety of professionals and trades that have a significant impact on the global economy (Gosling et al. 2012). The amount and forms of residential, commercial, industrial, and heavy construction throughout the world are extremely diverse, especially in technologically advanced nations. Regardless of the type of Construction

Company in this industry, they are increasingly presented with a market that expects the timely and cost-effective completion of projects (Magalhaes et al. 2012). In the construction industry, the most common approach for supply chain management (SCM) and integration of supply chains is to examine each separate project and consider what is required for that project as one supply chain, i.e., as "the extended enterprise," implying the integration of all "tiers" and the activities and actors involved in the project. Construction businesses have recognized supply chain management as a means to minimize costs, improve manufacturing quality, shorten project execution time, and boost scheduling flexibility. Risk is an unavoidable aspect of building projects. As a result, proper risk allocation in construction contracts has risen to prominence, as risk identification and risk allocation have a direct impact on risk management decisions. Road construction projects are exposed to numerous risk sources and are categorized as Technical & Contractual risks (e.g., insufficiency of the preliminary bill, changes imposed by the engineer, defective design, late handing over of the site, tentative drawing and scope change), Economical, Financial & Political risks (e.g., delayed payment, reliance on foreign funds, regulations & difficulty in obtaining permits, inflations and legislative changes), and Managerial risks (e.g., incompetence of the project manager (e.g., acts of God, adverse weather conditions & unforeseen site ground conditions). There is no single optimal response to a risk, and diverse risk management strategies should be employed to deal with hazards effectively (Parera et al. 2009). Identification of risks is the first and most important phase in the risk management process. It describes the competitiveness conditions and the elucidation of risk and uncertainty factors, as well as the identification of potential sources of risk and responsibility for uncertainty-related events. There are three kinds of project risks: external (political, economic, social, and weather), project (time, cost, work, construction, and technological), and internal (Resources, Project members, Construction site & Documents, and Information). A risk analysis is an evaluation of risk and uncertainty that identifies the significance of the sources of risk and uncertainty for the project's objectives. Estimating the probability of occurrence and severity of risk impact constitutes risk assessment. Risk management is a five-step process consisting of identification, analysis, evaluation, response, and monitoring. Risk control provides a plan that reduces or eliminates the influence of sources of risk and uncertainty on the deployment of the project.

Effective risk management encourages construction companies to identify and quantify hazards, as well as to adopt risk containment and risk reduction programs. Effective and efficient construction risk management results in cost savings, increased productivity, increased new project success rates, and enhanced decision-making. The construction industry needs to incorporate risk management into its project management. In construction organizations, qualitative methods of risk assessment are utilized more frequently than quantitative approaches. In construction project risk management, hazards can be compared using a matrix that plots risk impact versus likelihood. To assure the building company's risk tolerance and appetite, mitigation solutions are afterward created from the set limits. The framework for building project risk management can be enhanced by combining qualitative and quantitative approaches to risk analysis (Iqbal et al. 2015). Construction projects can be extraordinarily complicated and riddled with unpredictability. Risk and uncertainty can have potentially negative effects on construction projects. In order to successfully deal with uncertainty and unanticipated events and to ensure the success of a project, analysis, and management of risk are the essential components of the project management of construction projects.

3. Study Framework

The outlines of the present study involved two stages. The first stage includes the identification and listing of risks involved in road construction projects based on a literature review and inputs from domain experts. The second stage includes the analysis of data for identification of the impact of risks and finally, results are discussed and concluded. The various phases used in this study are demonstrated in Fig. 61.1.

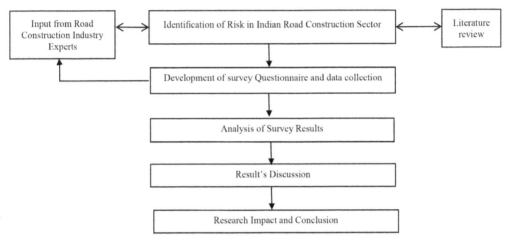

Fig. 61.1 Various phases in the study

Source: Author's compilation

Through a review of the literature and discussions with fifty experts in the Indian Road Construction Industry, ten risks were nominated. These risks are further divided into two clusters, internal risk, and external risk. Internal risks are related to the execution of the project at the site and usually come into the command of the project developers, on the other hand, external risks are influenced by external factors such as political, social, environmental, and legal; these are beyond the control of the project developers (Fang et al. 2004; Wand and Chou 2003; Aleshin 2001). Internal risks are further broken down into five categories, such as technical, site, project cost, supply of resources, and project management risk. Similarly, external risks are further divided into five categories such as contractual or legal, political, social, environmental, and economic risks.

Technical risks are concerned with the technical aspects of the project, such as a lack of details in the drawings, poor design quality, unanticipated changes to the design, a delay in the design process, poor workmanship, a change in the way the project is built, a need to finish the project quickly, etc. The risks associated with a construction project site are called "site conditions risks." These include things like unanticipated site conditions, a lack of supporting infrastructure, an insufficient site investigation, unexpected underground utilities, delay in getting land for right of way, and a bad choice of site location. Cost-related risks are those that cause the cost of a project to change, such as when the price of a material goes up, when an error needs to be fixed, when the scope of the project is reduced, or when a skilled worker leaves the project. Resource-related risks are those that have to do with the supply of people, materials, plants, and equipment. For example, there may not be enough aggregate, cement, steel, and bitumen, there may be a delay in the supply of resources, there may be a delay in the acquisition of resources, there may not be enough good subcontractors, and the failure of a subcontractor could have serious consequences. Management risks are risks that come from a lack of experience on the part of the management team, bad or insufficient project planning, a bad organization structure, bad quality assurance, and quality control, bad coordination and communication between stakeholders, etc. Legal risks come from a contract that isn't clear, a change in the project's scope, the possibility of a claim, a change in codes and regulations, and too many variations in the contract. The political risks are caused by changes in the government, changes in government laws and rules, political instability, and delays in project approvals. The term "social risk" refers to problems with obtaining land and paying compensation for it, public opposition to the project, and social and spiritual differences. The environmental risks are caused by things like "acts of God," pollution caused by construction, and not being able to get environmental approval for the project. The biggest economic and financial risks come from unanticipated changes in the inflation rate, problems with project funding, unanticipated changes in bank loan interest rates, late payments, changes in tax laws, and a bad economy in the country. A detailed survey has been carried out to quantify the impact of the above-identified risk on the Indian road construction project.

4. Development of Survey Questionnaire and Data Collection

Generally, the study methodology largely depends on the survey questionnaire and the way the questionnaire is designed. The survey questionnaire in this study was distributed in two parts. The first part consists of general information such as the name of the respondent, type of company, relevant years of experience, designation and value of project-bond, etc. The second part contains the construction risk factors for evaluation of the risk assessment. The questionnaire was tested with a pilot survey for clarity, ease of use, and value of information that can be collected (Jayasudha et al., 2014). The questionnaire for the pilot study was developed after reviewing the literature in the field of construction risk with freehand to ask extra questions related to the issues that come during the process of data collection. Based on the preliminary survey, 15 risk variables were listed. The questionnaire-based survey served as the primary data collection method. Following discussions with knowledgeable specialists in the Indian highway construction area, the questionnaire was designed in accordance with local requirements. Respondents were requested to indicate the significance of these risks using the Likert Scale (1–5), with "1" representing "very low", 2 representing "low", 3 representing "moderate", 4 representing "high", and 5 "very high" influence (Nerija et al., 2012).

5. Results and Discussion

The research was conducted utilizing an information-based approach of sample selection and focuses on highway building projects in various sorts of construction companies. Public and private Indian construction companies having a minimum yearly revenue of one billion rupees were included in the study. The study imposes severe requirements on the required yearly revenue and minimum years of industry experience in order to ensure that the sample dataset includes only the most important and sustainably minded, rapidly expanding enterprises. Smaller organizations and start-ups that do not yet execute sufficient project value or have insufficient construction project experience in the competitive Indian market are not included in the study sample. This is due to the fact that corporations will prioritize getting construction contracts and completing projects in order to preserve their survival rather than pursuing sustainable procurement procedures. The selection of the 45 Indian construction firms satisfies the aforementioned criteria and ensures that only the most successful and rapidly expanding firms with sustainable procurement practices are recognized. Domain experts and key decision-makers have been identified for each of the 45 companies. Then, the survey questionnaire was distributed to each domain expert from the sample firms.

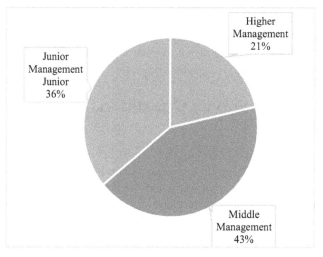

Fig. 61.2 Response classification on the basis of management level

Source: Author's compilation

Figure 61.2 reveals that 21% of respondents are from Higher Management (i.e., Directors, CEO, CFO, Sr VP, etc.), 43% of respondents are from Middle Management (i.e., AGM, DGM, CPM GM & AVP, VP, etc.), and 36% of respondents are from Junior Management (i.e., SPM, PM, DM and below). This graph indicates that the majority of the respondents are from Middle Management.

Figure 61.3 reveals that 13% of respondents are Clients, 10% of respondents are concessionaires, 24% of respondents are consultants, 50% of respondents are contractors and 3% of respondents are Academics so the majority of the respondents are contractors.

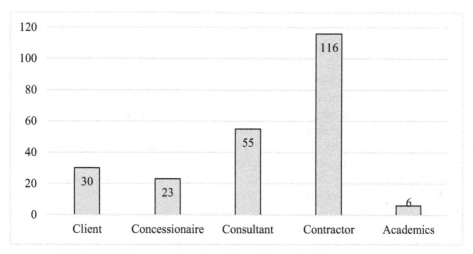

Fig. 61.3 Response classification on the basis of type of industries

Source: Author's compilation

Table 61.1 Response classification on the basis of financial capacity

S No	Capacity	Number	%
1	Small Scale	79	34%
2	Medium Scale	84	37%
3	Large Scale	67	29%
	Total	**230**	

Source: Author's compilation

Table 61.1 reveals that 34% of respondents are from Small Scale Industries (i.e., Annual Turnover is below 500 Cr), 37% of respondents are from Medium Scale Industry (i.e., Annual Turnover is between 500–1000 Cr) and 29% of respondents are from Large Scale Industry (i.e., Annual Turnover is Over 1000 Cr) so the majority of the respondents are from Medium Scale Industry.

Table 61.2 Response classification on the basis of working experience

S No	Range	Number	%
1	1-12 Years	31	13%
2	13-24 Years	116	50%
3	25-36 Years	74	32%
4	36-48 Years	9	4%
	Total	**230**	

Source: Author's compilation

Table 61.2 reveals that 13% of respondents are 1 to 12 years of working experience, 50% of respondents are 13 to 24 years of working experience, 32% of respondents are 25 to 36 years of working experience, and 4% of respondents are 36 to 48 years of working experience so the majority of the respondents are 13-24 years of working experience.

Risk management is the most important in terms of outcome priority, with 81% of respondents believing it has a high to very high impact. The main factors that contribute to technical risk are a lack of experienced project management, poor project planning, a lack of sufficient professionals, an inadequate project organization structure, poor quality assurance, poor coordination and communication among stakeholders, and legal disputes among stakeholders. The second risk is political and social, which 78% of respondents believe will have a high to very high impact. The main factors contributing to political risk are changes in government laws, political instability caused by government delays in project approvals, and policies affecting the project. Other external risks, such as environmental, social, and economic risks, are prioritized by 70% of respondents over internal risks, such as resource cost and site risk. Other external risks, such as environmental, social, and economic risks, are also prioritized by 70% of respondents. Other internal risks, such as resource, cost, and site-related risks, are weighted later. This demonstrates that cumulative external risk factors are far more important for Indian road projects than internal risk factors.

6. Conclusion

The assessment of risks in a road-building project enables stakeholders to take the necessary measures to mitigate its unintended consequences. Consequently, risk identification and evaluation is a crucial risk management activity. On the basis of this study, it can be concluded that project management risk has a significant impact on the Indian road construction project. Although the contractor is the primary stakeholder in establishing the project's construction milestones, the consultant and client must work with the contractor to ensure the project is completed on time and under budget. This study also concludes that external risks, including political, social, and economic concerns, have a significant effect on the Indian road construction business. External risks pose a significantly greater threat to Indian road construction projects than internal hazards, according to extensive research. It is also observed that the relationship between the road construction project's parties is extremely strained. Diverse parties, including contractors, consultants, subcontractors, and resource suppliers, are keen to engage in discussions to meet the client's specifications. This action by stakeholders increases the possibility that more hazards may materialize. Therefore, to reduce the increased cost impact due to time extension, emphasis should be placed on enhancing relationships between government authorities and other project stakeholders. It is normal to practice delegating the majority of risks to the contractor, while clients assume very few risks directly. This is primarily due to the construction industry's established ethnic principles and weak contractual agreements with the client. Government officials are expected to share risks in a fair and judicious manner. This study is useful for identifying and assessing the hazards in the current Indian road construction business. Stakeholders in Indian road construction may now assess the risks associated with the various phases of the project, which can be analyzed periodically. This study reveals the paper of future work for the correct planning of risk mitigation to lower the cost and length of the Indian road construction project. In the future, both the mitigating measures and the reaction strategy can be investigated in depth.

REFERENCES

1. Ahmed, Syed Mahmood, Salman Azhar, and Irtishad Ahmad. "Supply chain management in construction: Scope, benefits and barriers." *Delhi Business Review* 3.1 (2002): 1–6.
2. Aleshin, Artem. "Risk management of international projects in Russia." *International Journal of Project Management* 19.4 (2001): 207–222.
3. Bankvall, Lars, et al. "Interdependence in supply chains and projects in construction." *Supply chain management: an international journal* (2010).
4. Fang, Dongping, et al. "Risks in Chinese construction Market-Contractors' perspective." *Journal of construction engineering and management* 130.6 (2004): 853–861.
5. Gosling, Jonathan, Mohamed Naim, and Denis Towill. "Identifying and categorizing the sources of uncertainty in construction supply chains." *Journal of Construction Engineering and Management* 139.1 (2013): 102–110.
6. Gustavsson, Tina Karrbom, Olle Samuelson, and Örjan Wikforss. "Organizing it in construction: present state and future challenges in Sweden." *Journal of Information Technology in Construction (ITcon)* 17.33 (2012): 520–534.
7. Jayasudha, K., B. Vidivelli, and ER Gokul Surjith. "Risk assessment and management in construction projects." *International Journal of Scientific & Engineering Research* 5.8 (2014): 387–396.
8. Lee, Namhun, and John E. Schaufelberger. "Risk management strategies for privatized infrastructure projects: Study of the build–operate–transfer approach in East Asia and the Pacific." *Journal of management in engineering* 30.3 (2014): 05014001.
9. Magalhães-Mendes, J. O. R. G. E., MARIA FERNANDA Rodrigues, and L. M. Ferreira. "Construction supply chain management: a Portuguese Case Study." *Proceedings of the 3rd European Conference of Civil Engineering Recent Advances in Engineering, Paris, France.* 2012.
10. Manu, Emmanuel. "Supply chain management practices in construction and inter-organisational trust dynamics." (2014).
11. Marques, Rui Cunha, and Sanford V. Berg. "Risks, contracts and private sector participation in infrastructure." *Journal of construction engineering and management* 137.11 (2011).
12. Michalski, Paweł. "The Application of the Concept of Supply Chain Management in the Construction Industry." *Logistics and Transport* 1.41 (2019).
13. Nerija, B., and A. Banaitis. "Risk Management in Construction Projects, Risk Management Current Issues and Challenges." *ISBN* (2012): 978–953.
14. Nielsen, Kris R. "Risk management: Lessons from six continents." Pipeline Engineering and Construction: What's on the Horizon? 2004. 1–10.
15. Okate, Anmol, and Vijay Kakade. "Risk management in road construction projects: high volume roads." *Proceedings of Sustainable Infrastructure Development & Management (SIDM)* (2019).
16. Perera, B. A. K. S., Indika Dhanasinghe, and Raufdeen Rameezdeen. "Risk management in road construction: the case of Sri Lanka." *International Journal of Strategic Property Management* 13.2 (2009): 87–102.
17. Wang, Ming-Teh, and Hui-Yu Chou. "Risk allocation and risk handling of highway projects in Taiwan." *Journal of management in Engineering* 19.2 (2003): 60–68.
18. Zavadskas, Edmundas Kazimieras, Zenonas Turskis, and Jolanta Tamošaitiene. "Risk assessment of construction projects." *Journal of civil engineering and management* 16.1 (2010): 33–46.
19. Zoysa, Sanjaya De, and Alan D. Russell. "Knowledge-based risk identification in infrastructure projects." *Canadian Journal of Civil Engineering* 30.3 (2003): 511–522.

Handbook of Evidence Based Management Practices in Business – Satyendra Kumar Sharma et al. (eds)
© 2023 Taylor & Francis Group, London, ISBN 978-1-032-54216-4

Chapter

Analysis of Impetus for Formal E-Waste Management System in India

Varun Kumar[1], Om Ji Shukla[2]
Department of Mechanical Engineering,
National Institute of Technology, Patna, India

Saurabh Tripathi[3]
Department of Mechanical Engineering,
Rajkiya Engineering College Banda, India

ABSTRACT: Low efficient management of e-waste in developing countries, despite consistent increments in recycling centres, legislation framework and organizing systems, become a point of concern. It is high time to identify the causes and the contributing factors that can improve the performance. The study consists of the identification of impetuses as driving factors for the formal E-waste management system in developing countries. An ISM (MCDM) approach is applied to the eight impetus which is identified by literature survey and expert opinion. The final model is fabricated in which the impetuses are designed in hierarchy form as per their rank secured by the ISM method and later the model is validated using MICMAC analysis. The result shows that the impetuses "Incentives for depositors," "E-waste generation and collection monitoring," and "Integration of informal sector to formal sector" are found to be dependent impetus with low driving power. Factors "Technical and infrastructure support" and "Training and empowerment for formal recyclers employees" are the factors having strong driving power with low dependency on another factor. The research has the potential to help e-waste collection policymakers and efficient e-waste management systems in a developing nation.

KEYWORDS: E-waste, ISM, Impetus, MICMAC

1. Introduction

As people and civilizations advance, so do the extent and breadth of their resource consumption and asset use. Industrial activities have compounded the difficulties of waste management,

[1]varunk.ph21.me@nitp.ac.in, [2]omjishukla.me@nitp.ac.in, [3]tripathi096@gmail.com

DOI: 10.4324/9781003415725-62

ecological balance, and the availability of finite resources. With the middle of the twentieth century, and particularly since the emergence of contemporary information and communication technologies, the ubiquity and significance of electronic and electrical gadgets in daily life have increased dramatically. Rapid technological progress and ongoing invention have accelerated the pace of obsolescence, resulting in a shorter lifetime for a variety of electrical and electronic devices. As a consequence of its excessive manufacturing, processing, and disposal, e-waste causes problems (Prakash and Barua, 2016). The predicted worldwide buildup of e-waste in 2018 was 50 Mt, up from 44.7 Mt in 2016, and is anticipated to increase by multiples in the next years. Asia generated the greatest electronic trash, 18.2 Mt, among all continents (Garg 2021, 281). The worst aspect is that approximately 15–20% of the entire amount of e-waste produced globally gets processed, documented, and recycled.

In December 2021, India had 468 formal recyclers for e-waste of 1.38 million tonnes of quantity recycling (Sengupta et al., 2022). In April 2022, it increased to 472 authorized recyclers handling 1.42 million tonnes quantity of e-waste (CPCB, 2022). This means there is an equal 3% rise in recyclers and the amount of e-waste recycling is increasing yearly, still, the circulation of electrical and electronic equipment production to waste to return to authorized industries and recyclers is not that much efficient. Global monitoring report shows that 95% of e-waste generated globally is handled by informal sectors in various countries, especially in developing countries (Singh et al., 2022). The present Indian informal system is based on poor recovery techniques, which has severe effects on the environment and the long-term survival of the country's animal and plant life (Ilankoon et al., 2018). It is necessary to extract and analyse the key factors which can help developing countries to enhance their efficiency in existing e-waste management systems. The following objectives of this research help to identify and prioritize the key drivers which enhance the performance of existing e-waste management systems in developing countries:

(a) To identify the impetus which affects the existing e-waste management system in developing countries.
(b) To create a model for ranking and analysing the driving and dependence power of factors using Interpretative Structural Modelling (ISM).
(c) Using MICMAC (cross-impact matrix multiplication applied to classification) to validate the fabricated model for removal of any biasness and robustness test of the fabricated model.

The following part of the paper is structured as follows: Section 2 consists of a methodology description of the study. Section 3 includes the implementation of ISM and MICMAC for model formation and validation. The findings of the research are discussed in section 4. In the end, section 5 provides the conclusion of the study along with the limitation and future scope.

2. Methodology

The study aimed to identify the critical success factor (drivers/impetus) which helps to enhance the efficiency of the existing formal e-waste management system in developing countries like India. The material used for the research is the extensive literature review of the past decade with few experts in relevant fields and institute members working in the same domain.

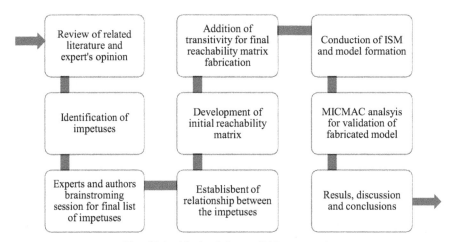

Fig. 62.1 Methodology of this research

Source: Author's compilation

After identification of the impetuses (drivers/critical success factors), ISM was implemented for model fabrication and rank distributed to the factors. A hierarchy was fabricated as per the structure of the model. Later, MICMAC analysis is performed for the reduction in the decision-making process and robustness of the fabricated model. The methodology of this study is mentioned in Fig. 62.1.

Identification of Impetuses—There are eight major impetuses are identified, mentioned in Table 62.1. Initially, more than eight impetuses were identified from the literature survey and expert opinion. The impetus used for the study in this research was the combination of those identified factors which come under similar sectors e.g., regular updates or regulation of data related to e-waste generation and collection data updates combined into E-waste collection and monitoring.

Table 62.1 Identified Impetuses

Code	Impetus	Description	Reference
I1	Awareness initiatives	Programs raise awareness about the proper disposal of e-waste, its impact on human health, and the recovery of valuable elements.	(Singh et al., 2022)
I2	Incentive for depositors	The government-provided financial incentive for e-waste depositors to deposit e-waste at formal collecting points and facilities.	Expert opinion
I3	E-waste generation and collection monitoring	Regular updates facilitate the adoption of a flexible formal e-waste management system.	(Kashyap et al., 2022)
I4	Integration of informal sector into formal sector	To overcome the inadequate amount of supply of e-waste to formal recyclers.	Expert opinion
I5	Stakeholders Responsibility	To ensure and clarify the responsibility of each actor and organization of the e-waste supply chain.	(Shukla et al., 2019)

Code	Impetus	Description	Reference
I6	Technical and infrastructure support	To provide a secure environment and smart infrastructure for the recycling of e-waste.	(Jangre et al., 2022)
I7	Legal and regulatory framework	To provide a legal and government obligation framework for the development of a streamlined e-waste management system.	(Prakash and Barua, 2016)
I8	Training and empowerment for formal recyclers employees	To create an appropriate foundation for a structured staff training programme at a recycling facility.	(Ramzan et al., 2019)

Source: Author's compilation

3. ISM Implementation

The model formed by using the ISM, an MCDM technique contains various steps. This section includes all those steps with a detailed description. After the identification of the drivers for the study where a scale was used to full fill the relation among the impetus is, mentioned in Table 62.2.

Table 62.2 Symbols with their meaning

S. No.	Symbol	Meaning
1.	K	Factor c helps to achieve d but not vice versa.
2.	L	Both factors (c & d) help each other to achieve.
3.	M	Factor d helps to achieve c but not vice versa.
4.	N	There is no relation between both (c & d) factors.

*c (vertical) and *d (horizontal) are the impetus mentioned in SSIM (Table 62.3)
Source: Author's compilation

Formation of structural self-interaction matrix (SSIM)—The interrelation between the impetuses is used to formulate the SSI matrix. The brainstorming session between experts and authors helps to generate the matrix in K, L, M, and N form, shown in Table 62.3.

Table 62.3 Structural self-interaction matrix (SSIM)

Impetus	I1	I2	I3	I4	I5	I6	I7	I8
I1	L	K	K	K	L	N	L	K
I2		L	N	L	N	N	M	N
I3			L	K	N	M	M	N
I4				L	N	M	M	N
I5					L	N	L	L
I6						L	K	M
I7							L	N
I8								L

Source: Author's compilation

Table 62.4 The rule for replacement of symbol to numeric form

S. No.	Symbol in SSIM	Value for RM for (c, d)	Value for RM for (d, c)
1.	K	1	0
2.	L	1	1
3.	M	0	1
4.	N	0	0

Source: Author's compilation

By using the replacement rule mentioned in Table 62.4. The initial reachability matrix is formed, shown in Table 62.5. Transitivity provides a mutual relation between the criteria under the MCDM technique.

Table 62.5 Initial reachability matrix

Impetus	I1	I2	I3	I4	I5	I6	I7	I8
I1	1	1	1	1	1	0	1	1
I2	0	1	0	1	0	0	0	0
I3	0	0	1	1	0	0	0	0
I4	0	1	0	1	0	0	0	0
I5	1	0	0	0	1	0	1	1
I6	0	0	1	1	0	1	1	0
I7	1	1	1	1	1	0	1	0
I8	0	0	0	0	1	1	0	1

Source: Author's compilation

Table 62.6 Final reachability matrix

Impetus	I1	I2	I3	I4	I5	I6	I7	I8	Driving Power
I1	1	1	1	1	1	1*	1	1	8
I2	0	1	0	1	0	0	0	0	2
I3	0	1*	1	1	0	0	0	0	3
I4	0	1	0	1	0	0	0	0	2
I5	1	1*	1*	1*	1	1*	1	1	8
I6	1*	1*	1	1	1*	1	1	0	7
I7	1	1	1	1	1	0	1	1*	7
I8	1*	0	1*	1*	1	1	1*	1	7
Dependence Power	5	7	6	8	5	4	5	4	

Source: Author's compilation

Here, if impetus A affects another impetus B, also impetus B affects C then A affects C too. The addition of transitivity to the initial reachability matrix by 1* representation, is mentioned in "Table 62.6". The matrix also consists of driving power and dependence power by the addition of all values of rows and columns of each impetus which support further analysis of the research.

Level distribution to Impetus The level partition provides an idea about the driving and dependence factors with their progressive stage or position. the level partition of this research is distributed total in five levels, mentioned in Table 62.7. The factor having a similar set of impetus with reachability and intersection set is considered at the top level in the diagraph hierarchy. After ranking the factor, it gets hidden for the further ranking process and the same steps follow till the end. The level partition finally indicates the final ISM model for this study, refer to Fig. 62.2.

Table 62.7 Level partition of impetus

Impetus	Reachability Set	Antecedent Set	Intersection Set	Levels
I1	1,2,3,4,5,6,7,8	1,5,6,7,8	1,5,6,7,8	3
I2	2,4	1,2,3,4,5,6,7	2,4	1
I3	2,3,4	1,3,5,6,7,8	3	2
I4	2,4	1,2,3,4,5,6,7,8	2,4	1
I5	1,2,3,4,5,6,7,8	1,5,6,7,8	1,5,6,7,8	3
I6	1,2,3,4,5,6,7	1,5,6,8	1,5,6	4
I7	1,2,3,4,5,7,8	1,5,6,7,8	1,5,7,8	3
I8	1,3,4,5,6,7,8	1,5,7,8	1,5,7,8	5

Source: Author's compilation

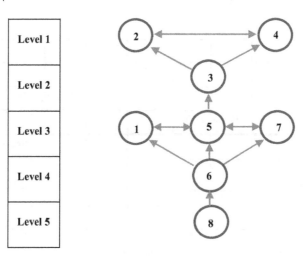

Fig. 62.2 Diagraph for the relationship of impetus

Source: Author's compilation

MICMAC analysis—The analysis used to validate the ISM method and help to examine the robustness of the fabricated model. Driving power and dependence power are identified by the multiplication principle of matrices. The key impetus and mitigation strategy are mainly pointed out using this analysis. The hierarchy model fabricated by the level partition in Fig. 62.3 is validated by the MICMAC analysis region distribution of the impetus, shown in Fig. 62.4.

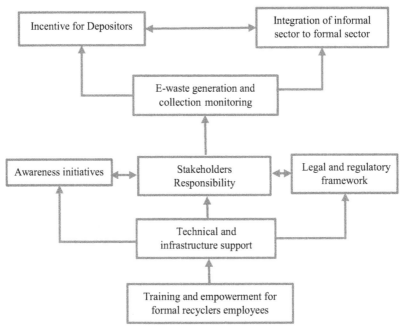

Fig. 62.3 The hierarchical model of impetuses

Source: Author's compilation

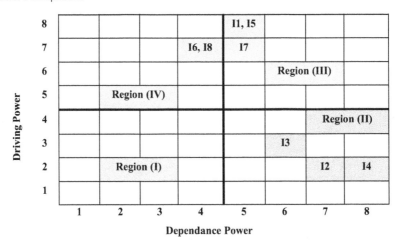

Fig. 62.4 MICMAC analysis (region distribution)

Source: Author's compilation

According to the analysis, the overall region parted into four regions, in which the elements or factors under region 1 indicate the autonomous elements which have less contribution and effect on the system or model, generally disconnected from the model. The strongest and the highly effective region comes under the 3rd region which has strong driving and dependence power. Minor changes in the elements of this region cause disturbance to other factors. For this study, the impetuses I2, I3, and I4 are found dependent on impetus. Another side, I1, I5 & I7 found strong dependence and driving factors of the model. I6 and I8 are the factors having strong driving power and independence.

4. Findings and Discussions

An increase in formal recycling centres and a proper management handling system needs to focus on the factors which enhance their performance and restrict the elements which act as barriers for them. This study focused to identify and create a model with their effective levels so can the existing management system can easily increase their efficiency. For this study, the impetuses I2 (Incentives for depositors), I3 (E-waste generation and collection monitoring), and I4 (Integration of informal sector to formal sector) are found to be dependent impetus with low driving power which mainly depends on other factors to get influenced. Another side, I1 (Awareness initiatives), I5 (Stakeholders' responsibility) & I7 (Legal and regulatory framework) impetuses are found to equal dependence and driving factors of the model. I6 (Technical and infrastructure support) and I8 (Training and empowerment for formal recyclers employees) are the factors having strong driving power with low dependency on another factor. For the validation, The MICMAC analysis shows the exact result as the hierarchy fabricated by the ISM method.

5. Conclusions, Limitations, and Future Scope

Factors in form of drivers and barriers are especially key elements for a supply chain of any management system or industry. It also helps society to maintain sustainability in the environment. This paper has considered an emerging economy or developing country like India as the region for the analysis of the driving factors in the proper E-waste management system. The identified impetuses are further used to fabricate a model for the analysis purpose using an MCDM technique i.e., ISM and validated by MICMAC analysis.

The limited expert and author opinion can be found as a biased perspective on the factors taken for the model formation. The decision can be uncertain in some cases which can be removed by a fuzzy technique like Fuzzy-ISM. Also, more impetus factors can be considered for further investigation into the factors affecting formal e-waste management systems.

There is also various MCDM technique like the Best-Worst method (BWM), TOPSIS, and DEMATEL and for removal of uncertainty, research can be used by researchers using the fuzzy form of these techniques.

REFERENCES

1. Central Pollution Control Board (CPCB), 2022. List of E-Waste Recyclers/Dismantlers. https://cpcb.nic.in/uploads/Projects/E-Waste/List_of_E-waste_Recycler.pdf, (Accessed April 29, 2022).

2. Garg, Chandra Prakash. 2021. "Modeling the e-waste mitigation strategies using Grey-theory and DEMATEL framework." Journal of Cleaner Production, 281, p.124035. https://doi.org/10.1016/j.jclepro.2020.124035

3. Ilankoon, I.M.S.K., Ghorbani, Y., Chong, M.N., Herath, G., Moyo, T. and Petersen, J. (2018). E-waste in the international context–A review of trade flows, regulations, hazards, waste management strategies and technologies for value recovery. Waste Management, 82, 258–275. https://doi.org/10.1016/j.wasman.2018.10.018

4. Jangre, J., Prasad, K., Patel, D. (2022) Analysis of barriers in e-waste management in developing economy: an integrated multiple-criteria decision-making approach. Environmental Science and Pollution Research. 1–15.

5. Kashyap, A, Kumar, C., Kumar, V., & Shukla, O. J. (2022). A DEMATEL model for identifying the impediments to the implementation of circularity in the aluminum industry. Decision Analytics Journal, 100134. https://doi.org/10.1016/j.dajour.2022.100134

6. Kashyap, Abhishek, & Shukla, Om Ji. 2022. "Analysis of critical barriers in the sustainable supply chain of MSMEs: a case of Makhana (Foxnut) industry." Benchmarking: An International Journal.

7. Kumar, A., Gaur, D., Liu, Y. and Sharma, D. (2022). Sustainable waste electrical and electronic equipment management guide in emerging economies context: A structural model approach. Journal of Cleaner Production, 336, p.130391. https://doi.org/10.1016/j.jclepro.2022.130391

8. Prakash, Chandra, and Barua, Mukesh Kumar. 2016. "A multi-criteria decision-making approach for prioritizing reverse logistics adoption barriers under fuzzy environment: Case of Indian electronics industry." Global Business Review 17(5), 1107-1124. https://doi.org/10.1177/0972150916656667

9. Ramzan S, Liu CG, Munir H, Xu Y. (2019). Assessing young consumers' awareness and participation in sustainable e-waste management practices: a survey study in Northwest China. Environmental Science and Pollution Research 26, 20003–20013. https://doi.org/10.1007/s11356-019-05310-y

10. Singh, S., Dasgupta, M. S., Routroy, S. (2022). Analysis of Critical Success Factors to Design E-waste Collection Policy in India: A Fuzzy DEMATEL Approach." Environmental Science and Pollution Research 29, 10585-10604. https://doi.org/10.1007/s11356-021-16129-x

11. Shukla, O.J., Joshi, A., Soni, G. and Kumar, R. (2019). Analysis of critical drivers affecting implementation of agent technology in a manufacturing system. Journal of Industrial Engineering International 15, no. 2, 303-313. https://doi.org/10.1007/s40092-018-0293-3

12. Sengupta, D., Ilankoon, I.M.S.K., Kang, K.D., Chong, M.N. (2022). Circular economy and household e-waste management in India: Integration of formal and informal sectors. Minerals Engineering 184, 1–11. https://doi.org/10.1016/j.mineng.2022.107661

Biography

Varun Kumar is a student in a doctor of philosophy (PhD) in the Department of Mechanical Engineering, National Institute of Technology Patna. His research interests are E-waste management, Rotary ultrasonic machine, and Additive manufacturing.

Dr. Om Ji Shukla is presently an Assistant Professor at the Department of Mechanical Engineering, NIT Patna. He has received his doctorate from MNIT Jaipur and master's from BITS Pilani. During his PhD, he worked in the area of multi-agent-based manufacturing systems that involves real-time production scheduling problems. His research interests are Agent-based modelling, AI in manufacturing, Operations Management, Supply Chain Management, and E-waste management. He is heading the Entrepreneurship Cell at NIT Patna as Professor in Charge. Presently his research team at NIT Patna is working on the Makhana supply chain network design and healthcare supply chain with a focus on vaccines and e-waste management issues.

Mr. Saurabh Tripathi is presently an Assistant Professor at the Department of Mechanical Engineering, Rajkiya Engineering College Banda. His research interests are materials, composites, and operations management.

Chapter

Long Term Business Planning to Mitigate Ill-effects of Natural Calamities

Rajkumar Sharma[1]

Research Scholar, Department of Management, BITS Pilani

Satyendra Kumar Sharma[2]

Associate professor, Department of Management, BITS Pilani

ABSTRACT: Understanding the impact of natural calamities on small scale businesses in big cities. Focusing the study on Mumbai its geographical and economical characteristics were explored. Effort was put into understanding why Mumbai attracts a lot of people in the city which is already overcrowded and faces 4-5 months of extreme rainfall every year which sometimes even leads to flooding. Comparisons were made with other emerging business centres or small cities in India which can be a good option for setting a business. Hence a framework was suggested after analysing the literature and data to make a long-term plan to avoid the uncertainty in business arising from natural calamities. The framework contains some suggestions which can be implemented with the help and coordination from the government incorporating the use of Geospatial data to mitigate losses in a disaster.

KEYWORDS: MSMEs business plan, GIS based disaster management, Business continuity plan, Mumbai's vulnerability

1. Introduction

The US, being a wealthy nation, has invested in measures to assist and lessen the impact of major natural disasters. Its economic strength, strong infrastructure, disaster readiness programs, fast response time and high insurance penetration rates help it revive quickly.

[1]p20210038@pilani.bits-pilani.ac.in, [2]satyendrasharma@pilani.bits-pilani.ac.in

DOI: 10.4324/9781003415725-63

Whereas China, Philippines, India, and Indonesia are emerging economies whose major focus relies on economic development and in its quest for overpowering developed economies it is compromising on the fact that it has limited capacity to withstand the impact of major disasters. This leads to making these countries become most vulnerable to natural disasters.

The short and long-run economic impacts of natural disasters cannot be ignored be it economic growth, development, and poverty reduction. Can't these negative impacts be avoided with in-time disaster preparedness? [17]. So why we are not becoming self-reliant in handling the disasters and minimizing its impacts. Vulnerability is changing quickly in rapidly developing countries. Natural disasters cause significant impact on the economy of the country, it can cause short or term fiscal deficits. In a country like India, whenever a disaster hits, hundreds of crores go into relief and rehabilitation efforts from the government, businesses get shop, people get unemployed and production suffers. Hence, it's not just their people who get affected but it also affects the economy of the country by highly impacting small and medium sized enterprises.

Direct as well as Indirect impacts are devastating on business activities and continuity in those times as these disasters totally disrupt the supply chains, affect procurement of raw materials and laborers. Although it affects all businesses but it is mostly the Micro, Small and Medium Sized Enterprises (MSMEs) that are mostly affected [16]

In India, during 1990- 2017 floods accounted for more than half of climate related disasters in India causing a damage of $54.63 billion [2]. In the coming time there is going to be an increase in the intensity and frequency of natural disasters as a result of global warming and climate change.

2. Literature Review

As per the data of National Institute of Disaster Management (NIDM) Between 1980 to 2010 some major disasters struck India which incurred huge cost to life and property [20]. Figure 63.1 depicts the major disasters and the areas they occurred in.

Table 63.1 summarizes the maximum damage brought to life, fields, property, and food between 1953 to 2004 in India as per (2006-07) data.

What could be the scale of impact of these disasters on MSME businesses would depend on their vulnerability and exposure. The data that the government portrays about loss is basically a lower-bound estimate because of the presence of a large informal economy and the difficulty of monetizing indirect impacts. Various socioeconomic factors also intensify the impacts such as

• Population explosion,

• High rate of urbanization,

• Infrastructure expansion in high-risk zones and

• Larger proportions of people living in informal settlements in poor and destitute conditions [2].

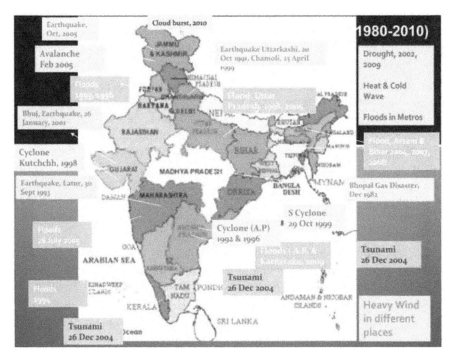

Fig. 63.1 Major disaster between 1980 and 2010 in India [20]

Table 63.1 Maximum damage between 1953 and 2004 in India

Item	Unit	Average during 1953-2004	Max. damage (Year)		Damage during 2004
Area affected	Million hectares	7.63	17.50	(1978)	8.47
Population affected	Million	32.92	70.45	(1978)	34.19
Human lives cost	No.	1,597	11,316	(1977)	1,650
Cropped area affected	Million hectares	3.56	10.15	(1988)	2.92
Value of damaged crops	Rs. billion[a]	7.086	4.26	(2000)	7.55
Value of damaged houses	Rejeski, 1993	2.51	1.308	(1995)	8.707
Value of damaged public utilities	Rs. billion	8.137	56.04	(2001)	22.28
Value of total damage to houses, crops and public utilities	Rs. billion	18.17	88.645	(2000)	38.54

Notes: [a]1 USD ~ 44 Rs (year 2008)
Source: CWC (2006-2007)

These lead to a need to understand the long-term impact of these natural disasters on businesses and hence plan accordingly to minimize costs.

The impacts on small businesses can be broadly classified as-

1. Damage to physical structure (production/operation plant, doors, windows, roof, flooring, and physical structure)
2. Damage to operating equipment (electrical and communication systems, air conditioning)

3. Damage to material (inventory, raw materials, finished products)
4. Disruptions of Supply Chain
5. Loss of Personnel
6. Loss of clientele [2]

Immediate costs to disaster-

1. Cleaning their premises
2. Restarting operations
3. Temporarily moving production elsewhere [2]

2.1 Mumbai—The Dream City and Financial Capital of India

We will concentrate our study on Mumbai, a city which turns dreams into reality. The dream city Mumbai extends between $18.00°–19.20°N$ and $72.00°–73.00°E$ with a total area of 437.79 km^2 which accommodates an average population density of $27209/\text{km}^2$ as per the Government of Maharashtra 2006. There are two revenue districts in the city – Mumbai City district (67.79 km^2) and Mumbai suburban district (370 km^2) from 9.93 million in 1991 to 11.91 million in 2001 [3]. But the city officials estimate that there is a floating population of an additional 2-3 million that also resides in Mumbai [18]. Its geographical location makes it vulnerable towards various natural and human-induced hazards, including floods, cyclones, earthquakes, landslides, fires, and industrial and chemical accidents. Rains are something that happen heavily every year for around 4-5 months mostly leading to floods. Initially Mumbai consisted of a cluster of seven islands but as the population pressure increased many areas were reclaimed from sea to meet the demand of space. This all has led to increased vulnerability of Mumbai towards floods. The most devastating floods hit Mumbai on 26 July 2005, when it received 944 mm of rainfall measured in 24 hrs along with a simultaneous high tide of 4.48 m; that claimed around 500 lives [3]. In order to accommodate its inhabitants that are increasing at an exponential rate, it is also expanding at an exponential rate in terms of infrastructure and urbanization [3].

3. Methodology

The study adopts a qualitative approach combined with study of available quantitative data to derive insights and capture root causes of problems. The primary source of data for this research was obtained from literature review and informal interviews with various households and small-scale business owners residing in low lying areas of Mumbai. Contextual Enquiry was done to empathize with end users who regularly face the problems arising from heavy rains in Mumbai every year. Justification of selection of Mumbai for the research is primarily its role in economic contribution in GDP of India, its geographical location, it being the first choice of every Indian who wants to achieve big in their life. This research collated the statements and opinions of various researchers and geologists who have conducted research on Mumbai and have derived certain quantitative results using GIS [13].

3.1 Vulnerability of Mumbai

Induced hazards like sea-level rise, storm surge, flooding and coastal erosion make the city vulnerable and the vulnerability proportion is almost 24%. These regions include frequently flooded inland coastal areas, built up, barren, forest, vegetation, and mangrove regions. This city also has the maximum population density in the world exposed to disasters and there are unaccounted groups of floating population that keep flooding the city hence risking its vulnerability. Mumbai city, the financial capital of India, was just seven isolated islets as Isle of Bombay, Mahim, Colaba, Parel, Mazagon, Worli, and Little Colaba. A single land mass was created by merging these islets by reclaiming land mass from the sea. Fig. 63.2 provides the geographical map of the Mumbai region also highlighting the areas affected by flood on 26 July 2005 [19].

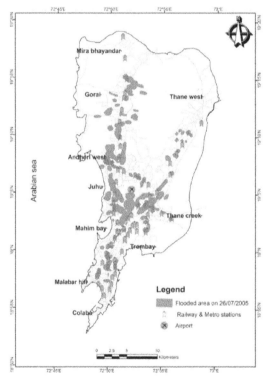

Fig. 63.2 Geographical map of Mumbai highlighting the impact of 2005 Floods

Source: EIS India [19]

As per the Canadian research the city may experience acute water shortage if the current predicted rate of the annual precipitation decreases by 2%. Flooding along coastal and low-lying areas would increase dramatically endangering the slums located there [10].

3.2 Damage Due to Disasters

In 2005, a lot of damage was reported to electrical appliances, wirings, water pipes and household structure and vehicles.

In a city like Mumbai where floods are a recurring phenomenon, they face problems because of-

* Disrupted transportation,
* Power supply failure,
* Food, drinking water and other supplies get scarce.
* Also fuel availability and storage get scarce [11].

Hence, it can be said that extreme rainfalls sometimes leading to floods bring a grave damage to households in monetary terms whereas recurrent floods cause recurrent problems of inconvenience and survival issues [8][9].

Loss of Workdays: Workers lose their effective work days every year depending on the scale of rainfall during monsoons. The reason being unavailability of transport services, water logging on roads and danger to life in walking on those potholes covered roads [15].

Health and well-being: Perhaps we already know that water logged areas are a home to mosquitos and other water borne diseases. Conditions of government health centres are already bad and they get worsened during floods [15].

The need of the hour is forming a result oriented preventive response plan in coordination with government officials, fire stations, engineers, architects, and others which can lead to a better future where we not be worried about devastating impact of natural disasters.

3.3 MSMEs in India

MSMEs can be best defined by Figure 63.3 which states the definitions as per the provisions of Micro Small & Medium Enterprises Development (MSMED) Act,2006. In India, the MSME sector provides the maximum employment after agriculture and offers an unprecedented growth opportunity. Despite this fact, this sector is excluded from the nation's institutional and policy framework of disaster management as well as recovery plans. In the event of disasters, institutional funding towards emergency assistance to enterprises is clubbed under general livelihood support measures, with little thought for specific considerations that affect MSME recovery [6]. Further, more than 90 percent of micro firms in India exist in the informal economy. They must rely on their ingenuity to adapt and carry on (even in the formalized MSME sector, insurance penetration rests at 1 percent)

According to the latest Census of 2011, the registered **MSME sector has an estimated 1.56 million enterprises (45.23 percent of 4 them in rural areas), of which 94.94 percent are micro businesses (67 percent in manufacturing and 32.9 in services)** [7]. The labour to capital ratio and overall growth in the MSME sector is far greater than in large 5 industries. These figures pale in comparison to the number of informal enterprises and their workforce. **More than 94 percent of Indian MSMEs fall in the informal or unorganized 7 sector**. According to the National Commission for Enterprises in the Unorganized Sector, which describes an unorganized sector enterprise as employing less than 10 workers, there were 58 million informal enterprises in India in 2006-2007 with a workforce of 104 million.

Manufacturing Sector	
Enterprise Category	**Investment in plant & machinery**
Micro Enterprises	Does not exceed twenty five lakh rupees
Small Enterprises	More than twenty five lakh rupees but does not exceed five crore rupees
Medium Enterprises	More than five crore rupees but does not exceed ten crore rupees
Service Sector	
Enterprise Category	**Investment in equipment**
Micro Enterprises	Does not exceed ten lakh rupees:
Small Enterprises	More than ten lakh rupees but does not exceed two crore rupees
Medium Enterprises	More than two crore rupees but does not exceed five crore rupees

Fig. 63.3 Definitions of MSMEs as per MSMED Act

Source: https://samadhaan.msme.gov.in/WriteReadData/DocumentFile/MSMED2006act.pdf

Activity Category	Estimated Number of Enterprises (in lakh)			Share (%)
	Rural	Urban	Total	
(1)	(2)	(3)	(4)	(5)
Manufacturing	114.14	82.50	196.65	31
Electricity*	0.03	0.01	0.03	-
Trade	108.71	121.64	230.35	36
Other Services	102.00	104.85	206.85	33
All	324.88	309.00	633.88	100

*Non-captive electricity generation and transmission

Fig. 63.4 Estimated Number of MSMEs in India [7]

India's MSME Sector comprises 633.88 lakh units as per National Sample Survey 73rd Round (2015-16)- Manufacturing 360.41 lakh, Trade 387.18 lakh, Total 1109.09 lakh, Other Services 362.29 lakh [7].

47.78 lakh MSMEs in Maharashtra employ 90.77 lakh employees of which 17.97 lakh are women Source: NSS 73rd Round, 2015–16.

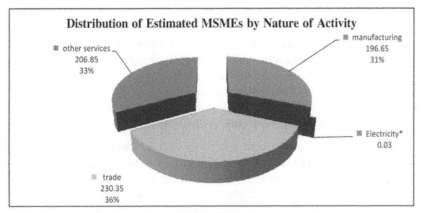

Non-captive electricity generation and transmission

Fig. 63.5   Distribution of estimated Number of MSMEs

Source: https://www.industrialautomationindia.in/articleitm/11484/MSMEs-and-Industrial-Safety/articles

3.4 Vulnerability of MSMEs

Due to resource, knowledge, planning and experience gaps, MSMEs' vulnerability towards natural hazards are greater than large MNCs. **Informal operations in major parts of India** keeps MSMEs away from availing insurance etc. The lack of compliance with norms and regulations further increases disaster risk. The challenges faced during calamities have a domino effect on the involved supply chain still MSMEs do not have proper business continuity plans in place. Huge financial burdens on MSMEs after disasters through resources spent for physical reconstruction of lost infrastructure and lost demand etc. All these factors suggest an increased vulnerability of MSMEs in post-disaster situations.

The factors responsible for MSMEs vulnerability towards natural hazards are [15]:

1. Their operations are in sub-optimal locations;
2. The MSMEs are small in working capacity as well as are financially weaker;
3. Their financial and technical capacity are also limited;
4. The absence of effective business continuity plans;
5. The local market is mostly their target market;
6. Does not include Disaster Risk Reduction (DRR) measures and
7. Mostly get excluded from recovery programs.
8. Take longer to recover hence losing customer satisfaction
9. Use personal funds or borrow at high interest rates to build back to pre-flood levels.
10. No government compensation and insurance

The chief factor determining the impact of a disaster on MSMEs is their vulnerability related to aspects such as their degree of formalization and financial integration into the economy, and the extent to which they have access to risk insurance mechanisms. Simply put, greater the integration of MSMEs into the formal economy, lesser their vulnerability. Formal MSMEs technically have a social security net and access to government support programs such as start-up support, general advice, access to credit and, more importantly, financial support in times of crises. Informal MSMEs are bereft of these advantages. Context-specific factors such as location and type of business also influence an MSME's degree of vulnerability to disaster risk, apart from factors such as pre-existing levels of disaster preparedness and post disaster recovery decisions. These, in turn, depend on how far the sector is recognized as part of the overall framework of DRR and recovery support in a policy and institutional context.

MSMEs can be affected by disasters but differently. **Type of hazard, risk exposure as well as characteristics of MSMEs affect the MSMEs vulnerability to natural hazards** [1]. MSME's should take steps now to plan their business to eliminate the recurrent losses in business every year combined with their physio-psycho stress.

3.5 Framework to Cope with Disasters

Understanding the impact of disasters on MSMEs we understand that recurrent problems often impact the performance of businesses by hampering the infrastructure, eliminating the labour availability, and disrupting the supply chain every year. Hence a long-term plan in coordination with the government can be put to action to promote a sector which plays a major role in the economy but is ignored constantly on large scale. The suggestions made based on data and root-cause analysis provides a framework to be adapted by businesses to mitigate ill-effects of disasters.

1. From the Government side, an analysis of topology, climatic variations and impact of slow onset disasters should be done for the cities that attract businesses like MSMEs. Collaborating with geologists and engineers, a guideline needs to be mandated for constructing a business infrastructure and a committee to keep a check on the implementation whenever any new establishment is created. Like in earthquake prone regions the building design should be earthquake resistant, the electrical and water supply lines should be able to withstand the tremors of the intensity faced by those areas in the past. The Draft Regional Plan for MMR Region 1996-2011 lays out a set of guidelines for the land use policies for the city [12]. The DMAP looks quite elaborate and practical on paper, but does not provide any specific time frame for achieving the mitigation measures. A list of alternate locations needs to be prepared which can be utilized to set up a production unit in order to level out the density from compact high-density locations to low density locations and for that provide some subsidies so that it's profitable to both parties. In Mumbai, this would help in spreading out the population from the main city of South and Central Mumbai to nearby locations like Vasai, Belapur etc.

2. The government's vision should be to prepare a long-range (30-year) vision and action plan for the Mumbai Metropolitan Region (MMR) for risk mitigation by actively engaging stakeholders and providing appropriate incentives. They should collaborate in setting up an efficient urban disaster response and recovery capacity in the city utilizing special agencies like hospital, fire service, police etc [18].

3. Use of GIS by the government of Maharashtra after 2005 floods has obviously enhanced urban planning and municipal governance. Mumbai Municipal Corporation can now identify anything in advance using Geo-Referencing. They have also incorporated Esri ArcGIS for a host of services for increasing transparency, ease of doing business and improving the quality of services. Similar steps need to be taken by the governments in Orissa, West Bengal, Kerala, Karnataka etc which are often hit by natural disasters and bring a lot of damage and destruction to lives and properties. GIS helps in speedy transmission of information and making people disaster ready by implementing the pre-disaster risk reduction guidelines. Figure 63.6 represents the various phases of disaster preparedness [5].

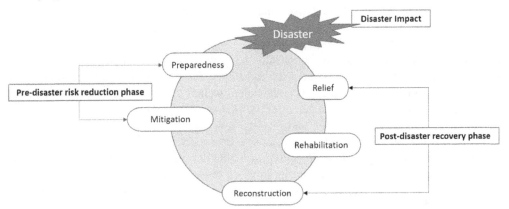

Fig. 63.6   Various phases of disaster risk preparedness

Source: Author's compilation

4. Close the gaps in the Government's current Risk Management Plan- Greater Mumbai Disaster Management Action Plan (DMAP) 2007 is implemented in Maharashtra [14]. In this specific relief and mitigation measures for Mumbai were suggested like - Infrastructure improvements (but every year we read reports of failure of roads, sewer disposal systems and storm water drainage systems that cost lives. No improvement in living conditions of slums, incidents of collapsing of old housings are common every year.

5. Build on the spirit of Mumbai and set an example for others to follow. Mumbai's geographical conditions, weather, sea-level rise, building conditions etc., create an enhanced vulnerability for the city. But Mumbai's informal coping mechanism – a strong social network and cooperation among people – is a key to the city's resilience and reduces vulnerability to some degree [14].

6. Public Investment in infrastructure restoration and socio-economic policies is necessary to promote MSMEs at times of post crisis recovery. This would involve restoring basic services necessary for seamless operation of businesses and would in term prevent migration of workers. Making sure adequate housing is there for the affected families, this would help them in keeping up with their productive activities. If the plan is for large scale restoration of infrastructure, then it should be designed in such a manner that not

a single affected business, no matter how small is excluded from the recovery benefits. This would in terms generate emergency employment opportunities and can support lives.

7. Governments can run programmes like Cash for Work or direct cash grants that would help restore MSMEs operations by providing some working capital for business continuity. It can play a pivotal role in short term economic recovery. Central and state governments should coordinate hand in hand to form policies for easy revival after disasters [4].

4. Conclusions

Implementation of suggested framework that involves long term and short-term vision in association with various stakeholders from government to businessmen will help to eliminate risk from natural calamities to MSMEs. Identification of alternate locations incorporated with subsidized facilities would help in establishing new business development centres and would spread out the load from high-risk areas to new centres. Use of the Geographical Information System (GIS) can help in accurate data collection as well as to develop strategy to frame early warning, rescue, and rehabilitation activities. GIS-based maps can be utilized for meeting the requirement of food, camps, water, and required relief shelter and help in fast post disaster recovery. It would also help higher authorities to keep a check on the level of rescue operations and verify the arrangements. Planning and prioritizing development efforts economically and in infrastructure needs a lot of relevant information regarding locations and level of damage in less time which can be provided by GIS tools. Government is most of the time engaged in framing policies but what is needed is implementation of those policies on ground level to eliminate risk in the long run. GIS can be utilized up to great extent in infrastructural improvement and provisioning of compensations to the affected at times of crises as well as frame strategies for implementation of rescue activities.

REFERENCES

1. The Impact of Natural Disasters on Micro, Small and Medium Enterprises (MSMEs): A Case Study on 2016 Flood Event in Western Sri Lanka by GunathilakaSamantha
2. Impacts of Natural Disasters on Households and Small Businesses in India https://reliefweb.int/sites/reliefweb.int/files/resources/ewp-603-disasters-households-small-businesses-india.pdf
3. Spatio-temporal analysis of sub-hourly rainfall over Mumbai, India: Is statistical forecasting futile? https://www.ias.ac.in/public/Volumes/jess/126/03/0038.pdf
4. Brouwer, Roy, Sonia Atker, Luke Brander, and Enamul Haque. 2007. "Socioeconomic Vulnerability and Adaptation to Environmental Risk: A Case Study of Climate Change and Flooding in Bangladesh." Risk Analysis 27 (2): 313–26.
5. Indian Space Research Organisation (ISRO). 2015. Chennai Floods 2015: A Satellite and Field Based Assessment Study. Hyderabad: National Remote Sensing Centre, ISRO.
6. Intergovernmental Panel on Climate Change (IPCC). 2012. Managing the Risks of Extreme Events and Disasters to Advance Climate Change Adaptation: Special Report of the Intergovernmental Panel on Climate Change. Cambridge University Press

7. Mercy Corps and Okapi. 2016. Transforming Chennai: A Research Report on Building Micro, Small and Medium Enterprise Resilience to Water-Related Environmental Change. http://www. indiaenvironmentportal.org.in/content/438669/transforming-chennai-building-micro-small-and-medium-enterprise-resilience-to-water-related-environmental-change/

8. Merz, Bruno, Heidi Kreibich, Reimund Schwarze, and Annegret Thieken. 2010. "Assessment of Economic Flood Damage." Natural Hazards and Earth System Sciences 10: 1697–1724.

9. Messner, Frank, Edmund Penning-Rowsell, Colin Green, Volker Meyer, Sylvia Tunstall, and Anne van der Veen. 2007. Evaluating Flood Damages: Guidance and Recommendations on Principals and Methods. http://www.floodsite.net/html/partner_area/project_docs/T09_06_01_Flood_damage_ guidelin es_d9_1_v2_2_p44.pdf

10. Patankar, Archana. 2015. "The Exposure, Vulnerability, and Ability to Respond to Poor Households to Recurrent Floods in Mumbai." World Bank Policy Research Working Paper 7481.

11. "Assessment of economic flood damage" B. Merz1, H. Kreibich1, R. Schwarze 2, 4, and A. Thieken 3, 4.

12. The Exposure, Vulnerability, and Ability to Respond of Poor Households to Recurrent Floods in Mumbai by Archana Patankar World Bank group Nov 2015.

13. GIS-based disaster management A case study for Allahabad Sadar sub-district(India) S. H. Abbas, R. K. Srivastava and R. P. Tiwari.

14. Schaer, Caroline, and Archana Patankar. 2018. "Promoting Private Sector Engagement in Climate Change Adaptation and Flood Resilience: A Case Study of Innovative Approaches Applied by MSMEs in Mumbai, India." In Theory and Practice of Climate Adaptation, Climate Change Management edited by F. Alves, W. Leal Filho, and U. Azeiteiro, 175–91. Cham: Springer.

15. World Bank. 2004. "Understanding the Economic and Financial Impacts of Natural Disasters." Disaster Risk Management Series 4. Washington, DC: World Bank.

16. KPMG -2016/05/Disaster-Management-Preparedness-SME.

17. Understanding the Economic and Financial Impacts of Natural Disasters Charlotte Benson and Edward J. Clay-World Bank.

18. October, L. U. (2005). DISASTER RISK MANAGEMENT PROFILE Last Update October 2005 Mumbai , India. Communication, October (https://www.alnap.org/system/files/content/resource/ files/main/cp-mumbai-09-05.pdf).

19. Murali, R.M., Riyas, M.J., Reshma, K.N. et al. Climate change impact and vulnerability assessment of Mumbai city, India. Nat Hazards 102, 575–589 (2020). https://doi.org/10.1007/s11069-019-03766-2

20. Tabish, A. (2017). Disasters in India: An Overview*. 8(1), 392–397.

Handbook of Evidence Based Management Practices in Business – Satyendra Kumar Sharma et al. (eds)
© 2023 Taylor & Francis Group, London, ISBN 978-1-032-54216-4

Chapter

Analyzing the Impact of Agri Supply Chain Management Strategies on Farmers' Incomes

C. V. Sunil Kumar[1]
Assistant Professor, Institute of Public Enterprise,
Osmania University Campus, Secunderabad, Telangana, India

M. L. N Rao[2]
Professor, Institute of Public Enterprise,
Osmania University Campus, Secunderabad, Telangana, India

ABSTRACT: The flow of money, information, and primarily agricultural produce can be streamlined by agricultural supply chains (ASCs) more successfully and efficiently. It is thought that ASCs can maximize the supply chain profits distributed among the stakeholders while objectively growing the pie of revenue generated by the supply chain. The ASC configurations, in contrast, are quite distinctive because supply and demand do not match exactly as they do in conventional manufacturing supply chains. Farmers in particular are frequently thought to be losing out because they don't receive the proper value for their agricultural produce. On the other hand, consumer tastes are also significantly changing and frequently becoming more health conscious, leading to consumers being willing to pay more for high-quality produce. The development of crucial supply chain systems has advanced well, but there is still a gap between the abilities of small farmers and the shifting demands, which is constantly widening. The consumption patterns of customers and small stakeholders would be impacted by the shifting power dynamics along with the ASCs and large retail organizations. The proposed study is concentrated on analyzing how the ASC processes can boost the farmers' income in an effort to reduce this gap and better meet the needs of the end customers. According to the authors, farmers' incomes can rise in tandem with their efforts to meet the demands of consumers by providing high-quality produce. In cognizance to these objectives, the proposed study was carried out to investigate potential Agricultural Supply Chain Management Strategies (ASCMSs) in boosting the earnings of different stakeholders along the ASCs, particularly the farmers.

KEYWORDS: Agricultural supply chains, Increasing farmers' income, Agri supply chain management strategies, Kano model

[1]cvenkata_sunil@yahoo.com, [2]mlnrao@ipeindia.org

DOI: 10.4324/9781003415725-64

1. Introduction

The well-being of rural India where the majority of the population resides can be enhanced by strategically developing the ASCs (Anupindi, R. and Sivakumar, 2007). Agriculture is the major source of income for many people in rural India, there have to be well-developed supply chain systems in place to exercise standardized practices, overcome the root causes of the shortcomings and continuously improve the supply capabilities to meet the increasing demand expectations of the customers (Goyal et al., 2013). On one hand, the supply side is constrained by numerous challenges viz. coordination along the upstream processes (lack of information), standardization of supply management processes, compliance to the best input quality standards (that enhance the value of the outputs for the end customers), availability of resources (fertilizers, credit-based capital, and equipment) and so and so forth. While on the other hand, the end customers are increasingly expecting for fresh and safe agricultural produce, better availability, affordable prices and so and so forth. Certainly, it is a challenge to maximize the income for small farmers along the ASCs as well as to timely offer fresh, healthy, and safe agricultural produce to the end customers. In this regard, the current study has focused on exploring the current ASCMSs with an objective to increase incomes for the stakeholders along the ASCs specifically the farmers. The study will attempt to examine the prominent ASCMSs that can enhance the value for the end customers as well as make the processes cost-effective for the small farmers. The current paper is organized as follows: section 2 presents the literature review; section 3 presents the methodology of implementing the Kano model; section 4 presents the results and discussions; and section 5 provide the concluding remarks and scope for future research.

2. Literature Review

Agriculture sector has been recognized as one of the important areas contributing towards the Indian economy and source of employment for more 50% of the population in India the Government of India has taken up many initiatives. Some of the latest initiatives taken are soil health card scheme, Pradhan Mantri Krishi Sinchai Yojana (PMKSY): for improved water efficiency, Paramparagat Krishi Vikas Yojana (PKVY): for organic farming, unified national agriculture market: for increasing the farmer's income, and Pradhan Mantri Fasal Bima Yojana (PMFBY): for reducing risk (Annual Report, 2016-2017). Although there has been good progress achieved in matching the supply side capabilities and demand side requirements of the Agricultural Supply Chains (ASCs), the demand expectations are growing ever increasingly (Chandrasekaran and Raghuram, 2014). Even the ASCs pose serious challenges to handle viz. with regards to the scale of production (volume), seasonality (nature of demand), perishability (type of products) and longer supply lead times. Often the scale of production is bulkier along the ASCs; the uncertainties along the various stages of the ASCs would greatly affect all the stakeholders but specifically those who are towards the supply side. This is because the stakeholders on the supply management side may have to deal with larger quantities compared to those on the demand side of the ASCs. In support to this, (Chopra and Meindl, 2007) also mentioned that the ordered quantities from the upstream to downstream processes of ASCs would get reduced. Although the production of agricultural produce is limited to certain seasons nonetheless the demand for the produce many at times last throughout the year posing huge requirement for production, sustainability and availability (Chandrasekaran and Raghuram, 2014). Moreover, often the ASCs are also lengthier with regards to widely scattered demand points and demographically focused farm production centers. Since the ASCs are lengthier often it is difficult for the supply management stakeholders to understand the dynamic requirements of the customers (Routroy and Sunil Kumar, 2014). It has become much more complex with globalization where the customers' preferences are diverse and have differences in the various economies. Besides to these constraints since the agricultural produce are mostly perishable they have to be shipped through these lengthy ASCs timely, in right quantity and exactly matching the requirements of the end customers. But though the agricultural produce is moved to the right market places, in right quantity and right quality they have to be more competitive than other suppliers (Agarwal, 2017). Internationally the markets are no longer looking for homogeneous commodities rather differentiated products (Reardon et al., 1999). Hence the rural economies should be able to competitively link with the urban and export economies. Thus the variations and the levels of uncertainties are severe in the case of ASCs compared to conventional supply chains (Behzadi et al., 2017). If the supply side management processes are better conducted and capitalize on the dynamic requirements of the end customer (urban and export economies) certainly the income of the small farmers can greatly enhance. As mentioned above the ASCs are complex to handle nonetheless in the process of better management there can be large number of employment opportunities explored for the society at large.

3. Methodology

The current study has adopted the Kano quality model as a methodology for analyzing the ASCMSs. It is a two-dimensional model coupled with a satisfaction matrix. Because the authors wanted to investigate the role that ASCMSs play in raising farmers' incomes, they applied the Kano model in this situation. Considering which ASCMSs should be given top priority and which ones they cannot afford to ignore can be useful for practitioners as well as policymakers. The steps that must be taken in order to adopt the Kano quality are described below.

The Kano quality model divides a product's or service's characteristics into five general categories: (1) Must-have characteristics; (2) One-dimensional characteristics; (3) Attractive characteristics; (4) Indifferent characteristics; and (5) Reverse characteristics. The ASCMSs are categorized and prioritised according to these criteria in the current study so that practitioners can carefully select the best ASCMSs to raise stakeholder incomes along the ASCs, particularly for farmers.

The effectiveness of the ASCMSs in raising farmers' incomes is measured using the Kano quality model. A Kano survey questionnaire, which is typically developed along two ways of questioning, one in the form of positive/functional and the other in the form of negative/dysfunctional, can be used to achieve the aforementioned classification under the quality characteristics. As a result, two sets of questions are constructed in accordance with the ASCMSs to gather opinions. Additionally, these inquiries are combined to obtain the qualitative opinions using the Kano evaluation table (Kano, 1984). The GAEs were contacted after creating the survey questionnaire in order to gather the responses.

Table 64.1 Positive and negative forms of questions

Functional Question	Dysfunctional Question
What is your opinion regarding the influence on increasing farmers' incomes with the presence of an ASCMS? Choose one of the options given below? We like it ☐ We expect it must be that way ☐ We live with it that way ☐ We are neutral to it ☐ We dislike it that way ☐	What is your opinion regarding the influence on the manufacturer with the presence of a PSE? Choose one of the options given below? We like it ☐ We expect it must be that way ☐ We live with it that way ☐ We are neutral to it ☐ We dislike it that way ☐

Source: Author's compilation

The above-mentioned questionnaire's responses should be further combined using the Kano evaluation table, as shown below.

Table 64.2 Kano evaluation table

		Dysfunctional				
		MLK	MMT	MLI	MNT	MDS
Functional	MLK	Q	A	A	A	O
	MMT	R	I	I	I	M
	MLI	R	I	I	I	M
	MNT	R	I	I	I	M
	MDS	R	R	R	R	Q
Manufacturer Like it (MLK); Manufacturer expects it Must be that way (MMT); Manufacturer Live with it that way (MLI); Manufacturer is Neutral (MNT); Manufacturer Dislike it that way (MDS)						
Note: Q, A, R, I, O, and M denote "Questionable", "Attractive", "Reverse", "Indifferent", "One-dimensional", and "Must-be" attributes, respectively						

Source: Author's compilation

Based on the data collected the satisfaction and dissatisfaction coefficients are determined by using the following equations.

Satisfaction Coefficient (SCF) = $(A + O)/(A + O + M + I)$

Dissatisfaction Coefficient (DSCF) = $-(O + M)/(A + O + M + I)$

4. Results and Discussions

As per the methodology detailed in the previous section, the ASCMSs were analyzed to obtain the classification of ASCMSs into Kano Quality attributes. The following Table 64.3 provides the summary of data analysis conducted in analyzing the ASCMSs.

Table 64.3 SCF and DSCF values of ASCMSs

Agri Supply Chain Management Strategies	A	O	M	I	R	Q	Category	SCF	DSCF
Regulatory Controlled Operations (RCO)	0	0	37	13	0	0	M	0	-0.74
Institutional Quality in Processing firms (IQP)	0	0	31	19	0	0	M	0	-0.62
Reduced Obsolescence at Stakeholders (ROS)	38	0	0	12	0	0	A	0.76	0
Cold Chain Infrastructure (CCI)	0	0	12	38	0	0	A	0	-0.24
Material Handling and Maintenance (MHM)	8	0	31	11	0	0	M	0.16	-0.62
Cooperative Marketing of Supplies (CMS)	36	0	0	14	0	0	A	0.72	0
Connected to E-Commence Platforms (CEP)	35	0	5	10	0	0	A	0.7	-0.1
Value Chain Transparency (VCT)	12	0	26	12	0	0	M	0.24	-0.52
Agri-Supply chain Aggregation (ASA)	40	0	9	1	0	0	A	0.8	-0.18
Supply Chain Coordination (SCC)	32	0	10	8	0	0	A	0.64	-0.2
Revenue and Risk Sharing contracts (RRS)	35	0	0	15	0	0	A	0.7	0
Agri-supply Chain Integration (ACI)	36	0	0	14	0	0	A	0.72	0
Information Sharing Along Stakeholders (ISS)	37	0	1	12	0	0	A	0.74	-0.02
Accessibility to Demand Locations (ADL)	18	0	21	11	0	0	M	0.36	-0.42
Sustainable and Efficient Agri-logistics (SEA)	37	0	4	9	0	0	A	0.74	-0.08
Technology Enabled Operations (TEO)	33	0	4	13	0	0	A	0.66	-0.08
Socially Enterprising Practices (SEP)	33	0	4	13	0	0	A	0.66	-0.08
Legitimate Supply chain Financial flows (LSF)	32	0	12	6	0	0	A	0.64	-0.24
Diversification of Agriculture Produce (DAP)	11	0	4	35	0	0	A	0.22	-0.08
Knowledge about Value Addition (KVA)	41	0	0	9	0	0	A	0.82	0
Traceability along the Supply Chains (TSC)	44	0	0	6	0	0	A	0.88	0

Source: Author's compilation

The SCF indicates the potential for increasing incomes for stakeholders along the ASCs, particularly farmers. While the DSCF shows how failure to pursue an ASCMS can lead to stakeholder dissatisfaction as opportunity costs rise, effectively resulting in income loss. The higher the SCF, the more effective the ASCMS would be in increasing farmers' income, while the higher the DSCF, the more negative the ASCMS would be for farmers. In terms of values, SCF is considered to be higher when it tends to one, whereas DSCF is considered to be higher when it tends to minus one. The satisfaction matrix plot should be developed by plotting the ordered pairs such as (SCF, DSCF) on the Cartesian coordinate system, with SCF along the X-axis and DSCF along the Y-axis and lines drawn parallel to the X and Y axes and passing through the averages of satisfaction and dissatisfaction coefficients. The ASCMSs are classified into four quadrants based on this plot (I-quadrant: low satisfaction and low dissatisfaction coefficient ASCMSs; II-quadrant: high satisfaction and low dissatisfaction coefficient ASCMSs, III-quadrant: High satisfaction and high dissatisfaction coefficient ASCMSs, IV-quadrant: low satisfaction and high dissatisfaction coefficient ASCMSs). The

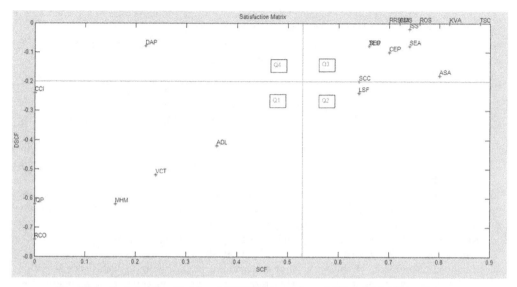

Fig. 64.1 Satisfaction Matrix of ASCMSs based on SCF and DSCF Coefficients

Source: Author's compilation

ASCMSs in the III-quadrant have a large influence on increasing farmer incomes, whereas those in the I-quadrant have little influence on increasing farmer incomes. ASCMSs in the II and IV quadrants have a one-way influence on farmer income, respectively.

5. Conclusions

The ASCMSs identified in this study are essentially significant for increasing farmer incomes along supply chains. Serval studies have mentioned the importance of increasing farmers' incomes, but objective studies in this regard are scarce, so the current study can be regarded as one of the important contributions to the research directions aimed at increasing farmers' incomes. The current study has also revealed that by focusing the ASCMS, farmers not only generate higher incomes, but customers on the receiving end can also receive high-quality produce. Customers, in general, are willing to pay higher prices for high-value produce, which increases income for farmers and other stakeholders along the supply chain. Further the current study also distinguished between ASCMSs that significantly increase income and those that we cannot afford to overlook because they may increase opportunity costs. This can help the policy makers, and practitioners to make impactful decisions in improving farmers' incomes along the ASCs.

REFERENCES

Note: **Funding:** The Authors would also like to express deep sense of gratitude and acknowledge the financial support received from the Indian Council for Social Science Research (ICSSR), New Delhi, India [File No. IMPRESS/P1899/2018-19/ICSSR] for carrying out the current research.

1. Agarwal, S. (2017), "Issues in supply chain planning of fruits and vegetables in agri-food supply chain: A review of certain aspects", *IMS Business School, Kolkata, India.*
2. Anupindi, R. and Sivakumar, S. (2007), "Supply chain reengineering in agri-business", *Building Supply Chain Excellence in Emerging Economies*, Vol. 3, pp. 119–122.
3. Behzadi, G., O'Sullivan, M. J., Olsen, T. L., Scrimgeour, F. and Zhang, A. (2017), "Robust and resilient strategies for managing supply disruptions in an agribusiness supply chain", *International Journal of Production Economics*, Elsevier, Vol. 191, pp. 207–220.
4. Chandrasekaran, N. and Raghuram, G. (2014), *Agribusiness Supply Chain Management*, CRC Press.
5. Chopra, S. and Meindl, P. (2007), *Supply Chain Management: Strategy, Planning & Operation*, *Supply Chain Management: Strategy, Planning & Operation*, Pearson Education Inc., Upper Saddle River, NJ.
6. Goyal, A., Rajagopalan, C., Goedde, L. and Nathani, N. (2013), "Harvesting golden opportunities in Indian agriculture: from food security to farmers' income security by 2025", *Journal of Chemical Information and Modeling*, Vol. 53 No. 9, pp. 1689–1699.
7. Kano, N. (1984), "Attractive quality and must-be quality", *Hinshitsu (Quality, The Journal of Japanese Society for Quality Control)*, Vol. 14, pp. 39–48.
8. Reardon, T., Codron, J.-M., Busch, L., Bingen, J. and Harris, C. (1999), "Global change in agrifood grades and standards: agribusiness strategic responses in developing countries", *The International Food and Agribusiness Management Review*, Elsevier, Vol. 2 No. 3–4, pp. 421–435.
9. Routroy, S. and Sunil Kumar, C.V. (2014), "Analyzing supplier development program enablers using fuzzy DEMATEL", *Measuring Business Excellence*, Vol. 18 No. 4, available at: https://doi.org/10.1108/MBE-08-2013-0046.

PART

EVIDENCE BASED STRATEGIC MANAGEMENT AND ENTREPRENEURSHIP

Handbook of Evidence Based Management Practices in Business – Satyendra Kumar Sharma et al. (eds)
© 2023 Taylor & Francis Group, London, ISBN 978-1-032-54216-4

Chapter

Winner-Take-All Strategy in Digital Platform Market: A Theoretical Exposition

Shatakshi Bourai[1]
Research Scholar, Department of Management,
Birla Institute of Technology and Science, Pilani – Pilani Campus, Rajasthan, India

Neetu Yadav[2]
Assistant Professor, Department of Strategy and Management,
Management Development Institute, Gurgaon, India

Rahul Arora[3]
Assistant Professor, Department of Economics and Finance,
Birla Institute of Technology & Science, Pilani – Pilani Campus, Rajasthan, India

ABSTRACT: Industries are witnessing the growth of and transition to digital platform marketplaces from traditional network markets. These markets offering products as varied as smartphones, credit cards among others and services as varied as ride-hailing, food delivery among others are influenced by network effects and other factors unique to these markets. The literature on these unique factors has popularized a hypothesis that competition in the digital platform market pushes firms to adopt a get-big-fast strategy which is likely to result in winner-take-all outcome. However, the unconditional, winner-takes-all hypothesis has perplexed many practitioners as several standards of products and services have prevailed in recent competitions in some IT platform industries. This leads to the research question of our study: do these findings suggest a shift in the platform market dynamics such that winner-take-all is no longer the standard? To achieve the objective of this paper existing research papers on digital platforms from the field of strategic management and case studies from Harvard Business Review, Fortune and Business Week were referred. The present study will help managers to employ significantly different strategies than those that were successful in the past.

KEYWORDS: Digital platforms, Winner-take-all, Platform strategy, Platform competition

[1]p20200040@pilani.bits-pilani.ac.in, shatakshibourai0703@gmail.com; [2]neetu.yadav@mdi.ac.in;
[3]rahul.arora@pilani.bits-pilani.ac.in, rahulphdeco@gmail.com

DOI: 10.4324/9781003415725-65

1. Introduction

The increased prominence of digital platforms makes it clear that it has become the core and backbone of today's economy as they our lives are made easier by them (Kenney & Zysman 2016; de Reuver et al., 2018; Stummer et al., 2018). Be it products or services, it is supplied more quickly and affordably. Additionally, these platforms have made it simpler to link businesses and consumers. For instance, Uber brings together drivers and passengers who would never have met otherwise, Google helps us find information we would have never known about, LinkedIn helps us make valuable connections, and Amazon lets us buy almost anything more cheaply and conveniently while also allowing third parties to sell products alongside Amazon's regular selection. Imagine that 50 Ubers, Googles, LinkedIns, and Amazons were in direct competition with one another, each serving a distinct internet niche, profession, or product category. It would lead to frustration and inefficiencies. Therefore, these large digital platforms tend to benefit us as consumers.

Markets for digital platforms have typically been fiercely contested arenas. Usually, a dominant market leader with much more than 50% of the market share emerges from these competitions (Kemerer, et. al., 2017). It is exceedingly challenging to compete for businesses that started later once a platform has established itself as the industry leader. For instance, Microsoft and Intel continue to rule the personal computer processor and software markets, respectively, after 60 years in business. Meanwhile, it appears like Google, Amazon, and Facebook will continue to rule the search and social media industries for some time to come. The result of one digital platform gaining market domination is known as "Winner-Take-All" (hereinafter "WTA") (Arthur 1996, Kelly 1999, Shapiro & Varian 1999).

In a digital platform market, winner-take-all scenarios have been defined by numerous authors. There isn't, however, agreement on a definition. So, the question of how to define a winner-take-all market scenario still stands. According to the Cambridge Dictionary, a winner-take-all scenario is one in which "the entire prize goes to the one competitor who wins" (Cambridge Dictionary, 2019). While a winner-take-all scenario is viewed by Ruutu, Casey, & Kotovirta (2017) as a competition outcome where one platform can lock-in clients and be able to drive competitors out of the market due to superior resource allocation, this is not the case in reality. Although they provide room for interpretation, these definitions nonetheless pose more queries.

These digital platforms, which provide services and goods as diverse as ride-hailing, food delivery, and credit cards among others, are driven by network effects and other factors particular to these industries. According to the literature on these distinctive variables, enterprises are pushed to pursue a get-big-fast strategy in the digital platform market, which is likely to lead to a winner-take-all outcome (McIntyre & Subramaniam, 2009; Zhu & Iansiti, 2012; Cennamo & Santalo, 2013). In other words, successful digital platforms have the property that they develop extremely quickly and that, in the end, there is only one winner left. Many practitioners, however, are baffled by the unconditional, winner-takes-all premise as a number of standards of goods and services have emerged in recent contests in several IT platform industries (Kemerer *et. al.*, 2017). Microsoft, for instance, arguably controlled the information technology sector from 1990 until 2010. The organisation lost the war for mobile, despite having won the desktop market with the launch of Windows in 1985 and enjoying the first-mover advantage by releasing a mobile operating system years before Apple or Google as it was unable to secure the support of the three parties it required for a mobile platform: device manufacturers, app developers, and consumers. This leads to the research question of our study: do these findings suggest a shift in the platform market dynamics such that winner-take-all is no longer the standard? To achieve the objective of this paper existing research papers on digital platforms from the field of strategic management and case studies from Harvard Business Review, Fortune and Business Week were referred. The authors also capture this phenomenon evident in the industrial world to strengthen the relevance of the article for both academicians and practitioners.

To pursue the task, the entire paper is organized into 6 sections including the present introductory one. Section 2 describes the characteristics of a winner-take-all market. Section 3 discusses the key factors determining winner-take-all outcome in digital platform markets. Section 4 sheds light on the paradigm shift from winner-take-all outcome in digital platform market. Section 5 and 6 cover the discussion and conclusion of the study respectively.

2. Characteristics of Winner-take-all Market

Digital platform firms should adopt aggressive strategies to grow both their installed user base and complementors, according to a WTA model for multisided markets, such that gains earned on each side of the market reinforce one another. More specifically, a "get-big-fast" strategy (Eocman et al., 2006) would compel digital platform firms to (1) lock in their users by hastening the growth of their platform's installed base; and (2) weaken the capacity of rival platforms to adopt a similar strategy in order to lock them out of the market, causing the market to tip in their favour.

2.1 Lock-in of Customer

Customer lock-in provides winner-take-all market dynamics a particularly urgent flavour. If a company enters the market too slowly or without enough vigour, the installed base of locked-in consumers will grow slowly, providing competitors the chance to overtake them. The main issue is that substantial investments are necessary to build up an installed base. In essence, the companies building digital platforms are placing a sizable amount of money on the slim possibility of enormous success, with a very high likelihood of unfavourable results (McGrath, 2015). Therefore, it's essential to consider carefully how the provider of the digital platform might lock in users and how much funding it will require to reach critical mass. For instance, Google's advertising business, which charges advertisers to post advertisements on websites featuring chosen keywords, benefits from lock-in in three different ways. First, website owners are locked in since they have registered and get paid every time a visitor clicks an ad. They are encouraged to stick with Google because the cost per click-through may rise as the network of advertisers expands. Second, the fact that Google has access to the greatest variety of websites and searches encourages advertisers to work with it. And finally, Google provides the most comprehensive access to search results that are dynamically priced and tailored to their interests, which locks in website visitors.

Customers can also be locked in by switching costs. Customers do not want to go through the same steps with a different provider after making an initial commitment in learning, training, developing relationships, or capital. Switching costs are caused by idiosyncratic learning, transaction-specific programming, capital inputs, and simply basic familiarity and comfort. The more a customer is locked in the higher the switching cost. Switching costs are such a potent barrier to free competition that regulators occasionally insist that businesses reduce them. For instance, recent law on mobile number portability aims to make it simpler for phone users to switch carriers. Network externalities are not necessary for switching costs, but their impact is significantly increased when they are. Lock-in can occasionally result from utilising product portfolios and related assets as well. Microsoft, for example, has faced numerous legal challenges for what may have been unfair business practises because it attempted to force users who were accustomed to using its operating system to use its web browser, Explorer, and its office productivity software. Lock-in is also at its most potent when several of these components may be used together. For instance, switching costs and network externalities are both utilised by online marketplaces and auctions. A shopping website like eBay will see an increase in customers because there are more sellers there and the resultant transactions are likely to be more profitable than those made on other websites. Customers are further locked in by the addition of additional components like dynamic pricing, searching, connecting, or other interactive features to the offering.

2.2 Lock-out of Competitors

According to the legal definition of "natural" monopolies, this is how monopolists traditionally control markets. Early movers can do a lot to discourage later entry by rivals when faced with a high fixed cost to enter a category and low marginal costs to expand it. Of course, the easiest thing to do is to reduce prices below actual costs, with the understanding that rising volumes and the impacts of the learning curve will eventually cause the cost-price curves to cross and produce profitability. If rivals are resolute, such a tactic might be quite dangerous. It might resemble an attrition-based war in business. In this situation, both businesses make significant investments that may last for years before they start to pay off in an effort to build a larger installed base than their competitor (McGrath, 2015).

Competitors may be excluded through customer complementarity or co-production. A co-produced or co-evolving category lowers a customer's incentive to change partners and start over. For instance, once a user creates a "group" on the Yahoo portal, it becomes difficult for other service providers who also provide group functionality to advance very far because the user has made unique investments in the Yahoo group location. There may also be times when working with many providers is impossible due to a lack of resources (such as time, money, energy, or physical space). This is frequently referred to as "pre-emption of scarce assets". Lock-outs may sometimes be the result of intentional government policy. Businesses operating globally would obviously like as few barriers to competition as feasible, but protecting preferred competitors is sometimes a point of dispute in globalising industries when governments wish to offer their home competitors some benefits.

3. Factors Determining Winner-take-all Outcome in Digital Platform Market

3.1 Network Effects

In digital platform markets, winner-take-all is a phenomenon that is fuelled by network effects (direct and indirect). The notion of network effects was created by economists in the 1970s, refined in the 1990s, and then entrenched as one of the cornerstones of the new economy by business gurus, entrepreneurs, and the tech media. The literature on network effects claims that when a business enters a new market incredibly quickly, it draws clients, and those clients draw even more clients, and so on. The first mover consequently sees rapid expansion, seizes a commanding position in the market, and generates fantastic profits. The same logic has been applied to digital platforms, which businesses with network effects; for example, if a fast mover attracts customers to one side of its platform, such as video game players, it draws customers to the opposite side, such as video game developers, increasing the value of its business to the first side's customers. Once more, the notion is that the strength of network effects will result in rapid expansion and perpetual, winner-take-all supremacy (Evans, and Schmalensee, 2016)

The advantages that each customer receives when other customers make purchases are a potent source of consumer lock-in as the value of an offering rises as more people join the network of users. For instance, video games are more valuable to the extent that more people play video games, and so on. Network externalities have strong effects that are frequently non-linear in nature. Due to this, many businesses commit large resources to either launch new user networks or capitalise on existing ones, frequently without a clear business plan in place. When the internet bubble was in its heyday, this sort of behaviour was expected. For instance, Excite@ Home spent $780 million to buy the free online card store www.Bluemountainarts.com in order to gain access to its base of millions of loyal users, only to give it back to the company's founders for pennies after declaring bankruptcy. Another example is the recent $580 million purchase of the well-known social networking site Myspace by News Corp. Businesses that can foresee renewing content, setting prices, allowing consumers to co-create information, or trading dynamically benefit greatly from access to a network of users.

3.2 Homing Tendencies

Numerous authors stress the significance of user groups not being confined to a single platform. Multi-homing is the term for this situation which as opposed to single-homing, describes users who interact with various platform ecosystems (Choi, 2010). Eisenmann, Parker, and van Alstyne (2011) contend that multi-homing costs must be significant for at least one of the user sides in order for a winner-take-all scenario to develop. The amount users infer when using a platform are referred to as "costs connected to homing" and comprise opportunity costs for using the platform as well as costs associated with platform adaptation and operation (Eisenmann et al., 2006). Users are highly unlikely to pay the same fees repeatedly and join many platforms if joining one is pricey for them. Schmalensee and Evans (2014) concur with this statement. They also draw the conclusion that both single-homing and multi-homing scenarios can produce various market results. They argue that if actors single-home on one side of the platform, they are then limited to communicating with actors on the other side of the platform exclusively through that platform. As additional transaction partners become accessible via the platform, platforms compete in this scenario by recruiting more players from both sides and displacing them from the competing platform. They argue that if actors single-home on one side of the platform, they are then limited to communicating with actors on the other side of the platform exclusively through that platform. As additional transaction partners become accessible via the platform, platforms compete in this scenario by recruiting more players from both sides and displacing them from the competing platform.

Another setting of the market is where one side of the digital platform multi-homes, while the other side single-homes. As a result, Armstrong (2006) refers to the single-home section of the platform as a "competitive bottleneck." Practically speaking, if a multi-homing agent wants to communicate with a single-homing agent, the agency must join the platform that the single-homing agent has selected. For instance, if a user wants to watch movies from The Walt Disney Company and only Netflix has the right to do so, that user cannot choose to join another streaming service like Amazon Prime or HBO but must instead sign up for Netflix.

As a result, platforms have monopoly power over the single-homing consumers they serve on the multi-homing side. Because the platform competes with other providers for single-homing actors, it is likely that price premiums will be necessary. As a result, this monopoly power may result in higher pricing for the multi-homing side (Belleflamme & Peitz, 2019). In the worst-case scenario, the single-homing actors do not profit from the larger income of the multi-housing side (Armstrong, 2006, pp. 669–670). The "competition bottleneck" idea does not, according to some authors, always predict how the described price structure will behave (Evans & Schmalensee, 2014, p. 16). From the perspective of the platforms, digital platforms compete on both sides of the platform wherein both the sides single-home, but in the market environment characterised as a "competitive bottleneck," platforms battle on the side that is single-homing, forcing the multi-homing side to pay monopolistic rates (Peitz & Belleflamme, 2019).

3.3 Complementors

Apps exclusivity describes the degree to which a platform denies its competitors access to its complementary products, i.e., those created for and offered just on that one platform. The main goal of exclusivity is to give users access to premium products and services that they won't be able to find on other platforms (Lee, 2007; Mantena et al., 2008). This strategy can improve a system's ability to compete since customers with strong preferences for particular (exclusive) items are forced to conduct business on the platform that manages them. A platform may also restrict access to complementary goods and services by exclusive agreements or contracts, reducing the actual participation of its rivals in the content and consumer markets (Armstrong & Wright, 2007; Mantena et al., 2008). This will also help the platform firm to establish long-lasting connections with complementary products and services producers making it easier to coordinate release dates and the type and quantity of products and services that complementors create (Yoffie & Kwak, 2006; Stennek, 2007).

4. One Winner Does Not Take All: A Paradigm Shift

The notion that only one winner emerges in the digital platform competition has recently been challenged by many researchers as many digital platform firms have been found to coexist with a significant installed base because of: (1) network effects that are asymmetric; (Shankar and Bayus; 2003; Suarez, 2005) (2) low charge of associating with a number of platforms; or (3) differentiated consumer choice that may limit the benefits of individual platforms. This has called into question the unconditional logic of the WTA hypothesis.

Network effects can also overturn and quickly destroy value. For instance, the two social networks that expanded rapidly and "won" the social networking market in their respective nations in the 2000s were MySpace in the U.S. and Orkut in Brazil and India. But once some users switched to Facebook, others did likewise, and both websites experienced a precipitous decline. Officially, Orkut was shut down in September 2014. The fact that Time, Inc. acquired what little of MySpace was left in February 2016 may say it all. The issue is that network effects aren't as strong as they once were. Historically, network effects were difficult to reverse in digital platform industries. The winner-take-all model of the first mover digital platform firm is threatened by current technology, which makes it easy for a challenger to enter the market at a minimum cost (Evans, and Schmalensee, 2016).

Recent theoretical models suggest that many platforms can coexist if the quality and positioning of their ecosystems are sufficiently distinct, which could prevent the market from favouring one dominant platform (Eisenmann, 2007; Eocman et al., 2006; Mingchun & Tse, 2007). Choosing platform content that appeals to the preferences of the greatest number of users is part of a "get-big-fast" approach. This will place the digital platform in the running to lead the mass market and position it to fully dominate the market if it amasses the largest installed base of users (Katz & Shapiro, 1994; Shapiro & Varian, 1999). The heterogeneity of consumer choices for the type of food, the variety of food items available in specialised niches, and their quality, for example, are distinguishing characteristics of the restaurant industry. These factors may lead users with various tastes to group around distinct market niches.

In an incredibly interesting empirical study, Huotari et al. (2017) analysed how consumer interactions at the micro-level lead to platform competition at the macro-level. In their study, the authors challenge the winner-take-all theory, contending that consumers are selectively attentive and locally biased rather than valuing a network's overall connection. Their research analysed various agent-based models with various presumptions about the behaviour of consumer agents, and then compared the predictions to actual data from the PlayStation 3 vs. Xbox 360 battle. The findings demonstrated that it is only possible to explain actual market sharing between the specified platforms when consumers are presupposed to be selectively attentive and locally biased. Despite the fact that an early entrant has established a winner-take-all situation for itself by having a larger initial installed base, a larger pool of complementary products, and a lower starting price, it is shown in practise how a late-entrant platform can still be embraced by the majority of customers in the market.

Winner-take-all circumstances can occasionally be constrained by regional dependencies, which can lead to the emergence of many local winner-take-all situations. The example of

Hungry.dk demonstrated how the level of competition depends on the variety of options available in a given market. Similar outcomes were observed with MyHammer. The supply side's ability to meet service requests is constrained in both situations. These two instances also demonstrate how regional dependencies vary depending on the business and are a feature of all industries. They also demonstrate how users in the same industry can have different regional dependence. The competition between platforms is related to an area as a result of this knowledge, and the competition results follow suit. The tangibleness of the good or service might also be connected to this regional dependence. Digital services like those offered by Fiverr are not necessarily location-based way actual goods and services like food and craftsman services are. However, governing authorities can intervene in regulations to create their regional dependencies. An illustration of this is the necessity of filing taxes in various nations when offering services worldwide.

The markets for mobile operating systems, digital media files, digital image files, and flash memory cards are examples of a distinct type of rivalry where no clear winner is revealed (Bresnahan, Orsini, & Yin 2015). A "Winners-Take-Some" (hereinafter "WTS") outcome, in which numerous platform owners survive the competition and each earn a sizeable but non-dominant portion of the market, has instead occurred in these markets. In the existence of low-cost conversion technologies, a WTS outcome is more probable. For instance, no tipping to one format or standard was shown in the market for digital flash memory cards. The widespread use of converters serving as "gateway technology" between various formats is credited with this WTS result (David, &Bunn, 1988). By enabling users to select a flash memory card format with a smaller installed base and not worry about compatibility costs, the availability of converters lowers consumers' perception of the value of network effects (Liu et al., 2012Another explanation for "winner-takes-some" situations is "asymmetric" regulation, which refers to regulation put in place to favour domestic platforms or to aggressively limit the market dominance of foreign platforms by regulatory or antitrust measures. Customers in Lebanon, for instance, can sign up for "Match.com" or "IslamicMarriage.com" according on their unique religious convictions and cultural preferences (Rossotto et. al., 2018)

5. Discussion

Winner-take-all markets have a number of significant drawbacks. The creation of new companies and businesspeople with innovative ideas is essential for economic development and creativity. Industries stagnate when the creative destructive gale stops blowing. When a small number of market leaders have complete control, they may put off potential competitors who cannot match their resources and industry clout. Startups are reportedly failing more frequently and more quickly than in the past. Investors prefer well-established businesses that offer safe short-term profits. Even when a startup is successful, it frequently gets bought out by a bigger organisation for instance each year, firms like Apple, Amazon, Facebook, and others buy hundreds of others.

Markets where the winner takes all tend to discourage cooperation and collaboration. The winners are motivated to keep their new information and knowledge to themselves. Copyright and patents are extensively employed to stifle any real competition. When they graduate from college, skilled professionals are immediately in demand and the winners offer strong incentives for them to stay on as employees. The circumstance is akin to a prisoner's dilemma as a result. Although working together may be great for everyone, being selfish is advantageous for each organisation separately. As a result, nobody works together; instead, they all compete.

As a result, there is what Warren Buffett refers to as a "moat"—a substantial barrier to competition. There are several types of business moats. An example of a moat in a better brand identity is Apple. It has required significant resource commitments to establish, and newer businesses are unable to compete. The level of significance Apple has in our cultural consciousness cannot be replicated by any number of Facebook advertisements or billboards. The moat for other winners can be the capacity to offer a good or service at a cheaper cost than rivals, as with Amazon and Alibaba. Each of these has a considerable amount of market power and the ability to affect prices. If Amazon lowers its pricing, rivals are forced to follow suit and earn less money. Consumers won't likely shop elsewhere for their phones and computers if Apple decides to boost its costs, and they will pay more. Market power thus, can make markets inefficient because it keeps the price and quantity out of the equilibrium of supply and demand, according to Greg Mankiw in Principles of Microeconomics (Street, n.d)

The concept of a winner-take-all market had to be clearly defined. The lack of agreement among scholars in characterising this competition outcome gives rise to the necessity. Scholars cannot analyse the situation with a consistent understanding in the absence of a precise definition, and practitioners cannot outline tactics for reaching a winner-take-all conclusion without first comprehending what that term entails. The winner-take-all outcome is not the only method for dominance and persistence, as recent research has shown, which makes it even more important to discover the other potential strategies for persistence for digital platform firms and the factors influencing it.

6. Conclusion

Will "creative destruction," or capitalism's capacity to develop, annihilate, and remake itself, eventually end the market dominance of the tech giants? Due to the potent combination of winner-take-all variables, this looks unlikely. For instance, a competitor to Google in the search market would need to provide customers with an incentive or a notably superior experience over a length of time sufficient to break their habit of using Google. With little likelihood of success, this would take years and cost tens of billions of dollars. In 2013, it was reported that Microsoft had lost $11 billion overall in search. Therefore, it is difficult to imagine the tech giants' ever ceding control of their primary markets. Apple is the lone exception. Apple, which is still the most lucrative corporation in the world, is now facing difficulties as its price advantage over high-end Android devices is eroding and it is more pushed to integrate Google services into its ecosystem. At the periphery of their primary markets, the other IT behemoths also see some competition. As more people shop directly on Amazon, perhaps using its Echo smart speaker and Alexa voice assistant, the primary immediate threat to Google is the company's expanding search business. Similar to this, users of social media can multi-home leading towards an outcome where rivals coexist alongside Facebook. However, based on the trend already mentioned, it appears unlikely that Google, Amazon, Facebook, or Microsoft would lose their global market domination in the near future.

Successful platforms can be "eclipsed," but not "displaced," according to a general principle (Barwise & Watkins 2018). For instance, Kodak had 85% market dominance in camera sales and a 90% market share in film sales. The transition to digitization, not the presence of direct competition, was what led to Kodak's demise. Digital cameras, which themselves were surpassed by smartphones, overtook the conventional camera industry. Why do widely known platforms eventually become into monopolistic ones where one firm gets everything? In sum, there are a number of causes for this (Shapiro & Varian 1999; Stummer et al., 2018).

First, the standard economy of scale is applicable. Large fixed costs and low marginal costs are frequently associated with digital goods and services. For instance, creating machine learning methods that scale properly is quite expensive. However, it is inexpensive to use the learned model on a fresh group of customers. Take note that Uber and Airbnb have marginal transaction costs that are almost nil. Losses, if any, are brought on by fixed costs. Second, there are frequently referred to as "network effects." The platform gains value as more individuals or groups sign up. The platform is less valuable than when practically all of your friends are on Facebook if only one of your colleagues uses it. Airbnb loses value when it just offers one room in Amsterdam, but the value improves when it offers thousands of rooms. Also, more data makes machine learning approaches more effective. As a result, the quality of the platform naturally improves as platform utilisation grows. In addition to these network effects, technology companies employ a variety of user retention tactics (e.g., not trying to reducing switching costs).

It is always possible that a rival with a dominant market share could overtake a company with less market share. To counter this risk, the big tech businesses make significant investments in new goods and technology, whether through their own R&D, the purchase of start-ups that show promise or pose a danger, or the duplication of unattainable technologies. Self-driving technology is an excellent example, with businesses like Tesla, Google, and Apple vying for the top spot in a competitive new market (Barwise, 2018).

REFERENCES

1. Armstrong, Mark, and Julian Wright. "Two-sided markets, competitive bottlenecks and exclusive contracts." *Economic Theory* 32, no. 2 (2007): 353–380.
2. Armstrong, Mark. "Competition in two-sided markets." *The RAND journal of economics* 37, no. 3 (2006): 668–691.
3. Arthur, W. Brian. "Increasing returns and the new world of business." *Harvard business review* 74, no. 4 (1996): 100.
4. Barwise, Patrick, and Leo Watkins. "The evolution of digital dominance." *Digital dominance: the power of Google, Amazon, Facebook, and Apple* (2018): 21–49.
5. Barwise, Patrick. "Nine reasons why tech markets are winner-take-all." London Business School. July 10, 2018. https://www.london.edu/think/nine-reasons-why-tech-markets-are-winner-take-all.

6. Belleflamme, Paul, and Martin Peitz. "Platform competition: Who benefits from multihoming?." *International Journal of Industrial Organization* 64 (2019): 1–26.
7. Bresnahan, Timothy, Joe Orsini, and Pai-Ling Yin. "Demand heterogeneity, inframarginal multihoming, and platform market stability: Mobile apps." In *Proc. 9th IDEI-TSE-IAST Conf. Econ. Intellectual Property, Softw. Internet.* 2015.
8. *Cambridge Dictionary.* Cambridge: Cambridge University Press, 2019
9. Cennamo, Carmelo, and Juan Santalo. "Platform competition: Strategic trade-offs in platform markets." *Strategic management journal* 34, no. 11 (2013): 1331–1350.
10. Choi, Jay Pil. "Tying in two-sided markets with multi-homing." *The Journal of Industrial Economics* 58, no. 3 (2010): 607–626.
11. David, Paul A., and Julie Ann Bunn. "The economics of gateway technologies and network evolution: Lessons from electricity supply history." *Information economics and policy* 3, no. 2 (1988): 165–202.
12. De Reuver, Mark, Carsten Sørensen, and Rahul C. Basole. "The digital platform: a research agenda." *Journal of information technology* 33, no. 2 (2018): 124–135.
13. Eisenmann, Thomas R. "Winner-take-all in networked markets." In *Harvard Business School Background Note*, vol. 806, pp. 1–15, 2007.
14. Eisenmann, Thomas, Geoffrey Parker, and Marshall Van Alstyne. "Platform envelopment." *Strategic management journal* 32, no. 12 (2011): 1270–1285.
15. Evans, D., R. Schmalensee, and A. Hagiu. "Invisible Engines: How Software Platforms Drive Innovation." (2014).
16. Evans, S David and Schmalensee Richard. "Why winner-takes-all thinking doesn't apply to the platform economy." Harvard Business Review. May 04, 2016. https://hbr.org/2016/05/why-winner-takes-all-thinking-doesnt-apply-to-silicon-valley
17. Farnam Street. "Winner takes it all: How markets favour the few at the expense of the many." n.d. https://fs.blog/mental-model-winner-take-all/.
18. Huotari, Pontus, Kati Järvi, Samuli Kortelainen, and Jukka Huhtamäki. "Winner does not take all: Selective attention and local bias in platform-based markets." *Technological Forecasting and Social Change* 114 (2017): 313–326.
19. Kelly, Kevin. *New rules for the new economy: 10 radical strategies for a connected world.* Penguin, 1999.
20. Kemerer, Chris F., Brian Kimball Dunn, and Shadi Janansefat. "Winners-take-some dynamics in digital platform markets: A reexamination of the video game console wars." *University of Pittsburgh, PA* (2017).
21. Kenney, Martin, and John Zysman. "The rise of the platform economy." *Issues in science and technology* 32, no. 3 (2016): 61.
22. Lee, Eocman, Jeho Lee, and Jongseok Lee. "Reconsideration of the winner-take-all hypothesis: Complex networks and local bias." *Management science* 52, no. 12 (2006): 1838–1848.
23. Lee, Robin S. "Vertical integration and exclusivity in platform and two-sided markets." *American Economic Review* 103, no. 7 (2013): 2960–3000.
24. Liu, Charles Zhechao, Chris F. Kemerer, Sandra A. Slaughter, and Michael D. Smith. "Standards competition in the presence of digital conversion technology: An empirical analysis of the flash memory card market." *MIS Quarterly* (2012): 921–942.
25. Mantena, Ravindra, Ramesh Sankaranarayanan, and Siva Viswanathan. "Platform-based information goods: The economics of exclusivity." *Decision Support Systems* 50, no. 1 (2010): 79–92.

26. McGrath, R. "And the winner takes it all? Necessary conditions and entry strategies in winner-take-all markets." *Strategy, Innovation and Change–Challenges for management* (2005): 57–68.

27. McIntyre, David P., and Mohan Subramaniam. "Strategy in network industries: A review and research agenda." *Journal of Management* 35, no. 6 (2009): 1494–1517.

28. Parker, Geoffrey, and Marshall W. Van Alstyne. "Platform strategy." (2014).

29. Rossotto, Carlo Maria, Prasanna Lal Das, Elena Gasol Ramos, Eva Clemente Miranda, Mona Farid Badran, Martha Martinez Licetti, and Graciela Miralles Murciego. "Digital platforms: A literature review and policy implications for development." *Competition and Regulation in Network Industries* 19, no. 1–2 (2018): 93–109.

30. Ruutu, Sampsa, Thomas Casey, and Ville Kotovirta. "Development and competition of digital service platforms: A system dynamics approach." *Technological Forecasting and Social Change* 117 (2017): 119–130.

31. Shankar, Venkatesh, and Barry L. Bayus. "Network effects and competition: An empirical analysis of the home video game industry." *Strategic management journal* 24, no. 4 (2003): 375–384.

32. Shapiro, Carl, Hal R. Varian, and Shapiro Carl. *Information rules: A strategic guide to the network economy.* Harvard Business Press, 1999.

33. Stummer, Christian, Dennis Kundisch, and Reinhold Decker. "Platform launch strategies." *Business & Information Systems Engineering* 60, no. 2 (2018): 167–173.

34. Sun, Mingchun, and Edison Tse. "When does the winner take all in two-sided markets?." *Review of Network Economics* 6, no. 1 (2007).

35. Yoffie, David B., and Mary Kwak. "With friends like these: The art of managing complementors." *Harvard business review* 84, no. 9 (2006): 88–98.

36. Zhu, Feng, and Marco Iansiti. "Entry into platform-based markets." *Strategic Management Journal* 33, no. 1 (2012): 88–106.

Chapter

Business Networks and Strategic Orientation Help Firms Navigate the Dynamic Nature of Business, Leading to Product Innovation

Amit Kumar Gupta*

Management Development Institute Gurgaon,
Sukhrali, Mehrauli road, Gurgaon, Haryana, India

ABSTRACT: Innovation is of utmost necessity for firms to be able to compete in the market and survive. Organizations use strategic business networks to multiply their capabilities and increase product innovation. In this ever-changing world, networking, strategic alliances, and the firm's ability to adapt to the dynamic nature will help the companies compete. Thus, this study examines whether Business Networks and Strategic Orientation help firms navigate the Dynamic nature of business in India, which can further lead to Product Innovation. The study surveyed respondents working in the manufacturing and service sectors. The study worked on 270 sample responses. The hypotheses are tested using Covariance-based structural equation modeling. Business networks and strategic orientation, directly and indirectly, affect a company's product innovation. Strategic orientation directly influences dynamic capability, while business networks indirectly influence dynamic capability mediated through strategic orientation. Further, it is also noted that developing dynamic capabilities provide companies with a competitive edge in the market by ensuring more robust product development.

KEYWORDS: Product innovation, Business networks, Strategic orientation, Dynamic capabilities, SEM

1. Introduction

Organizations use strategic business networks to multiply their capabilities and increase product innovation. Innovation is of utmost necessity for firms to be able to compete in the

*amitkgupta@mdi.ac.in; amitg56@gmail.com

DOI: 10.4324/9781003415725-66

market and survive. In this ever-changing world, networking, strategic alliances and the firm's ability to adapt to the dynamic nature will help the companies compete. Technology is one field that has seen rapid advancements in the past few decades. The growth is exponential. Firms relevant a few decades ago are obsolete now, and the relevant firms may be obsolete in a few years if they don't adapt to changes. With innovation, the product life cycle can be longer, and the firms can be in the growth stage for a longer time, otherwise moving to the maturity and decline phase in no time. There was a time when a firm was self-sufficient with all the upstream and downstream activities done by the company itself. But this era of globalization requires businesses to form networks and be able to compete with competitors all over the globe. If a firm can reduce its expenses by outsourcing, it will readily do it. The smaller firm's competitive advantage may be in that field and hence can produce or provide the service at a lower cost. New methodologies in research have led companies to come up with product innovations. Consumers are also becoming increasingly quality-conscious, making firms develop new products regularly with innovations that please the customers. Consumers want the product value to outdo the monetary value of the product. A business network is a network of companies working to accomplish specific objectives and dynamic capabilities by integrating their core competencies, another network, and the power of suppliers and human resources to tackle the fast-paced changing environments in which the firms currently function. There have been innumerable instances of this happening, and every firm in the market, in one way or another, follows the business network to benefit from that. It is mutually beneficial for the firms involved and potential clients and customers. It's a win-win situation for the companies who are forming a network. The firms also need to concoct the company's long-range vision for daily work, starting from a simple understanding of the concepts to complex cognizance of the impact of thinking and actions. Expanding a business involves setting milestones regularly that depict the critical stages in the future that a firm aspires to reach by utilizing its resources and capabilities more often, planning and achieving short-term goals will help in capturing the long-term goals. The long-term goals can be broken down into short-term goals that will keep the company on the right track. The Strategic Orientation needs effective implementation by the firm's top management, followed by the middle and bottom management. It has been successfully integrated into the company. In this changing environment, organizations need to develop new products and changes to the design of the established product or use new materials to reduce the cost of manufacturing without compromising on quality through product innovation.

2. Business Networks

Business Networks are the ability of a business to align with other firms working in the same space or in the position of its supplier to extract competitive advantage by using each other's core competency for mutual benefit (Morales-Alonso et al. 2020; Trequattrini, Russo, and Lombardi 2012). This helps the firm save on cost and future investments in R&D. Networks are part of a firm's resources. For successful management of networks, it was also found that managing intra-firm relationships is crucial as these are ultimately the individuals who network with the partners (Ritter et al., 2004). Bengtsson and Kock (2000) argue that "coopetition" is the most beneficial form of relationship with competitors that involves cooperating and simultaneously competing with the other firm. However, Networks give greater collaboration opportunities for product innovation but may also hamper the internal change required to exploit this opportunity (Håkansson and Ford 2002).

Dynamic Capability

A firm can create flexibility in its business process which will help them fight against the environmental changes that continuously distort its operations. A firm also has to ensure that flexibility is continuous and evolves as the changes evolve. In this VUCA (Volatile, Uncertain, Complex, Ambiguous) world, a firm that adapts to the dynamic nature of the environment will be the one successful in the industry (Eisenhardt and Martin, 2000; Vu, 2020). The term "Dynamic Capability" was introduced by (Teece and Pisano 1994) to describe what allows firms to gain a competitive advantage over others, which could be done through enhancing the capabilities, i.e., functional capability, integrative capability, and innovation capability (Lawson and Samson, 2001). Winter (2003) states that new product development is itself an example of "dynamic capability" as it is different from the ordinary routines performed to serve the customer in the present.

Product Innovation

It is the process by which an organization continuously updates its services/ products to have that competitive edge over its competitors. The updating could be incremental or a complete overhaul. The customers will buy those products which are convenient for them. They readily accept any innovation which will increase their convenience. Lukas and Ferrell (2000) define product innovation as "bringing new technology into use" and thus breaking product innovation into three categories, extensions, imitating competitor products, and creating entirely new products. Un et al. (2010) explore the effect of R&D Collaboration with different stakeholders on product innovation. Partnering with suppliers in R&D was found to have the most positive impact on innovation. On the other hand, Zhou and Wu (2010) state that technological capability has a direct effect on exploitative innovation, but when it comes to exploratory innovation, this capability has an inverted U-shaped relation

Strategic Orientation

Every company has a strategy. It'll follow these strategies to achieve its overall mission. The strategy has to make use of its competitive advantage. The firm can organize its processes, system, human resource, and external connections to leverage the company's set strategy in the best possible way (Schweiger et al., 2019). Venkatraman (1989) gives a six-dimensional model to measure strategic orientation, i.e., Aggressiveness, Defensiveness, Proactiveness, Futurity, Risk Aversion, and Innovativeness. It is found that strategic orientation is firm and environment dependent. The same orientation may not work for all firms. Its structure and culture dictate what suits it (K. Z. Zhou et al., 2005).

The study examines the effect of business networks and strategic orientation on a firm's ability to handle the highly vulnerable and changing environment by developing dynamic capabilities like upcoming technologies, flexible strategies, and strategic partnerships, which leads to Product Innovation. The hypotheses are tested using Covariance-based structural equation modeling. The study surveyed respondents working in the manufacturing and service sectors. The study worked on 270 sample responses.

2. Literature Review and Theory Development

Narrative literature reviews are done to draw the required hypothesis and develop the conceptual model.

2.1 Impact of Internal Strategy and External Collaborations on an Organization

In this changing world, every company or firm requires a competitive edge over the other players to ensure they remain profitable and have the most significant piece of the pie. This involves having the most powerful, technologically advanced, and efficiently priced product/ service available in the market. This might seem easy at first, but it requires overhauling multiple departments. Spending a huge sum of money to develop such a specialized department means a loss of efficiency and competitive advantage (Zhang and Wu, 2017). Instead, integrating with other companies specializing in these departments and partnering with them to provide these services means a more cost-efficient and quicker way of reaching the firm's goal. A direct correlation between the capabilities achieved from outside integration and the firms' sustainable conduct in the VUCA world (Eikelenboom and de Jong 2019).

Firms come together to leverage the skill and techniques that the other player has developed and pitch in for the player's transformation so that the firm can survive the changes coming up in the market and ensure they can secure themselves from the vulnerabilities going to hit it. This further entails that the benefit the firm gains goes into making its product and service more conducive to changing customer preferences (Kollmann et al., 2021). Though the picture looks beneficial for both parties in the partnership, The partnership might start initially like well-oiled machinery but soon enough is slowed down due to the other partner's constant bickering and feeling of deceit (Zhang and Wu, 2017). With the growth in vertical integration, there has been an increase in profitability with more efficient sharing of ideas simultaneously. Thus, filigree tasks among companies and their associates significantly affect novelty accomplishment (Eggers et al., 2020).

Unlike the 19th century, the 20th century has created yet another challenge for companies. The companies can no longer survive with a fixed strategy. The need is not just to alter its strategy but to have a strategy that differentiates it from the competition, giving them that extra edge over the competition. It not only depends on the company's strategy but also on the communication that goes from the top management to the low-level workers and their understanding that ensures success (Adams et al., 2019). How effectively strategic orientation works depends on the market forces at work. A company might have a winning strategy, but how the customers and the market sentiment react to it also control the success of the company's product/ service and financial performance. When a market is highly uncertain, it isn't easy to gauge the consumer's preferences and the way the market will react to the new product/ services. Adaptive skills in such a situation are more driven by technology orientation than customer orientation, as they give an overall advantage by reducing the cost while increasing the performance of the product/services. It also reduces the time to enter, ensuring that the product/ service is launched before the customer's preferences alter (Zhu et al., 2019). Another factor that improves the chance of success for a product/ service is the autonomy to make decisions. Giving freedom to mid and low-level employees leads to higher morale and better involvement. It also helps to surface research directly gathered from the customers by the employees communicating with them. It also brings better synergy in the various levels of the organization, which means better acceptance of the strategy devised. All this increases the chances of delivering product innovation, which not only is innovative but is according to market requirements and competitively priced and featured (Beugelsdijk and Jindra, 2018). However, partnerships lead to a better method of handling the changing world by fulfilling the capabilities that the firm misses out on. However, in the current world, partnerships don't end with firms with interdependent capabilities; they also extend to competitors. When the pie representing the customers doesn't increase, competition can lead to a new player in a price war; however, creating synergies between competitors can mean a better strategy for handling this situation. But it doesn't mean that the effect of partnership with competitors was not linearly correspondent to product innovation. Instead, a bell-shaped relationship can be seen between such partnerships and product innovation. Though the partnership looks attractive, factors like technological capability and firm structuring (A part of dynamic capability) also weaken this relationship (Wu, 2014). The capability of a firm to integrate with other firms, whether partner firms or competitors, also depends on the culture of the organizations, the technology they use, and the mindset of the management handling the organizations. The organizations' strategies should intermix in a cohesive bond to work towards mutual benefits. Thus the new capabilities they develop out of the bond depending on the type of synergy they have and the strength of their bond (Jiang et al., 2015). Effectively using the existing resources in a changing environment (Coordination flexibility) has been shown to positively affect product innovation. This effect is more critical in a higher-competition scenario (Yuan et al., 2010). Thus more important than the people and the technology of the firm is how the organization strategies and then translates it to process task and resource management controls the product/ service innovation it can develop. Efficient Business Management strengthens the positive effect of organizational Innovation depth (Zhu et al., 2019). Therefore, we hypothesize:

H1. Firm business networks improve firms' strategic orientation

H2: Firms' Strategic Orientation and Business Networks affect Indian firm's Dynamic capabilities

H3: Strategic Orientation mediates the influence of the Business Networks on Dynamic capabilities

2.2 Adapting Business to the Changing Environment

As technology, political environment, regulations, and consumer preferences change, companies have this requirement to evolve constantly and keep themselves ahead of the competition. In addition to being ahead, with the continually depleting resources and public sentiment increasing towards being eco-friendlier, companies must constantly evolve their practices to make their services and products eco-friendly (Zhu et al., 2019). Companies must continuously move forward by developing their skillset, investing in human resources, and utilizing a new technology. In addition, a company needs to be on the lookout for partnering with organisations that can be a value add, improving their process and cost-efficient. Developing capabilities that will help firms develop plans to steer through the stormy atmosphere will help them make their products/ services better and cheaper while ensuring earlier entry into the market. Firms making better exploratory and exploitative product innovation in a stormy atmosphere is known for combinative skills since such products will help them beat their competitor and ensure customers stay attracted to their product, ensuring their lead in the market (Sheng, 2017). A crucial factor in today's world that affects market perception is the company's practices. Since the depleting resources have pushed consumers to purchase products that ensure future existence, developing green product advances can improve a firm's attractiveness in the mind of consumers (Chen and Liu, 2020). Thus creating a strategy that combines an eco-strategy with the firms existing strategy and communicating the strategy to the employees working at each level of the organization would ensure success in today's market. The efforts don't end at communicating executive backing, and morale-boosting are essential practices that ensure that the low-level workers believe in the company's plans. The ability of a company to develop practices and engineer products that are not only eco-friendly but also have the required features at similar pricing would mean that the product is successful and ensures customer loyalty. These practices directly correlate with the market value and the green products for companies (Dangelico et al., 2017).

A growing population and increasing purchasing power mean no shortage of opportunities for a firm to excel. Still, not every opportunity can align with how a firm functions. Thus, dynamic capabilities directly correlate with the firm's intent of adopting a newly available opportunity. The secret behind the firm's success is its ability to track the changes they are about to encounter quickly and mold its strategy and skillset through technology or human resources as promptly as possible so that it can stay competitive in the market (Zhou et al., 2018). Another power that companies today possess is the power of data, the companies that understand this power quickly are the ones that have the highest probability of success. With a huge information database, firms today can understand trends and patterns that indicate how the market is changing, giving the firm a fighting chance and the ability to alter its offering according to the demand. Thus higher the data higher the probability of success. (Zhou and Li, 2012). Therefore, researchers have used the different dimensions in the "Dynamic Capabilities" to show that it helps in the organization's product and service innovation. But not much research has been done exploring the mediating effect of dynamic capabilities when business networks and a firm's strategy support innovation. (Laforet, 2008) analyses the relationship between product innovation and strategic orientation for South Korean SMEs. SMEs generally don't have the budget to invest as much in R&D. Still, strategic orientation affects product innovation. Do capabilities matter if the organization has strategy available and the partners needed to support innovation? Therefore, we hypothesize the following:

H4: Strategic orientation, Business networks, and The ability to handle dynamic environment leads to product innovation

H5: Dynamic capabilities positively mediate the influence of Strategic orientation and Business networks on Product innovation.

Based on the above literature review and hypothesis formation, the study proposes the theoretical model shown in Fig. 66.1.

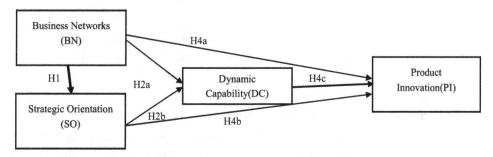

Fig. 66.1 Proposed conceptual diagram

Source: Author's compilation

3. Research Methodology

3.1 Questionnaire and Measures

Questionnaires were developed using well-rounded constructs taken post-literature review: business networks, strategic orientation, dynamic capability, and product innovation. We measured these questions on a seven-point Likert scale, where 1 is defined as low/ don't agree and 7 as high/ agree. Measures are adopted from (Jiang et al., 2020) and (Gupta 2021; Gupta and Gupta 2019).

3.2 Sample Design

Samples were collected from individuals, including male and female individuals with diverse qualifications, working in the manufacturing and service sector of Indian companies at various Positions. 270 samples were received. Data received were cleaned, and multivariate normality and outlier tests were performed using (Mahalonabis 1936). 197 data were obtained after cleaning.

3.3 Reliability and Validity Test

The constructs' reliability or consistency was estimated using Cronbach's Alpha on all the constructs using SPSS. Validity of the constructs is ensured using a measurement model (CFA) using AMOS. The output of the test is summarized in Table 66.1. Cronbach's values greater than 0.7 signify the constructs' measures are reliable (J F Hair et al., 2018). Similarly, values of AVE and CR for each construct greater than 0.5 and 0.7, respectively, signify convergent validity, and AVEs greater than MSVs of all constructs indicate discriminant validity (Joseph F. Hair et al., 2014; Fornell and Larcker 1981).

Table 66.1 Outcome of the reliability and validity test

	DC	SO	BN	PI
AVE	0.55	0.54	0.62	0.58
CR	0.83	0.82	0.83	0.80
MSV	.495	.495	.435	.48
Sqrt(AVE)	0.74	0.73	0.79	0.76
α-Values	0.755	0.766	0.747	0.771

Source: Author's compilation

3.4 Hypotheses Testing- Structure Equation Modeling

The hypotheses are tested using Covariance based structural equation modeling in AMOS. The fit and valid measurement model is converted into a structural equation model, and estimation for path coefficients is done, as shown in Fig. 66.2.

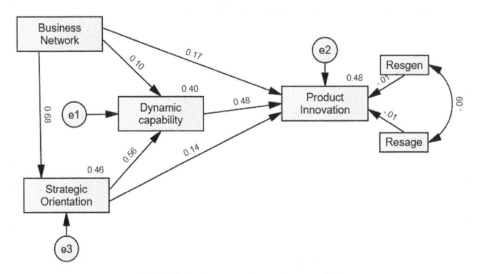

Fig. 66.2 Structural equation model

Source: Author's compilation

The estimated values and results of direct, indirect, and total effects are summarized in Tables 66.2 and 66,3.

Table 66.2 Results of direct effect

	BN	SO	Resgen	Resage	DC
SO	0.68***				
DC	0.103	0.562***			
PI	0.166**	0.143*	-0.006	-0.01	0.48***

Source: Author's compilation

Table 66.3 Results of indirect and total effect

Indirect effect			Total effect					
	BN	SO		BN	SO	Resgen	resage	DC
SO			SO	0.68***				
DC	0.382***		DC	0.485***	0.562***			
PI	0.33***	0.27***	PI	0.497***	0.413***	-0.006	-0.01	0.48***

Source: Author's compilation

Resgen (respondent gender) and Resage (respondent age) are the model's control variables. The standardized direct effect of Resgen and Resage on endogenous variable Product innovation (PI) is insignificant. Thus, it indicates the robustness of the model.

4. Results and Discussion

The outcomes of the Hypotheses are summarized in Tables 66.4 and 66.5

Table 66.4 Outcome of the hypotheses (direct)

Hypothesis	Standardies effect	p-values	R-square	Outcome
H1. Firm business networks improve firms' strategic orientation	0.68	0.002	0.46	Accepted
H2a: Firms' Business Networks affect Indian firm's Dynamic capabilities	0.103	0.201	0.4	Not accepted
H2b: Firms' Strategic Orientation effect on Indian firm's Dynamic capabilities	0.562	0.001		Accepted
H4a: Business networks influence product innovation	0.166	0.019	0.48	Accepted
H4b: Strategic orientation influences product innovation	0.143	0.09		Accepted
H4c: The ability to handle dynamic environment influences product innovation	0.48	0.001		Accepted

Source: Author's compilation

Table 66.5 Outcome of the hypotheses (indirect)

Hypothesis	Standardies effect	p-values	Outcome	Mediation effect	Mediation type
H3: Strategic Orientation mediates the influence of the Business Networks on Dynamic capabilities	0.382	0.001	Accepted	79%	Full
H5a: Dynamic capabilities positively mediate the influence of Strategic orientation on Product innovation.	0.27	0.001	Accepted	66%	Partial
H5b: Dynamic capabilities positively mediate the influence of Strategic orientation on Product innovation.	0.16	>0.05	Accepted	32%	Partial

Source: Author's compilation

Business networks directly influence strategic orientation and product innovation while fails to influence dynamic capability at a 95% confidence level directly. Thus, H1 and H4a are accepted, while H2a is not accepted. Similarly, Strategic orientation directly affects dynamic capability and product innovation at 99% and 90% confidence levels. Thus, H2b and H4b are accepted. The dynamic capability of firms leads to Product innovation. Thus, H4c is accepted.

The strategic orientation fully mediates the effect of business networks on dynamic capability. Though business networks do not directly influence dynamic capability, in the presence of the firm's strategic orientation, it affects dynamic capability. Thus H3 is accepted. Similarly, Dynamic capability partially mediates the effect of Business networks and strategic orientation on Product innovation.

REFERENCE

1. Adams, Pamela, Isabel Maria Bodas Freitas, and Roberto Fontana. 2019. "Strategic Orientation, Innovation Performance and the Moderating Influence of Marketing Management." *Journal of Business Research.*
2. Bengtsson, Maria, and Sören Kock. 2000. "'Coopetition' in Business Networks - To Cooperate and Compete Simultaneously." *Industrial Marketing Management.*
3. Beugelsdijk, Sjoerd, and Björn Jindra. 2018. "Product Innovation and Decision-Making Autonomy in Subsidiaries of Multinational Companies." *Journal of World Business.*
4. Chen, Jiawen, and Linlin Liu. 2020. "Customer Participation, and Green Product Innovation in SMEs: The Mediating Role of Opportunity Recognition and Exploitation." *Journal of Business Research.*
5. Dangelico, Rosa Maria, Devashish Pujari, and Pierpaolo Pontrandolfo. 2017. "Green Product Innovation in Manufacturing Firms: A Sustainability-Oriented Dynamic Capability Perspective." *Business Strategy and the Environment.*
6. Eggers, Fabian, Thomas Niemand, Matthias Filser, Sascha Kraus, and Jennifer Berchtold. 2020. "To Network or Not to Network – Is That Really the Question? The Impact of Networking Intensity and Strategic Orientations on Innovation Success." *Technological Forecasting and Social Change..*
7. Eikelenboom, M., and G. de Jong. 2019. "The Impact of Dynamic Capabilities on the Sustainability Performance of SMEs." *Journal of Cleaner Production.*
8. Eisenhardt, Kathleen M., and Jeffrey A. Martin. 2000. "Dynamic Capabilities: What Are They?" *Strategic Management Journal.*
9. Fornell, Claes, and DF Larcker. 1981. "Evaluating Structural Equation Models with Unobservable Variables and Measurement Error." *Journal of Marketing Research.*
10. Gupta, Amit Kumar. 2021. "Innovation Dimensions and Firm Performance Synergy in the Emerging Market: A Perspective from Dynamic Capability Theory & Signaling Theory." *Technology in Society.*
11. Gupta, Amit Kumar, and Narain Gupta. 2019. "Innovation and Culture as a Dynamic Capability for Firm Performance: A Study from Emerging Markets." *Global Journal of Flexible Systems Management.*
12. Hair, J F, R E Anderson, R L Tatham, and W C Black. 2018. *Multivariate Data Analysis, Multivariate Data Analysis. Multivariate Data Analysis, Multivariate Data Analysis B2 - Multivariate Data Analysis, Multivariate Data Analysis.*
13. Hair, Joseph F., William C. Black, Barry J. Babin, and Rolph E. Anderson. 2014. *Multivariate Data Analysis Seventh Edition. Pearson New International.*

14. Håkansson, Håkan, and David Ford. 2002. "How Should Companies Interact in Business Networks?" *Journal of Business Research.*

15. Jiang, Wei, Felix Tinoziva Mavondo, and Margaret Jekanyika Matanda. 2015. "Integrative Capability for Successful Partnering: A Critical Dynamic Capability." *Management Decision.*

16. Kollmann, Tobias, Christoph Stöckmann, Thomas Niemand, Simon Hensellek, and Katharina de Cruppe. 2021. "A Configurational Approach to Entrepreneurial Orientation and Cooperation Explaining Product/Service Innovation in Digital vs. Non-Digital Startups." *Journal of Business Research.*

17. Laforet, Sylvie. 2008. "Size, Strategic, and Market Orientation Affects on Innovation." *Journal of Business Research.*

18. LAWSON, BENN, and DANNY SAMSON. 2001. "DEVELOPING INNOVATION CAPABILITY IN ORGANISATIONS: A DYNAMIC CAPABILITIES APPROACH." *International Journal of Innovation Management.*

19. Lukas, Bryan A., and O. C. Ferrell. 2000. "The Effect of Market Orientation on Product Innovation." *Journal of the Academy of Marketing Science.*

20. Mahalonabis, Prasanta chandra. 1936. "Proceedings of the National Institute of Science of India." In *On the Generalised Distance in Statistics*, 49–55.

21. Morales-Alonso, Gustavo, Guzmán A. Vila, Isaac Lemus-Aguilar, and Antonio Hidalgo. 2020. "Data Retrieval from Online Social Media Networks for Defining Business Angels' Profile." *Journal of Enterprising Communities..*

22. Ritter, Thomas, Ian F. Wilkinson, and Wesley J. Johnston. 2004. "Managing in Complex Business Networks." *Industrial Marketing Management.*

23. Schweiger, Simone A., Tatiana R. Stettler, Artur Baldauf, and César Zamudio. 2019. "The Complementarity of Strategic Orientations: A Meta-Analytic Synthesis and Theory Extension." *Strategic Management Journal.*

24. Sheng, Margaret L. 2017. "A Dynamic Capabilities-Based Framework of Organizational Sensemaking through Combinative Capabilities towards Exploratory and Exploitative Product Innovation in Turbulent Environments." *Industrial Marketing Management.*

25. Teece, David, and Gary Pisano. 1994. "The Dynamic Capabilities of Firms: An Introduction." *Industrial and Corporate Change.*

26. Trequattrini, Raffaele, Giuseppe Russo, and Rosa Lombardi. 2012. "Defining Business Network." *International Journal of Business Research and Management.*

27. Un, C. Annique, Alvaro Cuervo-Cazurra, and Kazuhiro Asakawa. 2010. "R&D Collaborations and Product Innovation." *Journal of Product Innovation Management.*

28. Venkatraman, N. 1989. "Strategic Orientation of Business Enterprises: The Construct, Dimensionality, and Measurement." *Management Science.*

29. Vu, Hieu Minh. 2020. "A Review of Dynamic Capabilities, Innovation Capabilities, Entrepreneurial Capabilities and Their Consequences." *Journal of Asian Finance, Economics and Business..*

30. Winter, Sidney G. 2003. "Understanding Dynamic Capabilities." *Strategic Management Journal.*

31. Wu, Jie. 2014. "Cooperation with Competitors and Product Innovation: Moderating Effects of Technological Capability and Alliances with Universities." *Industrial Marketing Management.*

32. Yuan, Li, Su Zhongfeng, and Liu Yi. 2010. "Can Strategic Flexibility Help Firms Profit from Product Innovation?" *Technovation.*

33. Zhang, Junfeng, and Wei ping Wu. 2017. "Leveraging Internal Resources and External Business Networks for New Product SuccessA Dynamic Capabilities Perspective." *Industrial Marketing Management.*

34. Zhou, Kevin Zheng, Gerald Yong Gao, Zhilin Yang, and Nan Zhou. 2005. "Developing Strategic Orientation in China: Antecedents and Consequences of Market and Innovation Orientations." *Journal of Business Research.*

35. Zhou, Kevin Zheng, and Caroline Bingxin Li. 2012. "How Knowledge Affects Radical Innovation: Knowledge Base, Market Knowledge Acquisition, and Internal Knowledge Sharing." *Strategic Management Journal.*

36. Zhou, Kevin Zheng, and Fang Wu. 2010. "Technological Capability, Strategic Flexibility, and Product Innovation." *Strategic Management Journal.*

37. Zhou, Yu, Jin Hong, Kejia Zhu, Yang Yang, and Dingtao Zhao. 2018. "Dynamic Capability Matters: Uncovering Its Fundamental Role in Decision Making of Environmental Innovation." *Journal of Cleaner Production.*

38. Zhu, Xiaoxuan, Zhenxin Xiao, Maggie Chuoyan Dong, and J. Gu. 2019. "The Fit between Firms' Open Innovation and Business Model for New Product Development Speed: A Contingent Perspective." *Technovation.*

Chapter

Sustainability Practices:
A Case Study of State Bank of India

Yatisha Kalia*

Research Scholar, Guru Nanak Dev University

ABSTRACT: Corporate Sustainability is visualized as a directing force adding acceleration for achieving long-term success. It is a bridge that is heading towards persistence (Padmanabhan, 2014). Financial System is a backbone of an economy and no development is possible without the assistance of it. In present scenario, inclination of banks' is towards incorporating sustainable practices. With the emergence of sustainable development, companies are required to disclose more of the financial and non- financial nature of information commonly known as sustainability reporting. With time, there have been many guidelines governing the business on how to inculcate sustainable issues in their overall corporate performance. Global Reporting Initiatives (GRI) established in 1977 has been adopted by 93% of corporate houses across the globe. United Nation Global Compact Principles which are based on ten principles focusing on paramount values of environment, anti-corruption, human rights, labour standards of sustainable reporting. Government of India has also established a framework known as National Voluntary Guidelines (NVGs) providing a podium for Indian firms to comply with Sustainable Reporting (Kumar & Prakash, 2019). The case of SBI has been studied to identify and differentiate various sustainability practices of State Bank of India for the year 2020-21on the basis of GRI and Business Responsibility Reporting (BRR). It aims to fill the gap in literature by comparing GRI standards with BRR principles. The data has been collected from the sustainability report and annual report with the help of content analysis. To quantify the results of content analysis, four points scale has been framed ranging from "No Evidence" to "Full Compliance of Standard". The results show that GRI standards are vaster in terms of environment and governance in comparison to BRR. Moreover, SBI practices 38.89% of environmental, 44.73% of social and 18.18% of governance on the basis of GRI standards. Further it practices 35.71% of environmental, 20.12% of social and 34.09% of governance on the basis of BRR. Overall, SBI practices 33.05% of GRI practices and 25.75% of BRR practices.

KEYWORDS: Global responsibility reporting, Business responsibility reporting, Content analysis

*Yatisha.kalia@gmail.com

DOI: 10.4324/9781003415725-67

1. Introduction

Mankind possesses the potential to head towards sustainable development i.e. meeting the need of the present without compromising the need of future generations (Burton,1987). The incorporation of sustainability in the course of Indian business is not a new concept. Vedanta, one of the six schools of Hindu Philosophy also preaches 'Sarva Loka Hitma' meaning 'well-being of stakeholders'. In the era of globalisation and privatisation, there was a huge shift in capital investment, asset creation, market expansion from local to national to even global levels leading to the worst impact of industrial development on the environment and sooner it becomes a global concern with the signing of Kyoto Protocol in 1997 (Gandhi, 2016). Sustainable Development is fetching importance globally and nationally as well. Internationally many summits have directed the global interest towards achieving Sustainable Development Goals such as Pittsbury Summit held in September, 2009. From Indian perspective, the Twelfth Five-Year Plan has highlighted the urge for speedy, comprehensive and sustainable growth (Charkrobarty, 2013).

Corporate Sustainability is visualized as a directing force adding acceleration for achieving long-term success. Corporate Sustainability is a bridge that is heading towards persistence (Padmanabhan, 2014). India has taken various steps like mandatory two per cent CSR on average net profits, carbon tax, clean energy cess and also the government of India has proposed various projects like Wind Energy, Water and National Mission, etc, indicating its steps towards sustainable development (Gandhi, 2010).

Financial System is a backbone of an economy and no development is possible without the assistance of it. Therefore, the need of the hour is to align the financial institution with sustainable development goals. RBI has kept an eye on the role of banks in facilitating sustainable development practices. Banks are drifting apart from cushioned role where human and climatic influence is viewed as an added liability to sustainable banking (Gwin & Libman, 2007). With the growing awareness, banks have started giving weightage to clean production projects, corporate governance and sustainable energy which ultimately enhance their brand image as well as manage socio-environment aspects of their investments. Reserve Bank of India is playing a pivotal role in motivating and guiding the banks towards sustainable development. In its circular dated December 20, 2007, it has drawn the attention of banks towards their role play in Corporate Social Responsibility, Sustainable Development, and Non- Financial Reporting. A major move by RBI is to abreast banks to have financial inclusion plans, making non- financial reporting mandatory (Chakraborty, 2011).

With the emergence of sustainable development, companies were required to disclose more of the financial and non- financial nature of information commonly known as sustainable reporting. With time, there have been many guidelines governing the business on how to inculcate sustainable issues in their overall corporate performance. Global Reporting Initiatives (GRI) established in 1977 has been adopted by almost 93% of corporate houses across the globe. United Nation Global Compact Principles which are based on ten principles focusing on paramount values of environment, anti-corruption, human rights, labour standards of sustainable reporting. Government of India have also established a framework known as

National Voluntary Guidelines (NVGs) providing a podium for Indian firms to comply with Sustainable Reporting (Kumar & Prakash, 2019).

2. Literature Review

Singh and Ahuja (1983) considered the Indian scenario of firms and concluded that apart from size and industry, financial performance had also showed positive association with voluntary disclosure. Branco and Rodrigues (2006) studied the four dimensions of social responsibility information that are related to community involvement, employees, product and consumers, and environment. They observed that Portuguese banks gave more weight to annual reports as a medium of disclosure in comparison to internet. Community disclosure emerged as a vital part of the social responsibility disclosure in the study. Khan (2010) examined the corporate social responsibility reporting practices in Bangladeshi banking industry by using the mode of annual report disclosure and observed that the scope of CSR reporting practices was at its infant stage. Mahadeo et al. (2011) considered environmental disclosure, human resource disclosure and community involvement disclosure and found that size had positive association with human resource and environment disclosure, and financial performance showed no association. Kansal et al. (2014) further added to the literature of Indian firms' determinants on CSR disclosure by reporting that third party recognition i.e. awards and social rating shows significant positive impact on disclosure. Jain et al. (2015) evaluated the CSR reports of six large banks of India, China, Australia and Japan. They had created disclosure assessment framework considering sixty indicators grouped under eight heads. After analysing the information of over seven years, they observed that CSR disclosure improved in quantity and quality, and also reported the maximum improvement of Indian banks after the best score of Australian banks. Krasodomska (2015) identified information on CSR related information provided in management report of twelve banks under study for a period of 2005-2011. He stressed upon social and environment disclosure and to quantify these disclosures he has adopted an index which considered weights given on the basis of importance as well as a simple binary index. Finally, he concluded that banks had initiated to include CSR disclosure in management commentary and showed improvement in quality of CSR in 2011 in comparison to 2005. Bhatia and Kaur (2016) had thrown a light upon the emerging new way of Internet Technology for companies to communicate information to the stakeholders. They had examined the web-based reporting practices on the basis of 144 elements differentiated by nine broad heads. The results showed the dominance of website in comparison to RTI and Technology related information in case of both Public and Private sector banks. Ahmed et al. (2018) conducted a study considering thirty private commercial banks of Bangladesh with the objective of finding the drivers for considering Environment, Social and Governance (ESG) criteria in bank lending process and they prepared the questionnaire to calculate the ESG score and resulted that banks which consider ESG factor in lending are benefited with high financial performance. Kumar and Prakash (2019) conducted a study to measure the sustainability banking performance they constructed a framework inspired by GRI, NVG and BRR guidelines that focuses mainly on environment and social aspect; which are sub-divided in five groups. The study concluded that Indian banking sector is at very initial stage with regard to adopting sustainability tools and focused more on social dimensions rather than on key areas like financial inclusion, financial literacy and energy efficiency.

3. Objectives of the Study

1. To measure various sustainability practices of State Bank of India for the year 2020-21 on the basis of GRI and BRR.
2. To compare various sustainability practices of State Bank of India for the year 2020-21 on the basis of GRI and BRR.

4. Methodology

Sustainable practices are measured by an index using prominent sustainability code of conduct (Global Reporting Initiative (GRI) guidelines and Business Responsibility Reporting (BRR) principles). From these indices environmental, social and governance parameters have been considered for the study. The data has been collected from the sustainability report and annual report with the help of content analysis for the year 2020-21. To quantify the results of content analysis, four points scale has been framed denoting '0 as no evidence','1 as little evidence' i.e. only qualitative information, '2 as some evidence' i.e. both qualitative and quantitative information, '3 as moderate evidence' i.e. monetary information as required by guidelines or elaborated quantitative information, '4 as significant evidence' i.e. complete compliance of guidelines. The collected data is statistically analyzed using percentages.

5. Results and Conclusion

The sustainability practices are analyzed on 59 and 66 ESG principles of GRI and NVG respectively.

Table 67.1 Total number of guidelines of ESG under GRI and NVG

	GRI	NVG
ENVIRONMENT	18	14
SOCIAL	19	41
GOVERNANCE	22	11
Total	59	66

Source: Author's compilation

From the above Table 67.1, it is evident that GRI standards are vaster in terms of environment and governance in comparison to NVG.

To measure the sustainability, ESG parameters of both the indices have been quantified on four point scale. For instance, according to GRI, governance practices one of the guidelines (102-21) of GRI requires to report process for communication between stakeholders and the top level management on economic, environmental, governance and social topics. While measuring this guideline there was no evidence hence allotted '0 point' to it. Moreover, in case of BRR, one of the guidelines as per principle 1 of NVG requires reporting details of complaints, bribery, and corruption cases registered in the financial year, which have significant evidence. For instance, in 2020-21 sustainability report of SBI, there were 55 complaints reported on the 'garima platform' including 10 pending of previous year out of which resolved complains were 49, therefore allotted '4 points'.

Further, if we consider environmental practices one of the guidelines (302-1) of GRI requires reporting total consumption of different types of fuels in joules or multiples from non-renewable sources within the organization, which have significant evidence in bank's report. For example in 2020-21 SBI reported energy consumption of 7,90,806 GL and 50,70,995 GL in diesel and grid electricity respectively therefore, allotted '4 points' to it. In case of BRR, one of the guidelines requires to report strategies or initiatives to address global level environmental issues such as climate changes, resource scarcity, health pandemics and emergencies, natural disaster etc., which have little significance in banks' report. For example in sustainability report of SBI for the year 2020-21, it has reported the identification of climate risks and is in process of devising a framework for integrating ESG risk assessment in overall credit risk assessment, therefore, allotted '1 point' to it.

Table 67.2 Comparison between GRI and NVG practices

(Figures in percentages)

	GRI	NVG
ENVIRONMENT	38.89 (28/18)	35.71 (20/14)
SOCIAL	44.73 (34/19)	20.12 (33/41)
GOVERNANCE	18.18 (16/22)	34.09 (15/11)
Overall	33.05 (78/59)	25.75 (68/66)

Source: Author's compilation

To compare sustainability practices on the basis of GRI and NVG, percentages have been calculated. For instance in case of environment, total guidelines was 18 and 14 for GRI & BRR respectively. As per the highest point on 4 point scale, maximum score bank can get is 72 (18*4) for GRI guidelines and 56 (14*4) for BRR guidelines. Hence, the percentage is 38.89 and 35.71 for GRI and BRR respectively. Similarly, from the above table, it is clear that SBI practises 44.73% of social and 18.18% of governance guidelines on the basis of GRI standards. Further it practises 20.12% social and 34.09% governance guidelines on the basis of BRR.

To conclude, overall SBI practises 33.05% of GRI guidelines and 25.75% of BRR principles. Henceforth, to measure sustainability practices of an Indian financial institutions combination of both indices is desirable as one is internationally accepted (GRI) and other is mandatory at national level for top 1,000 listed companies by market capitalisation. Moreover, GRI makes voluntary for organization to disclose some material topics on which reporting are required whereas NVG makes it mandatory.

REFERENCES

1. Ahmed, S. U., Ahmed, S. P., & Hasan, I. (2018). Why banks should consider ESG risk factors in bank lending?. Banks & Bank Systems. 13(3):71-80.
2. Bhatia, M. R. K., & Kaur, J. (2016). Online corporate reporting practices of indian public and private commercial banks. Gian Jyoti E-Journal.6(2):64-75.
3. Branco, M. C., & Rodrigues, L. L. (2006). Corporate social responsibility and resource-based perspectives. Journal of Business Ethics. 69(2):111-132.
4. Burton, I. (1987). The world commission on environment and development. Environment Science and Policy for Sustainable Development. 29(5):25–29.
5. Chakrabarty, D. K. (2013). Environmental and social sustainability: key issues and concerns. Yes Bank–GIZ–UNEP Sustainability Series event on Environment and Social Risk Management, Mumbai, April.
6. Chakrabarty, K. C. (2011, June). Non-financial reporting–what, why and how–indian perspective. In Proceedings of the National Conference on Non-Financial Reporting and Risk Management for Financial Institutions, Mumbai, India (Vol. 6).
7. Gandhi, R. (2016). Green finance–early initiatives. Delivering a Sustainable Financial System in India, BIS central bankers' speeches.
8. Gwin, C., & Libman, M. L. (2007). Banking on sustainability: financing environmental and social opportunities in emerging markets. Washington, D.C., World Bank Group.
9. Kansal M., Joshi M., & Batra G.S. (2014). Determinants of corporate social responsibility disclosures: evidence from india. Advances in Accounting, Incorporating Advances in International Accounting. 30(1):217–229.
10. Krasodomska, J. (2015). CSR disclosures in the banking industry empirical evidence from poland. Social Responsibility Journal.11 (3):406-423.
11. Kumar, K., & Prakash, A. (2019). Developing a framework for assessing sustainable banking performance of the indian banking sector. Social Responsibility Journal.15 (5):689-709.
12. Mahadeo J, Oogarah-Hanuman V, Soobaroyen T. (2011). A longitudinal study of corporate social disclosures in a developing economy. Journal of Business Ethics. 104(4):545–558.
13. Padmanabhan, G. (2014). Corporate Sustainability a Panacea for Growth: Values, Convictions and Acrions. Working paper id: 6209, https://ideas.repec. org/p/ess/wpaper/id6209.html (assessed August28, 2020).
14. Singh DR, Ahuja JM. (1983). Corporate social reporting in india. The International Journal of Accounting.18 (2):151–169.

Handbook of Evidence Based Management Practices in Business – Satyendra Kumar Sharma et al. (eds)
© 2023 Taylor & Francis Group, London, ISBN 978-1-032-54216-4

Chapter

Value Appropriation in Inter-firm Coopetitive Alliances: Case of the Indian Pharmaceutical Industry

Roopesh Kumar*, Anil Bhat[1]
Department of Management, Birla Institute of Technology and Science,
Pilani, Rajasthan, India

Neetu Yadav[2]
B-20, Scholars, Management Development Institute,
Gurgaon, 122007, India

ABSTRACT: Coopetition research is evolving in management practice, with an increasing number of firms relying on collaborating with competitors to boost up their product development and foster innovation. The competition and collaboration dualism in coopetitive alliances has led to a lot of coopetition research on value creation and value appropriation in strategic coopetitive alliances. Though inter-firm value appropriation has been studied in diverse settings, and the assortment of theoretical perspectives has been adopted, most research on inter-firm value appropriation has concentrated around either the firms' bargaining power, or the isolating mechanisms deployed by firms to exploit or defend appropriation streams.

Our research approach is a qualitative study, intending to inform research about configurations of value appropriation by identifying the determinants of value appropriation in interfirm coopetitive alliances. We conduct a context interview with a senior leader from the Indian pharmaceutical industry (IPI) to propose a framework based on determinants influencing value appropriation in coopetitive interfirm alliances in the IPI. Overall, our results provide unique insights into how pharmaceutical firms in a coopetitive dyadic alliance perceive value appropriation, how different factors influence the value appropriation and provide guidance to managers on what factors or mechanisms can help in appropriating value in a coopetitive alliance. Further, we identify a set of opportunities for future research studies that may inspire the advancement of research on value appropriation in coopetitive alliances.

*Corresponding Author: roopeshkamaltilak@gmail.com
[1]anilkbhat@pilani.bits-pilani.ac.in, [2]neetu.yadav@mdi.ac.in

DOI: 10.4324/9781003415725-68

KEYWORDS: Value appropriation, Value capture, Coopetition, Relational factors, Knowledge sharing

1. Introduction

With the increase in strategic interfirm coopetitive alliances, an issue that has been attracting wide attention is how firms might improve their performance through strategic partnerships as well as the conflicts and various trade-offs this entails (Chiambaretto and Maurice., 2020; Gnyawali et al., 2006; Gulati, 1998; Wassmer, 2010). Researchers dealing with this issue have largely focused on two interconnected key questions: (1) how value is created by firms; and (b) how value is appropriated by firms' partnering in a strategic alliance. Though value creation and value appropriation shape the outcome of strategic alliances, both of them are considered as separate processes and concepts (Coff, 1999; Lepak et al., 2007). The concepts of value appropriation presents less definitional variety in comparison to that of value creation. Researchers have increasingly advocated the need to study value capture utilizing interfirm strategic alliances (Dyer and Singh, 1998; Oxley and Silverman, 2008). Instead of value appropriation, the majority of study has, however, concentrated on the process of value creation (Lavie, 2007) and it is only lately that researchers started to devote attention to the process of value appropriation.

When two firms' partner, they co-create value by accessing each other's resources and sharing risks & costs. The value created by this alliance is generally appropriated among the alliance partners based on various factors such as contractual agreements (Gulati & Singh 1998), investments and contributions by each partner towards the alliance (Dyer, 1997; Dyer & Singh, 1998; Dyer et al., 2008), factual inter-dependencies (Khanna et al., 1998; Dyer et al., 2008), degree of fairness (Luo, 2008), power relations (Lavie, 2007), and opportunistic behaviour of the alliance partners (Lavie, 2006) etc. The objective of this paper is to offer a better understanding of coopetitive alliances in the context of value appropriation mechanisms in inter-firm dyadic alliances. In more detail, the purpose of the paper is to investigate determinants of value appropriation in the pharmaceutical industry alliances. Further, the authors aim to supplement existent research by looking into value appropriation characteristics deploying a real-world case study to provide additional insights.

The remainder of the paper is organised as follows:

In the next section, the value appropriation mechanisms from the existent literature on strategic alliances are identified and conceptualised. In the following section we describe the methodology used while the next section uses a qualitative case study approach by having a case interview to gather more evidence on value appropriation in the dyadic alliances from the perspective of a specific industry Viz. IPI. Then in the final section, based on the pilot qualitative case study, we provide managerial and theoretical implications of the research.

2. Conceptualization of Value Appropriation

Since 1996, when Brandenburger and Nalebuff used the keyword "coopetition", researchers have focused more on examining the paradoxical nature and outcome of coopetition (Bouncken et al., 2020, 2016; Fernandez et al., 2014; Gnyawali et al 2016; Hoffman, 2005; 2007; Le Roy and Czakon, 2015; Ritala, 2019; Ritala and Hurmelinna-Laukkanen, 2009; Santos, 2021). Coopetition is defined as "a paradoxical relationship between two or more actors simultaneously involved in cooperative and competitive interactions, regardless of whether their relationship is horizontal or vertical" (Bengtsson & Kock, 2014). Coopetition, owing to its dichotomy of co-operative and competitive behaviours (Bengtsson and Kock, 2000; Lado et al., 1997), is anticipated to produce better performance and create more value in contrast to other relational modes. Numerous studies show that coopetition increases value and has a favourable effect on innovation (Bouncken and Kraus, 2013), the market (Robert et al., 2018), or stock-market performance (Wu et al., 2015). However, a few studies emphasize a contrasting view indicating a mixed impact of coopetition in terms of the market performance (Ritala, 2018) or innovation performance standpoint (Gast et al., 2018). This indicates value appropriation playing a part in the coopetitive alliance.

It is well known that firms enter into an alliance in order to produce more value and that they subsequently compete with their alliance partner(s) for capturing that value (Bengtsson & Kock, 2000; Gnyawali et al., 2006, Gnyawali and Madhavan, 2001, Walley, 2007). However, a number of empirical studies highlight that the process of value creation and appropriation can overlap, and the respective emphases might keep on shifting backwards and forward during coopetitive engagement (Gnyawali and Park, 2011; Ritala et al., 2009). The benefits associated to a specific collaboration might not always be perfectly in-line with the unique strategic goals of each partnering firm (Dyer et al., 2008; Khanna et al., 1998). Firms entering a coopetitive alliance will probably use their resources and capacities to secure and appropriate value (Czakon, 2009; Lavie 2009; Le Roy and Czakon, 2015; Le Roy and Guilletreau, 2010; Ritala and Tidström, 2014). To stay competitive as individual entities, the firm must, however, simultaneously follow their respective value appropriation goals and consider the relational factors that maximise the value creation in their coopetitive partnerships (Dyer and Singh, 1998).

There has been a lot of research on coopetition as a result of the duality of competition and collaboration and there are multiple views on how value is appropriated. Table 68.1 indicates some of the literature on mechanisms and theoretical underpinnings on how firms' appropriate value from alliances. Firms in an alliance will each have a unique set of skills for capturing value through their experience base of coopetition and strategies (Anand and Khanna 2000; Czakon, 2009; Le Roy and Czakon, 2015; Lavie, 2009) and by managing internal and external coopetition tensions (Bengtsson et al. 2016), as depicted by the tension-based view of coopetition (Bengtsson and Kock, 2000; Fernandez et al., 2014; Rai, 2016).

Khanna et al. (1998) associated value appropriation with private benefits. According to them, a company can obtain private benefits by picking up new abilities from a partner company and applying them to situations that fall outside the purview of the current alliance. Consequently, the concept of value appropriation emphasises the following two aspects:

Table 68.1 Research studies with a focus on value appropriation mechanisms in coopetitive alliances

#	Paper	Theoretical underpinnings	Key findings	Value appropriation mechanisms
1	Adegbesan, Higgins (2010)	Strategic Factor Market Theory	A firm's value appropriation depends on how strong its negotiation power is, and how scarce and more valuable it is in comparison to the other firm in the alliance	Scarcity premium, bargaining ability, and greater complementarity
2	Gimeno (2004)	Transaction Cost Economics, Social Exchange Theory	Alliance co-specialization demands greater relational exclusivity while alliance co-specialisation reduces intra-network competition	Competition exclusivity
3	Khanna, Gulati, Nohria (1998)	Organizational Learning	Relative scope in the alliance leads to defining the ratio of common (shared/co-created) benefits and private (competition) benefits accrued by a firm	Relative scope of a firm within an alliance
4	Kim (2015)	Evolutionary Theory, New Institutional Economics	Value can be derived from the spatial scope of information capture in an alliance	Isolating Mechanisms
5	Lane et al. (2001)	Organizational Learning	An organization's ability to understand and assimilate outside knowledge influences the value they capture	Absorptive Capacity
6	Lavie (2007)	Game theory and Bargaining power	The bargaining power of a dominant partner in the alliance can affect firm performance because of disproportionate value capture	Bargaining Power
7	Lepak et al. (2007)	Resource Based View, Bargaining Power Theory	Competition and isolating mechanisms determine how the newly created value is captured and how slippage happens	Isolating Mechanisms, Bargaining Power
8	Silverman, and Baum (2002)	Transaction Costs Economics, Resource	Competitive intensity affects value appropriation	Competition
9	Vasudeva, and Anand (2011)	Organizational Learning	Asymmetrical learning and isolation mechanisms influence value appropriation	Absorptive Capacity

Source: Author's compilation

1. Common benefits distribution among the partnering firms and
2. The ability of partner firm to leverage the skills and capabilities of other partner, learn from it and use the learnings outside the alliance's boundaries

We have used the definition of value appropriation above, which is quite similar to other descriptions of value appropriation in diverse contexts (Di Minin and Faems, 2013). Henceforth, we will consider the mechanism of appropriation of value as a process that determines the distribution of mutual benefits among each partner and the ability of partners to unilaterally obtain private benefits that are not available to other partner firms (Lavie, 2007).

3. Methodology

The research setting is the Indian pharmaceutical sector. The IPI is a fast-growing industry that has contributed to India being considered the pharmacy of the world by building cost-efficient processes and delivering pharmaceuticals across the world. The high-growth industry comprises a very competitive environment that has firms with advanced technical capabilities operating in a stringently regulated environment. The high level of globalization and high cost of drug development means these companies need to collaborate to innovate and gain market while ensuring a high level of secrecy to protect in-house intellectual properties.

Our research approach is a pilot qualitative study, focusing on domestic and MNC players in the IPI. We conducted this pilot study to collect data from the Head, Business Development and Licensing (Asia pacific), of a large pharmaceutical company operating in India. The interviewee has been selected due to his vast experience and engagement in various types of coopetitive alliances over the last one-and-a-half decade of his career in IPI. The interview focused on identifying the background and need for the alliance, the objectives of firm-specific value appropriation with special emphasis on determinants of value appropriation in interfirm coopetitive alliances.

4. Case Description

In recent years, strategic alliances have become key to success in sectors such as the pharmaceutical and high-tech industry (Dadfar et al., 2014). In the wake of shorter product life-cycles owing to long development timelines and huge investments to bring innovative medicines, pharmaceutical firms prefer strategic alliances to overcome resource and competence limitations. The dichotomy of competition plus collaboration enable firms in high-tech sectors like pharmaceuticals to share research and development (R&D) in order to lower the costs of developing new products, increase market share through co-marketing, achieve economies of scale (Miotti and Sachwald, 2003), utilise synergistic effects by locating and combining complementary resources (Ancarani & Costabile, 2010; Mariani, 2009), distribute and reduce risks (Meyer, 1998), and provide value to customers (Hitt et al., 2000; Townsend, 2003).

The case here concerns a dyadic alliance that started in 2011 between two major pharmaceutical firms (One of the top 10 US pharma with a top 10 Indian pharma) in IPI. Both these firms manufacture pharmaceutical products and supply them in India as well as overseas markets. The US pharma firm had an innovative molecule, a first in class dipeptidyl peptidase-4 (DPP4) inhibitor and was selling it in the Indian market since 2009 while the Indian Pharma MNC had a strong presence in the Indian market. Considering that the current market sales for this molecule and its combinations are around ₹1,000 crores (~10% of the overall oral anti-diabetes drug market), both companies had a strong and competing presence. Further, considering this collaboration was for over a decade from 2011 to 2022, makes this a perfect alliance for studying value appropriation in coopetition inter-firm alliance. Table 68.2 provides the background and strategic objective of alliance formation, while Table 68.3 highlights the findings of contextual case interview on identified value appropriation factors apart from tension managing mechanisms in a dyadic interfirm alliance.

Table 68.2   Brief background, strategic objective, and value appropriation objective of the Interfirm dyadic alliance from the case interview

Coopetitive alliance	Firm-A (Leading US Pharmaceutical firm)	Firm-B (Leading Indian Pharmaceutical firm)
Timelines	Started in 2011 and concluded in 2022	
Background	Firm A launched an innovative DPP4 inhibitor in India in 2008 and commercialized it alone till 2010. However, with upcoming competition from Novartis's vildagliptin that was to be commercialized with three co-marketing partners, it evaluated and entered a coopetitive partnership from 2011 with Firm-B wherein Firm-B shall co-market its secondary trademark product (in-licensed from Firm-A) and acquire rights to the trademarks at the end of the deal in 2022. (Co-marketing deal) The deal was for private reimbursed market/ out-of-pocket market while firm-A kept reimbursed tender market with themselves.	
Strategic Objective	To bring the DPP4 inhibitor and shape the patient behaviour and the customer (Healthcare practitioner) behaviour to switch patients on DPP4 making it the first line of therapy supported by its rigorous scientific data on safety and efficacy parameters	
Value Appropriation Objective	• To learn from the complementary competencies of the partner • To make the best use of each other's resources and abilities to have a solid footprint when it comes to geospeciality coverage (more penetration and more share of voice to the healthcare practitioners)	

Source: Author's compilation

The case study indicates that absorptive capacity, prior experience in alliances management, governance mechanisms (formal and informal), knowledge management and bargaining power influences value appropriation in interfirm coopetitive alliances. Further, various tension and conflict reducing mechanisms such as building trust, empathy, and regular communication might be moderating value appropriation.

Based on the interview the identified determinants of value appropriation are shown in Fig. 68.1.

5. Implications, Limitations and Future Research

This study seeks to close the research gap in the academic literature on value appropriation and advances academic knowledge by identifying important elements determining value appropriation in a regulated industry like pharmaceuticals. The results of our pilot study contribute to knowledge of how a co-marketing coopetitive alliance functions in the pharmaceutical industry and suggests further testing the empirical model via exploratory research. Consistent with previous research, our pilot study supports various firm level and relational determinants of value appropriation. Further, the study brings an integrated perspective on the determinants of value appropriation in coopetitive alliances. Our results provide some

Table 68.3 Findings of the case study interview

Coopetitive alliance	Firm-A (Leading US Pharmaceutical firm)	Firm-B (Leading Indian Pharmaceutical firm)
Firm-specific Value Appropriation Objectives	• To increase the market share for its DPP4 inhibitor, which benefits the firm's bottom-line • Jumpstart commercial capabilities, which are already proven in the diabetes space for the Indian market • Launch the product at 1/6th of the US price and showcase to Indian policymakers and HCPs that the firm is serious to bring innovative yet affordable drugs to India • Understand and learn how a generic Indian pharmaceutical company works	• Emphasis on learning from giving the other firm access to its salesforce • Learn the regulated market way of marketing – Preparing the scientific data package and presenting the right data i.e., firm B realized and learned how to create high science inputs for innovator products and for regulated markets • Learn segmentation, targeting and promotion-related best practices • Getting a lot of exposure to US compliance processes which helps in redesigning their organization and practices • Getting access to trademarks after the deal successfully gets over after the agreed period and start selling the generic molecule that gives you a lot of headway over other generic companies
Determinants of Value appropriation		• The absorptive capacity of firms: Though alliance managers are assigned from both firms who manage alliances are expected not to share information back to the parent organization, informal learnings and deployment happens to other parts of the organization through workshops, training, and compliance mechanisms • Coopetitive alliance experience contributes to value appropriation as prior experience helps in tension management and setting up better information and knowledge-sharing mechanisms. • Alliance management capability: Experience and involvement of alliance managers in managing and driving alliance and setting up strategic objectives influences value appropriation • Governance mechanisms and contractual rights: Alliance managers along with the respective firm's finance team, compliance team, regulatory team, and pharmacovigilance team setup contracts that define cooperative value appropriation • Inter-organizational trust and communication: Training and workshops provide avenues for informal meetings that help build trust and lead to informal knowledge sharing leading to private value appropriation • Relative bargain power (depends on the availability of alternatives and superior complementarity) influences value appropriation
Mechanisms to reduce tension		Three types of tensions experienced during the coopetitive alliance 1. Operational (supply, payment, KPIs and overlaps) 2. Strategic including commercial and IP: (e.g., is there a repeat audit finding, misalignment on #of HCP visits etc.) 3. Compliance: Complying with laws and guidelines like MCI and OPPI Here are the ways used to manage tensions arising in the alliance. Formal/Contractual Management: • Non-poaching agreements and Noncompeting contractual agreements • Escalation mechanisms and committees to manage issues • Early warnings systems Empathy and Trust: leading to sharing of information and tension management Regular communication and workshops The intervention of top management with prior experience in managing alliances

Source: Author's compilation

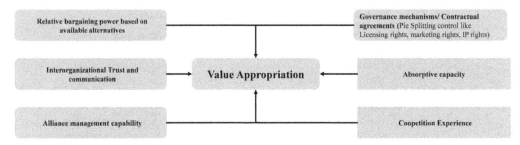

Fig. 68.1 Determinants of value appropriation in a coopetitive inter-firm alliance

Source: Author's compilation

direction to leaders managing alliances in the pharmaceutical industry. The study suggests that the alliance managers should emphasise on strengthening top leadership support for the alliance and strive to develop relationship-based governance apart from formal contractual governance mechanisms. Further, they should focus on developing a better absorptive capacity to ensure a win-win situation and better value appropriation for their firm.

There are some limitations to the study. First, it was conducted in a highly regulated industry sector and employed an exploratory research design, limiting its generalizability. Further, the study only covers one type of coopetition deal in a dyadic inter-firm alliance, which is based largely on co-marketing. This implies that the dynamics of value appropriation for other kinds of competitive alliances (e.g., R&D alliances) may be different.

More generalizable techniques, such as survey studies, should be used in future study to get beyond the aforementioned constraints. In addition, future studies could also concentrate on carefully analysing and contrasting problems connected to value appropriation techniques on various levels (for e.g., dyadic relationship between two partners, or an alliance coopetitive network comprising multiple partner firms). Finally, research that concentrate on different industry sectors could uncover diverse objectives of coopetitive alliance formation, and this could offer further insights on the internal dynamics of value appropriation in inter-firm coopetitive alliances.

REFERENCES

1. Adegbesan, J. A., and Higgins, M. J. (2010). "The intra-alliance division of value created through collaboration." Strategic Management Journal, 32, 187–211.
2. Anand, B. N., and Khanna, T. (2000). "Do firms learn to create value? The case of alliances." Strategic Management Journal, 21, 295–315
3. Ancarani, F., and Costabile, M. (2010). "Coopetition dynamics in convergent industries: Designing scope connections to combine heterogeneous resources." In S. Yami, S. Castaldo, G. B. Dagnino, & F. LeRoy (Eds.), Coopetition: Winning strategies for the 21st century (216–237).
4. Bengtsson, M. and Kock, S. (2000). "Coopetition in business networks - To cooperate and compete simultaneously." Industrial Marketing Management, 29(5), 411–426. Doi: 10.1016/S0019-8501(99)00067-X

5. Bengtsson, M. and Kock, S. (2014). "Coopetition - Quo vadis? Past accomplishments and future challenges." Industrial Marketing Management, 43(2), 180-188. Doi: 10.1016/j.indmarman.2014.02.015

6. Bengtsson, M., Raza-Ullah, T., Vanyushyn, V. (2016). "The coopetition paradox and tension: The moderating role of coopetition capability." Industrial Marketing Management 53, 19–30

7. Bouncken, R. B. and Kraus, S. (2013). "Innovation in knowledge-intensive industries: The double-edged sword of coopetition." Journal of Business Research, 66(10), 2060–2070. doi: 10.1016/j.jbusres.2013.02.032

8. Bouncken, R.B., Fredrich, V., (2016) Good fences make good neighbours? Directions and safeguards in alliances on business model innovation. Journal of Business Research 69 (11), 5196–5202

9. Bouncken, R. B., Fredrich, V., Kraus, S. (2020). "Configurations of firm-level value capture in coopetition." Long Range Planning, 53(1), 101869. doi:10.1016/j.lrp.2019.02.002

10. Brandenburger, A.M., Nalebuff, B.J., (1996). Co-opetition. Doubleday, New York

11. Chiambaretto P., Maurice J., Willinger M. (2020). "Value Creation and Value Appropriation in Innovative Coopetition Projects." M@n@gement, 23(2), 20–41. https://doi.org/10.37725/mgmt.v23i2.4622

12. Coff, R.W. (1999). "When competitive advantage doesn't lead to performance: the resource-based view and stakeholder bargaining power." Organization Science, 10, 119–133.

13. Czakon, W. (2009). "Power asymmetries, flexibility and the propensity to coopete: an empirical investigation of SMEs' relationships with franchisors." International Journal of Entrepreneurship and Small Business 8 (1), 44–60

14. Dante, D. G. (2013). "Value Creation and Value Appropriation: An Integrative, Multi-Level Framework." Journal of Applied Business and Economics, 15 (1), 39–53

15. Di Minin, A., and Faems, D. (2013). "Building Appropriation Advantage." California Management Review, 55(4), 7–14.

16. Dyer, J.H. (1997). "Effective interfirm collaboration: How firms minimize transaction costs and maximize transaction value." Strategic Management Journal, 18(7), 535–56.

17. Dyer, J.H., and Singh, H. (1998). "The relational view: cooperative strategy and sources of inter-organizational competitive advantage." Academy of Management Review, 23 (4), 660–679.

18. Dyer, J. H., Singh, H., Kale, P. (2008). "Splitting the pie: Rent distribution in alliances and networks." Managerial and Decision Economics, 29, 137–148.

19. Fernandez, A.-S., Le Roy, F., Gnyawali, D.R., 2014. "Sources and management of tension in co-opetition case evidence from telecommunications satellites manufacturing in Europe." Industrial Marketing Management 43 (2), 222–235

20. Gast, J., Hora, W., Bouncken, R. B., Kraus, S. (2018). "Challenges and merits of coopetitive innovation." In A. Fernandez, P. Chiambaretto, F. Le Roy & W. Czakon (Eds.), The Routledge Companion to Coopetition Strategies (pp. 283–297). Abingdon: Routledge.

21. Gimeno, J. (2004). "Competition within and between networks: The contingent effect of competitive embeddedness on alliance formation." Academy of Management Journal, 47 (6), 820–842

22. Gnyawali, D. R., He, J., Madhavan, R. (2006). "Impact of co-opetition on firm competitive behavior: an empirical examination." Journal of Management, 32 (4), 507–530.

23. Gnyawali, D.R., Madhavan, R., (2001). "Cooperative networks and competitive dynamics: A structural embeddedness perspective." Academy of Management Review 26 (3), 431–445.

24. Gnyawali, D.R., Madhavan, R., He, J., Bengtsson, M., (2016). "The competition-cooperation paradox in inter-firm relationships: A conceptual framework." Industrial Marketing Management 53, 7–18.

25. Gnyawali, D. R., and Park, B. J. (2011). "Co-opetition between giants: Collaboration with competitors for technological innovation." Research Policy, 40(5), 650–663.
26. Gulati, R. (1998). "Alliances and networks." Strategic Management Journal, 19: 293–318
27. Gulati, R. & Singh, H. (1998). "The architecture of cooperation: Managing coordination costs and appropriation concerns for strategic alliances." Administrative Science Quarterly, 43(4), 781–814.
28. Hitt, MA. Dacin, MT., Levitas, E., Arregle JL., and Borza A (2000). "Partner selection in emerging and developed market contexts: Resource-based and organizational learning perspectives." Academy of Management Journal, 43(3), 449–467
29. Hoffmann, W. H. (2005). "How to manage a portfolio of alliances." Long Range Planning, 38(2), 121–143.
30. Hoffman W.H. (2007). "Strategies for managing a portfolio of alliances." Strategic Management Journal, 28: 827–856.
31. Dadfar, H., Dahlgaard, JJ., Staffan Brege & Arzaghi, BJ. (2014). "International strategic alliances in the Iranian pharmaceutical industry: an analysis of key success and failure factors." Total Quality Management & Business Excellence, 25: 7–8, 812–826, DOI:10.1080/14783363.2014.906109
32. Khanna, T., Gulati, R., Nohria, N. (1998). "The dynamics of learning alliances: competition, cooperation, and relative scope." Strategic Management Journal, 19 (3), 193–210.
33. Kim, M. (2015). "Geographic scope, isolating mechanisms, and value appropriation." Strategic Management Journal. DOI: 10.1002/smj.2356.
34. Lado, A. A., Boyd, N. G. & Hanlon, S. C. (1997). "Competition, cooperation, and the search for economic rents: A syncretic model." Academy of Management Review, 22(1), 110–141. Doi: 10.5465/amr.1997.9707180261
35. Lane, P. J., Salk, J. E., & Lyles, M. A. (2001). "Absorptive capacity, learning, and performance in international joint ventures." Strategic Management Journal, 22, 1139–1161.
36. Lavie, D. (2006). "The competitive advantage of interconnected firms: An extension of the resource-based view." Academy of Management Review 31 (3), 638–658
37. Lavie, D. (2007). "Alliance portfolios and firm performance: a study of value creation and appropriation in the U.S. software industry." Strategic Management Journal, 28, 1187–1212.
38. Lavie, D. (2009). "Capturing value from alliance portfolios." Organizational Dynamics 38 (1), 26–36.
39. Le Roy, F., Czakon, W. (2015). "Managing coopetition: the missing link between strategy and performance." Industrial Marketing Management 53, 3–6
40. Lepak, D. P., Smith, K. G., & Taylor, M. S. (2007). "Value creation and value capture: a multilevel perspective." Academy of Management Review, 32 (1), 180–194
41. Luo, Y. (2008). "Consumption dynamics under information processing constraints." Review of Economic Dynamics, 11(2), 366–85
42. Mariani, M. M. (2009). "Emergent coopetitive and cooperative strategies in interorganizational relationships. Empirical evidence from Australian and Italian operas." In G. B. Dagnino, & E. Rocco (Eds.), Coopetition strategy: Theory, experiments and cases (pp. 166–190). Oxon: Routledge.
43. Meyer, H. (1998). "My enemy, my friend." Journal of Business Strategy, 19(5), 10–16.
44. Miotti, L., and Sachwald, F. (2003). "Co-operative R&D: Why and with whom? An integrated framework of analysis." Research Policy, 32(8), 1481–1499
45. Oxley, J. E., and Silverman, B. S. (2008). "Inter-firm alliances: a new institutional economics approach." In New Institutional Economics: A Guidebook, E. Brousseau & J. M. Glachant (Eds). New York: Cambridge University Press.
46. Rai, R. K. (2016). "A co-opetition-based approach to value creation in interfirm alliances: Construction of a measure and examination of its psychometric properties." Journal of Management 42 (6), 1663–1699

47. Ritala, P. & Hurmelinna-Laukkanen, P. (2018). "Dynamics of coopetitive value creation and appropriation." In A.-S. Fernandez, P. Chiambaretto, F. Le Roy & W. Czakon (Eds.), The Routledge companion to coopetition strategies (pp. 58–67). Abingdon: Routledge.

48. Ritala, P. (2019). "Coopetition and market performance." In: A.-S. Fernandez, P. Chiambaretto, F. Le Roy, W. Czakon (Eds.), The Routledge Companion to Coopetition Strategies pp. 339–347. Routledge, New York, NY

49. Ritala, P., Hurmelinna-Laukkanen, P. (2009). "What's in it for me? Creating and appropriating value in innovation-related coopetition." Technovation 29 (12), 819–828

50. Ritala, P., Hurmelinna-Laukkanen, P., Blomqvist, K. (2009). "Tug of war in innovation - Coopetitive service development." International Journal of Services Technology Management, 12, 255–272.

51. Ritala, P., Tidström, A. (2014). "Untangling the value-creation and value-appropriation elements of coopetition strategy: a longitudinal analysis on the firm and relational levels." Scandinavian Journal of Management 30 (4), 498–515.

52. Robert, M., Chiambaretto, P., Mira, B. & Le Roy, F. (2018). "Better, faster, stronger: The impact of market-oriented coopetition on product commercial performance." M@n@gement, 21(1), 574–610.

53. Santos, J. N. (2021). "Linking joint value creation to the interplay of competition and cooperation: A fuzzy set approach." Industrial Marketing Management, 92, 45–54. doi:10.1016/j.indmarman.2020.10.015

54. Silverman, B. S. and Baum J. A. (2002). "Alliance-based competitive dynamics." Academy of Management Journal 45(4): 791–806.

44. Townsend, J.D. (2003). "Understanding alliances: A review of international aspects in strategic marketing." Marketing Intelligence & Planning, 21(3), 143–155

45. Vasudeva, G. and Anand, J. (2011). "Unpacking absorptive capacity: a study of knowledge utilization from alliance portfolios." Academy of Management Journal, 54 (3), 611–623.

46. Walley, K. (2007). "Coopetition - An introduction to the subject and an agenda for research." International Studies of Management & Organization, 37, 11–31.

47. Wassmer, U. (2010). "Alliance portfolio: A review and research agenda." Journal of Management, 36, 141–171

48. Wu, Q., Luo, X., Slotegraaf, R. J. & Aspara, J. (2015). "Sleeping with competitors: The impact of NPD phases on stock market reactions to horizontal collaboration." Journal of the Academy of Marketing Science, 43(4), 490–511.

Handbook of Evidence Based Management Practices in Business – Satyendra Kumar Sharma et al. (eds)
© 2023 Taylor & Francis Group, London, ISBN 978-1-032-54216-4

Chapter

DIVA'S of Enterprise:
A Study of Constraining Factors
Affecting Women Entrepreneurs in India

Kirti Malik[1]
Research scholar, Bhagat Phool Singh Mahila Vishwavidyalaya,
Khanpur Kalan, Sonipat

Pooja Yadav[2]
Research Scholar, K. R. Mangalam University, Gurgaon, Haryana

Sonam Sachdeva[3]
Research Scholar, GD Goenka University, Sohna

Harshika Sondhi[4]
Research Scholar, BITS, Pilani

ABSTRACT: Purpose: The aim of the study the challenges and barrier faced by women entrepreneurs in India while setting up their businesses.

Design/methodology/approach: For this study, an exploratory research methodology has been adopted. A literature review of 125 research articles were done and ten themes (challenges and barriers) faced by women entrepreneurs were found.

Findings: The study identifies barriers such as lack of possibilities of training and education and experience; spatial mobility and lack of family support; lack of institutional support; lack of entrepreneurial management; and issues related to financial resources.

Practical Implications: Government and society should collaborate in order to remove barriers that prevent entrepreneurs from succeeding in their endeavours in order to advance Indian women in the field of entrepreneurship. This paper will help women entrepreneurs to know the issues they can face and then they can prepare themselves to solve those problems.

Limitations: In future researcher can do empirical research as this paper is based on secondary data. Hence there is need to test empirically and see what are factors that affect women entrepreneurs. Mixed method or qualitative research method can be used in further analysis.

[1]mkirti76@gmail.com, [2]py29041995@gmail.com, [3]Sonamsachdeva287@gmail.com,
[4]p20220035@pilani.bits-pilani.ac.in

DOI: 10.4324/9781003415725-69

Originality and value: On the basis of review of the literature, this study aims to find the main challenges faced by female entrepreneurship in India.

KEYWORDS: Women entrepreneurs, Challenges, Barriers, Obstacle, Inhibitors, Constraint etc.

1. Introduction

An effort related to commercial and industrial activity can be used to define the term "business" throughout the 1700s Anggadwita et al. (2017); Fichter and Tiemann (2018); Leonidou et al. (2020). Although founders and entrepreneurs come from very different backgrounds, economists and scholars have noted that most founders go on to become entrepreneurs Schumpeter (1947). Prior to the 1990s, experts and influential media outlets observed that women's entrepreneurial activity were limited to modest lifetime jobs and property ownership Baker et al. (1997).The education paper on the topic of women entrepreneurs was first published in 1976.Schwartz (1976) and "The bottom line: unequal enterprise in America" was the title of first policy which were reported in 1979. The first textbook on women entrepreneurs was published in 1985. Goffee and Scase (1991). Nowdays entrepreneurship as topic of research or in field is growing globally. Among that entrepreneur topics like their challenges, success stories, struggles of women entrepreneurs is widely in demand. Henry et al. (2016).Women entrepreneurs are not only contributing to the economy by creating jobs but also boosting economic growth. Kelley et al. (2010).

Women entrepreneurs are becoming increasingly important in developing countries by creating jobs, surpassing their male contribution to the economy by making a significant contribution and making significant advances in various fields including banking, restaurants, cosmetics, education etc. Baker et al. (1997); Kelley et al. (2010); Ramaswamy, (2013). There is an increase in women's representation at the beginning of India's natural business growth with Prime Modi's focus on self-employment through strong initiatives, skills development programs, training institutions, and flexible credit policies Rajvanshi, (2017). Indian ranking on Master card Index of women Entrepreneurs is 57th while USA rank 29th and China is 4th. Limited [Press Trust of India], (2017), for women entrepreneurs in the country. It pointed out that the "basic conditions" of women entrepreneurs in India are relatively poor compared to high-scoring countries. In contrast, this study aims to answer the question: 'What discourages women in society or the economy from becoming entrepreneurs?' Clearly, this study examines factors that affect the business acumen of Indian women.

2. Review of Existing Literature

Insufficient business skills and the mismatch between work and household responsibilities, according to Maina (2015), have an impact on the performance of women-owned businesses. In their 2014 survey of 31 women business owners in Malaysia's retail and service industries,

Kiambu et al. also noted a variety of difficulties, including ruthless competition, dishonest suppliers, overwhelming household obligations, poor debt management, and a lack of qualified labour.Cho et al. (2020) concludes challenges such as gender stereotypes as the dominant factor in the growth of women entrepreneurs context. The perception of risk discourages women from becoming entrepreneurs as identified by Arafat et al. (2020) in a study by Social and Cognitive Aspects of Women Entrepreneurs. Thomas & Jose, (2018) in the study of involvement and development of young women entrepreneurs: The social work challenge posed by the barriers that women entrepreneurs face in their immediate environment, such as family commitment and a lack of positive attitudes on the part of the women themselves is exit. Despite the fact that Jamaican women are more educated than males, Saner & Yiu (2019) found that the country's economic status and the role of women as domestic carers make it difficult for women to enter the workforce. Women are still deprived of employment opportunities. Chaudhuri et al., (2020) in the article entrepreneurial risk assessment concludes with a view to failure, a work-life balance, and limited social support for business needs as major barriers to women's entrepreneurship. Study titled "Businesses in the Women Entrepreneurs and emerging markets in Pakistan", Khan et al. (2021) claimed that internal factors such as the need for success, risk-taking, and self-reliance and external factors such as economic and social factors have a positive and significant impact on women's success. Nguyen et al. (2021) in a research of the Challenges and allowing progress of women entrepreneurs in the Vietnamese coffee business discovered that the majority of respondents were "driven by demand" or "forced" entrepreneurs in interviews with women entrepreneurs in the coffee industry. All of the comments alluded to a personal problem and the demand for additional income to pay for family obligations. They face various challenges caused by their lack of knowledge. It has been that there was a significant shortage of systems that support live and certified coffee products. Women entrepreneurs and family conflict in the workplace: a review of previous studies Poggesi et al. (2017) in Italy shows that both work and family disruption (WIF) and family and work disruption (FIW) play an important role in explaining the work-family conflict experienced by women entrepreneurs. Panda, 2018, draws the conclusion that gender discrimination, family conflict, financial difficulties, a lack of infrastructure, unstable businesses, differences in economic and political status (BEP), a lack of education and training, and personality traits are among the challenges that women entrepreneurs in developing countries face. Welsh et al. (2018) confirmed that family moral support is linked to improved firm performance in Turkey, a country with a more developed economy. Gender-related personal concerns appear to be impeding Turkish women entrepreneurs' ability to succeed in business. Hasan & Almubarak, (2016) in the study Factors influencing the performance of women entrepreneurs in Bahrain-driven SMEs highlighted a number of challenges women entrepreneurs face such as lack of access to financial services, difficulty finding qualified staff, domestic conflict and downsizing profit. Reusult of previous study shows that the most influencing factor is industry (SMEs) characteristics followed by entrepreneurial goals and motivations (EGM), and legal factors. Sharma, (2013) identified the following barriers to women's entrepreneurship: family obligations, male domination, middle class exploitation, inadequate education, social barriers, inadequate raw materials, limited access to financial services, intense competition, high production costs, legal, travel limitations, lack of business acumen, insufficient management skills, low risk-taking capacity and lack of confidence. Gill and Mand, (2013) found that women entrepreneurs in India has financing issues, market challenges, regulatory issues and a lack of infrastructure, which negatively affects the growth of MSMEs. Ratten et al. (2018) have found that business activities are heavily influenced by the gender firms of Bosnia and Herzegovina, which are related to innovation, activism and risk taking.

3. Methodology

For this study, an exploratory research methodology has been adopted. With the help of a thorough literature study, this technique is determined to be suitable for addressing the "what" questions related to barriers faced by women's entrepreneurship. The terms "barriers to women entrepreneurship," "inhibitors of women entrepreneurship," "challenges to women entrepreneurship," "constraint to women entrepreneurship," and "obstacle to women entrepreneurship" were used as keywords in seven publisher-managed databases: Emerald, Wiley, Sage, JSTOR, Elsevier, ProQuest, and Scopus to find relevant literature for this study. There were many papers available from these databases. Ten significant hurdles were found among the 125 academic publications that were shortlisted.

4. Findings

Based on the literature review, we identified ten obstacles listed below:

1. **Lack of motivation**: Indian women lack the drive which is needed to become company owners from their homes and communities, Indian women have low levels of motivation across the board. Indian women must overcome a number of inspiring obstacles (Mbithi, 2015).

2. **Infrastructure and technology issues**: Infrastructure is important for the development of female businesses. Rahman, (2010) highlighted that rural women's ability to expand their businesses will be hindered by a lack of infrastructure. In some rural areas of India, access to power is limited, and even in suburban areas, technology prevents women from beginning their own enterprises.

3. **Work and family life Balance:** Work and family life balance is one of the biggest obstacles that women entrepreneurs must overcome. It is simple for single women without children to adjust to the business requirements of Al-Ghamri, (2016). Compared to male entrepreneurs, women entrepreneurs must choose between their occupational health and family health, according to Peeters et al. (2005).

4. **Lack of market experience**: Another significant barrier is that starting a new business is very dependent on education and prior work experience, which is related to marketing a product or service Martins et al. (2004). Customer acquisition and product delivery are difficult for women. Lack of awareness about tactics that can quickly sell a product is another issue with marketing for female business owners.

5. **Employee-related difficulties**: Performance is a crucial factor in running a successful business. It might be difficult to find and retain qualified employees. When workers seek

promotions, management controls related to the employee business are enhanced, and the expense of representation rises, this practise becomes a barrier.

6. **Monetary problem:** Finance related problems are the one of the most pronounced barrier to business. Many entrepreneurs need to discard their ideas for a new firm because of financial problems Sandhu et al. (2012).

7. **Lack of regulation/law and directives**: The majority of women entrepreneurs have made it clear that there is an inevitable lack of belief in the legal and governmental framework of the country. (Kirkwood, 2009).

8. **Lack of understanding, talent and experience**: Due to their lack of business management knowledge and abilities, female entrepreneurs struggle to manage firm operations. All facets of corporate management require educated, capable women. Indeed, in many circumstances, possessing the requisite abilities will encourage women to pursue entrepreneurial initiatives, Niazkar and Arab-Moghaddam, (2011)

9. **Fear of failing**: Fear is a common phenomenon in people and also applies to new entrepreneurs. Previous researcher has found that there are more fears in women entrepreneurs than male entrepreneurs. Thus Fear act a major problem for women entrepreneurs Chaudhuri et al. (2020)

10. **Lack of societal awareness of entrepreneurship:** In India, social issues are very important for female business owners. It can be difficult for women to use business models, interact with them, and manage these issues Revathi and Krishnan, (2013).

5. Discussion

Women entrepreneurship can help India to create more jobs for the people and can becomes crucial factor in removing unemployment in India. The economy will gain from having more company leaders and more jobs will be created. In order to advance Indian women in business, society and the government must collaborate, and efforts must be made to remove obstacles to entrepreneurship since a number of obstacles impede women's commercial operations. The impediments to female entrepreneurship have been examined in our study. Less research has been done in the Indian setting to remove barriers in the area of women's entrepreneurship.

6. Theoretical and Practical Implications

The results of the study are similar to those of a study conducted in this regard as (Solanki, 2019) states that 20% of women living in rural areas are found to lack confidence in entrepreneurship due to a lack of business literacy. The primary barriers preventing women from starting their own businesses were found to be fear of failure, a lack of family support, a lack of resources, and family obligations. 40% of women reported being 10 out of 10 happy after starting their own business. Women's enterprises are successful because they provide satisfaction, pleasure, fulfillment, success, and community contribution through employment. Raghuvanshi et al. (2017) recognizes a lack of possibilities for education, experience, and training, space travel, as well as a lack of family support, institutional support, business management, and financial resources. Reports from government departments and financial institutions highlight the challenges facing women entrepreneurs in their immediate environment, such as family obligations and the lack of a positive attitude towards women themselves concludes (Thomas & Jose, 2018). When the focus is on women's participation in the economy and society, it is very helpful to be reminded of some important facts. UN Women informs us that "women make up 66 per cent of the world's work, produce 50 per cent of food, but earn 10 per cent of income and own one per cent of assets" (UNICEF, 2012). We should not only emphasize the unique challenges faced by Indian women entrepreneurs, but also suggest improvements for how to include leadership development programs for these devoted women. Innovation, economic growth, and job creation are three areas of the Indian economy where the contribution of female entrepreneurs has not yet been completely tapped. Financing is a major problem that women entrepreneurs are facing. Therefore, the government and other financial institutions should provide free loans to encourage women entrepreneurs. Another major problem women entrepreneurs is facing in selling their goods, therefore marketing support should come to help them in selling their products successfully at reasonable prices.

7. Limitations

The future researcher can test the findings of the study by doing a empirical research and see whether these are only barriers or there are some others themes. They can used mixed method approach to generalise the findings.

8. Conclusion

The difficulties and limitations faced by Indian women who want to become business owners were examined in the current study. Ten restrictions were discovered as a result of the exploratory research approach used for this study, which focused on the barriers. Knowing the specific barriers that have prevented Indian women from succeeding as entrepreneurs would be useful for practitioners and academics. By concentrating on and addressing these specific obstacles, we may break down barriers and encourage more women to pursue entrepreneurship. For female business owners, the Indian government, investors, and business advisors, this discovery will be very helpful.

REFERENCES

1. Al-Ghamri, N. (2016), "Challenges facing business women and their negative impact on the performance of small businesses in the province of Jeddah in Saudi Arabia", International Journal of Business and Management, Vol. 11 No. 9, pp. 96–116.
2. Anggadwita, Grisna, Bachruddin Saleh Luturlean, Veland Ramadani, and Vanessa Ratten. 2017. Socio-Cultural Environments and Emerging Economy EntrepreneurshipWomen Entrepreneurs in Indonesia. Journal of Entrepreneurship in Emerging Economies 9: 85–96.
3. Arafat, M., Ali, J., Dwivedi, A., & Saleem, I. (2020). Social and Cognitive Aspects of Women Entrepreneurs: Evidence from India. Vikalpa: The Journal For Decision Makers, 45(4), 223–239. https://doi.org/10.1177/02560909211015457.

4. Baker, Ted, Howard E. Aldrich, and Liou Nina. 1997. Invisible Entrepreneurs: The Neglect of Women Business Owners by Mass Media and Scholarly Journals in the USA. Entrepreneurship and Regional Development 9: 221–38.

5. Chaudhuri, S., Ghosh, R., & Abichandani, Y. (2020). Exploring the Risky Terrain of Entrepreneurship With Support From Developmental Relationships: Narratives From Indian Women Entrepreneurs. Advances In Developing Human Resources, 22(2), 137–149. https://doi.org/10.1177/1523422320907044

6. Cho, Y., Park, J., Han, S., Sung, M., & Park, C. (2020). Women entrepreneurs in South Korea: motivations, challenges and career success. European Journal of Training and Development, 45(2/3), 97–119. https://doi.org/10.1108/ejtd-03-2020-0039

7. Fichter, Klaus, and Irina Tiemann. 2018. Factors Influencing University Support for Sustainable Entrepreneurship: Insights from Explorative Case Studies. Journal of Cleaner Production 175: 512–24.

8. Gill, A. and Mand, H.S. (2013), "Barriers to the growth of small business firms in India", International Journal of Business and Globalisation, Vol. 10 No. 1, pp. 1–13.

9. Goffee, Robert, and Richard Scase. 1991. Proprietorial Control in Family Firms: Some Functions of 'Quasi-Organic' Management System. Family Business Review 4: 337–52.

10. Hasan, F., & Almubarak, M. (2016). Factors influencing women entrepreneurs' performance in SMEs. *World Journal Of Entrepreneurship, Management And Sustainable Development*, *12*(2). https://doi.org/10.1108/wjemsd-09-2015-0037.

11. Henry, C., Foss, L., & Ahl, H. (2016). Gender and entrepreneurship research: A review of methodological approaches. International Small Business Journal, 34(3), 217–241.

12. Hisrich, Robert D., and Marie O'Brien. 1981. The Woman Entrepreneur from a Business and Sociological Perspective. Frontiers of Entrepreneurship Research 21: 19–23.

13. Jyoti, J. (2011). Factors affecting women entrepreneurship in J & K (India). *Journal of Services Research*, *11*(1), 1–21.

14. Kelley, D. J., Bosma, N., & Amoros, J. E. (2010). Global entrepreneurship monitor: 2010 global report. Santiago: Universidad del Desarrollo, Babson College.

15. Khan, R., Salamzadeh, Y., Shah, S., & Hussain, M. (2021). Factors affecting women entrepreneurs' success: a study of small- and medium-sized enterprises in emerging market of Pakistan. Journal Of Innovation And Entrepreneurship, 10(1). https://doi.org/10.1186/s13731-021-00145-9

16. Kirkwood, J. (2009), "Is a lack of self-confidence hindering women entrepreneurs?", International Journal of Gender and Entrepreneurship, Vol. 1 No. 2, pp. 118–133.

17. Leonidou, Erasmia, Michael Christofi, Demetris Vrontis, and Alkis Thrassou. 2020. An Integrative Framework of Stakeholder Engagement for Innovation Management and Entrepreneurship Development. Journal of Business Research 119: 245–58.

18. Loveline, A.A., Uchenna, O.I. and Karubi, N.P. (2014), "Women entrepreneurship in Malaysia: an empirical assessment of the challenges faced by micro and small business owners in Kuching-Sarawak", International Journal of Humanities Social Sciences and Education, Vol. 4 No. 1, pp. 48–58.

19. Maina, W. (2015), "Factors influencing performance of women owned micro and small enterprises in Kikuyu sub county, Kiambu county Kenya", Doctoral dissertation, University of Nairobi, pp. 1–67.

20. Martins, S., Couchi, C., Parat, L., Federico, C. and Doneddu, R. (2004), "Barriers to entrepreneurship and business creation", ECC-European Entrepreneurship Cooperation, pp. 1–49.

21. Mbithi, L.M. (2015), "Barriers faced by women-owned businesses: perspectives of women from east African community: pathways to African feminism and development", Journal of African Women's Studies Centre, Vol. 1 No. 1, pp. 105–123.

22. Nguyen, G., Hoang, T., Nguyen, T., & Ngo, T. (2021). Challenges and enablers of women entrepreneurs' career advancement in Vietnam's coffee industry. *Journal Of Enterprising Communities: People And Places In The Global Economy*, *15*(1), 76–95. https://doi.org/10.1108/jec-04-2020-0075

23. Niazkar, F. and Arab-Moghaddam, N. (2011), "Study of barriers to women's entrepreneurship development among Iranian women (case entrepreneur women)", World Academy of Science, Engineering and Technology, Vol. 60, pp. 1115–1119.

24. Panda, S. (2018). Constraints faced by women entrepreneurs in developing countries: review and ranking. *Gender In Management: An International Journal*, *33*(4), 315–331.https://doi.org/10.1108/gm-01-2017-0003

25. Peeters, M.C., Montgomery, A.J., Bakker, A.B. and Schaufeli, W.B. (2005), "Balancing work and home: How job and home demands are related to burnout", International Journal of Stress Management, Vol. 12 No. 1, pp. 43–65.

26. Poggesi, S., Mari, M., & De Vita, L. (2017). Women entrepreneurs and work-family conflict: an analysis of the antecedents. *International Entrepreneurship And Management Journal*, *15*(2), 431–454. https://doi.org/10.1007/s11365-017-0484-1

27. Press Trust of India Limited. (2017, March 8). India rank low among countries with women entrepreneurs: Survey. *The Economic Times*. https://economictimes.indiatimes.com/smallbiz/entrepreneurship/a-mothers-love-inspires-a-whole-new-eco-friendly-category-of-diapers/articleshow/69784791.cms

28. Rahman, M. (2010), "Barriers to women entrepreneurship in Bangladesh BRAC Development Institute (BDI)", pp. 8–37.

29. Raghuvanshi, J., Agrawal, R., & Ghosh, P. (2017). Analysis of Barriers to Women Entrepreneurship: The DEMATEL Approach. The Journal Of Entrepreneurship, 26(2), 220–238. https://doi.org/10.1177/0971355717708848

30. Rajvanshi, A. (2017). Women entrepreneurs in India: Challenges and opportunities. *IOSR Journal of Humanities and Social Sciences*, *22*(4), 1–9. https://doi.org/10.9790/0837- 2204050109.

31. Ramaswamy, G. (2013). Psychosocial and psycho-entrepreneurial predictors—An exploratory study on Indian women entrepreneurs. *Women's Studies*, *42*(2), 163–192. https://doi.org/10.1080/00497878.2013.747380

32. Ratten, V., Dana, L. P. and Ramadani, V. (Eds) (2018a), Women Entrepreneurship in Family Business, Routledge, London.

33. Ratten, V., Ramadani, V., Dana, L. P., Hisrich, R. D. and Ferreira, J. (Eds) (2018b), Gender and Family Entrepreneurship, Routledge, London.

34. Revathi, D.S. and Krishnan, J. (2013), "Economic and social issues of women entrepreneurs in microenterprise",International Journal of Economic Research, Vol. 10 No. 2.

35. Saner, R., & Yiu, L. (2019). Jamaica's development of women entrepreneurship: challenges and opportunities. Public Administration And Policy, 22(2), 152–172. https://doi.org/10.1108/pap-09-2019-0023

36. Sandhu, N., Hussain, J. and Matlay, H. (2012), "Barriers to finance experienced by female owner/managers of marginal farms in India", Journal of Small Business and Enterprise Development, Vol. 19 No. 4, pp. 640-655.

37. Schumpeter, Joseph A. 1947. The Creative Response in Economic History. The Journal of Economic History 7: 149–59.

38. Schwartz, Eleanor Brantley. 1976. Entrepreneurship-New Female Frontier. Journal of Contemporary Business 5: 47–76.

39. Sharma, Y. (2013), "Women entrepreneur in India", Iosr Journal of Business and Management, Vol. 15 No. 3, pp. 9–14.

40. Solanki, N. (2019). Women Entrepreneurship: A Paradigm Shift. Humanities & Social Sciences Reviews, 7(1), 501–504. doi: 10.18510/hssr.2019.7157

41. Thomas, P., & Jose, S. (2018). Engaging and promoting young women's entrepreneurship: A challenge to social work. International Social Work, 63(1), 69–75. https://doi.org/10.1177/0020872818783243

42. Tripathi, K., & Singh, S. (2018). Analysis of barriers to women entrepreneurship through ISM and MICMAC. Journal Of Enterprising Communities: People And Places In The Global Economy, 12(3), 346–373. https://doi.org/10.1108/jec-12-2017-0101

43. Welsh, D., Kaciak, E., Memili, E., & Minialai, C. (2018). Business-family interface and the performance of women entrepreneurs. *International Journal of Emerging Markets*, *13*(2), 330–349. https://doi.org/10.1108/ijoem-03-2017-0095

Handbook of Evidence Based Management Practices in Business – Satyendra Kumar Sharma et al. (eds)
© 2023 Taylor & Francis Group, London, ISBN 978-1-032-54216-4

Chapter

Bibliographic Analysis and Strategic Management Research in India

B. S. Rathore[1]
Professor, School of Business,
Mody University of Science and Technology,
Lakshmangarh, Dist. Sikar, Rajasthan, India

Nardeep Kumar Maheshwari[2]
Professor, and Dean-Admin,
Mody University of Science and Technology,
Lakshmangarh, Dist: Sikar, Rajasthan, India

Sunita Verma[3]
Associate Professor, School of Business,
Mody University of Science and Technology,
Lakshmangarh, Dist: Sikar, Rajasthan, India

ABSTRACT: The purpose of this study is to examine the existing literature regarding strategic management research in India based on the bibliometric approach used as a means of supplementing the subjective evaluation of bibliographic literature reviews. A total of 245 research publications were extracted from the Scopus database and bibliometric techniques using the Vows viewer, which includes sources, authors, organisations, keywords, and citation analysis. Publication growth in strategic management research in India gradually increased, but a rapid increase was found from 2017 to 2021. The most productive year for strategic management research in India was 2021, during which a total of 33 research documents were published. The Department of Management Studies, Indian Institute of Technology Delhi, is at the top and the only institute that published over 2 research publications and received citations totaling 50, followed by the Department of Strategic Management, National Institute of Industrial Engineering Mumbai, which received 30 citations. Dhir S. emerged as a top author with 5 publications and 86 total citations. Emerald Emerging Markets Case Studies journal is at the top, publishing 87 documents and 42 citations, followed by Strategic Entrepreneurship, a journal that published 3 documents and 181 citations. The result shows a co-occurrence

---
[1]bsrathore.sob@modyuniversity.ac.in, [2]dean.admin@modyuniversity.ac.in, [3]sunitaverma.sob@modyuniversity.ac.in

DOI: 10.4324/9781003415725-70

network of authors' keywords, elaborated with a minimum occurrence of five keywords and 26 items containing five clusters.

KEYWORDS: Bibliometric analysis, Citations, Research, Research productivity, Strategic management

1. Introduction

Emerging markets have attracted significant interest from academics and professionals over the last few decades. This increased focus, which is not unjustified, is centered on the fact that developing markets account for more than half of the global population and a sizable portion of strategic management operations (Mukherjee et al., 2022). India is one of the most significant emerging markets and has the sixth-largest nominal gross domestic product (GDP) in the world. Foreign direct investment (FDI) in South Asia climbed by 20% to $71 billion in 2020, according to the World Investment Report 2021, primarily due to a 27% ($64 billion) rise in FDI into India (UNCTAD, 2021). Given this dynamic economic environment, it makes sense that strategic management studies in India have expanded quickly. Consequently, a large and rich body of strategic management literature has been produced by scholars using India as their research laboratory (Dheer et al., 2015).

The recent special editions of prestigious business journals like Management Decision, Management Research Review, Strategic Entrepreneurship Journal, and Strategic Outsourcing: An International Journal are devoted to India and demonstrate this rising interest. Researchers have also made a strong case for utilising the diverse Indian context more effectively for the development of strategic management theory. Nevertheless, despite the increased attention, only a small number of studies have carefully examined the underlying organisation of the knowledge issues in this field. In other words, a closer look at the literature on India is justified given its centrality and significance as a significant emerging economy. In fact, to the best of our knowledge, no study has been published to date that maps the philosophical foundations of this rich and developing body of research. This oversight suggests a sizable gap in the literature and presents a chance for a thorough and in-depth scholarly project.

By conducting a descriptive bibliometric analysis, the study reveals patterns in journals, articles, and authors that will aid future research. The application of bibliometric analysis is widespread in a variety of disciplines, including social science, engineering, library science, agriculture, economics, medicine, and management disciplines including entrepreneurship, and strategy. In addition to having a broad range of applications, bibliometric analysis is pertinent to strategic management research in India, which is characterized by major research constraints.

The current aim of the study is to identify and evaluate Strategic Management Research in India publishing patterns and trends from 2006-2022 by considering the most productive authors, organizations, key journals, collaborative networks, and authorship patterns for helping future researchers in identifying gaps especially strategic management research in India.

The following research questions have been considered to answer the research objective:

1. What are the publishing trends in strategic management research in India?
2. What are the top strategic management research publishing journals?
3. Which of the authors, journals, and organizations are most productive in strategic management research?

2. Methodology

The first step in a bibliometric analysis is to establish the database in order to obtain the articles used for the analysis. In this study, we used information provided by journals indexed in the Scopus database.

Data were retrieved from the software Scopus using the title search "Strategic Management" AND "India" AND "Research," and it generated 245 academic records. The data was retrieved and downloaded on December 9, 2022, and refined by document type, which consists of (i) articles, (ii) proceeding papers, (iii) reviews, and (iv) book chapters. The bibliometric research study presents network analysis, publishing trends, the most productive authors, journals, and countries (Su et al., 2019), author keywords, etc. by utilising VOSviewer software for the literature published during 2006–2022.

3. Data Source and Search Strategy

On December 9, 2022, a search query was used to get information from the software Scopus. The database has 245 bibliographic records.

3.1 Data Analysis

This session provides a comprehensive analysis of the bibliometric study. After sorting each record and screening each bibliometric record by reading the title and abstract, 245 unique records were verified and used for current studies.

3.2 Total Publication Growth Trend

The publications of the articles we looked at ranged from 2006 to 2022. Figure 70.1 illustrates year-wise research publications on Strategic Management Research in India from 2006-2022. The research publishing trend indicates a significantly increasing from 2006 to 2022 with little fluctuation whereas the boom in the publication of Strategic Management Research in India has been observed from 2018 to 2021. The most research productive year in Strategic Management Research in India was 2021 in which a total of 33 research documents were published. The increase in papers produced over time indicates that the subject is moving to a more advanced level. As a result, various study directions may be pursued.

3.3 Most Research Contributing Institutions

The top research contributing organizations in the field of strategic management research in India are shown in Table 70.1 which indicated Department of Management Studies (DMS),

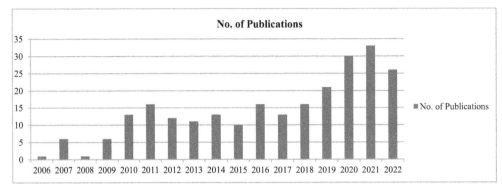

Fig. 70.1 Publication growth trend

Source: Author's compilation

Table 70.1 Most Research contributing institutions

S.N.	Organization	Documents	Citations	Total link strength
1	Amity Institute of Psychology and Allied Sciences, Amity University, Noida, India	1	46	258
2	Department of Geology, Andhra University, Visakhapatnam, Andhra Pradesh, India	1	70	57
3	Department of Geology, ML Sukhadia University, Udaipur, Rajasthan, India	1	70	57
4	Department of Management Studies, Indian Institute of Technology Delhi, New Delhi, India	2	50	117
5	Department of Management Studies, Indian Institute of Technology Roorkee, Roorkee, India	1	45	64
6	Department of Management, Dav University, Jalandhar, India	1	111	131
7	Department of Management, Lovely Professional University, Phagwara, India	1	111	131
8	Department of Mechanical Engineering, University College of Engineering, Punjabi University, Patiala, India	1	73	143
9	Department of Organisational Behaviour and Human Resource Management, International Management Institute New Delhi, India	1	46	258
10	Department of Strategic Management, National Institute of Industrial Engineering, Mumbai, India	2	30	39
11	Institute for International Management and Technology, Haryana, India	1	84	4
12	Management Development Institute (MDI), Gurgaon, India	1	98	114
13	Mechanical Engineering Department, Baba Banda Singh Bahadur Engineering College, Fatehgarh Sahib, India	1	73	143
14	Prasar Bharati, Government of India, New Delhi, India	1	40	89

Source: Author's compilation

IIT Delhi, is at the top and the only institute that published over 2 research publications and received 50 citations followed by Department of Strategic Management, National Institute of Industrial Engineering, Mumbai and received 30 citations. Department of Management (DoM), Dav University Jalandhar, and DoM, Lovely Professional University Phagwara received the highest number of citations 111 followed by Management Development Institute, Gurgaon received 98 citations.

3.4 Most Productive Authors

The list of most productive authors and their affiliation with strategic management research in India is compiled in Table 70.2. The author's publication range varies from 2-5. Dhir S. emerged as a top author with 5 publications and 86 citations.

Table 70.2 Most productive authors

S.N.	Author	Documents	Citations	Total link strength
1	Bhattacharyya S.S.	5	36	0
2	Chaudhary S.	2	3	0
3	Dhir S.	5	86	5
4	Doh J.P.	2	55	3
5	Gupta A.	5	7	6
6	Jain S.	2	40	0
7	Koul S.	2	8	0
8	Kumar J.	2	3	3
9	Kumar V.	3	22	2
10	Mor R.S.	2	29	1
11	Parameswar N.	3	40	5
12	Satar M.S.	2	8	0
13	Sawhney S.	3	4	3
14	Setia R.	2	18	2
15	Shankar R.	2	9	3
16	Sharma K.	2	6	1
17	Sharma S.	4	5	1
18	Sharma V.	3	8	0
19	Singh A.	3	14	5
20	Singh S.	2	27	1
21	Singhania M.	5	3	1
22	Sinha P.	3	10	2
23	Srivastava A.	2	7	0
24	Stumpf S.A.	2	55	3
25	Sushil	2	63	2
26	Vrat P.	2	9	3

Source: Author's compilation

3.5 Most Publication Journals

We restricted the visualization to 24 journals that have at least 50 citations. The results as per the number of documents and citations indicate that Emerald Emerging Markets Case Studies journal is at the top in publishing 87 documents and 42 citations followed by Strategic Entrepreneurship Journal published 3 documents and 181 citations.

Table 70.3 Most Publication Journals

S. N.	Source	Documents	Citations	Total link strength
1	Asia Pacific Journal of Human Resources	1	22	0
2	Benchmarking	1	46	0
3	Critical Perspectives on International Business	1	15	0
4	Emerald Emerging Markets Case Studies	87	42	0
5	Global And Planetary Change	1	15	0
6	Global Journal of Flexible Systems Management	3	36	0
7	Groundwater for Sustainable Development	1	70	0
8	Human Resource Management	1	98	0
9	International Journal of Business Performance and Supply Chain Modelling	1	24	0
10	International Journal of Educational Management	2	89	0
11	International Journal of Integrated Supply Management	1	17	0
12	International Journal of Manpower	1	18	0
13	International Journal of Organizational Analysis	2	30	0
14	International Journal of Productivity and Performance Management	2	111	0
15	International Journal of Productivity and Quality Management	2	27	0
16	Journal of Business Ethics	1	49	0
17	Journal of Cleaner Production	1	47	0
18	Journal of Manufacturing Technology Management	1	17	0
19	Journal of Operations Management	1	176	0
20	Journal of Organizational Change Management	1	45	0
21	Landscape and Urban Planning	1	19	0
22	Management Decision	2	91	0
23	Management Research Review	2	31	0
24	Strategic Entrepreneurship Journal	3	181	0
25	Strategic Outsourcing: An International Journal	1	15	0

Source: Author's compilation

3.6 Keywords Occurrences

According to Su and Lee (2010), publication keyword analysis in bibliometrics is considered the basic representation of knowledge concepts to explore and reveal the research domain's knowledge structures. The keywords analysis reveals that 26 different keywords were used by authors for strategic management research. Table 70.4 shows a co-occurrence network of authors' keywords that elaborated with a minimum occurrence of five keywords and Figure shows 26 items containing five clusters.

Table 70.4 Keywords occurrences

S. N.	Keyword	Occur-rences	Total link strength	S.N.	Keyword	Occur-rences	Total link strength
1	Article	7	7	14	Management	5	9
2	Change Management	5	7	15	Marketing	5	5
3	Corporate	5	12	16	Planning	6	16
4	Competition	5	7	17	Social Enterprise	9	19
5	Competitive Advantage	9	12	18	Stakeholder Management	6	10
6	Competitive Strategy	14	24	19	Strategic Management	56	66
7	Corporate Strategy	9	15	20	Strategic Management/ Planning	21	24
8	Critical Success Factors	5	13	21	Strategic Planning	5	6
9	Diversification	7	7	22	Strategy	28	35
10	Dynamic Capabilities	5	7	23	Supply Chain Management	5	14
11	Entrepreneurship	17	21	24	Sustainability	10	20
12	India	67	80	25	Sustainable Development	8	15
13	Innovation	14	14	26	Value Chain	5	9

Source: Author's compilation

The node with the most keywords (seven), Cluster 1 displayed in red, includes the keywords "competitive strategy" "entrepreneurship" "marketing" "social enterprise" "stakeholder management" "strategic management/planning" and "value chain". Cluster 2 (6 items) displayed in green, includes the keywords "competition" and "competitive advantage" "critical success factors" "planning" "strategic management" and "strategic planning". Cluster 3 (5 items) displayed in Blue, includes the keywords "corporate strategy" "diversification" "dynamic capabilities" and "innovation". Cluster 4 (5 items) displayed in yellow, includes the keywords "corporate" and "management" "supply chain management" "sustainability" and "sustainable development". Cluster 5 (3 items) displayed in purple includes keywords "article" "change management" and "India".

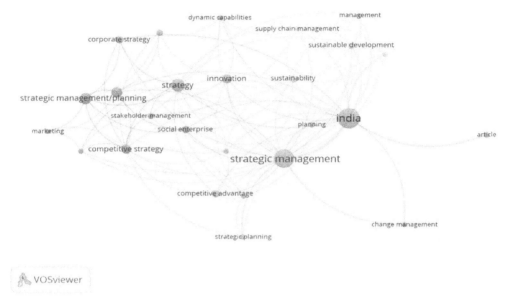

Fig. 70.2 Keyword occurrences

Source: Author's compilation

4. Conclusion and Limitations of the Review

This study has done an investigation and provided an overview of the existing literature in the field of strategic management research in India. It aimed to identify various historical and actual contexts regarding these research 245 articles, retrieved through the Scopus database. The most research productive year in strategic management research in India was 2021 in which a total of 33 research documents were published. Department of Management Studies, Indian Institute of Technology New Delhi, is at the top and the only institute that published over 2 research publications and received citations 50 followed by the Department of Strategic Management, National Institute of Industrial Engineering, Mumbai which received 30 citations. Dhir S. emerged as a top author with 5 publications and 86 total citations. Emerald Emerging Markets Case Studies journal is at the top in publishing 87 documents and 42 citations followed by Strategic Entrepreneurship journal published 3 documents and 181 citations. The result shows a co-occurrence network of authors' keywords that elaborated with a minimum occurrence of five keywords and 26 items containing five clusters.

This Bibliometric study will help the researchers better grasp the direction and scope of strategic management research in India. However, this study has several limitations, just like every other scientific study. This bibliometric analysis can be regarded as thorough but not exhaustive because it only used Scopus, which may have limited our ability to retrieve articles, and because our filtering procedure may have missed some pertinent studies. Other databases like the Web of Science could be used for extracting more relevant articles in this field. Even comparison of both can also be conducted. This study included only academic articles whereas it can also include, conference proceedings, review electronic copy, and early access articles.

This paper would be a pioneering work in the field of management research as it would fill the gap and provide management researchers with quality research. Also, it fills a gap in the literature on research methods, which helps management students and junior members of faculty advance in their careers.

REFERENCES

1. Dheer, R., Lenartowicz, T., and Peterson M. (2015), "Mapping India's regional subcultures: Implications for international management", Journal of International Business Studies volume 46, pages 443–467.
2. Kumar, S., Pandey, N. and Mukherjee, D. (2022), "Cross cultural and strategic management: A retrospective overview using bibliometric analysis", Cross Cultural & Strategic Management, Vol. 29 No. 1, pp. 171-194. https://doi.org/10.1108/CCSM-08-2021-0147.
3. Mukherjee, Debmalya., Kumar S., Mukherjee, Deepraj., and Goyal K. (2022), "Mapping five decades of international business and management research on India: A bibliometric analysis and future directions, Journal of Business Research, Volume 145, June 2022, Pages 864–891, https://doi.org/10.1016/j.jbusres.2022.03.011.
4. Su, Hsin-Ning, and Pei-Chun Lee (2010). "Mapping knowledge structure by keyword co-occurrence: a first look at journal papers in Technology Foresight, Scientometrics 85, no. 1 (2010): 65–79.
5. Su, Xinwei, Xi Li, and Yanxin Kang (2019). "A bibliometric analysis of research on intangible cultural heritage using CiteSpace." Sage Open 9, no. 2 (2019): 2158244019840119.

Handbook of Evidence Based Management Practices in Business – Satyendra Kumar Sharma et al. (eds)
© *2023 Taylor & Francis Group, London, ISBN 978-1-032-54216-4*

Chapter

71

Enabling Sustainable Entrepreneurial Intentions Through the Fintech Ecosystem and Entrepreneurship Education Ecosystem: Does Sustainable Orientation Matter?

Manpreet Rajpal[1]
Research scholar,
Indian Institute of Information Technology, Lucknow, India

Bindu Singh[2]
Assistant Professor,
Indian Institute of Information Technology, Lucknow, India

ABSTRACT: Academicians and researchers continue to acknowledge the significance of entrepreneurial ecosystems (EEs) in fostering an entrepreneurial environment and building an entrepreneurial culture. Despite the notion that EEs are essentially interaction networks of hierarchically independent yet mutually dependent entities, only a small body of research has examined how interactions across ecosystem actors in fintech and entrepreneurial education influence entrepreneurial aspirations. Moreover, with the growing consideration of sustainability in the current business world, sustainable entrepreneurship has also gained great attention. However, a roadmap to a sustainable entrepreneurial career remains unexplored. To address and bridge this gap, this paper adopts the lens of knowledge spillover theory and empirically investigates how ecosystem actors of the fintech industry (blockchain, venture funding, crowdfunding) impact the entrepreneurship education ecosystem (EEEs) determinants (institutional settings, curriculum structure, incubators) to influence youth's sustainable intention to pursue an entrepreneurial career path. While bridging the pathway of sustainable entrepreneurship, this paper also measures the impact of sustainable orientation on the boundary conditions of EEEs and sustainable entrepreneurial intentions (SEIs).

KEYWORDS: Entrepreneurship education, Sustainable entrepreneurial attitude, Sustainable entrepreneurship, Sustainable entrepreneurial intention, Sustainable orientation

[1]rmh21201@iiitl.ac.in, [2]bindu@iiitl.ac.in

DOI: 10.4324/9781003415725-71

1. Introduction

Expansion and gradual upliftment of emerging economies emphasises on exploring the numerous economy boosters (Liu Y et al., 2022). One such booster is entrepreneurship, which transforms the employment search scenario into an employment generation platform, which is recognized as a critical enabler of economic growth (Sahut JM et al., 2021; Stock T et al., 2018; Bag S et al., 2020; Elia G et al., 2020). Founders of new ventures are known for their inventive and innovative approaches to solving such problems and probing for new opportunities (Shepherd and Patzelt, 2011). Values and aspirations distinguish business practises and, as a response, shape entrepreneurship in diverse forms. Likewise, sustainable entrepreneurs aim to create value for others by uncovering and grasping economic venture opportunities emerging from environmental and social concerns that have been overlooked or unsuccessfully addressed by the community, corporate, or societal entities (Schaltegger and Wagner, 2011). Thus, for the future entrepreneurs, the focus is placed on the triple bottom line - incorporating economic, social, and environmental gains (Sung and Park, 2018). Such audacious manifesto calls for a strategy that prioritises the cultivation of sustainable behaviour as a device in the creation of venture models and practices. In this context, entrepreneurial studies explored on devising drivers to shape and influence sustainable behaviour among the youth. Intention for entrepreneurial career choice is viewed as significant and rapidly emerging research area due to its substantial role in venture formation, survival, and development (Belz and Blinder 2017). Even though business world is becoming increasingly focused on corporate social responsibility and environmental accountability (Reyes-Rodrguez et al., 2020), yet less is known about factors stimulating youth for career development in sustainability inbuilt entrepreneurship (Agu et al., 2021; Arru, 2020; Majid et al., 2017; Vuorio et al., 2018). This study takes this call and focus on intentions to become sustainable entrepreneurs (Vuorio et al., 2018). The question is thus how sustainability intention can really sprout among students enrolled in academic institutions. Prior literature stresses on the individuals' aspirations towards the formation of a sustainable firm (Ahmad et al., 2020). Counting on sustainable entrepreneurship, previous research has yet underestimated the role of *sustainable entrepreneurial orientation* that do affect sustainable entrepreneurial career intentions (Kuckertz & Wagner, 2010; Hörisch, Kollat, & Brieger, 2019; Dickel, P., & Eckardt, G. 2021).

The theoretical lens of present conceptual study is based on knowledge spillover theory (Acs et al. 2013)) that reflects the pertinent role of academic institutions and universities as a source of knowledge creation, knowledge management and further focusing on commercialisation, yet its potent role in framing sustainable intention for entrepreneurial career journey is under covered. Knowledge management of financial technology (fintech) and its ecosystem perspective is critical for the arrangement and management of finance designed for the further entrepreneurial journey. Thus, it highlights the role of appropriate channel for knowledge transformation blended with entrepreneurship education framework concerning the fintech ecosystem actors (venture fund, crowdfunding, blockchain etc.).

On the other hand, ecosystem perspective is instrumental in nurturing entrepreneurial talent among youth. Consequently, the increased emphasis on entrepreneurial ecosystem has led to the emergence of numerous unknown and understudied areas; consequently, experts have advocated for theoretical and empirical research to fill the resulting gaps in the literature (Audretsch et al., 2018; Brown & Mason, 2017; Stam, 2015; Maysami AM et. al., 2020). In context with entrepreneurial education the academic institutions and universities are well known as a medium of knowledge transformation and thus it magnifies the need to adopt tailor made curriculum and institutional climate to spur entrepreneurial mindset among university students. The government policies are inculcating and boosting incubator setups in academic institutions to instil entrepreneurial culture and sustainable goals aligning the triple bottom line of sustainable development (Ray P et al., 2022). Yet there is a need of exploring ecosystem perspective of entrepreneurial education more specifically the role of academic incubators.

In order to address this research gap, this conceptual research framework contributes towards the role of entrepreneurial education actors along fintech actors with ecosystem perspectives to build intentions among youth for sustainable business formation. Based on the aforementioned, this study extends Bandura's SCT (Social Cognitive Theory) throwing light on a formal blend personal attributes and with significantly contributes to the existing literature on sustainable entrepreneurial intention. The study aims to support the ecosystem perspective of EE as a useful method for enhancing students' entrepreneurial aspirations.

2. Conceptual Paper Design

The proposed research model (refer Fig. 71.1) draws on the blended framework of knowledge spillover theory, social cognitive theory of Bandura and the contribution of scholars such as **Vuorio** in the context of blending sustainable development goals in entrepreneurship. The mechanism of environmental (fintech ecosystem and education ecosystem of entrepreneurship), personal attributes (sustainable entrepreneurial orientation), and behavioural (sustainable entrepreneurial intention) facets of sustainable entrepreneurship is introduced into the Bandura's SCT (Social Cognitive Theory) model in response to the rising emphasis on the significance of education in achieving sustainable development goals (Frank et al., 2019; Vuorio et al., 2018; Walmsler, 2020), and the current study framework highlights sustainability-oriented ecosystem of entrepreneurship education (institutional settings, curriculum, academic incubators). The proposed research finds a gap in the literature by establishing a conceptual insight into the role of sustainability-focused entrepreneurial study where the role of academic institutions and universities is magnified through the lens of ecosystem to promote entrepreneurial culture with a motive to address and adopt sustainable developmental goals.

RQ1. Does entrepreneurial education ecosystem significantly influence the intention of university-enrolled students to engage in sustainable entrepreneurship?

RQ2. Does perception and knowledge management of fintech ecosystem assist in developing intention for sustainable oriented entrepreneurial career among university enrolled students?

On the other hand, as personal attributes, sustainability orientation denotes an individual's concern for environmental conservation as well as social responsibility (Kuckertz & Wagner, 2010; Sung & Park, 2018). Despite these valuable findings, we know little about impact of sustainable orientation on entrepreneurial attitude with sustainable goal, also the moderating impact of SEO on the relationship of sustainable oriented attitude and sustainable entrepreneurial intention is a unique and uncovered aspect.

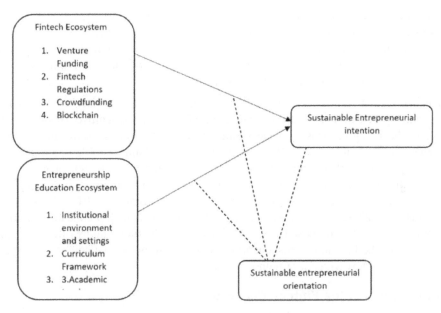

Fig. 71.1 Proposed model based on present conceptual study

Source: Author's compilation

3. Literature Review

3.1 Sustainability Driven Entrepreneurship

Sustainability-driven entrepreneurship builds on the preceding ideas of social, environmental, and institutional entrepreneurship and emphasises the use of creative/innovative commercial efforts to address concerns relating to environmental and social sustainability while concurrently pursuing economic success (Abrahamsson, 2007; Schaltegger, 2002). According to Hockerts and Wüstenhagen (2010), Nicolopoulou (2014), and Vuorio et al. (2018), an entrepreneurial activity emphasises the triple bottom line when it combines comprehensive economic, social, and environmental goals that endure through time.Along with this recent literature reviews (Fellnhofer et al., 2014; Munoz and Cohen, 2018) call for studies to elucidate SE, claiming that these emerging issues require to be researched, structured, and synthesised. (Hockerts & Wüstenhagen, 2010; Nicolopoulou, 2014; Vuorio et al., 2018).

3.2 Ecosystem Perspective of Entrepreneurship Education

It is widely accepted that entrepreneurial culture can be built through cohesive learning ecosystem. Thus, for entrepreneurship, to deal with the factors affecting entrepreneurial culture among the young generation, favourable learning environment is much needed to promote innovative culture and sprout entrepreneurial behaviour among youth studying in academic institutions. It is an accepted thought that entrepreneurship can be taught through adopting well-structured education system. (Yang, Chen, Yang, & Liu, 2021) points out that education is a renowned framework to fabricate entrepreneurial attitude and behaviour and to build innovative entrepreneurial capabilities and skills. In the words of Agu et al. (2020), education for sustainable entrepreneurship (ESE) refers to advancement of entrepreneurial knowledge, skills inclination and intention that are much needed to successfully launch and retain a sustainability-oriented entrepreneurial venture.

The mechanism of environmental, cognitive, and behavioural facets of sustainable entrepreneurship is introduced into the Bandura's SCT (Social Cognitive Theory) model in response to the rising emphasis on the significance of education in achieving sustainable development goals (Frank et al., 2019; Vuorio et al., 2018; Walmsler, 2020), and the current study framework highlights sustainability-oriented ecosystem of entrepreneurship education considering the academic intuitional settings(climate), the curriculum and most importantly the role of academic incubators (Arumugam, B., & Ravindran, S. 2014). Prior literature placed a major emphasis on the function of general entrepreneurship education and related programmes. The current proposed research fills a gap in the literature by offering empirical understanding of the function of sustainability-focused entrepreneurial education in the SCT model in Indian context which is still undercover.

3.3 Impressions of the Fintech Ecosystem

There has been a significant shift in the corporate world's working culture and requirements toward being technologically driven. As 'finance' and 'technology' merge, interest has grown in studying financial technology (fintech). As defined by Leong and Sung (2018), fintech refers to innovative ecosystems incorporating technology into a business setting and adopting transformative business models. According to Bofondi and Gobbi (2017), FinTech provides all of the services that banks previously provided, albeit with a small profit margin. Given the rise in market participants in a variety of industries, including digital payments, wealth management, crowdfunding, lending, capital markets, and insurance, it is crucial to research the fintech phenomenon (Lee & Shin, 2018). According to Autio et al. (2018), digitalization influences both the type of entrepreneurial opportunities that emerge and how founders seek such opportunities. While fintech encompasses not only new ventures but also traditional financial institutions and technology firms, this study focuses on start-ups because of their economic impact and disruptive innovations (Palmié et al., 2019).

4. Conclusions, Implications and Limitations

The purpose of this study was to explore the ecosystem structure of entrepreneurial education and construction of knowledge capitals, as well as to understand the perception about the financial technology(fintech) ecosystem. Building on the Bandura's SCT (Social Cognitive Theory) and the knowledge spillover theory of entrepreneurship (Acs et al. 2013) we argue that entrepreneurial culture and building knowledge capitals are at the heart of university ecosystem and that need to be compatible in the way to spur intention for entrepreneurial career and knowledge spillover to further university enrolled students (Audretsch, DB., & Belitski, M. 2021). This study suggested that well-structured ecology of entrepreneurial university or entrepreneurial course structure can be adopted when all stakeholders (students, community, university, market players) are interrelated and persistently put efforts along the process of the knowledge building, transformation and commercialization. Furthermore, the special focus on the institutional climate, the curricular structure of education for entrepreneurship as well as academic incubators to pave the way to sprout favourable attitudes towards venture formation adopting sustainable development goals (UN SDGs 2030).

5. Abbreviations

EEE- entrepreneurship Education Ecosystem

SEI – Sustainable Entrepreneurial Intention

SEO – Sustainable Entrepreneurial Orientation

EE – Entrepreneurial Education

FE – Fintech Ecosystem

REFERENCES

1. Abrahamsson, Anders. "Researching Sustainopreneurship–conditions, concepts, approaches, arenas and questions." In *Proceedings of the International Sustainable Development Research Conference*. 2007.
2. Acs, Zoltan J., Pontus Braunerhjelm, David B. Audretsch, and Bo Carlsson. "The knowledge spillover theory of entrepreneurship." *Small business economics* 32, no. 1 (2009): 15–30.
3. Agu, Agu Godswill, Okwuagwu Okuu Kalu, Chidadi Obinna Esi-Ubani, and Paul Chinedu Agu. "Drivers of sustainable entrepreneurial intentions among university students: an integrated model from a developing world context." *International Journal of Sustainability in Higher Education* (2021).
4. Ahmed, Waqar, Muhammad Saeed Ashraf, Sharfuddin Ahmed Khan, Simonov Kusi-Sarpong, Francis Kow Arhin, Horsten Kusi-Sarpong, and Arsalan Najmi. "Analyzing the impact of environmental collaboration among supply chain stakeholders on a firm's sustainable performance." *Operations Management Research* 13, no. 1 (2020): 4–21.
5. Arumugam, B., and S. Ravindran. "Success factors of incubatee start-ups and the incubation environment influencers." *International Journal of Applied Business and Economic Research* 12, no. 4 (2014): 1179–1193.
6. Audretsch, David B., and Maksim Belitski. "Three-ring entrepreneurial university: in search of a new business model." *Studies in Higher Education* 46, no. 5 (2021): 977–987.
7. Audretsch, David, Colin Mason, Morgan P. Miles, and Allan O'Connor. "The dynamics of entrepreneurial ecosystems." (2018): 471–474.
8. Autio, Erkko, Satish Nambisan, Llewellyn DW Thomas, and Mike Wright. "Digital affordances, spatial affordances, and the genesis of entrepreneurial ecosystems." *Strategic Entrepreneurship Journal* 12, no. 1 (2018): 72–95.
9. Bag, Surajit, Lincoln C. Wood, Sachin K. Mangla, and Sunil Luthra. "Procurement 4.0 and its implications on business process performance in a circular economy." *Resources, conservation and recycling* 152 (2020): 104502.
10. Bandura, Albert. "Social cognitive theory of self-regulation." *Organizational behavior and human decision processes* 50, no. 2 (1991): 248–287.

11. Bandura, Albert. "Social cognitive theory of self-regulation." *Organizational behavior and human decision processes* 50, no. 2 (1991): 248–287.
12. Belz, Frank Martin, and Julia Katharina Binder. "Sustainable entrepreneurship: A convergent process model." *Business Strategy and the Environment* 26, no. 1 (2017): 1–17.
13. Bofondi, Marcello, and Giorgio Gobbi. "The big promise of FinTech." *European economy* 2 (2017): 107–119.
14. Covin, Jeffrey G., and William J. Wales. "Crafting high-impact entrepreneurial orientation research: Some suggested guidelines." *Entrepreneurship theory and practice* 43, no. 1 (2019): 3–18.
15. Dickel, Petra, and Gordon Eckardt. "Who wants to be a social entrepreneur? The role of gender and sustainability orientation." *Journal of Small Business Management* 59, no. 1 (2021): 196–218.
16. Elia, Gianluca, Alessandro Margherita, and Giuseppina Passiante. "Digital entrepreneurship ecosystem: How digital technologies and collective intelligence are reshaping the entrepreneurial process." *Technological Forecasting and Social Change* 150 (2020): 119791.
17. Hockerts, Kai, and Rolf Wüstenhagen. "Greening Goliaths versus emerging Davids—Theorizing about the role of incumbents and new entrants in sustainable entrepreneurship." *Journal of business venturing* 25, no. 5 (2010): 481–492.
18. Hörisch, Jacob, Jana Kollat, and Steven A. Brieger. "Environmental orientation among nascent and established entrepreneurs: an empirical analysis of differences and their causes." *International Journal of Entrepreneurial Venturing* 11, no. 4 (2019): 373–393.
19. Kalawapudi, Komal, Ojaswikrishna Dube, and Renuka Sharma. "Use of neural networks and spatial interpolation to predict groundwater quality." *Environment, Development and Sustainability* 22, no. 4 (2020): 2801–2816.
20. Kuckertz, Andreas, and Marcus Wagner. "The influence of sustainability orientation on entrepreneurial intentions—Investigating the role of business experience." *Journal of business venturing* 25, no. 5 (2010): 524–539.
21. Lee, In, and Yong Jae Shin. "Fintech: Ecosystem, business models, investment decisions, and challenges." *Business horizons* 61, no. 1 (2018): 35–46.
22. Liu, Yang, Yanlin Yang, Huihui Li, and Kaiyang Zhong. "Digital economy development, industrial structure upgrading and green total factor productivity: Empirical evidence from China's cities." *International Journal of Environmental Research and Public Health* 19, no. 4 (2022): 2414.
23. Majid, Izaidin Abdul, Aziz Latif, and Wei-Loon Koe. "SMEs' intention towards sustainable entrepreneurship." *European Journal of Multidisciplinary Studies* 2, no. 3 (2017): 24–32.
24. Maysami, Amir Mahdi, and Ghanbar Mohammadi Elyasi. "Designing the framework of technological entrepreneurship ecosystem: A grounded theory approach in the context of Iran." *Technology in Society* 63 (2020): 101372.
25. Palmié, Maximilian, Joakim Wincent, Vinit Parida, and Umur Caglar. "The evolution of the financial technology ecosystem: An introduction and agenda for future research on disruptive innovations in ecosystems." *Technological Forecasting and Social Change* 151 (2020): 119779.
26. Ray, Pradeep, and Rajib Shaw. "Technology Entrepreneurship and Sustainable Development." (2022).
27. Reyes-Rodríguez, Juan Felipe, Jairo González-Bueno, and Gladys Rueda-Barrios. "Influence of organisational and information systems and technologies resources and capabilities on the adoption of proactive environmental practices and environmental performance." *Entrepreneurship and Sustainability Issues* 8, no. 2 (2020): 875.
28. Sahut, Jean-Michel, Luca Iandoli, and Frédéric Teulon. "The age of digital entrepreneurship." *Small Business Economics* 56, no. 3 (2021): 1159–1169.

29. Schaltegger, Stefan, and Marcus Wagner. "Sustainable entrepreneurship and sustainability innovation: categories and interactions." *Business strategy and the environment* 20, no. 4 (2011): 222–237.

30. Schaltegger, Stefan. "A framework for ecopreneurship: Leading bioneers and environmental managers to ecopreneurship." *Greener management international* 38 (2002): 45–58.

31. Shepherd, Dean A., and Holger Patzelt. "The new field of sustainable entrepreneurship: Studying entrepreneurial action linking "what is to be sustained" with "what is to be developed"." *Entrepreneurship theory and practice* 35, no. 1 (2011): 137–163.

32. Stock, Tim, Michael Obenaus, Sascha Kunz, and Holger Kohl. "Industry 4.0 as enabler for a sustainable development: A qualitative assessment of its ecological and social potential." *Process Safety and Environmental Protection* 118 (2018): 254–267.

33. Sung, Chang Soo, and Joo Y. Park. "Sustainability orientation and entrepreneurship orientation: is there a tradeoff relationship between them?" *Sustainability* 10, no. 2 (2018): 379.

34. Vuorio, Anna Maija, Kaisu Puumalainen, and Katharina Fellnhofer. "Drivers of entrepreneurial intentions in sustainable entrepreneurship." *International Journal of Entrepreneurial Behavior & Research* 24, no. 2 (2017): 359–381.

35. Wamsler, Christine. "Education for sustainability: Fostering a more conscious society and transformation towards sustainability." *International Journal of Sustainability in Higher Education* 21, no. 1 (2020): 112–130.

36. Hörisch, Jacob, Jana Kollat, and Steven A. Brieger. "Environmental orientation among nascent and established entrepreneurs: an empirical analysis of differences and their causes." *International Journal of Entrepreneurial Venturing* 11, no. 4 (2019): 373–393.

37. Dickel, Petra, and Gordon Eckardt. "Who wants to be a social entrepreneur? The role of gender and sustainability orientation." *Journal of Small Business Management* 59, no. 1 (2021): 196–218.

38. Nicolopoulou, Katerina. "Social entrepreneurship between cross-currents: toward a framework for theoretical restructuring of the field." *Journal of Small Business Management* 52, no. 4 (2014): 678–702.

Chapter

72

Opinion of Students Pursuing Higher Education on Online Learning During COVID-19 Pandemic: Review of Literature and a Sample Survey

Deepti Shetty[1]

Department of Management Studies,
Visvesvaraya Technological University, Belagavi

Vidya S. Gurav[2]

Department of Management Studies,
D.K.T.E.S's Textile and Engineering Institute, Ichalkaranji

ABSTRACT: COVID-19 pandemic situation has disturbed teaching and learning process in a many of institutions. This situation has tested the efficiency of higher academic institutions to deal with such abrupt and unwanted situations and crisis. Online teaching and learning have become the main way of being in contact with students during the pandemic everywhere. There has been a significant amount of research conducted on how students perceive the learning process that occurred during the period when there was no in-person, offline education. In this paper it has been tried to know the students' perceptions of online learning by reviewing the literature of research done by different researchers. The chosen research papers for review examined the pros, cons, and overall effectiveness of online education in various institutions. This paper analysed that the most widely and well-known online applications were Zoom, Microsoft Teams, Google meet etc platforms were used to offer online interactive classes and whats app is being used as a communication medium to communicate with students outside the class. Several studies have shown that both teachers and students believe that online education has been helpful during the COVID-19 pandemic. But along with positive response there were negative response too. Many have felt that online education is not as effective as face-to-face learning and teaching. According to student feedback, online learning has presented challenges such as a lack of interaction and motivation, technical and internet issues, data privacy concerns, and security risks. But students also opined about the positive side of online

[1]deeptishetty@vtu.ac.in, [2]vsgurav@dkte.ac.in

DOI: 10.4324/9781003415725-72

learning. Mainly self-learning, low costs, convenience, and flexibility were the positive factors of online education. Despite being a useful temporary solution during the pandemic, online learning cannot fully replace in-person instruction. But on the contrary it is also true that there is no other option for online learning in this situation.

KEYWORDS: COVID-19, Online learning, Students, Effectiveness

1. Introduction

The World Health Organization declared the COVID-19 outbreak as a global pandemic in March 2020. It has drastically impacted all walks of life and all sectors including education. The effect is so hard that many institutions have closed down. This situation has put all the institutions to have unpredicted shift from traditional to online learning. This unimagined outbreak triggered new ways of teaching and learning online. Some institutions opposed and many institutions accepted the required change. Due to the COVID-19 pandemic and the resulting lockdowns, many countries around the world have had to shift from in-person to online education. In order to control the spread of the virus, universities and schools were closed and instruction moved to online platforms. This transition to online learning has been necessary in over 190 countries worldwide.

Many institutions have adopted both synchronous and asynchronous online teaching methods in response to the COVID-19 pandemic. Synchronous online learning involves real-time interaction between faculty and students, while asynchronous online learning allows students to access course materials on their own time without direct interaction with the instructor. However, some universities in developing countries may not have the resources or training to effectively teach online, and Internet connectivity can be a barrier for disadvantaged students. It is generally acknowledged that in-person instruction is more effective than online learning, but the COVID-19 pandemic has necessitated a shift to online education, highlighting the need to understand students' perceptions of this learning modality in order to identify its advantages, disadvantages, and challenges.

The COVID-19 pandemic has had a significant impact on online learning, both for faculty and students. While online learning has many benefits, such as time flexibility, it can also present challenges such as a lack of real-time interaction and peer learning. These challenges can affect students' engagement and personal development. Additionally, faculty play important roles in teaching, monitoring, and advising students in both academic and personal matters. The current crisis highlights the importance of the internet and technology in education and the role of online learning in responding to unforeseen challenges. It is therefore crucial to understand the perspectives of both faculty and students on online classes.

2. Objectives of the Study

1. To study the various views of the students about the online learning in this situation of COVID 19 through reviewing the research papers

2. To explore the advantages as well as disadvantages of online education through the review of literature

3. To understand the impact of shift of education from online to offline on students.

4. To analyse the perception of students about online learning through the review of papers

3. Review of Literature from Selected Research Papers

Total 5 research papers have been studied to understand the perception of students seeking higher education about online learning and the impact of online learning on the students.

T. Muthuprasada, S. Aiswarya, K. S. Aditya, Girish K. Jhaa (January, 2021) have studied on "Students' perception and preference for online education in India during COVID-19 pandemic". This paper shows the efforts needed to be put by the higher education institutions to shift from offline to online teaching to adjust with the critical situation arose and fight against the pandemic situation and survive and continue giving education to the students. The efforts are being taken by universities and institutions for shifting to online platforms to catch up with the curriculum. This paper tries to put the perception and readiness of teachers and students for online education.

The findings of this study revealed that most of the students gave positive outlook towards online learning in the worst situation of COVID-19. Online learning provided various advantages like it provided flexibility to the learner and provided easy and comfort way for learning to the learner. Students wished for having recorded videos of lectures to be uploaded on their university websites with quality content. Students also pointed out that, in order to have interactive sessions, activities like having quiz at the end of class and giving assignments to students, should be planned. Also, many students said that online classes might be little more challenging than offline classes because of technology constraints, delayed feedback and lack of physical person to person interaction. So, while developing such online platforms or applications, consideration of all the possible scenarios and various factors is very important for learners to have better and effective learnings. There are higher chances that education system may adopt and continue the online teaching system, even after COVID-19 pandemic settles down. Also, for more effective learning education system can combine traditional teaching methods with online teaching methods. Hence this study will prove helpful for rethinking and rebuilding new learning models which includes new online components to make learning fun and effective.

Shivangi Dhawan (2020) in her research titled "Online Learning: A Panacea in the Time of COVID-19 Crisis" concluded that natural disasters always make human beings to change accordingly. Higher education giving institutions are not exceptions. COVID-19 situation has given motivation for making use of new emerging online communication technologies and e-learning tools. In order to make best use of e-learning during such difficult times, stakeholders of educational field should majorly focus on, how to make use of these new online learning technologies effectively and efficiently. Technologies must be providing maximum benefit and should have minimum maintenance. The author suggests to consider all the advantages and disadvantages of the tools to be used in e learning before implementing them. Institutions should consider various factors and should do research before brining any technology. Once a technology is adopted then, there should be a proper and valid reason for adopting that technology. Different factors like security issue, speed of internet, availability of internet, any requirement of special online application, availability of laboratories and their conditions etc., should be taken into consideration before deciding the technology. As per the authors view such systems need to be developed in educational institutions that make sure that no student is getting deprived of education due to their location, social class, ethnicity, and so on. Pandemic like Covid-19, creates chaotic and fearful situation; therefore, there is an necessity of having deep study of technology and with due diligence to balance these fears and tensions amidst such crisis.

Kari Almendingen, Marianne Sandsmark Morseth, Eli Gjølstad, Asgeir Brevik, Christine Tørris (2021) in their research paper "Student's experiences with online teaching following COVID-19 lockdown: A mixed methods explorative study" found that students were able to have firm hold over online education and did not face much difficulties in shifting from offline to online mode of learning. Most of the common problems students faced were lack of social interaction, spiking the feeling of loneliness while studying alone, uneven bandwidth caused trouble during learning, uncomfortable environment made them less motivated and made them to put in less efforts. Data analysis showed that face-to-face contact was being missed greatly during this time-period, students adapted with the urgent requirement of having online education to complete their academics. The study also revealed that the students expressed that they wanted more structure in future digital courses and the students started feeling comfortable with online education which could be a bit threaten for continuation of off line education.

Shyam Sundar Sarkar, Pranta Das, Mohammad Mahbubur Rahman and M S Zobaer (July 21) in their research paper "Perceptions of Public University Students Towards Online Classes During COVID-19 Pandemic in Bangladesh" have denoted these points. From many past year, Bangladesh's education system practices traditional in-class schooling method in almost all educational institutions. It doesn't matter whether it a school or university, same method is practiced. But after COVID-19 pandemic, the government of Bangladesh has focused on online learning system. So, teachers as well as students, both are trying hard to get comfortable with this newly introduced practice. Though most of the teachers and students have got comfortable with this new learning system but still, there are various problems which is limiting stakeholders to utilize 100% of the online teaching. However, there is no other way to continue the education system, but online classes.

With the help of this study, researcher made an attempt and tried to get to know, what perspective do students of public university have towards online schooling. Researchers found the combined results. There are many students who have been benefited by this system and there are also students who faced many issues while learning. Because of online schooling discrimination in between rural living and urban living students, user using laptop or PC and user using mobile, user using WI-FI and users using mobile network. So, because of this there is a huge impact on learners in their learnings and teachers in their teaching. And there is no effective interaction between students with their teachers and classmates. The opportunities of group activities in between students has also been restricted. Also, there is no constant proper internet speed outside city area. So, stakeholder living in rural areas are facing many issues because of unstable internet connectivity. Therefore, such stakeholders are affected the most in such learning system. Additional burden of electricity issue is being faced by stakeholders living in rural areas. Moreover, there are students who are not having any electronic gadgets for attending the school. Such stakeholders also get affected. Nonetheless, research showed that considering virtual classes, female students had more positive attitude than male. The study also revealed that to overcome various problems government is trying various methods like broadcasting lectures through television as well as on radio which can be beneficial to many people and such for taking such actions by government is appreciated. But still there is room for improvement.

Mohammed Arshad Khan, Vivek, Mohammed Kamalun Nabi, Maysoon Khojah and Muhammad Tahir (December 2020) did the study on "Students' Perception towards E-Learning during COVID-19 Pandemic in India: An Empirical Study." The university students being the sample, the researcher tried to find out the perception of the students on online learning during COVID. The feedback of the students was to the surprise was much positive about online sessions as they gave the opinion that the online education provided them the free environment to study at any time and at their own pace. They also added that online education gave them the chance to connect with their teachers more comfortably. The students also felt that the online education gave them much of extra time to learn more stuff as it saved time of travelling, waiting and the rigid schedule. E learning gave the students availability of study material easily. E notes also helped them to save the cost of stationery. Online education also fulfilled the social issue of wasting paper. This paper comes out with the finding that the students of India are being comfortable with the online sessions. Though there are various problems related with technology the students have taken this online education very positively. Many situations like COVID may come in the future. Such situations are hurdle to the face to face interaction. Students feel that rather than being away from learning though there is absence of face to face interaction education should continue with the way of online. Digitalisation in education field could be the revolution in coming years. With this view all the stakeholders related with education field should seriously think of improving the online education methods and strongly support and provide all the necessary requirements of online education to consistently give the service of education successfully. Education should never stop though the situations like COVID hinder is what the strongest opinion of the students which has been taken as conclusion of this research paper.

4. Methodology

The researcher followed the systematic method to carry the study. Hypothesis was set for the study. The data has been collected by both primary as well as secondary way. The testing of hypothesis has been done through suitable statistical tools.

4.1 Primary Data

The study is carried out by collecting data through primary method. The well-structured questionnaire is prepared having 20 statements related with online learning for which the respondents gave their fed back. Also the respondents have been asked 4 basic questions related with online learning the answers for which have been collected.

4.2 Secondary Data

The researcher read various research papers related with online education and the response of higher education students and selected some of them for literature review and tried to know the overall feedback of higher education seeking students' feedback on online education. With the help of this the researcher framed the related twenty statements to get the feedback of the students on online education.

5. Sampling Method

The researcher adopted probability sampling method. The researcher further adopted simple random method to have the final sample. The researcher chose the students seeking higher education like MA, M.Com, M.Sc and MBA

5.1 Sampling Area

The researcher chose Kolhapur city to select the students of higher education to be the part of sample.

5.2 Sample Size

100 students of seeking higher education have been randomly chosen for the study.

6. Data Collection Tool

The well-structured questionnaire having 4 basic questions of yes or no type and 20 statements related with the opinions about the online education was prepared and the data has been collected.

The statements in the questionnaire were rated with 7 points Likert scale from strongly disagree to strongly agree. 1 being strongly disagree and 7 being strongly agree. 4 has been considered as neutral that is neither agree nor disagree.

6.1 Statistical Tool Used

To test the hypothesis z-test and chi square tests are performed.

7. Scope of the Study

The research study has surveyed the students' pursuing higher education. The geographical area chosen is Kolhapur city in Maharashtra. Though the study is made in Kolhapur city the result can be applied to the students pursuing higher education, especially the students pursuing M.Com, MA, M.Sc and MBA. The study made will be helpful to know feedback of the students about online teaching and learning. This would also help the stakeholders who are into education field to take the major decisions about blended education. The feedback of the students may help to make improvements in the online sessions conducted by the teachers. If in the future there arises any situation like COVID this feedback of the students may help to improve the overall system and may help in technologically innovate new tools and methods in online teaching and learning.

8. Analysis, Interpretation and Discussion

Table 72.1 showing Z-test results:

Table 72.1 Z-test results

Sr.No.	Alternative Statements (H1)	SD 1	MD 2	JD 3	N 4	JA 5	MA 6	SA 7	Weighted Total	Weighted Avarage	Weighted S.D.	Coeff.Variation	Rank	Z Test	Significance	P value	Decision on H0
1	I accepted online learning during COVID as an alternative learning	6	6	4	24	15	20	25	496	17.7143	8.9947	50.7766	11	0.8434	5%	0.05	Reject the null hypothesis and accepted the alternative hypothesis
2	I missed the offline lectures during COVID	7	5	6	22	10	25	25	498	17.7857	9.2685	52.1119	13	0.8411	5%	0.05	Reject the null hypothesis and accepted the alternative hypothesis
3	I faced the issue of connectivity while taking online lectures	5	7	6	18	14	27	23	502	17.9286	8.7505	48.8076	8	0.8646	5%	0.05	Reject the null hypothesis and accepted the alternative hypothesis
4	Online lectures would have been made more interesting by giving some extra effects to the presentations	3	9	7	17	12	29	23	505	18.0357	9.2505	51.2898	10	0.8583	5%	0.05	Reject the null hypothesis and accepted the alternative hypothesis
5	Offline lectures are more effective than the online lectures	2	2	3	27	14	30	22	527	18.8214	12.2299	64.9788	21	0.8368	5%	0.05	Reject the null hypothesis and accepted the alternative hypothesis
6	Online lectures provided an opportunity to be home and learn	2	4	3	22	17	25	27	531	18.9643	11.0108	58.0608	18	0.8695	5%	0.05	Reject the null hypothesis and accepted the alternative hypothesis
7	I prefer blended education than pure offline or pure online learning	3	7	2	18	17	28	25	523	18.6786	10.4517	55.9556	17	0.8669	5%	0.05	Reject the null hypothesis and accepted the alternative hypothesis
8	Online education during COVID improved my digital knowledge	4	9	4	17	18	24	28	532	19.0000	9.4944	49.9703	9	0.8758	5%	0.05	Reject the null hypothesis and accepted the alternative hypothesis
9	I improved the skills of being individual learner because of online education	6	6	4	24	15	20	25	496	17.7143	8.9947	50.7766	12	0.8434	5%	0.05	Reject the null hypothesis and accepted the alternative hypothesis
10	I faced bit difficulties to interact with the teachers during online sessions	9	7	8	28	6	21	21	462	16.5000	8.8264	53.4931	14	0.7466	5%	0.05	Reject the null hypothesis and accepted the alternative hypothesis
11	It was bit difficult to concentrate in online lectures	12	14	12	22	10	18	12	406	14.5000	4.2314	29.1821	3	0.5533	5%	0.05	Reject the null hypothesis and accepted the alternative hypothesis
12	I could know and learn online courses while having online education	2	2	6	18	30	20	22	520	18.5714	10.9805	59.1258	20	0.8491	5%	0.05	Reject the null hypothesis and accepted the alternative hypothesis

13	My technical skills improved because of online education	12	16	10	20	18	10	14	402	14.3571	3.9036	27.1893	2	0.5193	5%	0.05	Reject the null hypothesis and accepted the alternative hypothesis
14	At the beginning I felt stressful, depressed and demotivated to attend the online sessions	6	6	12	28	20	15	13	447	15.9643	7.8042	48.8851	7	0.7153	5%	0.05	Reject the null hypothesis and accepted the alternative hypothesis
15	Its very difficult to learn numerical related subjects and practical subjects online	10	16	14	20	12	16	12	404	14.4286	3.3523	23.2339	1	0.5449	5%	0.05	Reject the null hypothesis and accepted the alternative hypothesis
16	I faced some health issues because of online education	8	8	8	20	24	21	11	451	16.1071	7.0879	44.0046	5	0.7517	5%	0.05	Reject the null hypothesis and accepted the alternative hypothesis
17	I am completely satisfied with all the online session I attended	6	7	11	22	22	11	21	464	16.5714	7.1581	43.1953	4	0.8009	5%	0.05	Reject the null hypothesis and accepted the alternative hypothesis
18	I missed all the activities, practical sessions, group work with friends, connection with classmates and my college	2	2	2	2	12	35	45	605	21.6071	18.1725	84.1039	22	0.8568	5%	0.05	Reject the null hypothesis and accepted the alternative hypothesis
19	I feel teachers should be trained well to conduct online sessions	6	4	4	18	28	20	20	498	17.7857	9.5519	53.7053	16	0.8338	5%	0.05	Reject the null hypothesis and accepted the alternative hypothesis
20	I am self motivated and ready for forth coming online sessions if any	6	6	14	26	18	17	13	447	15.9643	7.0407	44.1028	6	0.7359	5%	0.05	Reject the null hypothesis and accepted the alternative hypothesis

Source: Author's compilation

From the above table it can be interpreted that the respondents who are the students pursuing higher education have given mixed feedback about online teaching and learning at the time of COVID. Most of the respondents agreed that online education was the best alternative at the time of pandemic instead of not learning anything. They felt that online education could save their years of education than having gap though most of the respondents missed the offline lectures. As it was all about the new experience of online education, many respondents faced various problems and problem of connectivity was the major one. Respondents felt that online lectures could have been made more effective and more interesting. They added that the online learning gave them an opportunity to be at home and learn in their comfort zone and with flexible timings. Not only the online education improved the respondents' digital knowledge but also it helped them to improve their technical skills. On the other hand the respondents felt bit difficult to concentrate in the online sessions. They also felt that they could not comfortably communicate with their teachers during online sessions. Many respondents took the situation as opportunity and completed some online certification courses which added values in their educational career.

Respondents also shared that they could come out of their comfortable zone of group learning and learn to be individual learner. Respondents shared that at the beginning they felt stressful, depressed and demotivated to attend the online sessions but eventually got habitual to online learning. Many respondents gave feedback as it was very difficult to learn numerical related subjects and practical subjects online and in this case they preferred only offline lectures. Many respondents faced some health issues because of online education like eyes irritation, back pain and head ache. Respondents missed all the activities, practical sessions, group work with friends, connection with classmates and their college life which made them sad. Though the situation was not favourable at the time of pandemic respondents could attend the online lectures and learn. Most of the respondents shared that new education system should have blended system of teaching and learning having both offline as well as online sessions as per the requirement of the courses.

In the above Table 72.1 it is found that the z value of all the statements is

Responses tested under chi square test:

Observation Table			
Sr. No.	**Particulars**	**Yes**	**No**
1	Feeling completely happy, satisfied and comfortable with online education	30	60
2	Online education completely improve the employability skills	15	85
3	Extraordinary activities are completely missed because of online education	80	20
4	Online education can replace the offline education in some field of education	40	60

Expected Frequency Table			
Sr. No.	**Particulars**	**Yes**	**No**
1	Feeling completely happy, satisfied and comfortable with online education	34.5	65.5
2	Online education completely improve the employability skills	34.5	65.5
3	Extraordinary activities are completely missed because of online education	34.5	65.5
4	Online education can replace the offline education in some field of education	34.5	65.5

Sr. No	Null Hypothesis	Level of Significance	Degree of Freedom	Test Value	P value	Decision
1	Higher education students significantly are not fully satisfied with online education	5%	3	1.9637	7.8147	Accept the Null Hypothesis

Source: Author's compilation

From the above tables reading it can be clearly interpreted that the students pursuing higher education in Kolhapur are significantly not fully satisfied with online education. When it comes to choose between offline and online education these students would prefer off line education over online. There may be consent for blended education system but not for complete online education. As we can see in the above table the P value is much in higher range the null hypothesis is accepted.

9. Conclusion

The review of literature done on "Opinion of students on online teaching and learning in higher education in COVID-19 Pandemic: A review of literature" based on six research papers shows one common point that the covid situation has hit the education line in a different way. Online teaching and learning have emerged with some advantages and some disadvantages. It has put a great challenge in front of higher education institutions, teachers and students. The quality of education now has a question mark as this online education has come with abundant problems of getting adapted with this new environment and facing the technical problems too. But if the institutes have to survive in the future there is no other way than the online education. As it is said survival of the fittest, the institutes which will strive hard and take efforts to make online education successful they will survive in the future and those won't may face problems. It can be concluded that though there are hurdles for online education in higher education it has to be continued with by maintaining quality as natural calamities may hit anytime.

REFERENCES

1. Mohammed Arshad Khan, Vivek, Mohammed Kamalun Nabi, Maysoon Khojah and Muhammad Tahir (December 2020), Students' Perception towards E-Learning during COVID-19 Pandemic in India: An Empirical Study, Sustainability 2021, 13, 57. https://dx.doi.org/10.3390/su13010057

2. T. Muthuprasada, S. Aiswarya, K. S. Aditya, Girish K. Jhaa, Students' perception and preference for online education in India during COVID -19 pandemic. Social Sciences & Humanities Open, ISSN (Print): 2590-2911, ISSN (Electronic): 2590–2911, 4 January 2021, Volume: 3, Issue: 1

3. Shivangi Dhawan, Online Learning: A Panacea in the Time of COVID-19 Crisis, Journal of Educational Technology Systems, 2020, Vol. 49(1), 5–22

4. Kari Almendingen, Marianne Sandsmark Morseth, Eli Gjølstad, Asgeir Brevik, Christine Tørris, Student's experiences with online teaching following COVID-19 lockdown: A mixed methods explorative study, https://doi.org/10.1371/journal.pone.0250378, August 2021

5. Shyam Sundar Sarkar, Pranta Das, Mohammad Mahbubur Rahman and M S Zobaer, Frontiers in Education, Brief Research Report, doi: 10.3389/feduc.2021.703723, 16th July 2021

6. Claudiu Coman, Laurentiu Gabriel Tîru, Luiza Mesesan-Schmitz, Carmen Stanciu, and Maria Cristina Bularca, Sustainability 2020, 12, 10367; doi:10.3390/su122410367, December 2020

7. Basilaia G., Kvavadze D. (2020). Transition to online education in schools during a SARS-CoV-2 coronavirus (COVID-19) pandemic in Georgia. Pedagogical Research, 5(4), 10. https://doi.org/10.29333/pr/7937\

8. Dhawan S. (2020). Online learning: A panacea in the time of COVID-19 crises. Journal of Educational Technology, 49(1), 5–22. https://doi.org/10.1177/0047239520934018

9. Doucet A., Netolicky D., Timmers K., Tuscano F. J. (2020). Thinking about pedagogy in an unfolding pandemic (An Independent Report on Approaches to Distance Learning during COVID-19 School Closure). Work of Education International and UNESCO https://issuu.com/educationinternational/docs/2020_research_covid-19_eng

10. Maurin E., McNally S. (2008). Vive la révolution! Long-term educational returns of 1968 to the angry students. Journal of Labor Economics, 26(1). https://doi.org/10.1086/522071

11. Murgatrotd S. (2020, March). COVID-19 and Online learning, Alberta, Canada. doi:10.13140/RG.2.2.31132.8512

12. Petrie C. (2020). Spotlight: Quality education for all during COVID-19 crisis (hundrED Research Report #01). United Nations. https://hundred.org/en/collections/quality-education-for-all-during-coronavirus

13. Ravichandran P., Shah A. K. (2020 July). Shadow pandemic: Domestic violence and child abuse during the COVID-19 lockdown in India. International Journal of Research in Medical Sciences, 08(08), 3118. https://doi.org/10.18203/2320-6012.ijrms20203477

14. Sintema E. J. (2020 April 7). Effect of COVID-19 on the performance of grade 12 students: Implications for STEM education. EURASIA Journal of Mathematics, Science and Technology Education, 16(7). https://doi.org/10.29333/ejmste/7893

15. Subedi S., Nayaju S., Subedi S., Shah S. K., Shah J. M. (2020). Impact of e-learning during COVID-19 pandemic Among nurshing students and teachers of Nepal. International Journal of Science and Healthcare Research, 5(3), 9.

Handbook of Evidence Based Management Practices in Business – Satyendra Kumar Sharma et al. (eds)
© 2023 Taylor & Francis Group, London, ISBN 978-1-032-54216-4

Chapter

Exploring a Mediating Role of Entrepreneurial Passion Between Individual Entrepreneurial Orientation and Social Entrepreneurship Linkage: A Conceptual Framework

Shefali Srivastava[1], Bindu Singh[2]
Department of Management & Humanities,
Indian Institute of Information Technology, Lucknow, India

ABSTRACT: The significance of entrepreneurship in the development of a country cannot be overstated. The Indian government has undertaken a number of supportive initiatives to encourage entrepreneurship in the nation. However, the findings were less encouraging, particularly among university students. Therefore, in order to promote entrepreneurship, it is crucial to understand the factors that affect students' intentions in this regard. An extensive amount of evidence, as revealed by a thorough assessment of the literature, demonstrates how entrepreneurial orientation fosters entrepreneurial intention inside an organization. However, the entrepreneurial inclination of an individual toward social entrepreneurship and their connections were not thoroughly addressed in earlier studies. Hence, this study analyzes the connections between Individual Entrepreneurial Orientation (IEO) and Social Entrepreneurial Intention (SEI) and presents a theoretical framework to fill this gap by utilizing the conceptual viewpoints of Indian university students. Additionally, Entrepreneurial Passion (EP) was established as a mediator for the relationship between IEO and SEI. Therefore, this study gives an apparent explanation of the effect of IEO on SEI that is theoretically supported and suggests that IEO is the eventual foundation of entrepreneurial intention. Further, this research contributes significantly to the burgeoning entrepreneurial literature. Additionally, the managerial ramifications are discussed.

KEYWORDS: Individual Entrepreneurial Orientation, Social Entrepreneurial Intention, Entrepreneurial Passion.

[1]rmh22102@iiitl.ac.in, [2]bindu@iiitl.ac.in

DOI: 10.4324/9781003415725-73

1. Introduction

The current age demonstrates the growing interest in research in Social Entrepreneurship (SE) (Nicolás, Rubio, and Fernández-Laviada, 2018). Research on SE demonstrates a solid theoretical underpinning as well as empirical studies pertaining to its causes and effects. The fundamental idea behind SE is to use it as a tool to solve problems that neither the public nor the private sector can solve in order to create economic value and address social challenges. It is a cutting-edge strategy for generating social value while securing a sizable financial gain. Tran and Von Korflesch, (2016) asserts that SE is drawing scholarly interest as a means of addressing societal issues, particularly in underdeveloped economies. By eradicating economic, social, and political inequities, it can be seen as a catalyst for a society to experience tremendous economic and social progress.

Furthermore, researchers asserted IEO as being particularly essential in amplifying entrepreneurial intention (Sahoo and Panda, 2019) and emphasized its significance by relying on the SEI idea that orientation acts as an influential factor in establishing an individual's intentional behavior. The core concept is that IEO creates favourable settings for improving purposeful behavior and activities that influence an individual's intention and contribute to EP (Sahoo and Panda, 2019; Martins and Perez, 2020; Huyghe, Knockaert, and Obschonka, 2016; Tran and Von Korflesch, 2016). However, a study on entrepreneurial literature suggests that prior investigations have not thoroughly confirmed the IEO perspective on SEI (Sahoo and Panda, 2019; Martins and Perez, 2020). Consequently, there is a dearth of empirical research that examines the relationships between IEO and SEI and looks at how IEO aspects affect the purpose of social entrepreneurship. As a result, solving this issue is an essential line of inquiry.

With the aim to shed light and further contribute to the entrepreneurial literature, the primary novelty of the proposed framework is to examine how IEO drives SEI, via mapping EP as a mediator between IEO and SEI relationship. The proposed framework highlights the mechanism which hasn't been explored yet in context to the university students. There is a scant of literature which shows the explanation of EO from individual perspective and their impact on intention towards SE (Martins and Perez, 2020), which limit the generalization of already published results. This emphasizes the need to justify the connection between IEO, EP, and SEI. A conceptual framework that examines the connection between IEO and SEI has been attempted. Further, the methodological and theoretical underpinnings of the connection are explained. Finally, this paper analyzes the study's consequences for practitioners.

2. Theoretical Perspective

Numerous authors (Huyghe et al., 2016; Tran and Von Korflesch, 2016) have proposed different models that explained the process of IEO. Following Lumpkin and Dess (1996) IEO comprises of five dimensions: innovativeness, risk-taking propensity, pro-activeness, autonomy, and competitive advantage. The paper examines how IEO (i.e., Innovativeness, Risk-taking, and Pro-activeness) and SEI are closely linked in such a way that EP act as a mediating factor to transfer the impact of IEO on SEI of university students. The theoretical framework of the study is presented in Fig. 73.1.

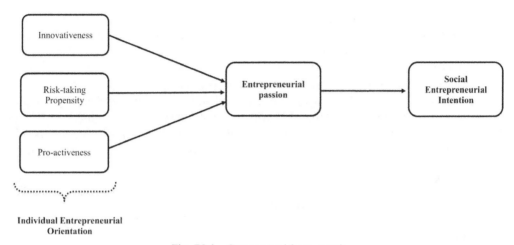

Fig. 73.1 Conceptual framework

Source: Author's estimation

The researchers highlight the significance of IEO in developing EI (Taatila and Down, 2012; Karimi, Biemans, Lans, Chizari, and Mulder, 2016; Maresch, Harms, Kailer, and Wimmer-Wurm, 2016; Sahoo and Panda, 2019; Martins and Perez, 2020; Huyghe et al., 2016; Tran and Von Korflesch, 2016) as EO act as primary mechanisms to influence individuals' intention (Sahoo and Panda, 2019). Literature suggest how IEO comprised of three dimensions, innovativeness, risk-taking propensity, and pro-activeness, enhances SEI (Tran and Von Korflesch, 2016; Sahoo and Panda, 2019; Martins and Perez, 2020), via incorporating EP into the study to enhance the understanding (Huyghe et al., 2016; Biraglia and Kadile, 2017). Based on the review, the following paragraphs discuss how each one of the dimension has an impact on EP that further enhances the SEI.

3. Research Approach

The initial stage of the investigation seeks to obtain pertinent literature in order to explain the hypothesized linkages and accomplish the goal. The process begins with the use of the search engines Proquest, Google scholar, and Ebscohost, and publications relating to social entrepreneurship are prioritized. 30 papers were analyzed during this process. Further, the analysis and methodical integration procedure starts with the final synthesis after the identification of the literature. Later in this work, the hypothesized relationships are discussed.

4. Proposed Framework

With the goal of illuminating the links between IEO and SEI, a thorough evaluation of relevant literature was conducted, and a theoretical framework examining the links between IEO and SEI was proposed, as shown in Fig. 73.1. The proposed framework will shed light on how individuals can effectively develop social entrepreneurial intention by promoting entrepreneurial orientation and indicates that entrepreneurial passion plays a vital role in advancing the link between IEO and SEI. In this proposed framework, IEO is viewed as a precursor to SEI (Satar and Natasha, 2019; Hassan, Anwar, Saleem, Islam, and Hussain, 2021; Bolton and Lane, 2012; Sahoo and Panda, 2019; Koe, 2016; Mohammadi, 2021; Alarifi, Robson, and Kromidha, 2019) through encouraging attributes such as innovativeness, risk-taking behavior, and pro-activeness in individuals (Weerakoon, McMurray, Rametse, and Arenius, 2019). Further, according to researchers, innovativeness, risk-taking behavior, and proactiveness increase individuals' aim to grow, produce, and improve their entrepreneurial expertise. The proposed framework will provide answers to the question as how IEO can develop passion effectively by practicing social entrepreneurship.

5. Theoretical Underpinnings

5.1 IEO

The concept 'Individual Entrepreneurial Orientation (IEO)' was introduced by Miller (1983), and popularized by Covin and Slevin (1989), which defines IEO as the summation of three dimensions, namely Innovativeness, risk-taking propensity, and pro-activeness. Further, Lumpkin and Dess (1996) redefined and suggested a five-dimension model via adding Autonomy and Competitive Aggressiveness in the concept. Taatila and Down, (2012) defined as the ability, competency, and motivation of an individual to start their own business. Numerous studies have looked at the "intend to act" as the key element in the development of an enterprise because it appears to be the primary motivator in the entrepreneurship process (e.g., Karimi et al., 2016; Maresch et al., 2016). IEO is seen as an entrepreneurial skill that can be acquired through hands-on training (Sahoo and Panda, 2019). Various researchers established the favourable association between IEO and EI (Karimi et al., 2016; Martins and Perez, 2020; Sahoo and Panda, 2019). Studies on the relationship between EO and company performance are widely available in the literature, but because IEO is a more recent conception, there is comparably little research on the construct (Martins and Perez, 2020).

5.2 EP

The term "Entrepreneurial passion" refers to the 'consciously available, intensely happy sensations that are experienced when engaging in entrepreneurial activities connected to roles that are significant to the entrepreneur's sense of self' (Cardon, Wincent, Singh, and Drnovsek, 2009). Moreover, different authors emphasized the complex nature of EP by proposing three unique entrepreneurial identities associated with various components of the entrepreneurial process. These are: an inventor, a founder, and a developer. These different components of passion are related to identity-related passions affect goals-related cognitions and lead to specific business results (Cardon et al., 2009). Hence, EP is a fundamental motivator of entrepreneurial behavior, especially when resources are scarce and the environment is unpredictable, acting through its features of intense positive feelings connected to significant identities (Cardon et al., 2009; Huyghe et al., 2016). Moreover, Biraglia and Kadile, (2017) highlighted the crucial role of passion in entrepreneurial motivation and success.

5.3 SEI

According to Mair and Noboa, (2006), SEI is an individual's psychological activity that encourages them towards becoming social entrepreneurs by accumulating knowledge, developing ideas, and putting the social business plan into action. Developing intention towards entrepreneurship is one's state of mind that drives them to establish a venture. Tran and Von Korflesch, (2016) mentioned SEI can be viewed as a person's belief in and desire to launch a new social enterprise initiative. Researchers are building on a long tradition in psychology study that connects empathy, or responsively to another's experiences, to the display of helping behaviors in an effort to explain the "social" part of SE intentions. In fact, social entrepreneurs pursue social missions with the intention of assisting those in need rather than pursuing their own interests.

6. Discussion and Implications of the Study

Though there is unquestionable fact that research on entrepreneurial intention has made certain advancement the role of individual's entrepreneurial orientation and entrepreneurial passion has not been fully explored in relation with social entrepreneurship. The review of the entrepreneurial literature reveals that there have been relatively few attempts in this direction and calls for further, in-depth investigation of this phenomenon. The primary goal of this inquiry is to develop the state of understanding. Based on a review of IEO and SEI literature, following are some key topics to consider when creating a conceptual framework; (a) Theoretical understanding of the concepts already in existence, (b) which clarifies the connections between IEO, EP, and SEI, (c) with the intention of contributing towards the factors that enhance social entrepreneurship.

The theoretical analysis shows a substantial relationship between IEO and entrepreneurial intent. Findings of the study reveal that the IEO factor enhances creativity and fosters risk-taking behaviour, facilitates the integration of information and societal processes inherent in individuals, helps replicate solutions in new and different contexts, which in turn encourages passion for entrepreneurship and develops entrepreneurial intention. In summation, findings demonstrate that IEO promotes social entrepreneurship. Hence, the ramifications for professionals, academic institutions, and decision-makers are evident. Universities hoping to boost entrepreneurial intent should focus on IEO because, from a strategic perspective, IEO influences people's motivations, actions, and passions, all of which impact SEI.

Additionally, the study contributes by developing and testing a conceptual framework with the view to examine personal context (i.e. IEO) and Behavioral context (i.e. EP) as an antecedent of SEI and exploring EP as a mediator, using a secondary dataset. Despite the fact that there is ample research on how IEO affects EI, no study has looked at how this relationship is strengthened by other factors like organizational, personal, and behavioral factors, as a mediators, and moderators. The proposed model is expected to be the guidance for researchers and practitioners on how to develop a sustainable organization. In terms of how to provide adequate support and guidance through IEO, EP, and SEI, this research offers significant implications to IT sector and to emerging markets as well. Further, this work throws light on how the working conditions may effectively increase the productivity, efficiency, and creativity of individuals. Therefore, universities and industries should look forward to studies which guide them to achieve a sustainable outcome.

7. Limitations and Future Aveneues

While the study contributes to the literature on entrepreneurship, it is not without flaws. Foremost, while researching IEO and SEI links, a few EO variables got attention in the theoretical framework on an organizational level. Therefore, future research should make an effort to address the entrepreneurial orientation on an individual level. Furthermore, empirical research is necessary to provide statistical proof of links in terms of methodology. In order to convey a complete picture of the SEI phenomena and to offer a useful insight to managers, governments, and universities currently grappling with the issue's unsatisfactory level of knowledge, other factors and intentional outcomes may be included to the framework as well.

8. Conclusion

In conclusion, this research advances the field by arguing that there are connections between IEO and SEI and that IEO improves SEI. Additionally, the role of EP as a mediator is highlighted in the study which strengthens the linkages between IEO and SEI. Therefore, more debate is necessary to improve our comprehension of the connections and so add to the entrepreneurship literature. Moreover, the linkages between IEO and SEI proposed in this framework should be tested and validated in order to acquire broader applicability and credibility in theorization. These studies should be empirical and longitudinal with reference to the Indian context.

9. Acknowledgement

Authors are grateful to academic Institution for their consistent support. With the submission of this manuscript, we would like to undertake that, a. All authors of this research paper have directly participated in the planning, execution, or analysis of this study, b. All authors of this paper have read and approved the final version submitted, and c. My Institute's representative is fully aware of this submission.

REFERENCES

1. Satar, M. S., & Natasha, S. (2019). Individual social entrepreneurship orientation: Towards development of a measurement scale. *Asia Pacific Journal of Innovation and Entrepreneurship*, *13*(1), 49–72. https://doi.org/10.1108/apjie-09-2018-0052.
2. Hassan, A., Anwar, I., Saleem, I., Islam, K. M. B., & Hussain, S. A. (2021). Individual entrepreneurial orientation, entrepreneurship education and entrepreneurial intention: The mediating role of entrepreneurial motivations. *Industry and Higher Education*, *35*(4), 403–418. https://doi.org/10.1177/09504222211007051.
3. Langkamp Bolton, D., & Lane, M. D. (2012). Individual entrepreneurial orientation: Development of a measurement instrument. *Education + Training*, *54*(2/3), 219–233. https://doi.org/10.1108/00400911211210314.

4. Sahoo, S., & Panda, R. K. (2019). Exploring entrepreneurial orientation and intentions among technical university students. *Education + Training, 61*(6), 718–736. https://doi.org/10.1108/et-11-2018-0247.

5. Weerakoon, C., McMurray, A. J., Rametse, N. & Arenius, P. (2019). Knowledge creation theory of entrepreneurial orientation in social enterprises. *Journal of Small Business Management.* https://doi.org/10.1080/00472778.2019.1672709.

6. Koe, W.-L. (2016). the relationship between individual entrepreneurial orientation (IEO) and entrepreneurial intention. *Journal of Global Entrepreneurship Research, 6*(1). https://doi.org/10.1186/s40497-016-0057-8.

7. Mohammadi, S. (2021). The relationship between individual entrepreneurial orientation (IEO) and entrepreneurial bricolage: Exploring passion and perseverance. *Asia Pacific Journal of Innovation and Entrepreneurship, 15*(1), 75–86. https://doi.org/10.1108/apjie-01-2021-0002.

8. Alarifi, G., Robson, P., & Kromidha, E. (2019). The manifestation of entrepreneurial orientation in the social entrepreneurship context. *Journal of Social Entrepreneurship, 10*(3), 307–327. https://doi.org/10.1080/19420676.2018.1541015

9. Lumpkin, G. T, & Dess, G.G. (1996). Clarifying the entrepreneurial orientation construct and linking it to performance. *Academy of Management Review, 21*(1), 135–172.

10. Miller, D. (1983). The correlates of entrepreneurship in three types of firms. *Management Science, 29*(7), 770–791.

11. Taatila., V. & Down, S. (2012). Measuring entrepreneurial orientation of university students. *Education þ Training, 54*(8/9), 744–760.

12. Karimi, S., Biemans, H.J.A., Lans, T., Chizari, M. & Mulder, M. (2016). The impact of entrepreneurship education: a study of Iranian students' entrepreneurial intentions and opportunity identification. *Journal of Small Business Management, 54*(1), 187–209.

13. Maresch, D., Harms, R., Kailer, N., et al. (2016). the impact of entrepreneurship education on the entrepreneurial intention of students in science and engineering versus business studies university programs. *Technological Forecasting and Social Change, 104*, 172–179.

14. Martins, I., & Perez, JP. (2020). Testing mediating effects of individual entrepreneurial orientation on the relation between close environmental factors and entrepreneurial intention. *International Journal of Entrepreneurial Behavior & Research, 26*(4), 771–791.

15. Cardon, M. S., Wincent, J., Singh, J., & Drnovsek, M. (2009). The nature and experience of entrepreneurial passion. *Academy of Management Review, 34*(3), 511–532.

16. Huyghe, A., Knockaert, M., & Obschonka, M. (2016). Unraveling the "passion orchestra" in Academia. *Journal of Business Venturing, 31*(3), 344–364. https://doi.org/10.1016/j.jbusvent.2016.03.002.

17. Biraglia, A., & Kadile, V. (2017). The role of entrepreneurial passion and creativity in developing entrepreneurial intentions: Insights from American home brewers. *Journal of Small Business Management, 55*(1), 170–188.

18. Mair, J., & Noboa, E., (2006). Social Entrepreneurship: How Intentions to Create a Social Venture are Formed. *In Social Entrepreneurship*, edited by J. Mair, J. Robinson, and K. Hockerts, 121–135. London: Palgrave Macmillan UK.

19. Tran, A. T., and Von Korflesch, H., (2016). A Conceptual Model of Social Entrepreneurial Intention Based on the Social Cognitive Career Theory. *Asia Pacific Journal of Innovation and Entrepreneurship, 10* (1), 17–38.

20. Nicolás, C., Rubio, A., & Fernández-Laviada, A., (2018). Cognitive Determinants of Social Entrepreneurship: Variations According to the Degree of Economic Development. *Journal of Social Entrepreneurship, 9*, 154–168. https://doi.org/10.1080/19420676.2018.1452280.

21. Maresch, D., Harms, R., Kailer, N. & Wimmer-Wurm, B. (2016). The impact of entrepreneurship education on the entrepreneurial intention of students in science and engineering versus business studies university programs. *Technological Forecasting and Social Change, 104*(3), 172–179.

Handbook of Evidence Based Management Practices in Business – Satyendra Kumar Sharma et al. (eds)
© 2023 Taylor & Francis Group, London, ISBN 978-1-032-54216-4

Chapter

Evidential Insights:
Factors Affecting Higher Education Readiness

Tanu Shukla[1], Virendra Singh Nirban[2], Deepanjana Chakraborty[3]
HSS Birla Institute of Technology & Science (BITS) Pilani,
Pilani Campus, Jhunjhunu, Rajasthan, India

ABSTRACT: The modern world has transformed industry-education partnerships towards skill-based contributions to society. Productivity emerges as the new indices of harnessing human potential in the current age of science and technology. This need has propelled the need for immediate transformation within the higher education system to imbibe skills and capacities in the transitioning population for preparation towards STEM-dominated higher learning programs. Contrastingly, the current evidence of preparation for higher learning is not strongly situated in the context of the Indian education system. *The objective of this paper is to introduce a framework of Higher Education Readiness with the conceptualization of skills that can foster STEM learning in the transitioning young population of India. It aims to investigate the differences in the readiness ability along the demographic lines of gender and spatial reference by using the Higher Education Readiness test. Data from the district with a high literacy rate was collected to address the objectives of the study. The results demonstrate that female students compete equally with male students on performance in Higher Education Readiness abilities yet fail to pursue STEM disciplines in their higher learning programs.* The paper is expected to provide the factors associated with readiness for higher education. Based on the data enabled evidence, the findings demand influential changes in the policies related to STEM education for stronger educational management at the secondary level. The findings of the study would help in the transformation of the educational management towards vocationalisation and increasing productivity levels in the learning individual.

KEYWORDS: Higher education readiness, Higher education, STEM learning, Productivity, Skills

[1]tanushukla8@gmail.com, [2]nirban@pilani.bits-pilani.ac.in, [3]deepachakraborty1234@gmail.com

DOI: 10.4324/9781003415725-74

1. Introduction

The latest transformations in the industry-education relationship, are based on the requirement of an educated, skilled, and qualitatively productive workforce. This mutual interest has pushed the existent educational administrations and human resource management communities to decide over 'the most profitable type of human capital' for developing and sustainable economies of the world. Following the global commitment of reaching the Sustainable Development Goals by 2030, international economies need to invest more in the youth for research and innovation areas along with sustainable skills (Abuzyarova et. al, 2019; Gugliemi, Neumeister & Jones, 2021). According to the Seventh Edition of UNESCO's Science Report subtitled 'The Race Against Time for Smarter Development' majority of the countries today have accepted the reliance on the successful management of the transition to digital and scientifically viable societies for future economic competitiveness and sustainability (Lewis, Schneegans & Straza, 2021).

Employability paves the way for economic growth quantitatively (Croak, 2018). This is further supported by the large-scale assessments like PISA and TIMSS that have reflected positive links of the completion of formal education to the possibility of attaining employability in the later years (Papadakis, 2020). Thus, the meaningfulness of attaining secondary education and higher education is narrowly understood as the 'ability of the students, after completion of the course or program, in terms of comprehending and making powerful use of the acquired knowledge to enhance their lives and effective contribution in society through scientific, technological and innovative abilities' (Cai, Ma & Chen, 2020).

Various Asian studies have contemplated that the best form of education is possible only through institutional learning (O' Brien & Howard, 2020). Furthermore, countries like India have constantly found the empirical evidence to support the importance of formal institutions in the learning process, for imparting secondary level education to the prodigies (Bandyopadhyay & Chugh, 2020). The recent data of Gross Enrolment Ratio (GER) at the secondary level education could reach only 51.40% compared to GER of primary education at 92.39% (UDISE 2017-18). It is compounded by the gap in foundational literacy levels of various states (Banerji, 2021). Meanwhile, the expansion of the equity measures in higher education through the establishment of over 900 higher education institutions has reflected the Gross Enrolment Ratio (GER) of 26.3% in higher education as compared to the presence of 243 million youth population in India (AISHE, 2019). Simultaneously in the gender context, the GER of 26.4% female population poses a huge threat to the egalitarian aspiration of creating highly skilled workforce in terms of both males and females in India (AISHE, 2019). Furthermore, the inclination of the learning population (23.3 lakh) continues to stagnate in pursuing non-scientific streams (AISHE, 2019). These concerns pose the biggest question towards education reforms about what particular 'skill set' can be developed in the transitioning population to enhance their preparation for higher education? Also, when government efforts have expanded in elevating the quality of the enrolled population within elementary learning, why are the participation levels at STEM learning massively variant in higher education? The study examines the various frameworks for preparedness to higher education against the backdrop of the Higher Education Readiness Framework persistent globally and explores various attributes that measure Higher Education Readiness. The paper addresses these concerns with the inclusion of Indian males and females of the district with a high literacy rate in Rajasthan.

2. Rationale

The managerial inefficiency of the country in raising its transition rate to higher education through policy interventions have consequently widened the gap between the industrial demands and the supply of the young workforce. Based on the success of the Sarva Shiksha Abhiyan (SSA) and Rashtriya Madhyamik Shiksha Abhiyan (RMSA), the initiative of Rashtriya Uchchtar Shiksha Abhiyan (RUSA) aimed at improving the quality of higher education. However, the discrepancies of the transition rate, low percentage of youth opting for STEM learning in higher education, and existing gender disparities in pursual of STEM professions after the completion of higher learning programs have emerged to be the most important questions of the needed reform for our trillion-dollar economy aspirant country. Additionally, despite the efforts of the government towards the upliftment of the science and technological skills in the form of VIGYAN JYOTI and KIRAN initiatives, the current educational reforms addressed in the New Education Policy (2020) are not sufficient to catalyze the competencies that foster the choice of STEM learning in the higher education programs.

The study centralizes on examining the various frameworks and related attributes for preparedness to higher education against the backdrop of the Higher Education Readiness Framework. It explores whether accessibility of secondary education results in Higher Education Readiness (HER) abilities of the students along the demographic lines of gender and place within the school systems.

3. Review of Literature

3.1 Higher Education Readiness (HER)

Many studies have consistently evinced the importance of higher education citing its contribution to encouraging economic development (Tilak & Choudhury, 2018) and skilled and knowledgeable population by promoting the growth of logical and critical thinking abilities (Suleman, 2018). The earliest definitions of higher education have theoretically portrayed post-secondary programs as 'programs of knowledge acquisition after the total learning tenure' (Everwijn, Bomers & Knubben, 1993). Other definitions have expanded on 'meticulously curated program' that facilitates the process of transformation from school competencies to employability competencies, in a relatively complex learning environment, to foster multi-dimensional achievement of well-being" (Maclean & Pavlova, 2013). Similarly, readiness has been conceptualized as a synthesis of cognitive, emotional, and motivational qualities, that psychophysiologically facilitate the direction or opportunities to perform in the industrial areas (Seryapina, 2018). Repetuyeva (2009) has defined readiness as an array of attitudes and relevant associations for the performing activities irrespective of any industry/profession.

With the emergent need for science and technology embedded in educational reforms, the period of 1998 to 2014 defined STEM education as an 'interdisciplinary field based on the synthesis of Science, Engineering and Technology education' (Hasanah, 2020). Despite the continued ambiguity of a well-defined definition of a field with multiple disciplines, majority of the parallel existent educational reforms continue to support the idea of STEM education by being fixated only on the core disciplines (US National Science Foundation, 1998; Vasquez, Sneider & Comer, 2013). Drawing by these definitions, the operational definition of Higher Educational Readiness can be understood as: degree of preparedness in terms of key competencies possessed by an individual to assimilate science, technology, engineering, and mathematics at the transition level for the preparation of higher educational experiences within and outside the classroom (Vasquez, Sneider & Comer, 2013). The expansion of the scope of higher educational experiences beyond the classroom is understood as employability and real-life problem-solving.

3.2 Conceptual Frameworks

The complete idea of readiness is theoretically situated in developing learning strategies within the students that can help them in the development of higher learning skills. Since education is closely related to the 'ability of acquisition and application', scholars support the incorporation of 'assessment' as an integral part of student development (Tolstova & Levasheva, 2019). In this regard, the theoretical underpinning of Pascarella's Model of Student Development shapes the growth and development through: "(i) Student's precollege traits (ii) University's structural characteristics (iii) Organizational environment (iv) Present socializing agents and (v) student's quality of effort put" (Pascarella & Terenzini, 1991). Although the model portrays the need for balancing individual traits with institutional variables, the value of individual traits remains higher than organizational variables. Thus, considering the importance of 'precollege traits' and the 'quality of effort' within the students, the study predominantly bases its understanding on readiness as a capability or skill. Derivatively, the current frameworks of Higher Education Readiness (HER) are based on the available understanding of readiness at different levels: (i) School readiness (ii) University Readiness (iii) Professional Readiness. The earliest recognition of readiness at the federal policy-making level was demonstrated by the U.S. National School Readiness Indicators Initiative (2005) through school readiness which considers learners to be ready for formal learning until precisely under the domains of physical, cognitive, affective, and social development (Gilbert, 2011). Similarly, Gutkina's university readiness framework (2006) has identified cognitive components, personal components, and Voluntary Behaviour Regulation that further add to problem-solving skills and acceptance of different viewpoints as the preparatory skills of university education (Nisskaya, 2018).

The literature also demarcates the concept of professional readiness in terms of 'socially significant activity requiring special knowledge, skills, and professional qualities (Simonova et. al, 2016). Scholars have believed professional readiness to be prominent in 2 domains- (1) Practical readiness consisting of personal qualities, knowledge, and abilities, and (2) Theoretical readiness including profound professional knowledge, individual aptitude for the chosen profession, and planning skills (Seryapina, 2018). While theoretical readiness has taken a backstep, practical readiness has soared high in terms of industrial demand, because of its focus on developing sustainability skills as a part of practical readiness within the higher learning systems. In this regard, the Framework on Sustainable Skills has focused primarily on readiness through problem-solving skills required at the higher education level for sustainability (Wiek et. al, 2015). The framework is inclusive of: (1) Systems thinking competence pertaining to the ability to collectively analyze complex systems. (2) Anticipatory competence pertaining to the ability to collectively analyze, evaluate, and craft rich "pictures" of the future. (3) Normative competence pertaining to the ability to collectively map, specify, apply, reconcile, and negotiate sustainability values.

All these frameworks develop a particular aspect of readiness at different levels of the developmental phase. However, the reiteration of the requirement of a comprehensive readiness continuum is met by the World Bank's Skills Toward Employment and Productivity (STEP) Framework to enable policymakers and researchers to design systems in obtaining jobs. It lays out five interlinked stages extending from Early Childhood Development to matching skills with labor market demand at later stages in life, inclusive of (1) Getting children to the right start (2) Ensuring that all students learn (3) Building job-relevant skills (4) Encouraging entrepreneurship and innovation (5) Facilitating labor mobility and job matching (Banerji et. al, 2010).

3.3 Attributes of Higher Education Readiness (HER)

Drawing from these frameworks, Higher Education Readiness can be understood through a multidimensional perspective that rests upon Career Aspiration, Academic Buoyancy, Flexibility, and Entrepreneurial Activities Based Learning. The scientific evidence of the inclusion of these components is discussed as follows:

(1) Career Aspirations are understood as a strong determiner to pursue STEM learning after secondary education. Specifically, career aspiration can be illustrated as 'the mindset characterized by a need to give selective attention to activity, goal, or subject in terms of professional choice, the interest of disciplines and orientation to the career (Mau & Li, 2018). It relates to career interest, orientation, and making STEM-governed academic choices in the course of learning. Social scientists have considered the amount of interest, through Social Cognitive Career Theory, held by an individual towards a related career to determine the intensity of the efforts put (Kaleva et. al, 2019).

(2) Academic Buoyancy is operationalized as the capacity to deal with everyday academic hardships, performance setbacks, and learning challenges in the higher education context. This definition is further used for the constructs to be assessed, including academic coping, academic hardiness, and academic adaptability (Martin and Marsh, 2009). Research studies portray the gender disparity in pursuing STEM subjects despite higher mathematical abilities (Kaleva et. al, 2019).

(3) Flexibility is operationally understood as "condition of willingness in intention to procure adjustment to a relatively novel environment" (Mellander & Lind, 2021). It is measured by the extent of belief held by the individual in his/her ability to imbibe the existent information along with using innovativeness as a consequent behavior in the related industry. Studies have highlighted the importance of flexibility in the acquisition of higher education as a component of gaining occupational opportunities (Mellander & Lind, 2021).

(4) Entrepreneurial Activity Based Learning Originally, the definition of Entrepreneurial Activities Based Learning (EABL) is synonymous with the tendency of fostering positive effects through harboring services as well as products that catalyze the solution-finding requirement to the challenges in society (World Bank, 2018). The basic premise of defining entrepreneurial activities within the learning context is the thought of inculcating social change or social value creation rather than wealth creation by supporting the marginalized people devoid of recognition and fundamental rights throughout the learning phase (World Bank, 2018).

4. Methodology

The paper follows a quantitative research design for the research objective. The study for this paper is specifically conducted with quantitative data collection, in the district of Rajasthan with high literacy rates. It investigates the research questions as whether the students of both gender and spatial reference differ in the performance of Higher Education Readiness (HER) at the secondary level? The sample consists of representative data collected from four divisions of the Jhunjhunu district in Rajasthan. Two schools were randomly visited in each of the four divisions, making a total of 8 schools. The total number of students' responses collected was 31 of which 18 were male students and 13 were female students. Similarly, for spatial reference, responses were collected from 20 students of urban setting and 11 students from rural setting. For data collection, the questionnaire of Higher Education Readiness was formed. The total questionnaire consisted of 20 items. Each dimension was allotted 5 items. The Cronbach Alpha value for Higher Education Readiness is 0.7 which indicates acceptable internal consistency.

5. Results

The study addresses the issue of Higher Education Readiness competency scores in female students. Attempts are made to calculate the performance on the ability of readiness in the female students enrolled in schools in comparison to their male classmates. Also, the performance on the ability of readiness is computed based on the students enrolled in schools according to the spatial reference. *t*-test was used to assess the difference in the performance in both demographics (gender and spatial reference) at the secondary school level.

Table 74.1 *t*-test table for ability on higher education readiness of gender and spatial reference demographics

Demographics	Category	N	M	S.D.	*t*-value
Gender	Male	18	79.36	14.42	2.82*
	Female	13	81.31	19.48	
Spatial Reference	Urban	20	86.16	19.20	5.75*
	Rural	11	74.80	11.66	

*$p < .01$ level

Source: Author's compilation

In the context of the gender demographic, table 1 includes the data of students depicting that the differential value of the mean Higher Education Readiness (HER) ability scores between the male and female students is significant at the 0.01 level. This indicates that male and female students differ significantly in the scores of Higher Education Readiness (HER) ability. In the context of Spatial Reference demographic, Table 74.1 is indicative of the data of students depicting that the differential value of the mean Higher Education Readiness (HER) ability scores between the urban residence and rural residence is significant at the 0.01 level.

6. Discussion

STEM as an educational reform has long been researched upon, among both gender in preparation of the students for higher learning to gain access to better chances of employability. Our study results show that the average Higher Education Readiness performance scores for females (81.31) are greater than the average performance scores for males (79.36). The study confirms that females have better orientation towards HER performance than males. The study examined the discrepancies in the Higher Education Readiness scores which impacts learning outcomes at the secondary level. Various research studies substantiate the relationship between female schooling and development in terms of scientific and technological professions (Bisht & Pattnaik, 2020).

The gender parity seem to have reduced greatly in recent times. Most of the research studies favorably portray the likelihood of students with higher academic competencies to be inclined to STEM careers (Kaleva et. al, 2019). However, secondary grade females in the majority of the countries happen to demonstrate less favorable attitudes to STEM-related opportunities than their male companions (Kaleva et, al. 2019). The findings of this study aptly reflect that girls are better in the performance of Higher Education Readiness abilities than boys. Contrastingly, they appear negligent in opting for STEM inclined higher education specializations and later stage careers despite performing well in the readiness abilities.

In the district under study, there are differences in school enrolment rates between both genders, where higher number of male students are enrolled as compared to female students. This leads to criticism that formal secondary learning institutions promote learning opportunities for the students, without maintaining equality of enrolments at the secondary level. It can be opined that the overall proportion of the females transitioning in secondary education is itself very unevenly distributed to all schools of the district. In this regard, some research studies in the USA have further explored the reasons for less participation of women in STEM education, right from the secondary learning period (Casad et. al, 2018; Wang et. al, 2016). In addition to low enrolments, other reasons observed were (a) lifestyle or family expectations (b) gender-related stereotypes and biases (Wang & Degol, 2017). By Vroom's Social Expectation Theory, it can be understood that 'available information of social position or achievement' constitute an intertwining human agency process to shape 'performance, self-efficacy, and outcome expectations of others, in this case females (Cano et. al, 2018). In this regard, the research studies based on gender differences, especially in mathematical domain have consistently shown the absence of female role-models and career growth opportunities in the STEM fields for females. Deductively, the Expectation Theory and Social Cognitive Career Theory become instrumental in understanding that females do not prefer STEM professions as their sole choice because of the intertwined effect of gender stereotypes for maintaining domestic occupations, interest towards child centric careers like teaching etc. in shaping the perceived lower ability to choose STEM inclined higher learning programs for wider arena of professions later (Kaleva et al., 2019).

The results demonstrate that the average Higher Education Readiness performance scores for students in the urban residence (86.16) are greater than the average performance scores for students in the rural residence (74.80) in the data. Our study examines whether there are discrepancies in the Higher Education Readiness scores between the spatial reference demographic that facilitate learning outcomes at the secondary level. The current study highlights that there exists a significant difference between students of urban and rural settlements in terms of Higher Education Readiness abilities. Students in urban settings demonstrate higher ability on their readiness skills than their peers in rural settings. This poses a serious question on what obstructs the transitioning learning population in the rural spaces from being ready for higher learning? The stark difference can be explained firstly through the underrepresentation of the students in the secondary classes at the rural level.

Furthermore, it is observed that the motivation level of the students towards higher learning is highly individualistic in the academic learning process. We explain this through the Self-Determination Theory that serves as an extension of the learning dynamics of adolescent students (Ryan & Deci, 2017). Through our study, the significance of this theory can be ascertained in terms of (a) 'support' in terms of guidance services towards the development of the psychological needs of competence, relatedness, and autonomy (b) 'support' in terms of access to pre-vocational and vocational opportunities in the rural areas. We observe that students at the urban level experience abundance of support through educated parents, school-level guidance through school counselling services, peer interaction, and digital accessibility to assess the importance of higher learning programs in the current employability scenario. Contrastingly, students in the rural spaces are highly devoid of the exposure to the importance of gaining higher education to meet the demands of employability other than the primary occupations (mostly agriculture). Researchers have argued that 'support' in terms of availability of pre-vocational and vocational opportunities typically include internships, job fairs, simulated short-term employments, and work-related exposures that facilitate better connections with the scope and skill demands at the employability level (Bisht & Pattnaik, 2020). Thus the rural spaces lack the basic awareness towards the growth of various employment opportunities that are revolutionizing the labor market today.

7. Conclusion

Based on these evidential insights, gender and spatial differences emerge as the most promising factors in scientifically determining the existent variations in the preparedness of higher education at the secondary level. Other factors embedded macroscopically in these two demographics are equity, geographical, and socio-economic factors that happen to be unevenly managed at the educational resource front, thereby being causes of low preparedness in the secondary level students. Within the student group, female students enrolled at the school, overcome these barriers to outperform male students. It is evident in the studied district that female students are outnumbered in the enrolment to secondary classes as compared to the males yet, the performance on Higher Education Readiness (HER) ability is higher than the male students. Drawing from this study, we conclude that the microscopic constraint for students in the significant achievement of preparedness to higher learning is their failure to attend secondary schooling. It can involve a myriad of reasons, starting with the mere absence of parental coercion for secondary education to the lack of pre-vocational and vocational opportunities within the school environments in providing the opportunities to the young students for gaining preparatory skills required in higher education systems today. In India, where attainment of education remains a persistent phenomenon among the lower socioeconomic classes, secondary education involving orientation to skill-based higher learning remains a far-fetched privilege. Hence, the study paves the way for the requirement of strong policy management that can enhance the realistic preparatory skills at the secondary level to promote the increased selection of higher education programmes for the future world of work.

REFERENCES

1. Abuzyarova, D., Belousova, V., Krayushkina, Z., Lonshcikova, Y., Nikiforova, E., and Chichkanov, N. .2019. The Role of Human Capital in Science, Technology and Innovation. 13(2 (eng)), 107–119.
2. Bandyopadhyay, M., and Chugh, S.2020. Status of secondary education in India: A review of status, challenges and policy issues. *Universal secondary education in India*, 17–49.
3. Banerji, A., Cunningham, W., Fiszbein, A., King, E., Patrinos, H., Robalino, D., and Tan, J. P.2010. Stepping up skills: For more jobs and higher productivity. Washington, DC: World Bank.
4. Banerji, R. 2021. Learning for All: Lessons from ASER and Pratham in India on the Role of Citizens and Communities in Improving Children's Learning. In Powering a Learning Society During an Age of Disruption (pp. 181–194). Springer, Singapore.
5. Bisht, N., and Pattanaik, F. 2020. Youth labour market in India: education, employment, and sustainable development goals. In International perspectives on the youth labor market: Emerging research and opportunities (pp. 172–196). IGI Global.
6. Cai, Y., Ma, J., and Chen, Q. 2020. Higher education in innovation ecosystems. Sustainability, 12(11), 4376.
7. Cano, F., Martin, A. J., Ginns, P., and Berbén, A. B. G. 2018. Students' self-worth protection and approaches to learning in higher education: predictors and consequences. *Higher Education*, 76(1), 163-181.
8. Casad, B. J., Oyler, D. L., Sullivan, E. T., McClellan, E. M., Tierney, D. N., Anderson, D. A., and Flammang, B. J. 2018. Wise psychological interventions to improve gender and racial equality in STEM. Group Processes & Intergroup Relations, 21(5), 767–787.
9. Croak, M. 2018. The effects of STEM education on economic growth.
10. Everwijn, S. E. M., Bomers, G. B. J., and Knubben, J. A. 1993. Ability-or competence-based education: bridging the gap between knowledge acquisition and ability to apply. Higher education, 25(4), 425–438.
11. Gilbert, J. L. 2011. Purposeful Play Leads To School Readiness.
12. Guglielmi, S., Neumeister, E., and Jones, N. 2021. Adolescents, youth and the SDGs: what can we learn from the current data?

13. Hasanah, U. 2020. Key definitions of STEM education: Literature review. Interdisciplinary Journal of Environmental and Science Education, 16(3), e2217.
14. India. Ministry of Human Resource Development. Department of Higher Education. 2019. All India Survey on Higher Education 2018–19.
15. Kaleva, S., Pursiainen, J., Hakola, M., Rusanen, J., and Muukkonen, H. 2019. Students' reasons for STEM choices and the relationship of mathematics choice to university admission. International Journal of STEM Education, 6(1), 1–12.
16. Lewis, J., Schneegans, S., and Straza, T. 2021. UNESCO Science Report: The race against time for smarter development (Vol. 2021). UNESCO Publishing.
17. Martin, A. J. and Marsh, H.W. 2009. Academic resilience and academic buoyancy: multidimensional and hierarchical conceptual framing of causes, correlates and cognate constructs, Oxford Review of Education, 35: 3, 353–370
18. Mau, W. C. J., and Li, J. 2018. Factors influencing STEM career aspirations of underrepresented high school students. The Career Development Quarterly, 66(3), 246–258.
19. Mellander, E., and Lind, P. 2021. Context and Implications Document for: Recruitment to STEM studies: The roles of curriculum reforms, flexibility of choice, and attitudes. Review of Education, 9(2), 399–404.
20. Nisskaya, A. K. 2018. School readiness outcomes of different preschool educational approaches. Psychology in Russia: State of the art, 11(1), 43–60.
21. O'Brien, Catherine and Howard, P. 2020. Living Schools: Transforming Education. Education for Sustainable Well-Being Press: Winnipeg, MB, Canada.
22. Papadakis, N. 2020. Education, Training, LLL and Youth Employability in Europe, today: Trends, political priorities, benchmarks, challenges and the state of play. 2020, 217–233.
23. Pascarella, E. T., and Terenzini, P. T. 1991. How college affects students: Findings and insights from twenty years of research. Jossey-Bass Inc., Publishers, PO Box 44305, San Francisco, CA 94144–4305 (ISBN-1-55542-304-3--$75.00, hardcover).
24. Repetuyeva. G. N. 2009. Formation of Readiness for SelfControl in Educational and Professional Activity of Future Vocational Training Teachers in the Process of Studying Psychological and Pedagogical Disciplines. Abstract of Cand. Diss
25. Ryan, R. M., and Deci, E. L. 2017. Self-determination theory. Basic psychological needs in motivation, development, and wellness.
26. Seryapina, Y. S. 2018. The concept of "readiness for pedagogical activity": motivational readiness, psychological readiness, readiness to innovative activity. 10(4), 77–86.
27. Suleman, F. 2018. The employability skills of higher education graduates: insights into conceptual frameworks and methodological options. Higher Education, 76(2), 263–278.
28. Tilak, J. B., and Choudhury, P. 2018. Inequality in Access to Higher Education in India between the Poor and the Rich An Analysis of 64th and 71st Rounds of NSSO Data (2007-08 and 2013–14). India: Social Development Report, 187–202.
29. Tolstova, O., and Levasheva, Y. 2019. Humanistic trend in education in a global context. In SHS Web of Conferences (Vol. 69, p. 00121). EDP Sciences.
30. Vasquez, J. A., Sneider, C. I., and Comer, M. W. 2013. STEM lesson essentials, grades 3-8: Integrating science, technology, engineering, and mathematics (pp. 58–76). Portsmouth, NH: Heinemann.
31. Wang, J., Hong, H., Ravitz, J., and Hejazi Moghadam, S. 2016. Landscape of K-12 computer science education in the US: Perceptions, access, and barriers. In Proceedings of the 47th ACM Technical Symposium on Computing Science Education (pp. 645–650).

32. Wang, M. T., Ye, F., and Degol, J. L. 2017. Who chooses STEM careers? Using a relative cognitive strength and interest model to predict careers in science, technology, engineering, and mathematics. Journal of youth and adolescence, 46(8), 1805–1820.

33. Wiek, A., Bernstein, M., Foley, R., Cohen, M., Forrest, N., Kuzdas, C., Kay, B., and Withycombe Keeler, L. 2015. Operationalising competencies in higher education for sustainable development. In: Barth, M., Michelsen, G., Rieckmann, M., Thomas, I. (Eds.) (2015). Handbook of Higher Education for Sustainable Development. Routledge, London. pp. 241–260.

34. World Bank. 2018. World development report 2019: The changing nature of work. The World Bank.

Handbook of Evidence Based Management Practices in Business – Satyendra Kumar Sharma et al. (eds)
© 2023 Taylor & Francis Group, London, ISBN 978-1-032-54216-4

Chapter

Choice of Expansion Modes: A Capabilities Perspective

Arun Kumar Tripathy*

Assistant Professor, Strategic Management,
Management Development Institute Gurgaon, India

ABSTRACT: This paper focuses on the choice of expansion modes of a firm. The capability perspective defines the expansion strategy of a firm as a process of creating capabilities that allow an organization to respond best to future market opportunities. Prior literature has talked about firms creating strategic advantage through the deliberate and effective development of capabilities. The choice of expansion mode is an essential part of the expansion strategy that helps organizations to build different capabilities. This paper argues that the choice of expansion mode of firms is based on the firm's present level of capabilities and the level of capabilities required to address its future market opportunities. A framework is developed to link a firm's expansion mode to its capability creation process.

KEYWORDS: Expansion modes, Capabilities, Real options

1. Introduction

To create long-term competitive advantages, organizations need to focus on developing and nurturing capabilities (Marsh & Stock, 2003). Helfat & Peteraf (2003) have argued that we need to include all organizational capabilities and generate heterogeneity in capabilities required for sustainable competitive advantages. This paper seeks to develop a capability-based framework for choosing expansion modes. Different expansion modes help firms exploit their current capabilities or build new ones. Capabilities are classified at different levels (Collis, 1994) depending upon the outcome of processes (like providing flexibility, learning, and efficiency); it helps an organization build. Different expansion modes are distinguished based on the

*arun.tripathy@mdi.ac.in

DOI: 10.4324/9781003415725-75

options they create, thereby linking them to the different levels of capability creation. For example, Joint Ventures help firms create capability because it provides high flexibility and external learning options. Similarly, acquisitions provide high growth and learning options but are found to be low in providing flexibility. Greenfield projects provide medium option value for flexibility, learning, growth, and operating options. In this paper, the capability as real options view is taken to determine firms' choice of expansion modes. *Capabilities* are defined as a bundle of resources (technological and organizational) that permits the firm to respond best to future market opportunities. The advancement in technology and its increased acceptability in society are causing firms to rethink their productive bundle of assets, the locus of competition, and how to compete and manage in this new environment. The capability view of the firm (an extension of the RBV) focuses on the present capabilities of the firm. It also needs to emphasize how these capabilities can be created. Increased competition and shorter product life cycles have increased the importance of flexibility and learning in strategic growth investments. The research on strategic flexibility has focused predominantly on the study of strategic flexibility and its consequences (how it is) rather than on how strategic flexibility is built (how to). This paper tries to answer the above two questions, i.e., how do firms create or develop capabilities considering the increased importance of strategic flexibility and learning? Real Option values the flexibility provided by an investment. A firm can build capabilities that better utilize future market opportunities by choosing the suitable expansion mode for growth investments. Baldwin and Kim (1994) state that Japanese firms with better operating performance had capabilities that allowed them to exploit market opportunities more effectively than their American counterparts. The learning for firms is that they should invest in long-term capability enhancement to achieve sustainable competitive advantage. Capability-based advantages are further being valued in the new economy, as the business landscape shifts to knowledge-based competition, where the winners appear to be rewarded in the market place not only by their present earnings but also by the future options embedded in their strategies.

In the context of expansion mode, the capability perspective would suggest that the best choice of expansion mode for an organization is one that allows it to effectively utilize its resources and capabilities to identify and pursue growth opportunities. In this paper using the capability perspective we theorize a framework that helps decision makers in deciding the appropriate expansion mode given their current and future capability requirements.

2. Theoretical Development

An organisation's resources and capabilities are described as technological and organisational investments. Kim and Kogut (1996) describe a firm's technological and organisational investments as building platforms that correspond to the firm's prediction regarding the evolution of the external environment. These platforms allow an organisation to enter a broad range of future markets. Hence, a capability is defined as *"A bundle of resources (technological and organisational) that permits the firm to respond best to future market opportunities."*

Winter (2003) classifies capabilities as dynamic and operational capabilities. We use this classification of capabilities for the framework. Building a higher-level capability, also known as a dynamic capability, is a path-dependent process that arises through an evolutionary process of experience gathering and learning (Teece et al., 1997, Helfat and Winter, 2011; Winter, 2003). The path chosen by a firm is vital as it not only defines the current growth options open to the firm based on its past decisions leading to the areas of competence but also the capabilities that are likely to be developed in the future. Winter (2003) argues that dynamic capabilities are higher-order capabilities necessary to initiate innovation and change. Flexibility and learning are the outcomes of dynamic capabilities. These higher-order capabilities are limited by the increasing costs (Winter 2003) involved at each higher level. On the other hand, lower-order capabilities are Operational capabilities developed for exploiting the available capabilities. The organisational theory has slowly embraced the idea that organisations can proactively exploit risk rather than absorb it (Kogut and Kulatilaka 2001). Nevertheless, firms and their environment are engaged in a coevolutionary dynamic (Koza and Lewin 1998). In that case, it is helpful for a firm to contemplate the match between its future capabilities and future environments. Kogut and Kulatilaka (1994) defined *Capabilities* as platforms that create a generic set of resources representing investments in future opportunities. Real options theory helps firms to identify and value these capabilities. Thereby, real option valuation helps a firm to analyze the value of capabilities by a market test (Kogut and Kulatilaka 2001).

The expansion mode of a firm is a process of creating capabilities. The capabilities a firm wants to create depend on how it foresees its future opportunities. Many investments a firm makes, such as acquiring new technologies, entering into joint ventures, and setting up a new manufacturing plant, create future investment opportunities and benefit the organisation from their current uses. For example, investing in an emerging technology may bring short-term cash flows. However, it can also create valuable growth opportunities should the market develop favourably.

The capability development process is path dependent and requires investments in technological and organisational assets. Expenditures on education and training, specialised information, physical infrastructure, and processes for coordination and integration are essential to achieve better performance in quality, speed, learning and flexibility. Different expansion mode helps a firm to build different levels of capability. When firms decide on the modes of expansion, they commit to long-term, nearly irreversible investments in developing specific capabilities. The degree to which businesses can leverage and redeploy their resources and capabilities depends on their chosen ex-ante mode of investment (Teece et al., 1997; Luo, 2002). In this paper, three types of expansion modes have been studied for long-term growth investments: joint ventures (or alliances), mergers and acquisitions, and Greenfield (or internal).

The following section discusses the relative degree and level of capabilities and hence the type of options embedded in each of these three expansion modes. A framework is developed to choose the type of expansion mode based on the current capability level and the future capability requirement.

3. Framework

In this paper, a firm's choice of expansion mode is a process of creating firm capabilities. The framework considers the difference between the current firm's capabilities and the capabilities required to exploit future opportunities as an essential factor in deciding the expansion mode. If there is a difference between the two, then the firm must create (explore, develop or acquire) the necessary capabilities to compete successfully in the market. If the firm perceives no gap, it depends on the value of the existing growth opportunities to exploit its capabilities. The capabilities are classified into different levels/orders of capabilities. Winter (2003) differentiates higher-level -dynamic capabilities from lower-level -operational capabilities. He argues that dynamic capabilities are higher-order capabilities necessary to initiate innovation and change. The increasing costs associated with dynamic capabilities limit these higher-order capabilities. Operational capabilities are differentiated from dynamic capabilities in terms of "ordinary or zero-level capabilities that enable short-term survival of a firm." Thus, effective utilization of higher-order capabilities-described as exploration involves search, variation, risk-taking, experimentation, play, flexibility, discovery and innovation. Effective utilization of lower or zero-level capabilities-described as exploitation primarily involves refinement, choice, production, efficiency, selection, implementation and execution.

According to the organisation theory perspective, organisations rely on other organisations in their environment to obtain the scarce resources they require (Pfeffer and Salancik, 1978). By creating joint ventures, businesses may stabilise the flow of resources they require and lessen the unpredictability they face (Pfeffer and Nowak 1976). In brief Joint Ventures (JV) are beneficial because they may lead to the pooling of resources to spread risk, increase the efficiency of the process through economies of scale, or eliminate duplication of effort, or disseminate knowledge (Kogut 1988), achieving synergy from respective capabilities, and leveraging one another's experience. Joint ventures may also be established to overcome or adhere to the regulatory pressures of a particular country (Sinha and Cusumano, 1991). However, joint ventures are complicated, and there is potential for conflicts of responsibilities, liabilities and rewards if they need to be delineated.

Kogut (1991) applied real options approach to analyse JVs. He argued that JVs could be viewed as a real option for firms to expand in response to future technological and market developments; the acquisition of ventures accompanies the exercise of such an option. In a volatile environment, switching strategies is very important as a market can grow up or down, requiring investment or divestment. In joint ventures, the collaborating firms can expand capacity if there is unexpected growth in the market, and if one of the firms wants to increase commitment further, they can buy out the partner. The option is also to reduce commitment by selling out to the partner. The collaborating firm provides a ready market for assets created that an ordinary direct investor needs to do. Janney and Dess (2004) have talked about the learning value of the joint venture, which accrues to both parties. JVs provide the structural mechanisms for fostering more intimate interaction for the interchange of knowledge between firms (Kogut, 1988). JVs are an attractive expansion mode for enhancing firms' capabilities when the in-house development of all the necessary know-how will take a long time, and licensing of it is considered relatively inadequate in terms of the more subtle and tacit aspects of the know-how and firms' bounded rationality in absorbing it.

Joint venture mode of expansion will help firms build capabilities by exogenous learning and provides flexibility by providing the option to expand or exit. This form of expansion mode (B) (Table 75.1) will be applied where both learning and flexibility are essential. Joint ventures will also be seen where complementary resources will be required to build new capabilities. But all these benefits come at a cost, like coordinating costs, appropriation issues, and sharing of technology. As Collis (1994) states, a firm goes from one level of capability to another. Joint venture being the highest level (as it provides flexibility and exogenous learning along with growth), the firms with the lower level of capability can only have the option of going for this strategy. This form of expansion mode is typically not suitable for a new enterprise. The higher the level of capability, the more value will be created by a firm. From the above description, it follows that a joint venture form of growth strategy is suitable for firms that are at the higher end of value creation, like new product development. Firms at a higher level of capability can acquire lower-level capabilities for various other reasons, but the opposite will not be suitable. Therefore, the JV (B) form of expansion mode will be used by firms with dynamic capabilities and the need to develop new capabilities further to meet future market requirements.

Table 75.1   Choice of expansion mode

Dynamic	Acquisition (A)	Alliance/Joint Venture (B)
Current Capability Level		
Operational	Greenfield/Internal (C)	Acquisition (D)
	Exploitation	Exploration
	Future Capability Requirements	

Source: Author's compilation

Mergers and acquisitions (M&A) are the most popular approach to diversification and are defined as combining two distinct organisations through partnering or purchasing. Two important reasons for firms to go for an M&A activity are to attain growth and synergy. Mergers and acquisitions may improve the organisation's performance due to increased market power, limiting competition, better utilisation of capacity or resources, building up economies of scope and scale, providing access to a growing and more profitable industry, managing government regulations or gaining excess to a foreign market. Acquisitions may help firms acquire new capabilities to address future growth opportunities. Some acquisitions help firms strengthen administrative control and avoid agency problems. From the above characterisation of the acquisition process, it is observed that acquisition helps a firm to acquire new capabilities. It loses out to joint ventures in terms of providing flexibility since the total investments have been committed upfront only. It also provides growth options. This form of expansion mode will be adopted when the technology has stabilised, i.e. the premium on flexibility has reduced. In terms of the level of capability creation, it comes next to joint ventures since it does not provide flexibility. However, it is higher than greenfield form because it helps bring in exogenous learning. The acquisition form of expansion mode (A) will help in capability creation only when the firm has a lower level of capabilities. If the firm does not have the lower level capabilities or the acquired firm has a higher-level capability, then it will become difficult for it to manage and integrate the acquired firm. The managing and coordination costs will increase, thereby reducing the benefits of the acquisition. Hence, firms with dynamic capability will go for acquisition (A) to exploit their current capabilities, or those with operational capability will choose acquisition (D) to acquire new capabilities.

A company's entry into a new business sector or geographical setting is called "greenfield" or "internal expansion." Greenfield subsidiaries typically form close ties with their parent companies and sister subsidiaries through a path-dependent process from initial formation to subsequent management (Harzing, 2002; Luo, 2002). MNEs typically use greenfield subsidiaries as pipelines for their multi-country networks to gain economies of scale and scope because this investment mode makes it simpler to incorporate the technologies and organisational practices of the parent company and integrate with the parent's global network (Chung and Beamish, 2005; Harzing, 2002). The parent companies typically exercise greater control through greater use of their employees and a higher percentage of equity ownership. According to Luo (2002), greenfield subsidiaries are well-suited to employing practices comparable to those of the parent company's network regarding managerial expertise, knowledge, technology, and experience. For a firm that has developed certain capabilities, it is much easier to develop those skills from scratch at a new establishment (Greenfield) than to transfer that knowledge to a new partner, as most of that knowledge is embedded in organisational practices and labour skills. The costs of imparting knowledge in a new venture are lesser than transferring knowledge in a company that has been taken over or included as a partner. In those situations, old practices will have to be unlearned, and these present a challenge.

Some firms may go into greenfield ventures in related/ unrelated areas in order to better utilise firm assets that cannot be sold due to transaction costs and other imperfections. These include brand loyalty, specific skills, and narrow technological focus. When the firm has entered a greenfield venture in a related field, it can share a lot of resources and knowledge to start the business. The firm also benefits from learning curve advantages, economies of scope, product/ process technology diffusion and internal markets for capital. It is advantageous, especially when the opportunity is one for which information is scarce, and so funding is not readily available. The main advantage of Greenfield investments is that along with proprietary control of the new capabilities and high growth options; it provides some flexibility (due to staging) and endogenous learning options also. Greenfield expansion mode is best suited when a firm has exploitation capabilities in a growth market. The main characteristic of Greenfield investments is that it provides little of everything, i.e. growth, learning and flexibility options, along with proprietary control of the new capabilities. This strategy implementation has the lowest cost and capability creation among the three growth strategies studied. This type of expansion mode is best suited for exploiting a firm's present capability because of its low cost. The firm will not have to pay a premium as required for an acquisition or incur coordination costs as in a joint venture. Firms with operational capabilities(C) will opt for this expansion mode.

4. Conclusion

This study is to help managers in deciding the choice of expansion modes. By linking the current capabilities to the future required capabilities of a firm, the developed framework will help decision-makers choose an appropriate expansion mode. The expansion mode of a firm is considered to be a process of capability creation. In the present scenario, companies in India are scouting for growth opportunities. This mapping may help the managers decide the appropriate mode for their growth investments. Some of the limitations of this classification are that it may not be that useful for the short-term realization of available opportunities. Moreover, the study has been limited to three types of expansion modes. It can be further expanded to include other forms like outsourcing, franchising, and licensing.

REFERENCES

1. Baldwin, Carliss Y., and Kim B. Clark. "Capital-budgeting systems and capabilities investments in US companies after the Second World War." *Business History Review* 68, no. 1 (1994): 73–109.
2. Chung, Chris Changwha, and Paul W. Beamish. "Investment mode strategy and expatriate strategy during times of economic crisis." *Journal of International Management* 11, no. 3 (2005): 331–355.
3. Cohen, Wesley M., and Daniel A. Levinthal. "Absorptive capacity: A new perspective on learning and innovation." *Administrative science quarterly* (1990): 128–152.
4. Collis, David J. "Research note: how valuable are organizational capabilities?." *Strategic management journal* 15, no. S1 (1994): 143–152.
5. Harzing, Anne-Wil. "Acquisitions versus greenfield investments: International strategy and management of entry modes." *Strategic management journal* 23, no. 3 (2002): 211–227.
6. Helfat, Constance E., and Margaret A. Peteraf. "The dynamic resource-based view: Capability lifecycles." *Strategic management journal* 24, no. 10 (2003): 997–1010.
7. Helfat, Constance E., and Sidney G. Winter. "Untangling dynamic and operational capabilities: Strategy for the (N) ever-changing world." *Strategic management journal* 32, no. 11 (2011): 1243–1250.
8. Hill, Charles. W. L., Hwang, Peter, and Kim, W. Chan. 1990. An Eclectic Theory of the Choice of International Entry Mode, Strategic Management Journal, 11: 117–128.
9. Kogut, Bruce. "Joint ventures: Theoretical and empirical perspectives." *Strategic management journal* 9, no. 4 (1988): 319–332.
10. Kogut, Bruce. "Joint ventures and the option to expand and acquire." *Management science* 37, no. 1 (1991): 19–33.
11. Kogut, Bruce, and Nalin Kulatilaka. "Operating flexibility, global manufacturing, and the option value of a multinational network." *Management science* 40, no. 1 (1994): 123–139.
12. Kogut, Bruce, and Nalin Kulatilaka. "Capabilities as real options." *Organization Science* 12, no. 6 (2001): 744–758.
13. Kogut, Bruce, and Udo Zander. "Knowledge of the firm and the evolutionary theory of the multinational corporation." *Journal of international business studies* 24, no. 4 (1993): 625–645.
14. Koza, Mitchell P., and Arie Y. Lewin. "The co-evolution of strategic alliances." *Organization science* 9, no. 3 (1998): 255–264.
15. Kulatilaka, Nalin, and Enrico C. Perotti. "Strategic growth options." *Management Science* 44, no. 8 (1998): 1021–1031.
16. Luo, Yadong. "Contract, cooperation, and performance in international joint ventures." *Strategic management journal* 23, no. 10 (2002): 903–919.
17. Marsh, Sarah J., and Gregory N. Stock. "Building dynamic capabilities in new product development through intertemporal integration." *Journal of product innovation management* 20, no. 2 (2003): 136–148.
18. Parkhe, Arvind. "Strategic alliance structuring: A game theoretic and transaction cost examination of interfirm cooperation." *Academy of management journal* 36, no. 4 (1993): 794–829.

19. Pfeffer, Jeffrey, and Phillip Nowak. "Joint ventures and interorganizational interdependence." *Administrative science quarterly* (1976): 398–418.

20. Pfeffer, Jeffrey, and G. R. Salancik. "A resource dependence perspective." In *Intercorporate relations. The structural analysis of business.* Cambridge: Cambridge University Press, 1978.

21. Sinha, Deepak K., and Michael A. Cusumano. "Complementary resources and cooperative research: a model of research joint ventures among competitors." *Management science* 37, no. 9 (1991): 1091–1106.

22. Teece, David J., Gary Pisano, and Amy Shuen. "Dynamic capabilities and strategic management." *Strategic management journal* 18, no. 7 (1997): 509–533.

23. Winter, Sidney G. "Understanding dynamic capabilities." *Strategic management journal* 24, no. 10 (2003): 991–995.

Chapter

ESG Disclosures and Firm Performances— Evidence from India Inc.

Tulika Bal[1]
Department of Business Administration, DDCE,
Utkal University, Bhubaneswar, India

Ashutosh Dash[2]
Associate Professor, Management Development Institute
Gurugram, India

ABSTRACT: Corporate reporting is witnessing a paradigm shift from numbers to narratives. Corporate non-financial disclosures have gone through many reforms, specifically in environmental, social and governance areas. Sustainable practices, generally associated with ESG and CSR, have become key non-financial indicators of financial and non-financial performances, quality of management and risk management. The purpose of this research work is to examine whether the ESG performance (proxied by ESG and governance score), a supposedly contributors to shareholder wealth creation, is leading to better financial performance of the firms. Though a vast majority of extant research has been done in developed countries, the impact of ESG performances in emerging markets like India is yet to be explored systematically. With help of Governance and ESG Score of the BSE 500 constituent companies in India and employing panel regression model, the study attempts to test the two research hypotheses. The market performance is measured through Tobin's Q while ROA and net profit margin are used as measures of operating/accounting performance. The analysis of data shows that accounting performance is negatively correlated with ESG and governance score when a year fixed effects regression was conducted, and market performance is not correlated with ESG and governance score.

KEYWORDS: Corporate governance, ESG, Financial performance, Operating performance, Sustainability, Value creation

[1]tulikabal@gmail.com, [2]ashutosh@mdi.ac.in

DOI: 10.4324/9781003415725-76

1. Introduction

Corporate reporting and disclosures have witnessed many reforms as the risks associated with a company is not necessarily limited to financial events but dependent on several non-financial events linked mainly to environmental, social and governance areas. In 21st century, with changing corporate orientation from stockholders to stakeholders, the practice of reporting non-financial disclosures has been rising to increase visibility, avoiding the risk associated with firm performance and achieving sustainability. The stakeholders are also very vocal about climate change, labour laws, depletion of natural resources, standard working conditions for workers, etc. These issues have given rise to corporate social, ethical and environmental responsibilities. Due to the alertness on the social and environmental issues, the customers expect the companies to follow the sustainable practices. Thus, sustainable business practices have become an important part in decision making process of the investors. This has led to study the impact of the ESG disclosure on the performance of the business entity. Reporting of ESG performance can be considered as a risk management tool for disclosure of the quality of governance of the firm and its sustainable strategy. With ESG disclosures, the firms create a clean and green image to attract more investors, hence the roles of ESG disclosures on corporate performance are mainly analysed on market base and/or accounting base. Because of the value creation potential of ESG disclosures, the corporate entities take voluntary steps to embed environmental and social aspects in their operating activities and in many cases, they integrate sustainability issues into their strategy. One of the important questions that arises is whether the good governance and sustainable activities have been rewarded by the market and reflected in their financial performances.

2. Literature Review

A wide range of literature can be found on CSR and corporate sustainable practices across the disciplines. In the finance domain a significant number of researchers have attempted to investigate the relationship between sustainable practices, reporting and corporate performance be it operating, financial or market performances. The reviews of literatures presented below are not unidirectional rather show a mixed result. While a section of studies found positive relationship between social/environmental performance and financial performance, many others found contradictory results.

Buallay, et al. (2022) conducted a study to examine the impact of sustainability reporting on the the operational, market and financial performance of firms in the tourism industry. The study concluded with a positive outcome that sustainability reporting has a significant influence on the assets return and market valuation. The authors also advocated that the relationship between sustainability activities and the firm's performance is nonlinear and nonlinear models are better fit over the linear models. The authors recommended that the firms in tourism sector should emphasize more on non-financial disclosures for enhancing their value and return on assets.

Buallay (2022) studied the sustainability practices and its impact on the performance of the retail sector. The firm's operational performance, financial performance and market performance were measured by ROA, ROE and Tobin's Q respectively. With help of multivariate regression analyses the study concluded that the ESG positively and significantly influences the firm performances when measures by return on assets and return on equity. The study also highlighted that sustainability disclosure has a positive influence on the valuation of the firm measured by Tobin's Q.

Buallay, et al. (2021) examined the relationship between the sustainability reporting and the firm's performance of top 20 smart cities The multiple regression analysis revealed that the impact of sustainability practices on ROA and ROE is positively significant, however it is negatively significant for TQ. By limiting the negative impact and increasing the positive impact the companies can transform the cities with ESG at the leading edge of innovation. They suggested forming a legislature for mandatory spending of certain amount or portion of profit on sustainable activities. The authors emphasised that the corporate leaders should adopt the sustainable development goals of UN to achieve sustainability.

Bahadori, et al. (2021) studied the impact of ESG factors on the financial performance in emerging markets. They gave a more generalized view by taking a large sample of 600 firms from various countries and different sectors spanning over 5 years from 2014-18. They found that the social and environmental component have positive and significant effect on return on assets and return on equity. However, governance component has negative and/or no significant impact on the firm performances. Weak governance practices, lack of proper legal system might be some of the reasons of not having good firm performance as suggested by the author.

Dakhli (2021) studied the relationship between board attributes and CSR and also the moderating effect of financial performance on the aforementioned relationship. Multiple regression showed that the board size and CEO duality has a significant negative relation with CSR whereas female representative in board and board independence has positive relation with CRS. Apropos the influence of good governance on firm performance, the findings of the study confirm that various governance facets like CEO-duality, board size and board independence significantly influence the financial performance of firms.

Caiazza, et al. (2021) studied the effect of CSR on merger and acquisition performance. They collected data of 6562 merger and acquisition deals in hospitality sector from the years 2000 to 2019. By using the regression and event study they found that sustainability factors in merger and acquisition are significantly correlated with long term performance as there were improvements in financial ratios in the long run, however the short term effects were irrelevant. After the deals there was also development in ESG scores in the companies involved in merger and acquisition.

Buallay et al. (2021) analysed the sustainability reporting in banking and financial sector's performance. They studied the effect of ESG scores on the return on asset, return on equity and Tobin's Q. The dependent variables taken were the Bank's operational (ROA), market (Tobin's Q) and financial (ROE) performance. The independent variables taken were the environmental scores, social scores and governance scores. They carried out multiple regression and concluded that there was significantly negative relationship between ESG and the bank's performance for the whole sample.

Sharma et al. (2021) studied the role of ESG performance in profitable investments for sustainable future. The study finds that the top 10 percent firms on ESG scores have 14% excess return on equity as compared to their counterparts. The authors employed machine learning technique for predicting the net profit margin and return on assets. Contrary to many findings, the study revealed that the companies with the lowest ESG scores have higher net profit margins and ROA but the authors confirm the existence of a positive relationship between ESG performance and financial performance when financial performance is measured through ROE.

Pekovic and Vogt (2020) explored the moderating role of corporate governance on sustainable firm's financial performance measured through the valuation ratio Tobin's Q. The authors found that the CSR firm's financial performance is moderated positively by the board size and gender diversity. However, ownership concentration negatively moderates the same. Further, the independence of board members does not support the positive moderating effect on CSR firm's financial performance.

In a unique study Buallay (2019) investigated the costs and benefits of ESG to the reporting firms. On examining the relationship between ESG and the firm performance, the results reveal ESG positively impacts the market performance but bears a negative relationship with the financial performance of firms. So it can be concluded that while capital market rewards the firms with sustainable performances, the product market does not do so.

Various empirical research has attempted to examine the connection between ESG disclosure and operational performance (Buallay, 2019; Buallay et al., 2021; Bahadori et al., 2021; Pekovic et al., 2021; and Minutolo et al., 2019) but have delivered different and mixed findings.

While some researchers discovered a positive association between financial performance and sustainability reporting and confirmed that sustainability reporting improved the firm performance (Chauibi et al., 2020; Saleh et al., 2021; Sharma, 2022; Buallay, 2022A; Buallay, 2022B; Buallay et al., 2021; Bahadori et al., 2021, Pekovic et al., 2021; Minutolo et al., 2019), many other studies revealed a negative relationship between firm performance and sustainability reporting (Buallay A., 2019; Buallay A., 2021; Buallay, A., Fadel, S. M., Alajmi, J., and Saudagaran, S., 2020; Buallay, A., Fadel, S. M., Al-Ajmi, J. Y., and Saudagaran, S., 2020).

The most objective way to assess the impact of ESG disclosure is to examine its value creation potential in stock price or stock market value. Many researchers have connected ESG with market valuation measured through Tobin's Q (Buallay, A., 2021). A section of literature reveals that sustainability reporting has significant positive relationship with the firm market performance (Buallay et al., 2021; Karim et al., 2020, Buallay, 2022A; and Minutolo et al., 2019). These studies revealed that sustainability reporting improves the market performance of the firm. On the other hand, sustainability reporting and market performance are found to have an inverse relationship in many studies (Buallay, 2019; Buallay 2021; Buallay, 2022B).

The growing body of literature with inconsistent finding on the relationship of ESG disclosure provokes the researchers in delving with the topic more systematically. Moreover, the data on ESG scores of companies was difficult to assess in emerging markets like India. The study considers a longer horizon of time that probably has not been used by many researchers in Indian context.

Given the gap in prior literature, we have developed two hypotheses to completely study the effect of ESG disclosure mechanism on shareholder wealth creation.

H1: Market Performance is positively correlated with ESG Score.

The paper tries to measure this hypothesis by looking at the governance score of BSE 500 companies and their market performance (by using Tobin's Q ratio).

H2: Accounting Performance is positively correlated with ESG Score.

For the firm's accounting performance, the variables like ROA and net profit margin will be used.

3. Research Methodology

The Research is designed in four steps. With help of an in-depth literature review in the first step, the authors identified proxy parameters for dependent and independent variables to examine the causal relationship of ESG closure and firm performance. In the step further, the data for the study have been gathered on the identified variables and in the final step a multivariate regression analysis have been carried out to test the hypotheses and conclude on the relationship of ESG disclosures and firm performances.

After thoroughly reading the research papers related to this topic, we have chalked out these dependent variables as a proxy for value creation which are already used in many papers.

Table 76.1   List of variables and measures

Variables	Measures	Explanation
Social/Sustainable Performance	ESG Score	Provided by Bloomberg
Market Performance	Tobin's Q	Tobin's Q = Market Value/Intrinsic Value
Accounting or Operating Performance	Return on Assets (ROA) Net Profit Margin	ROA = NOPAT/ Total Assets NOPAT = Net Operating Profit after tax or EBIT * (1-t) Net Profit Margins = Net Income/Total Sales
Control Variables	Leverage	D/E = Total Debt/Total Equity

Source: Author's compilation

3.1 Data Collection

With an intent to cover a broad range of firms, the study collected data of 500 companies that are the constituents of the broad-based BSE 500 index. The independent variable ESG scores have been gathered from the Bloomberg Terminal. Considering 120 sustainability indicators across environmental, social and governance factors, Bloomberg provides ESG scores and overview of various companies from ESG perspective. The market performance, accounting performance and control variables of the 500 firms have been collected for 13 years from the

Bloomberg LLP. Period of study is taken as 13 years because ESG parameters keep on varying over the years.

3.2 Regression Models

Expected outcome will be derived by verifying or denying the hypotheses using regression analysis in Stata between dependent variables and independent variables. The fixed effects regression models have been used which is an analysis tool employed in a panel data setting. By including year fixed effects which is important because year fixed effects (also known as "year dummies" or "dummies for each of the years in your dataset [excluding the first year]") acknowledge the influence of aggregate trends happening because of time series.

Tobin's $Q = b_0 + b_1$ Vector of ESG Score $+ b_2$ ROA $+ b_3$ Margin $+ b_4$ D/E $+ b_5$i.year

ROA $= b_0 + b_1$ Vector of ESG Score $+ b_2$ Tobin's Q $+ b_3$ Margin $+ b_4$ D/E $+ b_5$i.year

4. Result and Discussion

The study makes the analysis of hypotheses by two methods, first by including a year fixed effects which is important because year fixed effects acknowledge the influence of aggregate trends happening because of time series. Then the second model is employed without taking time series effects. The results presented below include hypothesis which is checked, independent and dependent variable, control variables and type of analysis used, and finally the results and screenshot of Stata output.

The relationship between the market performance and ESG score has been analysed through a multivariate panel model (without year effect) and the results are presented in the Table 76.2.

Table 76.2 Regression results without year effect

Tobin's Q = $b_0 + b_1$ ESG Score + b_2 ROA + b_3 Profit Margin + b_4 D/E						
Fixed-effects (within) regression				Number of obs = 2414 Number of Groups = 301		
R-sq: Within = 0.1200 Between = 0.4606 Overall = 0.3654				Obs per group: Min = 1 Avg = 8.0 Max = 14		
Corr(u_i, xb) = 0.4165 (Std. Err. Adjusted for 301 clusters)				F (4, 300) = 8.04 Prob > F = 0.0000		
Tobin Q ratio	**Coefficient**	**Robust Std. Err**	**t**	**P > |t|**	**95% Conf.**	**Interval**
ESG Score	0.0193	0.0103	1.87	0.062	-0.001	0.0396
ROA	0.0989	0.0193	5.13	0.000	0.061	0.1369
Profit Margin	-0.0063	0.0032	-1.94	0.053	-0.0128	0.00008
D/E ratio	-0.00005	0.00005	-0.91	0.361	-0.0001	0.00005
_cons	0.8896	0.5490	1.62	0.106	-0.1908	1.9700

Source: Author's compilation

Tobin's Q, the proxy for market performance, is used as the dependent variable in the regression model and ESG disclosure score is considered as independent variable. The control variables used in the study included Return on Asset, Profit Margin, Total Debt to Equity ratio. Fixed effect regression without year fixed effects reveals a positive correlation with governance score and market performance. From above results it can be observed that Tobin's Q ratio is positively correlated with governance score at 10% significance level and 1 unit increase in governance score led to .019 unit increase in the ratio. However, return on asset is significant at 1% level with 1 unit increase in return on asset lead to .09 unit increase in the ratio.

The relationship between the market performance and ESG score is again analysed through a multivariate panel model (with year effect) and the results are presented in the Table 76.3.

Table 76.3 Regression results with year effect

Tobin's Q = b_0 + b_1 ESG Score + b_2 ROA + b_3 Margin + b_4 D/E + b_5 i.year i.year _Iyear_2007-2020 (naturally coded; _Iyear_2007 omitted)						
Fixed-effects (within) regression				Number of obs = 2414 Number of Groups = 301		
R-sq: Within = 0.2315 Between = 0.4839 Overall = 0.3852				Obs per group: Min = 1 Avg = 8.0 Max = 14		
Tobin Q ratio	**Coefficient**	**Robust Std. Err**	**T**	**P>|t|**	**[95% Conf.**	**Interval]**
ESG score	-0.0039	0.0092	-0.43	0.668	-0.022	0.0141
ROA	0.9991	0.0204	4.90	0.000	0.0597	0.1400
Profit Margin	-0.0040	0.0023	-1.75	0.081	-0.0086	0.0005
D/E Ratio	-0.0001	0.00007	-1.46	0.144	-0.0002	0.00003
_Iyear_2008	0.1614	0.3280	0.49	0.623	-0.4842	0.8070
_Iyear_2009	-0.4003	0.3153	-1.27	0.205	-1.0208	0.2202
_Iyear_2010	0.0825	0.343	0.24	0.810	-0.5923	0.7572
_Iyear_2011	0.1500	0.3600	0.42	0.677	-0.5584	0.8586
_Iyear_2012	0.3010	0.3949	0.76	0.447	-0.4762	1.0782
_Iyear_2013	0.222	0.3978	0.56	0.577	-0.5609	1.005
_Iyear_2014	1.181	0.4607	2.56	0.011	0.2744	2.0878
_Iyear_2015	1.1605	0.4653	2.49	0.013	0.2448	2.0761
_Iyear_2016	1.1648	0.4607	2.53	0.012	0.2581	2.0715
_Iyear_2017	1.1748	0.4532	2.59	0.010	0.2829	2.067
_Iyear_2018	1.1811	0.4607	2.56	0.011	0.2744	2.0878
_Iyear_2019	0.9576	0.4807	1.99	0.047	0.0116	1.9035
_Iyear_2020	0.4994	0.4731	1.06	0.292	-0.4316	1.4304
Cons	1.189731	0.5513	2.16	0.032	0.1048	2.2746

Source: Author's compilation

The Fixed effect regression considering the year fixed effects reveals an insignificant relationship between ESG score and market performance. From above results it can be observed that Tobin's Q ratio is not correlated with ESG scores of the entities. This helps to conclude that good governance does not necessarily improve the market valuation of the companies under study. The ROA seems to have a significant relationship at 1% level. Both the models though contradict on the influence of ESG on market performance, they converge on the fact that ROA is an influential factor in enhancing the valuation of the firms.

The relationship between the accounting performance and ESG score has been analysed through a multivariate panel model and the results are presented in the Table 76.4.

Table 76.4 Regression results without year effect

ROA = b_0 + b_1 Vector of ESG Score + b_2 Tobin's Q + b_3 Margin + b_4 D/E						
Fixed-effects (within) regression				Number of obs = 2414 Number of Groups = 301		
R-sq: Within = 0.2866 Between = 0.1733 Overall = 0.3920				Obs per group: Min = 1 Avg = 8.0 Max = 14		
Corr(u_i, xb) = 0.0557				F (4, 300) = 17.65 Prob > F = 0.0000		
Return on asset	**Coefficient**	**Robust Std. Err**	**T**	**P>|t|**	**95% Conf.**	**Interval**
ESG Score	-0.1018	0.0326	-3.12	0.002	-0.1659	-0.0376
Tobin Q ratio	1.10999	0.1710	6.49	0.000	0.7734	1.4466
Profit Margin	0.1544	0.0619	2.49	0.013	0.0325	0.2764
D/E Ratio	-0.0014	0.0007	-1.87	0.062	-0.0029	0.00007
_cons	8.5299	1.8048	4.73	0.000	4.978	12.081

Source: Author's compilation

Return on Assets is used as the dependent variable in the regression model and ESG disclosure score is considered as independent variable. The control variables used in the study included Tobin's Q, Profit Margin, Total Debt to Equity ratio. Fixed effect regression without year fixed effects reveals a negative correlation with governance disclosure score and operating performance. From above results it can be observed that return on asset (accounting performance) is negatively correlated with governance score at 1% significance level and 1 unit increase in governance score led to (-0.1) unit decrease in the return on assets.

The relationship between the operating performance and ESG disclosure score is again analysed through a multivariate panel model (with year effect) and the results are presented in the Table 76.5.

The Fixed effect regression considering the year fixed effects reveals an insignificant relationship between ESG score and operating performance. From above results it can be observed that ROA is not correlated with ESG disclosure scores of the entities. This helps to conclude that sustainable activities do not necessarily improve the operating profits of the companies under study. But the Tobin's Q and profit margin are positively associated with the ESG performances.

Table 76.5 Regression results considering year effect

ROA = b_0 + b_1 Vector of ESG Score + b_2 Tobin's Q + b_3 Margin + b_4 D/E + b_5i.year						
Fixed-effects (within) regression Group variable: gvkey2			Number of obs = 2414 Number of Groups = 301			
R-sq: Within = 0.3127 Between = 0.1974 Overall = 0.4296			Obs per group: Min = 1 Avg = 8.0 Max = 14			
Return on Asset	**Coefficient**	**Robust Std. Err**	**T**	**P>|t|**	**95% Conf.**	**Interval**
ESG Score	-0.0516	0.0329	-1.56	0.119	-0.1165	0.0133
Tobin Q ratio	1.236	0.1828	6.67	0.000	0.8760	1.596
Profit Margin	0.1465	0.0605	2.42	0.016	0.0274	0.2656
D/E Ratio	-0.0011	0.0007	-1.59	0.113	-0.0026	0.00027
_Iyear_2008	-0.5365	1.4886	-0.36	0.719	-3.466	2.393
_Iyear_2009	-2.275	1.666	-1.37	0.173	-5.554	1.003
_Iyear_2010	-1.686	1.574	-1.07	0.285	-4.785	1.4123
_Iyear_2011	-2.124	1.592	-1.33	0.183	-5.257	1.009
_Iyear_2012	-2.911	1.603	-1.82	0.070	-6.066	0.2438
_Iyear_2013	-3.1057	1.618	-1.92	0.056	-6.290	0.0788
_Iyear_2014	-3.7299	1.7564	-2.12	0.035	-7.186	-0.2734
_Iyear_2015	-4.3109	1.6849	-2.56	0.011	-7.626	-0.9952
_Iyear_2016	-3.739	1.758	-2.13	0.034	-7.199	-0.2786
_Iyear_2017	-3.883	1.733	-2.24	0.026	-7.2948	-0.4723
_Iyear_2018	-3.7299	1.7564	-2.12	0.035	-7.1864	-0.2734
_Iyear_2019	-3.1393	1.827	-1.72	0.087	-6.735	0.4564
_Iyear_2020	-3.4987	1.753	-2.00	0.047	-6.949	-0.0482
Cons	9.118	2.325	3.92	0.000	4.542	13.694

Source: Author's compilation

Table 76.6 Results and analysis

Hypotheses	**Results**
Market performance has a positive correlation with governance score and ESG score.	Market performance when measured through Tobin's Q is not related to ESG score.
Accounting Performance has a positive correlation with governance score and ESG score.	Accounting Performance as measured by Return on Assets is negatively correlated with ESG score.

Source: Author's compilation

5. Conclusions

ESG is a topic in demand and the reason is that the performance of a firm is directly or indirectly depend on sustainable practices of the firm. The main reason for this research is to analyse the impact of sustainable practices on firm's performance and value creation. We have mentioned in the literature review a lot papers providing contradictory views to the same hypotheses. There are not many research papers written in context of Indian companies maybe because ESG is still in developing phase and a lot of shady practices happens in Indian firms, and data is also not easily available. However, we have chosen BSE 500 companies and they include large corporates as well as medium and small firms. The conclusions that were found out during the study are contradictory to the observations mentioned in the papers earlier written. Few of the observations were accounting performance is negatively correlated with ESG score and governance score when a year fixed effects regression was conducted. Market performance is not correlated with ESG score and governance score.

REFERENCES

1. Athma, P. and Rajyalaxmi, N. 2019. "Integrated reporting in India: An analysis of selected companies." Indian Journal of Accounting: 28–46.
2. Bahadori, N., Kaymak, T., & Seraj, M. 2021. "Environmental, social, and governance factors in emerging markets: The impact on firm performance." Business Strategy & Development 4, no.4: 411–422.
3. Blowfield, M. and Murray, A. 2011. Corporate Responsibility. Oxford University Press.
4. Boerner, S. and Jobst, J. 2011, "Stakeholder management and program planning in German public theaters", Nonprofit Management and Leadership 22, no.1: 67–84.
5. Buallay, A. 2019. "Between cost and value: Investigating the effects of sustainability reporting on a firm's performance." Journal of Applied Accounting Research 20, no. 4: 481–496. doi 10.1108/jaar-12-2017-0137.
6. Buallay, A. 2021. "Sustainability reporting in food industry: an innovative tool for enhancing financial performance." British Food Journal 124, no.6: 1939–1958. doi 10.1108/bfj-01-2021-0053.
7. Buallay, A., Al-Ajmi, J., & Barone, E. 2021. "Sustainability engagement's impact on tourism sector performance: linear and nonlinear models." Journal of Organizational Change Management 35, no. 2: 361–384. doi 10.1108/jocm-10-2020-0308.
8. Buallay, A. 2022. "Toward sustainability reporting in the MENA region: the effects on sector's performance." Managerial Finance. doi 10.1108/mf-09-2021-0422.
9. Buallay, A., El Khoury, R., & Hamdan, A. 2021. "Sustainability reporting in smart cities: A multidimensional performance measures." Cities. https://doi.org/10.1016/j.cities.2021.103397
10. Buhr, N. 2007. "Histories of and rationales for sustainability reporting." Sustainability Accounting and Accountability: 57–69
11. Caglio, A., Melloni, G. and Perego, P. 2020. "Informational content and assurance of textual disclosures: Evidence on integrated reporting" European Accounting Review 29, no. 1: 55–83.
12. Caiazza, S., Galloppo, G., and Paimanova, V. 2021. "The role of sustainability performance after merger and acquisition deals in short and long-term" Journal of Cleaner Production, 314, 127982.
13. Chouaibi, S., Chouaibi, J., & Rossi, M. 2021. "ESG and corporate financial performance: the

mediating role of green innovation: UK common law versus Germany civil law." EuroMed Journal of Business 17, no.1: 46–71.

14. Clayton, A. F., Rogerson, J. M. and Rampedi, I. 2015. "Integrated reporting vs. sustainability reporting for corporate responsibility in South Africa" Bulletin of Geography. Socio-Economic Series, 29: 7–17.

15. Crane, A. and Matten, D. 2010 "Business ethics: Managing corporate citizenship and sustainability in the age of globalization" Oxford University Press.

16. Dumay, J., Bernardi, C., Guthrie, J. and Demartini, P. 2016. "Integrated reporting: a structured literature review" Accounting Forum 40, no. 3: 166–185.

17. Dakhli, A. 2021. "Does financial performance moderate the relationship between board attributes and corporate social responsibility in French firms?" Journal of Global Responsibility.

18. Eccles, R.G. and Serafeim, G. 2014. Corporate and integrated reporting: a functional perspective. Harvard Kennedy School.

19. Elkington, J. 2004. "Enter the triple bottom line." The triple bottom line: Does it all add up?: 1–16.

20. Esch, M., Schnellbacher, B. and Wald, A. 2019. "Does integrated reporting information influence internal decision making? An experimental study of investment behaviour" Business Strategy and the Environment, 28: 599–610.

21. GRI (Global reporting initiative). 2013. "Carrots and sticks: Sustainability reporting policies worldwide- Today's best practice, tomorrow's trends." Amsterdam: Global reporting initiative.

22. GRI (Global reporting initiative), 2011. Sustainability Reporting Guidelines, Version 3.1, Amsterdam: Global reporting initiative.

23. Guthrie, J and Abeysekera, I. 2006. "Content analysis of social, environmental reporting: what is new?",Journal of Human Resource Costing and Accounting, 10: 114–126.

24. Hill, C.W.L. and Snell, S.A. 1988. "External control, corporate strategy and firm performance in research- intensive industries" Strategic Management Journal 9, no.6: 577–590.

25. Jonikas, D. 2013. "Conceptual framework of value creation through CSR in a separate member of value creation chain" Bulletin of Geography: Socio Economic series, 21: 69–78.

26. Kahloul, I., Sbai, H., and Grira, J. 2022. "Does Corporate Social Responsibility reporting improve financial performance? The moderating role of board diversity and gender composition" The Quarterly Review of Economics and Finance, 84: 305–314.

27. Lai, A., Melloni, G. and Stacchezzini, R. 2018. "Integrated reporting and narrative accountability: the role of preparers" Accounting, Auditing and Accountability Journal, 31: 1381–1405.

28. Leedy, P. D and Ormord, J. E. 2001. Practical Research: Planning and Design. 7th Edition. Merrill Prentice Hall and SAGE Publications, Upper Saddle River, NJ and Thousand Oaks, CA.

29. Lenhard, J. and Leach, H. 2022. Start Up and Smell the ESG. Economic Times, 24th August 2022, 8.

30. Maniora, J. 2017. "Is integrated reporting really the superior mechanism for the integration of ethics into the core business model? An empirical analysis." Journal of Business Ethics, 140: 755–786.

31. Pekovic, S., & Vogt, S. 2021. "The fit between corporate social responsibility and corporate governance: the impact on a firm's financial performance" Review of Managerial Science 15, no.4: 1095–1125.

32. Richardson, B.J. 2009. "Keeping ethical investment ethical: regulatory issues for investing for sustainability" Journal of Business Ethics 87, no.4: 555–572.

33. Saggi, M.S. 2016. "Recent trends in corporate reporting practices in India" International Journal of Applied Research. 2. No. 9: 880–883.

34. Sharma, U., Gupta, A., & Gupta, S. K. 2022. "The pertinence of incorporating ESG ratings to make investment decisions: a quantitative analysis using machine learning" Journal of Sustainable Finance & Investment 26: 1–15.

35. Shleifer, A. &Vishny, R.W. 1997. "A survey of corporate governance" Journal of Finance 52, no.2: 737–783.

36. Singh, J., Sadiqb, M. and Kaur K. 2019. "Integrated Reporting: Challenges, benefits and the research agenda." International journal of innovation, creativity and change. 7: 1–16.

37. Singhania, M. and Saini N. 2022. "Quantification of ESF regulations: A cross country benchmarking analysis" 26, no.2: 163–171.

38. Williams, C. 2007. Research Methods, Journal of Business Economics, 5: 65–72.